Dynamics of Ascent: A History of the American Economy

Foreword to the First Edition by Arthur S. Link

❋ Dynamics of Ascent: A History of the American Economy

SECOND EDITION

W. Elliot Brownlee

University of California, Santa Barbara

Wadsworth Publishing Company
Belmont, California
A Division of Wadsworth, Inc.

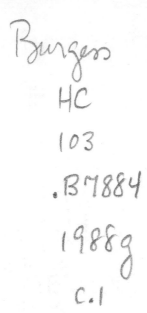
© 1974, 1979 by Alfred A. Knopf, Inc.

© 1988 by W. Elliott Brownlee

ISBN 0-534-10497-5 (previously ISBN 0-256-03739-6)

Library of Congress Catalog Card No. 87-72839

Printed in the United States of America

3 4 5 6 7 8 9 0 DO 4 3 2 1 0 9

For My Mother and Father

※ Foreword to the First Edition

It is altogether possible that *Dynamics of Ascent: A History of the American Economy* will revolutionize the teaching of American economic history. Until the publication of this book, the only history textbooks covering the entire field have been descriptive; that is, they have told us what happened—when depressions occurred, for example, or when the economy prospered—without attempting to tell us why in a comprehensive or general fashion. Students encountering *Dynamics of Ascent* in their courses in economics and history will find no conventional descriptive history, nor, for that matter, will they find turgidly written economic analysis opaque beyond comprehension. On the contrary, they will discover a vigorous, coherent, gracefully written, and breathtaking survey covering the full span of the subject, from the European background to the present day, one that is unique in its masterful organization around the themes and the whys of the dynamics of economic growth, stability, and the distribution of wealth and incomes characterizing the development of the American economy. Students will also find that economic history can be as exciting as rewarding, for in structuring his survey, Professor Brownlee has constantly stressed the interrelationships of changes within various sectors of the economy to expose and elucidate their mutual impact. One happy result has been to greatly enlarge our knowledge of the complexities of the processes of development.

As I have said, *Dynamics of Ascent* is unique in the field for its analytical character and emphasis upon the whys of economic development. In fact, it invites comparison with only one other book—Douglass C. North, *The Economic Growth of the United States, 1790–1860* (1961). However, this is of course a particular study. Moreover, Professor Brownlee does not confine his focus to growth, as Professor North does, and he offers a more comprehensive explanation of the causes and consequences of the industrial revolution.

In unraveling the complexities of the American economic experience from Jamestown to the Nixon era, Professor Brownlee displays a thorough grasp of the voluminous "new" work in American economic history that has been produced since the 1950s, as well as the more traditional scholarship stretching back into the nineteenth century. The digestion of this recent work is a prodigious feat for an historian to accomplish, since economists, publishing in journals of their own discipline, have accounted for most of the recent work in American economic history. For many members of the historical profession, this work has been as obscure and unknown as the large new literature on Minoan culture. This obscurity is certainly understandable given the ignorance of the broader cultural setting of American economic development displayed and sometimes stubbornly adhered to by many of the "new" economic historians. However, they have contributed a great deal of immense value to the noneconomic historians even within the narrow marketplace analysis to which they have largely confined themselves. *Dynamics of Ascent* bridges the gap between economics and history. Historians can no longer use the excuse of disciplinary purity to remain aloof from the influence of the "new" economic history. And those historians who appreciate the insights that it can provide now have a superb means of introducing their students to the subject.

Despite the extent to which economic analysis appears throughout *Dynamics of Ascent,* history students of all ages will be swept along in its swiftly flowing story told in uncommonly clear English. In his economic analysis, Professor Brownlee does not apply formal, explicit mathematical models, nor does he clutter up his pages with arcane charts and tables. His method is simply to define problems in terms of economic concepts and to explain economic change in terms of economic variables. Since he knows how to write clear English prose, he has the capacity to make the results and methods of quantitative research, which has become so characteristic of contemporary economic history, intelligible to the uninitiated.

Moreover, readers will soon discover and be grateful that Professor Brownlee does not confine his enterprise to application of economic analysis alone. While he uses economic concepts as tools to define historical problems—for example, the coming of the American Revolution, the industrial revolution, the causes of the Great

Depression, or the emergence of our own ecological crisis—he also deals with these problems in terms of traditional historical categories and analysis. Many of his original interpretations may well stimulate new interdisciplinary research by economists and historians. Given the underlying rigor and integrity of this work, economists can now in good conscience provide their students with a textbook that is sensitive to large historical issues. They may even discover that Professor Brownlee has taken an important step in fostering the kind of cooperation that once existed between economists and historians in a past generation when the discipline of political economy flourished.

Finally, reading *Dynamics of Ascent* will be vital not only to an understanding of the development of the American economy but also to an appreciation of the economic context in which the American society, culture, and political institutions and practices evolved. This is not to suggest that Professor Brownlee is an economic determinist. On the contrary, he has a firm understanding of the complexity of historical experience and an ironic detachment that will not please those persons who believe that history should be written with a strong and explicit commitment to contemporary political assumptions and persuasions. It is in an undogmatic, unideological, and original fashion that he attributes a central role to the marketplace in the American experience.

Arthur S. Link

Princeton University

September 1973

❖ Acknowledgments

In writing this book, I have incurred heavy obligations to the generations of scholars, both historians and economists, who have lent the field of American economic history its rather unique interdisciplinary quality. Of those debts, the largest is to Eric E. Lampard, who demonstrates how an historian should function on disciplinary intersections. In writing the first edition, I benefited from the advice of Morton Borden, Stuart Bruchey, Stanley Coben, Otis L. Graham, C. Warren Hollister, and Arthur S. Link. Criticism provided by Alan Anderson, Carl V. Harris, Diane Lindstrom, Lloyd Mercer, Irene Neu, James H. Soltow, and Jeffrey G. Williamson was especially helpful in preparing the second edition. Also I should thank three graduate students in history at the University of California, Santa Barbara —Charles A. Keene, Otto H. Reichardt, and Philip L. Solodkin—for their assistance, particularly in the identification of errors in the first edition. Mary Margaret Brownlee continued to offer the most thoroughgoing and valuable criticism of all aspects of the project. David C. Follmer and Linda Sinsheimer Moser lent their highly professional editorial expertise to the project. To all these individuals, I am grateful. Once again, however, I must point out that their advice often fell upon barren ground; responsibility for error is solely mine.

W.E.B.

ix

❋ Contents

❈ Maps and Charts

※ Photo Credits

Alexander Graham Bell, 1892 *The Granger Collection*

Propaganda for Bimetalism, 1894 *Culver Pictures*

Audit Division of the Metropolitan Life Insurance Company, 1897 *Courtesy, Metropolitan Life Insurance Co.*

Child Tending Spindles in a North Carolina Textile Mill, 1909 *Culver Pictures*

Samuel Gompers *The Bettmann Archive*

Anti-Chinese Rioting in Denver, 1880 *The Bettmann Archive*

Combines on a Pacific Northwest Wheat Farm, 1908 *Courtesy, The National Archives*

Barn Raising in Ohio, 1888 *The Massillon Museum*

Women Working on Fuses for Artillery Shells *Courtesy, The National Archives*

One Family Who Owned a Radio in 1929 *Courtesy, RCA*

A Run on a New York City Bank *Brown Brothers*

The Human Dimension of Migration *New York Public Library, Picture Collection*

Shipyard of Henry J. Kaiser, Portland, Oregon *Courtesy, Kaiser Aluminum & Chemical Corporation*

Women Assembling a Dive Bomber *Wide World Photos*

The Marshall Plan's Setting *UPI*

Head Start Classroom, 1966 *Marilyn Silverstone/Magnum*

Cars Lined Up for Scarce Gasoline, February 1974 *Dennis Brack/Black Star*

Long Island, New York, 1950s *Charles Harbutt/Magnum*

Solar Heated Home, Corrales, New Mexico *Tom McHugh/Photo Researchers*

❈ Introduction
At the Juncture of Economics and History

During the 1970s, awareness of the costs of economic growth has intensified. Nonetheless, the history of economic growth remains well worth telling. For one thing, economic growth, or the process by which a society becomes more productive, is still one of the most remarkable discontinuities in recorded history and a central determinant of the fabric of contemporary society. On just that ground the story of how economic growth became sustained in both Europe and North America deserves the same degree of scrutiny as other striking episodes in the development of Western civilization—the rise of the modern national state, the Reformation, the Enlightenment, and the development of the "modern" family, for example. Moreover, it is reasonable to propose that each of the historical developments just mentioned is better understood when placed in the context of concomitant economic change. Even if Western society came to judge, for whatever reasons, that economic growth had become a thoroughly distasteful and short-sighted goal, the process should remain intensely interesting to students of history.

A secondary set of reasons for scholarly preoccupation with economic growth arises from the capacity of gains in economic productivity to aid in the solutions of contemporary problems. Many historians correctly view such problem-solving considerations as ephemeral and illusive. Nonetheless, objections to the importance that I attach to economic growth should come more from those who would emphasize the environmental costs of economic growth. To them, I would recommend the proposition that economic growth has proved the most effective means of raising large numbers of people above a subsistence level of living, of freeing people, both physically and spiritually, from total absorption with the stark necessities of survival. That suggestion may imply to some that a trade-off exists between solutions to the "environmental crisis" and solutions to the poverty problem. Certainly if it were true, as many environmentalists maintain, that no-growth solutions are required to unravel the tangle of environmental problems, it would be exceedingly difficult to launch a successful war on poverty. But in reality no-growth solutions are neither the sole nor the most efficacious answers to impacted environmental problems. Most centrally, economic growth, properly conceived, measures the quality, as well as the quantity, of the productive capacity of a society. Indeed, it is as an indicator of quality of life—not as an end unto itself—that economic growth has been valued by American society. As I discuss in the concluding chapter, resolution of the "environmental crisis" can be sought effectively within the context of explicitly recognizing environmental costs in calculating national product, within the context of reliance on profit-maximization behavior for reducing and eliminating dependence on exhaustible natural resources, and within the context of the invocation of economic incentives for the world-wide limitation of population.

While this survey of American economic history focuses most directly on the phenomenon of increasing economic productivity, it also emphasizes two other aspects of economic change: (1) the distribution of national income and wealth and (2) the inability of the American economy to employ its productive capacity at consistently high levels—in other words, the persistence of episodes of high unemployment for people and capital resources. To expose the implications of economic growth for the welfare of the population as a whole it is imperative to move beyond a discussion of per-capita national income or product to consider how that income has been distributed among various economic and social groups and to determine how consistently people have been able to enjoy the fruits of their labor or capital in the face of the often severe fluctuations of the business cycle. Consequently a fundamental task of this survey is to define rigorously the historical patterns of economic change with respect not only to economic growth but also to the distribution of income and economic instability.

Beyond tracing the leading elements of change in the American economy over the last three centuries and providing explanations in terms of available economic theory, this study seeks to place economic change in the context of institutional developments that are not strictly economic in character. In so doing, I have meant to secure the new economic history of the last two decades in the context of more traditional approaches to the discipline and to create a more significant environment for the narrow economic interpretations which, in recent years, have become popular among economic historians. While I question the implicit assumption often made in the new economic history that a marketplace is able to stand on its own, independent of supportive social institutions (including appropriate political decisions), I do attribute to the marketplace a highly central role in explaining economic and social change in the United States. More sharply, I have devoted this survey in large part to explicating the marketplace conditions that shaped the historical patterns of growth, distribution, and stability and, simultaneously, lent American society much of its distinctive character. Accordingly, I would describe the core of the American experience as an encounter between a highly mobile, restless, acquisitive population and a continent of incredibly abundant natural resources during the pinnacle of enthusiasm for marketplace capitalism. For better or for worse, that is the historical experience within which American society must define its future.

W. Elliot Brownlee

Santa Barbara, California
February 1978

part one

THE EXPANSION OF THE COLONIAL MARKETPLACE

The American economy has always been a dynamic one. As a part of the expansive and vigorous Atlantic society endowed with an abundance of natural riches, America became the vehicle for material advancement for aggressive and acquisitive European settlers. The fullness of landed resources, combined with a dearth of labor to exploit them, and the demand in the Atlantic economy for American goods and services guaranteed sustained opportunities for transplanted European society to reap strong economic gains. And as the American economy expanded in its colonial period, it also increased in efficiency. In the eighteenth century, even before the transformations of the industrial revolution, the institutions ordering economic life enabled European immigrants to improve their standards of living. Under institutional arrangements designed to release capitalist energies, the population of preindustrial America appeared fundamentally similar to the later generations who industrialized the nation.

1

The Origins and Character of European Interest in North America

THE MIGRATION OF HUMAN POPULATIONS

The formal economic history of the United States usually begins with the North American probes by various Europeans in the fifteenth century. Increasingly, however, historians have recognized the significance of the populations of Asian origin that reached North America perhaps 20,000 years earlier. Regardless of the chronological emphasis, the origins of American economic life were clearly part of the migratory history of human populations. Thus, the movement of Asians, Europeans, and Africans to North America ought to be understood in the context of the general history of geographically mobile peoples.

Of all the animals on our planet, Homo sapiens has achieved the widest distribution of any. No full explanation exists for the uniquely wide and rapid distribution of the species, but at least two significant factors have been involved: (1) the ability of humans to adapt to new environments and, as a consequence, to survive and reproduce in them without having to undergo substantial evolutionary changes, and (2) the tendency of human adaptations to the environment to occur unevenly around the globe. Relying on this theory of technological imbalance, one would explain the migrations of the earliest peoples to develop agriculture and animal husbandry—perhaps 10,-000 to 12,000 years ago—in terms of the technical advantage that farmers gained over hunters and gatherers. Farmers, with their greater concentrations on the land, could mobilize more manpower at any given point and effectively displace hunters from good agricultural land. This interpretation would suggest, further, that the subsequent displacement of some groups of cultivators and herders by other farmers resulted from the massive population explosion produced by this first agricultural revolution and the uneven spread of improved weaponry among farming societies.

By 2500 B.C. these farming economies had spread throughout Europe and had achieved a degree of geographic stability. But as metals gradually came into use for tools and weapons, new geographic and technical imbalances arose. Town-based civilizations, founded on metal-using technology, developed and became foci for population growth. These town-based civilized centers acted as economic magnets, drawing peasants and artisans from the hinterland and various migrant groups from beyond. Among the distant groups, ironically, were peoples who appeared less civilized but who possessed a superior military technology. Confronting established Europe were the northern tribes who subjugated Rome, Arabs who spread the Islamic world from Spain to India by the middle of the eighth century, and the Turks who pushed both east and west, conquering Constantinople in 1453. These migrating groups often were aided by important allies in the microorganisms of disease. The fact that some migrating groups acquired immunities to certain diseases helped them to survive and to conquer other groups that were not immune to those diseases. This advantage was, in effect, another form of technological imbalance. Smallpox in the second century, measles in the third, and bubonic plague in the sixth appear to have contributed significantly to the reduction of the highly concentrated Roman populations and to a weakening of their ability to withstand invasion.

By the fall of Rome a wide variety of human migrations had become evident. Some were voluntary; others were compulsory. Some resulted from attractions of the areas that received migrating groups; others resulted from forces of push exerted by the areas from which migrating groups left. But all were shaped in a fundamental way by inequalities in the distribution among geographic areas and related unevenness in human adaptation to the physical environment.

AN ECONOMY IN FLUX: EUROPE, 1000–1500

Expansion, 1000–1350

Following the demographic crisis that accompanied the decline of Rome, Europe's population remained relatively stable until the tenth century. But from the end of that century through the early fourteenth century, the High Middle Ages, Europe experienced a renewed population explosion. That population explosion increased pressures for territorial expansion. The amount of land under tillage increased; the period between the eleventh and thirteenth centuries was one of prodigious dyking and draining, construction of great irrigation canals, and founding of settlements on former wasteland in forest clearings. And a vigorous colonization movement carried Europeans east of the Elbe River into eastern Germany and Poland and into the previously Moorish districts of the Iberian Peninsula.

The population growth and the colonization movements of the High Middle Ages were accompanied by a definite widening of the marketplace. Interregional trade grew rapidly and extended over increasingly longer distances. Indeed, from the tenth century trade expanded to reach virtually all of central and eastern Europe. European trade embraced new raw materials, including wool from Britain, lumber from France and the Baltic area, grain from the Baltic, and salt from Spain. Like the expansion of the European economy under the Romans, this later widening of the marketplace included geographical thrusts designed to capture new sources of raw materials. When Europeans would turn to North America in the late fifteenth century they would be engaged primarily in the same quest for raw materials.

The population growth and redistribution of the High Middle Ages contributed to and was, in turn, furthered by important changes in the organization of economic life. The widening of the marketplace produced by population growth induced specialization, and hence efficiency gains, by bringing areas with varying endowments of natural resources and factors of production (land, labor, and capital) into close contact. These efficiency gains were often the results of efforts of an emerging mercantile plutocracy that grew as the number and size of European towns increased. The new merchants were socially mobile; that is, their status derived increasingly from personal property rather than from landownership. Frequently, the new merchants functioned not only as commercial entrepreneurs but also as landlords and feudal officials, spreading their control over economic activity in rural areas and promoting a more efficient use of land. Local landowners produced more than the local market could absorb. The new merchants exported this surplus, chiefly cloth from northern France and Flanders, metal goods from western Germany, and wool from England.

These powerful commercial interests also led the way in introducing a set of technological and organizational changes that ultimately provided a foundation for the flood of initiatives that carried Europeans to North America to establish permanent colonies. Key technological innovations included the horse collar, the compound plow, and the windmill, all permitting more extensive cultivation, and improvements in navigational aids and in shipbuilding, resulting in ships that were larger, more maneuverable, and more seaworthy. An important organizational change occurred when mercantile groups seeking greater efficiency increased the scale of their operations, employed resident agents in distant ports, and developed banking and insurance services. They also sought political security for their enterprises, negotiating treaty arrangements with foreign officials which gave the foreigners a share of new earnings, gained more support from their governments in suppressing piracy, and encouraged the enlargement of their national states in order to provide a greater degree of order and security in expanding markets.

Responding to the needs of commerce, the European political economy moved to guarantee the exclusive, private ownership of property—the kernel of modern capitalism. That development was a response to the increasing pressure of population on the land. Rapidly growing populations raised the price of land relative to that of labor and thereby increased incentives for landownership and reduced the interest of employers in control over labor. As a result of the development of private ownership and a labor force less constrained by feudal obligations, production increased in efficiency, thus stimulating the further extension of trade, the continued growth of population, and, in turn, a prolonged search for new ways of increasing productivity. No direct measures exist of the productivity gains produced during this era of economic ferment. One indirect index is the building of massive cathedrals. The large capital investment essential for cathedral building testifies not only to religious enthusiasm but also to a high rate of economic growth. Without this high rate of economic growth towns probably would have been unable to generate the large accumulations of savings necessary for cathedral building.[1]

The technological and organizational innovations characteristic of the High Middle Ages were typical results of a widely felt impulse to use resources more productively, in a fashion that would enhance returns to both private individuals and society at large. They, as well as vigorous population movement and the expansion of trade, were central to the European economy at least two centuries before the sustained exploitation of the New World began and four centuries before the West entered an industrial revolution.

Decline, 1350–1500

Europe's economic expansion stalled during the first half of the fourteenth century with marked declines in population, production, and most probably standards of living. In England the output of the nation's mines and farms waned. On the Continent the textile-producing regions entered a period of adversity, with both declining supply of and weakening demand for the finished product. At the heart of Europe's general contraction was a Malthusian process—a decline in population stemming from the demands of population on scarce resources and the related advent of chronic epidemics. As population grew during the High Middle Ages, pressure on the land to produce increased, profits in agriculture consequently declined, real wages then declined, and, eventually, famine spread and epidemic disease returned to riddle the weakened populations throughout Europe. With high population concentrations and improved communications throughout western Europe, the onslaught of epidemics was even more dramatic than it had been in Roman times. The most severe epidemic was the Black Death, or bubonic plague, which reached its peak in 1348. Between that year and 1350 it claimed as much as 20 percent of England's population, and its impact was even greater on the more urban (and more commercial) Continent. Epidemics of various kinds returned frequently in the next half-century, causing Europe's population to decline further. In England, as a result, the population in 1400 was only about one-half as great as that in 1348.

The demographic crisis contributed to an erosion of "law and order," which, in turn, reinforced the pressures of excess population. Wars, peasant uprisings, urban revolts, and conflicts between feuding elites, such as the Wars of the Roses in England, increased in intensity and destructiveness, during the fourteenth and fifteenth centuries. These conflicts were largely the result of tensions created by competition for shrinking resources. Much of the peasant unrest, for example, stemmed from the fact that in response to the scarcity of labor and the increase in real wages that followed population declines, lords tried to reimpose feudal obligations. The social unrest, in turn, aggravated the contraction by inhibiting the desire to invest in commercial enterprise. The disruption of Eastern trade routes also stifled extensive commerce; in 1368, the Mongols and Europeans found themselves expelled from China with the establishment of the Ming dynasty and, at the same time, the Arabs recaptured Middle Eastern trading posts, denying the Italians their privileges which had given them direct access to the East.

Europe's economy resumed expansion only toward the end of the fifteenth century, and levels of living did not return to their former heights until perhaps as late as the seventeenth century. It was near the end of the period of economic contraction that Europeans turned toward the North American continent. And it was during the subsequent period of expansion in the sixteenth and seventeenth centuries that Europeans made their massive commitment to the North American enterprise.

The English Setting

To connect European contraction and expansion with the development of North America it is helpful to examine the changing character of trade and production in England. An organizational change in the conduct of business, involving the elimination of foreign control over England's trade, and, later, the rise of the native merchant-venturers were crucial to the reorientation of economic life, and indirectly laid the foundation for North American expansion. Men from the Continent, predominantly Italian, entered England during the twelfth and thirteenth centuries as collectors of papal taxes; later they moved into the trading of English wool and the financing of English royalty. (Wool trading and royal finance became intertwined as the energetic Italian traders provided loans for the crown and collected customs in return for receiving a monopoly in the wool trade.) By 1300 the great Italian trading houses of the Ricardi, the Frescobaldi, the Bardi, and the Peruzzi dominated wool exports from England, simultaneously exercising a large measure of control over the royal customs. Despite their preeminence during the expansion of the High Middle Ages, the Italians had virtually disappeared from England, with the exception of Southampton, by 1350. Social and political pressure from rising English merchants, the financial difficulties faced by the large Italian houses during the contraction of trade, and the failure of the Italians to provide a continuing line of credit to the crown during the Hundred Years' War cost them their protected position in the wool trade, which English merchants now sought to win control over. First a group of the wealthier independent English wool traders formed a consortium to manage wool exports; shortly afterward another group, known as the Company of the Staple, received a formal monopoly in the wool trade in return for guaranteeing to advance loans and collect customs duties for the crown, just as the Italian trading houses had done.

Hard on the heels of the Staplers the merchant-venturers rose to prominence, forming their first fellowship in York in 1356. Their emergence marked a larger structural transformation of the English economy, a measure of which was a shift in the composition of English exports—from wool to cloth—and an expansion of exports during the fourteenth century.[2] Production of English cloth for export originated in the newly growing hinterland behind small port cities, and partly as a consequence of that geographical shift, London as an exporter lost ground to cities like Liverpool, Hull, York, Exeter, and

Bristol, which were better able to tap the cloth-producing backlands. The businessmen who captured the cloth trade resided not only in London but also to a very large extent in the lesser ports. While the wool merchants of the Staple served only the well-established, centralized market for wool in the cloth-producing cities of the Low Countries, such as Antwerp, the new cloth merchants, the merchant-venturers, attempted to meet the rapidly growing but widely dispersed markets for cloth in France and Spain. The wool merchants of the Staple, regulated by law in 1363 to confine their activities to exporting from the English base in Calais and chary by disposition of risky enterprise, were not able to meet the demand for cloth. The merchant-venturers, less organized than the merchants of the London Staple, operated under much less regulation and received far less protection from the crown in coping with the exigencies of war and diplomacy. But their flexibility was of the highest necessity in the initially uncertain export trade in cloth.

These cloth merchants were of inferior social position with origins frequently in the countryside, close to the production of cloth. At first the venturers were employees or apprentices to artisans and small merchants but, in the course of the fifteenth century, they formed their own companies, putting themselves in position to ride on the crest of England's export wave. By 1500 the wisdom of their enterprise made them men of substance, rather than men on the margin of trade, replacing landholders in local community power. In some places, such as York, the merchant-venturers had achieved significant political power even by the end of the fourteenth century. By 1500 they had become firmly entrenched in the English ruling class. Reinforcing their position was the Tudor dynasty (from 1485) with its clear financial and political dependency on the merchant-venturers.

Merchant-Venturers Look Westward

The activities of merchants in Bristol, on the west coast of England, exemplify the kind of changes that transformed the export trade and led to an interest in the Western Hemisphere. Bristol was the second largest port of England during the period and of critical importance for the development of an English North American interest.[3] By the 1460s the merchant-venturers controlled not only the external trade of the town but the town itself. Organized as a fellowship, they fixed prices and licensed trade to their major metropolitan markets in France, Spain, and Portugal. They also established Bristol as a transshipment center for regional exchanges between the hinterland and the metropolitan markets, stationing agents in the hinterland to finance the collection of forest products, food for Bristol's own citizens, alabaster and metals, as well as the essential components of Bristol's exports—hides, wool, and cloth. Trading not only with Portugal, Spain, and France but with Iceland, Ireland, and the Mediterranean as well, the merchants exported these products in exchange for fish, wheat, coal, iron, and wine, which they sold, in part, to people in their town and in its hinterland. Basically the men of Bristol had to ferret out trade areas that were marginal or complementary to the areas of influence (including the Low Countries) created by the still-powerful Italian merchants and the merchants of the German cities organized in the Hanseatic League.

The merchant-venturers of Bristol, as flexible and creative merchants with a solid export base, enjoyed expanding markets as European populations once again began to increase during the last half of the fifteenth century. Nonetheless, toward the end of the century they found themselves insecure about the future growth of markets and sources of supply. Bristol's Irish connections were firm, despite the persistent political chaos among the warring Irish tribes. However, the Irish trade, consisting of exchanges of Irish cattle, timbers, linens, grains, and fish for salt, iron, and exotic products from the East, was small compared with the whole of Bristol's activities, as was its trade with the Mediterranean, due to the fact that the Genoese insisted on carrying cloth from England. Bristol's most important trading areas were France, Spain, and Iceland. (See Figure 1.) In sizable exchanges with Gascony (in the extreme southwest of France), Bristol merchants sent fish, cloth, hides, and grain to Bayonne and Bordeaux in return for wine. This trade was growing, though slowly, and was periodically in jeopardy from the king of France or from the English settlers in Gascony who defied British rule. When Bristol's ties with Gascony weakened during the 1480s, the Bristol merchants attempted to strengthen their relationships with Castile, exporting fish and cloth there in exchange for a wide range of products, including wine, oil, salt, dyes, tallow, cork, hides, leather, fruit, southern delicacies (figs, raisins, dates, almonds, honey, saffron, licorice, and vinegar), and iron. To secure this trade, the merchants agreed to admit some Spaniards to their fellowship and obtained the support of the English crown in suppressing the Mediterranean pirates who raided the Spanish trade.

Thus Spain and France were the two most important trade centers the Bristol merchants were able to tap. To have strength in this Continental trade, however, Bristol had to rely heavily on its trade with Iceland through which it obtained fish for Catholic Europe. Furthermore, Bristol's position in the Iceland trade depended upon England's relationship with the Hanseatic League. The Bristol mer-

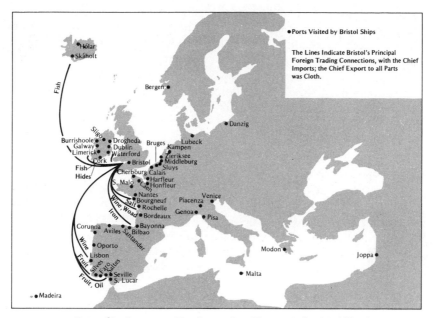

FIGURE 1: *Bristol's Overseas Trade at the Close of the Middle Ages*

chants had been accustomed to interloping in the Icelandic fish trade, avoiding the regulations of the Norwegians. However, in the mid-fifteenth century, the aggressive German ports, aided by the financially weakened Danes, intervened to shut off this trade, and the English crown, now seeking an accommodation with Denmark against France during the Wars of the Roses, declined to support the merchants. Bristol resumed this trade in the latter part of the century only with the greatest difficulty and found its foothold extremely precarious.

As the future of Bristol trade became threatened, its merchant-venturers and those of other English ports turned away from traditional medieval trade routes. Eventually Bristol merchants looked beyond Ireland and even beyond Iceland, at first sending expeditions to the seas west and south of Ireland to search for new supplies of fish for their Continental trade. This response was a very natural one, since Atlantic-coast fishermen worked the waters around Iceland and very probably had already sailed in North American waters. Further, their knowledge of these waters was far wider than was that of either of the traditional sea powers of Europe. (The domain of the Italians was the Levant to the Channel and that of the Hanseatics was the Channel to the Baltic and Iceland. The Bristol merchants' main arena was the Atlantic.)

In the summer of 1480 two ships under one John Lloyd set out from Bristol, not for trade, but to sail "to the island of Brasylle in the western part of Ireland" in search for new sources of fish. Although Lloyd's mission failed, the Bristol merchants continued to send out parties, one of which may have reached Newfoundland in 1494. A syndicate of Bristol merchants helped finance John Cabot's successful voyage to Newfoundland in 1497, after Christopher Columbus had failed to sell his services to Henry VII for the same voyage because he asked too high a price. Upon return from Newfoundland Cabot's companions reported that they "could bring thence so many fish that they would have no further need of Iceland." Thus the fish trade itself, coupled with the information obtained in these early voyages, laid the basis for the development of transatlantic trade. By the beginning of the sixteenth century, England had a well-established trading tradition carried on by a group of innovative, flexible, and powerful merchants who searched vigorously for new markets and, most significant for the development of British America, for new sources of supply.

The Portuguese Analogue

Other European trading nations similarly developed an interest in North America, especially Portugal. Defeated in its desire to conquer Moslem Africa at the Battle of Tangiers in 1437, blocked by the Venetians and the Genovese in the Mediterranean, and opposed by the Arabs in the Indian Ocean, Portugal, like England, turned to the Atlantic in search of new trading areas. The Algarve province in southern Portugal, home of Henry the Navigator, was a seedbed of new schemes and ventures, just as was the west of England. The Portuguese engaged in vigorous exploration and preliminary exploitation of sub-Sahara Africa, trading in slaves as well as ivory and gold. They sought opportunities in the Atlantic islands, including the Canaries, the Azores, and the Cape Verde Islands, initiating settlement there and establishing new crops, especially wines and sugar. The Portuguese acquired Atlantic expertise through their voyages down the African coast, early probes toward the coast of Brazil (perhaps reaching Brazil prior to Cabral's voyage of 1500), and, ironically, the expeditions of Columbus, who relied very heavily on the accumulated experience of fifteenth-century Portuguese western expeditions, and whose mission was to lay the basis for Spain to compete successfully with the Portuguese. The Portuguese state was more vigorous in promoting Atlantic initiatives than was the English but, as with the English, at the core of Portuguese endeavor was an ambitious, flexible group of merchants motivated by dissatisfaction with the capacity of medieval trade routes to maintain a growing volume of trade and, especially, a distrust of the reliability of the old sources of raw materials for trade.[4]

The resurgence of population, markets, and interregional trade in the last quarter of the fifteenth century led mercantile groups in virtually all European nations to expand their horizons, to seek out the centers of most rapid growth, and to search for innovations that would lead to more efficient commerce. England and Portugal, however, finding themselves excluded from the foci of growth, strove to develop new areas for trade, areas more remote from the forces of international economic and military competition. In the process they turned to what was then the margin of the European economy, the Atlantic.

NORTH AMERICAN COLONIES, 1500–1630

The interest of the English in seeking new sources of raw materials in the Western Hemisphere widened the scope of England's commerce but did not lead to an immediate concern for planting colonies in the New World. A century elapsed between the voyage of John Cabot and the establishment of the first permanent English colony, at Jamestown, in 1607. This delay resulted primarily from the character of opportunities that were initially available to the English in North America. Certainly the English possessed sufficient resources and abilities to engage in extensive colonization activity in North America, had such efforts held prospects for earning adequate returns. However, none of their attractive North American opportunities required permanent settlement in order to be exploited.

The English did not enjoy the advantages realized by the Spanish, who found in South America the fortunate conjunction of a large, advanced native population that they could employ or easily subjugate and the availability of precious metals that they could easily mine. At first unpromising, the Spanish empire, stretching from Florida and California through Chile, became the most rewarding of all in the sixteenth century; gold and silver bullion filled Spain's coffers and became the chief elements in the increase in the West's money supply—leading to a long-term, persistent inflation (the *price revolution*) and a prolonged stimulation of economic activity. As in England and Portugal, the Spanish expansion was headed by a mercantile elite—centered in Seville, commercialized in part by an infusion of Genovese migrants, and supported politically by the monarchy—which responded to opportunities in a way designed to maximize their profits. Their English competitors envied them for their success.[5]

While the Spanish enjoyed their position at the center of expansion, Englishmen waited on the periphery. In North America, they confronted a resistant native population, and rarely in the sixteenth century did they find agricultural or mining opportunities that they could exploit easily. (The English discovery of deposits of Bermuda ambergris, which the English had only to shovel onto their boats, was useful to perfume manufacturers and an exception to the general pattern of failure, but it was hardly the same as finding precious metals.) Inasmuch as depression struck the Continental cloth trade during the 1530s and again during the 1550s, prompting public and private concern for finding new markets for cloth and more activity in the Russian, Baltic, and Mediterranean areas, the English certainly would have made substantial investments in North America if it had presented new markets for cloth exports. However, given the dismal prospects for North American markets, the more intensive quest for markets, during the first half of the century, imposed a higher requirement for potential returns upon proposed North American enterprises. In addition, in the latter half of the sixteenth century, turmoil in the Low Countries and the growing conflict between England and the states of the Iberian Peninsula created new incentives for eliminating European middlemen, and a group of recently emergent import merchants based in London promoted a search for new trade routes that would directly tap the spices, silks, and other exotic products of the East. Although this redirection of trading initiative created some interest in the discovery of a Northwest Passage, the anticipated new route to the Orient, its more significant impact was to raise even higher the minimum return required for investment in North American ventures.

Prelude to Colonization

An impressive set of voyages, expeditions, and preliminary, rather tentative North American settlements did, however, open England's pocketbook during the period between Cabot and Jamestown. Many expeditions were designed purely to expand fishing in North American waters to meet the European demand which was growing at least as rapidly as the population; by the 1530s the fishing industry of the Grand Banks was well established. By the late sixteenth century, perhaps as many as fifty fishing and exploring expeditions struck out each year from Bristol and the seaport towns of Devonshire toward the Newfoundland banks, Nova Scotia, and the Maine coast. To secure this enterprise Sir Humphrey Gilbert, in 1583, claimed Newfoundland for Elizabeth. Also, the various probes for a Northwest Passage, including that of Martin Frobisher (1576–1578), explored the Arctic zone. Although unsuccessful in their primary purpose, these efforts did contribute to the development of whaling and sealing industries in the Arctic during the seventeenth century.

A new and far more compelling English objective in the late sixteenth century was the looting of the Spanish and Portuguese in South America. That interest had been subdued during the earlier part of the century, England then being unwilling to challenge the papal bull of 1494 which divided the New World between the Spanish and the Portuguese. By the middle of the sixteenth century, however, a nationalistic and religious rivalry between Spain and England reinforced the sense of economic competition already strongly felt by English merchants. While Henry VIII (ruling 1509–1547) had concentrated upon the search for allies against France, Elizabeth (ruling 1558–1603) by the 1560s had become persuaded that Catholic Spain was a dire threat to England's survival as a Protestant nation. Elizabeth sought allies among French Huguenots and in the Low Countries; and when she supported the revolts against the Spanish that occurred there in 1568, full war with Spain ensued.

In the Western Hemisphere the military conflict with Spain gave certain English merchants an opportunity to harass Spanish trade routes and interlope in Spanish trade. These merchants were West Country traders who had been absorbed in Anglo-Spanish trade, including exchanges with Spanish America. During England's Reformation, led by Henry VIII, they remained intensely loyal to their royal benefactor and had faced persecution under the Spanish Inquisition and disruption of their trading opportunities. Suffering from the waxing political and religious rivalry between Spain and England and having observed at firsthand, covetously, the flow of treasure from Spanish territories in the Americas, they had long urged the crown to be more aggressive on behalf of commerce. Although these merchants sponsored raiding as early as the 1540s, only in the 1560s were they able to undertake raiding and interloping as instruments of the state.[6]

In interloping, Sir John Hawkins, son of a Brazil trader, registered the sole English success—by smuggling slaves into Haiti in the 1560s. Hawkins had hoped to make his trade regular by offering to protect the Spanish against piracy, but the Spanish regained control of the slave trade by the 1570s. Thereafter, the English focus was primarily on the raiding expeditions—open attacks on Spanish cities and treasure ships, that were missions of piracy legalized by the crown, for which the returns were exceptional. Sir Francis Drake, for example, the most notable looter of Spanish-American trade routes, earned a return of over 4,500 percent on the investment made in his 1577–1580 American mission.

With such returns from raiding and with the onset of a war with Spain in 1585, a new interest developed in colonization, specifically in colonies that would support privateering expeditions. Sir Walter Raleigh received a royal charter to establish such a colony and, in fact, in 1584 and 1585, created in what is now North Carolina the Roanoke settlement, which was designed as a base for penetrating Spanish trade routes. To propagandize on behalf of Raleigh, Richard Hakluyt, in a *Discourse Concerning Western Planting* (1584), argued that such a colony would permit tapping the West Indian trade of the Spanish, help to eliminate middlemen in West Indian trade, and provide a base for promoting slave revolts in Spanish domains. However, it soon became apparent that the costs of establishing colonies that had no significant means of support and were staffed by soldiers expecting to live in a garrison supplied largely by Indians would be too high; Raleigh had to resettle the colony in 1587, and, by 1591 it had disappeared virtually without a trace.

In addition to praising colonies as instruments against the Spanish, Hakluyt promised that colonization would relieve population pressures at home. The English must colonize, he wrote, because "through our long peace and seldom sickeness, we are grown more populous than ever heretofore; so that now there are of every art and science so many, that they can hardly live one by another, nay rather they are ready to eat up one another." Hakluyt's concern was common, since England's population had resumed growth during the late fifteenth century and since, by 1550, agricultural returns had fallen and wages had declined. Actually, however, the rate of population increase was rather small, perhaps as little as 0.5 percent annually (judging from the period 1570–1600). Furthermore, the English, and Europeans in general, were better able to feed new populations at this time than during the expansion of the High Middle Ages, thanks chiefly to municipal grain storages, a greater availability of food surpluses from distant regions, and a much larger volume of fish coming from the Grand Banks. In addition, commerce rapidly increased in efficiency at the same time as it expanded, compensating in part for declining returns from agriculture. As a result, during the sixteenth century, interest in colonization (outside of the British Isles) as a way of reducing population density, although real, was marginal to the primary thrust toward the expansion of traditional trade and the looting of the Spanish empire.

The North American probes of the sixteenth century, although producing no permanent colony, established English territorial claims and provided a settler class. The men interested in colonization and those engaged in the raiding activity were bound together both by kinship and origins in the west of England: Men like Drake,

Hawkins, Raleigh, and Gilbert were frequently related and were all younger sons of gentry families who traditionally would have followed careers in agriculture, government, and the church, which rested on the ownership of large estates. Finding these avenues blocked by primogeniture, population pressures, and the breakup of the monasteries, many young men turned to the sea, for both excitement and business, engaging in exploration, fishing off Newfoundland, raiding the Spanish, Irish warfare and settlement, and finally, North American settlement with its opportunities for re-creating a landed interest. During the period of initial colonization these men who had become familiar with the coasts of North America, especially New England, formed the basis of a colonizing class and carried English society across the Atlantic.

Central to the eventual success of the British colonies was the business experience acquired by merchants during the long period of North American probes and expanding trade. They developed the conviction that the investment required and the risks incurred in promoting and fostering settlement were far too large for individual enterprise, as had been characteristic of the sixteenth-century efforts. Thus at the beginning of the seventeenth century, sponsors of North American settlement were wedded to the notion that colonization would have to take place within the bounds of joint-stock companies.

In the late sixteenth century Englishmen had refined the joint-stock company to meet the needs of far-flung commercial activity; once again, expanding trade induced efficiency-minded innovation. The joint-stock company was similar to a medieval trading company such as the Company of the Staple in that it provided for a delegation of the sovereign's power in a distant realm to a private business group in return for their performance of a public obligation. But the joint-stock company also offered economies to those seeking to redirect commerce. Most important, the joint-stock company, while not providing limited liability in the strict sense, did allow some sharing of the risk to permit acquisition of more resources and provision of a greater degree of freedom from public regulation. That the joint-stock company had wider powers than a medieval trading company had can be seen in the 1606 charter of the Virginia Company: it allowed local councils to advise the governor, extended to the company the power to coin money, and granted the company the right to establish land grants and create a military structure. Broad powers were necessary to support a society and an enterprise that were far removed from the seat of ultimate authority; and they were especially necessary to attract investors to such undertakings. By the end of Elizabeth's reign the state had chartered some fifteen joint-stock companies, directed mainly toward the search for Asian markets. They included the Muscovy Company (1555), chartered to find a Northeast Passage to Asia, the Eastland Company (1579), to develop the Baltic trade, the Africa Company (1588), to participate in the slave trade, the Levant Company (1592), to by-pass the Constantinople middlemen, and the East India Company (1600), to reach India and points beyond (including the American West Coast). The success of these giant companies—bringing a new group of merchants to the heights of wealth and power, thus eclipsing the merchant-venturers in the seventeenth century—and the difficulties that had faced the more individualistic North American enterprises of the same period assured the application of the joint-stock company to future projects in the New World.

Almost two decades after the conclusion of the war with Spain in 1588, a new incentive to North American colonization appeared in the buoyant demand for furs—those of the beaver, in particular—to satisfy the craving for fur hats. The English, unable to compete successfully with the Dutch in obtaining higher-quality furs from the Russian trade, turned to North America as a second choice, just as they had done earlier in the fish trade, launching this sequence of North American ventures under the aegis of assorted new joint-stock companies. Between 1606 and 1630 eleven such companies appeared, including the first and second Virginia companies, the Newfoundland Company, the New Plymouth Company, the New Scotland (Nova Scotia) Company, the Adventurers to Canada Company, the Massachusetts Bay Company, and the Providence Islands (the Carolinas) Company. These companies were not only organized on the model of the great Eastern trading companies but were funded, at least initially, to a large extent by the rising Levant–East India merchants as well as the well-established merchant-venturers. Their purpose was primarily to exploit the furs of North America and, to a lesser extent, to follow the Spanish example by discovering accumulations of precious metals. Although commanding far fewer resources than the Levant–East India pursuits, these enterprises led the English to develop permanent colonies in North America.

Permanent Plantations

The history of the Jamestown colony, founded by the Virginia Company, graphically reveals the interplay between European tastes, expectations, institutions, and technology and the realities of the North American environment. Consequently, it is representative of the successful planting of all the North American colonies. At the time of the creation of the Virginia Company, interest in raiding the

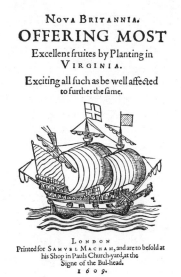

Nova Britannia.
OFFERING MOST
Excellent fruites by Planting in
VIRGINIA.

Exciting all such as be well affected
to further the same.

LONDON
Printed for SAMVEL MACHAM, and are to besold at
his Shop in Pauls Church-yard, at the
Signe of the Bul-head.
1 6 0 9.

TITLE PAGE OF AN EMIGRATION TRACT, 1609. Despite the "Starving Time" in 1607, this promotional literature advertised the abundance of food and resources.

Spanish had waned. The group of incorporators, including West Country gentry localized in Plymouth and a clique of wealthy London merchants, had to convince the king that their activities would pose no threat to Spain, since the king of Spain was now a cousin to the English sovereign. Their objective was to create a set of trading posts that would collect furs and fish or perhaps engage in the simple manufacture of forest products such as potash. The company received substantial political autonomy, certain tax incentives, and permission to ship its products duty-free into London. Subsequently, in 1607, the London group founded a colony in Jamestown.

Despite the earlier refinement of the joint-stock company, the Virginia Company survived only after undergoing further modification to perfect the autonomy of the company, establish firm financial backing, and ensure the availability of an adequate labor force. The latter objective was particularly central. The first group attracted to Jamestown were primarily adventurers. Viewing their expedition as a military mission modeled upon the Irish campaigns, they were easily distracted by futile searches for gold and quick riches, tried to rely on commerce with Indians for obtaining supplies, and were disinterested in the long-term future of the colony. Their distaste for agricultural labor, coupled with the hardships of the woods and the group's limited provisions to sustain their health, resulted in the death of 67 of the original 105 settlers during the colony's first year.

In 1609 the company obtained a new charter, providing the means to attract more-serious settlers. Now the company, renamed the Virginia Company of London, was able to offer stock in the venture for the labor of settlers as well as for capital by creating planter memberships. The planters received a headright of stock and were promised a dividend of one hundred acres of land per share after seven years; some 200 planters bought into the company immediately. And to manage Jamestown affairs more effectively the company obtained greater power from the crown, including the right to replace the governor by an act of the general court of shareholders. After these reforms and a successful appeal for additional capital, nine ships sailed for Jamestown (1609) with 800 new settlers.

Still, the colony only limped along, with rather dim prospects for permanent success. Rather than cut losses by abandoning it, however, the company obtained additional institutional reforms in 1612, again tending to give those actually in Jamestown greater control over their destinies. Under the new charter, control of the company passed almost wholly to the company itself and a deputy governor was established to serve in America to provide for more effective leadership in meeting the demands of a hostile environment. Under the new deputy governor individuals received plots of land outside the headright system, leasing plots in return for their labor and portions of their corn crop (thus introducing a system of local taxation).

These changes meant that the company reduced the pressure from abroad for quick profits and that the colony was better able to cope with the real problems of survival. Although about 500 investors, including some of the wealthiest and best established in London, ceased supporting the company, the main problem was not so much the lack of risk capital as Virginia's lack of an export commodity. The company experimented with a variety of solutions, including the development of manufacturing—futile, indeed, in the face of inaccessible markets. Nonetheless, at the time of the 1612 reforms the problem was on the verge of resolution because, in 1612 or 1613, John Rolfe successfully cured tobacco. A change in English tastes, promoted largely by Sir Walter Raleigh, created a very large demand for tobacco, a "new" product introduced from the Americas, despite the efforts of King James I to discourage his citizens from engaging in "so vile and stinking a custom." Even at the time of Rolfe's successes England imported more than £200,000 worth of tobacco annually. Thus Virginia producers had a clear opportunity for selling in a large metropolitan market and, on the other side of the Atlantic, mercantile groups and the crown had an attractive new source for a major import. England had been obtaining almost all her tobacco from the Spanish empire, and both English merchants and the crown were eager to stabilize the nation's balance of payments and the consequent drain of specie to Spain. The combination of these interests led directly to the success of the Virginia settlement and to its emergence as the locus of most rapid growth on the continent during the seventeenth century.

Tobacco production for the English market soared—so much so that a severe fall in prices and incomes resulted from bumper crops. After company and royal experimentation with production controls and taxes to restrict output, which were met by stiff colonial resistance in 1620, the Privy Council extended to the company a tobacco contract that recognized the primacy of Virginia tobacco production for the English market. It required all Virginia tobacco to be sold in England but, in return, gave Virginia producers a monopoly on the English market by banning tobacco production in England and by guaranteeing to ban tobacco produced elsewhere.

Under the favorable terms of this contract, production rose, incomes earned in tobacco growing increased, and the population of the colony burgeoned. The importation of women in large numbers and the purchase of slaves from the Dutch were promoted by the managers of the colony to cope with the mobility and expense of the labor force transplanted from England. In 1618, for example, the company shipped to the colony one hundred "young and uncorrupt maids to make wives to the inhabitants and by that means to make the men more settled and less moveable." And the introduction of slaves offered the possibility of reducing reliance on the free and indentured labor of restless and costly Englishmen.[7] Simultaneously, however, the company granted more of Virginia's plentiful land, in fifty- and one-hundred-acre parcels, to the settlers in an effort to attract more free labor to Jamestown. Further, the company made extensive grants to subsidiary groups within the colony. Although the colony retained the right to limit crops, organize the fields, and regulate the terms of conveyance, the terms of land tenure were extremely liberal by the standards of the day (it took New England a century to match them). Another change in 1618–1619 extended the principle of greater freedom for the company to greater freedom for the planters—by specifying that the plantation ought to be under the governance of the participants, as was the company. Thus at this point the House of Burgesses appeared as a legitimate force representing the freemen, while there was a commensurate decline of the old company in the administration of the colony. By 1622 a royal commission reported that the company was guilty of negligence and mismanagement and that it was on the verge of bankruptcy. Subsequently, the crown assumed administration of the colony, making it a royal colony in 1624 and thus ending the Virginia Company of London.

As the reforms of the company brought about the transference of the marketplace and supporting institutions to Virginia, the company became obsolete. Its original backers, predominately of the established merchant-venturer or Levant–East India groups, withdrew their support from continued colonization.[8] Capital for the plantations of Virginia, and North America generally, now came, not from the great merchants who found easy profits in monopolizing the exporting of cloth or the importing of Eastern exotica, but from a new group. To be sure, they had strong ties to the century-old interest of the West Country ports in North American enterprise and strengthened the connections between those outports and North America. But they were to a large extent men who had not been engaged previously in the financing of foreign trade, tending to be, rather, shopkeepers or sea captains.[9] Thus the beginnings of permanent colonization of North America were based on the energies of a flexible, competitive, and rather large entrepreneurial class and, more fundamentally, on a social order in England that had consistently, from perhaps as early as the fourteenth century, produced a significant group of individuals with an inclination to take economic risks and to respond to the changing patterns of economic opportunity in a way that enhanced both private and social income.[10]

While the power of English capital over North American development weakened, the individuals actually engaged in production won a very large measure of control over their own activities, subject only to regulation by the crown in the public interest (as defined by the crown). The Jamestown experience proved that to maximize colonial opportunities, both from the standpoint of the colony and of the mother country, it was necessary to ensure a large measure of decentralization and individual authority in the colonizing venture, the most important element being the individual settler's stake in the land and in the public affairs of the colony. Those with an interest in developing North America, whether they were merchants, landowners, or the political authority, united in rejecting a monopolistic approach to colonization as inappropriate to a sector of the English economy that was highly complex in its social requirements and growing rapidly. As a result, the autonomy of the companies tended to yield to the authority of the state, before which all subjects were more equal.

Each of the mainland colonies developed distinct patterns of production, but in their initial period all underwent a similar process of adjustment. Regardless of the unique objectives of any particular group of promoters, the overriding requirement for permanent colonization was an essentially autonomous set of institutions to order the domestic marketplace. In the case of the Massachusetts Bay Colony, the settlers had eliminated the absentee, armchair venturers from their enterprise by controlling the Massachusetts Bay Company themselves and carrying their charter with them to the New World. Hence, from the outset, they had protected themselves from the desires of English investors for colonies to show an immediate profit. Even in the proprietary Maryland colony the principle of colonial autonomy prevailed as Cecilius Calvert (Lord Baltimore), in order to promote the long-term survival of the colony, disposed of his American acres in a highly liberal fashion. In addition, Maryland's original charter called for the creation of a colonial assembly which met as early as 1635 and, by 1650, was able to initiate legislation as well as to approve that proposed by the proprietor. In the Dutch New Amsterdam colony the settlers chose to surrender peacefully to the English in 1664, for the English promised them a large measure of local freedom, assuring that the colony would be open to future immigrants from the Netherlands, that the present settlers would be free to leave, and that Dutch traders would be allowed to ignore the Navigation Acts and thus have free access to New York.

For ultimate prosperity settlers, as in Virginia, had to develop export commodities that were in demand in foreign markets, primarily in England. Some had greater natural endowments than others, but every colony managed to produce a commodity in demand in Europe and thus ensured its survival as a permanent settlement. Virginia and Maryland discovered tobacco—of all the staples produced on the North American mainland, the one in greatest demand in Europe. They were the only two colonies so fortunate. Georgia and South Carolina turned instead to rice and indigo; North Carolina had no choice but to concentrate on exporting naval stores. While religious cohesion enabled the New England communities to grow rapidly during their first years, drawing some 20,000 immigrants by the early 1640s, shipbuilding and trading provided the fundamental source of growth in the long run. However, some localities, such as Plymouth, never participated sufficiently in those activities to prosper. The wealth of the Middle Atlantic colonies came from their provisioning of the West Indian planters with foodstuffs. It was the establishment of an economic base in each successful colony and the development of a decentralized institutional framework, including a competitive marketplace, that permitted the planting of Englishmen and English society in the New World.

NOTES

1. See H. Thomas Johnson, "Cathedral Building and the Medieval Economy," *Explorations in Entrepreneurial History,* 4 (Spring–Summer 1967), 191–210.

2. E. M. Carus-Wilson and Olive Coleman, *England's Export Trade, 1275–1547* (Oxford: Clarendon Press, 1963), pp. 122–123.

3. See E. M. Carus-Wilson, *Medieval Merchant Venturers: Collected Studies* (London: Methuen, 1967). For studies of related developments elsewhere in England see J. N. Bartlett, "Expansion and Decline of York in the Later Middle Ages," *Economic History Review,* 12 (1959), 17–33; E. M. Carus-Wilson, *The Expansion of Exeter at the Close of the Middle Ages* (Exeter: University of Exeter, 1963); Eileen Power and M. M. Postan, *Studies in English Trade in the Fifteenth Century* (London: Routledge and Kegan Paul, 1933); Alwyn A. Ruddock, *Italian Merchants and Shipping in Southampton, 1270–1600* (Southampton: University College, 1951); Maud Sellers, *The York Mercers and Merchant Adventurers* (London: Andrews, 1918).

4. Frédéric Mauro, *Le Portugal et l'Atlantique au XVIIe siècle* (Paris: S.E.V.P.E.N., 1960); Edgar Prestage, *The Portuguese Pioneers* (New York: Barnes and Noble, 1967).

5. On Seville's expansiveness in the sixteenth century see Ruth Pike, *Enterprise and Adventure: The Genoese in Seville and the Opening of the New World* (Ithaca, N.Y.: Cornell University Press, 1966).

6. On the early looting enterprise and its basis in the difficulties of the West Country merchants in Spain see Gordon Connell-Smith, *Forerunners of Drake* (London: Longmans, Green, 1954).

7. On the origins of slavery in North America see below, pp. 42–43; and Edmund S. Morgan, "The Labor Problem at Jamestown, 1607–18," *American Historical Review,* 76 (June 1971), 595–611.

8. The only long-term interest of the Levant–East India group in Virginia was their control of the Magazine, the subsidiary company that had a monopoly of importing and exporting to the colony but did not invest in production in the colony. However, the company dissolved the Magazine in 1619.

9. With the rapid growth of profits from American commerce these new traders, as early as the 1640s, penetrated even the great companies, particularly the East India Company, and began to restructure traditional English commerce on a more competitive basis. And building on their political strength with Parliament, in contrast with the royalist allegiance of the merchant-venturer and Levant–East India establishment, the new merchants began in the 1650s to turn English foreign policy toward an expansion of commercial opportunities in North America at the expense of the Dutch (see Chapter 4). For a discussion of the rise of the Levant–East India traders and their subsequent challenge by

the American traders see Robert Brenner, "The Social Basis of English Commercial Expansion, 1550–1650," *Journal of Economic History,* 32 (March 1972), 361–384.

10. For the suggestion that the increase of the pool of businessmen who were willing to innovate in the organization of production and trade during the sixteenth century was a result of the diffusion of an "achievement norm," reflected in patterns of child rearing and formal education, see Richard H. Brown, "The Achievement Norm and Economic Growth: The Case of Elizabethan England," *Review of Social Economy,* 27 (September 1969), 181–201.

SUGGESTED READINGS

Books

Andrews, Charles M. *The Colonial Period of American History.* Vol I. *The Settlements.* New Haven: Yale University Press, 1934.

Brebner, John B. *The Explorers of North America, 1492–1806.* London: Black, 1933.

Carus-Wilson, E. M. *Medieval Merchant Venturers: Collected Studies.* London: Methuen, 1967.

Cell, Gillian T. *English Enterprise in Newfoundland, 1577–1660.* Toronto: University of Toronto Press, 1969.

Elton, Geoffrey R. *England Under the Tudors.* London: Methuen, 1955.

McNeill, William H. *Plagues and Peoples.* Garden City, N.Y.: Doubleday, 1976.

Morison, Samuel E. *Admiral of the Ocean Sea, A Life of Christopher Columbus.* Boston: Little, Brown, 1942.

———. *The European Discovery of America, the Northern Voyages.* New York: Oxford University Press, 1971.

Parry, John H. *The Age of Reconnaissance, 1415–1650.* London: Weidenfeld and Nicolson, 1963.

Postan, M. M., and E. E. Rich (eds.). *Trade and Industry in the Middle Ages.* Vol. II of *The Cambridge Economic History of Europe.* Cambridge, Eng.: Cambridge University Press, 1952.

Reynolds, Robert L. *Europe Emerges.* Madison, Wis.: University of Wisconsin Press, 1961.

Rich, E. E., and C. H. Wilson. *The Economy of Expanding Europe in the Sixteenth and Seventeenth Centuries.* Vol. IV of *The Cambridge Economic History of Europe.* Cambridge, Eng.: Cambridge University Press, 1967.

Thrupp, Sylvia L. *The Merchant Class of Medieval London, 1300–1500.* Chicago: University of Chicago Press, 1948.

Articles

Brenner, Robert. "The Social Basis of English Commercial Expansion, 1550–1650," *Journal of Economic History,* 32 (March 1972), 361–384.

Morgan, Edmund S. "The Labor Problem at Jamestown, 1607–18," *American Historical Review,* 76 (June 1971), 595–611.

North, Douglass C., and Robert P. Thomas. "An Economic Theory of the Growth of the Western World," *Economic History Review,* 23 (April 1970), 1–17.

❀ 2
Preindustrial Growth
in a Colonial Economy

From the collection of British trading posts, fishing stations, and simple agricultural communities on the mainland of North America developed an economy on the verge of the industrial revolution, shaped by a complex interaction of European and domestic conditions that had prevailed for at least two centuries. The predominating factor of this development was the demand created by European capitalism for the products of colonial enterprise. By the seventeenth century the trading interest of certain European and English ports, including London, Bristol, Plymouth, and Liverpool, had led to a series of New World conquests, particularly in Latin America, and the formation of European outposts designed to provide the mother ports with continuing supplies of colonial goods. In return, those ports shipped the colonies simple manufactured items and provided them with trading and other services. The pattern of trade under the control of trading centers in the mother countries formed a departure from the existing network of world trading relations: instead of a set of exchanges of surpluses of primary products such as fish, fur, timber, wool, and grain among regions of comparable economic bargaining power, trade as Europe expanded overseas was increasingly exchange between economically dominant regions, tending to specialization in simple processing and the provision of services, and less powerful regions—the colonies—tending to specialization in primary production. Within this complementarity of exchange the continuous search for sources of raw materials constituted the driving element; Europeans valued the colonies far less as markets for goods

and services than as provisioners of goods that were in strong demand in Europe.

The export of fish, furs, and agricultural products provided the
basis for American economic expansion during the colonial period.
During the seventeenth and early eighteenth centuries as much as
one-third of American production of goods may have gone into exports. The colonies were new, small, and simple in social organization. Time was required for the growth and development of more
complicated forms of enterprise that would supplement agricultural
exports with manufactured goods and commercial services. During
the colonial period, Americans found they could purchase the services of shippers and middlemen and manufactured goods, particularly textiles and metal goods, from Europeans more cheaply than
they could provide them for themselves. Imports of goods and services from Europe thus furthered American expansion and contributed to enhancing the American standard of living. The colonies
benefited from a transatlantic division of labor that enabled them to
make the most of their abundant lands, forests, and ocean resources
while relying on the more efficient provision of capital, mercantile
services, and manufactured goods by Europeans.

To achieve success as a colonial enterprise settlers first and foremost had to produce commodities that were in strong demand elsewhere in the world, preferably in the large European home market,
and they had to adapt or develop institutions that enabled them to
expand and effectively utilize their stock of land, labor, and capital.
The one region deficient in landed resources, New England, was
fortunate enough to develop a distinctly different capability, that of
managing commerce and all its related functions. Such enterprise,
promising as it was for future development, remained secondary to
the agricultural interest of the colonists.

Products of the forests and the seas remained important exports
throughout the colonial period. As late as 1770 they accounted for
over one-quarter of the value of American exports. Fishing, which
had been so critical to the initial English interest in North America,
grew in importance along northern coasts. Fishermen preserved
mackerel and cod by salting and drying and then sent the best grades
to markets in southern Europe while keeping the lowest grades to
sell to Caribbean sugar plantations. The fishing industry was concentrated in New England, specifically in Massachusetts. (See Figure 2.)
Its significance to that colony is clear; the fishermen of Boston and
the outports accounted for about 90 percent of Massachusetts' exports to Continental Europe and three-quarters of that colony's total
exports to the West Indies at the time of the Revolution. At the end
of the colonial period, fishing accounted for about 10 percent of all

American exports (including those of Newfoundland, Quebec, and the Maritime Provinces).

Whaling was another important maritime industry. It began as a local industry with small boats operating in local waters from many ports in New England and eastern Long Island. But in the eighteenth century, as the supply of whales declined, whalers invested in larger, well-equipped ships that had a wider range and increasingly concentrated their home bases in a few ports, such as New Bedford and Nantucket. Whales yielded a wide variety of products, but most important was whale oil, the most popular fuel oil for lamps.

European demand for furs had contributed to the need for permanent colonies, but the influence of that demand on the develop-

A View of a Stage, also ye manner of Fishing for, Curing & Drying of Cod at NEW FOUND LAND. A. The Habit of the Fishermen. B. The Line. C. The manner of Fishing. D. The Dressers of the Fish. E. The Trough into which they throw the Cod when dressed. F. Salt Boxes. G. The manner of carrying the Cod. H. The Cleansing of the Cod. I. A Press to extract the Oyl from the Cods Liver. K. A Cask to receive the Water and Blood that comes from the Livers. L. another Cask to receive the Oyl. M. The manner of drying the Cod.

CATCHING, DRESSING, AND DRYING CODFISH, 1738. During the fishing season, this industry generated substantial demands for labor.

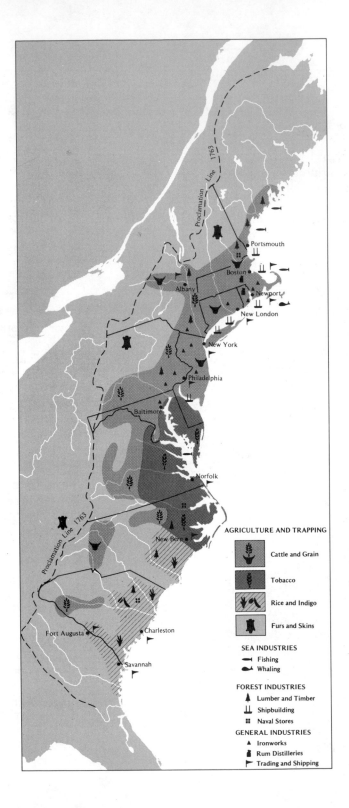

AGRICULTURE AND TRAPPING

	Cattle and Grain
	Tobacco
	Rice and Indigo
	Furs and Skins

SEA INDUSTRIES
Fishing
Whaling

FOREST INDUSTRIES
Lumber and Timber
Shipbuilding
Naval Stores

GENERAL INDUSTRIES
Ironworks
Rum Distilleries
Trading and Shipping

Portsmouth

Boston
Albany
Newport
New London

New York

Philadelphia

Baltimore

Norfolk

New Bern

Fort Augusta
Charleston
Savannah

Proclamation Line 1763

Proclamation Line 1763

ment of those colonies quickly waned. Extensive trapping virtually exhausted New England's fur resources by 1650; fur exports to Britain from the American colonies stagnated by the end of the seventeenth century. However, New York's trade remained vigorous. During all of the seventeenth century furs remained the colony's most important export, despite the growing importance of agriculture, and through the 1720s furs were the only commodities produced in New York that found a market in England. From 1700 to 1750 furs made up nearly 20 percent of all shipped goods (including transshipped West Indian goods) from New York. During that period, England obtained about one-quarter of the furs imported from New York. But New York furs were in relative decline as other New York exports increased more rapidly. Consequently, by 1770 fur exports accounted for just slightly more than 1 percent of all colonial exports. Substantial profits remained to be made from fur trading, however, and large fur trading interests, such as the Hudson's Bay Company, had a great influence on policy governing the disposition of western lands. Nonetheless, by the end of the colonial period the seaboard colonies were unable to use exploitation of fur animals as a significant source of economic expansion.

AGRICULTURAL EXPANSION: THE BASIS OF EMPIRE

The quest for fish and fur determined the character of English interest in the mainland of North America only in the early period of settlement, and only then did the colonies rely primarily on these exports. The powerful European demands for agricultural products, joined with the ability of Europeans in the New World to take advantage of the factor of production in greatest supply (and, therefore, the least expensive)—land—soon made agriculture the leading element in the growth of the North American colonies.

Patterns of Production: Regional Differentiation

The colonial exports that found the most buoyant markets in Europe were agricultural products of tropical or subtropical origin. Within the British colonial sphere sugar exports met the most dynamic markets in England, with tobacco, rice, and indigo next. But only colonists in the West Indies succeeded in cultivating sugar for export, with the result that Jamaica, the Bahamas, and certain of the Leeward Islands served as the focus of England's empire in the West, while the mainland colonies occupied a lesser position.[1] Thus, the

FIGURE 2: *Distribution of Colonial Production*

mainland colonies expanded less rapidly than they might have with a more favorable physical endowment, and they most certainly had to be innovative in a search for avenues of endeavor that would provide more vigorous growth. To become more than exporters of subtropical staples the mainland colonies turned to supplying West Indian plantations with foodstuffs, a function deemed highly desirable by the English, and, ultimately, to exporting grain products to southern Europe—a colonial kind of enterprise, although one theoretically in violation of the spirit of nationalistic mercantilism, which emphasized the virtues of a closed empire.

Success in meeting English demands for agricultural goods varied markedly among the mainland colonies. The ones closest to the ideal colonial model were those in the southern zone; the colonies from Maryland and Virginia south through Georgia were best equipped to provide England with commodities having strong European markets, especially the Chesapeake Bay area, including Maryland and Virginia, which specialized in tobacco production, and the Charleston area of South Carolina, which cultivated rice and, after the early 1740s, to a lesser extent, indigo. However, despite their highly commercial production, southern farmers produced a large but unmeasured volume of diversified crops for domestic consumption. In fact, corn grown on both large plantations and small farms was the South's chief crop—at least in terms of acreage. Almost all plantations in the upper South, despite their specialization in the staple crops, provided beef and pork to the Middle Atlantic colonies and both livestock and flour to the West Indies.

Tobacco was the most significant southern export; although grown in only a few counties, by 1750 it accounted for at least half of the value of all exports from the mainland. Tobacco exports were always the basis of the growth of Virginia and Maryland, but their most dynamic influence came after 1720. Before that the Chesapeake planters experienced grave difficulty in estimating future European demands for their tobacco and in obtaining labor in the face of the scarcity of freemen and the ability of the wealthier West Indian sugar planters to outbid tobacco planters for slaves. As West Indian sugar production soared in the 1660s, expansion of tobacco production slowed; by the eighteenth century the Chesapeake industry was stagnant. Nonetheless, by the outbreak of the Revolution, tobacco shipments from the Chesapeake had tripled from their 1725 level.

The success of the Chesapeake planters after the 1720s is a case study of the sensitivity of the colonial economy to European conditions and the crucial role played by European demand and European commercial services in encouraging colonial agricultural expansion.

The crucial element was the dynamic growth of the French demand for tobacco. The most populous nation in Europe, France demanded massive amounts of tobacco but lacked adequate sources of supply within its empire. Turning to purchases of tobacco from the British colonies, which grew as much tobacco as the rest of the Western world, France created a national tobacco monopoly—the United General Farms—designed to bargain effectively for low prices and raise revenue for the state.

The quest of French tobacco monopolists for American tobacco coincided with the efforts of middlemen in the Chesapeake to improve commercial services. Prior to the 1720s either independent merchants residing in the Chesapeake or larger planters who shipped tobacco themselves controlled tobacco exports. The larger planters, maintaining ownership of the tobacco until it was sold by London, Bristol, and Liverpool merchant houses, had severe difficulty in coping with price fluctuations. In contrast, the local independent merchants lacked sufficient capital to compete in this direct trade to Britain and consequently traded with the West Indies and southern Europe. Beginning in the 1720s, however, a group of shrewd Scottish merchants, based in Glasgow and taking advantage of the upsurge in French demand, reorganized the Chesapeake trade. They established chains of permanent stores in the Chesapeake and bought their tobacco directly from planters. They offered planters a full range of services, collecting tobacco in central warehouses, supplying plantations with European imports, extending credit, introducing inspection systems to control tobacco quality, taking over bad accounts, guaranteeing markets, and developing a rudimentary futures system—a market for commodities to be delivered at a future time—to stabilize prices and incomes. With their efficiencies, the Scots undercut English merchant houses and obtained the lion's share of the French business. The French, in turn, were willing to pay cash for guaranteed supplies of cheap tobacco, and this cash allowed the Scots to introduce further efficiencies. As a result of their efficiencies the Glasgow merchants quadrupled their trade in tobacco between the late 1730s and the early 1750s. By the 1750s they were providing the French monopoly with 40 percent of tobacco, in contrast with the 12 percent provided by the English.

Most Chesapeake tobacco continued to go to Great Britain and the West Indies; the French took only about one-quarter of American production. But the impact of the French monopoly on the Chesapeake was proportionately much greater. The French demand was highly buoyant and dependable. Consequently, the Scottish merchants could buy large volumes of tobacco, even of lower quality, without fear of overbuying. The French demand accelerated the

PRODUCING TOBACCO. Tobacco production involved a complex set of stages, including pressing, curing, storing, inspecting, and transporting.

extension of production onto new, more fertile land in the Piedmont as Scottish merchants by-passed the older, well-established planters along the tidewater to deal directly with smaller planters in the interior. Moreover, the French demand maintained older, less efficient areas in active production. And the cash payments of the French carried the vast credit structure that supported the tobacco economy. The expansion of credit generated by French demand drew subsistence settlers into the market economy and enhanced their economic welfare. It reduced the need for savings to protect farmers from disasters, allowed farmers to bid more successfully for slaves, and enabled them to reach the market and the larger incomes it provided. Thus, the French demand and the services of the Scottish merchants sustained the expansion of the tobacco economy after the 1720s. It was an expansion that would continue until the French Revolution, when the leading tobacco monopolists would be guillotined, the monopoly abolished, and the planting of tobacco in France legalized.[2]

The Middle Atlantic colonies—New York, New Jersey, Pennsylvania, and Delaware—did not attain the commercial success of the Southern colonies. General farming in small grains and livestock predominated, with home consumption far more important than in the South. However, New Jersey and Pennsylvania produced wheat surpluses for export from virtually the first years of settlement, and their agricultural sectors were greatly stimulated in the eighteenth century, when the international demand for wheat surged. Their trade with the West Indies, an area in need of food as a result of its specialization in sugar, was vigorous, and in the 1760s trade with southern Europe, especially Portugal and Spain, gave an additional boost to wheat production. Exports of wheat, flour, and bread made the Middle Atlantic colonies the breadbasket of the West Indies as well as a provisioner of southern Europe, thus adding significantly to the development of a region that was unable to produce the tropical crops most in demand in Europe. By the 1760s colonial exports of bread and flour, primarily from the Middle Atlantic region, exceeded those of any crop except tobacco.

Of the three groups of colonies, New England was the least successful in developing an agricultural sector that conformed to imperial expectations, despite the fact that relatively more immigrants to New England had a useful background in farming. With an inhospitable climate and land, and despite experiments with virtually every crop that might have served as a staple, New England failed to develop any crop in extensive international demand. New Englanders adapted wheat successfully during the seventeenth century, but a fungus, the black stem rust, destroyed its future for almost all of the region. Corn production predominated by 1700, its short growing season and high yield per acre suiting it to the more hostile New England environment. The cultivation of other grains, apples, and vegetables and the raising of livestock for food, clothing, and transport rounded out the pattern of general farming. Commercial agriculture was centered in only two river valleys: the Narragansett, in Rhode Island, where livestock production, including horses for powering West Indian sugar mills, prevailed, and the Connecticut, where grain, along with livestock and dairy products, provided a modest agricultural export base. As early as 1650 New England had limited surpluses of cattle, horses, and salted meat available for export.

The uneven success of the colonists in developing commercial agriculture implied that they acquired the resources for production in different ways and utilized them in different combinations. However, relatively speaking, all the colonies faced essentially the same scarcities of human and material resources. They all possessed abundant supplies of land, although that land varied in quality and, when defined broadly to include the entire physical environment, varied in its capacity to sustain crops that were in European demand. Also, all the colonies had to deal with deficiencies of labor, capital, and, during the early period of settlement, knowledge of the most appropriate modes of production. Thus, during the seventeenth century, colonists in all regions made quite similar experiments in developing staple crops; the British planters tried tobacco planting in Barbados while another group experimented with the crop in Plymouth. Most of their experiments, including attempts at silk and tropical fruits, failed everywhere, and to a very large extent the colonists had to rely on the skills and techniques of the native Indian population for developing successful first crops: among others, corn, tobacco, potatoes, pumpkins, squash, peanuts, beans, and tomatoes were all of Indian origin—as, indeed, were perhaps more than half of the crops in cultivation in the United States in the twentieth century.[3]

Technology and the Land

Although the colonists exploited, in a fairly costless fashion, the knowledge of the Indian population, they failed to improve European agricultural techniques in any significant way. By the middle of the eighteenth century some farmers, especially the Germans and English in Pennsylvania and the English in Rhode Island, had introduced fertilizers, more-careful crop rotation, and improved livestock husbandry. However, these innovations made virtually no impact on common practice. Perhaps the colonists' most telling shortcoming was their lack of interest in the selective breeding of native plants

—especially corn, tobacco, and potatoes. Further, the tools and tillage of tobacco culture hardly changed in the eighteenth century: as late as the 1760s, only one farmer in five used a plow. Such interest as there was in improving agricultural technique and in adapting methods of intensive, land-saving European cultivation rested with the educated elite. As a result, neither per-capita nor per-acre crop production registered significant gains as a result of technological change during the eighteenth century.

Agricultural historians have often criticized this lack of technological advance, judging the colonists poor farmers by European standards of the day. Specifically, the colonists have been scored for their "wasteful" use of land, for their encouragement of "soil exhaustion." Such criticism, however, ignores the fact that many of the "primitive" techniques used by the colonists were appropriate to the American environment. For example, it is highly dubious that the plow could have been of any great value to the first generation of American farmers. In cultivating a sandy loam soil under conditions of heavy rainfall, their main problem was the leaching of minerals; plowing and clean cultivation would have destroyed more rapidly the natural humus and weeds, which held minerals initially. Also, plowing was impractical on new lands until old roots had decayed and, in the piedmont areas, plowing encouraged erosion.[4] Further, the girdling and burning of trees, criticized for promoting erosion, provided mineral supplements, especially potassium, in addition to providing potash, a cash crop, during the first season of settlement. Instead of improving agriculture on the European model, the colonists chose to expand production—to develop a commercial agriculture—in the most economical way available to them. Lacking the necessity imposed by the European environment to use land efficiently, they took advantage of the great availability of land and looked for ways to use labor more effectively. One approach was to develop institutions that would facilitate the exploitation of an increasing, flexible supply of new, fertile land to replace that which had been "wasted." In short, conserving labor and capital brought higher returns than conserving land would have.

Systems of Land Distribution

The abundance of land was not just a physical fact but an institutional reality as well. Partly in response to the economic incentive provided by large quantities of land, colonists created systems of land distribution that permitted them to develop new land rapidly. Their powerful economic motivation was bound up with a pervasive social factor derived from Europe: landownership as a determiner of social status and power. Moreover, liberalizing the conditions of land possession was an effective tool for attracting settlement to a labor-scarce economy.

Consequently, the institutional development of land distribution in all the colonies shared a trend toward increasing openness and opportunity.[5] Initially the king had ultimate discretion, stemming from the rights of discovery, over the distribution of land, and the granting of land was tied closely to crown policy; royal grants required an oath of allegiance to the king and a stipulation of the recipient's obligations in return for the land grant. Because these grants were made primarily to the large trading companies, this period, varying in length from colony to colony, can be called the trading-company era. After initial settlement, however, the distribution of land became more closely associated with the specific interests of the intermediaries, who having received crown grants and being less responsive to crown policy, devised provisions for the development of the land to fit local conditions. This second phase was one of power granting, or the placing of great powers of land distribution and government in the hands of settlement agencies and leading colonists. During the Stuart Restoration (1660–1688) the crown reduced the power of the intermediaries, but throughout the remainder of the colonial period, power granting characterized royal policy. During that extended period of decentralized control over land distribution, land policy moved toward greater homogeneity and liberality, making land more available to a growing and dispersing population, regardless of the form of colonial political organization.

Within the fundamental similarity of land systems there were differences among the large groups of colonies, differences that reflected variations in community structure, the availabilities of good lands, and agricultural opportunities.

In the Southern colonies, which contained the greatest abundance of good agricultural land, possessed the most fruitful opportunities for commercial agriculture, and lacked strong communal institutions, the forms of land distribution came to be the most liberal. In the seventeenth century the commonest form was the headright, which meant the extension of control over large tracts to individuals, with grants as large as 10,000 acres not unusual, but the average being 300 to 500 acres.

When the production of tobacco became more profitable after 1720, the average size of landholdings tended to increase as did the number of large planters. But during the eighteenth century, in contrast to much of the seventeenth century, acquisition of large holdings came to have less to do with political connections than with the ability to purchase land in the marketplace. The initial period of land grants undoubtedly tended to create a quasi-aristocracy based in land, but a vigorous land market soon provided the most common means for the distribution of southern land among large and small planters alike. Land sales were either to individual settlers for immediate occupancy or to land dealers who resold parcels to settlers. In Virginia, the largest colony, the basis of this market was the provision by the House of Burgesses, in 1699, that the granting of land for the purpose of attracting settlers should cease and that as much of the land as possible should be disposed of by sale. In 1705 the legislature set the price of land and introduced the notions of prior survey, a grid system of surveying to order the disposition of public land, and land offices to conduct sales. Anyone wishing to purchase land would obtain a certificate and turn it over to a surveyor who would lay out the land and make a report to a land secretary who would then issue a patent and receive payment.

In the seventeenth century, southern grants commonly avoided swamps and rough country. While this practice promoted a more productive use of the land, it frequently resulted in irregularly shaped grants that were not always contiguous, leaving pockets of undistributed land. Boundaries thus often lacked sharp definition, continually complicating the transfer of property and engendering social costs (not the least of which were lawyers' fees). But the refinement of the marketplace resulting from the liberalizing of land policy lent a large measure of order to land distribution. Indeed, when the newly independent national government sought to develop a program for the orderly allotment of western lands in the Land Ordinance of 1784, it drew heavily on southern experience. The principles of prior survey and title, rectangular survey, and decentralized land sales emerged from the unfolding of the land-tenure system in the South as well as from precedents established in New England.

The Middle Atlantic colonies shared a good measure of the expansiveness of the Southern colonies, holding an ample supply of land and realizing solid commercial opportunities. Both as cause and effect, those colonies developed generally flexible land systems, similar in form to the South's. The fundamental legal distinction arose from the more general status of the Middle Atlantic colonies as proprietary rather than royal (Pennsylvania and Delaware until 1776, New Jersey until 1702, and New York until 1685). Thus the proprietor rather than the crown, a trading company, or a colonial legislature made grants of land. But as in the Southern colonies of the seventeenth century, the grants tended to be large and to reinforce the development of an indigenous aristocracy. In Pennsylvania, for example, the family of William Penn retained the larger parcels of land, and in New York the patroonships granted under Dutch rule persisted, carried forth by the English under both proprietary and royal government. However, as in Virginia, the colonies to the north liberalized their land systems under the pressure of expansion. The proprietors made generous grants to attract immigrants, allowed the quitrents due them as owners to go largely uncollected, and frequently used headrights, on the southern pattern, to stimulate settlement. Further, the proprietary goverment granted rights of preemption, or the right to first purchase, to those settlers, especially Germans, who merely squatted on undeveloped land. The headrights, along with preempted land, formed the basis of a vigorous marketplace in land which, with the creation of a land office in 1769, Pennsylvania organized along the line of Virginia's. But, because of the importance of family-farm production of wheat in the Middle Atlantic colonies, the landholdings exchanged on the market were smaller and more evenly distributed than in the Southern colonies. Only in New York, especially in the Hudson River valley, did a restrictive land system retard agricultural growth; elsewhere in the region, the land system moved in a decidedly liberal direction with access to land becoming even easier than in the South.

The New England land system, although fundamentally similar in its evolution to the other two, exhibited certain distinguishing characteristics. Without the imposition of royal control the initial pattern of land distribution was haphazard. The Massachusetts Bay Company made large land grants to private parties while others in Massachusetts and Rhode Island occupied land without title, or after having gone through the Anglo-Saxon pretense of purchasing it, with a transfer of title from the Indians. After 1635 the Massachusetts legislature granted land to town corporations (analogous to the grants of the Virginia Company or the Pennsylvania proprietors), and those grants became the most important vehicle for parceling out land.

The town corporations, led by town proprietors, organized parishes, or communities, frequently already in existence, by scheduling a program of land occupation, overseeing the division of land, and establishing a system of agriculture based upon not only home plots but also community fields, grazing land, and woodlots. The town proprietors distributed the land unequally—initially, largely according to the extent of the grantee's participation in the organization and development of the town; later, according to the size of the original home plot. Although fairly large accumulations resulted, they were far smaller than those in either the Southern or Middle Atlantic colonies. In Dedham, Massachusetts, for example, the average member of the first community received a holding of 150 acres from the common land.[6]

In the course of the seventeenth century the communal order eroded. Increasingly towns divided their communal arable land among smaller groups, and, finally, among individuals. By the eighteenth century New England was held largely in individual parcels, but the transition was slow, probably slower than the trend toward openness elsewhere, its pace depending on the course of marriages, barters, and numerous purchases. It was, for instance, some fifty years after the founding of Andover, Massachusetts, in 1630, before the familiar family-farm pattern emerged; not until the 1660s did some members of the community begin moving their homes from the nuclear village and the town begin selling small (20-acre) plots of land.[7] Despite the close control of the distribution and use of land by local elites and a somewhat rigid social structure, New England did develop, like the other mainland colonies, a set of liberal institutions for the distribution of land. It released its communal fields to individuals, provided for the inclusion of new settlers in the community, and, in the process, created a market, albeit a highly structured one, for the allocation of land. Most striking in the utilization of land in New England was not the forms but the results. The sharp limitations imposed by the environment on commercial agriculture in combination with a rapidly growing population that had easy access to the land brought about a rapid decline in the average holding of land. By 1786 the average accumulation in Dedham, a typical community, amounted to only 50 acres, in contrast to its seventeenth-century average of 150 acres, and was no larger than that in comparable English and French villages of the eighteenth century. This dramatic increase in the man-land ratio represented significant pressure on the arable land of New England and suggested the potential for the rapid swarming of migrants from that region onto new lands to the west.

The Scarcity of Labor

Although transplanted Europeans discovered an abundance of land on the mainland of North America, they faced an acute shortage of labor to unlock the wealth of the continent. However, the wide availability of land was a powerful magnet for attracting Europeans and for importing Africans and provided the basis for sustaining a rapidly expanding population. Both immigration and the reproduction rate of the established population brought about a growth in population and the labor force far greater than in the European zone of the Atlantic economy. Still, labor, both skilled and unskilled, remained scarcer and more expensive than in contemporary Europe. While clearly handicapping the growth of American manufacturing, the scarcity was insufficiently acute to preclude the development of a remarkably buoyant, market-oriented agriculture.

The colonies relied in varying degrees on reproduction and immigration to relieve labor shortages, with the Southern colonies and even more so the Middle Atlantic colonies making chief use of immigrants. In New England, where the rate of immigration fell off rapidly after the Cromwellian revolution, family labor predominated. However, immigration and reproduction failed to provide enough labor to supply the highly commercial Southern colonies; consequently they turned to sources of involuntary labor, primarily forcibly acquired Africans.

During the eighteenth century the commitment to slavery grew strong, especially after the demand for tobacco increased rapidly during the 1720s and southern planters were able to compete with West Indian sugar planters in the slave market. In 1720 only 25 percent of all planters in the Chesapeake region were slaveholders but by 1770 over half owned slaves. By the time of the Revolution the slave population amounted to well over one-third of the total population of the South, as the exceptionally heavy demands of the rice planters for unskilled labor came to reinforce the requirements of the tobacco growers. At the same time, the number of slaves supplied by American and European traders increased rapidly, beginning in the third quarter of the seventeenth century.

Economic conditions throughout much of North America appeared conducive to the spread of slavery. The great scarcity of labor and the wide availability of land existed not only in the Southern colonies but in the Middle Atlantic colonies as well. Yet, while white men owned slaves in all the colonies and almost 15 percent of the black population, most of which was slave, lived north of Maryland in 1780, slavery spread extensively only in the Southern colonies. Clearly the employment of southern slaves in crafts and in grain cultivation suggests their potential for more northerly employment. But no satisfactory, complete explanation exists for the localization of slavery in the South. A highly plausible answer would include the higher costs of clothing and sheltering slaves in the more northerly colonies and the less expansive character of agriculture in the North for much of the colonial period. Both these economic facts would have placed northern landowners at a disadvantage in bidding for slaves. In addition, northern landowners and craftsmen disagreed as to the desirability of slaveowning, resulting in a failure of government to support slavery in the North. That disunity could have arisen from some combination of not only discouragement over the high price of slaves and fears that wealthy employers would widen their competitive edge by being able to employ slaves in great numbers but also racial phobias and hatreds, along with doubts of conscience fed by the efforts of Quakers and certain Baptist and Methodist clergymen in the eighteenth century.

The Scarcity of Capital

The scarcity of capital proved less constraining to the growth of commercial agriculture than did the scarcity of labor. Capital was more scarce in the colonies than in Europe and more scarce than land in North America, but an abundance of capital resources was not necessary for agricultural expansion. Where, as a result of inadequate physical resources, agriculture could under no circumstances provide more than the sustenance of healthy life, the colonists found their own energies a sufficient source of capital goods. They fashioned their tools themselves, raised their own farm buildings, and contributed their labor, in lieu of taxes, to the building of community roads. The more commercial farm enterprises often also provided their own capital services, but they usually had additional, more sophisticated needs for capital. Beyond the capital necessary to satisfy the rather simple technological requirements of agriculture everywhere, the larger colonial farmers demanded extensive short-term financing of the marketing of current crops and the production of future crops. But where commercial agriculture for foreign markets was economical, the necessary capital was forthcoming. In the central linkages between Great Britain and colonial staple producers, commercial credit flowed readily from British mercantile houses to southern planters, especially after the rise of the Glasgow interest in American tobacco. In the coastal trade and the traffic with the West Indies and southern Europe, capital, also of a short-term variety, originated with the colonial merchants who specialized in exporting of products of temperate America. One of the reasons Philadelphia and New York merchants were strongly attached to domestic monetary stability, much more so than their Boston counterparts, was their financial stake in the agricultural interior. To protect their creditor position those merchants opposed inflationary policies that would diminish the value of their assets, while, in contrast, their Boston cousins, along with economic elites in the staple-producing areas, were absorbed in easing the burden of their debtor position, with respect to the British.[8]

A shortage of capital by no means restricted the pace and character of colonial growth. A strong trading tradition and considerable institutional sophistication provided adequately for the needs for short-term credit. However, the British mercantile world probably would have been unable to meet any significant demands for long-term capital. But commercial farmers would not require such amounts until they passed through an industrial revolution of their own—a development that was, at the end of the colonial period, at least two generations distant.

In summary, by the eighteenth century the mainland colonies had not only established a sustenance agriculture but had also developed a vigorous commercial sector. Commercial production expanded in direct response to strong European demands for tobacco, rice, indigo, and wheat, and, secondarily, to the West Indian need for foodstuffs. This commercialization primarily involved the Southern and Middle Atlantic colonies, with the tobacco market consistently the most important. Their responses to the European demands succeeded because of the favorable physiography in the Southern and Middle Atlantic regions, the abundance of land, the most important resource for agriculture, the increasing availability of labor (as a result of a fertile and highly mobile population, European immigration, and the introduction and elaboration of African slavery), and the strong interest of British commercial groups in extending the necessary short-term capital.

MANUFACTURING: EXPANSION AND BRITISH COMPETITION

Under the economic logic of empire, which fostered the complementary development of colony and metropolis, the colonists could hardly compete with British manufacturers in reaching the wider Atlantic marketplace. Imperial policy might well have inhibited an industrial revolution if British rule had extended into the nineteenth century, but during the colonial period the basic determinants of the development of manufacturing were those more narrowly economic —the extent of the marketplace and the availability of appropriate resources, both human and material.

The only industry in which the colonists obtained significant competitive success, shipbuilding, began in Massachusetts when the Puritan immigration brought master builders to Boston, Charlestown, Salem, Newbury, and Ipswich. By 1660 the plentifulness of oak and pine had made the construction of large ships for export to the English market a thriving industry. By 1698 well over half of all vessels owned in London and registered to trade in Massachusetts were built in Boston or Charlestown on direct orders from overseas shipowners. In 1784 a Bristol merchant estimated that almost one-third of all British-owned ships had been built in the colonies. Also, the colonies themselves provided a substantial market for ships. New England, for example, had a large fleet by 1698—as many as 2,000 vessels, exclusive of fishing boats, virtually all of them of colonial origin. Indeed, the domestic market probably outweighed the overseas market for most of the colonial period; yet the latter was of significant, growing strength. Between 1697 and 1714 almost 30 percent of the tonnage constructed in Massachusetts had its destination in overseas British ports. By 1771, Massachusetts shipwrights were selling as much as 60 percent of their tonnage abroad.

New England—especially Boston and Charlestown—was the focus of this industry, although the shipwrights toiled in Baltimore, New York, and Philadelphia as well. Shipbuilding provided an early stimulus to Boston's growth; at the same time, the related production of naval stores (pitch, tar, resin, turpentine, hemp, masts, yards, and bowsprits) in New England and the South stimulated dynamic, resource-based activities, thus providing considerable employment. The heavy reliance of shipbuilders on forest products was, in fact, the basis for the success of the industry. The costs of raw materials to colonial producers of ships, who had access to abundant timber close to the tidewater, were far less than to shipwrights in Great Britain, who had to import timber products from the Baltic. Indeed, from the outset the English, through the Navigation Acts, encouraged shipbuilding on American shores to take advantage of low raw-material costs and to promote self-sufficiency within the empire. They also allowed experienced shipwrights to immigrate freely to America. Despite the influx of skilled workers, labor costs remained higher in North America than in Britain, but the cheapness of raw materials enabled colonial manufacturers to build ships at about two-thirds of the expense incurred in Britain.[9]

The success of the shipbuilding industry was unusual. In most industries the colonists lacked an advantage in raw-material costs sufficient to offset high labor costs, particularly of skilled labor, and were consequently unable to develop an export market. For instance, iron production, a more typical industry, had no edge over its counterpart in the mother country and failed to find a significant foreign outlet for its products anywhere in the Atlantic community.

The domestic market for the colonial iron industry, however, was quite large; with the high costs of transporting iron and iron products across the Atlantic, colonial producers operated behind a natural tariff barrier which protected against British competition. Growth in the colonial industry was quite impressive in that it kept pace with the expansion of population and agriculture. Beginning in 1644 with Governor John Winthrop and his works at Lynn, Massachusetts, colo-

Construction in Philadelphia of a frigate that fought in the Tripolitan War (1803). Shipbuilding expertise contributed to the new nation's naval power.

nists produced crude and wrought iron. The former, pig or cast iron, was used in fashioning pots, kettles, and pans and the wrought iron was applied to the manufacture of edged tools. The furnaces were small-scale and were operated by a handful of skilled laborers; they produced for only a limited local market. As the population expanded, so did the number of furnaces. Pennsylvania led the pace for the better part of the eighteenth century, as the fastest-growing colony and as the colony most successful in attracting skilled immigrants. By 1700 the American colonies produced about 1,500 tons of iron annually, or about 2 percent of world production. By the eve of the Revolution, colonial iron production for the domestic market reached a high of 15 percent of world production, a proportion unequaled until much later, toward the mid-nineteenth century. The advances made in the British iron industry in the last quarter of the eighteenth century enabled British producers to overcome high transport costs with productivity gains, to penetrate American markets, and to dampen the expansion of the less advanced American producers.

The success of the colonial iron industry shows how manufacturing activity could thrive even without the foundation of an industrial revolution. Although production was either in very small-scale factories, as in iron manufacture, or, in the case of the textile industry, largely in households, output was buoyant. The level of production depended upon the demand created by the collection of local markets, the amount of skilled labor available, and the degree of protection from lower-cost foreign producers. Because of the predominance of handicraft labor, the resources of the colonists themselves, particularly the colonial merchants, were usually sufficient to finance the vast range of manufacturing, including the shipbuilding industry. Town and colony governments made loans to craftsmen, exempted their property from taxation, and granted them bounties. But these subsidies appear to have been far less important than private capital. The higher price of capital in the colonies, in contrast to that in Britain, proved not to be an important cost differential. The British overcame the high cost of transport and overwhelmed colonial producers only in the Southern colonies, where the rewards for specialization in agriculture reduced the capital available for manufacturing and where the skilled immigrants, so advantageous to preindustrial manufacture, found the social environment created by slavery inhospitable. Outside of the South, the geographic distribution of production often followed the distribution of population. (See Figure 3 for the example of glassmaking.) Each colonial industry—iron, textiles, flour milling, rum distilling, hat making, glass fabrication, brickmaking, or paper manufacture, to mention the most important—produced a large, sustained volume of goods, given the size of the domestic market, thus demonstrating that vigorous manufacturing activity was profitable in the preindustrial economy.

PATTERNS OF COMMUNICATIONS AND EXCHANGE

Transportation and Commerce

Transporation and commerce on the North American mainland both reflected and shaped the fundamental structure and performance of the internal colonial economy. Like manufacturing activity and most agricultural production for domestic consumption, internal transportation and commerce were local in focus. A central element in this pattern of restriced commerce was road transportation that was even more primitive than in western Europe. It prevented organization of widely scattered local markets, limited extensive, lengthy exchanges within colonies to those communities that could communicate over water, and, in particular, made transport by road between

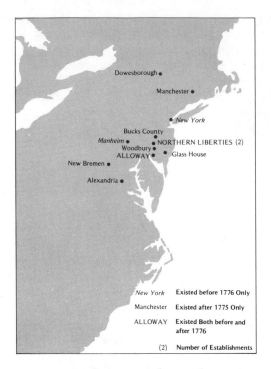

FIGURE 3: *Distribution of Glassworks, 1760–1790*

the tidewater and the back country extremely expensive. As a result of the failure of land transport to improve during the colonial period, the organization of domestic trade did not change, with the exception of the penetration of the Scottish merchants into the tobacco interior. The bulk of goods that were exchanged internally was transported only short distances and, to a large extent, traded, often through barter, by storekeepers in "general stores."

Ocean transportation, on the other hand, improved markedly, providing an institutional basis for expanded international and intercolonial communication, and perhaps even making possible increases in North American productivity. Improvement sprang not so much from technological change (the first truly significant such development was the introduction of the clipper ship to America in the 1830s), but from improvements in market organization and the British rise to naval supremacy in the Western Hemisphere. Both factors permitted shippers to employ smaller crews and more limited armaments, to spend less time laying over in port, and to enjoy lower insurance costs. With ship size, seamen's wages, shipbuilding costs, and the speed of ships remaining roughly stable throughout the colonial period, overall productivity of ocean shipping increased 1.35 percent per year, on an average, during the one hundred years prior to the Revolution. Thus, on some routes, the colonists could ship more than twice as many goods, in physical terms, for the same price in 1775 as in 1675.[10] Declining transportation costs brought the corners of the empire into closer contact, made clearer the comparative advantages of the various trading zones, advanced regional specialization and the division of labor, permitted output to increase, and may well have raised living standards throughout the empire. Most important, increasing productivity in trade tied new, growing regions more tightly to the market economy and swiftly augmented the demand for labor and, consequently, the returns to labor in those outlying regions. The extension of international and intercolonial commerce, then, served as a dynamic element in the expansion and differentiation of the colonies.

Ocean trade for the most part was dominated by a small body of merchants located in the larger ports that maintained close commercial ties to the mother country and that were rather unspecialized in their trading activities. In fact, the degree of specialization was so slight that such merchants failed to comprise a coherent group with well-defined, common interests. Merchants often combined wholesaling and retailing. The Scottish firms in Virginia, for example, although engaged primarily in the marketing of tobacco and goods of European manufacture, also handled country goods, operated cooperages to pack the tobacco for shipment, and themselves owned plantations. For that matter, larger planters frequently served as middlemen, not only in local economies but in the foreign marketing of their tobacco as well. Other large merchants were manufacturers too. The Brown family of Providence, for instance, primarily involved in the whale-oil trade and the supplying of Narragansett Bay horses to the West Indies, diversified into the production of pig iron and candles. The whaling activities of the Browns provided oil for the manufacture of sperm candles, which they in turn marketed in the mainland colonies and the West Indies. Another example was the New York merchant Peter T. Curtenius, the Browns' pig-iron agent, who combined general mercantile business with an extensive ironworks for processing pig.[11]

Despite their overall lack of specialization, the colonial merchants did develop considerable specialization within the realm of their transatlantic connections and thereby increased the efficiency of commercial services, contributing to the expansion of trade and production. In particular the concept of the colonial merchant as a highly diversified trader, tramping from port to port in triangles or even shifting polygons of trade, has proved to be incorrect. To the contrary, colonial merchants succeeded in establishing shuttle routes that created a trading pattern of links between two points, with ownership of the vessels resting in the home region, either Great Britain or the colonies. (The colonies dominated in the coastal trade, the trade between Great Britain and the Northern colonies, and the southern European trade. British merchants, however, controlled trade with the staple-exporting Southern colonies and dominated in the West Indian trade.) In limiting ship movements to shuttle patterns, colonial merchants sought to reduce several sources of cost and risk. For one thing, even though they spread ties of kinship throughout their transatlantic networks, sending a nephew as supercargo, or a son as ship's captain, or a cousin as resident agent, they were still insufficiently protected against unexpected, rapid market reversals. Concentrating on a few markets and using shuttle traffic maximized contact and speeded communications between armchair merchants and their agents. The advantage of centralized control reinforced the domination of trade routes by home ports. At the same time these shuttle movements reduced the high cost of skilled labor by allowing merchants to discharge crews during layovers in home ports, rather than having to maintain them in a series of outlying ports. Such savings were particularly evident in the trade between Britain and the Chesapeake as a result of the effort of the Scottish merchants to make their services more efficient and less costly. Consequently, Virginia tobacco production expanded further, thereby encouraging even more intense commercial specialization.

In creating their own sphere of interest in the intercolonial trade and the southern Europe market, the North American merchants consequently provided the income base for the expansion of port cities and promoted the expansion of agricultural production. The commercial sector in the leading cities of the colonies created demands for goods and services that stimulated the growth of those cities and naturally resulted in heightened demands for the agricultural products of their hinterlands. The coastal trade grew in volume until, by the second quarter of the eighteenth century, it was as great as the ocean trade, and the southern European trade provided a source of rapid commercial expansion during the third quarter. The loci of the impact of this expansionary force were Philadelphia, Boston, New York, and Baltimore. Quite apart from the development of an agricultural export sector, the growth of these cities, by the end of the colonial period, had become in itself, because of the specialization of the ports in commerce, a strongly expansive force in colonial society. Rapidly growing colonies usually contained not only a vigorous primary sector but intense commercial activity as well.

Throughout the colonial period (and very far beyond) Americans conducted most of their Atlantic trading with Great Britain. However, until the last quarter of the seventeenth century, British trade was small in absolute terms, reflecting the initial difficulties faced by the colonists in developing staple products for the metropolitan market. Only with the growth in the tobacco trade after 1675 did trade with England increase rapidly. By the 1690s tobacco accounted for about two-thirds of colonial exports to England, with at least half of those tobacco exports reexported for the European market. The tobacco-trade bonanza shifted the balance of trade during the last quarter of the seventeenth century to one decidedly favorable for the colonists; the average annual colonial sales to England at the end of the century were almost £400,000 as contrasted with comparable purchases in the English market of slightly less than £350,000. In the eighteenth century that trade with England continued to be dynamic, but the balance of trade with England again shifted from a slightly favorable position in the first half of the century to a clearly unfavorable excess of imports by the fifth and sixth decades of the century.

Regional variations within the general trends of Anglo-American trade reveal the significant differences in the ability of the colonies to conform to the expectations of empire. In the Southern colonies the volume of English trade was much larger than elsewhere, accounting for roughly 80 percent of exports to Britain and just under 50 percent of imports from the mother country during the colonial period. The South's favorable balance of trade with England lasted much longer than did the colonies' overall, although a reversal eventually appeared there too, and by the 1760s the southern balance had become unfavorable, due in part to strong increases in per-capita imports, including imports of slaves.

As indicated, the Middle Atlantic colonies had rapidly growing demands for English imports, but with the exception of New York's furs, developed no export commodity that had significant demand in Great Britain, and their balance of trade with England became increasingly unfavorable throughout the eighteenth century. As per-capita consumption of imported manufactured goods increased, imports expanded far beyond exports to England. By the 1760s Middle Atlantic imports of British goods were almost seven times as large as exports, which themselves amounted to less than 10 percent of all colonial exports to England.

New England's position with respect to the mother country was similar to that of the Middle Atlantic colonies: limited production of exportable primary products—about 10 percent of total colonial exports to England—and high demands for English imports. However, significant differences did exist. New England's shipping industry, the related production of naval stores, and her fishing fleet—all of which accounted almost entirely for that region's exports to England —did find sufficiently vigorous markets to make New England a larger exporter to England than the Middle Atlantic region throughout the eighteenth century. In addition, slower-growing New England had fewer per-capita imports, and a better balance of trade, than did the Middle Atlantic colonies, and the trend did not worsen. Throughout the eighteenth century, imports from England remained about three times as large as exports to it.

The Middle Atlantic and New England colonists made up their trade deficit with England by departing from the imperial orthodoxy of trade relations. First, their traditional ties with the West Indies, involving the export of foodstuffs and livestock to the sugar plantations, redounded to the favor of the colonists. However, they still purchased high levels of imports from the West Indies, primarily sugar and slaves, and the favorable margin was not sufficient to make up for the English deficit, particularly as the eighteenth century wore on. Indeed, it was southern Europe that was the real growth sector of colonial trade. The Middle Atlantic colonies, followed at a distance by New England and the Piedmont region of the upper South, developed into strong exporters of wheat and flour to Europe south of Cape Finisterre, with New England adding exports of dried fish. During the 1760s, for the Middle Atlantic colonies, total exports to southern Europe were almost ten times as large as imports from southern Europe. In that trade the colonists acquired specie, or hard money, with which, together with the specie and bills of exchange from the West Indian trade, they paid for almost all of the excess of imports from England. Even at the end of the colonial period, despite the swiftly growing demand for English imports, the overall trade account of the colonists was roughly in balance as a result, primarily, of the exceedingly dynamic southern European traffic.[12]

The merchants of Philadelphia and Baltimore were most vigorous in taking advantage of these new export opportunities, largely because of their access to dynamic wheat-producing hinterlands. In the process of participating successfully in this newer, more risky trade outside of conventional mercantilistic paths, these Middle Atlantic merchants strengthened habits of flexibility that would prove invaluable once the ties of empire were dissolved by the Revolution. New York's merchants lacked a large wheat-producing hinterland but were no less creative. Indeed, they became even more cunning, making New York the privateering capital of America. New York merchants led the way in the lucrative activity of raiding the French in the West Indies. The prizes brought a substantial flow of revenue. The value of enemy ships taken by New Yorkers between 1689 and 1763 equaled the value of New York's exports to England during the same period. And New York merchants sharpened tastes for risk taking and extralegal activity that would prove valuable during and after the Revolution.

The trade with southern Europe constituted the colonists' most striking departure from the strict dictates of an ideal imperial system, but it was necessary for development of the Northern colonies: in order to grow by increasing their exports and at the same time meet their obligations to English merchants, they had to seek outlets other than Great Britain. This was so because beginning with the eighteenth century the Northern colonies, for reasons of geography, largely had to replicate the pattern of English development. Their staples in demand in England, such as furs, fish, and naval stores, provided no lasting basis for growth and had begun to wane in the seventeenth century. Wheat production gave the Northern colonies a new opportunity to expand their export market, but they had to look beyond the English, who were amply supplied from domestic sources. Southern staples, in contrast, continued in high English demand and therefore received primary attention from commercial farmers in the South. The incentives for specializing in growing tropical and subtropical commodities remained powerful until well into the twentieth century, and the strong ties would continue as well, although weakened by the industrial revolution in the United States. Despite the intimations of maturity—the new export trade with southern Europe in a nontropical product, the growth of grain agriculture in the Middle Atlantic colonies, the increase in per-capita demands for imported manufactured goods, and the vigor of the colonial merchants—the fundamental pattern of commerce remained unaltered at the end of the colonial period.

The Money Supply

Although to some extent the colonists financed their purchase of British imports with bills of exchange obtained elsewhere, sale of shipping services to Englishmen, British military expenditures, and credit extended by British merchants to American producers, a net flow of hard money from the colonies persisted because of the unfavorable balance of trade with England. The drain was particularly large in the Middle Atlantic colonies, which lacked the ships, naval stores, and fish of New England and the ability to attract British capital that the South possessed. It might be tempting to conclude, as many colonists did, that such specie shipments retarded the expansion of the colonial economy by restricting the growth of the colonists' money supply, or by promoting experimentation with highly unstable systems of domestic design, and worked inequities by promoting deflation (a decline in the general price level) burdensome to debtors of all types, not the least of which were those planters obligated to British merchants. The colonists, indeed, had their monetary difficulties, but their record in the manipulation of money, despite the loss of specie, was basically a successful one.

Certainly the colonies did not suffer from deflation. On the contrary, prior to the Revolution prices in the colonies moved upward; in fact, in Philadelphia, where they were the most stable, prices rose 57 percent during the fifty-four years following 1720. This inflation, however, occurred at the very reasonable annual rate of 0.8 percent. Pennsylvania was able to provide an expansive yet stable money supply, despite absorbing balances of both trade and payments with Great Britain more unfavorable than those of any other colony. Like all the other colonies, Pennsylvania provided for its money needs through the creation of paper money. Beginning in Massachusetts in the 1690s, the British allowed colonies to create paper money if they contributed to their own defense, and colonies initially used paper money to pay their wartime debts. Under the same principle, the colonial legislatures expanded note issues during the eighteenth-century French wars. They experimented with a wide variety of issues, but their fundamental choices were bills of credit, or governmental promissory notes in anticipation of tax collections, and issues of land banks, which provided farmers with notes upon the security of land or crops (in Virginia for example, the land banks issued notes on tobacco so that planters might withhold the crops from market and obtain the best price possible). In Pennsylvania, the other Middle Atlantic colonies, and the South, the legislatures controlled the money supply so as to maintain a stable exchange rate between colonial legal tender and sterling, and thus create a medium of exchange that would be widely accepted in the colonies. Their success in creating viable money is suggested by the fact that New York and Pennsylvania paper money accounted for about half of the money supply at the end of the colonial period.

The New England colonies, particularly Massachusetts and Rhode Island, had much greater difficulty managing the colonial money supply than other colonies did. And their problems were of their own making, as demonstrated by the comparative success of Pennsylvania and New York, which faced greater obstacles to effective monetary control as a result of incurring a less favorable balance of payments. The laxness of New England management, exemplified by the failure of Massachusetts to make any significant effort to redeem its bills of credit, meant a mushrooming supply of paper money which depreciated rapidly in value and brought about excessive inflation.[13] In contrast to the small 0.8-percent rate of annual price increase in Philadelphia, the annual inflation rate in Boston from 1720 to 1774 was 4.0 percent. And during the same period, while the sterling exchange rate of colonial currency depreciated 13 percent in Virginia, 12 percent in New York, and 27 percent in Pennsylvania, it depreciated 330 percent in Boston and 1,340 percent in Rhode Island. Consequently paper money accounted for probably little more than 4 percent of the real value of the money supply of New England at the end of the colonial period. The face value of the voluminous issues of Massachusetts and Rhode Island had been high, but public trust in and use of such issues were, consequently, very slight.

Monetary management in the colonies, despite the excesses and instability in New England, was fundamentally sound and contributed to the strong growth of the Southern colonies and, more strikingly, the Middle Atlantic region by sustaining the expansion of marketplace exchanges. Such problems as there were stemmed not nearly so much from the unfavorable balance of trade with England as from the incompetency of colonial legislatures, particularly their tendency to tie the size of the money supply more to needs of wartime finance or an effort to redistribute wealth toward debtors than to commercial requirements. The basic success in issuing paper money would lead to the vigorous protest against English regulation that emanated from the conservative Philadelphia mercantile community when England stymied Pennsylvania's monetary policy with the Currency Act of 1764.[14]

NOTES

1. Consequently British mercantile policy favored the West Indies. See Chapter 4 for a discussion of the impact of mercantilism on the development of the mainland.

2. For the definitive history of this critical episode in the development of American trade, see Jacob M. Price, *France and the Chesapeake, a History of the French Tobacco Monopoly, 1674–1791, and of Its Relationship to the British and American Tobacco Trades* (Ann Arbor, Mich.: University of Michigan Press, 1973).

3. Everett E. Edwards, "American Agriculture—the First 300 Years," in U.S. Department of Agriculture, *Farmers in a Changing World* (Washington, D.C.: U.S. Government Printing Office, 1940), p. 174.

4. Conway, Zirkle, "To Plow or Not to Plow: Comment on the Planters' Problems," *Agricultural History,* 43 (January 1969), 87–89.

5. For a comprehensive survey of colonial land policy see Marshall Harris, *Origin of the Land Tenure System in the United States* (Ames, Iowa: State University of Iowa Press, 1953).

6. See Kenneth A. Lockridge, "Land, Population, and the Evolution of New England, 1630–1790," *Past and Present*, 39 (April 1968), 62–80.

7. See Philip J. Greven, Jr., "Old Patterns in the New World: The Distribution of Land in Seventeenth Century Andover," *Essex Institute Historical Collections*, 101 (1965), 133–148.

8. See pp. 53–55 for a discussion of colonial monetary policy.

9. For data on the colonial shipping industry and its significance see Bernard and Lotte Bailyn, *Massachusetts Shipping, 1697–1714* (Cambridge, Mass.: Harvard University Press, 1959); James F. Shepherd, "Commodity Exports from the British North American Colonies to Overseas Areas, 1768–1772: Magnitudes and Patterns of Trade," *Explorations in Economic History*, 8 (Fall 1970), 5–76; John J. McCusker, "Sources of Investment Capital in the Colonial Philadelphia Shipping Industry," *Journal of Economic History*, 32 (March 1972), 146–157.

10. For this estimate see Gary Walton, "Sources of Productivity Change in American Colonial Shipping, 1675–1775," *Economic History Review*, 20 (April 1967), 67–78. See also Douglass C. North, "Sources of Productivity Change in Ocean Shipping, 1600–1850," *Journal of Political Economy*, 76 (September–October 1968), 953–970; and James F. Shepherd and Gary M. Walton, "Trade, Distribution, and Economic Growth in Colonial America," *Journal of Economic History*, 32 (March 1972), 128–145.

11. See James B. Hedges, *The Browns of Providence Plantations* (Cambridge, Mass.: Harvard University Press, 1952).

12. The importance of another export, that of rum of New England manufacture, in compensating for the unfavorable balance of trade with Britain has not been determined. Exported rum appears to have been destined largely for Africa, where it was exchanged for slaves. However, given the importance of slave purchases and the fact that rum exports probably accounted for less than 10 percent of New England's exports, the colonists could not have earned a significant amount of foreign exchange in that trade. Rum distilling was an important New England enterprise, but the production was almost entirely for consumption within the colonies. See Shepherd, *op. cit.*, pp. 55–56, 64–65; and U.S. Bureau of the Census, *Historical Statistics of the U.S. from Colonial Times to the Present* (Washington, D.C.: U.S. Government Printing Office, 1965), pp. 761–769.

13. An explanation for the monetary excesses of New England may rest in the relatively greater degree of political power held by farmers in Massachusetts and Rhode Island and their continuing efforts to reduce the value of their debts and, thereby, their obligations to the mercantile community. For suggestions of this, still not successfully challenged, see Curtis P. Nettles, *The Roots of American Civilization* (New York: Appleton-Century-Crofts, 1938), pp. 530–537.

14. For useful data on exchange rates and the volume of the colonial money supply see Roger W. Weiss, "The Issue of Paper Money in the American Colonies, 1720–1774," *Journal of Economic History*, 30 (December 1970), 770–784. See also Curtis P. Nettles, *The Money Supply of the American Colonies Before 1720* (Madison, Wis.: University of Wisconsin Press, 1934); E. James Ferguson, *The Power of the Purse* (Chapel Hill, N.C.: University of North Carolina Press, 1961); and Richard Lester, "Currency Issues to Overcome Depressions in Pennsylvania, 1723 and 1729," reprinted in Ralph L. Andreano (ed.), *New Views on American Economic Development* (Cambridge, Mass.: Schenkman, 1965), pp. 73–118.

SUGGESTED READINGS

Books

Bailyn, Bernard. *The New England Merchants in the Seventeenth Century.* Cambridge, Mass.: Harvard University Press, 1955.

Bidwell, Percy W., and John I. Falconer. *History of Agriculture in the Northern United States, 1620–1860.* Washington, D.C.: Carnegie Institution, 1925.

Bruchey, Stuart (ed.). *The Colonial Merchant: Sources and Readings.* New York: Harcourt, Brace and World, 1966.

Gray, Lewis C. *History of Agriculture in the Southern United States to 1860.* 2 vols. Washington, D.C.: Carnegie Institution, 1933.

Harris, Marshall. *Origin of the Land Tenure System in the United States.* Ames, Iowa: State University of Iowa Press, 1953.

Nettles, Curtis P. *The Roots of American Civilization.* New York: Appleton-Century-Crofts, 1938.

Russell, Howard S. *A Long, Deep Furrow: Three Centuries of Farming in New England.* Hanover, N.H.: University Press of New England, 1976.

Shepherd, James F., and Gary M. Walton. *Shipping, Maritime Trade, and the Economic Development of Colonial North America.* New York and London: Cambridge University Press, 1972.

Articles

Land, Aubrey C. "The Tobacco Staple and the Planter's Problems: Technology, Labor, and Crops," *Agricultural History*, 43 (January 1969), 69–81.

Mauro, F. "Towards an Intercontinental Model: European Overseas Expansion Between 1500 and 1800," *Economic History Review*, 14 (August 1961), 1–17.

North, Douglass C. "Sources of Productivity Change in Ocean Shipping, 1600–1850," *Journal of Political Economy*, 76 (September–October 1968), 953–970.

Price, Jacob M. "The Economic Growth of the Chesapeake and the European Market, 1697–1775," *Journal of Economic History*, 24 (December 1964), 496–511.

Shepherd, James F. "Commodity Exports from the British North American Colonies to Overseas Areas, 1768–1772: Magnitudes and Patterns of Trade," *Explorations in Economic History*, 8 (Fall 1970), 5–76.

————, and Gary M. Walton. "Trade, Distribution, and Economic Growth in Colonial America," *Journal of Economic History*, 32 (March 1972), 128–145.

Taylor, George R. "American Economic Growth Before 1840: An Exploratory Essay," *Journal of Economic History*, 24 (December 1964), 427–444.

Walton, Gary. "Sources of Productivity Change in American Colonial Shipping, 1675–1775," *Economic History Review*, 20 (April 1967), 67–78.

Weiss, Roger W. "The Issue of Paper Money in the American Colonies, 1720–1774," *Journal of Economic History*, 30 (December 1970), 770–784.

3

Colonial Population and Labor Force

PATTERNS OF POPULATION DISTRIBUTION, COMPOSITION, AND GROWTH

The fundamental characteristics of the population—its distribution, composition, and growth—provide yet another avenue for exploring the essential patterns of the colonial economic experience. The ways in which people marry, reproduce, and move about the countryside are profoundly influenced by variations in the contours of economic opportunity and are reflective of them. Further, characteristics of the population, particularly those which condition the rates of mortality and fertility, themselves mold the development of economic opportunity by determining the potential size of the labor force.

Colonial people lived and worked almost entirely on the countryside. Even after the end of the colonial period, in 1790, roughly only 200,000 people out of a total of 3.7 million lived in urban places (defined by the United States census standard as having more than 2,500 population). Only two places (Philadelphia and Boston) contained over 25,000 people, only three (New York, Charleston, and Baltimore) had between 10,000 and 25,000, and only nineteen others held enough people to be designated urban. It is true that most urban dwellers lived in the Northern colonies (of the largest five cities, only Charleston was in the South) and that the percentage of the urbanized colonial population may have been growing toward the end of the colonial period primarily as a result of the rapid expansion of Philadelphia. That city, which contained some 40,000 inhabitants by

1775, had overtaken Bristol and, in fact, was larger than any English town with the exception of London, its growth resulting in large part from the buoyancy of agriculture in the Middle Atlantic colonies created by new European demands for wheat and the productivity of Philadelphia's hinterland.

The central characteristic of this predominantly rural population was its exceptional rate of growth. Of course, in the seventeenth century, the period of colony formation, the rate of population increase was rapid; between 1640 and 1700, for example, the population increased almost ten times in size, reaching about 250,000. The rate of increase declined after the colonies became well established, but the eighteenth-century rate of 2.5 percent per year was sufficient to add about 1 million people between 1700 and 1750. Put in other terms, during the eighteenth century the population increased by more than one-third every decade (at an average rate of 34.5 percent), or, it more than doubled every twenty-five years (see Table 1),

TABLE 1   CHARACTERISTICS OF COLONIAL POPULATION

| | Rate of Decennial Increase | | | |
	New England	Middle Atlantic	South Atlantic	Total
1700–1710	20%	53%	29%	30%
1710–1720	20	36	41	33
1720–1730	38	37	39	38
1730–1740	31	42	36	36
1740–1750	26	38	41	36
1750–1760	33	43	29	33
1760–1770	28	34	44	37
1770–1780	21	31	27	26
1780–1790	20	47	41	41
Average	28	40	35	34
	Distribution of Population, by Region			
1700	39%	19%	42%	100%
1710	35	23	42	100
1720	32	23	45	100
1730	32	23	45	100
1740	31	24	45	100
1750	29	24	47	100
1760	29	26	45	100
1770	28	26	46	100
1780	26	27	47	100
1790	25	28	47	100

Source: Jim Potter, "The Growth of Population in America, 1700-1860," in D. V. Glass and D. E. C. Eversley (eds.), *Population in History: Essays in Historical Demography* (London: Edward Arnold Ltd., 1965) p. 639.

a rate of growth at least *twice* that common in Europe during the early modern period.

The surprising characteristic of the growth of the colonial population was that even in this era of dynamic European expansion, its major source, at least for the white population, was the reproduction of the existing population rather than the direct transatlantic movement of people. The natural rate of increase of the white population was in the range of 26 to 30 percent per decade, in comparison with the overall decennial rate of 34.5 percent, and was considerably larger than that found in England at any time during the eighteenth and nineteenth centuries. As a consequence of the high rate of reproduction, only about one-tenth of the white population at the end of the colonial period was foreign-born.[1]

The relatively high birth rate (probably forty-five to fifty births per 1,000 colonial women per year, in contrast with the twenty-eight per 1,000 common in Europe) was implicit in the social facts that compared to Europeans, colonists married somewhat earlier, therefore tending to have more children over the course of a marriage, and had a higher percentage of population of childbearing age. The contrasts, however, between Europe and America were not dramatic in these respects. Scattered data suggest that the marrying age for colonial women was, on the average, between twenty and twenty-three—with surprisingly few teen-age marriages—throughout the colonial period, substantially below the average of at least twenty-five for European women. Colonial men were also marrying at a younger age, with their average being in the vicinity of twenty-four to twenty-six rather than the twenty-six to twenty-eight common in Europe. Instead of the average four or five births per marriage, as in Europe, the colonists probably had on the order of six or seven. Such differences were not overwhelming, but when cumulated over a large population and a long period of time, their impact was significant.[2]

An explanation for the high birth rate is rather plain. Most fundamentally, colonists found it easier to set up a household than did Europeans; more ample opportunities within an expansive agricultural sector made it possible and attractive for a younger man to acquire land, strike out on his own with a family, and establish a degree of economic independence. The interest of colonists in assuring such mobility was so strong that it worked to liberalize the division and distribution of the land. Further, such agricultural opportunity attracted Europeans, particularly those of a younger age. Immigration tended to raise the rate of colonial marriage over the European and thus increase the birth rate as well.

More important than the higher birth rate in accounting for the unusually rapid population increase in the colonies was the lowered mortality rate. In an average year, out of every 1,000 people, only twenty to twenty-five died. In Europe, however, the death rate was at least forty per 1,000 people. Quite obviously the colonial environment was a healthier one for the transplanted European, not for reasons of medical technology, which probably was more primitive in America than in Britain, but simply because conditions of land and climate were conducive to longer survival. Crops were more abundant on a per-capita basis, sharply reducing periods of famine, and although the winters were harsher in much of America, families were able to protect themselves against the winter more adequately as a result of the great availability of wood fuel for heating and cooking and for building of houses. While England had suffered an acute wood shortage, even for fuel, by the early seventeenth century over three-quarters of the adult, married freemen in the colonies may well have had their own houses. And, finally, it is possible that a general improvement in the American climate ensued during the middle of the eighteenth century. For many reasons, then, colonists avoided the extremes of disease and famine that afflicted Europe, and crises of mortality were far less frequent and not nearly as serious in North America as in Europe. (A diphtheria epidemic in New England in the late 1730s was the only striking break in a pattern of general stability of colonial mortality rates.) The infant mortality rate especially was lower, because pregnant and nursing women were better able to sustain their own health; likewise, the risks of childhood were less than in Europe. And those colonial males who survived childhood not only lived longer than European men; they lived almost as long as their mid-twentieth-century counterparts. Women, too, lived longer in America than in Europe, but because of the high mortality rates for those in childbirth, they could expect to live only until their forties—in contrast with the sixties for men. Thus the primary factors that explain natural increase were those that bore most directly upon mortality; disease, diet, and climate were much less burdensome in North America than in contemporary England and northern Europe.

The most striking variation from the general pattern of growth existed in the South, where the importation of Africans accounted for a more rapid population growth (about 90 percent of the North American black population lived in the Southern colonies by the time of the Revolution, and the vast bulk of this population were new immigrants or the children of immigrants). In 1700 there may have been as few as 5,000 blacks in the colonies, accounting for only 2 percent of the population, but by 1790 there were at least 675,000, accounting for about 20 percent.[3] Thus the black population was growing more rapidly than the white during the eighteenth century. Although reproduction rates for blacks were high, they were probably no higher than for whites.[4] But the rate of migration was sizable, with around 275,000 Africans coming to British North America between 1700 and 1790, including more than 75,000 arriving during the 1760s. Not very many more Europeans crossed the Atlantic during the same period, 1700–1790. The best estimate puts the number of European immigrants added to the population of British North America during those years at only 350,000. As a result of the heavy African migration the South's population grew at a rate about the same as the colonies as a whole, at a decennial rate of about 35 percent during the eighteenth century, and maintained a reasonably constant share of the population of the colonies—about 45 to 47 percent (see Table 1, p. 60). Without the black population, the decennial rate of increase for the South (for southern whites) would have been only about 29 percent—high by European standards but no greater than that for New England. Finally, the decades of highest slave importation (1710–1720, 1720–1730, 1740–1750, and 1760–1770) coincided with the decades of most rapid population growth in the South, and with periods of expansion of plantation agriculture.

Differences within the Southern colonies also reveal the importance of slave imports to southern growth and illustrate the importance of commercial agriculture to population growth. The most rapidly growing Southern colonies—South Carolina, Virginia, and Maryland—had the largest black populations: 70 percent, 47 percent, and 33 percent of their total populations, respectively, at the end of the colonial period. The striking ratio in South Carolina resulted from the high demands for heavy labor implicit in rice planting and meant a social profile, unique on the North American mainland, of a majority black population controlled by a compact elite of white plantation owners. The least successful of the Southern colonies in developing staple production was North Carolina, whose population was only 15 percent black. Filling the geographic vacuum created in North Carolina by inadequate harbors and infertile soils, a large influx of Scotch-Irish settlement moved southward along the Piedmont frontier. There they engaged in a family-farm style of subsistence agriculture or provided labor for the exploitation of the pine lands for naval stores.

Growth rates to the north, in the Middle Atlantic colonies, were much more rapid than for the colonies as a whole. The decennial rate of increase in their population was over 40 percent, well in advance of that of the colonies taken together. The Middle Atlantic colonies, particularly Pennsylvania and New York, attracted the most immigrants, especially of those who were non-English in origin. (See Figure 4.) By 1780 Pennsylvania was second only to Virginia in population size, and Philadelphia had become the largest city in North America. The lack of significant social barriers to immigrants of non-English stock and the expansiveness of agriculture, related to the boom of wheat exports, enabled these colonies to grow more rapidly than those to the north and south. In addition, the relative abundance of economic opportunity in agriculture may well have produced a rate of natural increase for whites greater than that

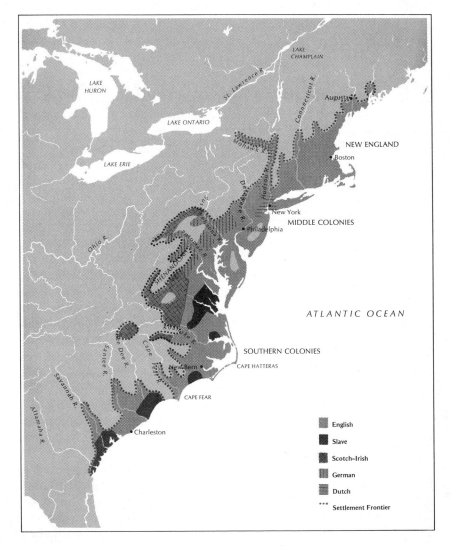

FIGURE 4: *Distribution of Major Immigrant Groups in Colonial America*

elsewhere. Students of historical demography have discredited, for New England at least, Benjamin Franklin's assertions, in his *Observations Concerning the Increase of Mankind and the Peopling of the Countries* (1751), that teen-age marriages were common in the colonies and that American marriages were usually followed by as many as eight births. But Franklin may well have made such observations with Pennsylvania in mind rather than Virginia or Massachusetts.

The poorest record of growth was in the New England colonies, where the decennial growth rate of 27 or 28 percent lagged far behind the colonial average. As a result, while 39 percent of the colonial population resided in New England in 1700, only 24 percent did so in 1790. Proportionally the loss was even greater in the largest state, Massachusetts—from one-quarter of the colonial population in 1700 to 10 percent in 1790. Massachusetts was a place of some religious and social intolerance, a collection of relatively homogeneous communities, and, as a result, immigration, especially of non-English people, was slight. The Scotch-Irish and Germans were careful to avoid the English-Puritan colonies. In fact, there was a net emigration, led by young, single men, out of Massachusetts after 1763, to both the Southern and Middle Atlantic colonies, bringing about a surplus of women in Massachusetts compared with a surplus of men in the colonies as a whole. Coupled with the social barriers to immigration was the relative lack of economic opportunity resulting from the stagnant agricultural sector; in particular, the latter factor shackled the growth of New England's largest city, Boston, thereby reducing opportunities for urban employment, especially jobs for skilled immigrants, although the vigorous sea trades compensated to a degree for those losses.[5] The narrower character of rural opportunities may have also slowed the rate of population growth by lowering the birth rate and by increasing mortality, in contrast to the pattern of natural increase in the colonies at large. For example, one study finds the crude birth rate in New England to have been as low as forty per 1,000, compared with the forty-five to fifty per 1,000 that pertained in the colonies at large.[6] Also, the marrying age was probably higher and average family size lower in New England than in the colonies as a whole. Nonetheless, the natural rate of increase was large by European standards, and in conjunction with limited economic opportunities in agriculture, it increased the pressure on the land (as in the example given of Dedham, Massachusetts, where the size of an average landholding fell by one-third, to only fifty acres, between the first seventeenth-century generation and the Revolution). The rapid post-Revolutionary surge of Massachusetts families into Vermont, New York, and, later, the Old Northwest was in large part a response to the limited character of economic opportunity in New England during the eighteenth century.

Despite New England's relatively poor growth performance, the rate of natural increase probably did not vary a great deal by region. The high rates of natural increase and population growth in the colonies as a whole arose from an abundance of land that colonists could easily turn into life-sustaining activity. Only in New England was there pressure on the capacity of the land to support a rapidly expanding population. The general pattern was quite distinct. Even if the colonial period was not yet one of dramatic intensive growth, or growth dependent on a more efficient use of human and material resources, it was certainly an era in which the ability of the American environment to sustain extensive growth was the most prominent economic fact. The markedly high rates of natural increase and, in the Middle Atlantic and South, the rapid influx of migrants, sustained for more than a century, testified to the dynamic quality of preindustrial life in North America, founded upon expansive agricultural enterprise. As a measure of the growth of the colonial economy, the rate of population increase indicates that the economy grew at least at the impressive rate of 2.5 percent per year; that is, it at least doubled in size every twenty-five years.[7]

The characteristics of population growth in colonial America suggest the existence of a thriving and prosperous people in the New World. Obviously the diminished risks of death and sickness were central elements of the social fabric. Additionally, the high geographic mobility of people and the related expansiveness of agriculture suggest the possibility that the real income of farmers increased as a result both of the rapid growth of demands elsewhere in the Atlantic community for American agricultural products and of the ability of colonists to move onto new lands that were more fertile and productive than older lands. However, even if real incomes of the colonists did not increase significantly, the continuing flow of immigration reflects the often-observed premium that American employers were willing to pay for labor, in contrast with their European counterparts, and the value that Europeans attached to freer access to land.[8] Further, the flexibility and growth of the population suggest a highly energetic, ambitious people inclined to make the most of their life chances for material gain.

THE QUALITY OF LIFE: THE CONDITIONS OF WORK

Free Labor

The work experience of Americans was set by a configuration of economic factors: the abundance of land, the scarcity of labor, and a level of technology that did not require a high degree of specialization. Those who labored as free people enjoyed a high degree of mobility, a lack of strong occupational identification, and a comparatively high level of material well-being.

For free people on the land, who accounted for most of the population in the New England and Middle Atlantic colonies, high rates of natural increase, expansiveness of production, transformation of systems of land distribution, and impressive geographic mobility speak eloquently of opportunity. The relative prices of the factors of production also favored the working conditions of the free urban population, particularly the large artisan class. For them, towns were clearly places of freedom and abundance. They enjoyed not only high wages but also rather leisurely working conditions. Hours were long, extending throughout the daylight hours, but the pace of work was relaxed. Meal and gin breaks were frequent, and the work atmosphere was highly social. The intensity of the work varied with the season, and each year artisans were able to take off several weeks for religious holidays and local celebrations. Moreover, the crafts were relatively open to the entry of new members. Apprentices were in great demand and received favorable remuneration in virtually all of the crafts. And established artisans and shopkeepers easily took up new crafts. Further, labor contracts became increasingly shorter in their duration. Free workers, even those who were common laborers, were able to insist on very short-term contracts, commonly no longer than a day. In short, the mechanisms of the labor market appear to have translated the fundamental scarcity of labor into highly favorable working conditions for free people.

It is possible that the marketplace did not work efficiently for a category of people whose freedom may have been only technical in nature: the women who were either independent or members of households headed by free men. The vast majority of free women worked within the context of households, outside of the marketplace in the sense that they did not receive direct payment for their economic contributions. It is estimated that in 1800 less than 5 percent of the female population over the age of ten worked outside their homes on a full-time basis. If measurable, the primary preoccupation of women within households during the seventeenth and eighteenth centuries would no doubt prove to be childbearing and child rearing. The larger size of the American family and the low infant mortality rate, which eased the psychological costs of child rearing, suggest that these responsibilities grew during the transplanting of European society. And not only did the investment in child rearing probably increase but it also became more concentrated in the hands of women. The powerful impulse to maximize the pecuniary returns to agriculture coupled with the acute labor scarcity contributed to a sharper specialization of economic roles within the family. Given the lower productivity of women in heavy agricultural labor, women devoted most of their energies to the lighter chores and to infant care and child training.[9] To be sure, throughout the colonies, women worked in the fields, particularly at harvest time. And, given the general short supply of labor, a much smaller percentage of American women (as well as men) were underemployed, or removed from any significant economic activity, than was the case in contemporary England. Thus, in agriculture, market forces simultaneously increased the labor input of women and the specialization of women in child-rearing activities. Although common assessments of the capabilities of women were usually biased, the specialization of women in child rearing was not a simple outgrowth of those attitudes. In an economy that lacked an adequate supply of skilled individuals, the economic contribution of child rearing and the need to raise sons and daughters capable of exploiting changing conditions were commonly regarded as important.

The increased participation of women in family enterprise meant that women became more deeply involved not only in agriculture but also in all of the diverse activities undertaken by the unspecialized households characteristic of the colonial period. Of the greatest long-run significance was their increased participation in the household manufacturing (spinning, weaving, sewing, for example) conducted by New England families. The brothers of New England women shunned such work; if young men were blocked by a lack of opportunity on the land, they usually sought their fortunes in other colonies or in the sea trades rather than in manufacturing. The consequent migration of young men out of New England left a surplus of women and an even larger pool of labor available to household manufacture.

A highly visible handful of women also contributed as farm managers and entrepreneurs. Where the large-scale management of agriculture relied heavily on family enterprise, a scarcity of competent male leadership created opportunities for women to move outside of roles prescribed by tradition. Such opportunities for the management of agriculture were particularly abundant in the South, since slave society viewed white women directing black men more tolerantly than free society viewed white women directing white men. Women who were members of wealthy families, which managed far-flung empires, were obviously unusual. But wherever business enterprises involved wives and daughters in a central fashion, opportunities existed for women to establish independent economic roles. The expansiveness of the eighteenth-century marketplace, the shortage of skilled people, the relatively unspecialized

The process of spinning and weaving in the eighteenth century was a cooperative effort. The family's work involved spinning yarn (left), reeling yarn onto yarnspools (center), and knitting stockings (right).

character of family enterprise—particularly within the crafts, and a high mortality rate (at least by twentieth-century standards) created opportunities for women who were full-fledged owners of mercantile establishments (sometimes in partnership with other women), members of skilled trades, and widows who were able to carry on their husband's enterprise as a consequence of the training they had acquired. Some of these women, on their own, entered skilled occupations such as millinery work, dress and mantua making, hairdressing, embroidery, and midwifery. But most were helpmates who had acquired a thoroughgoing knowledge of their husbands' craft and, therefore, were able to carry on after their husbands' deaths.

The independence of widows of craftsmen and tradesmen was enhanced because craftsmen and tradesmen commonly willed their property to their wives, and the courts respected those transfers. In the nineteenth century, when the line of distinction between work and home life became firmer, such transfers would become difficult. In the eighteenth century, however, American men valued the contribution of skilled women and placed no significant obstacles in the way of their continuing their husbands' crafts. Moreover, antenuptial contracts that were commonly drawn up between remarrying widows and their new husbands also found respect before the courts; these contracts guaranteed protection of the widows' property. Thus, colonial society used instruments of family law to advance the effective contribution of women to economic life.

The scarcity of labor clearly appears to have widened opportunities for women and to have increased their direct participation in economic life, despite cultural restrictions on women's social roles. And, although the economy suffered from the ideology that reduced opportunities for women outside the home and promoted the specialization of women in child rearing, child rearing was a vital part of the process by which society invested in future generations. During the colonial period, the rudimentary condition of educational institutions, the acute shortage of skilled labor, and the demands of the American environment for flexibility and adaptability in new generations lent an unusual urgency to child rearing as a central economic activity.

Bound Labor

For the immigrants who came to American shores during the colonial period, freedom was more the exception than the rule. This was so for Europeans as well as for Africans. Most Europeans who came to America arrived not as free individuals but in various conditions of voluntary servitude. For some groups, of course, the rate of indenture was quite low. Only about 10 percent of the Scotch-Irish, for example, were encumbered by a prior obligation. But, on the other hand, virtually all of the Germans from the Palatinate were indentured, and the average rate of indenture for all immigrants was over 50 percent. These immigrants had agreed to contracts of indenture prior to sailing for the New World. Planters and farmers, especially those in the Middle Atlantic colonies, were the largest employers of such labor. They worked through agents who recruited servants, wrote contracts of indenture, and arranged transport and transfer. The contracts included payment of food, shelter, clothing, and often a freedom bonus in return for an average of four to five years of bound service.

During the seventeenth century, indentured servants tended to be English, very young (with a median age of perhaps fifteen or sixteen), largely unskilled, and lacking in significant prospects for improvement. Their servitude was probably more arduous than it would have been in Europe. The labor demanded of them was more rigorous, they were subjected to harsh discipline, and their rate of mortality was high. If they ran away or violated the terms of their indentures, their owners could extend the terms of service. After fulfilling the terms of their initial contracts, many found themselves without the resources to buy land or otherwise obtain economic independence and consequently were compelled to extend their servitude. Most depressed of these servants were those who had been kidnapped, sold into servitude by a magistrate in order to pay off debts or fines, or pardoned for a felony in return for accepting indentured exile in America. They were almost completely without bargaining power and had to accept the terms of their employers. While they were predominantly male, there were women among their numbers. Indeed, during the early days of Jamestown, more women probably arrived as indentured servants than as members of established families. And some of these women were exiled felons or kidnap victims. During the initial years of Jamestown's growth, the English government looked dimly on kidnapping but for the most part prosecuted kidnappers only when they failed to restrict their activities to the poor. In 1618 the government executed one man because he had kidnapped a "rich yeoman's daughters ... to serve his Majesty for breeders in Virginia."

During the eighteenth century, however, the relative numbers of European immigrants who arrived in a condition of extreme dependence declined. The only significant dependents were the redemptioners, largely German, who arrived during the second quarter of the eighteenth century. They were displaced peasants who, lacking bargaining power, had boarded ship without payment. To pay for their passage they sold themselves and their children into service, often accepting unusually restrictive terms. The terms commonly provided for seven years' service and the most minimal freedom benefits. But the redemptioners and other highly dependent immigrants had become a minority of all immigrants. Convicts still came, to be sure. In 1692 English magistrates sent to Virginia "fifty lewd women out of the house of correction and thirty others who walked the streets at night." However, extreme colonial hostility to convict labor, initiated by Virginia after an uprising of servants in 1663 and fanned by Benjamin Franklin during the 1750s, reduced their numbers. At the most, no more than one-fifth (about 50,000) of the European immigrants during the colonial period came as convicts.

By the time of the Revolution most European immigrants to America experienced marked improvements in their levels of living. Central to the improvements was the shortage of labor. For those who were indentured, the terms of contracts had become significantly more favorable. A craftsman might receive exemption from unskilled manual labor or field work, receive clothing, tools, and even land after his period of indenture. Further, the colonial courts upheld the rights of servants, requiring agents to keep families together and ship captains to account for all the servants they transported as a way of preventing kidnapping. They also took a dim view of contracts entered into during the period of servitude and generally granted immediate freedom when the master failed to live up to his part of the contract. In New York colonial courts awarded freedom to the servant in virtually every breach-of-contract case.

While the terms of work under which Europeans emigrated to America improved, the terms of labor worsened for Africans who crossed the Atlantic. Even the redemptioners had some degree of control over the circumstances of their labor in the New World; Africans had virtually none. But it was, of course, the control over labor terms that made slavery so attractive to planters as an alternative to free labor.[10] That control, in addition to the advantages that slaves remained in bondage throughout their lives and bred more slaves, came at a price, however, and the price was too high for most planters until the early decades of the eighteenth century. Until then there was no massive shift to slave labor on southern plantations. The West Indian sugar planters earned a substantially higher rate of return on their slave investments and bid the price of slaves above what the tobacco planters could afford. By 1675 the English West Indies contained more than 100,000 slaves while the English mainland colonies held no more than 5,000. Even as late as 1700 the slave population accounted for no more than 15 percent of the people of the Southern colonies and perhaps as little as 5 percent. Thus, until well into the eighteenth century, Europeans, many of them indentured servants, did most of the labor on southern plantations.

The slave population was slow to grow but southern planters quickly recognized the potential benefits of owning slaves. By the end of the seventeenth century they had shaped slavery into forms that persisted, with only a few important changes, through Emancipation. As early as 1640 Virginia planters not only held blacks in lifetime servitude but also confined the children of slaves to the same status. After 1660 they wrote laws that defined slaves as property. In 1669 the Virginia legislature, while defining indentured servitude in liberal terms, determined that if a slave died as a consequence of punishment, his master was immune to felony prosecution. In the eyes of the legislature, it was inconceivable that a master would destroy his own property. Then in 1705 the legislature organized the assorted enactments of the preceding generation into a "slave code" closely defining the status of the slave as subhuman, to be regarded as nothing more than property. Thus, at the same time that the English colonies liberalized terms of indenture, they moved quickly to distinguish African slaves from European servants by stripping away whatever rights blacks had enjoyed.

The economic story of slavery in North America is one of a compelling need for a large stock of unskilled labor meeting a flexible supply of laborers available under terms that allowed their utmost exploitation by employers. The economic incentives that encouraged the spread of slavery in the New World were not unique. Throughout history, when very inexpensive land is joined with very expensive labor, slavery or its equivalent often flourishes. Under such economic conditions various forms of slavery and serfdom had arisen in the late Roman empire, in sixteenth-century Poland and Lithuania, in seventeenth-century Russia, in the Middle East, in the Aztec and Inca empires, and in some African societies.[11] But economic incentives alone cannot explain the rise of slavery in the English colonies. The process whereby Englishmen determined that particular groups of labor would remain free while others would become slave was distinct from the economic process shaping the rise of slavery. To fathom the former one needs to comprehend the intellectual characteristics of transplanted European society, especially its treatment of African racial and religious differences.[12] To some extent, certainly, racism simply provided a framework of rationalization for social arrangements profitable for the dominant classes. But the racism of the English in America appears to have been unusually intense. English slave codes appear to have been more restrictive than those in the Spanish and Portuguese colonies; regulation of manumission and specification of punishments, for example, tended to be more severe. Lacking the long history of contact with Africans that the Spanish and Portuguese had, Englishmen not only had more powerful assumptions of African racial and religious inferiority but also suffered from more compelling fears and anxieties about the potential for slave rebellion. Further contributing to English racism was the fact that the English colonies, with larger rates of immigration from Europe, had less need than the Spanish and Portuguese colonies for non-Europeans as skilled workers—artisans, overseers, and militiamen.[13] Therefore, in contrast with the Spanish and Portuguese, they did not foster the development of a class of free blacks. Such a class did develop in the English colonies, but it lacked significant size until the late eighteenth century and was never as large as its counterpart in the Latin colonies. For the English, the most pressing labor need was for unskilled labor. Thus, the English lacked economic incentives for providing blacks with a significant vehicle for economic and social improvement. The consequence was a confirmation of white racism and, in turn, a profound reinforcement of the institution of slavery.

THE QUALITY OF LIFE: PER-CAPITA INCOME AND THE DISTRIBUTION OF WEALTH

Rising Levels of Living

Despite the strongly positive implications of the characteristics of the population and the nature of working conditions for free labor, just how successful the colonists were in raising their standard of living remains unclear, because of the dearth of statistical information on preindustrial development. However, both statistical and more impressionistic evidence indicate that after the difficulties of initial settlement, colonists enjoyed a standard of living comparable to that of the wealthiest European countries, one which improved at a modest rate from at least as early as the first quarter of the eighteenth century. Thus, even before the changes associated with the industrial revolution, American society proved able to generate an increasing per-capita level of economic product.[14]

Given the difficulty of estimating income levels for the eighteenth century, it is hardly surprising that historians have invoked a wide range of values for per-capita income. With respect to the period around 1720, for example, after the colonies had succeeded in establishing a permanent social order, estimates range between £5 and £9. For the end of the colonial era, or the period around 1770, recent estimates extend from about £6 to £19. Assuming that the truth lies in the middle of each range, per-capita income in the colonies increased almost 80 percent during the half-century 1720–1770, or at a rate in excess of 2 percent per year. Thus an estimate that per-capita income increased by an annual rate of a least 1 percent during the period 1720–1770 seems plausible.[15] That rate of increase, although lower than the rate attained in the nineteenth century, and the levels of per-capita income attained in the eighteenth century were comparable with those achieved in contemporary England and Wales. And if it were possible to include the greater quantities of food and fuel that were available in America but were left out of income accounting because they never reached the marketplace, to reckon the value of a largely disease-free water supply in the colonies, to assess the value of the lower concentration of people (at least outside New England and the cities), and to determine the "psychic" income from the expectation of a longer life, the standard of living in the colonies might well be found to exceed that in the mother country.

These data on levels of living pertain, however, only to the free population. Not even the minimal measures of slave welfare that economic historians have developed for the nineteenth century are available for the colonial period. Demographic data, however, do suggest that slaves, like freemen, probably enjoyed a better diet and a longer life span than they would have experienced in their native lands. Certainly the mainland of North America was more free of the killer epidemics that routinely decimated the slave population of the West Indies and, more generally, tropical America. However, it is probable that the lower mortality rate on the mainland was less a product of better diets than the more salubrious climate. Moreover, a wide variety of impressionistic evidence suggests that slaves did not advance very far beyond the subsistence level during the colonial period; it is likely that this margin was even thinner in the colonial period than during the nineteenth century. This was so simply because the slave trade remained open throughout most of the colonial period. When the slave trade was open, planters could more readily obtain new supplies of slaves and had less incentive to maintain the health of their slaves. With high agricultural prices, closing the slave trade would have encouraged planters to protect their investment in slaves. Thus, even though the mainland climate was more favorable to slave health than that of the West Indies, the mainland economy of the colonial period was probably no more beneficent for slaves than the sugar plantations of the West Indies.

No comprehensive set of explanations exists to account for increasing productivity and higher levels of living enjoyed by the free people of the colonies. Recent studies have pointed to the organization of international trade within the Atlantic basin as an important source of productivity change during the seventeenth and eighteenth centuries.[16] Given the importance of agricultural production for export and the management of trade to colonial incomes, it is easy to visualize the potential significance of productivity gains in the distribution of goods. However, there has been virtually no systematic investigation of the relation of increased productivity to increased efficiency of production. The agricultural expansion that ensued in the Middle Atlantic and Southern colonies in the 1720s may have involved the cultivation of new, more fertile lands. At the same time, the refinement of regularized systems of land distribution in those regions in the course of the eighteenth century probably enhanced agricultural productivity. Institutional reform that made land more readily available also would have provided increased incentives for farmers to maximize their time, energies, and skills and, thus, to make themselves more productive. Further, the mid-eighteenth century saw advances in animal husbandry, modeled after English experiments, which produced larger sheep, cows, and bulls.

Another likely factor in productivity gains was the era of relative peace following the series of military encounters with the Indians, the French, and the Spanish that had absorbed colonial energies between King Philip's War in 1675 and the Peace of Utrecht in 1713. While the French wars of the eighteenth century were costly, they retarded the occupation of new land less than had the hostilities before 1713; by the start of the Revolution the agricultural population had moved into the Piedmont and even into the Mississippi valley. Occupation of more fertile land and perhaps a greater degree of confidence in a secure future could only enhance productivity.

Finally, it is worth considering the possibility that the restructuring of family relationships during the eighteenth century contributed to the development of a more productive labor force. While the transition from the extended family—which might include older children, single and married, grandparents, unmarried aunts and uncles, and servants, for example—to the nuclear conjugal group was slow, taking perhaps three or four generations, the process was no doubt well advanced everywhere by the mid-eighteenth century.[17] That transition meant the assuming of responsibility by sons at an earlier age, a fact reflected by lower marrying ages and the growing number of independent men who earlier would have been servants; the consequence was a labor force more responsive to the changing character of economic opportunities in trade and manufacturing as well as in agriculture and a society capable of yielding a larger economic product. That fundamental social change, often attributed to the forces of industrial revolution, emerged from the flux of the seventeenth and eighteenth centuries.

The initiation of a sustained gain in productivity often has been associated with the industrial revolution. So too has been the beginning of a sharply uneven distribution of wealth. But, like increasing productivity, the latter trend was visible during the eighteenth century. An estimate of the distribution of physical wealth (land, slaves, livestock, clothing, furniture, business equipment, inventories, and so on) for the Middle Atlantic colonies in 1774 indicates that the richest 10 percent of the wealth holders may have owned as much as 36 percent of all physical wealth while the poorest 10 percent owned only 0.4 percent and the poorer 50 percent held only 14 percent.[18] Although no comparable estimates exist for the earlier colonial period, studies of the changing distribution of wealth in areas of more limited scope, in Boston and in agricultural Chester County, Pennsylvania, strongly suggest that a trend toward a less equal distribution of wealth had set in no later than the early eighteenth century.[19]

Once again, the economic and social processes implied by this fundamental transformation are only partially understood, especially since the shift so obviously antedates the era of industrial revolution.

But it is possible to point to the various elements of colonial society central to the changing distribution of wealth.

For one thing, in the South the increasing use of slaves, led by a highly commercialized South Carolina, tended to narrow the distribution of wealth among the total population, both in the South and in the colonies as a whole. Uprooted Africans had virtually no opportunity to acquire property of any significance. Although slavery did not increase relative to free labor in the North during the eighteenth century, the number of slaves in northern cities such as Boston remained large enough to account for most of the poorest 10 percent of the population.

Among freemen everywhere in the colonies the distribution of wealth was becoming more uneven before the Revolution. Significant variations, however, did exist within that fundamental trend. Thus the distribution of income appeared to worsen less drastically in the Middle Atlantic colonies and to be consistently more favorable there than in New England.[20] Also, the distribution of wealth tended to be more unequal in urban areas than in rural ones. And, finally, wealth was distributed more evenly in the new agricultural areas than in older, well-settled districts.

These variations point out some of the factors behind the increasing polarization of wealth holdings in early American society. In the first place, as agricultural opportunities narrowed in New England and the more settled portions of the Middle Atlantic colonies, the distribution of income tended to become more uneven faster. Also, where society became more complex, as in the seaport cities, for example, the increasing specialization of economic life tended to concentrate income in fewer hands. That specialization included the growth of wage labor in the large cities and the refinement of mercantile elites promoting America's commerce. In Boston, for example, the middling group of artisans, shopkeepers, and traders that owned 21 percent of the city's wealth at the end of the seventeenth century owned only about half that a century later. With the flowering of transatlantic trade a small, fairly compact group of international traders had drawn apart from other property owners. While this trend was exaggerated in Boston, with a hinterland very possibly overpopulated and certainly stagnant in agricultural production, the basic development doubtless could be found in New York or Philadelphia as well.

The growing disparities among wealth holders were in part an outgrowth of the monopolization of certain opportunities by early-achieving generations of Americans. Town proprietors, beneficiaries of large land grants, and wealthy merchants tended to have wealth-

WESTOVER. One extreme of the colonial wealth distribution is illustrated by the Georgian-style home of the William Byrd family on Virginia's James River.

ier descendants than did their poorer contemporaries. Their accumulations of land, capital, expertise, and social influence tended to provide their heirs with a competitive edge. But such monopolization of opportunities and increased stratification of society implied by the increasing concentration of wealth provide misleading impressions of the quality of colonial economic life. Rather than reflecting a more rigid economy, the increasingly unequal wealth distribution suggests the growing mobility, diversity, and flexibility of colonial economic activity. With the loosening of traditional ties of authority due to the weakening of the extended family, the liberalization of institutions of land distribution, and the expansion of agricultural and commercial opportunities, society not only became more open but placed a higher premium on the accomplishments of those who pursued efficiency with aggressiveness and foresight. It is therefore no coincidence that the merchant groups that advanced their standing most rapidly during the eighteenth century also accounted for what were probably the most significant productivity gains. Also, the advance in economic position of the larger landholders in farming districts may well reflect their greater contributions to the enhancement of agricultural productivity.

Merchant Samuel Powel's parlor (1769) reflects Philadelphia's prosperity and the fact that not only planters had a taste for high consumption.

In sum, it is highly plausible that the increasingly uneven distribution of economic rewards resulted primarily from an expansion of new opportunities for the acquisition of wealth through productivity gains. If there had been no increase in such opportunities, it is much more likely that stability in the distribution of wealth would have prevailed and that total and per-capita social product would have been diminished. Whatever the source, however, an unequal distribution of wealth was a firmly established economic and social fact by the time of the Revolution, and the trend toward a less equal distribution which would characterize the early industrial revolution was already well under way.

LABOR MOVEMENTS AND CLASS CONSCIOUSNESS

The knowledge that the concentration of wealth was increasing during the eighteenth century readily leads to the question of whether or not Americans responded to that trend through any form of collective action designed to alter the distribution of wealth.

One form that a heightened class consciousness may assume is the development of a trade-union movement—a movement of workers who accept the likelihood of their long-run employment in a particular occupation and band together to collectively improve the conditions of their employment. The colonial period did, in fact, see the formation of organizations, located in the largest towns, which promoted the long-term economic interests of their members. The craftsmen who formed these associations were usually master craftsmen—small businessmen who employed journeyman craftsmen and apprentices and marketed their own manufactures. They sought to keep down wages they paid to their journeymen and to raise prices through a restriction of competition. For example, in 1724 ten carpenters founded the Carpenter's Company of the City and County of Philadelphia and proceeded to set a uniform scale of prices and wages. Carpenters in other towns followed suit. In the same year, thirty-two Boston barbers joined together to raise the prices of shaves and wigs. In 1760, thirty-nine masters formed the Cordwainer's Fire Company largely to recover runaway apprentices. In 1771 more than forty master tailors in Philadelphia banded together in the Taylor's Company with the explicit purpose of colluding to fix prices and limit the wages paid to journeymen.These companies were joined increasingly by benevolent or philanthropic societies, such as the Friendly Society of Tradesmen House Carpenters formed in New York in 1767. The latter specialized in mutual aid—providing sick benefits, lending money, paying funeral expenses, supporting widows, and so on. But they engaged in collusive trade practices as well, and it became increasingly difficult to distinguish their activities from those of the nascent trade unions.

The history of craft associations suggests that class consciousness among skilled workers was relatively weak during the colonial period, despite the widening gap between the wealth of an average master craftsman and that of a member of the mercantile elite. Permanent organizations of craftsmen were few in number and never represented more than a small minority of the masters in colonial towns. Craftsmen were aware of the opportunities afforded by the dynamic town economies of the eighteenth century and were reluctant to join restrictive associations. For their part, town governments wished to enlarge the ranks of the skilled workers. Consequently, associations did not follow the model set by the European guilds that tightly regulated crafts and restricted entry into them. Virtually the only guilds chartered were ephemeral, seventeenth-century organizations. And whatever minimal control the associations had over the crafts waned during the eighteenth century. For example, in 1769 the Philadelphia Carpenter's Company split with most of the members joining the new Friendship Carpenter's Company, which set its entrance fee at five shillings instead of the £4 of the parent association. In the eighteenth century, associations were generally powerless to enforce apprenticeship requirements, to block newcomers from entering their crafts, and to prevent artisans from practicing more than one craft at the same time or from shifting from one craft to another at will.

The founding of formal associations is not the only indicator of class consciousness. Craftsmen, for example, cooperated outside of organizations to advance their economic interests. Most active were the craftsmen who practiced trades that town and colony governments viewed as having a public interest and, therefore, licensed and regulated. These craftsmen and tradesmen, particularly the porters, carters, coopers, butchers, and bakers, often cooperated voluntarily to shape the regulations under which they worked. These regulations included not only the maintenance of quality but also the fixing of prices. And it was over the setting of prices that craftsmen and tradesmen became sufficiently exercised to engage in strike actions. Most visible were the strikes by licensed cartmen in New York in 1677, bakers in New York in 1741, and Savannah carpenters in 1746, but, overall, the incidence of such strikes was extremely small and the strikes themselves were highly disorganized affairs.

Artisans appear to have only cooperated across craft lines. The only example of broadly based union activity appears to have been the 1747 petition of building-trades workers to New York's governor against the competition presented by interlopers from New Jersey. The most significant informal cooperation among diverse craftsmen was of a political nature: pressuring town and colony governments to restrict the participation of slaves and freemen in the crafts. They supported taxing or closing the slave trade, taxing or prohibiting the use of slaves in the crafts, tightening the slave codes, and limiting the ability of masters to free their slaves.

In sum, the evidence of marketplace cooperation among craftsmen indicates that the American environment was infertile ground for the growth of class consciousness among craftsmen. The scarcity of skilled labor and the dynamic character of the colonial economy led craftsmen to augment their wealth by maximizing their flexibility in the marketplace. They developed only weak attachments to their social positions and, accordingly, tended to shun collective action.

The class movements of people less wealthy than the craftsmen resist full documentation. But it is clear enough that no organizations of any longevity resulted from whatever class solidarity people on the lower rungs of society developed. Even the journeymen who were squeezed by associations of their employers, the master craftsmen, failed to form organizations and only rarely withheld their labor in strike actions. Their first visible strike against their employers did not come until 1768, when journeyman tailors "turned out" in New York. In general, journeymen identified with the long-run interests of their master craftsmen and aspired to self-employment.

Even though no organized movements of employees existed during the colonial period, there were important instances of ad hoc, relatively spontaneous mass actions of colonial workers that were directed toward well-defined economic objectives. The most class conscious of all American workers were, no doubt, the slaves. There may have been as many as forty major slave revolts, including a massive New York rebellion in 1712, an uprising of at least one hundred slaves on the Stone plantation near Charleston in 1739, and a plot, discovered and suppressed, to seize Annapolis, Maryland, in 1740. The number and scale of slave revolts were substantially smaller in North America than in the West Indies during the eighteenth century, partly because of the more favorable material conditions enjoyed by North American slaves and, more importantly, because of the larger size of the free population, relative to the slave, and its consequently greater ability to deter rebellion. During the eighteenth century, the colonies generally tightened their restrictions on slaves and free blacks, including increasing the severity of punishment. After the 1712 rebellion, New York punished thirteen slaves by hanging, three by burning on the stake, one with starvation, and one with breaking on the wheel. With this kind of force available to the free community, slaves resisted far more by casual sabotage, malingering, and escape than by organized, large-scale violence.

The unusually acute, overtly expressed class consciousness of the slaves evolved from their highly constrained legal position—one which denied to them the ownership of their own earning capacity, or "human capital." Colonial law eliminated significant chances for improvement within the context of the free marketplace and slaves responded appropriately to their dismal prospects. In contrast, most indentured servants benefited from the scarcity of labor when they negotiated the terms of their indentures, and all, even the redemptioners and the exiled felons, could look forward to eventual freedom. With few exceptions, indentured servants did not engage in significant collective action to promote their economic interests. Most of the exceptions were found in the Chesapeake during the seventeenth century before the distinctions between slave and bound labor became sharp, and almost all of these involved organized escape attempts. There were, however, other exceptions, more serious in scale and purpose. One was an unsuccessful plot hatched by a group of Cromwell's soldiers, sent to Virginia under long terms of servitude, to marshal the support of the servant class to begin the creation of an independent commonwealth. In 1721, a group of exiled convicts conspired, also unsuccessfully, to capture the magazine at Annapolis. More spectacularly, in 1768 scores of Greek and Italian laborers began a rebellion against their masters in New Smyrna, located in east Florida. They were serving under extremely unfavorable terms in a colony that lacked resources adequate to support its 1,000 settlers. Military intervention was required to suppress the rebellion, but turmoil, fueled by the chaos of the Revolution, continued until the late 1770s when the settlement disintegrated and the servants either scattered or died. Such episodes were not only infrequent but resulted from unusual circumstances, typically involving concentrated numbers of servants laboring under highly restrictive terms that denied them the material rewards usually enjoyed by indentured servants.

The only group of servants that engaged in frequent collective protests were the American seamen of the Royal Navy. Their situation warrants close scrutiny. Colonial seamen (sailors, carpenters, cooks, and cabin boys), particularly those with skills, were, on the whole, well paid during the colonial period. They required compensation for the risks to health and survival that they incurred and for the restrictions that their labor contracts, the common law, admiralty law, and colonial legislation placed on their personal freedom while at sea. However, the sailors impressed into the Royal Navy did not receive the wage that their skills, risk taking, and personal loss of freedom warranted. They had been coerced into accepting lower wages than those that prevailed in the marketplace. Unable to afford labor at the going wages, treating its sailors more harshly than private employers did, yet enjoying the freedom of action befitting the central military institution of the modern British nation, the Royal Navy met its labor needs by impressment. During wartime periods, the navy swept through seacoast cities and captured scores of men. One raid in New York in 1757 took as many as 800 men, but the favorite targets were the towns of New England, particularly Boston. During the 1740s, when nearly continuous warfare produced intense impressment, seamen reacted with large-scale rioting. The climax came in 1747 when thousands of people took to the streets in Boston for three days after a large raid. Their objective was to gain the support of the town and of the colony for resisting impressment. However, they received only condemnation from the town meeting and the House of Representatives for threatening established order and the military strength needed for successful commerce.[21]

The protests of the seamen stand as obvious exceptions to the individualistic way in which colonial laborers usually pursued their economic self-interest. But this exception is hardly surprising. Impressment subjected seamen to coercion more severe than that encountered by any other group of laborers except for the slaves.

Moreover, seamen were accustomed to greater freedom and were able to communicate effectively with one another since they were concentrated in seaboard towns. They had both the disposition and the ability to organize under the threat of impressment. However, even their collective action did not reveal a fundamental class consciousness. It simply revealed an organized, appropriate response to a short-run threat to their economic freedom. When the seamen found themselves free of impressment threats, they exhibited the individualistic patterns of behavior typical of colonial labor in general. Indeed, the fact that the mob action of the seamen was so strikingly unusual underscores the individualistic nature of the colonial labor market. The seamen were simply resisting the circumvention of the free labor market by the Royal Navy.

NOTES

1. The best comprehensive survey of the sources of colonial population growth, from which this estimate is drawn, is Jim Potter, "The Growth of Population in America, 1700–1860," in D. V. Glass and D. E. C. Eversley (eds.), *Population in History: Essays in Historical Demography* (Chicago: Aldine, 1965), pp. 631–688.

2. Among the rapidly growing body of secondary sources for such data are Kenneth A. Lockridge, "The Population of Dedham, Massachusetts, 1636–1736," *Economic History Review,* 19 (August 1966), 318–344; John Demos, "Notes on Life in Plymouth Colony," *William and Mary Quarterly,* 22 (April 1965), 246–286; Philip J. Greven, Jr., "Family Structure in Seventeenth-Century Andover, Massachusetts," *William and Mary Quarterly,* 23 (April 1966), 234–256; Robert Higgs and H. Louis Stettler III, "Colonial New England Demography: A Sampling Approach," *William and Mary Quarterly,* 27 (April 1970), 282–294; Billy G. Smith, "Death and Life in a Colonial Immigrant City: A Demographic Analysis of Philadelphia," *Journal of Economic History,* 37 (December 1977); 863–889; Daniel Scott Smith, "The Demographic History of Colonial New England," *Journal of Economic History,* 32 (March 1972), 165–183; Maris A. Vinovskis, "Mortality Rates and Trends in Massachusetts Before 1860," *Journal of Economic History,* 32 (March 1972), 184–213.

3. The other major component of the "nonwhite" population in North America was, of course, the native American Indians. Although they contributed significantly to the adaptation of European agriculture to American conditions and engaged in the fur trade as trappers and middlemen, they cannot be said to have been an integral part of the developing colonial economy. In 1860, when the first census count of Indians occurred, the Indian population was comparable in size to only 1 percent of the black population. Indeed, Europeans commonly viewed the removal or extermination of the Indians as necessary for expansion, partic-

ularly when tribes were hostile or occupied desirable land. This was no small task; on the eve of the European invasion the Indian population north of Mexico was at least 1 million, and estimates for the total in North America and the New World range as high as 9.8 million and 90 million, respectively. See Henry F. Dobyns, "Estimating Aboriginal American Population: An Appraisal of Techniques with a New Hemisphere Estimate," *Current Anthropology,* 7 (1966), 395–449. For a recent survey of the salient literature concerning the confrontation between European and Indian populations see Wilbur R. Jacobs, "The Fatal Confrontation: Early Native-White Relations on the Frontiers of Australia, New Guinea, and America: A Comparative Study," *Pacific Historical Review,* 40 (August 1971), 283–309.

4. In the centuries to follow, sustained high rates of black natural increase would build an enormous black population in the United States. While the mainland of North America received only 4.5 percent of all slaves imported in the Atlantic slave trade down to 1861, by 1950 the United States contained fully one-third of the Afro-American (North and South) population. This is not necessarily to say that the United States slave system, and the caste system which followed Emancipation, were less harsh than counterparts in Latin America. But it does indicate that although slavery in the United States may have been more intellectually and psychologically brutalizing, its physical conditions, whatever their source—social or physiographic—were consistent with and favorable for high rates of reproduction and survival. For the best estimates of slave imports see Philip Curtin, *The Atlantic Slave Trade: A Census* (Madison, Wis.: University of Wisconsin Press, 1969), pp. 86–93.

5. Boston's hinterland may not have been growing rapidly enough to feed the city at the end of the colonial period. See David Klingaman, "Food Surpluses and Deficits in the American Colonies, 1768–1772," *Journal of Economic History,* 31 (September 1971), 553–569.

6. Higgs and Stettler, *op. cit.,* pp. 288–289.

7. This assumes that the percentage of people actively employed in the labor force remained more or less constant throughout the colonial period and that the productivity of labor did not decline as the labor force expanded. The first assumption is reasonable, but as yet untested, and the second is undebatable, at least for the eighteenth century, given the strong probability that intensive economic growth had set in before the end of the colonial period.

8. For instance, Richard B. Morris estimates that on the eve of the Revolution, American real wages exceeded English by 30 to 100 percent. See *Government and Labor in Early America* (New York: Columbia University Press, 1946), p. 45.

9. For emphasis on the significance of male-female productivity differentials in preindustrial agricultural systems, see Ester Boserup, *Woman's Role in Economic Development* (London: George Allen and Unwin, 1970), pp. 53 ff.

10. For suggestions of the difficulties faced by Virginia planters in using the indentured labor of Englishmen, see Edmund S. Morgan, "The Labor Problem at Jamestown, 1607–18," *American Historical Review,* 76 (June 1971), 595–611.

11. For an economic model designed to explain the rise of serfdom in Europe, see Evsey D. Domar, "The Causes of Slavery or Serfdom: A Hypothesis," *Journal of Economic History,* 30 (March 1970), 18–32.

12. For a masterly discussion of these issues, see Winthrop D. Jordan, *White over Black: American Attitudes Toward the Negro, 1550–1812* (Chapel Hill, N.C.: University of North Carolina Press, 1968), especially pp. 44–98.

13. Carl N. Degler, *Neither Black nor White: Slavery and Race Relations in Brazil and the United States* (New York: Macmillan, 1971).

14. Prominent examples of a rapidly growing literature concerning economic growth in the colonial period include Terry L. Anderson, "Wealth Estimates for the New England Colonies, 1650–1709," *Explorations in Economic History,* 12 (1975), 151–176; Marc Egnal, "The Economic Development of the Thirteen Continental Colonies, 1720 to 1775," *William and Mary Quarterly,* 32 (April, 1975), 191–222; Robert E. Gallman, "The Pace and Pattern of American Economic Growth: American Growth Before 1840," in Lance E. Davis, *et al.* (eds.), *American Economic Growth: An Economist's History of the United States* (New York: Harper & Row, 1972), pp. 17–32; Alice Hanson Jones, "Wealth Estimates for the American Middle Colonies, 1774," *Economic Development and Cultural Change,* 18 (July 1970), entire, and "Wealth Estimates for the New England Colonies About 1770," *Journal of Economic History,* 32 (March 1972), 98–127; Klingaman, *op. cit.;* and Jackson Turner Main, *The Social Structure of Revolutionary America* (Princeton, N.J.: Princeton University Press, 1965). The pioneering work on this problem is George R. Taylor, "American Economic Growth Before 1840: An Exploratory Essay," *Journal of Economic History,* 24 (December 1964), 427–444.

15. See Taylor, *op. cit.* For lower estimates, on the order of 0.5 percent per year, see Egnal, *op. cit.,* and Lance E. Davis, *American Economic Growth, an Economist's History of the United States.* (New York: Harper & Row, 1972), pp. 21 ff.

16. James F. Shepherd and Gary M. Walton, "Trade, Distribution, and Economic Growth in Colonial America," *Journal of Economic History,* 32 (March 1972), 128–145.

17. An already classic study of the slow transformation of extended, patriarchal families in New England is Philip J. Greven, Jr., *Four Generations: Population, Land, and Family in Colonial Andover, Massachusetts* (Ithaca, N.Y.: Cornell University Press, 1970).

18. Jones, *Wealth Estimates for the American Middle Colonies,* p. 119.

19. James A. Henretta, "Economic Development and Social Structure in Colonial Boston," *William and Mary Quarterly,* 22 (January 1965), 75–92; and James T. Lemon and Gary B. Nash, "The Distribution of Wealth in Eighteenth Century America: A Century of Changes in Chester County, Pennsylvania, 1693–1802," *Journal of Social History,* 2 (Fall 1968), 1–24.

20. The distribution of wealth among freemen in the South may have resembled that in the Middle Atlantic colonies, although adequate data on that region is lacking. In fact, in Virginia, which profited from an increasingly liberal and regular system of land distribution and reorganized tobacco marketing in the eighteenth century, the distribution of wealth may have been even more favorable and stable than in Pennsylvania.

21. On the mob activities of the seamen see Jesse Lemisch, "Jack Tar in the Streets: Merchant Seamen in the Politics of Revolutionary America," *William and Mary Quarterly,* 25 (July 1968), 371–407. For a fuller description of the economic and legal position of the seamen, see Morris, *op. cit.,* pp. 225–278.

SUGGESTED READINGS

Books

Bridenbaugh, Carl. *The Colonial Craftsman.* Chicago: University of Chicago Press, 1961.

Foner, Philip S. *History of the Labor Movement in the United States.* New York: International Publishers, 1947.

Jernegan, Marcus W. *Laboring and Dependent Classes in Colonial America.* New York: Frederick Ungar, 1960.

Lemon, James T. *The Best Poor Man's Country: A Geographical Study of Southeastern Pennsylvania.* Baltimore: Johns Hopkins Press, 1972.

Main, Jackson Turner. *The Social Structure of Revolutionary America.* Princeton, N.J.: Princeton University Press, 1965.

Morgan, Edmund S. *American Slavery, American Freedom: The Ordeal of Colonial Virginia.* New York: W. W. Norton, 1975.

Morris, Richard B. *Government and Labor in Early America.* New York: Columbia University Press, 1946.

Smith, Abbot E. *Colonists in Bondage: White Servitude and Convict Labor in America, 1607–1776.* Chapel Hill, N.C.: University of North Carolina Press, 1947.

Wells, Robert V. *The Population of the British Colonies in America Before 1776.* Princeton, N.J.: Princeton University Press, 1975.

Articles

Greven, Philip J., Jr. "Family Structure in Seventeenth-Century Andover, Massachusetts," *William and Mary Quarterly*, 23 (April 1966), 234–256.

———. "Historical Demography and Colonial America," *William and Mary Quarterly*, 24 (July 1967), 438–454.

Henretta, James A. "Economic Development and Social Structure in Colonial Boston," *William and Mary Quarterly*, 22 (January 1965), 75–92.

Jones, Alice Hanson. "Wealth Estimates for the New England Colonies About 1770," *Journal of Economic History*, 32 (March 1972), 98–127.

Land, Aubrey C. "Economic Base and Social Structure: The Northern Chesapeake in the Eighteenth Century," *Journal of Economic History*, 25 (December 1965), 639–654.

Lemisch, Jesse. "Jack Tar in the Streets: Merchant Seamen in the Politics of Revolutionary America," *William and Mary Quarterly*, 25 (July 1968), 371–407.

Lockridge, Kenneth A. "The Population of Dedham, Massachusetts, 1636–1736," *Economic History Review*, 19 (August 1966), 318–344.

Menard, Russell R. "From Servant to Freeholder: Status Mobility and Property Accumulation in Seventeenth-Century Maryland," *William and Mary Quarterly*, 30 (January 1973), 37–64.

Potter, Jim. "The Growth of Population in America, 1700–1860," in D. V. Glass and D. E. C. Eversley (eds.), *Population in History: Essays in Historical Demography*. Chicago: Aldine, 1965, pp. 631–688.

Vinovskis, Maris A. "Mortality Rates and Trends in Massachusetts Before 1860," *Journal of Economic History*, 32 (March 1972), 184–213.

4
Mercantilism and American Expansion, 1607-1815

The colonies matured not only in response to strictly economic conditions but also in response to the framework of British imperial law, considered loosely under the rubric "mercantilism." Thus the extension of the European marketplace to North America was more than the simple growth of complementary trade—exchange of manufactured goods and services for the products of fields, mines, woods, and waters—between metropolitan centers and colonial regions; it was also a result of empires competing vigorously: both metropolitan center and colonial population could find their development opportunities altered, either restricted or even enhanced, by the circumstances of international politics. The significance of such circumstances is worthy of special consideration in no small part because historians have often found the successful rebellion of the North American colonists against the obligations of empire as crucial to the maturing of the American economy.

IMPERIAL STRESS AND THE ELABORATION OF MERCANTILISM

The West Indies: The Center of Imperial Rivalries

The British mercantile system evolved from the interplay of imperial rivalries within the Atlantic economy, and the portions of it that had the greatest effect on the North American colonists were shaped by international competition for its most dynamic sector—the West Indian sugar complex.

In the sixteenth century the English had confined their West Indian interest to raiding the Spanish trade routes, but during the 1620s and 1630s they built colonies in the Leeward Islands, on Barbados and Antigua in particular. (See Figure 5.) During this period of settlement the English, along with the French, had to abandon privateering in order to gain the tolerance of the Spanish and the Dutch, and, as had the Southern colonies, these West Indian colonies secured their first economic base in the production of tobacco. But the English enterprise rested on a mere toehold in the empire created by Spain in the late fifteenth century and serviced by the Dutch, who by 1620 had come to dominate Caribbean trading.

Compatibility among the European powers in the West Indies persisted only so long as the English and the French were satisfied with their secondary roles. And the ambitions of the English, particularly the growing group of American traders and investors, mounted quickly, beginning with the effort to eliminate Dutch trade with the

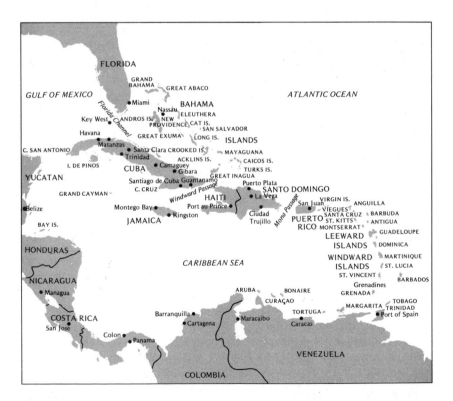

FIGURE 5: *The West Indies*

English colonies and, ultimately, with the entire West Indies. In the 1650s Cromwell, followed by the Stuart kings Charles II and James II, sought the destruction of the Dutch influence by a series of wars. The culmination of this policy came in 1674, when England, which had been supporting France during the Third Dutch War, negotiated a separate peace with the Dutch that included a division of imperial interest between East and West. From this point on in the Caribbean, the Dutch were willing to follow where the English led.

By the time of the English treaty with the Dutch the stakes of empire had grown considerably because of a sugar revolution that had begun in the tobacco islands. In the mid-seventeenth century, West Indian tobacco planters had experienced a price squeeze similar to the one that plagued the Virginia planters. Also, their soil was becoming depleted, and they lacked their Virginia competitors' easy alternative of moving production onto new lands. Then, too, Europeans found West Indian tobacco to suffer from an "earthy" aroma and preferred the Virginia product. Thus by at least 1650 the tobacco economy was ripe for rapid transformation. As early as the 1640s the Dutch had promoted a more vigorous agriculture by introducing and subsidizing techniques of sugar production (learned from the Portuguese in northern Brazil) in the British and French West Indies. In the third quarter of the century sugar production made rapid gains, and, by the last quarter, in the English and French islands, tobacco had given way entirely to sugar production, thanks to the European tastes for sweetened medicine, drink (especially raw, immature wine), and food. Pursuing this new opportunity, the English expanded their West Indian enterprises, beginning with the settlement of Jamaica under Cromwell's Western Design. Although the English were unable to conquer the Spanish Indies, suffering a defeat at Santo Domingo in 1655, Jamaica soon became the largest of the English colonies in the islands. A simultaneous increase in Caribbean trade occurred, not only in sugar, but in the commodities necessary to support the expansion of sugar production, including slaves. While the numerous small farmers in Jamaica could grow tobacco with family labor, sugar farmers required a large servile labor force. As a result, in the fifty years after 1670 the African population in Jamaica increased more than nine times, whereas the white population increased by little more than one-third.[1] Until the 1660s Dutch entrepreneurs dominated the provision of slaves for all the West Indian colonies, but by 1665 the Royal African Company, operating under a charter from the English crown, had driven the Dutch from trade with the English islands, and following the Third Dutch War, France became the legal supplier of slaves to the Spanish colonies.

The Initiation of the Navigation Acts and the Dutch Rivalry

As the English waged war both to reduce Dutch power in the West Indies and to advance the trading interests of the nation, they enacted imperial legislation to further the same ends. In 1651, shortly before the outbreak of the First Dutch War, Parliament initiated the first of the Navigation Acts, providing that only English ships could carry the exports of English plantations and that Continental goods could arrive in English colonies only in English ships or ships from countries in which the goods originated. The legislation thus protected the new English merchants with American commercial stakes by excluding the Dutch from the English colonial trade both in the West Indies and the Far East. Support for restriction gained particular force when a prolonged European trade recession became acute in 1649. The concern over sluggish trade, linked with the growing attractiveness of West Indian colonies and Cromwell's ambitions in the Caribbean, led directly to the first Navigation Act and contributed to the first of the Dutch wars.

Subsequent mercantile legislation pursued the same objectives of enlarging English commercial power, particularly in the colonial zones of the world, and of assuring the supply of tropical and semitropical products to England; in the process, the English designed the mercantile system to augment the competitive strength of their nation-state. To reduce expenditures on foreign middlemen and on imports of raw materials into the empire would also diminish, and perhaps reverse, the flow of specie out of the empire. And to the mercantilist world, specie and bullion were the measures of national wealth and, hence, national power.

The paradigm of success was the Spanish empire, which was based on the easy acquisition of precious metals in the New World. Unable to duplicate the Spanish success and finding only a limited future in plundering the Spanish trade routes, the English, in the seventeenth century, settled for the more prosaic benefits of commercial independence and a dynamic set of colonies producing primary products in strong European demand. The quest for an inflow of specie was made peculiarly intense by the assumption that the amount of the wealth—defined as the stock of precious metals—available in the world was fixed. Accordingly, the only way a nation-state could grow was by either extracting new precious metals or by encroaching on the wealth and power of its competitors. The notion of wealth as the capacity to grow, and the corresponding idea of many nations simultaneously becoming more wealthy, were at least a century distant.

Restoration Policy: Articulation of Mercantilism and the French Rivalry

The English mercantile system emerged full-blown during the Stuart Restoration, when the crown sought to augment and stabilize its own revenues. Much of the new legislation only reinforced the provisions of the Cromwellian acts. The Navigation Act of 1660, the first during the Restoration, reiterated the regulations imposed in 1651 and added the additional requirements that three-fourths of the crews of English ships engaged in the colonial trade had to be English and that certain colonial goods, the "enumerated" items, had to be shipped directly to England. By the latter addendum, England tried to ensure a supply of the most important primary products of tropical and subtropical origin, including sugar, tobacco, cotton, and indigo. (Rice and molasses were added in 1704, naval stores in 1705, and furs in 1724.) In 1663 Parliament complemented the act of enumeration with the Staple Act, which forced the use of English shippers in the conduct of the colonial trade by requiring that almost all foreign goods with colonial destinations be unloaded in England and subjected to a duty (the duty was remitted if the goods were then carried to the colonies by English shippers). The final act in the creation of the fundamental system of colonial regulation was one of 1673, which was designed to suppress evasion of the act of enumeration by colonial merchants, particularly of the port of Boston, that threatened to lead to the development of colonial trading centers rivaling the entrepôt of the mother country. That evasion was possible because the act of enumeration allowed captains to carry enumerated goods from one colony to another without paying customs or going to England; having obeyed the letter of the law, colonial captains often proceeded to carry their transshipped tobacco, sugar, or other staple to a Continental port. To close the loophole, the 1673 reform called upon merchants to bond themselves to take enumerated products only to England, Wales, or Berwick-on-Tweed (a receipt from the port of delivery was necessary for a refund of the bond). Under the original provisions of the 1673 act if colonial traders did not post bond, they had to pay a Plantation Duty, which was usually equal to the entrance tax that all merchants paid when bringing enumerated items to England. Thus if colonial merchants paid this duty and then took their goods directly to the Continent (in explicit violation of the law only after 1696), they would no longer have a tax advantage over English merchants in selling in Continental ports.

Restoration policy also involved the creation of an effective and uniform administration for the new body of colonial regulations. Previously the making of colonial policy rested with the king, ad hoc committees of the Privy Council, and the Council of Trade (established in 1650), although in fact they left it largely to the great trading companies. Under the Stuarts and the creation of a uniform framework of imperial law, the Privy Council appointed the Committee for Foreign Plantations (1660), which shifted power away from the large trading companies and the mercantile community of London toward the merchants dominating American commerce. In practice this committee at first shared responsibility for colonial affairs with a variety of other committees, but in 1675 an independent body was created, the Commission on Trade and Plantations (the Lords of Trade), an advisory body to the Privy Council. For about twenty years the Lords of Trade vigorously tightened enforcement of the Acts of Trade and Navigation and maximized the returns on the investments of the crown. In addition to sending customs commissioners into every major port to collect duties and prosecute illegal trade, the Lords of Trade attempted to drastically alter the colonial political structure in order to shape colonial economic development into a mold more amenable to English merchants. In direct response to the complaints of English merchants that the Massachusetts legislature was encouraging the formation of a rival entrepôt in Massachusetts Bay, the Lords created the Dominion of New England (1684), revoking the charter of Massachusetts, abolishing the Massachusetts General Court, and uniting New England and New York under the common management of Governor Edmund Andros. The Lords of Trade made similar if less radical attempts at reorganization and integration in the other colonies. But in a series of political disturbances, tenuously connected with the Glorious Revolution in England in 1688, entrenched aristocracies challenged the Lords of Trade and their American agents. Subsequently, in the face of such bitter opposition, the new sovereigns, William and Mary, abandoned centralization and authoritarian schemes. In 1691, Massachusetts received a new charter, restoring the essence of her previous political freedom, and in 1696 the Lords of Trade was replaced by the Board of Trade which, composed largely of paid officials, proved to be more responsive to political conditions in the colonies and uninclined to provide centralized executive administration for the colonies.

Tough reordering of the system of navigation and trade under the Stuarts, like the initial passage of the Navigation Acts, was in large part a response to an imperial rivalry—this time, with France. After the Dutch and English made peace in 1674, competition between France and England intensified in the Western Hemisphere. The English had already founded the Hudson's Bay Company (1670) to compete with the French for the lucrative Canadian and interior fur trade. And after the slaving concession for the large Spanish market passed to France following the destruction of Dutch commerce in the Third Dutch War, it became an object of competition. In addition, the French West Indies powerfully challenged British sugar production by growing a cane that not only surpassed the British in quality but yielded a lower-priced sugar. Further, the French West Indies offered attractive markets to New England merchants who sought to make up their unfavorable balance of payments with England. These colonial conflicts helped lead to a struggle between the Anglo-Dutch alliance and the French-Spanish entente—a struggle that included five conflicts on American shores (King William's War, 1689–1697; Queen Anne's War, 1701–1713; the War of Jenkins' Ear, 1739–1743; King George's War, 1743–1748; and the French and Indian War, 1755–1763). To build up its own power at the expense of the French, England tightened restrictions on the activities of the wide-ranging, ambitious New England merchants. In addition to attempting to control illegal trade by creating an effective enforcement bureaucracy, Parliament, hoping to force the merchants to rely on British-grown sugar, enacted the Molasses Act in 1733, effecting what was designed to be a prohibitory duty on the import of French and Spanish sugar into the British mainland colonies.

A New Interest: Regulation of Manufacturing

Thus the English at first had conceived a system of colonial control in order to exclude the Dutch from the West Indies, and later refined it both to compete more effectively with the French and to ensure a more rational and unified administration of the North American colonies. It was this system that persisted, without radical change, down to 1763. The one important departure that occurred, as mercantilism became somewhat more a means of industrial encouragement, was in the regulation of colonial manufacturing. During the eighteenth century the government began to place a greater emphasis upon domestic production as a means not only of creating a more favorable balance of trade—the objective of seventeenth-century industrial promotion—but also of increasing employment and reducing poverty (and thus public support for the poor). As part of that effort, England abolished export duties after 1720, placed bounties on domestic goods such as linen, paper, and sailcloth, and levied protective duties on competitive manufactures; it also attempted to prohibit the colonial manufacture, or at least export, of items such as woolens (1699), hats (1732), and certain kinds of iron and steel (1750). In addition, the Board of Trade and the Privy Council disallowed those acts of colonial assemblies that, manifesting independent mercantile policies, subsidized or protected, often through import duties, industries that might compete with British producers. At the same time, however, England promoted colonial manufacture of commodities badly needed at home but not sufficiently available (colonists received bounties for the production of naval stores in 1705, for example, and as early as 1662 found motherly encouragement in the shipbuilding enterprise). Nevertheless, if the British had lived up to mercantilist theory and if British rule had persisted into the nineteenth century, the net result of regulation would have been a retardation of the American industrial revolution.

MERCANTILISM AND AMERICAN DEVELOPMENT TO 1763

Although the mercantile system was largely produced by the narrow requirements of international, imperial competition, mercantilism did not interfere, in any compelling, fundamental way, with the character of North American development dictated by endowments of land, labor, and capital and the structure of European demand for goods and services. Given European resources and markets and the relative abundance of land in the colonies, the preeminent form of economic activity had to be specialization in semitropical agricultural products. The mercantile desideratum of complementary production in the mother country and colonies reinforced the basic pattern of development dictated by comparative advantage.

Of major importance to the development of agriculture in the North, which proved, ultimately, to be the most dynamic center of American growth, was the fact that the British system presented no obstacles to the export of wheat, wheat products, livestock, and articles of simple manufacture. The great significance that the British attached to the efficient provisioning of the West Indies allowed the free development of agriculture in the Middle Atlantic colonies, despite its similarity to that in England. Further, the English never interfered with colonial exports of grain and grain products to southern Europe, and that trade proved to be increasingly valuable in the mid-eighteenth century.

With regard to manufacturing, British restrictive policies failed to hinder the development of colonial capacities because of lax enforcement, and, as already mentioned, a few resource-based manufacturing enterprises, like shipbuilding and the processing of forest products into naval stores, actually received encouragement from the British. Consequently the colonists by 1763 had developed a well-diversified and extensive accumulation of preindustrial manufacturing activities. Although the British may have hampered the immigration of skilled labor in some cases, the shortage of skilled labor was, in fact, due more to the consistent liberalization of colonial land distribution, which widened alternatives for those with skills.

Further, the colonists clearly benefited from the military and naval protection afforded by the English. The contribution of the colonists to their own defense, even in the almost continuous warfare of the 1740s, was minimal. It is true that the colonists would probably have received protection from the center of any empire to which they might have belonged, but they were fortunate enough to receive protection from the nation that proved itself, in the course of the eighteenth century, to be the strongest in the Western Hemisphere and the most capable of providing security for economic activity. From a military standpoint, if independence had occurred before the defeat of the French in 1763, it would have been very expensive to the Americans, as was made clear during the Revolution and the War of 1812.

Finally, the mercantilism that emerged from the Restoration promoted the growth of North America by ensuring that its economic development lay not with great, monopolistic trading companies, but with relatively small, independent merchants on both sides of the Atlantic and by providing those merchants with a generally predictable body of imperial law and conditions remarkably close to those of free competition.

Nonetheless, in the conduct of commerce, if not the enterprise of manufacturing, the colonists did suffer certain liabilities of the English mercantile system. Colonial merchants undoubtedly faced narrowed opportunities and colonial producers received diminished incomes as a result of the Acts of Trade and Navigation, primarily from the distortions the acts imposed on colonial trade routes. If the colonists had been able to send their staple products directly to Continental markets, both planters and merchants would have realized larger incomes, especially in the case of tobacco. Similarly, colonial consumers and merchants would have realized savings if finished goods could have been imported directly from the Continent instead of first having to pass through England. Finally, those colonists who produced for and traded with the West Indies suffered losses as a result of being legally limited to the British islands. Offsetting these losses, however, were two considerations: the security that colonial staple producers received from having a guaranteed British market for their output and the very considerable, although as yet unmeasured, illicit traffic that transpired between the merchants of the northern colonies and the French and Spanish Caribbean. Taking these advantages and disadvantages into account, the consensus of economic historians is that the Navigation Acts proved only moderately burdensome to the colonial economy. The annual cost of distortions of trade routes imposed by the acts, at least from 1763 to 1775, was probably no more than 3 percent of colonial product, and that cost was offset, to an indefinite extent, by all the benefits of membership in the empire, including the subsidies, bounties, and military protection.[2] The Acts of Trade and Navigation slightly diminished colonial incomes, but they cannot be said to have either dramatically altered the pattern of colonial development or sharply reduced the returns available to the colonists in production for export or in the conduct of oceanic commerce.

IMPLEMENTING THE LOGIC OF EMPIRE: THE COMING OF REVOLUTION, 1763–1775

The limited impact of the Acts of Trade and Navigation on colonial economic development down to 1763 suggests that the Revolution and the attainment of political independence exerted little sway on the course of American economic life. However, it is doubtful that the conditions the British imposed upon American development would have remained unchallenged through the American industrial revolution of the nineteenth century. As American economic power grew, and her industrial development paralleled that of Britain, Americans would have resisted the spirit of mercantilism and tensions might well have disrupted the empire. Moreover, even as early as 1763, before American competition became a significant issue, the British altered the imperial framework in a capricious fashion that threatened to change the character of colonial development. Although those structural alterations did not impose an overbearing economic burden, they were significant in that they exposed the dangers inherent in an imperial system in which ultimate political control over economic development rested with the mother country.

New Imperial Priorities: New Costs

Beginning in 1763, with an intensity of purpose that they had lacked since the Restoration, the English turned their attention to the role of the North American colonies within the empire. In that year they decisively defeated the French in North America, gaining control over both much of the French West Indies (Guadeloupe, Martinique, and St. Lucia) and French Canada. The traditional logic of mercantilism should have led the English to keep the French sugar islands, whose essential raw material could have been used to create a more favorable balance of trade; but the British West Indian sugar planters, fearing the competition that would result from including the

French islands in the empire, successfully prevailed upon the government to turn the most important islands back to France at the Peace of Paris. As a result Britain concentrated its attention on the management of its enlarged continental holdings. (See Figure 6.)

Two major problems confronted the British in North America, the first being that of governing the newly acquired lands in the interior, to the west of the Appalachian ridge. With the French removed, exploiters of various sorts poured into new areas, arousing Indian hostility (including Pontiac's Rebellion), requiring protection, and embroiling themselves in internal conflicts for control of the new areas. Land-speculating organizations and commercial syndicates like the Ohio Company and the Loyal Company, with the support of colonial representatives in England (Benjamin Franklin among them), wanted the immediate extension of government and western settlement, while trading companies wanted to exclude settlers from the area between the Appalachians and the Mississippi in order to duplicate the French pattern of fur traffic. The second problem England faced was that of financing the protection of the old colonies and meeting the debts acquired during the Seven Years' War (the North American phase of which was the French and Indian War). The yearly cost to support British troops in North America during that war was between £300,000 and £400,000, and the debt incurred reached £1.5 million. The English government believed that it was politically impossible to increase property taxes at home, and that, in any case, the colonists themselves should bear a larger share of the costs of their own defense.

To settle the western question the British began by drawing the Proclamation Line of 1763, a victory for the fur traders, since it prohibited settlement west of the Appalachians and opened the fur trade to almost anyone. But the cutthroat competition of unregulated fur trade resulted in Indian disturbances which, reinforced by the continuing pressure of the colonial land developers in London, brought about a redrawing of the line in 1768 to suit the land companies. Then in 1774 the English reversed course once again by passing the Quebec Act (one of the Intolerable Acts), extending the boundary of Quebec to the Ohio, and causing seaboard colonists interested in western settlement to become fearful that Quebec's government would support the fur traders in the coveted northern Ohio valley. These actions clearly demonstrated British irresolution, and it seemed quite possible that Britain would halt the generous land policy, which almost all colonists saw as vital to continuing expansion and prosperity. Even if the western restrictions were not yet directly burdensome on a large portion of the colonists, the uncertain, unpredictable course of British policy created strong doubts

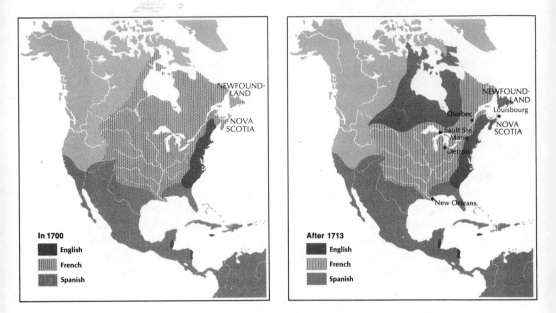

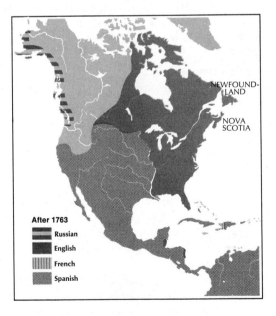

FIGURE 6: *North American Empires*

about the reliability and, ultimately, the legitimacy of British rule on behalf of colonial interests.

Reform: Administrative, Fiscal, and Monetary

The British response to the fiscal problems created by their protracted North American wars was to introduce new revenue measures, tighten the administration of the colonies, and, in general, force the mainland colonies to conform more closely to mercantile expectations. Like the legislation affecting the future of the western territory, impact of the measures was usually slight, but their potential cost was substantial, and the manner of their enactment highlighted the character of English rule.

Fiscal reform actually began in 1762, with the passage of a wartime measure that ordered absentee customs officials to their colonial posts, increased their cut of the revenues they collected, and gave the navy authority to seize cargoes suspected of customs violations. Parliament placed the act on a permanent basis in 1763 and the next year added the Revenue Act, which included a revision of the Molasses Act of 1733 (the Sugar Act) lowering the duty on molasses from the foreign West Indies but for the first time providing the means for strict enforcement. It also taxed wine imports from southern Europe; eliminated the refund of the tax on European goods transshipped from England to the colonies; tightened customs regulation by requiring cargo lists (cockets) that described every package; and increased the list of enumerated items to include iron and lumber. To make the collection of duties more effective, the British also altered the judicial aspects of the Navigation Acts in this 1764 program: the vice-admiralty courts received larger jurisdiction, customs officers were guaranteed freedom from retaliatory suits by those falsely accused (if a judge specified "probable cause" for the initial prosecution), a new vice-admiralty court was established in Halifax, and defendants in customs cases were obliged to prove their innocence.

The Currency Act of 1764, accompanying the revenue and administrative measures, caused the colonists to be seriously constrained for the first time in the management of their money supply. The act prohibited the creation of all new land banks throughout the colonies, demanded the phased withdrawal of previous land-bank issues, banned additional issues of bills of credit as legal tender, and required a scheduled retirement of all past issues of bills of credit. The colonists, in the future, could issue bills only when supported by rigid retirement schedules (a mere two years for those issued during peacetime) and could not declare them legal tender. Thirteen years earlier Parliament had applied similar restrictions to New England, but that measure was merely a temporary step to correct the exceptional excesses of Massachusetts and Rhode Island and reflected the opposition of part of the New England mercantile community to reckless money issues, especially through land banks. The 1764 act, however, was designed to exert uniform, massive downward pressure on prices in the colonies in order to reduce the exchange rate of colonial currency in terms of sterling, and it evoked vociferous protest from the conservative mercantile communities of Philadelphia, New York, and Baltimore.

In adopting the Currency Act, the English desired four specific results: (1) an increase in the value of the currency in which the colonists paid their taxes, both old and new; (2) an increase in the value of debts owed to English merchants; (3) an increase in colonial demand for English imports, as a result of the increased worth of colonial currency in terms of sterling; and (4) a decline in English demand for exports as a result of the falling value of sterling in terms of colonial currency. An increased valuation of colonial currency obviously reinforced the intent of the revenue and administrative reforms, while a decline in English purchase of colonial goods reinforced the British desire to improve their balance-of-trade position with regard to the colonies.

The desire to increase demands for English imports stemmed from the same factor that had influenced the British in giving up the French sugar islands: the English had begun to take colonies more seriously as markets and to de-emphasize the desirability of having colonies that served as sources of supply for primary products. While promoting English exports, British policy also aimed to increase the flow of specie into Britain, as well as merely to improve the balance-of-payments position of the entire empire. Both of these interrelated objectives had received forceful advancement from merchants with strong North American ties and from the West Indian sugar planters during the 1763 debates over the disposition of the territory seized from France.

As intended by the framers, the Currency Act produced a sharp appreciation in currencies of at least Pennsylvania, New York, and Virginia between 1765 and 1770. And, during the same period, throughout the colonies, the real value of colonial paper money issues, relative to the size of the population, contracted. By 1769, motivated by new revenue acts and the contraction of the money supply, with its deleterious impact on their balance of trade, the colonists tried to limit their purchase of British imports through the Nonimportation Agreements. Of all the reforms after 1763, currency restriction probably had the most profound economic impact on the colonies and posed the greatest threat to their domestic economic arrangements.[3]

Further revenue measures followed. As part of Prime Minister George Grenville's budget, the Stamp Act of 1765 placed a levy on legal and commercial papers, newspapers and the voluminous pamphlet literature, and playing cards and dice. Then, under a new ministry, the Chancellor of the Exchequer, Charles Townshend, sponsored a set of duties, enacted in the Townshend Acts, that taxed the colonists on their consumption of paper, glass, lead, paints, and tea imported from Britain. Parliament also authorized the superior courts of the colonies to issue general search warrants (writs of assistance), reorganized the vice-admiralty districts to provide for the rapid disposition of appeals, and established an American board of customs commissioners in Boston, in order to bring the whole weight of customs duties, including the Townshend levies, to bear on the colonies. (To the same general end, Parliament founded a colonial Department of State in 1768 to specialize in the administration of government in North America.)

Soon after their introduction, these potentially very costly enactments were repealed, the Stamp Act in 1766 and the Townshend duties (except for the tax on tea) in 1770. (Although the colonists welcomed such repeal, it did not enhance their esteem of British policy makers, who seemed all the more unsure of their course.) From these short-lived revenue measures and the ones that accompanied them resulted a steady but far from disastrous outward flow of colonial resources between 1764 and the outbreak of Revolution. More costly and threatening were the regulations on trade with the West Indies and southern Europe, the two most lucrative avenues of colonial commercial endeavor. (Those who were smuggling and trading illegally had the most to lose.) As a result of the 1764 trade duties and restrictions, coupled with the Currency Act of 1764, it became more difficult for the colonists to compensate for the unfavorable balance of trade with England and sustain the growth of the Middle Atlantic colonies.

Had they been enforced uniformly, the new regulations would have been even costlier. But their complexity and comprehensiveness precluded effective enforcement, despite the augmented bureaucratic apparatus. Enforcement became arbitrary, selective, and distinctly political in character, with the English singling out for particular attention the merchants, such as John Hancock of Boston, who were visible political opponents of the British. The arbitrariness of all the new regulations was an important contributor to the development of a revolutionary situation and, as such, was no doubt more significant than the direct economic burden the regulations themselves posed. The capriciousness and unpredictability of British rule, and the potential for substantial damage to colonial interests, fueled a growing lack of respect for British authority including, ultimately, the prerogatives of the crown.[4] Thus, while any strictly economic interpretation of the origins of the Revolution is inadequate, there was significant economic content in the issues surrounding movement toward political independence.

POLITICAL INDEPENDENCE AND ECONOMIC OPPORTUNITY, 1775–1815

The period between the Revolution and the end of the War of 1812, the period of the formation of an independent national government, provides additional basis for assessing the significance of mercantilism. Depending on whether the new nation experienced significantly enhanced or restricted opportunity, it could be said, other conditions remaining fundamentally unchanged, that participation in the British imperial system had been either significantly costly or beneficial.

The Revolution and the Extent of Revolutionary Change

The leaders of the Revolution clearly had economic objectives. The stable yet open and responsive system of government they sought promised distinct economic benefits and protections to a broad sweep of economic interests. But few supporters of the Revolution wanted radical changes in the economic structure of American society.

Even the considerable mob activity associated with the Revolution lacked radical economic focus. Surely, economic issues fueled rioting. The Stamp Act riots were in part protests against the potential economic burden of the legislation. Seamen participating in the Golden Hill Riot in New York (1770) and the Boston Massacre (1770) were agitated over impressment. The burning of the British revenue vessel *Gaspee* by Rhode Island citizens (1772) clearly expressed opposition to the enforcement of the Acts of Trade and Navigation. Certainly the depression that afflicted the shipbuilding industry during the 1760s sharpened the antagonisms felt by all the urban mobs. Rural rioters such the Regulators in South Carolina (1767) and North Carolina (1771) and the Paxton Boys in Pennsylvania (1763–1764) sought greater economic benefits, particularly protection against Indians, for frontier farmers. The New York antirent rioters who attempted to seize land in the Hudson River valley in 1766 attacked the prerogatives of their landlords.

The riots, despite their economic content, did not represent fundamental attacks on property. Even the antirent rioters were essentially conservative: they simply sought the kind of access to freehold tenure of land commonly enjoyed elsewhere in the colonies. The other rural rioters primarily desired fuller representation in the political system of the colonies and had no deep economic concerns. And the urban rioters were led by propertied individuals, including merchants, artisans, lawyers, and even large landowners, who expressed grievances, both economic and political, common to many Americans. Moreover, riots as a means of adjusting imbalances in the social order were well accepted in eighteenth-century America and should not be interpreted as fundamental challenges to the economic order.[5] Rather than a drastic redistribution of wealth or a change in the manner of holding wealth, the rioters sought the creation of a government that was more even-handed, more representative, and more protective of economic opportunity for Americans.

The Revolution left intact the basic forms of American society, including the institutions for ordering economic life. Even slavery, despite its violation of the libertarian spirit of the Revolution, survived the Revolution largely whole. Five states did outlaw importation of slaves after 1776 and Philadelphia Quakers formed the world's first antislavery society in 1775. But abolition only made modest advances, even in northern states. Slavery survived into the 1780s in Massachusetts, Pennsylvania, and Rhode Island; into the 1790s in Connecticut; into the first decade of the nineteenth century in Ohio and New Jersey; and into the 1810s in Illinois, Indiana, and New York. In the South, many planters, particularly in Virginia, had cast their lot with the Revolution largely because they believed the British to be the greater threat to the future of slavery. Primogeniture and entail, abandoned as legal institutions after the Revolution, had been outmoded earlier by the availability of cheap, fertile land outside the settled districts. Not only did the Revolution leave mercantile interests and large landowners firmly in place as the wealthiest economic groups,[6] the membership remained generally unchanged and was affected more by the warfare of the Revolution than by internal Revolutionary politics. Revolutionary governments did, of course, displace wealthy Loyalists, including merchants in Boston and New York who had profited from very close ties to England, such as in government contracting, and some of the largest land proprietors like the Penn family and the quasi-feudal barons in the Hudson River valley. Where this occurred, there were, of course, advancement opportunities for new men; the pace of upward mobility quickened. (In Boston, for example, the merchant families of Lowell and Cabot, among others, took advantage of this situation, particularly in contracting for new state governments.) But such opportunities did not alter the distribution of wealth appreciably. When New York publicly auctioned land confiscated from Loyalists, for instance, Robert Morris and other new merchants used their recently acquired wealth and public connections to maintain the landholdings more or less unaltered until they sold off small parcels after the war. Thus, in assessing the impact of the Revolution on economic opportunity, it is more important to consider the changing character of commerce than to examine fundamental structural change.

Commercial Opportunities, 1775–1793

In 1774 and 1775 the First Continental Congress had prohibited trade with Britain, Ireland, and the British West Indies. The British followed with the Prohibitory Act of 1775, banning almost all trade with the thirteen colonies and calling for confiscation of vessels that violated the act. Accordingly, the British sought to blockade the coasts of the United States. The result appears to have been a marked decline in the trade with Britain that had dominated American commercial activity before the Revolution. However, the available data on commerce during the Revolution are so weak that it is impossible to know the magnitude of the decline. The period was chaotic, and it is always difficult to gauge the magnitude of illegal trade, particularly with the West Indies during the eighteenth century.

The impact of the American restriction of trade and the British blockade was muted by the weakness of the blockade. To establish an effective blockade the British needed to occupy the seven major ports between Halifax and Charleston, but they never held more than four at any one time. They occupied New York throughout the war but gave up Boston in 1776, Philadelphia in 1778, and Newport in 1779. In the South, the British did not take Savannah until 1778 and Charleston until 1780. The problems of enforcement were compounded by the facts that ports occupied by the British were open to British goods and that Americans had the requirements for successful evasion: a large fleet of ships highly appropriate for the coastal and West Indian trade, far more knowledge than the British of North American waters, and a long experience, sharpened during the French wars, in illegal trade. Moreover, the British navy, especially after evacuating Newport, faced an impressive fleet of American privateers. With several thousand vessels ranging as far as the North Sea and the Atlantic coasts of France and Spain, the privateers seized 2,000 British vessels and took 12,000 British sailors. The value of British goods and ships taken and sold at auction (often in French ports) came to £18 million. This gain was as much as the total value of American imports from England from 1768 to 1774, and was acquired at a much lower cost. Privateering also stimulated colonial shipbuilding and provided American seamen with experience in handling the larger warships that would enhance American naval strength after the Revolution.

American merchants, with their large merchant marine remarkably unencumbered by the British blockade, innovated in developing new patterns of trade. The First Continental Congress opened American ports to all traders (except subjects of Great Britain) and consistently promoted a policy of commercial freedom with friendly European nations. After 1778, when the French formed an alliance with the United States and British naval power was focused on the southern seaboard, trade with the French West Indies and with Europe expanded rapidly. In the European trade Americans suffered from the loss of British bounties for indigo and naval stores, the disruption of the fur trade and the fishing industry, and British suppression of rice exports through Charleston and Savannah. But Americans were able to purchase high levels of European imports (including goods of English origin) with tobacco, West Indian sugar, subsidies and loans from France, Spain, and the Netherlands, and the proceeds from the considerable expenditures of the French military in America. This activity, carried on under the rigors of war, gave Americans not only experience and contacts that would prove invaluable after the Revolution but also a well-honed taste for adventure and risk taking.

Because of their conditioning in the habits of commercial innovation, Americans adapted easily to a new framework of enterprise during the 1780s. Ironically, Americans resumed reliance on Great Britain as their major trading partner and quickly restored that trade after the conclusion of hostilities in 1783. The Revolution had stimulated American manufacturing by reducing the supplies of British goods and creating demands for military supplies. But Americans retained a strong desire to purchase European goods that had remained less expensive. Moreover, wartime shortages and wartime destruction, particularly in the South where the British used terror most systematically, augmented American demand for British manufactured goods. Also, American consumers preferred British goods, given the decades of mutual adaptation of tastes. Responding to this demand, British merchants set aside wartime attitudes and risked a rapid extension of credit to American importers. As a result of the resumption of trade with Britain, commerce revived during the 1780s, although its volume was not as large as it had been at the end of the colonial period. But Americans were able to conduct international trade somewhat more favorably after 1784 than they had from 1770 to 1774. Prices for American exports were higher after the Revolution than before, and the ratio between export prices and the prices Americans paid for goods they imported—the terms of trade —was substantially higher during the period 1784–1792 than between 1770 and 1775. (See Table 2.)

Part of this improved trading position was a result of freedom from a mercantile system. Relieved of the restrictions of the Molasses and Sugar Acts, the ex-colonists could trade with greater freedom, and at lower cost, with the French West Indies. The French allowed all American products except flour to enter their islands, and admitted flour in times of scarcity. They imposed only modest duties on salt fish and salt beef from New England and the Middle Atlantic states. The overall demand for traditional southern staples declined. This trend, however, had little to do with the Revolution. The decline had ensued before the Revolution and was advanced most dramatically by the French Revolution and its abolition of the tobacco monopoly. Offsetting the income losses from this decline in demand were the gains Americans enjoyed from the freedom they now had to ship their tobacco directly to Europe. That new trade greatly augmented the incomes of both the merchants, who had been excluded from this trade previously, and the Chesapeake tobacco planters. One estimate is that between 40 and 70 percent of the increase in the price

TABLE 2   IMPORT-EXPORT PRICES AND THE "TERMS OF TRADE"

	Index of Import Prices (1790 Equals 100) (1)	Index of Export Prices (1790 Equals 100) (2)	Terms of Trade (2)/(1)
1770	110	69	63
1771	104	75	72
1772	102	83	81
1773	109	78	72
1774	108	73	68
1775	109	70	64
1784	103	115	112
1785	101	106	105
1786	101	97	96
1787	101	92	91
1788	99	87	88
1789	99	87	88
1790	100	100	100
1791	103	92	89
1792	110	86	78

Source: Gordon C. Bjork, "The Weaning of the American Economy: Independence, Market Changes, and Economic Development," *Journal of Economic History*, 24 (December 1964), 554.

of tobacco between 1770–1772 and 1785–1789 resulted from this increased trading flexibility, or the release from mercantilism.[7] Consequently the upper South enjoyed a period of significant prosperity during the last half of the 1780s.

American commerce profited in other ways from the demise of mercantilism. Americans gained the ability to export all goods, not just tobacco, directly to the Continent, and trade with northern Europe boomed as a consequence. Americans exported, without detour, grain, flour, rice, potash, and naval stores to France and the Netherlands. (Bad European harvests made this Continental trade even more valuable during the 1790s.) Americans also took advantage of their new freedom by developing a direct trade with Asia. As early as 1786 Americans began shipping beef, flour, and naval stores to French islands in the Indian Ocean. At the same time, they opened the China trade; the *Empress of China* returned to New England from her first voyage to Canton in 1785. The China trade developed quickly into a far-flung exchange of American manufactured goods for West Coast furs (including those of the sea otters harvested by California Indians) and the exchange of these furs for China's tea, silk, and ginseng. The trade was never significant in its total volume but had a disproportionately large impact on the organization of commerce. The movers of the China trade, particularly Robert Morris and John Jacob Astor, took great risks in innovating in the management of global business empires and reaped lucrative returns for their risks. The business techniques they developed and the capital they accumulated influenced heavily the growth of large-scale business enterprise in the nineteenth century. Finally, the release from British mercantilism opened America to new flows of foreign capital. Previously neither the French nor the Dutch had invested in American enterprise, but independence allowed capitalists in both countries to develop strong interest in commercial investments. They made their impact felt as early as the 1780s and eased the path of the new nation through its financial difficulties of the 1780s and 1790s.

To some extent, however, the loss of certain privileges and subsidies the empire had provided did offset the benefits of freedom. Except for limited periods when shortages threatened, the British now excluded American vessels from the carrying trade to the British West Indies—a leg of trade colonial merchants had dominated—and prohibited the importation of salt meat and fish from the independent colonies in order to protect such exports from Ireland and the Maritime Provinces. Consequently the official value of exports to the British West Indies fell by 1793 to little more than half their value in 1771–1773. Of course, the American merchants compensated for this loss, although to an unmeasured extent, by new trade with the

French islands and by their smuggling traffic with traditional customers on the British islands. Also suffering from exclusion from the empire were enterprises that had received British subsidies: Britain now encouraged its own producers, and the new government failed to continue a policy of special support. With regard to the American shipbuilding industry, for example, the proportion of foreign-built ships engaged in the North American trade between the Revolution and 1790 increased from about one-quarter to more than half of the total, most of the gains going to the British. Particularly hard hit from the loss of British aid were the producers of naval stores and indigo; in fact, so great was the importance of indigo to South Carolina and of naval stores to both Carolinas that the removal of bounties on these products, coupled with extensive wartime destruction, brought depression to the lower South, despite a buoyant market for rice. Growers of indigo as yet lacked the technical competence to cultivate short-staple cotton and lacked the resources to shift into rice production, with its high capital requirements. (One indicator of the difficulties of the period in that region was the unprecedented absolute decline of the slave population of South Carolina between 1775 and 1790.)

Other enterprises suffering reversals included the Massachusetts whale fishery, which now faced a prohibitive duty imposed by Britain, and the fur-trading industry of New York and Pennsylvania, which the British excluded from the interior by retaining seven key interior trading posts in violation of the Treaty of 1783. Finally, Americans engaged in the Mediterranean sector of the southern European trade were without the shield of the British fleet and British protection money paid to the commercial racketeers of Tripoli, Tunis, and Algeria. The result was a hiatus in extensive trade until 1805, when American naval power forced Tripoli to pledge not to molest American shipping in the Mediterranean. Diplomatic problems such as these undoubtedly contributed considerably to the movement for a stronger central government during the 1780s.

Aside from the particular inhibiting features mentioned, however, postwar British policy retained the more important aspects of its favorable treatment of the colonies. The British continued to give the same bounties, exemptions, and drawbacks on goods exported to the United States that they had extended to goods exported to British colonies; they allowed potash, pearlash, and bar iron to be imported from the United States duty-free and permitted American tobacco to enter duty-free if it was intended for reexport; and they cleared the way for the carrying of the most important American imports in either British or American ships. Thus the British trade policy was very favorable to continued United States–British trade, which was far more significant to the United States than its British West Indian traffic.

The Critical Period and the Federal Constitution

Freedom from British mercantilism brought net benefits to Americans through a fundamental, long-run improvement in the trading position of the former colonies. Even though the terms of trade worsened during the latter half of the 1780s they were still substantially more favorable than during the prewar period. As a consequence, the level of prosperity enjoyed by Americans during the decade after 1783 was higher than might be inferred from the political turmoil of the period. Contemporary observers often remarked on the improvement in basic commercial conditions. In 1786, for example, Benjamin Franklin declared that "America was never in higher prosperity, her produce abundant and bearing a good price, her working people all employed and well paid."[8]

The post-Revolution economy did face, however, significant short-run problems. The most serious of these problems had its roots in the arrangements used to finance the Revolution. The states and the Continental Congress, which lacked the legal authority to tax, financed the war effort almost entirely through borrowing and paper currency that lacked any backing except promises by the states to levy taxes sufficient to redeem them sometime in the future. Congress and the states issued nearly $440 million of such money, and a runaway inflation resulted. By mid-1781, the Continental dollar had depreciated to less than 1 percent of its face value. In 1781, however, the prominent Philadelphia merchant Robert Morris became superintendent of finance and was able to stabilize the nation's financial situation by drawing on foreign loans and by establishing the responsibility of the Congress for liquidating domestic and

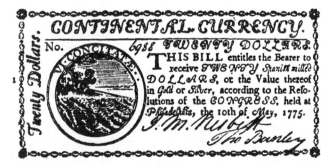

This $20 bill issued by the Continental Congress in 1775 was almost worthless by 1781; hence, the expression, "not worth a continental."

foreign debts. Nonetheless, the combination of a stock of highly depreciated paper money, a large burden of debt, the inability of the Congress under the Articles of Confederation to tax, and the inability of Americans to cover their purchases of European imports with sales of their own exports meant that in the 1780s specie flowed out of the country in large quantities. That outflow produced a severe decline in the price level—one that continued from 1785 into 1789. Like all serious deflations, it weighed heavily on debtors. Debtor farmers, particularly the small farmers of New England who were crowded on unproductive land, reacted most bitterly. Their discontent found expression in the 1786 rebellion of almost 2,000 western Massachusetts farmers led by Daniel Shays and aimed at preventing the collection of debts. Although the rebellion failed, Shays' supporters won an electoral victory in 1787 that enabled them to achieve passage of drastic debtor-relief legislation.

Shays' Rebellion precipitated the movement for a stronger national government—the movement that led to the drafting of the Constitution. The Congress had been ineffective in aiding Massachusetts' suppression of the rebellion since the Articles of Confederation had given Congress no substantial authority to act. Some men of property viewed the difficulty the Confederation faced in defending property against the threat of civil insurrection as absurd and dangerous and consequently promoted a stronger national government. But concern over the weakness of the Confederation extended far beyond the wealthiest classes. Farmers themselves saw value in a strong national government—one that could act more vigorously to expand foreign markets, shore up the nation's credit and promote price stability, insure American control over the trans-Appalachian West, protect slavery more effectively, and establish duties on trade that could pay off the nation's debts and provide property-tax relief to farmers. The interest in tax relief appealed even to some influential Boston merchants, who recognized that farmers needed tax relief but knew that only a national government could pass the excise taxes necessary to generate the new revenues required. Of greater significance to merchants was the desire for more effective monetary policy, the creation of a large, national free-trade area, and the development of more potent foreign economic policy. Manufacturers and artisans looked toward more bountiful subsidies and a national tariff to protect industry. Land dealers and veterans who held Confederation script redeemable in western lands sought a stronger federal presence in the West. All of these groups, and others, had become *national* interest groups, had developed a sense of the importance of America's national economic needs, and desired a government that could meet those needs. They contributed heavily to the convocation of the Philadelphia Convention in 1787 and the ratification of the Constitution in 1789.

Economic interest alone, however, does not explain the movement to draft the Constitution. Most fundamentally, the nationalists were logically concluding the Revolutionary process by replacing the British central government with an American counterpart. Moreover, while all of the writers of the Constitution were men of property, tending to be heavy owners of public securities, the opponents of the Constitution had strikingly similar holdings. They dwelt more heavily on the economic successes of the Confederation government, represented more local and regional perspectives, and feared the abuses of power that a stronger national government might engender. Nonetheless, the ratification of the Constitution clearly opened the way for more forceful participation of government in economic development.[9]

Sources of Prosperity and Depression, 1793–1815

Few of the economic benefits accruing to Americans from political freedom had revealed themselves in the 1780s. The margin of improvement had been slight. However, because the period to follow, particularly between 1793 and 1808, was so clearly one of enhanced prosperity, it suggests the possibility that the favorable results of political freedom came only after the formation of a strong central government under the Constitution. Alexander Hamilton's fiscal restructuring, which included a import tariff, national excise taxes, and the federal funding of the national debt (including state obligations), no doubt contributed to prosperity by promoting domestic stability and economic strength abroad. Doubtless the heightened strength of the government, augmented by a national army and navy funded by the new federal revenues, contributed to obtaining promises from the British (Jay's Treaty of 1794) that they would permit enlarged American trade with the British West Indies and would remove themselves from the western forts; to ending the quasi-war with France in 1800; and to curbing the Barbary pirates in 1805.

In truth, however, the growth realized during the period had far less to do with public policy or the creation of a vigorous nation-state than with the fact that during the Napoleonic Wars the ships of every combatant nation except England disappeared from international trade, leaving Europe's all-important ocean trade largely in the hands of neutrals, including the United States. These carriers imported and then reexported goods both to and from Europe, thereby protecting them from interception by a belligerent. With only minor breaks—in 1797–1798, during the height of an undeclared naval war with France, and in 1802–1803, after the conclusion of the Treaty of Amiens between France and England—the United States became increasingly active in this trade, showing a dramatic upsurge of total exports, which acted as a stimulus to other commercial activities. Despite a decline in export prices after 1797, exports more than tripled in value between 1793 and 1807, reexports accounting for over half the total. The primary beneficiaries of this dynamic growth were, of course, the large commercial cities and mercantile groups, with great mercantile fortunes accruing to individuals such as Archibald Gracie, E. H. Derby, John Jacob Astor, George Crowninshield, William Grany, and Stephen Gerard. In the late 1790s net international earnings from all service activities (primarily accounted for by activities in support of trade) were double those of the early 1790s; by 1807 such earnings were triple the early 1790s level. These swollen trade earnings permitted the purchase of an increasingly large volume of imports (both in absolute and in per-capita terms) during the period and even produced a favorable balance-of-payments position in 1793–1794 and again in 1801–1804. Finally, the carrying trade stimulated the growth of shipbuilding, reviving the industry from the doldrums of the 1780s, and enhanced the growth of complementary industries, such as insurance and banking. Some thirty-three insurance companies were active by 1800, including the Insurance Company of North America (in Philadelphia, 1790), the Massachusetts Fire and Marine Company (1795), and the Insurance Company of New York (1796). (By 1798 the Philadelphia company had more than quadrupled its 1793 volume of premiums.) During the same period, state-sponsored commercial banks proliferated, supported in part by the heightened level of commercial activities.

In response to the thriving commercial sector, the cities of Boston, New York, Philadelphia, and Baltimore accelerated in growth, especially during the 1790s, with overall urbanization in the United States increasing from 5.1 percent of the population in 1790 to 7.3 percent in 1810. In other words, during those two decades the urban population grew more rapidly than the rural population, and that growth probably promoted some modernization of colonial manufacturing since larger, more compact markets offered opportunities to exploit the efficiencies possible with larger-scale production. Beginning in 1793, New England wool manufacturers introduced carding machines and founded wool-spinning factories; by 1803 Oliver Evans had created the first automated mill of any kind, a flour mill in Philadelphia. And before 1807 New England textile manufacturers established about a dozen large-scale mills utilizing Richard Arkwright's spinning machine. The first clearly delineated movement of the American industrial revolution had appeared.[10]

Rapid commercial growth could continue only so long as the United States remained aloof from the European wars. That became impossible after the establishment of the French Continental System and Britain's Orders in Council in 1807, both designed to limit neutral trade. Subsequently, Jefferson's embargo policy put a virtual end to all foreign trade. In 1809 the Nonintercourse Act loosened American self-regulation by permitting trade with all nations except England and France, but the revival was modest and the onset of war in 1812 once again dampened trade. As a result of the privileged neutral position it had held earlier, the United States emerged even from the War of 1812 as a stronger competitor for the world's carrying trade. But with the resumption of European vigor in that enterprise, it had no chance to regain rapidly the position it had enjoyed from 1793 to 1807.

American manufacturing had received a fillip from the period of neutral trade and from the War of 1812, which cut off American consumers from British producers, in effect protecting American manufacturers. But the long-run benefits to manufacturing are difficult to measure. The experience that American manufacturers gained undoubtedly proved useful in the 1820s, when they began to compete seriously with the British for the first time. However, soon after 1815, cheap English imports wiped out large portions of the expanded American manufacturing, including some of the new textile firms, with urbanization actually declining slightly between 1810 and 1820—the only decade to show such a reversal.

The Revolution and Political Independence: Long-Run Effects

The fact that general prosperity was independent of the creation of a new government by no means implies that the national programs of a more unified central government were inconsequential for the pattern of economic development and the pace of economic growth. In the long run, the government established under the Constitution lived up to the expectations of the national interest groups formed during the 1780s. And the policies of the early national administrations proved to be consequential elements in long-run economic growth. Influenced by Secretary of the Treasury Alexander Hamilton, the administration of George Washington strengthened the customs union established by the Constitution and assured the fiscal independence of the national government by passing a tariff for revenue and low national excise taxes. To firm the nation's credit in world markets, the first Congress assumed all the debts of the states and adopted a program of funding the federal and state debts on terms favorable to the nation's creditors. And to assist in the mobilization of capital as well as to facilitate the government's business, Washington sponsored the creation of a national bank. Thomas Jefferson's administration also promoted economic development, especially through the purchase of Louisiana and the liberalization of land policy. Jefferson thereby stimulated agricultural expansion, gains in agricultural productivity, and, indirectly, the growth of the manufacturing sector. But the benefits of the new national government to industrial development were perceived only dimly at the end of the eighteenth century.[11] Also incompletely foreseen was the impact of the new government on the future of slavery. Building on the prohibition of slaveholding in the Northwest Territory included in the Northwest Ordinance, the Constitutional Convention of 1787 allowed the close of the international slave trade and Congress ended that trade in 1807. That step proved to be an important instrument in the containment of slavery in the southern states and, quite likely, in the victory of the Union in 1865.[12]

Any determination of the long-run benefit that the American Revolution provided the economy rests upon assumptions about the hypothetical alternative of continued membership in the British empire and, most crucially, upon very heroic assumptions about probable English policy toward continued westward expansion, slavery, and an American industrial revolution. It is undoubtedly true that serious mercantilist policy would have restrained American industrialists, but mercantilist theory was already well on the wane in England, and in any case, the English would probably have lacked the political and military force to impose significant restrictions—as, in fact, the Revolution demonstrated. In addition, English policy in the long run would have been likely to favor settlers over fur traders in the interior, thus retaining the liberal land policy developed by the colonists. And those in America who wanted containment of slavery might well have played successfully on abolitionist sentiment in England. However, all such speculation is inherently disorderly; it is much more informative to observe that for more than three decades after the conclusion of the Revolution, there was no fundamental change in the character of the American economy.

NOTES

1. Philip Curtin, *The Atlantic Slave Trade: A Census* (Madison, Wis.: University of Wisconsin Press, 1969), p. 59. See, also, Richard B. Sheridan, "The Wealth of Jamaica in the Eighteenth Century," *Economic History Review*, 18 (August 1965), 297.

2. A classic work in the estimation of the impact of trade distortions on colonial development is Lawrence Harper, "The Effect of the Navigation Acts on the Thirteen Colonies," in Richard B. Morris (ed.), *The Era of the American Revolution* (New York: Columbia University Press, 1939), pp. 3–39. Recent economic historians have scaled down his calculations of the costs of the redistribution of transatlantic trade resulting from the Navigation Acts. See especially Robert P. Thomas, "A Quantitative Approach to the Study of the Effects of British Imperial Policy upon Colonial Welfare: Some Preliminary Findings," *Journal of Economic History*, 25 (December 1965), 615–638; and Peter McClelland, "The Cost to America of British Imperial Policy," *American Economic Review*, 59 (May 1969), 370–381.

3. Although in 1769 Parliament allowed New York to issue a limited amount of paper money acceptable in payments for taxes, only in 1773 did Parliament extend the act to the other colonies (still with the exception of New England).

4. For an explication, in constitutional and intellectual terms of the deepening crisis of confidence in the long-accepted framework of imperial law see Bernard Bailyn, *The Ideological Origns of the American Revolution* (Cambridge, Mass.: Harvard University Press, 1967).

5. On the controlled character of mob violence, see Pauline Maier, "Popular Uprisings and Civil Authority in Eighteenth-Century America," *William and Mary Quarterly*, 27 (January 1970), 3–35.

6. For discussion of the literature on the pattern of wealth distribution during the Revolutionary generation and evidence that it became marked by greater inequality see Allan Kulikoff, "The Progress of Inequality in Revolutionary Boston," *William and Mary Quarterly*, 28 (July 1971), 375–412; and James T. Lemon and Gary B. Nash, "The Distribution of Wealth in Eighteenth Century America: A Century of Changes in Chester County, Pennsylvania, 1693–1802," *Journal of Social History*, 2 (Fall 1968), 1–24. For a view that the Revolution reversed the trend toward greater inequality, at least for a time, see Jackson Turner Main, *The Social Structure of Revolutionary America* (Princeton, N.J.: Princeton University Press, 1965).

7. Albert Fishlow, "Comment," *Journal of Economic History*, 24 (December 1964), 561–566.

8. Quoted in Merrill E. Jensen, *The New Nation: A History of the United States During the Confederation, 1781–1789* (New York: Knopf, 1950), p. 249.

9. For an emphasis on the ideological sources of the Constitution movement, see Gordon S. Wood, *The Creation of the American Republic, 1776–1787* (Chapel Hill, N.C.: University of North Carolina Press, 1969). For an introduction to the problem of the significance of the property holdings of the Constitution writers, see Charles Beard, *An Economic Interpretation of the Constitution of the United States* (New York: Mac-

millan, 1913), and Forest McDonald, *We the People: The Economic Origins of the Constitution* (Chicago: University of Chicago Press, 1958).

10. Discussion of the sources of the industrial revolution follows below in Chapters 5 through 8.

11. For an excellent survey of the implications of the Constitution and the legislation of the 1790s for economic growth, see Stuart Bruchey, *The Roots of American Economic Growth, 1607–1861: An Essay in Social Causation* (New York: Harper & Row, 1965).

12. For suggestions of the way in which these enactments concentrated the power of slavery in the lower South, see William W. Freehling, "The Founding Fathers and Slavery," *American Historical Review*, 77 (February 1972), 81–93.

SUGGESTED READINGS

Books

Bruchey, Stuart. *The Roots of American Economic Growth, 1607–1861: An Essay in Social Causation.* New York: Harper & Row, 1965.

Dickerson, Oliver M. *The Navigation Acts and the American Revo;ution.* New York: Barnes, 1963.

Ernst, Joseph A. *Money and Politics in America, 1755–1775: A Study in the Currency Act of 1764 and the Political Economy of Revolution.* Chapel Hill, N.C.: University of North Carolina Press, 1973.

Jensen, Merrill. *The New Nation: A History of the United States During the Confederation, 1781–1789.* New York: Knopf, 1950.

Main, Jackson Turner. *The Social Structure of Revolutionary America.* Princeton, N.J.: Princeton University Press, 1965.

Nettles, Curtis P. *The Emergence of a National Economy, 1775–1815.* New York: Holt, Rinehart, and Winston, 1962.

North, Douglass C. *The Economic Growth of the United States, 1790–1860.* Englewood Cliffs, N.J.: Prentice-Hall, 1961.

Pares, Richard. *Yankees and Creoles: The Trade Between North America and the West Indies Before the American Revolution.* Cambridge, Mass.: Harvard University Press, 1956.

Articles

Bjork, Gordon C. "The Weaning of the American Economy: Independence, Market Changes, and Economic Development," *Journal of Economic History,* 24 (December 1964), 541–560.

Harper, Lawrence. "The Effect of the Navigation Acts on the Thirteen Colonies," in Richard B. Morris (ed.), *The Era of the American Revolution.* New York: Columbia University Press, 1939, pp. 3–39.

Kulikoff, Allan. "The Progress of Inequality in Revolutionary Boston," *William and Mary Quarterly*, 28 (July 1971), 375–412.

Thomas, Robert P. "A Quantitative Approach to the Study of the Effects of British Imperial Policy upon Colonial Welfare: Some Preliminary Findings," *Journal of Economic History*, 25 (December 1965), 615–638.

Ver Steeg, Clarence L. "The American Revolution Considered as an Economic Movement," *Huntington Library Quarterly*, 20 (August 1957), 361–372.

❋ part two
THE EMERGENCE OF INDUSTRIAL REVOLUTION

This section is devoted to a description and explanation of how the American nation underwent that variety of economic changes suggested by the concept "industrial revolution." The departures from the economic experience of the colonial period are undeniable. But the message of these chapters is that such changes, defined in terms of economic performance, structural transformation, and institutional adaptation, were gradual in character, sharply distinguishing the era of industrial revolution only over the course of at least two generations. And, the institutions of economic America as we know it in the late twentieth century were more a product of the accelerating industrialization of the last decades of the nineteenth century.

5

The Character of Industrialization, 1815-1860

THE PACE AND STRUCTURE OF THE INDUSTRIAL REVOLUTION

Was the Pace Revolutionary?

In the eighteenth century, advances in levels of living in America were steady and impressive, both by the standards of the day and by comparison with earlier trends within the Atlantic economy. But more striking during that century was the economic expansion that resulted simply from the acquisition and utilization of more resources, both human and material, rather than from a more efficient use of resources.

During this century the burgeoning population consumed the vast bulk of the economy's rapidly growing production of goods and services. In short, most early expansion was extensive rather than intensive in character. Beginning perhaps as early as the 1790s and certainly within the first half of the nineteenth century, the character of economic expansion began to change. Increasingly growth became intensive as well as extensive, and as a result, rates of increase in per-capita product and income grew gradually larger. For the period after 1840 the pace of economic growth is quite clear. Reliable, well-accepted data indicate that there was a steady rate of growth in per-capita product by the 1840s. (See Table 3.) Moreover, the rates of growth in per-capita output were higher than those characteristic of the eighteenth century. For the decade 1844–1854,

TABLE 3 UNITED STATES COMMODITY OUTPUT, 1839–1859

| | (Value Added in 1879 Prices) | | |
	Output (billions)	Output per Capita	Output per Worker
1839	$1.094	$64	$244
1844	1.374	68	*
1849	1.657	71	268
1854	2.317	85	*
1859	2.686	85	330

Source: Robert E. Gallman, "Commodity Output, 1839–1899," in Conference on Research in Income and Wealth, National Bureau of Economic Research, *Trends in the American Economy in the Nineteenth Century: Studies in Income and Wealth,* Vol. 24 (Princeton, N.J.: Princeton University Press, 1960), p. 16.

* Not available.

for example, the annual increase in per-capita product approached 2.5 percent. For the period 1839–1859 as a whole the corresponding annual rate was 1.45 percent, somewhat in advance of that achieved during the late colonial period. Hence, it is likely that the acceleration in the rate of growth observed in the 1840s and 1850s was well under way, having begun at some point between 1790 and 1840.

Structural Change: Manufacturing

Although economic historians have no measures of either total output of goods and services or incomes between 1790 and 1840, data pertaining to structural change and the output of particular sectors and industries exist that reflect meaningfully on earlier patterns of growth. An estimate of the growth of the manufacturing sector between 1809 and 1839 strongly suggests that historians should de-emphasize the 1840s as the decade of significantly accelerating growth. Although there was an increase in the rate of growth of manufacturing during the 1840s, the performance of the three earlier decades, according to this estimate, was very strong. The total value of manufacturing output increased by 153 percent during the 1840s, but the average rate of decennial change was 59 percent between 1809 and 1839. This rate is virtually the same as that experienced during the 1850s, higher than that reached during the 1860s and 1890s, and close to the average rates attained late in the century (74 percent in 1869–1899).[1] The high rate of growth of manufacturing activities during the 1840s should be seen, consequently, not as a dramatic departure from a rather disappointing earlier pattern, but as a variation on a century-long trend.

The expansion of the manufacturing sector—in effect, a shift of capital and labor from agriculture to the more productive sector, manufacturing—provided the leading edge in the postcolonial acceleration in the rate of growth of output and productivity from 1790 to 1840. Agriculture remained the dominant form of economic activity in the United States as late as the Civil War, with some 56 percent of the nation's output derived from farms. In 1839, however, only twenty years earlier, 72 percent of output had originated in agricultural pursuits. The manufacturing share of total commodity output thus increased from only 17 percent in 1839 to 32 percent in 1859. (See Table 4.) The employment of the labor force underwent a similar if less drastic structural change, a shift from farm to nonfarm occupations. (See Table 5.) Nonfarm employment, including manufacturing occupations, continuously and rapidly increased from 1810 until it accounted for almost half of total employment in 1860. (The declining importance of nonfarm employment between 1800 and 1810 resulted from the collapse of trade that followed Jefferson's embargo.) And the manufacturing share of total employment increased as well, at least after 1840.[2]

The movement of the labor force into manufacturing was less marked than the change in the composition of national product: in 1849–1850 only about 20 percent of the labor force (that employed in manufacturing) produced about 30 percent of the national output.

TABLE 4   SECTOR SHARES IN UNITED STATES COMMODITY OUTPUT

	Agriculture	Mining	Manufacturing	Construction
1839	72%	1%	17%	10%
1844	69	1	21	9
1849	60	1	30	9
1854	57	1	29	13
1859	56	1	32	11

Source: Gallman, *op. cit.*, p. 26.

TABLE 5   UNITED STATES LABOR FORCE DISTRIBUTION BY SECTOR

	Farm	Non-farm	Primary*	Manufacturing and Construction	Other
1800	73.7%	26.3%	74.5%	**	
1810	80.9	19.1	81.6	**	
1820	78.8	21.2	79.6	**	
1830	68.8	31.2	69.7	**	
1840	63.1	36.9	64.1	13.9%	22.0%
1850	54.8	45.2	56.4	19.5	24.1
1860	52.9	47.1	54.9	18.5	26.6

Source: Stanley Lebergott, *Manpower in Economic Growth: The United States Record Since 1800* (New York: McGraw-Hill, 1964), p. 510.

*   Includes farming, fishing, and mining.
** Not available.

In short, America's factories were considerably more productive than her farms. According to one estimate, in 1839 workers in agriculture were only about 50 percent as productive as workers in nonagricultural employment (including construction and mining, as well as manufacturing). The calculation of this ratio includes as output much production that took place outside the marketplace, and is consequently quite favorable to the productivity of agriculture. The inclusion of "value added" (referring to the value which labor and capital add to the cost of raw materials) in home manufacturing and the value of improvements made in farmland exaggerate the relative efficiency of the farm sector. If these activities were ignored, the productivity of persons employed in agriculture would be even lower—less than 40 percent that of those engaged in manufacturing.[3]

The growth of the manufacturing sector and the relative decline of farming, accelerating slowly over the extended period 1790–1860, are part of a set of structural changes in the economy, changes in the distribution of various inputs (including people) and outputs among sectors of the economy, occupations, geographic regions, and kinds of product. While manufacturing activity was the central focus of these changes, the entire body can be described as the industrial revolution, and the other transformations contain significant infor-

AD FOR BLANDY'S PORTABLE STEAM ENGINE, 1850s. This example of modern machinery suggests that industrialization reached the country-side as well as the city.

mation regarding the pace and character of the growth of productivity.

Structural Change: Urbanization

One structural change closely linked with the growth of manufacturing is the growth of urban populations, those populations living in places with at least 2,500 people. Between 1790 and 1860, the era of fastest territorial growth, the land area of the United States tripled. However, during the same period the size of the population on the land increased at an even swifter pace, the population density increasing from 4.5 to 10.6 persons per square mile.[4] Although the increasing concentration of population is not necessarily identical with urbanization, inasmuch as the population may have become more concentrated on the countryside as well as in urban places, urbanization definitely did increase in a sustained fashion beginning in the crucial decade of the 1820s, and continuing until the 1870s. (See Table 6.) (The share of the population living in census cities [at least 2,500 in population] actually increased from as early as 1790 and grew appreciably between 1790 and 1810; and the decade between 1810 and 1820 was the only decade since 1790 to register a declining level of urbanization.)

Urbanization is obviously tied to economic growth, but the process by which it contributes to economic growth remains as yet undetermined. At various times urbanization may have been simply

TABLE 6   URBANIZATION OF UNITED STATES POPULATION, 1790–1890

	Level of Urbanization (U/P)	Incremental Urbanization: Change in (U/P)
1790	5.1%	
1800	6.1	1.0
1810	7.3	1.2
1820	7.2	–0.1
1830	8.8	1.6
1840	10.8	2.0
1850	15.3	4.5
1860	19.8	4.5
1870	25.7	5.9
1880	28.2	2.5
1890	35.1	6.9

Source: Eric E. Lampard, "The Evolving System of Cities in the United States: Urbanization and Economic Development," in Harvey S. Perloff and Lowdon Wingo, Jr. (eds.), *Issues in Urban Economics* (Baltimore: Johns Hopkins Press, 1968), pp. 108, 117.

a passive response to the organization of a factory labor force, the demand of the agricultural and manufacturing sectors for services best organized in a concentrated fashion, or the building of a transportation system linking regions. On the other hand, urbanization as a spatial process of organizing the marketplace in the most efficient manner possible may itself have exerted a positive influence on economic growth. Moreover, it may have meant the creation of a form of economic organization that was more receptive to innovation, due to vastly augmented opportunities for exchange of information: in an urban locus, owners of both capital and labor could more easily make decisions that worked to their best economic interest. And in the large cities inventors could take advantage of the conjunction of concentrated demand for their services and access to the best current technical information. As a consequence of their unusually great access to information, New York's inventors accounted for more than 12 percent of the patents granted in the United States during the 1820s, despite the fact that New York's population was less than 2 percent of the nation's population. It is arguable that in a period in which communication over long distances was extremely difficult, cities were the only areas in which the marketplace was fully effective.

Urbanization also served as a medium for the circulation of information *throughout* the economy. Urbanization included not just a concentration of population but also a developing system of cities that enhanced the exchange of new ideas. The cities, linked by an increasingly efficient transportation system, exchanged information through the mails and interurban passenger travel. Within the system, the larger commercial seaports, particularly New York with its assets of size and central place in transport arrangements, served as the central nodes. They collected news from Europe, from other large American cities, and from smaller-sized cities (especially the interior towns that were the loci of the industrial revolution in textiles) and then disseminated it throughout the system. Information about the full range of economic activity, from improved manufacturing technology to more effective banking practices, spread through this increasingly large and efficient network. Thus, by 1840, even before the extensive railroad building and the introduction of the telegraph, the nation had made major advances in the exchange of information through the development of urbanization.[5]

Regional Variations

Further important regional variations occurred in productivity and manufacturing, with the Northeast leading the way in productivity and industrialism. In 1840, per-capita personal income, a reasonable substitute for per-capita product, was about one-third greater than the national average in the northeastern states. (See Table 7.) In the states of the South, eastern Great Plains, and the western Great Lakes, however, income per person was significantly lower than in the United States as a whole. The exception to the regional pattern was one that proves the rule. Per-capita income was higher in the West South Central area (the area now containing Arkansas, Louisiana, Oklahoma, and Texas). Because this region contained New Orleans, it had high commercial incomes resulting from the role of the urban center in the trade of the Mississippi valley and especially of the cotton South. The very regions with the highest income levels in 1840, New England and the Middle Atlantic states, also were leaders in urbanization and industrialization, and those with lowest incomes were the least urban-industrial. (See Tables 7 and 8.) (Again, the exception is the West South Central region, where the intense commercial activity, the large accumulation of population in New Orleans, and the city's dominance in the economic profile of the region explain the variation.)

As industrialization intensified in the Northeast between 1840 and 1860, per-capita incomes for that region continued their ascent. Simultaneously the income gap between the Northeast and the rest of the nation widened. (See Table 7.) The old Northwest (the Great Lakes states) also enjoyed relative gains in income during the two decades before the Civil War, but these gains were not as impressive

TABLE 7 PERSONAL INCOME PER CAPITA BY REGION: PERCENTAGES OF UNITED STATES AVERAGE

	1840	1860	1880
United States	100	100	100
Northeast	135	139	141
New England	132	143	141
Middle Atlantic	136	137	141
North Central	68	68	98
East North Central	67	69	102
West North Central	75	66	90
South	76	72	51
South Atlantic	70	65	45
East South Central	73	68	51
West South Central	144	115	60
West	—	—	190
Mountain	—	—	168
Pacific	—	—	204

Source: Richard A. Easterlin, "Regional Income Trends, 1840–1950," in Seymour E. Harris (ed.), *American Economic History* (New York: McGraw-Hill, 1961), p. 528.

TABLE 8   LEVELS OF URBANIZATION AND INDUSTRIALIZATION BY
REGION, 1840 PERCENTAGES OF UNITED STATES AVERAGE

	U/P*	Nal/L**
United States	100	100
Northeast		
New England	180	185
Middle Atlantic	176	154
North Central		
East North Central	36	87
West North Central	36	73
South		
South Atlantic	42	49
East South Central	19	38
West South Central	217	68

Source: Lampard, *op. cit.*, p. 119.

* The portion of the population living in urban places.
** The portion of the labor force engaged in nonagricultural activity.

as those achieved by New England. The West North Central area
(that which included or would include the Dakotas, Iowa, Kansas,
Missouri, Minnesota, and Nebraska) declined relatively in terms of
real growth between 1840 and 1860. Their decline stems from the
inclusion of the new frontier states of Kansas, Nebraska, and Minnesota in the 1860 estimate. The South's decline, which occurred fairly
uniformly across the regions, suggests that the cotton-producing
slave economy was unable to compete with the long-term growth
potential of the northern states based upon manufacturing enterprise.

The Trade Thesis

In describing and explaining American development before 1860 we
are presented with a compelling nexus among industrialization, urbanization, and productivity growth. An alternative attempt to ana-
lyze the character and sources of growth, at least between 1790 and
1840, is one that rests on trade data and explanations of growth that
link economic development to the changing character of trade.
Largely on the basis of a continuing improvement in trade beginning
in the 1830s, the most important recent study that relies on trade
data chooses that decade, rather than the 1840s, the 1820s, or the
1790s, as the period of most significant acceleration.[6]

This trade thesis is founded on the dramatic increase of both
imports and, especially, exports in the 1830s, reversed only by the
general contraction that ensued in 1839. Not only did exports in-

crease almost 80 percent in value and imports more than double between 1830 and 1835 but the per-capita level of exports and imports, in terms of constant prices, was also increasing rapidly.[7] The increasing level of exports, with respect to the size of the population, suggests that possibly the productivity of Americans was growing. At the same time, the growth in imports, again relative to the rate at which population was increasing, implies that per-capita incomes were likewise growing and augmenting the demand for foreign goods and services. The 1830s also marked a change in the structure of trade. In particular, expansion of the international market for cotton led the dynamic growth of exports during the decade. Between 1831 and 1836 cotton exports almost trebled in value, and during approximately the same period their share of total exports (by value) grew from about 51 percent (1830) to about 65 percent (1835). American manufactured goods during the 1830s competed less successfully in world markets, however, increasing no more rapidly than American exports in general and accounting for only about 9 percent of all exports in 1835—a small piece of the pie and no larger than the slice of a decade earlier.

Based largely on the strongly improving position of the United States in international trade, relative to the fortunes of the preceding decade, one theorist weaves an interpretation of economic growth in this decade that not only places the 1830s in center stage but makes the cotton export trade the principal actor.[8] The growth of the demand for cotton implicit in the development of English textile mills initiated a chain of events in the United States, which, according to this schema, had been operating within a colonial framework with rather mixed success, chiefly because European demand for traditional American staples such as tobacco was stagnant. The burgeoning quest for raw cotton revived the sluggish economy, raising cotton prices, stimulating the use of unemployed and underemployed agricultural resources, and accelerating the expansion of cotton production. Aided by a growing network of internal improvements built upon river and canal transport and concomitant bank expansion, new areas marketed their crops and enlarged the marketplace. This growth of agriculture in the Southwest had a constellation of interregional effects. The expansion of facilities to market cotton and supply the needs of planters created a heightened demand in the East for services and manufactured goods, and, additionally, the East benefited from incomes earned in handling portions of the cotton trade. The West was likewise affected, particularly the Mississippi and Ohio valleys, as demand for foodstuffs stimulated both the expansion of wheat, corn, and hog farming and the quickening of North-South commerce on interior waterways. The increase of manufacturing and urbanization in the East enhanced the growth of western agriculture even more, especially in the upper Northwest, which, after the completion of the Erie Canal in 1825, had access to the eastern coast.

The notions crucial to this particular explanatory framework are regional specialization and regional interdependence. The theory emphasizes the market, stimulated by the cotton trade and facilitated by the development of effective national communications, as the agent providing the opportunity for regions to develop in new patterns. This development encompassed a recognition of comparative advantages and was most efficient for the economy as a whole. The widening market permitted the attainment of other efficiencies as well. First, manufacturing became less tied to local markets; with rapidly declining transfer costs, manufacturing became distributed according to a more complex consideration of cost factors. Second, it became less dependent on skilled labor as more efficient production techniques were devised that utilized relatively cheaper unskilled labor.

Although we postpone any detailed examination of the interregional trade data, which are the basis for stressing the role of regional specialization, we should emphasize that if the period of acceleration in economic growth occurred earlier or later than the 1830s, the whole trade thesis would tumble. Although exports were a rather constant fraction of the total value of goods and services produced domestically during the period in which we can measure both quantities (1839–1860), there is no compelling reason to believe that the constancy of the ratio was maintained during the 1830s. Moreover, it is highly probable that other measures are superior to exports as a means of gauging the early progress of the economy. For instance, the pace of urbanization exposes more facets of the developing supply capacity of the economy and, much more directly than trade, reveals the extent to which manufacturing, the leading element in modern economic growth, was becoming organized on a more efficient basis. And as we have noted, the most significant departure in the rate of urbanization occurred in the 1820s rather than the 1830s. Moreover, the 1820s also marked an acceleration in the incremental industrialization of the labor force. In other words, both the residential and occupational structures of the population were changing more rapidly than in earlier decades, with the population becoming more concentrated in urban places and in nonagricultural employment. However, in the 1830s, the decade suggested by trade data as the temporal locus of accelerated growth, the growth of the nonagricultural sector slackened, although urbanization did continue to accelerate. (See Table 9.) And given that the 1840s again witnessed the conjunction of accelerating urbanization and industrialization, the

TABLE 9 INCREMENTAL URBANIZATION AND INDUSTRIALIZATION
COMPARED, 1790–1860

Period	Change in Percentage of Population Urbanized	Change in Percentage of Population in Nonfarm Occupations
1790–1800	1.0	*
1800–1810	1.2	–7.2
1810–1820	–0.1	2.1
1820–1830	1.6	10.0
1830–1840	2.0	5.7
1840–1850	4.5	8.3
1850–1860	4.5	1.9

Source: Lebergott, *op. cit.*, p. 510; and Lampard, *op. cit.*, pp. 108, 117.

* Not available.

1830s seem, in fact, to have contained a significant break in the progress of the industrial revolution and economic growth rather than to have encompassed a period of acceleration.

Further evidence contrary to the findings of the trade theory is provided by the movement of real wages in Philadelphia, where real wages were rising strongly as early as the 1790s. A short-lived increase of about 3 percent annually occurred during the 1790s, followed by a period of little or no growth after 1800 through the War of 1812 (when cost-of-living increases outran money wages), and then, most interestingly, by a period of rapid and sustained growth from 1815 through the 1820s, with average annual growth rates between 3 and 4 percent. These were exceptionally high rates of increase; indeed, national real wages between 1840 and 1914 never exceeded an average annual rate of 2 percent.[9] It should be noted, however, that Philadelphia possessed an unusually modern manufacturing sector for this time; in addition, since wages cannot be taken as the equivalent of income, one should not be lured by these data into fixing the 1790s as the most significant ante-bellum period of acceleration in real income. Nonetheless, if real-income growth paralleled the growth of real wages, the strength and well-established character of the trend in Philadelphia lends weight to the selection of the 1820s rather than the 1830s as the decade of marked increase in the nation's rate of growth.

Finally, pinpointing a decade as containing the most striking rate of acceleration in the pace of economic activity provides only very modest information concerning the determinants of economic growth. The entire process of industrialization, involving increasing per-capita incomes and output, ought to be seen as a more gradual process involving the interaction of a vast complex of societal changes, with dramatic, exogenous changes such as a sharp increase in the demand for domestic cotton or the explosive growth of a particular industry playing a less important role. The effort to dissect each decade of the early nineteenth century to discover the locus of an industrial revolution is less fruitful than attempts to comprehend the structural and institutional changes, the changes in technology and social organization, that underlay the industrial revolution in the United States. It is the exploration of these changes which shall occupy our attention in the following chapters.

THE DISTRIBUTION OF INCOME AND WEALTH, 1790–1860

Increasing levels of per-capita income and product during the period 1790–1860 did not necessarily reflect changes that might have occurred in the standard of living for the population as a whole. It is quite possible that the enlarged social product was distributed in a fashion that meant only slight improvement in the levels of living for a large segment of the American people. Although a fuller discussion of the quality of early nineteenth-century urban life follows (Chapter 6), it is important to note now that the distribution of income and wealth was becoming less equal in the first half-century of industrial revolution.

The extent of inequality, the length of time over which wealth and income distributions grew more uneven, and the pace of movement within that period all remain obscure. But the weight of evidence currently available suggests that the drift toward greater income and wealth inequalities, which had begun during the colonial period, continued until at least the end of the nineteenth century. At the end of the eighteenth century, the 10 percent of families that were the wealthiest owned between one-third and one-half of the nation's wealth. Despite the large inequality of wealth holding implied, the share of the wealthiest 10 percent increased even further, to perhaps as much as 70 percent by 1860.[10] And there is evidence, although of a rather sparse and weak quality, that between 1815 and 1860 the average wage rate of skilled laborers tended to rise more rapidly than that of the unskilled.[11]

The sources of this increasing concentration of wealth in the hands of the wealthiest are poorly understood. One can begin by comparing, in a simple fashion, urban with rural trends. The distribution of wealth was less equal in northern urban areas than in northern agricultural districts or in the cotton South among free people. Moreover, the distribution of wealth in agriculture as a whole, and even among slaveholders, remained more or less constant through-out the period. Thus, the trend toward concentration was localized in urban areas, particularly in the largest northeastern cities.[12] As the urban population became a larger share of the total population, the distribution of wealth in the nation as a whole tended to become more uneven.

Behind the urban trend of concentration were several factors. First, the rate of technological change proceeded unevenly, both within the economy as a whole and within the urban sector. Key factory-based manufacturing industries led the way in creating productivity gains, with commerce, banking, and transportation following. Indeed, manufacturing never outstripped agriculture in its productivity growth more dramatically than during the period from 1815 to 1860. The pattern of technological change favored the intensive use of the services of both physical capital (such as machinery) and people with skills (or, put differently, with an accumulation of human capital). As the price of machines fell due to marked advances in the machine-tool industry, the demand for skills, including those of a managerial nature, that were required to use machines effectively grew even more rapidly. The high premium attached to the work of skilled individuals meant that the wages of skilled labor increased more rapidly than the wages of unskilled labor, which was used more intensively in the less productive industries and the agricultural sector. Consequently, the distribution of wealth among individuals became more uneven—concentrated in the hands of relatively fewer individuals. Second, unskilled workers, whose relative income position suffered, spent a larger share of their incomes than did skilled workers on goods that were produced less efficiently —food and fuel. In other words, the unskilled spent more of their incomes than did the skilled on goods whose prices were rising relative to the prices of manufactured goods. As a consequence, the cost of living for the unskilled increased more rapidly than for the skilled. This trend contributed directly to the increasing concentration of wealth; cost-of-living movements worked against the poor more than the rich. Third, during the 1840s and 1850s the expansive flow of immigrants, who tended to be less skilled and less well informed about marketplace opportunities than the native population, kept down the wages of unskilled labor. That retardation of the advance of unskilled wages meant a declining share of income and wealth in the hands of the unskilled. Although their relative importance remains undetermined, each of these factors enhanced the concentration of wealth and income.[13]

The increasing concentration of wealth and the growing prominence of economic elites should not be taken to imply a narrowing of economic opportunities. In fact, the incomes and wealth holdings of the vast bulk of the free population increased. The average wage rate of even an unskilled worker increased solidly—roughly 1 percent per year—between 1820 and 1860. Further, the expansion of the economy was highly dynamic. Even with wealth holdings becoming more concentrated, the rapid growth of jobs, particularly of a skilled nature, meant that the "average" individual enjoyed more opportunity for upward economic mobility than data on wealth distribution would reveal. Mobility upward to a wealthier class probably increased, despite the increasing concentration of wealth in the upper classes. As in the colonial period, American society supported groups of entrepreneurial individuals with unusual skills in their quest for profits in manufacturing, agriculture, commerce, and finance. It was only when such skills had become widely diffused throughout the population, through processes of education and learning from experience, that the distribution of urban incomes began to become more even and the early and mid-nineteenth-century trend reversed.[14]

POPULATION GROWTH, 1790–1860

While the American population was becoming more productive, it was growing dramatically in size. In vital ways, this growth both influenced and was influenced by the marked gains in economic efficiency. Consequently, the characteristics of the population's expansion illuminate the process of economic development.

During this era of industrial revolution American population growth was as strikingly rapid as it had been during colonial times. From 1790 to 1860 the population grew at a rate close to 3 percent per year—enough to produce a doubling of the population roughly every twenty-three years. The dominant source of that increase, as during the colonial period, was the reproductive power of the population. During the 1840s and 1850s immigration became considerably more influential than it had been during the seventeenth century. (See below, pp. 142–143.) Still, for the period as a whole, immigration failed to reach the significance it would attain later. Not until the 1840s did the immigration of Europeans assume levels, either absolute or relative to the total population, that were substantially larger than colonial levels. In fact, between 1810 and 1830, European immigration was of less consequence to American population growth than at any earlier time. Moreover, Congress ended the immigration of Africans with its 1808 ban on the slave trade, and, with abundant opportunities elsewhere for free labor, Europeans never came to the South in large numbers. By the beginning of the nineteenth century the South had acquired almost the entire base of population for its future growth.

The high rate of natural increase stemmed from patterns of birth and mortality similar to those of the eighteenth century. The birth rate was quite high (on the order of forty-five to fifty live births per 1,000 people per year), and the death rate was exceptionally low (about twenty deaths per 1,000 people per year). Contributing to both was the relatively abundant supply of good land, which led farm families to be rather optimistic in planning family size and which provided the basis for nurturing healthy infants. Despite the increase in population concentration and the greater risks of disease that attended that concentration, mortality rates appear not to have worsened even in highly urban places.[15] American health conditions were as good as, and quite likely better than, those common in western Europe.

Persistently high fertility rates clearly reflected economic opportunity. Most parents remained confident of the ability of a large number of offspring to lead effective, productive lives and felt no fundamental conflict between satisfying their own economic desires and equipping their children to enter the marketplace. The productivity and income gains of the industrial revolution augmented the ability of families to afford children—children as sources of direct satisfaction to parents and children as individuals to whom parents felt obligated to transmit human capital.

While some elements of the industrial revolution enabled parents to maintain or increase family size, others encouraged them to limit the number of children they produced. The high pecuniary returns that young people with skills could earn created incentives for parents to raise "higher quality" children by doing what they could to provide their children with more human capital. Parents spent more money on the education of their children, kept them in school longer (thus increasing the costs of support and reducing the earnings that children might contribute to family income), and simply devoted more effort within the home, providing children with a healthier environment, better food, basic academic skills, and the personal and social qualities appropriate to urban life. Added to the costs of these efforts was the increasing value attached to the marketplace work of women, who assumed most of these child-rearing responsibilities. Throughout the period women left homes at growing rates for jobs that paid them increasing wages. The enhanced value of their work meant that if wives stayed home to raise children their families would forego a source of income that was increasingly large. In short, mother's time was becoming more valuable. Given all of these costs —the cost of domestic and educational services, the opportunity costs of sending children to school, and the opportunity costs of home services provided by mothers, parents found it easier to undertake increased investment in their children if they had fewer children. Consequently, some parents began to limit the size of their families, to have fewer children than their parents had.

Urban upper- and middle-class families led in the movement for "higher quality" children and in the restriction of family size. They, more easily than lower-class families, could afford additional educational expenses and, most importantly, the loss of family income entailed in keeping children out of the work force longer. They, more often than rural families in that era of costly communication, knew of the exceptional value attached to urban-based skills. And, from their closer proximity to neighbors, urbanites felt more acutely the impact of rapidly rising "consumer aspirations," which conflicted with planned family size. Urban people may also have acquired more readily information on birth-control techniques. However, during this period, abstinence, coitus interruptus, and self-induced abortions were the most common means of birth control, and no compelling evidence indicates that knowledge of these methods was more common in urban areas. In fact, some rural parents began to limit family size early in the century. The rising price of land in older agricultural areas made it more difficult for farm families to endow each of their children with land that was comparable in value to or greater than the value of land they had received from their parents.[16] Moreover, parents in established agricultural regions shared with urban middle-class parents an awareness of the high returns to human capital available in urban employments. Further, like urban wives, farm wives in older areas found that their work in the marketplace was rewarded more fully. In growing numbers they took up employment, particularly of a part-time nature. As a consequence, significant numbers of farm families, especially in the eastern and Great Lakes states, began to practice birth control in the early decades of the nineteenth century. In contrast, the fertility rates in frontier areas declined little from the rates that had been characteristic of the eighteenth century. On the frontier, the labor of children retained greater relative value, the price of land remained low, and urban employments were less attractive.

The net effect of some people enlarging their families and others restricting them initiated a long-term decline in fertility that continued until World War II. The best, although imperfect, measure of fertility for the ante-bellum period is the number of children under ten years of age per 1,000 white women of childbearing age (from sixteen to forty-four). This "birth ratio" declined from 1,844 in 1800 to 1,308 in 1860, or by 29.1 percent.[17] The decline was not sharp. It

TABLE 10 GROWTH OF THE AMERICAN POPULATION, 1790–1860

	Total Growth (Millions)	Decennial Growth Rate	Share From Natural Increase
1790–1800	1.4	35.1%	96.9%
1800–1810	1.9	36.4	96.7
1810–1820	2.4	33.1	95.8
1820–1830	3.2	33.5	95.2
1830–1840	4.2	32.7	85.6
1840–1850	6.1	35.9	71.9
1850–1860	8.3	34.6	70.5

Source: Jim Potter, "The Growth of Population in America, 1700-1860," in D. V. Glass and D. E. C. Eversley (eds.), *Population in History: Essays in Historical Demography* (London: Edward Arnold Ltd., 1965),pp. 667-668.

slowed only moderately the rate of natural population increase. Even during the 1850s, after the fertility decline had been under way for a half-century, natural increase (births minus deaths) caused the population to increase about 25 percent every ten years. (See Table 10.) Moreover, the effect of the fertility decline on population growth was almost entirely offset after 1840 by the increase in immigration. The immigration that began in the 1840s quickly restored the population's overall growth rate to the levels prevailing in 1800. Finally, the fertility decline was substantially more modest than during the last decades of the century.

The association between industrial revolution and fertility decline is a reminder of the continuing close linkages between economic change and the central elements of family behavior. The historical investigation of these linkages has only just begun, but study of the nineteenth-century fertility decline has underscored the importance of the role of the family in economic life. Highlighted is the centrality of family life, not only in shaping population growth, but also in inculcating values, in training in the division of labor, in educating in altruism, in facilitating the intergenerational transfer of wealth, and in providing for the continuity of the social order.

FLUCTUATION IN ECONOMIC ACTIVITY
Emergence of the Industrial Business Cycle

All measures of economic activity fluctuate. Moreover, variations in rates of growth of output, income, trade, investment, or money supply tend to be cyclical in character, exhibiting a wavelike pattern of movement. These cycles, and the economic instability they represent, although important in themselves, are interesting as well for what they reveal about the character of the American economy.

The most striking characteristic of the early nineteenth-century business cycle, especially before the 1830s, is the relative gentleness of the fluctuations and the mildness of the depression years. Unemployment in the "crisis" year of 1819, for example, was as low as 3 to 5 percent, and in 1838 and 1858, also depressed years by early nineteenth-century standards, never rose above 6 to 8 percent. In contrast, during the much more severe crises of the 1870s and 1890s the unemployed laboring population was twice as large. These much lower rates in the first half of the century reveal an important structural difference in the economy of that period: the smaller role of the manufacturing sector despite the fact that the industrial revolution was well under way. In fact, in 1819 manufacturing was of such limited importance, in comparison with agriculture, that the panic that ensued during that year perhaps should not be considered part of a "business" cycle. Making such a judgment, the National Bureau of Economic Research begins dating American business cycles with the period 1834–1838. Not until the 1850s was there an "industrial" cycle, that is, one dependent primarily on nonagricultural investment rather than on the ups and downs in the world's market for agricultural produce, particularly cotton. But in 1819 agriculture still far outweighed industry in determining the ebb and flow of economic activity.

During the Panic of 1819 and the subsequent depression, manufacturers were in a severely depressed state; but this predated the panic. Large-scale factory production, particularly of cotton textiles, had developed during the sheltered years of the War of 1812, but after the cessation of hostilities it was, for the most part, unable to survive the inundation of English imports that immediately followed; only the most efficient operations, such as the factory of the innovative Waltham textile firm, succeeded. While the economy as a whole was booming, manufacturing stagnated. And when the panic struck, the difficult circumstances of the large manufacturers were only intensified and extended. Thus we cannot interpret as "industrial" either the boom that preceded the Panic of 1819 or the depression that followed. Instead they must be viewed as stemming from the fluctuations of world trade in agricultural products and a monetary stringency. After the War of 1812 British exporters unloaded their swollen inventories in their former colonies, and the price of imported goods fell drastically despite the existence of high levels of pent-up demand. Other factors also caused high import levels. State commercial banks, not constrained by any requirement to redeem their issues of bank notes in specie, expanded credit rapidly. The federal government, as well, encouraged imports by allowing payments of tariff duties on imports to be delayed—in some cases, for more than a year. English exporters aided the boom by extending short-term credit to American purchasers of European exports. At the same time, values of American exports rose, although not as swiftly. Increased exports, coupled with monetary and credit expansion, led to an increase in land purchases, a boom in land prices, and a marked growth in the indebtedness of landowners, especially farmers.

Expansion continued in 1819, encouraged by the laxness of the Second Bank of the United States (the federally sponsored commercial bank established three years earlier) and the Treasury. Beginning in the summer of 1818, the bank sought to protect its assets by sharply restricting its activities, thereby producing a sustained and severe monetary contraction, one that culminated in the Panic of 1819 and lasted through 1820. Reinforcing the monetary contraction was a sharp decline in foreign demand for American agricultural exports as a result of bumper European crops after 1817 and a business contraction in Britain. Markets for American staples collapsed, and production fell off. In all, American incomes declined, and unemployment in the cities reached a level that was acute for the times.

By 1821 the economy was exhibiting clear signs of recovery. Banks again extended credit and once again both the prices and values of American agricultural products swung upward in response to European demand. The period of expansion that followed in the 1820s was the most sustained since that of the 1790s, and, as has been suggested, the 1820s were probably the decade of fastest economic growth prior to the Civil War.

The expansion continued into the 1830s, augmented in 1832 by a boom in Britain that produced a lively interest in American investments (particularly in public improvements) and a desire to buy cotton. Americans maintained this influx of capital and high demand for cotton by increasing purchases of British imports. At the same time an increasing domestic money supply, provided by specie imports and the banking system, sustained capital inflows and pushed up domestic prices, a rise that made British imports even more attractive and offset the high demand for cotton.

The long boom and inflation came to an end in the Panic of 1837, as a result of two factors. The Bank of England, convinced that it was losing specie to the United States, in late 1836 curtailed the flow of capital. Concurrently, British demand for cotton declined, the price of cotton fell, and the credit structure, keyed to the use of cotton as security, collapsed. The situation was further aggravated by the overextended condition of state banking that had developed after 1834. However, the decline that followed was moderate, one reason being that the Bank of England resumed lending to Americans after accumulating a larger cushion of reserves, and another being that the conjunction of a short cotton harvest and American transactions on the cotton market revived cotton prices.

Then in 1838 came severe deflation. First of all, the English wheat crop proved to be very short, and to finance imports it was necessary for England to export specie. Again responding to the resulting specie drain, the Bank of England tightened credit in 1839. Next, a very large American cotton crop in 1839 drove down cotton prices and once again forced many banks to suspend specie payment. A number of states followed by defaulting on their bonds, and the British in turn ceased to export capital. At the same time United States banks raised their reserve ratios, and the public sought to increase its specie balances. The resulting contraction of the money supply, coupled with the hiatus in imports of British capital, extinguished the boom.

Although the deflation between 1838 and 1843 was severe, involving a fall of over 40 percent in the price level, it is unclear to what degree production declined. However, it is quite clear that investment suffered appreciably, falling almost one-quarter between 1839 and 1843, led by declines of two-thirds in railroad construction and nine-tenths in canal construction. Investment in cotton textile mills dropped sharply in response to falling profits, but investment in the modernizing sector of the iron industry was strong. (It should be stressed, however, that net investment in canals and railroads did not account for the turning points in the ordinary cycle of business activity until the 1850s. For it to have been an independent contributor a net-investment downturn would have to have preceded business collapse, and in the 1830s and 1840s net investment in transport facilities usually fell or increased *in response to* reversals of economic conditions, merely reinforcing downturns or upswings. For example, in the 1830s railroad investment continued after 1837 and 1839, and declined only in 1840. Then, too, despite the business expansion of the mid-1840s, investment in internal improvements remained in a depressed condition, not rising again strongly until the extremely vigorous boom of the 1850s.)

By the mid-1840s, recovery from the downturn was under way. Industry reinforced by foreign demand now led the expansion, while the Irish potato famine added strength to agricultural expansion in the Great Lakes states. After some tightness in money markets in 1848, the boom gathered momentum and by the early 1850s was characterized by buoyant land sales, high levels of internal and international migration, rising prices, and dynamic capital inflows. Then in the middle of the decade prosperity climaxed: domestic trade peaked in 1855; land sales reached a high point in 1854–1855; immigration fell off sharply in 1855; aggregate real output began to decline from a high point in 1856.

The clearly delineated decline of the 1850s preceded the financial crisis referred to as the Panic of 1857. The sequence of the business cycle during the 1850s clearly distinguishes it from that of the 1830s, when financial panic preceded deceleration and the crucial element of collapse was international in origin. Thus, for the first time, stability depended on nonagricultural investment rather than on the international market for cotton. Growth during the remainder of the 1850s was sluggish despite the South's continuing prosperity.

Nonagricultural investment exerted even more leverage on the economy in the 1850s, with railroads probably having a crucial degree of influence. Railroad investment accounted for about 10 percent of total capital formation between 1834 and 1858 and for 15 percent between 1848 and 1858, including a peak of 25 percent in 1854. In addition, the financial organizations of railroads were extremely large-scale for the 1850s; given the concentration of assets in the hands of a few firms, those companies had an even larger potential "autonomous" impact on stability than shares of capital formation reveal. Furthermore, railroad expenditures were not only large during the 1850s but largely indispensable, given their favored position in international security markets. As a result, rather than lagging behind other business-cycle measures, as in the 1830s, railroad investment clearly led the collapse in the mid-1850s. Railroad investment peaked in 1854 and then, having been pushed downward by the scandals involving the financial fraud of Robert Schuyler, president of the New York and New Haven Railroad, fell off sharply, ahead of other indicators. The decline of investment worsened in 1857, possibly hastening the financial crisis of that year. The industrial character of this business cycle indicates the extent to which the economy had been transformed before the Civil War and provides a clear portent of certain characteristics of the post-bellum economy, including the prominence of railroads in determining patterns of investment. Clearly the maintenance of economic stability would depend increasingly on domestic conditions of production rather than on foreign demand for the staples of agricultural enterprise.

The Significance of Long Swings

In discussing the business cycle, we have ignored many of the types of fluctuations that were shorter in cycle, or of higher frequency, than those surrounding the most visible expansions and contractions of the ante-bellum period. For any segment of time, one could discover, within the limits of available data, any number of variations in economic activity. Under the rubric "business cycle" we have considered only the most dramatic of those that were directly recorded by contemporary observers of the economic scene. But this kind of information mainly reflects conditions affecting the stability of the economy and reveals little about either the pace and timing of economic growth or the factors that might, on one level, explain those variations. In order to understand the dynamic process of economic growth it is essential to know more about patterns of investment, cycles of migration, changes in the productivity of capital and labor, to mention only a few of the important variables involved.

In order to provide such data it is possible to smooth short-term movements of economic indices and thus obtain a measure—an artificial construct—of underlying patterns of economic activity. This kind of measure varies as methods of smoothing out business-cycle movements differ, but the most commonly used data are long swings, or Kuznets cycles, named for their discoverer, Simon Kuznets. These wavelike movements in total output and other variables are from fifteen to twenty-five years in duration, making the Kuznets cycle two to five times as long as the ordinary business cycle.

The most basic observation to be made from the long-swings data is that economic growth took place in periodic surges, rather than at a steady pace. Furthermore, each swing in output has been accompanied by waves in the level of immigration, increments to the population, additions to the labor force, the net volume of fixed capital (especially from the construction of residences and utilities), territorial additions, levels of internal migration, and extent of suburban growth. The broader indices of resource growth, productivity growth, and the intensity of use of all resources underwent long swings as well.

Although data on the pre-Civil War period are incomplete or in other ways inadequate, long swings seem to have assumed a pattern that prevailed until the 1920s (when the nation placed restrictions on immigration, and the farm population in older agricultural areas began to decline). Typically, that pattern began with an upward thrust of economic growth and a demand for labor in excess of the available supply, resulting in increased migration from older farm areas and overseas. The swifter migration, in turn, enlarged growth rates for population, labor force, and households in the centers of economic opportunity. (That turning points of long swings in rate of output growth generally preceded those in the rate of immigration tends to confirm that immigration was responding to changed conditions in the United States, rather than abroad. If the contrary had been true, if the push had been greater than the pull, immigration should have either led or been concurrent with movements in the rate of output growth.) The new households in cities and in new agricultural areas then generated demands for new services, that required new investment. That investment itself created new needs, supported the level of total demand, and provided new opportunities. (One of the new services in the pre-Civil War period was the expansion in railroads during the late 1840s and 1850s, which although largely a response to preexisting demand, itself promoted internal migration and immigration by creating new opportunities for agriculture and by promoting these opportunities with publicity and special emigrant passenger service.) But when new additions to capital failed to maintain the growth of productivity, the rate of growth of output declined, the rate of growth of income and total demand fell as well, and depression ensued. The existence of these long-term variations in levels of economic activity probably stems from the fact that commitments to spend, whether made by households, firms, or governments, tended to be bunched. Discontinuity of expenditures meant that demand, income, output, and population also moved in uneven patterns.[18]

In conclusion, long swings are clearly observable in the first half of the nineteenth century and have the same basic structure and frequency as those following the Civil War. The expansive agricultural sector of the ante-bellum years did not make the long swing as distinct as it did the ordinary business cycle. While the business cycle (at least before the 1850s) was dominated by the international movement of agricultural prices, long swings were dominated by population expansions onto new lands, with demands for housing and transport. Later in the century, long swings would be shaped similarly by the urban development boom and concomitant demands. Furthermore, the character of these long swings in the early portion of the nineteenth century lends further support to the finding that economic growth characterized the economy before the dramatic surge of the 1840s and 1850s.

NOTES

1. Barry W. Poulson, "Estimates of the Value of Manufacturing Output in the Early Nineteenth Century," *Journal of Economic History,* 29 (September 1969), 522.

2. One should be careful to note, however, that "manufacturing and construction" employment was less than other types of "nonfarm" employment and that there is no data available on the size of the manufacturing sector as a clearly defined entity before 1840. Consequently we are certain that employment in manufacturing and construction, as a share of total employment, was increasing from 1840, although it is quite likely that gains in manufacturing employment began earlier.

3. These estimates are by Paul David, based largely on the data of Robert E. Gallman. Paul A. David, "The Growth of Real Product in the United States Before 1840: New Evidence, Controlled Conjectures," *Journal of Economic History*, 27 (June 1967), 168–169. For suggestions as to limitations in David's estimates, see Robert E. Gallman, "The Statistical Approach: Fundamental Concepts as Applied to History," in George R. Taylor and Lucius F. Ellsworth (eds.), *Approaches to American Economic History* (Charlottesville: University Press of Virginia, 1971), pp. 63–86.

4. U.S. Bureau of the Census, *Historical Statistics of the United States, Colonial Times to 1957* (Washington, D.C.: U.S. Government Printing Office, 1960), pp. 7–8.

5. For a specification of this system of cities and preliminary measurement of the rates of information flow, see Allan R. Pred, *Urban Growth and the Circulation of Information: The United States System of Cities, 1790–1840* (Cambridge, Mass.: Harvard University Press, 1973).

6. This is the now classic work of Douglass C. North, *The Economic Growth of the United States, 1790–1860* (Englewood Cliffs, N.J.: Prentice-Hall, 1961).

7. U.S. Bureau of the Census, *op. cit.*, p. 1; North, *op. cit.*, p. 233.

8. Once again we are referring to the interpretive framework of Douglass C. North.

9. Donald R. Adams, Jr., "Wage Rates in the Early National Period: Philadelphia, 1785–1830," *Journal of Economic History*, 28 (September 1968), 404–417.

10. The state of the literature on this problem can be assessed by consulting Robert E. Gallman, "Trends in the Size Distribution of Wealth in the Nineteenth Century: Some Speculations," in Lee Soltow (ed.), *Six Papers on the Size Distribution of Wealth and Income* (New York: National Bureau of Economic Research, 1969); Jackson Turner Main, "Trends in Wealth Concentration Before 1860," *Journal of Economic History*, 31 (June 1971), 445–457; Lee Soltow, "Economic Inequality in the United States in the Period from 1790 to 1860," *Journal of Economic History*, 31 (December 1971), 822–839, and *Patterns of Wealthholding in Wisconsin Since 1850* (Madison, Wis.: University of Wisconsin Press, 1971).

11. Jeffrey G. Williamson, "The Relative Costs of American Men, Skills, and Machines: A Long View," *Discussion Paper No. 289–75*, Institute for Research on Poverty, University of Wisconsin, Madison (July 1975). An older measure of wage inequality by skill for the 1840s and 1850s contradicts Williamson, but it appears to have defined skilled labor too narrowly. W. Randolph Burgess, *Trends in School Costs* (New York: Russell Sage Foundation, 1920), p. 70.

12. For a discussion of the implications of the trend in those cities, see Edward Pessen, "The Egalitarian Myth and the American Social Reality: Wealth, Mobility and Equality in the 'Era of the Common Man,'" *American Historical Review*, 76 (October 1971), 989–1034.

13. For an emphasis on technological imbalance and cost-of-living effects, see Jeffrey G. Williamson, "American Prices and Urban Inequality Since 1820," *Journal of Economic History,* 36 (June 1976), 303–333. For more on the role of labor-force growth, see Peter H. Lindert, *Fertility and Scarcity in America* (Princeton, N.J.: Princeton University Press, 1978).

14. On the growing importance of human capital, even in the early decades of the century, see Stuart Bruchey, *The Roots of American Economic Growth: An Essay in Social Causation* (New York: Harper & Row, 1965).

15. Maris Vinovskis, "Mortality Rates and Trends in Massachusetts Before 1860," *Journal of Economic History,* 32 (March 1972), 184–213.

16. For the argument that rural families reduced fertility in the nineteenth century under pressure of declining land availability in order to provide their children with an adequate start in life, see Richard A. Easterlin, "Factors in the Decline of Farm Family Fertility in the United States: Some Preliminary Research Results," *Journal of American History,* 63 (December 1976), 600–614, and "Population Change and Farm Settlement in the Northern United States," *Journal of Economic History,* 36 (March 1976), 45–75; and Don R. Leet, "The Determinants of the Fertility Transition in Antebellum Ohio," *Journal of Economic History,* 36 (June 1976), 359–378.

17. Colin Forster and G. S. L. Tucker, *Economic Opportunity and White American Fertility Ratios, 1800–1860* (New Haven and London: Yale University Press, 1972), p. 3.

18. Closer examination of the mechanism as it operated before the Civil War is impossible, given the data available at present. One estimate of the patterns of long swings in the earlier portion of the nineteenth century places peaks at 1814, 1834, and 1846 and troughs at 1819, 1840, and 1858. See Moses Abramovitz, "Long Swings in United States Economic Growth," in National Bureau of Economic Research, *Thirty-eighth Annual Report* (May 1958), p. 48.
Given the averaging devices used to develop such data, it is difficult to make them conform in an obvious fashion with the normally observed fluctuations in economic activity. But, as a rule, the rate of growth of output tends to peak before the aggregate output of the ordinary business cycle peaks. This makes sense, given declining productivity experienced at the high levels of capital utilization and output near the peak of the long swing.

SUGGESTED READINGS

Books

Bruchey, Stuart. *The Roots of American Economic Growth: An Essay in Social Causation.* New York: Harper & Row, 1965.

Conference on Research in Income and Wealth, National Bureau of Economic Research. *Output, Employment, and Productivity in the United States After 1800.* New York: Columbia University Press, 1966.

————. *Trends in the American Economy in the Nineteenth Century.* Princeton, N.J.: Princeton University Press, 1960.

Easterlin, Richard A. *Population, Labor Force, and Long Swings in Economic Growth: The American Experience.* New York: Columbia University Press, 1968.

Fishlow, Albert. *American Railroads and the Transformation of the Ante-Bellum Economy.* Cambridge, Mass.: Harvard University Press, 1965.

Jerome, Harry. *Migration and Business Cycles.* New York: National Bureau of Economic Research, 1926.

North, Douglass C. *The Economic Growth of the United States, 1790–1860.* Englewood Cliffs, N.J.: Prentice-Hall, 1961.

Pred, Allan R. *Urban Growth and the Circulation of Information: The United States System of Cities, 1790–1840.* Cambridge, Mass.: Harvard University Press, 1973.

Smith, Walter B., and Arthur H. Cole. *Fluctuations in American Business, 1790–1860.* Cambridge, Mass.: Harvard University Press, 1935.

Temin, Peter. *The Jacksonian Economy.* New York: Norton, 1969.

Thomas, Brinley. *Migration and Economic Growth.* Cambridge, Eng.: Cambridge University Press, 1954.

Articles

Abramovitz, Moses. "The Nature and Significance of Kuznets Cycles," *Economic Development and Cultural Change,* 9 (April 1961), 225–248.

David, Paul A. "The Growth of Real Product in the United States Before 1840: New Evidence, Controlled Conjectures," *Journal of Economic History,* 27 (June 1967), 151–197.

Easterlin, Richard A. "Economic-Demographic Interactions and Long Swings in Economic Growth," *American Economic Review,* 56 (December 1966), 1063–1104.

————. "Population Change and Farm Settlement in the Northern United States," *Journal of Economic History,* 36 (March 1976), 45–75.

————. "Regional Income Trends, 1840–1950," in Seymour E. Harris (ed.), *American Economic History.* New York: McGraw-Hill, 1961, pp. 525–547.

Gallman, Robert E. "Trends in the Size Distribution of Wealth in the Nineteenth Century: Some Speculations," in Lee Soltow (ed.), *Six Papers on the Size Distribution of Wealth and Income.* New York: National Bureau of Economic Research, 1969.

Hughes, J. R. T., and Nathan Rosenberg. "The United States Business Cycle Before 1860: Some Problems of Interpretation," *Economic History Review,* 15 (April 1963), 476–493.

Lampard, Eric E. "The Evolving System of Cities in the United States: Urbanization and Economic Development," in Harvey S. Perloff and Lowdon Wingo, Jr. (eds.), *Issues in Urban Economics.* Baltimore: Johns Hopkins Press, 1968, pp. 81–139.

Macesich, George. "Sources of Monetary Disturbances in the United States, 1834–1845," *Journal of Economic History,* 20 (September 1960), 407–434.

Taylor, George Rogers. "American Economic Growth Before 1840: An Exploratory Essay," *Journal of Economic History,* 24 (December 1964), 427–444.

Temin, Peter. "The Causes of Cotton-Price Fluctuations in the 1830's," *Review of Economic Statistics,* 49 (November 1967), 463–470.

Williamson, Jeffrey G. "American Prices and Urban Inequality Since 1820," *Journal of Economic History,* 36 (June 1976), 303–333.

6

The Structure and Dynamics
of Economic Growth, 1815-1860

NORTHEASTERN INDUSTRIALIZATION

Manufacturing led economic growth in nineteenth-century America, even though early in the century modern manufacturing was limited to a handful of states in the Northeast. It is true that manufacturing activity increased steadily and dramatically throughout the United States, but in the West and South most manufacturing grew without becoming more efficient. The northeastern states, on the other hand, contained a disproportionate share of industries that made important productivity gains during the first half of the century. As the locus of the structural changes associated with industrialization, the region enjoyed significantly higher levels of income. In 1840 personal income per capita was 35 percent higher in the Northeast than in the nation as a whole; the margin increased to 39 percent by 1860. (See Table 7, p. 129.) The disparity was greatest in New England, where per-capita income increased dramatically from 32 to 43 percent of the national average between 1840 and 1860. The divergence of regional income that was linked with the modernization of manufacturing, although not as reliably quantifiable as after 1840, became manifest as early as the 1820s. That kind of regional divergence is a commonly observed characteristic of nations entering an industrial revolution, and in the case of the United States, the development of manufacturing in the Northeast is the logical point at which to begin analysis of the processes linking industrial revolution and economic growth.

Economies of Scale, American Technology, and the Rise of Competitive Manufactures

The story of the development of the industrial Northeast rests on the success of American manufacturers in competing with western Europeans, particularly the British, who were riding on a more advanced wave of the industrial revolution. Their achievements, in turn, depended on an expanding home market. With the reduction of internal transportation costs, continuing population growth, and rising incomes, the domestic market for manufactured goods widened. Increasingly firms reached more than the inhabitants of their home communities. As a consequence, competition intensified and firms and individuals, already wedded to profit maximizing, became more sophisticated in evaluating costs of production. In particular, firms chose plant sites with greater attention to the possible returns in various locations. With widening of markets, firms could take into account raw material, labor, and capital costs, for example, rather than just accessibility to a market, in determining the best locus of production. The aggregation of such locational choices supported the concentration of industry in the Northeast, the area that had already realized returns from its comparative advantage in commercial enterprise.

While American producers were becoming more efficient, however, the easier access to the American marketplace and the growing capacity of Americans to purchase manufactured goods were presenting Europeans with new opportunities to gain profits against American competition. The natural tariff barrier provided by the costs of transatlantic shipping became increasingly porous as those costs fell. Wherever and whenever transportation was sufficiently expensive, traditional, preindustrial manufacturing activity continued without disruption. As late as the Civil War, for example, an iron industry that utilized eighteenth-century methods thrived in Missouri, where the industry was sufficiently remote from the competitive threat posed by modernized American or European ironmasters. Furthermore, throughout the ante-bellum period, western industry tended to be preindustrial in character while the northeastern states experienced the dynamic changes of industrial revolution.

The growth of markets permitted changes in the organization of manufacturing that, in turn, augmented the effectiveness of manufacturers in utilizing the factors of production more efficiently. Most important was the increasing scale of production, which enabled manufacturers to combine labor and capital at a lower cost; in effect, employment of economies of scale increased the units of capital and labor available to a given manufacturing operation. In the New England textile industry, for example, the productivity of both labor and capital was strikingly higher for the largest firms than for an average-size firm. The largest firms were able to maintain specialized shop crews to continually modify equipment according to the best knowledge available, whereas smaller firms, once having committed themselves to one kind of equipment, were unable to purchase new equipment until the prospective costs of the output of the new equipment were not merely less than those of the equipment to be replaced but sufficiently lower to offset the investment already made in the older equipment. In the early stages of textile-industry growth, the larger firms also benefited from their monopoly of the production of textile machinery; even as late as the 1830s a small or average-size textile firm was too small to build, improve, and patent its own machinery and was forced to buy from its larger competitors. The first machine-producing factories were built in conjunction with the New England textile mills and then later became independent entities, splitting off from firms such as the Amoskeag Manufacturing Company in Manchester, New Hampshire, and the Lowell Mills, in Lowell, Massachusetts. This kind of differentiation was another result of the new economies of scale. The increasing scale of production permitted specialization that frequently allowed two or more firms to perform distinct but interrelated tasks that one firm had performed formerly.

ENGLISH POWER LOOM WEAVING. Americans adapted capital-intensive machinery such as this to their own market conditions.

Machine shops, whether they were part of firms that used machine tools or were independent producers of machine tools for the market, played a strategic role in the development of competitive American industry. Their role constituted a response to the scarcity of labor in the United States or rather, the fact that although both capital and labor were in shorter supply than in Britain, labor was the more scarce factor of production. The thrust of American technological development was toward the use of labor-saving, capital-using innovations. In other words, manufacturers in the United States learned how to use more capital per unit of labor than their British counterparts, thereby enhancing their own competitive position.[1]

Although American manufacturers imported heavy machine tools from England, they developed their own machines in most industries—notably in the production of cotton textiles, small arms, clocks and watches, and sewing machines. In the textile industry, for example, Americans eliminated a good deal of hand labor employed in cleaning by developing a device to crush burrs in raw wool. In the 1820s American manufacturers began using the Goulding automatic roving machine, which fed wool automatically from one carding machine to another and finally formed a strand of wool that could be transferred to spinning machinery, thus ending the need to have small children pass wool from one machine to another. English producers, in contrast, did not find it necessary to adopt this innovation for twenty-five years. (This particular invention was also capital-saving, because it permitted speeds to be increased by about one-third and allowed the machines to be placed closer together.) Another example within the textile industry was the device invented by two Americans in 1853 to clean carding machines of dirt and waste automatically, doing away with yet another hand operation. And in weaving the early adoption of the power loom in America enabled manufacturers to make a continuous series of improvements that were more potent in their ability to conserve labor resources than those in England.

Scarcity of labor had the greatest impact on technological adaptations in those fields that were amenable to the making of machines and finished products with identical parts to be used interchangeably. Although credit for the conception of the process should be extended to Europeans (and *not* to Eli Whitney or Samuel Colt), the flowering of this labor-saving notion in the United States accounts for its universal description as the American system. In attempting to fulfill a contract with the United States government for the manufacture of 10,000 rifles between 1798 and 1800, Whitney did seek to cut labor costs by using unskilled labor, and consequently he may have used some interchangeability. But interchangeability was not central to Whitney's effort, Whitney's techniques may well have been more

McCORMICK REAPER WORKS, 1850s. This scene illustrates the increasing importance of machinery and the machine-tool industry.

primitive than those employed at other armories, and in any case, Whitney failed rather decisively in meeting the terms of his contract. Nonetheless, the manufacturers of firearms were the first to perfect the American system, having done so by the 1840s. In their special field they combined the essential requirements of mass manufacture —the application of power machinery, the use of gauges, and a degree of interchangeability. The new techniques resulted from efforts to solve similar problems in various scattered places, including Colt's Armory, the government armories at Springfield and Harpers Ferry, and the Ames Manufacturing Company. The methods of the American system proved applicable to the production of a wide range of products, including screws, nuts, bolts, locks, clocks, agricultural machinery, boot and shoe machinery (especially after 1850), locomotives, and new machines such as the typewriter and the sewing machine.[2]

The competitive success of American manufacturers also depended to a large extent on rapid technical advance in the development of machine tools. British engineers invented most of the basic machine tools, but Americans devised the most important new machine tools of the nineteenth century, especially milling machines, grinding machines, and turret lathes. Americans used all of these tools to reduce reliance on "old-fashioned" skills and handcrafting and to make production both more rapid and more accurate. In turn, industries that abandoned hand manufacturing converged in their technological requirements, creating widening markets for machine-tool manufacturers, who reaped economies of scale. Certainly by the 1850s Americans had more-specialized machine tools than those available in England, especially those used in woodworking and small-arms manufacture; and the proliferation of specialized machine-tool manufacturers was greater in America than in England.[3]

Innovations in the early development of modern manufacturing saved capital as well as labor. This was especially true as long as the most important source of change was merely the transference of British technology to American shores. In the textile industry in the 1820s and 1830s firms used both capital and labor with increasing efficiency. But the pattern altered as the adaptation of British technology to American needs, specifically the relative scarcity of labor in general and of unskilled labor in particular, became the leading edge of change. Around 1840 innovation tended to become more labor-saving and capital-using, rather than capital-saving.[4] Capital then became less productive as manufacturers mobilized it to replace unskilled labor. To a growing degree the ability of American manufacturers to compete effectively depended on a steadily increasing supply of capital for creating large-scale operations and for seeking innovations to lessen the heavy nineteenth-century reliance on labor.

In this era of poorly developed formal capital markets, financing for America's industrial revolution came in large part from personal sources or from within the firm. Early industrialization took place without the support of the financial intermediaries that became so visible and significant after the Civil War. When banks or insurance companies invested in a long-term fashion, it was usually in non-manufacturing activity—transportation, banking itself, or even state government. Because of the inexperience of bankers in making manufacturing loans, the relatively modest assets of manufacturers, and the continuing profitability of traditional investments, bankers tended to disregard investment opportunities in manufacturing. Moreover, stock markets did not serve the long-term needs of manufacturers. Listings on the New York Stock Exchange, for instance, were predominantly governments, transportation companies, banks, and insurance companies, with very few manufacturing concerns represented.

In textiles, as in other industries that successfully adapted British technology to American needs, seed capital came from men who were relatively new to manufacturing enterprise. Many merchants, including a significant number of cotton traders, became the most important financiers and promoters of the industrial revolution in the textile industry, forming partnerships with small, innovative manufacturers. Mercantile wealth accounted for at least one-third of the total stock owned in the Massachusetts-type textile firms (large, multifactory firms usually capitalized at over $500,000) for virtually the entire period before 1860; and the proportion was substantially higher during the 1830s. Although some merchants were seeking a stable, guaranteed, controllable market for their cotton by investing in textile production, like other investors in textiles most were making a shrewd judgment as to the likely returns. Even during periods of commercial prosperity, mercantile capital flowed into textile manufacturing in response to expected high profits and to the supposed safety of textile investments. By the 1840s and 1850s, the soundness of textile investment had become widely apparent, with the result that financial institutions began to supplement, in a significant way, the funds provided by individual stockholders and lenders; between 1840 and 1860, savings banks and trust companies provided the bulk of the loans made to the Massachusetts-type firms.[5] Thus, the transfer of capital from trade to industry was not a short-run, dramatic phenomenon caused by a sudden sharp decline in profits earned in the cotton trade, but a gradual, long-run process lasting until the Civil War. The outcome was a gradual but impressive growth of profits that were available for further investment in textile firms and additional substitution of capital for labor.

The pace of labor productivity, as a measure of the rate of innovation, reflects the gradualness of the shift of capital into manufacturing. Despite the fact that the dramatic technological transformation of the cotton-textile industry had already occurred by the early 1820s, worker productivity, supported by capital substitution, grew strongly in the textile mills from the 1820s through the 1850s. As a result of the gradual flow of capital, by the end of that decade, the average worker in the largest textile mills produced twice as much as his counterpart had during the early 1830s.

For American manufacturers to effectively compete with the mill operators of Britain it was not enough for them merely to replace labor with capital, because both capital and labor were more expensive in the United States. One strategy would have been to develop a different technology, one that permitted American manufacturers to reduce the total cost of capital and labor below that of competitive producers. The evidence, however, reveals little of such an independent trend. Rarely did Americans devise a completely different technology; more commonly, they adapted British technology to their own distinctive pattern of relative factor scarcities. How, then, did American manufacturers compete?

The answer lies in the relative cheapness of the other fundamental input in the productive process, raw materials. Simply stated, the nation was favored by an abundant supply of natural physical resources. The availability of fertile land helped Americans become competitive by allowing them to compensate for the high costs of labor and capital with savings on raw materials. Consequently, as in Britain, industries specializing in the processing of agricultural products thrived, with the cotton textile, lumbering, boot and shoe, flour milling, and men's-clothing industries leading the way. (See Table 11.)

While the processing of food and fiber formed the basis of the industrial revolution in both the United States and Britain before the Civil War, it was more central to the American experience, given the crucial role of inexpensive raw materials and the consequent failure of the American iron industry to follow the example of other American industries, such as textiles, in adapting British technology. From the seventeenth century, American iron production, based on essentially preindustrial organization and technology, had been expansive and by the time of the Revolution may have accounted for as much as 15 percent of world production. Nonetheless, in the next fifty years, as the industrial revolution took hold in the United States, the fortunes of the iron industry reversed. Despite the imposition of tariffs to protect producers from foreign imports, by the 1820s America had become a net importer of iron after having been a net exporter of unfinished iron during the colonial period.

In this fifty-year period after 1775, American producers missed the technological revolution that reshaped the British industry. The key step in the British transformation was the substitution of coke for charcoal as a blast-furnace fuel. The changeover to coke eased the

TABLE 11   OUTPUT OF LEADING INDUSTRIES, 1859

Industry	Value Added (Millions)	Industry	Value Added (Millions)
1. Cotton goods	$54.7	6. Iron fabrication	$35.7
2. Lumbering	53.6	7. Machinery	32.6
3. Boot and shoe	49.2	8. Woolen goods	25.0
4. Flour and meal	40.1	9. Wagons	23.7
5. Men's clothing	36.7	10. Leather	22.8

Source: Secretary of the Interior, *The Eighth Census, Manufacturers of the United States in 1860* (Washington, D.C.: U.S. Government Printing Office, 1865), pp. 733–742.

pressure on Britain's depleted forests, enabled ironmasters to exploit abundant reserves of high-grade bituminous coal, and removed important bottlenecks to crucial technological innovations in production. Producers reaped particularly large productivity gains by adopting the techniques of puddling (the sustained melting of pig iron, to remove impurities) and rolling (the extrusion of the semi-molten wrought iron through rollers). As a consequence, Britain became a low-cost producer rather than a high-cost one, and found itself firmly established as a net exporter of iron. By persisting in the traditional charcoal technology, which involved the use of hammering to purify and shape pig iron, the United States, in contrast, became a high-cost producer. Although the output of the American iron industry did grow during the period, the expansion was no faster than the rate of population growth, which suggests that American producers were still tied mainly to local markets. One can safely assume that if tariffs had permitted unrestricted competition from Britain, ruin would have befallen the American industry. It was only in the 1830s that the iron industry began to modernize, and only in the 1840s that the economy reaped the rewards.

The revolution in iron technology was delayed in the United States by the cheapness of charcoal and the dearness of suitable coke, both in the East where only anthracite coal was available and in the West where the bituminous coal had a high sulfuric content that contaminated the iron. Development of methods to allow the employment of anthracite coal, which was difficult to ignite, in puddling and rolling and changes in the scale of blast furnaces used to smelt iron ore into pig iron were prerequisites to the successful adaptation of British technology.[6]

The dismal history of the iron industry during much of the antebellum period was by no means representative of the outcome of market forces. The structural shift of the economy to manufacturing enterprise reflected the abilities of American producers to engage in competition. The growth of American manufacturing, especially the substantial increments to productivity, developed rapidly in those industries in which it was easy to replicate British technology, substitute capital for labor within that technology, and take advantage of the cheapness of American raw materials. Indeed, the ability and proclivity of Americans to exploit their landed resources proved to be the foundation for the industrial revolution in America.

The Building of an Industrial Labor Force: Migration from the Countryside

Another factor that sustained modern manufacturing in the United States was the flexibility of the labor force, which grew and changed in response to the configuration of relative factor scarcities. Although the scarcity of all types of labor was not overcome in the nineteenth century, the labor force did respond to American needs; if it had been less flexible in structure, raising the costs of labor, successful adoption of British technology to an already labor-deficient economy would have been correspondingly more difficult. The most obvious example of flexibility was the massive shift of workers into nonagricultural employment.

The occupational redistribution of population, the shift from farm to factory, meant a rural-to-urban redistribution of population. During the first half of the nineteenth century, manufacturers recruited most of their labor force from the native-born people living on the countryside, particularly from younger women and children. Even as late as 1820 about half of the textile workers were children, but by the 1830s child labor was on the wane. (Although in 1832 some 60 percent of Rhode Island's textile workers were children, in Massachusetts only 10 percent were.) Instead, factories increasingly tapped the supply of female labor, which prior to the Civil War accounted for over 60 percent of employment in the cotton-textile and clothing industries, for about 40 percent of employment in woolen-textile manufactures, and for almost one-quarter of the employment in the boot and shoe industries.[7] Such heavy reliance on children and women underscores the importance of the shortage of unskilled labor to the development of American manufacturing, as well as the dependency on native sources of labor. The employment of women and children did not, however, constitute reliance on underemployed labor, because the labor of women and children on family farms brought a substantial economic return to both themselves and their families.

The meager profitability of New England agriculture, however, eased the mobilization of a new manufacturing labor force in the towns of New England's interior through the implementation of the Waltham system, relying on the labor of young, single women, or the Fall River plan, involving the employment of entire families. Even in the colonial period declining returns to New England's agriculture, which utilized inferior land and whose labor force lacked easy access to the West, had contributed to the increasing employment of young women in domestic manufacturing. Drawing on the labor of young women, New England households became the loci of what has been described as "proto-industrialization."[8]

The earlier participation of women in household industry paved the way for their participation in factories. For one thing, it created pressure for a widened social realm for women. Household manufacturing enhanced the value of children to their families and provided those children, including young women, with increased freedom from parental control. Such freedom weakened parental influence over the arrangement of marriages, delayed the age of marriage, and lengthened the period during which young women remained free of wifely obligations. Thus, household manufacturing enlarged the potential for the employment of women who wished to pursue a brief interval of independence before choosing familial confinement. For another, household manufacturing introduced young women to some of the basic technical problems and requirements of textile production. Before the 1840s the growth in the scale of factory operations was slow. In the small-scale factories that predominated until the 1820s and remained common until the 1840s, young women found that the skills they had learned at home enhanced their effectiveness.

For many of the women in the early factory labor force, industrialization meant a relatively smooth passage from market-oriented, household spinning or weaving to small-scale factory textile production. The early factory owners used forms of organization that were characteristic of proto-industrialization; the young women who were employed often had already won a greater measure of social independence from their families; and the new factories were set in the country (at the only available water-power sites) rather than in an urban milieu. Factory owners sought to make the factory work as attractive as possible by creating a social environment in the mills that was both protective of young women and conducive to the development of intellectual independence from parental authority. As a consequence, many factory women, whether they lived at home or in dormitories such as those made famous at Lowell, Massachusetts, experienced little change in their work patterns. For those farm girls who lacked previous contact with household manufacturing, the rural setting of the first factories and the fact that factory work was less demanding than farm chores eased the transition.

In addition to providing the social and psychological advantages of an independent income, the factory offered young women wages that were substantially above those possible from domestic service, the only real occupational alternative open to them. Higher wages not only provided young women with more economic independence but also might supplement family income, assisting a father to pay off a farm mortgage, a brother to acquire more schooling, or the family to accumulate a dowry for the daughter's marriage. Partly as a result of the high wages paid unskilled women, the relative significance of domestic service as an employer of women declined. Meanwhile, the growth of factory opportunities led to an overall increase in the rates at which women participated in the marketplace through full-time employment. In 1800, only 4.6 percent of the labor force consisted of women over the age of ten, and only 4.6 percent of women over the age of ten had full-time jobs. By 1850 those rates had doubled: 10.8 percent of the labor force were women, and 10.1 percent of women had full-time jobs. (See Table 12.)

The interest of young women in factory labor continued into the 1840s, but the combination of cultural barriers and changing economic opportunities brought a decline in women's factory work. Powerful cultural factors limited the upward mobility of women factory workers into the ranks of skilled labor and the managerial class. Young women only rarely aspired to factory careers of any length, and the turnover rate of women factory workers was higher than that of men.[9] This fact justified the reluctance of employers either to train women for highly skilled tasks or to promote them into supervisory positions. But in large part this lack of ambition reflected lack of opportunity. Where women did extend their employment beyond the customary age for marrying and leaving the factory, they found no greater opportunity than younger women workers and discovered that their chances for advancement were far narrower than for men with comparable experience and abilities. Employers were not solely responsible for such limitation of opportunity. If they ventured to place a woman in the position of supervising men, they invariably encountered the stern opposition of male employees. Although women had worked in factories for almost two generations and many had been supervisors in the first mills, by the 1850s they only occasionally served as supervisors and then almost always of other women. The conventional persuasion that women's appropriate social roles lay in the home remained powerful.

Partly as a consequence of the restrictions on upward mobility within the factory, many young New England women who sought

TABLE 12   PARTICIPATION OF WOMEN IN THE AMERICAN LABOR FORCE, 1800–1860

Year	Women's Share of Labor Force*	Working Women in the Female Population**
1800	4.6%	4.6%
1810	9.4	7.9
1820	7.3	6.2
1830	7.4	6.4
1840	9.6	8.4
1850	10.8	10.1
1860	10.2	9.7

Source: W. Elliot Brownlee and Mary M. Brownlee, *Women in the American Economy, a Documentary History, 1675 to 1929* (New Haven: Yale University Press, 1976), p. 3.

* Includes females over age ten and only free women.
** Population of women defined on same basis as women workers.

social independence before marriage turned to teaching and other urban, middle-class occupations. Beginning in the late 1830s, after the Panic of 1837 had restricted public credit, school boards filled positions with young women rather than young men, who would draw higher wages and strain school budgets. In so doing, school boards recognized both the extent to which the number of educated women had grown and the degree to which limited outlets for women's skills in the private sector had depressed their wages. The demands of the school boards and other urban employers significantly reduced the numbers of women available for factory work. Also depleting the available pool of women factory workers was the rapid expansion of highly productive agriculture and the rapid growth of urban, nonfactory employment for young native American men. Both factors enhanced the economic appeal of early marriage.

By the 1840s the growing labor needs of the textile manufacturers had initiated the first of the great waves of European immigration. Employers quickly found that they preferred the immigrants from Ireland, Germany, and Canada (the French Canadians) to American women because the immigrants were willing to work for lower wages, for longer periods of time, and with fewer complaints about conditions of work—particularly the speeding up of production that employers began in the 1840s in order to maximize returns on their capital investment. Many young, native American women, both skilled and unskilled, went on strike or protested in response to the factory speed-up. And some took advantage of the more attractive economic opportunities available to them but not to the unskilled immigrants. Consequently, immigrants replaced native Americans in the unskilled labor force, beginning in the 1840s. Although many of the new factory workers were women, the immigrant population was predominantly male, and the ratio of men to women among the factory labor force increased sharply during the 1850s, contributing to the overall decline in the importance of women's employment recorded for that decade.[10] (See Table 12.)

Thus, during the 1840s people began to move in great numbers into American towns from the European countryside. By 1860 more than one-quarter of the free, white, adult males in the nation and more than one-third of those in the northern states were immigrants. This transatlantic redistribution corresponded closely with the common phenomenon of industrialization mobilizing an underemployed, rural labor force. But the substantial contribution of immigrants to the growth of both the population and the labor force came late: new immigrant arrivals accounted for no more than 3 to 4 percent of the decennial increase in population in the decades between 1810 and 1830, and not until the 1840s did net arrivals come close to constituting one-third of decennial increase in population. Even then, immigrants sold their labor more to the construction industry, with its requirement for heavy labor in the building of canals, roads, and railroads, than to manufacturers. Most of the immigrants lacked skills. During the 1840s and 1850s nearly three-quarters of the immigrants were either common laborers or farmers (a category that included most immigrants of peasant background). (See Table 13.) Earlier, when immigrants were much less numerous, the proportion of immigrants who had professional or commercial occupations or had manual skills was substantially higher. During the 1820s nearly two-thirds and during the 1830s almost one-half fell in those categories.

The occupation of immigrants varied greatly by national group. On one extreme was found the British immigrants, who numbered three-quarters of a million between 1820 and 1860—making them less numerous than only those from Ireland (about two million) and Germany (about one and a half million). Among them was a high percentage of professionals, former landowners, and skilled laborers. On the other extreme was found the Irish, whose massive immigration began in the late 1840s. Like the British, the Irish also played a prominent part in the development of manufacturing activity.[11] But the Irish immigration was different in that it received a forceful, almost violent push in the homeland as a result of the potato famine of the 1840s. The force of the dislocation meant that the Irish were not discriminating in their initial choice of residence and occupation; although locating throughout much of the Northeast, to a large extent, by accident of shipping schedules, they gravitated to New England and to factory employment in Boston and its suburbs. By using this Irish work force, Boston industrialists were able to press labor costs even lower than was possible through the employment of native women, helping them to compete with those manufacturers in

TABLE 13   EMPLOYMENT BACKGROUND OF IMMIGRANTS

	1820s	*1830s*	*1840s*	*1850s*
Professional	3.2%	1.7%	0.9%	0.5%
Commercial*	28.1	16.3	6.3	8.7
Skilled labor	30.5	31.5	23.2	18.1
Farming	21.2	30.5	32.7	31.1
Domestic service	2.1	1.0	3.1	1.7
Common labor	14.9	19.0	33.8	39.9
Total	100.0	100.0	100.0	100.0

Source: Bureau of the Census, *The Statistical History of the United States from Colonial Times to the Present* (Washington, D.C.: U.S. Bureau of the Census, 1965), p. 61.

* Includes agents, bankers, hotelkeepers, manufacturers, and merchants.

the hinterland. By 1850 Irish workers made up over one-third of the total work force in the Hub city, and almost half of them were employed as unskilled laborers. At the same time, during the late 1840s and early 1850s, the Irish, despite being the largest national group of immigrants, made only a modest contribution to the farm population. Ironically, the Irish were of highly rural origin, but because they had usually been only tenant farmers, most lacked the minimal capital necessary for taking up new land in America.

More representative of nineteenth-century immigrant populations than the British or the Irish were those from Germany. Certainly German immigrants had faced economic dislocations in Germany that created strident forces of push, but in deciding to emigrate, the Germans had placed American opportunities foremost. During the great German outmigration of 1830–1845, those who arrived in America tended to be small, independent farmers, skilled artisans, and village shopkeepers. In contrast with the Irish, they frequently owned property and exercised discretion in planning their futures. (The propertyless classes of Germany tended to move about the German countryside rather than emigrate.) Although later German immigrants, those forming the large wave of the early 1850s, had less property than their predecessors, most were able to draw on their own savings in financing travel and some had sufficient resources to buy land in America. Consequently, to a greater extent than was the case for the Irish, the Germans were able to join the ranks of skilled urban labor or take up land in the West. These later immigrants responded to changes in American conditions. In the mid-1850s news of unemployment and the intensification of American antiforeign political agitation sharply reduced the volume of net immigration from Germany. But by that time, thousands of acquisitive Germans had joined the growing populations of the cities both on the seaboard and in the West, and the fertile lands of the interior.[12]

Thus, more generally, immigrants were highly sensitive to the relative patterns of economic opportunity in Europe and the United States: they tended to move where they could be more productive and earn higher returns on their labor. Although such moves did not eliminate wage differentials, the flexible labor market that they constituted certainly reduced them in general and perhaps virtually eliminated them for skilled labor.

The strong and relentless influx of people from both the European and American countryside into nonagricultural employment argues that laborers in this sector were better off in terms of real incomes than their counterparts in agriculture and more traditional occupations despite the fact that the distribution of income worsened at the same time. It would be otherwise difficult to explain the attraction that the factory and urban service occupations held for people on the countryside; certainly living conditions were less attractive in the developing industrial cities, with their minimal provision of social services and their slender efforts to confront the diseconomies of urbanization, such as the costs resulting from the pressure of high concentrations of people on rudimentary systems of transportation and sanitation. But the fact is that factory labor, as contrasted with employment in the more prosperous American countryside, meant significant advantages in real income, typically amounting to a real wage differential of over one-third during early industrialization.

It does not necessarily follow, however, that the structural shift from an undifferentiated labor force to a more specialized nonagricultural labor force meant real improvement in the levels of living enjoyed by *all* members of the labor force. Skilled artisans especially could have suffered from finding their skills outmoded by the machine and factory organization. But for most native American artisans, with their diversified talents, industrialization probably offered an opportunity to proceed to more profitable occupations, given the demand for skilled labor in factories, generally rising incomes, a growing supply of unskilled immigrant labor, and the continuing prosperity of the agricultural sector. Perhaps most displaced artisans had a variety of new life chances: they could acquire new skills through experience, set themselves up as small manufacturers, become foremen or plant superintendents, become shopkeepers, or move West to turn to farming or perhaps even to practice their crafts in a portion of the nation less subject to the rigors of industrial revolution and consequently more in need of their skills. Many artisans, however, failed to penetrate the new urban middle class, enter agriculture, or preserve their skills in the West. In the process of losing status (but not necessarily real income) by declining to unskilled occupations, these artisans resorted to unionization and labor politics to protect their position.

Another group potentially exposed to economic setbacks was, obviously, the native, unskilled laborers who came into direct competition with immigrants, particularly after 1840. Nonetheless, the initial contribution of the immigrant to the labor force was not as significant in manufacturing as in other areas of nonfarm activity, such as the flourishing construction industry, and even in this case the waxing of economic opportunity promoted by immigration muted any detrimental impact of immigration on manufacturing job opportunities and wages for unskilled native Americans. However, contemporary perceptions do not always conform to reality: many native Americans, including members of the old artisan class and unskilled laborers, may well have seen an economic rationale for supporting the waves of nativism that swept through industrial cities during the 1850s.

Finally, it has been suggested that immigration may have had a negative impact on the native population growth; that is, native Americans may have been unwilling to compete in the lowest orders of labor with immigrants and therefore limited their family size. Given our retrospective view that competition with native labor was minimal, we would be much surprised if this were the case. Indeed, the decline in birth rates occurred around the beginning of the nineteenth century, well in advance of large-scale immigration. An examination of individual states also fails to reveal any relationship between immigration and declining birth rates.[13] Acceleration of immigration in the 1840s is better understood as a partial response to this deceleration in the rate of natural increase than as the factor bringing on the decline. The rate of overall population growth had fallen after 1810, but the increased level of immigration in the 1840s returned that rate to a level more closely approximating the one realized during the opening years of the century.

In assessing the impact of immigration on economic growth it should be pointed out that before the 1870s, immigration probably led the long swings of investment and growth in the United States. Certainly population increments lifted requirements for railroad investment and social-overhead investment in general. Nonetheless, it is impossible to assert a firm causal relationship between immigration and long swings of growth. All we can do is note that before 1870 variations in the level of immigration preceded variations in the cycle of investment. Immigration, in addition, contributed to economic growth by meeting the nation's need for unskilled labor. For instance, the influx of Irish into Boston, with the resulting provision of cheap labor, permitted modernization and growth of areas such as the boot and shoe, the clothing, and the sugar-refining industries. That supply of unskilled labor did enable American manufacturers to improve their competitive position by reducing the costs of unskilled labor. Nonetheless, despite a flood tide of immigration, the supply of unskilled labor never grew fast enough to prevent wages from rising or to reverse entrepreneurs' long-term strategy of substituting capital for unskilled labor.

Emphasis on the contribution of immigration to the nation's supply of unskilled labor should not lead one to ignore the large share of immigrants who arrived with skills. (See Table 13.) In the early decades of the century many immigrants were highly competent in the techniques practiced by the most advanced British manufacturers. Given the rudimentary character of machine specification, they easily transmitted knowledge of British technology to America. The impact of skilled workers, not to mention merchants and others who brought physical as well as human capital to America, was magnified by the concentration of immigration in large cities, particularly New York. In the 1820s and 1830s that city often received over one-half of immigrant arrivals. During the 1830s and 1840s over three-quarters of all immigrants arrived in New York, Philadelphia, Boston, and Baltimore. This concentration enhanced communication among new immigrants and between the immigrant and native American communities, thus facilitating the flow of new, useful information to the American economy and to American capitalists. Centers of opportunity attracted skilled immigrants, and the process of urbanization augmented the impact of these immigrants on the economy beyond the significance of their numbers to overall immigration. Skilled immigrants, in turn, enhanced economic efficiency in the large cities. New York owed no small debt for its dynamism to its domination of immigrant traffic and, thus, transatlantic information flows.[14] And the American economy took advantage of this new information without first having had to bear the burden of developing the human capital responsible for it. American society reaped, at a very low cost, the benefits of the investments that the European nations, particularly Great Britain, had made in the education and training of their emigrants.

In sum, the willingness and capacity of men and women, native-born and immigrant alike, to move themselves, their families, and their possessions to locations offering greater economic promise were significant elements in the success of the nineteenth-century economy. Economic growth and the industrial revolution on the enormous North American land mass would have been far more difficult without a highly mobile population. It is necessary, then, to place labor mobility, the flexibility of the labor supply in response to changing patterns of economic opportunity, in a prominent place in building any explanation of nineteenth-century growth.

The Labor Movement

The vast majority of workers who participated in the burgeoning industrial revolution did so without the benefit of organization. Labor unions were more common now than in the colonial period; yet by 1830 only 26,000 people, or slightly more than 0.5 percent of the labor force, had joined them, and by 1860 union members had fallen sharply to only 5,000, or about 0.1 percent of the labor force.

No increase in union activity of any kind appeared until the 1820s and 1830s, the decades that saw the first sustained expansion of industry based on the factory system. Before the 1820s union activity resembled that of the colonial period—limited to organizations of independent master craftsmen, involving very few organizations of employees, and rarely utilizing the weapon of the strike. Further, virtually no traces of organization can be found among unskilled laborers—even the cotton-mill workers who numbered some 100,-000 by 1815. Nonetheless, organizations of skilled workers grew steadily, although very slowly, as the economic expansion created new demands for skilled workers and led them to organize in order to exploit the shortness of their supply. Moreover, the advance of the factory system threatened the economic position of artisans whose skills were becoming obsolete, and they, too, turned to organization.

During the economic expansion of the 1820s and 1830s, the shortage of skilled labor and the obsolescence of traditional skills stimulated the labor movement. The rapid urbanization of the 1820s created strong demand for the labor of skilled workers in the building trades, and this demand intensified the efforts of those workers to organize. House carpenters, house painters, stonecutters, nailers, and cabinetmakers developed stable organizations with particular success. They focused on shortening the working day and sponsored strike activity to further that end. In 1825, for example, some 600 Boston house carpenters struck until their contractor-employers agreed to a standard ten-hour day. In 1827, a group of Philadelphia building trades launched a similar strike for a ten-hour day. By the time the strike was concluded successfully, they had initiated coordinated action by groups of unions. They had founded the first effective city-wide organization of wage earners, the Mechanics' Union of Trade Associations, and spawned a political party, the Working Men's party. The union sought the establishment of the ten-hour day while the party labored more for expanded public school systems that would enable the children of workers to advance more readily into the ranks of the skilled and to acquire skills that would be less subject to technological obsolescence. Both goals were characteristic of a rising urban middle class; they represented the desire to acquire more leisure and education.

The building-trades unions received support from unions representing artisans who faced declining incomes, unemployment, and loss of status in the wake of advancing machine technology and factory organization. Hatters, tailors, weavers, and shoemakers were heavily represented within craft unions growing in strength, particualrly during the 1820s. However, these artisans seemed to have been much more enthusiastic about political action, which offered some hope, however vague and insubstantial, of returning America to a simpler era than they were about the ten-hour-day movement. They shared the interest of the building trades in public education but were most enthusiastic about programs that promised to protect their eroding social position through the destruction of concentrations of economic power. They promoted antimonopoly legislation, antibanking regulations, the abolition of imprisonment for debt, the introduction of general property taxation (which was designed to tax concentrations of wealth more heavily and to reduce taxes on small property-holders by applying the same tax rate to all categories of property), and President Andrew Jackson's veto of the rechartering of the Second Bank of the United States. Artisan efforts to reverse or restrain the industrial revolution were less significant than in nineteenth-century Europe but, nonetheless, shaped the political involvement of the labor movement in a decisive fashion.

The contribution to the labor movement made by artisans who were threatened by industrial revolution began to decline during the early 1830s. Already large numbers of these artisans had abandoned their occupations and the labor movement as well. Their departure was offset only to a limited extent by the growing participation of unskilled factory workers. The unskilled began to engage in sporadic strike activity, generally against wage reductions or production speed-ups, but did not organize formally and only hesitantly supported the political activity of the established unions. During the 1830s, reflecting the loss of the displaced artisans, unions moved away from political activity and concentrated more exclusively on the issues of greatest interest to skilled workers: shorter working days and higher wages. They refined tactics of strike and boycott with an increasing degree of success that led to further concentration on narrow economic issues. Following the example of the Philadelphia model, coalitions of unions formed and often engaged in strikes. Numbering nearly two hundred, these strikes focused union energies on achieving the ten-hour day, and, by the end of 1835, these efforts, along with employer initiatives, had established the ten-hour day as the standard day's work for most skilled workers in the largest cities and virtually all of the skilled workers in the building trades. With the ten-hour day behind them, the unions turned to boosting wages. Their campaign grew to include more than fifty strikes in 1836 before the Panic of 1837 and the subsequent depression intervened.

The precise contribution of union activity of the 1820s and 1830s to rising income remains undetermined. Clearly, the impact of the unions was more on shortening the working day than on raising wages. But measurement of that impact defies analysis because most skilled workers achieved shorter hours without resorting to union activity. They simply used their bargaining power to take more real income in the form of leisure. In fact, a very small percentage of skilled workers unionized, and the localization of serious union activity in the old Atlantic seaports suggests that unions only modestly reinforced the general scarcity of labor.

The promise of unionization largely disappeared after the economic decline that began with the Panic of 1837. Even though the decline, which continued through 1843, was not especially steep by modern standards, the demand for skilled labor slowed enough to blunt the cutting edge of the movement for organization. Moreover, artisans who feared displacement learned the futility of organizing in the face of the forces of industrial change. But even when economic expansion resumed during the 1840s, unionization failed to recover its earlier position. The decade saw only a sluggish expansion of unions of skilled workers, limited organization of new workers, such as women textile workers in the Lowell Female Labor Reform Association (LFLRA), and scattered political agitation by labor groups, such as the promotion of a legislated ten-hour day by the New England Workingmen's Association and the LFLRA. Craft unionism did not resume a growth rate approaching the rate achieved earlier until the mid-1850s; not until after the Civil War did craft unionism attain either the level of participation or bargaining success reached during the early 1830s. The organization of women never effectively reached unskilled factory workers and collapsed with the acceleration of immigration. More generally, the organization of the unskilled made no progress in the face of massive immigration. During the late 1840s and early 1850s, the ten-hour-day movement produced legislative victories, especially in New England, but the protective laws contained crippling loopholes except in states where factories were few in number and significance.

To explain the extended hiatus in the development of unionism, one must turn to the impact of immigration. With the 1840s, workers, both American and foreign-born, became far more absorbed in ethnic and religious warfare than in collectively advancing their economic interests. The most dramatic expression of the heightened ethnic tensions was large-scale, protracted urban rioting that began in the 1830s. In Philadelphia violence peaked in 1844 following the organization of Native American Clubs by skilled workers (prosperous artisans, tradesmen, and some white-collar employees). These clubs called for a longer waiting period before naturalization, restriction of public offices to native-born Americans, and use of the Protestant Bible in public schools. In so doing the clubs provoked anti-Irish rioting that lasted for two months, escalated into open warfare between the Protestants and the Pennsylvania militia, and cost many casualties. By the end of the decade, the issues that had occupied street gangs became the province of politicians. By the 1850s, the national Know-Nothing movement dominated the anti-immigrant movement. Literally hundreds of thousands of people joined Know-Nothing lodges and engaged actively in anti-immigrant electoral politics. Heavily represented among the Know-Nothings were skilled workers of English or Ulster stock. Then, as the sectional crisis developed, their passions turned increasingly to the antiblack hysteria that fed the efforts of the Free-Soil movement to deny slavery, and thereby blacks, access to the territories and contributed to the swift growth of the Republican party after the Kansas-Nebraska Act of 1856.

The nativist and racist movements of the 1840s and 1850s resulted largely from the extraordinary growth of the American population, which brought together unusually diverse peoples within a society that was only loosely ordered. The flux of the dynamic 1840s and 1850s provided an opportunity for the eruption of ancient antagonisms and fears that divided peoples by ethnicity and religion.[15] But in addition to their deep cultural roots, the nativist and racist movements had their economic sources as well. The economic content of the anti-immigrant movement was more complex. It played on the concerns of unskilled workers that massive immigration would cost them their jobs. And it easily engaged the energies of artisans who had lost their jobs or feared their loss as a consequence of the encroachment of the factory system. From the 1840s their interest in turning back the economic clock—in recreating a community of farmers, small manufacturers, and tradesmen—moved from advocacy of antimonopoly legislation to agitation for restriction of immigration. During the 1850s, the increasing severity of the business cycle fed their concerns. Growing numbers of workers, both unskilled and skilled, found themselves unemployed for reasons that were understandably mysterious; they blamed their dislocations on cheap immigrant labor, seeking economic relief and psychic solace in nativism.[16] The economic concerns of skilled workers, however, are more difficult to isolate. Certainly the growing majority of skilled workers—skilled factory workers, skilled laborers in the building trades, and skilled white-collar employees—faced no direct threat from the immigrants. But the skilled workers did worry about competition from the immigrants that might develop after immigrants or their children acquired skills. Also, they feared that Catholic preferences for parochial schools would weaken the public schools, which they regarded as essential for economic success. Labor-union activists took particular exception to the proposals of Catholic clergy and Democratic legislators in many eastern states that school funds be divided so that the taxes Catholics paid would be used to support parochial schools. Thus, to many skilled workers, immigration represented a threat to their vision of the ideal society—not simply because it brought more Irish Catholics, but because it appeared to limit opportunities for wage earners to climb the economic ladder.

The history of the labor movement as a measure of class consciousness, 1790 to 1860, suggests that despite the onset of the industrial revolution, American workers retained their attachment to the ideal of a classless, open society. To a great extent that idea reflected reality because even with its increasing concentration of wealth the American social order remained highly fluid, and economic opportunity remained tied to individual flexibility and adaptability in the face of rapid social change. The most difficult challenges to the ideal of openness came from immigration and slavery. Immigration roused ancient hatreds and newer economic concerns, which, however irrational, powerfully shaped nineteenth-century social alignments. But opponents of immigration won no immediate victory; the nation's borders remained open until well into the twentieth century. Slavery was a more direct and blatant challenge to American ideals than was immigration (which, after all, resulted from a free labor market), and, consequently, it fell two generations earlier than did open immigration. When noting the lack of a powerful, organized labor movement one should also mark the contribution of many American workers to the demise of slavery. Both that contribution and the weakness of the labor movement demonstrated the commitment of American workers to individual economic freedom.

AGRICULTURAL EXPANSION

Although nonfarm labor increased steadily, most Americans were employed in agriculture before the Civil War. In 1840 over three-quarters of the labor force worked in agriculture, and although this proportion was declining, in 1860 almost two-thirds of all jobs remained agricultural. Because of its sheer size the agricultural sector had a significant bearing on the character of growth during the first half of the nineteenth century.

The central fact of American agriculture was the rapidity with which production was carried onto new lands. Beginning in 1790, three streams of population poured west of the Appalachians and accounted for a marked redistribution of population and economic activity. In the South there were two lines of expansion: cotton production spread from the older South to what would become Alabama and Mississippi, and people migrated into the Ohio valley from the upper South to specialize in the production of corn. To the north, a third major stream of population flow began during the 1830s, as settlers, primarily from New England and the Middle Atlantic states, carried wheat farming into the northern part of the Great Lakes basin—northern Ohio, northern Illinois, and southern Wisconsin. (See Figure 7 for the resulting geography of agricultural production in 1860.)

The population shifted westward so quickly that by 1840 the distribution of people over the countryside had been altered extensively in the favor of newer regions. Although the coastal states contained almost the entire citizenry in 1790, they contained about two-thirds of the total United States population in 1840 and about one-half in 1860. (See Figure 8.) The East South Central states (Kentucky, Tennessee, Alabama, and Mississippi) received most of the population shift out of the coastal states until 1830. After 1830, however, these states grew at approximately the same rate as the entire United States, maintaining their share of total population until the 1850s. As settlement grew along the Ohio valley after 1790, the East North Central states (Ohio, Indiana, Illinois, Michigan, and Wisconsin) also increased their share of population. With the opening of settlement in the upper Great Lakes in the 1830s and the slackening of population growth in the East South Central region, the largest thrust of population began. By 1850 these two eastern areas of the nation's geographic heartland accounted for more than one-third of America's population. Following the Louisiana Purchase the West Central states (almost exclusively Arkansas, Louisiana, and Missouri) began to increase in population, although somewhat sluggishly until the 1840s, when Iowa and Texas started to make their mark. During the 1850s Missouri, Iowa, and Texas continued to dominate the growth of the region, but Minnesota and Kansas were also gaining in numbers. By the 1850s, the West Central states had replaced the East North Central states as the most rapidly growing portion of the nation.

The thrust of people onto new lands was not limited to movements between regions. A considerable amount of relocation took place within states and within regions, particularly within New England and the Middle Atlantic states, and especially after the War of 1812 and during the 1820s. The spread of farmers into the backcountry of northern New England and upstate New York meant a reduction of agricultural productivity because their land was stony, difficult to clear, and lacking in adequate transportation services. A movement out of these areas soon developed; by 1830 most of the uplands of New England and the Middle Atlantic states had passed their population peaks. Abandoned farms and homes dotted the countryside, their owners having sought better lands and higher returns in western New York or the interior.

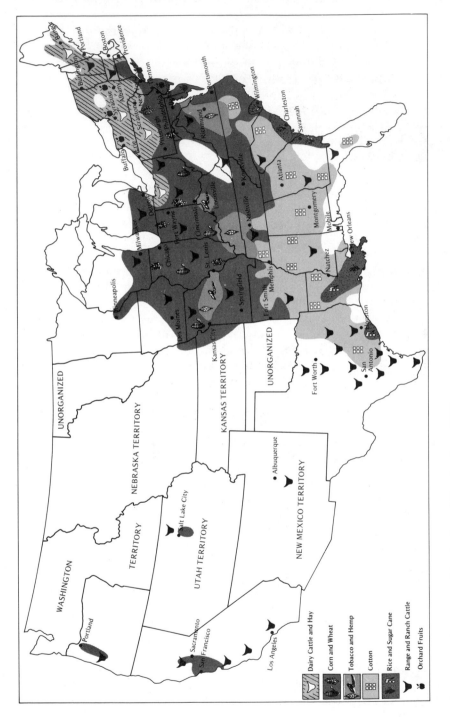

FIGURE 7: *Patterns of Agricultural Production, 1860*

Dairy Cattle and Hay

Corn and Wheat

Tobacco and Hemp

Cotton

Rice and Sugar Cane

Range and Ranch Cattle

Orchard Fruits

WASHINGTON

TERRITORY

UTAH TERRITORY

NEBRASKA TERRITORY

KANSAS TERRITORY

NEW MEXICO TERRITORY

UNORGANIZED

UNORGANIZED

Portland

Sacramento
San Francisco

Los Angeles

Salt Lake City

Albuquerque

Fort Worth

San Antonio

Houston

Minneapolis

Des Moines

Kansas City

Fort Smith

Memphis

Springfield

St. Louis

Chicago

Milwaukee

Detroit

Fort Wayne

Cincinnati

Louisville

Nashville

Knoxville

Natchez

New Orleans

Mobile

Montgomery

Atlanta

Savannah

Charleston

Wilmington

Richmond

Portsmouth

Pittsburgh

Philadelphia

Trenton

New York

Albany

Scranton

Syracuse

Buffalo

Erie

Boston

Providence

Portland

Bangor

It has been suggested that the westward movement, taken as a whole, retarded or even precluded economic growth in the country at large before 1840, just as settlement of the New England and New York backlands certainly inhibited the general improvement of agricultural productivity. Accordingly the westward movement might be described as the shift of people from market-oriented production to comparatively self-sufficient pioneer farming activities. Nonetheless, the evidence available indicates that the contrary was the case. For one thing, even as early as 1840, or before the achievement of marked advances in agricultural productivity during the 1840s and 1850s, the productivity of labor was higher on new, interior farms than on seaboard farms and plantations.[17] In the newly opened areas in the interior, East Central and West Central states, agricultural productivity was higher than in the United States as a whole.

Agricultural productivity in the older areas of New England and the South Atlantic states lagged behind that in the nation as a whole. Productivity in Middle Atlantic states was high by national standards, but was below that characteristic of the West Central and East North Central states. The pattern of greater productivity in the central interior can be better understood by the fact that grain production in the Western states in 1840 used labor more efficiently than such production in the South and Northeast. The westward movement resulted in sharp gains in agricultural productivity and the further extension of the marketplace.

Data on interstate migrations between 1830 and 1860 reveal a significant direct relationship between levels of migration and wage rates. For example, within New England during the 1830s, population tended to increase most rapidly as a result of migration into those states that offered highest wages for common labor. In the 1850s the North Central states offered the most attractive opportunities of productivity and wages—and they received the most voluminous flow of people during the decade. In addition, the states that gained the most population within that region tended to offer the highest levels of wages for common farm labor.[18] Hence, the continuing stream of population into the West meant an enhancement of the productivity of agricultural labor and increasing returns to farm labor.

The characteristics of people on agricultural frontiers between 1840 and 1860 also support the argument that the frontier rapidly reproduced the marketplace economy of older agricultural areas. Rather than a collection of young, single, adventuresome males, willing to cope with real deprivation and a marginal existence, frontier people were quite similar to those left behind. Looking at the first

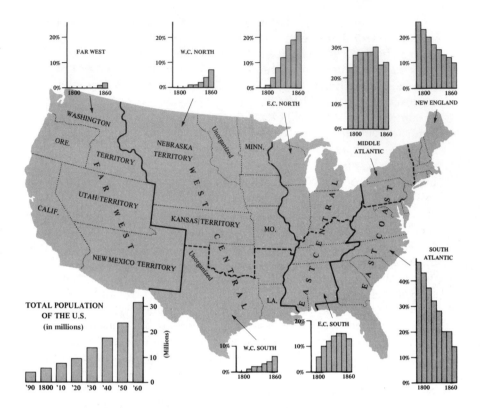

FIGURE 8: *Estimated Population of the United States, 1790–1860 (in percentages by regions)*

decade of settlement in portions of the North Central states, in Mormon Utah, and in the Oregon Territory, one analyst finds that the population compared to that of the nation contained only 10 percent more children under ten years of age; the same proportion of women in their twenties; only about 25 percent more men in their twenties; only 20 percent fewer men and 10 percent fewer women in their thirties; and only slightly fewer adults over forty. Furthermore, only about one-quarter of the adult males on the agricultural frontier were single. In addition, the vast majority of the population, or 85 percent, were native-born, coming from New England, the Middle Atlantic states, and states contiguous with the frontier.[19] To take another example, a second analyst, discussing the composition of population on the Illinois-Iowa frontier, concludes that the typical pioneer was married, between the ages of twenty-five and forty-five, and started a family before moving to the frontier.[20] It seems, then, that the family was probably the central institution in the movement of American society onto new lands; this social fact, in turn, strongly suggests that the institution of the marketplace, involving a high degree of sensitivity to economic opportunity, was also firmly entrenched in the process of new settlement. It is unlikely that these rather typical families were willing, in such large numbers, to sacrifice their economic capacities or undergo extreme risks for greater elbowroom. A strong reason for their mobility, while other families persisted in more established communities, was very probably the seductive opportunity that new, more fertile lands provided.

The augmented agricultural productivity generated by the occupation of virgin soil stemmed, not from increased yields per acre, but from the reduced number of man-hours required per acre under cultivation. The thinner and sparser forests in the prairie lands of the West reduced the cost of clearing farmland, and the greater fertility of the new land diminished the amount of labor necessary to produce a crop. Furthermore, important technological changes, mainly in farm machinery, sustained the growth of productivity in the West. Although the harvester, hay rake, and seed drill were used only rarely before 1850, the earlier spread of Jethro Wood's cast-iron plow reduced by about half the labor required in plowing, making it possible to till increased acreage. Similar technological changes favored the cultivation of cotton and corn as well: replacement of the scythe with the cradle in the harvesting of small grains, improved plant breeding, the use of timothy clover, and more capable animal husbandry contributed to the capabilities of the nation's farms.

After a period of declining productivity in northern farming, associated with migrations onto marginal land in New England and New York, labor productivity increased as a result of the settlement of more-fertile western lands. For the national economy this meant that between 1800 and 1840 the westward movement, facilitated by improved transport, produced almost a 10-percent increase in agricultural productivity. Thus gains in agricultural productivity served to reinforce gains realized in the nonagricultural sector even before the undisputed gains of the farm sector in the 1840s and 1850s.[21] In other words, the rapid extension of the agricultural frontier augmented the productive capacity of agriculture and stimulated real economic growth in the nation as a whole. If Jefferson's expansionary policy had been reversed and a latter-day Proclamation Line drawn to restrain agriculture behind the Appalachians, productivity could have been maintained only with an acceleration in technological change. To conserve land rather than men, it might be supposed, nineteenth-century America could have developed a land-intensive agriculture, one similar to that of modern Japan or the post-1940 United States. But such a development, of course, would have demanded rather enormous leaps in chemical and biological technology to augment the mechanical technology that yielded cultivators, threshers, and reapers. In contrast, although improved modes of transport and mechanical cultivation required some application of scientific knowledge, they demanded no scientific progress. Given the scientific and technological realities of the mid-nineteenth century, the more intensive path was virtually impossible.

After 1840 the impetus that expansion lent to the growth of agricultural productivity is unquestionable. Labor-saving technological change, primarily in the planting and harvesting of grains in areas bordering the Great Lakes, combined with the fertility and ease of cultivation of new lands, produced a remarkably efficient agriculture. John Deere's steel plow, superior to the cast-iron plow because of its scouring capacity and strength, found widespread acceptance during the 1850s. Most important were the various reapers—the McCormick, the Hussey, the Atkins, and the Manny—which increasingly dotted the plains, especially during the 1850s. Previously, one man, using a sickle, was able to cut one-half to three-quarters of an acre of wheat per day; using a cradle scythe, he could cut two to three acres per day. But with a self-raking reaper a farmer could cut twelve acres per day. In addition to saving labor and increasing the amount of acreage planted, the farmer with a reaper could cut his crop closer to the ideal time rather than having to harvest prematurely to avoid spoilage. Also, the trunk lines completed during the 1850s provided fast and smooth connections between the North Central states and urban eastern markets. During the 1850s, as a result of more-fertile and more-easily-cleared land, the adoption of labor-saving machinery, and reduced transportation costs, expansion augmented agricultural productivity—perhaps as much as 20 percent during that single decade.

The alacrity of expansion resulted from a variety of cultural and institutional factors as well. The growth of the American population, the cultural fixation on landownership, persisting from the colonial period, the availability of capital for investing in new lands, the improvements in communications that fostered new settlement, and the expansion of markets were all circumstances that shaped the general American economic experience of the nineteenth century, especially territorial expansion and the growth of agriculture.

Indispensable to all these factors, of course, was that the United

States government, which had virtually complete discretion over the disposal of unoccupied land, responded positively to the widespread conviction that settlement on new lands should be as liberal and unencumbered as was consistent with the preservation of order. Beginning with the Land Ordinance of 1785, which set a minimum price of $1 per acre, the terms of land acquisition were made increasingly favorable to the prospective settler. When the price was increased to $2 per acre in 1796, the buyer was granted a year to make full payment, and in 1800 the payment period was extended to four years. With the Panic of 1820 Congress abandoned the credit provision but reduced the price to $1.25, then in the Graduation Act of 1854 allowed lands that had long been on the market to be sold below the $1.25 minimum. Thus $200 would purchase 160 acres of federal land—not an overwhelming price by any means, in light of the estimate that between 1820 and 1850, under average wage and employment conditions, an individual could accumulate savings worth $500 in ten years. Moreover, available mortgage funds expanded more rapidly than the farm population in the North, as county school funds, life insurance funds, mutual savings bank funds, and the funds of wealthier individuals became available to new farm makers.[22]

The process of liberalizing land policy culminated in the Preemption Act of 1841 and the Homestead Act in 1862. Recognizing the frequent failure of government auctions to keep pace with the extension of settlement, the former permitted a squatter to have first rights to the purchase of the property he occupied, and provided that any settler who was a family head, widow, or person of age and an American citizen (or a person in the process of naturalization), and not an owner of 320 acres or more elsewhere could claim 160 acres of surveyed land prior to public sale if the settler had constructed a dwelling and made improvements. The Homestead Act allowed the same categories of people to obtain 160 acres after submitting a filing fee, improving the land, and living on the parcel for five years.

Although under these laws land frequently fell into the hands of large and small speculators (perhaps best described as absentee landlords), the outcome was often hastened settlement. Large, intermediate landowners could promote land sales, pay transportation costs, supply building materials, locate claims, provide some initial, social overhead investment, make a sizable tax contribution to a growing community, and, perhaps most important, provide credit. Examples of abuses of the system through the power of speculators are easy to uncover, but the success of the system in providing the majority of farmers with freehold tenure of the land they tilled is more striking.

The government subsidy provided to farmers is reflected in the fact that after one hundred years the government was in the red on its land program: despite monopoly power in the sale of new land, it had failed to realize consistent returns on land sales or even cover costs of what was an efficient administration. Yet this subsidy of land was probably the most important source of government promotion of economic growth prior to the Civil War.

Besides liberalizing the terms of land acquisition, the government encouraged settlement by specifying the creation of a dependable political and social environment in new territory. The use of a rectangular survey (the marking off of parcels with a grid) prior to settlement lent regularity to the system and reduced the social cost from litigation of land claims. The companion act to the Land Ordinance of 1785, the Northwest Ordinance of 1787, guaranteed stable political conditions in new regions and assured a new territory the attainment of statehood on equal terms after certain minimum conditions were met. By assuring self-government as well as providing readily available land resources, the federal government adopted an enlightened colonial policy, one that would augment the power of the marketplace and the landowning culture that swept families onto new lands.

Despite the significance of free labor to the expansion of agriculture, it was not necessary for the relentless occupation of new territory. Indeed, the southern economy, based on slave labor, conformed to the expansive national pattern. By 1801, only about a decade after the cotton gin permitted the culture of short-staple cotton (the only variety that could be carried onto the uplands), the United States produced almost one-tenth of the world's cotton supply. By the 1820s the United States was the world's largest cotton producer and the largest slaveholder in the Western Hemisphere. By 1850, as a result of the westward movement of plantations, the United States accounted for more than two-thirds of the world's output. (In 1821 South Carolina and Georgia had accounted for over half of American production. By 1859 their share had fallen to less than one-quarter of the total, while the share of Alabama, Mississippi, and Louisiana had increased from about one-quarter to almost two-thirds of American production.)

Thus, slavery did not drastically alter the expansionary quality of nineteenth-century agriculture and was not an exception to the pervasive search for newer, more productive land. Southern farmers were no different from their northern counterparts in making a sustained effort to maximize returns on their labor and capital through the occupation of fresh lands.

DOMESTIC AND FOREIGN COMMERCE: CHANGING PATTERNS OF TRADE

The international economy underwent a period of marked expansion during the nineteenth century, and the American economy profited from participation in that growth. Expansion promoted an international division of labor, and brought enormous volumes of foreign investment capital and labor to the United States in search of the higher returns that reflected its relative scarcities of capital and labor. As the factors of production became more mobile across the oceans and across national boundaries, international trade flourished. Nations were increasingly able to exploit their particular comparative advantages and develop, with adequate complements of labor and capital, their varying endowments of natural resources. The mobility of labor and capital promulgated the economic specialization of nations and more intense international exchanges of goods and services.

The expansion of the world marketplace required the innovation of many central economic institutions. Nations had to develop capital markets that could provide the medium for increasing levels of international investment. Credit had been extended in international commerce for centuries, but only in the nineteenth century did firms appear whose primary function was judging the returns on a wide assortment of noncommercial activities. Following the rise of international bankers, such as the Rothschilds and Baring Brothers, mobility of international funds increased. At the same time, investors grew more sensitive to the profit differentials of various economies.

Reinforcing the improvements in capital markets were institutional changes that enhanced the mobility of other resources, human and material. Sharply reduced tariffs were characteristic of the period and encouraged the extension and intensification of trade. In 1846 Britain repealed the Corn Laws that had imposed duties and quotas on grain imports; in the United States the free-trade movement gathered momentum in the 1840s and 1850s, resulting in consistently lowered tariffs, and appeared to be on the verge of victory before the Civil War intervened. In the late 1840s Britain eliminated a barrier to labor mobility by repealing the Navigation Acts. Besides encouraging the emigration of skilled artisans to the United States and partially relieving the shortage of skilled labor, repeal increased the flow to the United States of practical information concerning British technological advance. Americans, following the British in the development process, had naturally relied on British technology and had always found immigration of knowledgeable laborers to be the best channel of information; the removal of the legal obstacle to such information flows accelerated the process of technological adaptation. All movements of capital, men, and goods and services found real encouragement from a dramatic decline in the costs of ocean transport, which resulted from improvements in sailing ships that increased both average tonnage and efficiency. As a consequence of technological and organizational advances of all sorts, transport costs fell by more than 50 percent between the end of the War of 1812 and the 1850s, the sharpest decline within the nineteenth century.[23]

America's development of its particular set of comparative advantages was reflected in the growth and structure of the nation's exports. The trend of exports was strongly upward throughout the period, with the early 1830s marking a period of acceleration. From 1839, the first year for which estimates of production and income accounts are available, exports grew as rapidly as national product, maintaining a level of 6 to 7 percent of gross national product. Both national product and exports almost tripled in value during that twenty-year period. Despite the striking growth of exports, their structure remained fairly unchanged, primary products (food and fiber, including processed food, such as flour) constituting most of American exports throughout the ante-bellum period. Until the 1840s raw materials and crude foods (e.g., unmilled grains) made up at least two-thirds of exports. Finished and semifinished goods never formed even one-quarter of exports by value during the period, although they did begin to grow relative to total exports during the 1840s. Manufacturing exports hardly increased beyond the category of low-quality cotton textiles; no general increase in manufacturing exports took place until the 1850s.[24]

Nevertheless, the ability of the United States to compete in international manufactures markets was evident in the rapid growth of manufacturing exports in the 1840s and 1850s. By those decades the manufacturing sector was sufficiently developed, and tariffs and transportation were low enough, to permit successful competition in world markets. The United States relied primarily on the comparative advantage stemming from the cheapness of land; those exports that used the largest inputs of land, whether they were farm products or manufactured goods (such as textiles), were dominant.

Raw cotton dominated exports of agricultural goods throughout the period. Although cotton exports grew more slowly than exports as a whole after the 1830s, even in the 1850s cotton accounted for almost half of export values, lending a colonial cast to the structure of the export sector. Cotton had replaced the traditional colonial exports of tobacco, rice, lumber, and naval stores and thereby sustained the growth of the export sector. Exports of wheat and flour gained importance only in the 1840s and 1850s, when the Irish potato famine, the Crimean War, and the repeal of the Corn Laws increased European demands. Thus the colonial pattern of exports persisted well into the nineteenth century, until at least the 1840s, with a change only in export staples. Moreover, Great Britain persisted as the major recipient of exports, her share actually increasing to 50 percent of the total by the time of the Civil War.

Despite the dynamic export trade, the United States had an unfavorable balance of trade from the 1820s until the 1870s. During the periods of most rapid growth the demand of Americans for imported goods greatly intensified, exceeding the foreign demand for American exports by unusually large margins. More generally put, as national income moved, so did the merchandise trade balance, with import movements outweighing export fluctuations. The imported goods in high demand were diverse, although they were mainly manufactures and semimanufactures. They included finished textiles, railroad iron—a commodity in especially strong demand during the expansion of the 1850s—and primary products originating in the tropics, most notably sugar, coffee, tea, and cocoa.

Within its balance-of-payments account, the nation made up for the trading imbalance primarily through exporting specie and gaining returns on service-and-current items, such as immigrant remittances and shipping earnings. Within this latter category of payments, funds brought by immigrants to the United States roughly canceled out tourist expenditures made by Americans in Europe, up until the 1850s; then the latter became heavier as European travel became less expensive, more comfortable, and more popular. The sale of American shipping services in financing the trade imbalance was most significant as a result of the comparative advantage in carrying goods that America held until the Civil War. Earnings in the service-and-current account contributed to the ability of the United States to maintain substantial imports of gold and silver, which began in the 1820s, peaked in the 1830s, and continued into the 1840s. During the 1850s, as a result of the economic upsurge of that decade, the margin of imports over exports grew even more rapidly, supported by the California mining boom, which allowed an outflow of almost $400 million in gold and silver from the country during the decade.

The net debt position of the United States changed little over the course of the first six decades of the nineteenth century, except during the 1830s and the first half of the 1850s. While imports of foreign, primarily British, capital did not constitute a significant portion of American capital formation for the period as a whole, and although such imports did not dominate capital formation in even the transportation sector, foreign capital did make a significant impact on the building of the canal network in the 1830s and the railroad system in the first half of the 1850s by supplementing domestic savings that were available for such projects.

The international division of labor, made possible by flexible institutions of international trade, redounded to the benefit of Americans, who found they were able to purchase manufactured goods and other products that they could not have otherwise afforded. At the same time the high level of imports during the periods of expansion freed both labor and capital from consumer-goods production. Consequently the nation found it easier to shift resources into canal and railroad construction, which was to have a much greater, albeit indirect, impact on later development.

The trade thesis, which asserts that the most important influence on United States growth through the 1840s was the expanding international market for cotton, attaches even greater importance to international trade. In this interpretive framework the cotton-export sector led development in the West and North. The South, specializing in cotton production, needed the foodstuffs of the West for sustenance, particularly in the boom years of cotton, when even more of the land was put into cotton production. Also, merchants were looking for ways to diversify their activities: the income accruing to northern middlemen enabled them to turn to the financing of manufacturing in a capital-scarce environment. And the cotton mills could draw on inexpensive cotton from the South and the factory populations could rely on food from the West.

No alternative explanation for the early stages of nineteenth-century growth is as fully articulated or as broad in scope. Nonetheless, with regard to the patterns of trade, this thesis contains a number of flaws, which, when taken in sum, necessitate either a restructuring of the argument or the statement of an alternative hypothesis.

The most thoroughly criticized portion has been the notion that southern demand for western foodstuffs led western development in its earliest stages. Recent studies make historians reasonably certain that, at least during the 1850s, cotton plantations were largely self-sufficient in basic foods and that the cotton South as a whole usually was self-reliant in basic foods and, in fact, produced important surpluses in good years.[25] Cotton planters enjoyed the use of cheap land and, because of the high requirements of labor at the time of cotton harvesting and the limited opportunities to rent out slaves, maintained a surplus of labor. These factors, coupled with the high cost of transporting food, led them to extend production to foodstuffs. When a dynamic market for cotton induced expansion, planters carried production of both cotton and food onto new lands and chose to provide their own food requirements, thereby taking advantage of the underemployed slave labor force and the cheapness of land. Now, if the cotton South had also been self-sufficient in the 1820s and 1830s, creating no demands for western foodstuffs, there could have been no linkage between western and southern development of the character postulated in the trade thesis. There is no definite evidence for the earlier period, but in light of the greater proximity of the West and the cotton South during the 1850s and the consequently lower costs of interregional transport, it would seem likely that contact was greater during the *later* period than during the earlier.

In addition, interregional trade routes do not appear to have carried sufficient western agricultural exports, at least during the 1840s and 1850s, to support the trade thesis. In fact, the South, especially the grain belt of the upper South, probably should be seen more as a supplier of foodstuffs to a food-deficient Northeast than as a recipient of western produce.[26]

The clear capability for food production demonstrated by the South during the 1840s and 1850s indicates that proponents of a trade theory must seek new evidence to obtain credibility. Specifically, they must measure the magnitudes of interregional flows of foodstuffs during the 1820s and 1830s, both from West to South and from West to East, and must be able to compare the size of southern demands for western products with western production during the earlier period. Although the South was essentially self-sufficient in food, and although costs of transporting food from the Ohio valley to the cotton South were substantially higher in the 1820s and 1830s than in the following decades, it remains conceivable that the South, given the large size of the cotton economy, generated enough demand for western produce to stimulate western development in a critical fashion. But as yet no solid evidence has been presented to confirm such a hypothesis.

Rather than accept the unsubstantiated trade thesis, it is far safer to assume that western development depended to a much greater degree on the growth of demand for grains, grain products, and livestock in the industrializing Northeast. The link between Northeast and West may well have been as important during the industrial expansion beginning in the late 1820s as it became during the 1850s. In fact, the connection is much more probable now that we have placed the most significant acceleration of industrialization in the 1820s rather than the 1830s. Thus the growth of western settlement during that decade and during the 1830s is more likely to have been a response to the demands of newly forming urban-industrial populations for the products of agriculture, than if settlement had preceded industrialization, as suggested by the trade theory. Certainly a significant volume of west-to-east traffic was feasible and probably profitable during the 1820s, even before the completion of the Erie Canal in 1825, given the existence of trans-Appalachian roads, the ability of livestock to provide its own transportation to market from the West, and the tendency of western corn farmers to transform their crop into the less bulky form of whiskey before transport to the East.

And as previously noted, the fact that industrialization in the United States may have actually experienced a quickening of pace during the 1820s undermines another, even more important, part of the trade thesis, since, obviously, the boom in cotton exports during the 1830s could not have played a role in the initial, sustained acceleration of industrialization in the Northeast. Nevertheless, it is still unknown to what extent profits generated in the cotton trade financed the industrial revolution in the Northeast during and after the 1830s. Certainly the cotton merchants played a very important role. However, they contributed far less than a majority of the funds initiating modernization, because most cotton was shipped *directly* from southern ports to Europe, especially prior to 1840. This meant that the majority of the financing and the related services was provided, not by Americans, but by European importing houses.[27] The earnings from cotton exports mainly either went to Europeans or financed the extension of the cotton frontier. The South may have been functionally independent from the other two sections and, instead, tied almost exclusively to European capitalism, as were other plantation economies of the time.[28] American growth, then, should be explained in the context of complementary relationships between the industrializing Northeast and the highly productive agricultural Northwest, with Europe and the South playing a lesser role in the trading sectors.

In summary, trade, both international and interregional, promoted economic growth in that it permitted a fuller division of labor. Those institutional changes that widened trade encouraged greater regional and national productivity. Mushrooming trade with Europe permitted Americans to rely more heavily on foreign producers for articles of consumption, enabled southern farmers to specialize in profitable cotton production, and provided a small but growing foreign market for American manufactured goods. But internal commerce absorbed the vast bulk of western and northeastern production, and the specialization that resulted from this trade was more significant to the development and strengthening of industrialization in the United States than was the flourishing of international exchange.

NOTES

1. One qualification of this description of relative scarcities has often been made: Although both skilled and unskilled labor were scarcer in the United States than in Great Britain, skilled labor may have been relatively more available in the United States. This suggestion has been seriously questioned, but it is nevertheless possible that America possessed a relative abundance of skilled machinery makers; such an abundance also would have contributed strongly to the substitution of capital for labor. See Nathan Rosenberg, "Anglo-American Wage Differences in the 1820's," *Journal of Economic History,* 27 (June 1967), 221–229.

2. On the development of the machine-tool industry see Robert S. Woodbury, "The Legend of Eli Whitney and Interchangeable Parts," *Technology and Culture,* 2 (Summer 1960), 235–253; and Nathan Rosenberg, "Technological Change in the Machine Tool Industry, 1840–1910," *Journal of Economic History,* 23 (December 1963), 414–443.

3. On the comparative development of British and American machine tools see Nathan Rosenberg (ed.), *The American System of Manufactures* (Edinburgh: Edinburgh University Press, 1969).

4. Lance E. Davis and H. Louis Stettler III, "The New England Textile Industry, 1825–60: Trends and Fluctuations," in Conference on Income and Wealth, National Bureau of Economic Research, *Output, Employment, and Productivity in the United States After 1800,* Vol. 30, *Studies in Income and Wealth* (New York: Columbia University Press, 1966), p. 228.

5. Lance E. Davis, "Stock Ownership in the Early New England Textile Industry," in *Purdue Faculty Papers in Economic History, 1956–1966* (Homewood, Ill.: Irwin, 1967), p. 571; Davis, "The New England Textile Mills and the Capital Markets: A Study of Industrial Borrowing, 1840–1860," *Journal of Economic History,* 20 (March 1960), 1–30.

6. In the preceding discussion of the iron industry I rely heavily on Peter Temin, *Iron and Steel in Nineteenth-Century America* (Cambridge, Mass.: M.I.T. Press, 1964). Owners of anthracite coal fields appear to have taken a vigorous role in promoting the technological changes discussed by Temin in order to create a market for their hard coal. Alfred D. Chandler, Jr., "Anthracite Coal and the Beginnings of the Industrial Revolution in the United States," *Business History Review,* 46 (Summer 1972), 141–181.

7. Stanley Lebergott, *Manpower in Economic Growth: The United States Record Since 1800* (New York: McGraw-Hill, 1964), p. 70.

8. Franklin F. Mendels, "Proto-Industrialization: The First Phase of the Industrialization Process," *Journal of Economic History,* 32 (March 1972), 241–261.

9. A study of women employed at the Lyman Mills during the 1850s reveals that fewer than one-third remained as long as three years. Apparently

most married and left the labor force. Ray Ginger, "Labor in a Massachusetts Cotton Mill," *Business History Review,* 28 (1954), 83–85.

10. On the replacement of native American women by immigrants, see Edith Abbott, "History of the Employment of Women in the American Cotton Mills," *Journal of Political Economy,* 16 (November–December 1908), 602–621.

11. The leading work on the nineteenth-century Irish immigrants is Oscar Handlin, *Boston's Immigrants, 1790–1880: A Study in Acculturation* (Cambridge, Mass.: Harvard University Press, 1959). It should, however, be read in conjunction with Peter R. Knights, *The Plain People of Boston, 1830–1860* (New York: Oxford University Press, 1971).

12. On the sources of German immigration see Mack Walker, *Germany and the Emigration, 1816–1885* (Cambridge, Mass.: Harvard University Press, 1964).

13. Yasukichi Yasuba, *Birth Rates of the White Population of the United States, 1800–1860* (Baltimore: Johns Hopkins University Press, 1961).

14. For a discussion of these relationships, see Allan R. Pred, *Urban Growth and the Circulation of Information: The United States System of Cities, 1790–1840* (Cambridge, Mass.: Harvard University Press, 1973).

15. For the best summary of recent literature emphasizing the role of ethnic and religious issues in American politics, see Robert Kelley, "Ideology and Political Culture from Jefferson to Nixon," *American Historical Review,* 82 (June 1977), 531–562.

16. For suggestions of the significance of displaced workers to the Know-Nothing movement, see Michael F. Holt, "The Politics of Impatience: The Origins of Know Nothingism," *Journal of American History,* 60 (September 1973), 309–331.

17. Data by Richard A. Easterlin cited in Paul A. David, "The Growth of Real Product in the United States Before 1840: New Evidence, Controlled Conjectures," *Journal of Economic History,* 27 (June 1967), 179.

18. Lebergott, *op. cit.,* pp. 74–87.

19. Jack E. Eblen, "An Analysis of Nineteenth-Century Frontier Populations," *Demography,* 2 (1965), 399–413.

20. Allan G. Bogue, *From Prairie to Corn Belt: Farming on the Illinois and Iowa Frontier* (Chicago: Quadrangle, 1968), pp. 21–28.

21. A good estimate of overall improvement in agricultural productivity between 1800 and 1840 is 31 percent. David, *op. cit.,* p. 179.

22. Clarence H. Danhof, *Change in Agriculture in the Northern United States, 1820–1870* (Cambridge, Mass.: Harvard University Press, 1969), pp. 75–84.

23. Douglass C. North, "Ocean Freight Rates and Economic Development, 1750–1913," *Journal of Economic History,* 18 (December 1958), 537–555.

24. The trends of international exchange discussed in this section are defined by data developed by Douglass C. North. See his *The Economic Growth of the United States, 1790–1860* (Englewood Cliffs, N.J.: Prentice-Hall, 1961), pp. 284, 288, and "The United States Balance of Payments, 1790–1860," in Conference on Research in Income and Wealth, *Trends in the American Economy in the Nineteenth Century* (Princeton, N.J.: Princeton University Press, 1960), p. 581.

25. See primarily Robert E. Gallman, "Self-Sufficiency in the Cotton Economy of the Antebellum South," in William N. Parker (ed.), *The Structure of the Cotton Economy of the Antebellum South* (Washington, D.C.: Agricultural History Society, 1970), pp. 5–37. Also consult William K. Hutchinson and Samuel H. Williamson, "The Self-Sufficiency of the Antebellum South: Estimates of the Food Supply," *Journal of Economic History*, 31 (September 1971), 591–612.

26. For a discussion of western-southern trade see in particular Albert Fishlow, *American Railroads and the Transformation of the Ante-Bellum Economy* (Cambridge, Mass.: Harvard University Press, 1965), pp. 275–288.

27. European domination of cotton financing is underscored by the fact that fluctuations in the domestic cotton market during the 1830s resulted from fluctuations in the English cotton market rather than from disturbances of domestic origin. Peter Temin, "The Causes of Cotton-Price Fluctuations in the 1830s," *Review of Economic Statistics*, 49 (November 1967), 463–470.

28. For this suggestion see Morton Rothstein, "The Cotton Frontier of the Antebellum South: A Methodological Battleground," in Parker, *op. cit.*, pp. 149–165.

SUGGESTED READINGS

Industrialization

Books

Coleman, Peter J. *The Transformation of Rhode Island, 1790–1860*. Providence, R.I.: Brown University Press, 1963.

Habakkuk, H. J. *American and British Technology in the Nineteenth Century: The Search for Labour-Saving Inventions*. New York: Cambridge University Press, 1962.

Handlin, Oscar. *Boston's Immigrants, 1790–1880: A Study in Acculturation*. Cambridge, Mass.: Harvard University Press, 1959.

Hansen, Marcus L. *The Atlantic Migration, 1607–1860*. Cambridge, Mass.: Harvard University Press, 1940.

Kranzberg, Melvin, and Carroll W. Pursell, Jr. (eds.). *Technology in Western Civilization*. 2 vols. New York: Oxford University Press, 1967.

Lebergott, Stanley. *Manpower in Economic Growth: The United States Record Since 1800.* New York: McGraw-Hill, 1964.

McGouldrick, Paul F. *New England Textiles in the Nineteenth Century.* Cambridge, Mass.: Harvard University Press, 1968.

Norris, James D. *Frontier Iron: The Maramec Iron Works, 1826–1876.* Madison, Wis.: State Historical Society of Wisconsin, 1964.

Porter, Glenn, and Harold C. Livesay. *Merchants and Manufacturers: Studies in the Changing Structure of Nineteenth-Century Marketing.* Baltimore: Johns Hopkins University Press, 1971.

Purdue Faculty Papers in Economic History, 1956–1966. Homewood, Ill.: Irwin, 1967.

Schmookler, Jacob. *Invention and Economic Growth.* Cambridge, Mass.: Harvard University Press, 1966.

Soltow, Lee. *Men and Wealth in the United States, 1850–1870.* New Haven, Conn.: Yale University Press, 1975.

Strassmann, W. Paul. *Risk and Technological Innovation: American Manufacturing Methods During the Nineteenth Century.* Ithaca, N.Y.: Cornell University Press, 1959.

Taeuber, Conrad, and Irene B. Taeuber. *The Changing Population of the United States.* New York: Wiley, 1958.

Taylor, George Rogers. *The Transportation Revolution, 1815–1860.* New York: Holt, Rinehart and Winston, 1951.

Taylor, Philip. *The Distant Magnet: European Immigration to the U.S.A.* New York: Harper & Row, 1971.

Temin, Peter. *Iron and Steel in Nineteenth-Century America.* Cambridge, Mass.: The M.I.T. Press, 1964.

Thernstrom, Stephan. *Poverty and Progress.* Cambridge, Mass.: Harvard University Press, 1964.

Usher, Abbott P. *A History of Mechanical Inventions.* Cambridge, Mass.: Harvard University Press, 1954.

Walker, Mack. *Germany and the Emigration, 1816–1885.* Cambridge, Mass.: Harvard University Press, 1964.

Walsh, Margaret. *The Manufacturing Frontier: Pioneer Industry in Antebellum Wisconsin.* Madison, Wis.: State Historical Society of Wisconsin, 1972.

Warner, Sam Bass, Jr. *The Private City.* Philadelphia: University of Pennsylvania Press, 1968.

Yasuba, Yasukichi. *Birth Rates of the White Population of the United States, 1800–1860.* Baltimore: Johns Hopkins University Press, 1961.

Articles

Adams, Donald R., Jr. "Wage Rates in the Early National Period: Philadelphia, 1785–1830," *Journal of Economic History,* 28 (September 1968), 404–417.

Brito, D. L., and Jeffrey G. Williamson. "Skilled Labor and Nineteenth-Century Anglo-American Managerial Behavior," *Explorations in Economic History*, 10 (Spring 1973), 235–251.

David, Paul A. "The Growth of Real Product in the United States Before 1840: New Evidence, Controlled Conjectures," *Journal of Economic History*, 27 (June 1967), 151–197.

Jeremy, David J. "British Textile Technology Transmission to the United States: The Philadelphia Region Experience, 1770–1820," *Business History Review*, 47 (Spring 1973), 24–52.

Livesay, Harold C., and Glenn Porter. "The Financial Role of Merchants in the Development of U.S. Manufacturing, 1815–1860," *Explorations in Economic History*, 9 (Fall 1971), 63–87.

Potter, James. "The Growth of Population in America, 1700–1860," in D. V. Glass and D. E. C. Eversley (eds.), *Population in History: Essays in Historical Demography*. Chicago: Aldine, 1965.

Poulson, Barry W. "Estimates of the Value of Manufacturing Output in the Early Nineteenth Century," *Journal of Economic History*, 29 (September 1969), 521–525.

Agriculture

Books

Bogue, Allan G. *From Prairie to Corn Belt: Farming on the Illinois and Iowa Frontier.* Chicago: Quadrangle, 1968.

Danhof, Clarence H. *Change in Agriculture in the Northern United States, 1820–1870.* Cambridge, Mass.: Harvard University Press, 1969.

Gates, Paul W. *The Farmer's Age: Agriculture, 1815–1860.* New York: Holt, Rinehart and Winston, 1960.

Gray, Lewis C. *History of Agriculture in the Southern United States to 1860.* 2 vols. Washington, D.C.: Carnegie, 1933.

Lampard, Eric E. *The Rise of the Dairy Industry in Wisconsin: A Study in Agricultural Change, 1820–1920.* Madison, Wis.: State Historical Society of Wisconsin, 1963.

Parker, William N. (ed.). *The Structure of the Cotton Economy of the Antebellum South.* Washington, D.C.: Agricultural History Society, 1970.

Article

David, Paul A. "The Mechanization of Reaping in the Ante-Bellum Midwest," in Henry Rosovsky (ed.), *Industrialization in Two Systems: Essays in Honor of Alexander Gerschenkron.* New York: Wiley, 1966, pp. 3–39.

Commerce

Books

Atherton, Lewis E. *Main Street on the Middle Border.* Bloomington, Ind.: University of Indiana Press, 1954.

Clark, John G. *The Grain Trade of the Old Northwest.* Urbana, Ill.: University of Illinois Press, 1966.

Hidy, Ralph W. *The House of Baring in American Trade and Finance: English Merchant Bankers at Work, 1763–1861.* Cambridge, Mass.: Harvard University Press, 1949.

North, Douglass C. *The Economic Growth of the United States, 1790–1860.* Englewood Cliffs, N.J.: Prentice-Hall, 1961.

Williamson, Jeffrey G. *American Growth and the Balance of Payments, 1820–1913.* Chapel Hill, N.C.: University of North Carolina Press, 1964.

Woodman, Harold D. *King Cotton and His Retainers.* Lexington, Ky.: University of Kentucky Press, 1968.

Articles

North, Douglass C. "Ocean Freight Rates and Economic Development, 1750–1913," *Journal of Economic History,* 18 (December 1958), 537–555.

Rothstein, Morton. "Ante-Bellum Wheat and Cotton Exports," *Agricultural History,* 40 (April 1966), 91–100.

Temin, Peter. "The Causes of Cotton-Price Fluctuations in the 1830's," *Review of Economic Statistics,* 49 (November 1967), pp. 463–470.

⬧ 7

The Institutional Setting
of Industrialization and Growth:
Organization of the Marketplace,
1790-1860

The growth of the economy in the nineteenth century has been discussed in terms of its developing structure—the patterns of resource utilization and of the production of goods and services—and the relative scarcities of capital, labor, and land as shaped by changing technological capacities. Ultimately, however, all explanations of economic growth and industrialization must be couched in terms of social organization, that is, the modes of ordering economic life that led to the rise of modern manufacturing and the development of a more efficient economy. Focusing on a particular industry (such as textiles), or one sector (such as international trade), precludes development of a framework sufficient for describing and explaining a process that involves the entirety of society in its definition and elaboration. The institutional changes considered in this chapter are worthy of special attention because of their centrality in the economy and because they have received intensive investigation on the part of economic historians during recent years. In discussing key institutions it is essential to be sensitive to the interrelationships among such institutions and the impact institutional development had on the relative availabilities of capital, labor, and land, technological change, patterns of production and commerce, and, finally, the extent and timing of economic growth.

TRANSPORTATION

Analysis of every significant aspect of the nineteenth-century economy necessarily involves an assessment of the role of transport. If

America's economy had been more compact, like Great Britain's, with easy access to the seas and short land distances, one could safely minimize the contribution to growth made by roads, rivers, canals, and railroads. But in contrast to the nations of western Europe during the industrial revolution, the United States integrated great chunks of contiguous land into the economy as it took advantage of the abundance of cheap land and realized the gains of regional specialization. The achievement of these efficiencies required the building of large, complicated, and expensive transportation systems.

The timing of sustained economic growth during the first decades of the nineteenth century frequently has been explained in terms of improved railroad transport. Unfortunately for this notion, railroad systems were quite rudimentary before the Civil War. Virtually no mileage existed in 1830; even during the 1840s railroads at most formed small, unconnected systems which frequently transported only passengers. The first boom in railroad construction did not occur until the 1850s. So any reassessment of the role of the railroads must begin with the fact that the American economy attained high levels of growth in the nineteenth century without the services of a highly developed railroad network.

Roads: Looking Westward

During the initial stages of rapid economic growth roads, rivers, and canals served as the prime modes of transportation. Prior to the 1790s, river and ocean travel constituted virtually the only means of long-distance travel; roads tended to service commerce only within restricted regions (for example, the Philadelphia-Lancaster Turnpike, initiated in 1789 as the first turnpike, was designed solely to tap Philadelphia's agricultural hinterland). Another common characteristic of early roads was that they were funded by private capital, even though they operated within strictly framed charters granted by state governments. Despite the intraregional orientation of most roads and the lack of public financing for turnpike construction, enthusiasm for internal improvement during the 1790s created a basic road system linking the eastern seaboard states with the Ohio valley. (See Figure 9.) In New York, the Mohawk Turnpike and the Great Genesee Road provided the linkage. In Maryland and Pennsylvania, Forbes Road and Braddock's Road linked the coast with Pittsburgh. To the south, in Virginia, the Great Valley Road and Richmond Road led to the Cumberland Gap, where the Wilderness Road extended to Louisville and Frankfort, Kentucky. Finally, by 1796, Zane's Trace crossed Ohio. Although these roads were often little more than widened trails, they permitted large herds of cattle

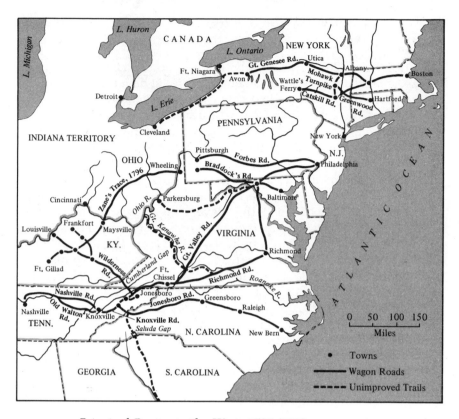

FIGURE 9: *Principal Routes to the West, 1795–1812*

and hogs to pass eastward from the frontier, and by 1800 enabled whiskey from Kentucky and Tennessee to replace rum as the national beverage.

When the War of 1812 demonstrated inadequacies in the nation's road system, the federal government, in cooperation with state governments in the Middle Atlantic and the West, established interregional linkages. Public revenues largely financed the construction, which continued through the 1830s. The greatest contribution was the National Road, a continuation of the old Cumberland Road, which extended to Wheeling, Virginia, by 1818, crossed the Ohio River by 1833, and reached Vandalia, Illinois, by mid-century. For the most part, however, construction of major interregional roads ceased by the 1840s, and there was virtually no improvement in the quality of road transportation until the age of the automobile and the introduction of the hard-surfaced road.

Waterways: Binding the Regions

During the 1820s waterways, both rivers and canals, became more important than roads to ante-bellum regional development. Serious interest in canal building had begun at the conclusion of the War of 1812, but the heavy capital investments needed and the lack of engineering expertise prevented the rapid completion of any major canal system. No canal longer than 28 miles existed when the New York legislature initiated the Erie Canal in 1817. Generously supported by an ambitious state government and facing rather benign terrain (the rise between the Hudson River at Albany and Buffalo amounting to only 650 feet), the lawyers who served as engineers on the project overcame the technical difficulties rather easily and opened the first segment to traffic by 1819. Even the first section of 75 miles proved highly successful, generating immediate profits that facilitated the completion of the canal in 1825. The Erie Canal, the first profitable major canal, became the critical link in the penetration of the Appalachians and the development of the upper Northwest. It provided the farmers of northern Ohio, northern Indiana, northern Illinois, Michigan, and Wisconsin, as well as those of upstate New York, with cheap access to the port of New York. Indeed, growth of traffic continued on the Erie until a peak was reached in 1880. Its quick profitability and demonstration of social benefit led to a canal boom, which by 1840 had resulted in a large network linking major natural waterways. As was the case with roads, most construction received heavy government assistance; between 1815 and 1860 almost three-quarters of all canal investment was made or sponsored by government. The resulting canals linked the upcountry and the tidewater in those states bordering on the Atlantic, joined the Atlantic states with the Ohio River valley and the Great Lakes region, and connected the Ohio-Mississippi network with the Great Lakes. (See Figure 10.)

Natural river waterways were essential to the success of the canals in providing interregional links. Steamboats on the Great Lakes linked the upper northwest and cities like Chicago, Milwaukee, and Detroit and their agricultural hinterlands with the Erie Canal. The steamboat also brought the Mississippi River into transportation networks by permitting upstream traffic, beginning in 1815; by the end of the 1820s steam travel dominated the major rivers as well as the lakes, bringing significant productivity gains to transport on the nation's waterways. These water-route improvements not only enhanced the flow of goods but also advanced the exchange of information provided by the mails as well as intercity passenger

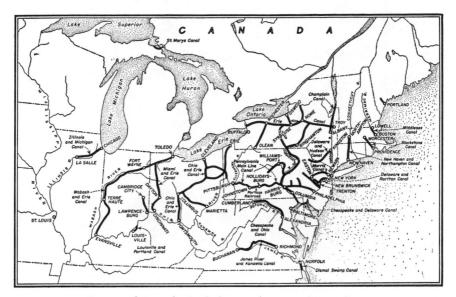

FIGURE 10: *Principal Canals Built by 1860*

traffic. By 1830, rates of travel had increased significantly over their levels in 1800 largely as a consequence of improvements in water transport. (See Figures 11 and 12.) A traveler from New York could go to Boston in a day and a half, to Charleston in five days, to New Orleans in two weeks, and to Detroit in two weeks. In 1800 the same trips would have required twice as much time. Business communication operated far more efficiently, and this, in turn, stimulated enterprise. In particular, the time saved in making and filling orders led to a more efficient use of working capital and a higher rate of profit on capital invested in inventories.

The canal boom subsided by the late 1830s, primarily because the best waterways for long-distance travel had been completed. Also, the Panic of 1837 and widespread defaults on canal-company debts inhibited canal building by weakening European confidence in state bond issues and by reducing state enthusiasm for extending credit to canal-building enterprises. Wisconsin, for example, in its constitution of 1848, prohibited state aid to public improvements. Despite the heavy capital requirements and the shock of 1837, substantial sums continued to be expended on canals into the 1840s. Most of the money was spent on extensions of old canals. (There were no new major canals constructed between 1840 and 1860.)

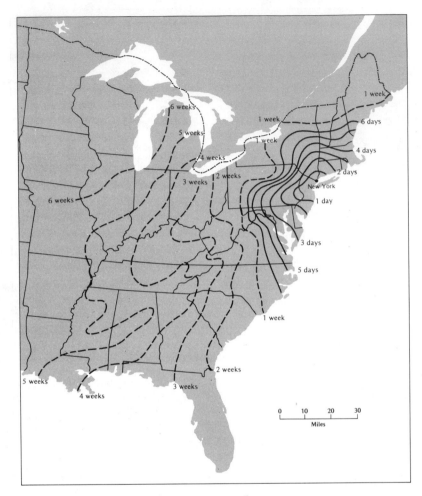

FIGURE 11: *Rates of Travel from New York, 1800*

Railroads: Direct and Indirect Benefits

Although the first railroad (the Baltimore and Ohio Railroad) had been chartered in 1838, the leadership position of canals was not successfully challenged until the 1850s. In 1852, according to one estimate, the tonnage carried on canals in the United States was still twice that borne by the railroads. But during the next five or six years a great diversion of goods to railroads occurred, as railroad mileage increased rapidly, trunk lines developed in New York and Pennsylvania, and railroad rates fell. (See Figure 13 for railroad building during the 1850s.) By 1859, according to the best estimate available, canals carried 1.6 billion ton-miles of traffic. (One ton of goods shipped one mile constitutes one ton-mile of traffic.) The railroads, on the other

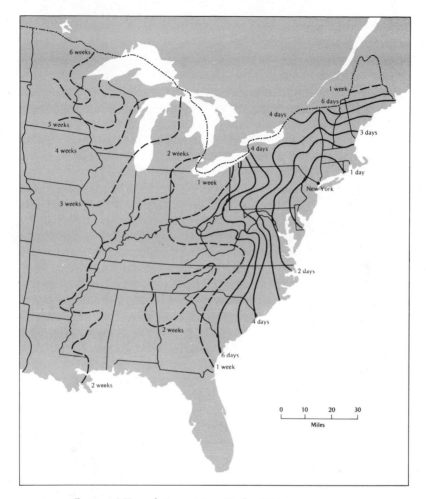

FIGURE 12: *Rates of Travel from New York, 1830*

hand, had increased their traffic to more than 2 billion ton-miles, or about one-quarter more than canals carried. And although the Erie Canal and the Ohio canal system continued to be quite successful in attracting growing amounts of western produce for eastern ship-ment, much of the gain in railroads' traffic amounted to business taken away from canal-river transportation.[1] Yet the clear competi-tive success of the railroads did not necessarily mean that the nine-teenth-century railroad system brought large savings in transportation costs. Even a very small price advantage favoring rail transport could have produced a very large shift in the volume of traffic away from water, as shippers sought to maximize profits. But, in fact, the railroad reduced appreciably the cost of transportation

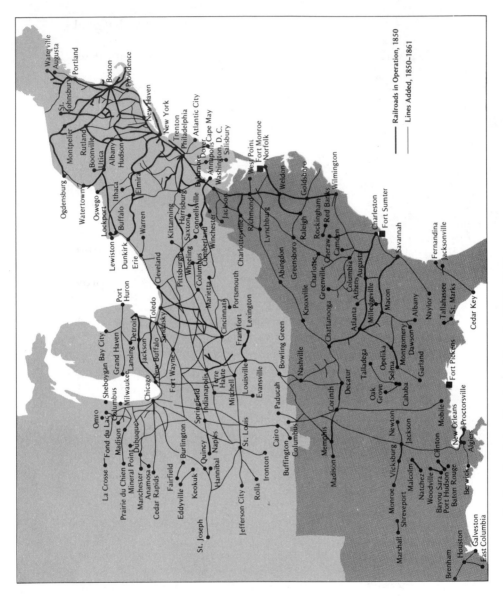

FIGURE 13: *Railroads of the North and South, 1850–1861*

services, accounting for a social saving, according to the best estimate, of between $150 million and $175 million by 1859. In other words, railroads enabled society to provide its transportation services more efficiently and thereby to enjoy a saving of resources that could be turned to purposes other than transport. Although the saving was only a modest portion of national product (about 4 percent), it was nevertheless important. In particular, it provided the basis for later, more impressive savings of resources—amounting to possibly 15 percent of national product by 1890.[2] It can safely be said the economy could not have sustained high rates of growth in the latter part of the century without the direct savings provided by a modern railroad system.

Railroads also contributed to economic growth in indirect ways, which although not so easily measurable, were very probably more significant for the development of the nineteenth-century economy than the direct benefits. Generally speaking, the expansion of railroads encouraged other developments that enhanced economic efficiency. Within this category of indirect benefits, the most important stimulus to the antebellum economy was the encouragement of the western extension of settlement and agriculture through the provision of flexible transportation services. Although railroad construction lagged behind agricultural demand for improved transportation, even behind settlement itself, the relentless building of railroads in settled areas contiguous to relatively unpopulated territory helped to push people to the frontier by creating the assurance of continued rail development. The construction of the late 1840s and early 1850s, in particular, responded to the demands of farmers for access to eastern markets and, in turn, supported the voluminous flow of land seekers ahead of the domain of the iron horse. The cycle was complete when these newly transplanted populations themselves demanded continued railroad extensions. Thus, although the building of railroads was not an example of social overhead capital (capital supporting basic social functions) being deployed before the existence of a demand for the services the capital was to provide, the impact of railroads on development was much the same.

As a result of strong demands for railroad services prior to railroad construction, the absence of severe technological obstacles to laying rails across the Midwest, and the refinement of capital markets and railroad business organization during the 1840s and 1850s, private sources were able to finance the railroad growth of this period. Until the Civil War as much as three-quarters of all railroad investment came from private sources—just the reverse of canal financing.[3] The risks to private entrepreneurs were higher in the latter case, given low population densities in the West and an array of technical problems; consequently, private capital markets were inadequate to provide the large amounts of money necessary.

By promoting new settlement, the rapid elaboration of railroad systems in the late 1840s and early 1850s raised the productivity of farm labor. The ability of farmers to produce more by moving to more fertile land brought them increases in real income and enabled the economy to support a larger urban-industrial population. The railroads reinforced the development of a progressive, market-oriented agriculture during a period of more general and more rapid industrialization. Furthermore, agricultural growth in the West, encouraged by the rapid proliferation of railroads, generated demands for increased commercial services and more-accessible processing facilities. In turn, these demands promoted indigenous urbanization and industrialization which themselves were supported by the externalities created by the railroads.

As might be expected, rail transport had little impact on the growth of manufactures in the Northeast. New England manufacturers found water transportation, in particular the river and canal system connecting manufacturing centers with the coast, more than adequate to meet their particular needs. The New England cotton-textile industry, for example, enjoyed its period of initial growth long before the completion of rail connections; its locational pattern, designed around water-power sites and water transportation, was unaffected by the coming of the railroad. Finally, none of New England's textile mills experienced increased prosperity due to the completion of its railroad system in the 1840s.

Industry in the Middle Atlantic states was likewise independent of railroads. The Erie Canal, the Hudson River, and the network of waterways surrounding the port of New York adequately served the needs of New York industry. In the same way in Pennsylvania, producers of coal and iron found the connections offered by the rivers and the Pennsylvania Canal sufficient throughout the period.

The background and objectives of early railroad entrepreneurs also indicate the disassociation of railroad development and the needs of early industry. For example, the group of Bostonian investors who financed railroads in western New England and the West were not manufacturers or merchant-manufacturers but general traders, many of them old China traders who turned from stagnating enterprises in the late 1830s and early 1840s to seek new areas of investment. For the most part the new rail lines constructed in New England in the 1840s were designed to augment passenger traffic and to tap the western trade, as Boston strove to compete with her rival cities as an outlet for the products of the developing interior, rather than to transport cloth and cotton.[4]

Although railroads did not promote industrial modernization through providing cheaper freight rates, they did contribute to it by creating new railroad-induced demands, chiefly for rail iron both in larger quantities and of higher quality. American iron makers responded to these demands by successfully introducing protection of their industry from foreign competition in 1842 and by modifying advanced British iron-making technology to account for the different availabilities and prices of American resources. To the benefit of American producers, the Tariff Act of 1842, reinforced by a coincidental expansion in British and European rail demands, reduced the amount of British rail exported to the United States. However, the induced demand for domestic production was short-lived: in 1846 the Walker Tariff lowered the import duties on bar iron, and cheap, high-quality, foreign iron again became available when English rail demands fell off in 1848. Consequently iron imports returned to high levels during the late 1840s, the period of important acceleration of American demand. Despite some modernization during the early 1840s, most American manufacturers until the late 1850s were simply unable to reduce costs enough to compete effectively with foreign producers; in fact, from 1849 until 1854 imports met fully 80 percent of all American needs.

(Nevertheless, iron production did increase in the 1840s, largely to meet the growing demands of other industries. Agricultural implements and consumer durables, plows and stoves, for instance, were the most important sources of overall expansion in iron production before 1860.)

Although the reliance of American railroads on imports meant that they absorbed a rather small share of total domestic pig-iron production—no more than about 20 percent—even during the peak years of the late 1850s, railroad demands for certain types of iron were large enough to stimulate American iron producers to meet more stringent specifications. In effect, the needs of the railroads directed the development of the most modern kind of iron production, and by 1860 the rail mills were the largest and most technically advanced iron mills in the country. Then after the Civil War, rail production initiated the Bessemer process.

Railroad demand for machinery yielded further impetus to modernization, even though the demand for train engines, just as for rails, was small compared to the needs of other industries. In much greater production were stationary engines, such as those used in rice and sugar mills, and even steamboat engines, partly as a result of their shorter life span. But the engineering requirements for train engines were more advanced, prompting greater technical competence in the machinery industry. Moreover, to service the relatively complex locomotives, the railroads built a large network of machine shops and thereby stimulated the dissemination of industrial skills and the enlargement of a skilled labor force.

In conclusion, it would seem fair to say that except for the results in increased agricultural productivity, the impact of the railroads on the industrial revolution was not dramatic. But it was, by the 1850s, substantial, and suggested the massive contribution railroads would make to economic growth in the last decades of the century.

COMMERCIAL BANKING AND THE SEARCH FOR ORDERLY FINANCE

Any banking system has two major purposes: (1) to promote economic stability, that is, to moderate the fluctuations of the ordinary business cycle, and (2) to promote the development of the economy through the provision of uniform yet flexible financial arrangements, including a supply of credit that leads or grows apace with the long-term requirements of economic expansion. The development of American banking before the Civil War, including its impact on economic growth, can be considered by analyzing how the system performed these two basic objectives.

The 1790s and the First Bank of the United States

Throughout the colonial period only the rudiments of banking institutions existed. Some private traders and trading companies performed banking functions in the normal course of conducting business, but the credit that was the basis of their trade was sharply limited at home, since the virtually exclusive source of capital was the English metropolis. After the Revolution the situation improved. By 1790 there were four commercial banks chartered by special acts of legislature in Pennsylvania, Massachusetts, New York, and Rhode Island, all of which sought to encourage the accumulation of private capital and managerial talent by lending public sanction and protection to banking enterprise. These banks provided short-term commercial loans, particularly in support of trade, purchased government securities, held and exchanged specie, accepted deposits which were withdrawable on demand, and issued paper notes based on capital and demand deposits. Their capital-mobilizing activities reinforced the expansion of trade, which generated heavy demands for working capital, and the urban growth of the 1790s so successfully that by 1798 twenty-two more such institutions had been founded, all but two in the Northeast (twelve were located in New England, five of them in Massachusetts).

Another commercial bank that appeared during the flourishing 1790s was the First Bank of the United States, which Congress had chartered in 1791 in response to the request of Secretary of the Treasury Alexander Hamilton for a bank to support the various activities of the federal government. In function the bank was no different from the state-chartered banks. It made loans to both the government and commercial borrowers, issued paper currency (one redeemable in specie and acceptable in payment of federal taxes), kept and moved government deposits among convenient seaport depositories, and, after 1800, collected customs as well. The government participated as a 20-percent stockholder in the bank, thus sharing in the returns from the bank's highly profitable operation. Also, the bank helped to uphold the price of federal government securities by requiring that 75 percent of the stock subscribed by private parties be purchased with United States securities. Insofar as it made credit more available and expanded the money supply through its currency issues, the bank reinforced and sustained the expansion of the 1790s, a growth that continued into the first decade of the 1800s. But it neither unified the nation's financial activities nor promoted stability within capital markets. For example, the custom of using this bank as a deposit center for outlying banks did not develop; nor was the bank under any obligation to come to the aid of other banks in times of distress. However, it did receive state bank notes, redeemable in specie, which the Treasury accepted in payment of taxes, and by presenting these notes to state banks for payment in specie, it could influence the ability of the state commercial banks to dispense credit. But it never used this power in a discretionary fashion, primarily because of the conservative administration of the bank. As a result, during its early history the bank never occupied a position of dominance among the nation's commercial banks.

Ignoring the economic benefits of the bank, politicians failed to recharter it in 1811. The Secretary of the Treasury Albert Gallatin and most state bankers approved of it, but two political facts caused the bank's demise. For one thing, the leadership of the bank was too closely affiliated with prominent unpopular Federalists. For another, popular distrust of banks as institutions beyond the pale of democracy, whose activities—particularly their creation of money—defied common-sense understanding, was too widespread for most Republican politicians to ignore.[5] Consequently the bill to recharter failed by a one-vote margin in both House and Senate.

State Banking and the Second Bank of the United States

Meanwhile state banks thrived. Encouraged by the success of the Bank of the United States and the other commercial banks, as well as the growing demands of trade and production, they numbered some eighty-nine in 1811, their note issues by that time having been so enlarged as to represent most of the nation's currency. The failure to recharter the First Bank of the United States further encouraged the growth of state banking and state note issues, with added acceleration provided during and after the War of 1812, when the Treasury permitted the suspension of specie payments to ease financing of federal wartime expenses. Concerned about impairing the popularity of the war, James Madison eschewed higher taxes. In response, state banks expanded to finance the war, but their capacity for mobilizing resources was limited. Their limitations, coupled with the inflationary impact of specie suspensions, revitalized the concept of a national bank and led to the chartering of the Second Bank of the United States in 1816.

The charter of the Second Bank of the United States was essentially the same as that of its predecessor; the bank was granted a twenty-year term; required to draw 80 percent of its capital from private sources; permitted to make loans and issue notes redeemable in specie and receivable for all obligations to the United States; and made responsible for handling government deposits. Of course, the federal government could have stabilized the nation's currency by insisting on specie payments and by financing the war through taxes, but the bank served to create a demand for government securities and thus made the war, and its aftermath, politically more acceptable. But no one had a more ambitious design in mind for the bank; between 1816 and 1823 it did little as a central bank apart from servicing the financial requirements of the federal government.

In the financial circumstances leading to the Panic of 1819 the bank made little or no contribution to maintaining economic stability; in fact, it may have aggravated the severity of the downturn. In the interests of promoting economic activity and of establishing a uniform currency, the bank allowed the notes issued by any one of its branches to be redeemed at any of the other branches. In conjunction with the fact that the West and South suffered a persistently unfavorable balance of trade, this right of redemption produced a steady flow of notes of western and southern branch banks to the East. Hence, to a large extent, the issues of the southern and western branches failed to return home for redemption, and there was as a consequence no effective check on the activities of these banks. Managers of the eastern branches asked for a curtailment of activity, but the southern and western managers failed to oblige. In the summer of 1818, with the necessity of paying off the Louisiana Purchase debt out of the specie reserves of the bank looming large, the threat to the bank's eastern reserves became clear, and the directors curtailed operations and decreed that all notes be redeemed at the bank of issue. At the same time, they required state banks to redeem large volumes of notes in specie. The result was a banking panic.[6]

The Second Bank, nonetheless, should be spared full blame for the crisis; the Treasury shared complicity in that throughout 1817 and early 1818 it had persuaded the bank not to press the state banks for effective return to specie payments. It is likely that the banking crisis, although postponed, was worse as a result. Also, the full panic was not so much a product of the banking collapse as the result of international deflation confronting internal inflation. As an unfavorable balance continued prior to 1819, specie was at a premium in terms of both United States bank notes and state bank issues; the bank could not continue to expand note issues and simultaneously pay out specie at increasing rates. In this instance the second bank was less fortunate than the first, which operated almost exclusively during periods of buoyant prices, when the integrity of the nation's credit structure went unchallenged.

The 1820s and the Leadership of Nicholas Biddle

The panic indirectly effected a change in the bank, however. By seriously questioning the capacity of the leadership of the bank, the panic paved the way for the appointment of Nicholas Biddle to its presidency in 1823. His concept of the proper role for the bank in stabilizing the economy was much more aggressive and positive than that of his predecessor, Langdon Cheves; he became the first to exploit the potential power, which the bank held by virtue of its legal and economic position, to regulate the banking system. At the same time more stringent regulation meant that, almost necessarily, the bank had to abandon much of the expansionary policy it had pursued prior to the summer of 1818.

Under Biddle the bank exerted considerable control over the activities of state-chartered banks. In addition to its traditional service functions, it took more-decisive action in providing central leadership in the interests of stability and regularity for the banking community. Biddle's bank did this, in part, through its power to decide whether any state institution was meeting the requirement that it redeem its notes in specie, a security required before it would accept state bank notes. More important, the bank took advantage of its receipts of state bank notes in payment of obligations. By consistently maintaining a creditor position in relation to the state banks, it returned notes to banks of issue on a regular basis. As a consequence of the leadership of a national bank, the nation moved toward the attainment of a uniform currency. In particular, the bank succeeded in enhancing the value that bank tellers attached to state bank notes circulating at a distance from issuing banks. Thus transactions of all sorts could take place within an atmosphere of greater monetary stability.

However, successful regulation of state bank issues was achieved at the cost of relinquishing effective discretionary control over the size of the money supply and at the cost of exercising a deflationary influence on the economy. To prevent state banks from retaliating by presenting United States notes at its windows, the bank had to exercise an unusual degree of restraint in increasing its own notes and deposits. The policy was even more deflationary because state banks frequently used the notes of the Second Bank of the United States rather than specie as reserves for new issues of their own. If the bank had allowed balances of state notes to accumulate, and thereby permitted an expansion of credit, it would have been failing to be an effective policeman. By keeping a tight rein on state banking, the bank retarded the growth of the money supply, actually leaving the determination of its size to external forces. Since external factors provided for a strong growth of money during the late 1820s, supporting the revival of economic activity after the Panic of 1819, the deflationary pressure of the bank posed no threat to expansion. Indeed, in a period of growing interregional connections the fostering of a uniform currency and a dependable financial environment for investors was the greatest contribution that a national bank could make to sustained growth. Furthermore, despite actions restricting the money supply, the Second Bank was the single largest creditor in the West and South, thereby promoting the expansion of those regions.

The policy of strictly regulating the issues of state banks, however, handicapped the bank in fulfilling another central bank function— that of acting as a lender of last resort (an institution for bailing out banks with emergency loans in periods of crisis). There is little doubt that Biddle was committed to the relief of state banks whenever the public lost confidence in their ability to redeem their notes in specie and lent some assistance to imperiled banks during a threatened crisis in 1825. But Biddle tied his hands by refusing to place the bank in the position of becoming a net debtor that would have jeopardized its service. In the context of the 1820s, nonetheless, it was most important that a central bank build a dependable, national financial structure rather than soften the impact of mild, preindustrial business cycles. Furthermore, the notion that a public bank could act as a lender of last resort or seek to moderate the business cycle was most uncommon during this period, even within the banking community; and at the same time an almost universal faith prevailed in the ability of international metallic standards to govern the fluctuations of the business cycle. Although Biddle's interest in managed countercyclical activity was modest by twentieth-century standards, it was ambitious by the standards of his day.

Destruction of Biddle's Bank

The charter of the Second Bank was allowed to lapse in 1836. As with the demise of the First Bank, the economic motivation behind this policy was obscure—possibly nonexistent. Even state bankers, who might have been expected to resent the restraint on profitable lending operations imposed by the bank and to dislike the direct competition posed by the most powerful commercial bank in the nation, supported the rechartering of the bank prior to its short-run but fatal political problems in the early 1830s. Their esteem of order, regularity, and stability apparently outweighed the desire for short-term profits. More specifically, western bankers appreciated the role of the bank in facilitating interregional product exchanges and the contribution of local branches of the bank in meeting short-term needs. The only source of systematic hostility or apathy was in the Northeast where state banking was sufficiently mature enough to provide financial order. Ironically, opposition to the bank tended to originate in the most conservative banking circles, particularly those of Boston and New York, whereas southern and western bankers usually regarded Biddle's bank with warmth.[7] In the end centralized banking was brought down by the widespread mass prejudice against banking and large corporations, and mass suspicions of mysterious paper money, skillfully fanned by President Andrew Jackson and his advisors and augmented by the willingness of Democratic supporters to place party loyalty to Jackson before economic conviction.

At the same time both facilitating the movement to destroy the bank and cushioning the impact of that demise was the lack of belief of the business community in the necessity of banking order at the *national* level. Business interest in interregional investment was minimal. Most American investors, including commercial bankers, preferred to keep their capital within their locality, state, or region. (And western areas frequently placed stringent regulations, often complete prohibition, on branch banking or, as in territorial Wisconsin, prohibition on the institution of commercial banking itself.) Demand for financial institutions to encourage interregional movement of domestic capital assumed large importance only in the 1850s, when the New York money market developed the ability to meet the short- and intermediate-term credit needs of western areas rapidly.

The termination of the bank was also cushioned by the moderate need, particularly in the West, for the long-term capital that commercial banks might provide. The bulk of long-term capital imported to the West in the 1820s and 1830s, largely for internal improvements, came from European sources. Personal relationships also served to mobilize long-term capital. The crucial western industries of flour milling, meat packing, oil refining, and agricultural-machinery production relied more on pools of retained earnings than on banking connections. Cyrus McCormick, for example, frequently brought in new monied partners to finance expansion, rather than resort directly to the money market. And the textile industry was financed mainly from internal capital sources. In agriculture demands for external, long-term capital through the 1840s were small. The greatest need was to finance land-clearing costs, a need usually met through savings retained from current income. Only in the 1850s, when farmers sought larger investments in agricultural machinery, such as reapers and threshers, did the demand for external capital become important and the utility of a national financial market become clearer.

Regional Initiatives

The failure of central banking was further muted by the rise of movements within states and within regions to make banking arrangements more regular. After all, the activities in which the Second Bank had engaged with the goal of regularity in mind could have been performed, in principle, by any large, powerful commercial bank. Although the bank admittedly occupied a strategic position by receiving all payments of government obligations, it was necessary only for a large bank to occupy a creditor position with respect to smaller, outlying banks. In New England, for instance, the private Suffolk Bank of Boston fulfilled the same function as the Second Bank of the United States by means of the *Suffolk system*. Established in 1824, this system arranged that the Suffolk bank act as agent for the six Boston banks, handling any notes they might receive issued outside of the city. In its capacity as a clearing house, the Suffolk bank received all the notes paid those banks and, in turn, could redeem or threaten to redeem these notes at the issuing "country" banks. It did this unless outlying banks maintained a permanent balance at the Suffolk to be used to cover redemptions. Because of the persistently unfavorable balance-of-trade position of Boston's hinterlands, the flow of "country" notes into Boston was unremitting. Despite this movement, the Suffolk system sharply reduced the discount placed on these notes. The public gained from the circulation of bank notes at par, or close to par, even at points distant from New England, and most New England banks profited from an improved credit reputation. In addition, the Suffolk bank provided the public with a flexible money supply. With fewer requests for redemption in specie as a result of enhanced public confidence in bank notes, specie could remain in banks as reserves, permitting expansion of notes and deposits. Even between 1834 and 1836 when western and southern banks followed expansive policies and reduced their holdings of specie relative to their note issues and deposits, the Suffolk system allowed New England banks to keep lower reserves than state banks elsewhere in the nation.[8] The New England experience bore witness that good banking practice, once public trust had been won, was entirely consistent with the rapid expansion of the money supply, the ready availability of credit, and low interest rates to borrowers.

The Suffolk system survived almost until the National Banking Acts of the Civil War years abolished state bank notes and eliminated the need for the specific kinds of regulatory functions provided by the Suffolk bank and the Second Bank of the United States. Other strong banks seeking to regulate credit markets followed the Suffolk bank. In New York, beginning in 1825, the largest New York City banks required country banks to maintain deposits with them before they would redeem their notes. These country banks obliged and, as a result, by 1826, circulated their notes in New York at discounts of only 1 to 3 percent. State regulation followed in 1829 with the passage of the Safety Fund Act, which lent greater stability and uniformity to the banking system of the region. Going beyond providing for a common fund to redeem the notes and discounts of member banks that had failed to subject banks to regular examination, the act required all member banks to pay in their capital stock before beginning operation, to restrict the issue of bank notes to no more than twice paid-up capital, and to hold loans and discounts to no more than two and one-half times paid-up capital. The ambit of the New York system widened; by the time of the expiration of the Second Bank of the United States, ninety of ninety-eight banks in the state and eighteenth of twenty-three New York City banks were included. As a result, New York bank notes improved markedly. And because New York was increasingly the center of money-market activities, the quality of banking enterprise rose in the entire Middle Atlantic region between 1819 and 1837.

In 1838, shortly after the demise of the Second Bank of the United States, New York legislated to make state bank notes an even more reliable credit instrument. First, the legislature set standards for bank-note security. Second, it required banks to hold a 12.5-percent specie reserve against circulation, a provision that many states, and the federal government in 1862, copied. In 1840 another act set a maximum discount for notes of country banks and required every country bank to name an agent in New York, Albany, or Troy with the responsibility of redeeming notes. In 1857 redemption of country notes was made even more regular by the requirement that any bank holding at least $10,000 in notes of another bank had to send those notes home for redemption.

Although the New York banking reforms worked to encourage the expansion of country banking by making adequate provision for the redemption of state notes, the money supply remained instable: note issues were closely tied to specie or securities whose volume varied with the business cycle, and that cycle was worsening by the 1850s. A few steps were taken, however, to attain greater stability, the most important being the founding of the New York Clearing House in 1854, which was designed initially as a way of easily settling interbank debts to eliminate the frequent accumulation of large adverse balances. Because the large New York City banks belonged to it, the clearing house had the potential to perform a true regulatory function, even though it was unprepared for the 1854 crisis. By 1857 it had developed emergency techniques of supporting credit, and its reaction to the panic of that year marked the beginning of a significant effort to manage the business cycle. By voluntarily agreeing to increase their loans simultaneously and proportionally, the member banks created some $6.5 million of additional credit. Also, the clearing house issued certificates against notes of country banks rather than insisting upon collection of specie. These clearing-house certificates, acceptable in the settlement of clearing-house balances, permitted city banks to continue to loan to country banks and keep them solvent during the crisis (these certificates were the forerunners of the clearing-house loan certificates initiated in 1860, which were used in every major panic through 1913). They represented specie that had been pooled by member banks and could be borrowed with a pledge of securities by banks suffering heavy specie demands. Further, after the 1857 panic, the clearing-house committee required that member banks keep a 20-percent reserve of specie against both deposits and circulation. These measures had a regularizing and stabilizing effect on all banking in the United States inasmuch as the New York money market came to occupy a central position in the national economy.

Before the Civil War, banking institutions reflected the persistent search of an industrializing nation for a system to replace personal relationships as the guiding force governing the flow of investment. This search received only a temporary setback as a result of the extinction of the Second Bank of the United States. The economy was not yet truly national in character; local and regional banking organization was in tune with the needs of investors. Thus the First and Second Banks of the United States were premature in conception. On the other hand, New England and the Middle Atlantic states, where demands for capital investment were most acute and where opportunities for new investment were most abundant, developed orderly banking structures long before the firm establishment of a national banking system during the Civil War. Furthermore, this banking system, held together by ad hoc regional and local arrangements, although it did not necessarily promote economic stability, encouraged the vigorous expansion of the late 1840s and early 1850s.

THE IMPACT OF URBANIZATION

Accompanying the nation's industrialization and rapid economic growth was an increasing urbanization of the population. The precise reciprocal influence of this urbanization on economic growth and industrialization is unknown, but certainly it did forcefully promote economic growth through the more efficient use of labor and capital it afforded. With access to concentrations of people and enterprises, investors and laborers could reduce costs of transactions that stemmed from inadequate information and high risk: they had fuller knowledge of real alternatives in the marketplace, and consequently could use their opportunities more successfully, with less risk to their resources of labor and capital.

Until the 1840s and 1850s, however, American cities grew more in response to the logic of the nation's transport system than as a result of the advantages offered by preexisting concentrations of population. Although the rate at which the nation was urbanizing increased from the 1820s on, and was accompanied by a rising rate of industrialization (with the exception of the 1830s), both these shifts, the urban and the industrial, did not reach their peak until the mid-1840s. It was then that the autonomous forces of urbanization dominated urban growth and became firmly meshed with the process of industrialization.

The great cities of the Atlantic seaboard first developed as focal points of commercial activity and remained such until the 1840s. They grew to significance because they were in the best position to serve as points of exchange between an agricultural hinterland and overseas trade areas. (Cities in the interior river valleys of the Mississippi and Ohio later underwent a similar pattern of development, when they functioned primarily as agricultural-service communities.) As populations grew within commercial cities, and the income of those populations grew as well, cities offered new attractions, ones generated by their very growth. Beginning in a significant way during the 1840s and 1850s, old commercial cities developed as markets and industrial centers. In an era of expensive land transport, concentrated populations lowered transportation costs appreciably by presenting compact marketplaces. They also fostered modern manufacturing by providing a large, mobile labor force, and, of course, urban markets encouraged large-scale manufacturing enterprises that could combine labor and capital in more productive ways. (Another important factor was that manufacturers could employ laborers who had received training earlier from other manufacturers in the same industry or in industries that demanded similar skills.) The laborer benefited as well from the enlargement of industrial opportunities within the city by enjoying a wider range of choices and a greater ability to improve his position by moving to an employer paying higher wages. The mobility of laborers among firms became increasingly easy as the development of large-scale factories and accompanying technological convergence made industrial skills more homogeneous.

The urban environment in the largest cities, especially the old coastal commercial cities, reduced the costs of mobilizing capital for new enterprises and effectively widened the opportunities available for new investment. At a time when financial markets and financial intermediaries (banks, insurance companies, etc.) were rudimentary, and when capital-investment decisions were made largely by individuals relying on personal, firsthand experience, an environment that put investor and enterprise in close physical proximity was essential for rational choice among competing capital users. Only as communications improved, financial markets became more sophisticated, and the methods for evaluating investment opportunities became more standardized within a more stable economic environment did cities loosen their hold on significantly large units of venture capital. The relaxation first appeared during the 1840s and 1850s in a very few locations, chiefly New York and Boston. It was investors from these cities, especially those interested in railroad enterprise, who first developed and refined the techniques for managing remote empires.

The Great Atlantic Seaports, 1790–1840

In the first half of the eighteenth century the commercial city, drawing on its favored position within an intercontinental nexus of communications, dominated the overall pattern of urbanization. (See

Figure 14.) The large agricultural sector and the consequently large demand for commercial services, both for exporting surpluses and for importing manufactured goods, account for the persistence of this colonial pattern of urbanization. Commercial development shaped the growth not only of smaller cities and towns but also of the largest cities, with New York, Philadelphia, Baltimore, and Boston, in particular, continuing as the preeminent urban centers during the early decades of the nineteenth century because of their fortunate positions within transportation networks. Until the 1820s these four largest seaports contained more than half of all urban people, and their share declined sharply only in the 1830s. (See Table 14.) Even then, relative to all cities, they grew more rapidly than the other, smaller coastal ports because of the advantages larger size provided

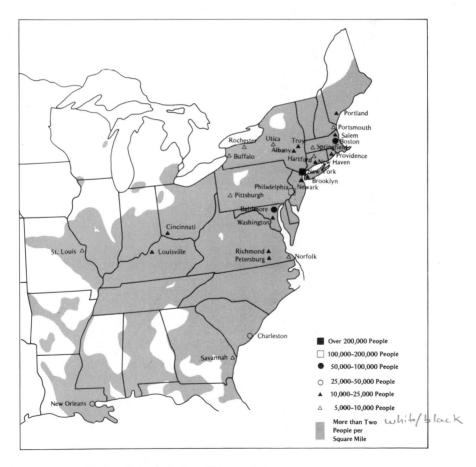

FIGURE 14: *Major United States Cities, 1830*

TABLE 14   SHARES OF URBAN POPULATION BY CITY GROUPS

	1790	1800	1810	1820	1830	1840
Four great Eastern seaports	54.1%	53.8%	52.0%	51.4%	48.1%	43.0%
Small Eastern seaports	36.0	32.0	26.8	22.3	17.9	15.9
Eastern interior cities	9.9	14.2	15:7	18.5	22.3	23.0
Western cities	—	—	5.5	7.7	11.6	18.0

Source: George Rogers Taylor, "American Urban Growth Preceding the Railway Age," *Journal of Economic History*, 26 (September 1966), pp. 322–323.

for the servicing of trade. They continued to control transatlantic trade and to function as the key centers in a domestic maritime trade that flourished as a result of the high cost of land transport along the seaboard.

Economic activity within these largest cities was predominantly mercantile in character. One measure, capital investment in the retailing and commission houses of the four largest cities, was five times as large as that in manufacturing as late as 1840. Even in Philadelphia, the most industrialized of these cities, the ratio of mercantile investment was more than three times that in manufacturing.[9] Their commercial function was reflected by their fairly sluggish growth, or rather, by their failure to grow dramatically in the fashion of large urban places later in the nineteenth century: their population growth was a function of growth of trade and the agricultural sector rather than of manufacturing enterprise, and they rarely grew faster than the national population. In fact, between 1790 and 1840 Boston, Baltimore, and Philadelphia often grew more slowly than the nation, which was increasing in population by approximately one-third per decade. If we examine the growth of the important central cities we see that in the case of Boston the rate of growth reached 40 percent only in the 1820s; in the case of Baltimore, after dramatic increases between 1790 and 1810, the rate of growth declined consistently to a point below the national rate; in the case of Philadelphia, after the decade of the 1790s, growth was extremely slow in contrast to the national rate. (See Table 15.) With the exception of the 1810–1820 decade, New York, alone among the larger cities, consistently grew faster than the nation as a whole, and its performance was, indeed, impressive.

The primary importance of the seacoast ports as trading centers explains the dramatic growth of New York, the disappointing performance of Boston, and the very slow growth of both Philadelphia and Baltimore. By measures of exports per capita, imports per capita, and

TABLE 15 POPULATION OF THE LARGEST CENTRAL CITIES, 1790–
1840: DECENNIAL RATES OF INCREASE

	1790–1800	1800–1810	1810–1820	1820–1830	1830–1840
Boston	36.1%	35.5%	28.1%	41.8%	38.5%
Baltimore	96.4	75.6	34.8	28.5	26.9
Philadelphia	44.5	30.3	18.8	26.1	16.4
New York	82.7	59.2	28.3	63.8	54.4

Source: Everett S. Lee and Michael Lalli, "Population," in David T. Gilchrist (ed.), *The Growth of the Seaport Cities, 1790–1825* (Charlottesville, Va.: University Press of Virginia, 1967), p. 29.

shares of registered shipping, the relative position of Boston in the period was essentially constant, while New York increased competitively at the expense of both Baltimore and Philadelphia.

The key to the continued growth of New York was the completion of the Erie Canal. From the late 1820s the agricultural hinterland of the city grew dramatically; people poured into the areas bordering the Great Lakes in the 1830s, and the advantages of having commercial linkages between the West, Northeast, and Europe grew even more important. New settlers in Ohio, Indiana, Illinois, and Michigan looked to New York as a market for the products of their farms and as a source of manufactured goods.

But the locational advantages of New York predated the Erie Canal. For one thing, its agricultural hinterland was growing rapidly well before 1825. While the population of Pennsylvania grew at about the national rate between 1790 and 1810 and that of New England increased at a rate of only one-third that of the nation as a whole, the population of New York State increased by almost three-quarters during the decade 1790–1800 and by almost two-thirds during the following decade. Besides access to a growing hinterland, New York City benefited from a natural advantage, the high quality of its harbor, which afforded ships unobstructed and protected access to Manhattan Island. The ports Baltimore and Philadelphia, on the other hand, suffered by being a long distance from the ocean and were further hampered by shoals, which made passage impossible for many ships except at high tide, and during winter by ice, which clogged the Delaware River. Ships entering Boston harbor had to endure heavy winter fogs. In addition, the Hudson River provided a broad channel for ocean vessels to sail 150 miles into the interior, an advantage offered by no other Atlantic port.

New Yorkers made important institutional innovations that gave them even greater leverage over the distribution of trade than that provided by a burgeoning agricultural hinterland and a superb port.

THE HUB OF NEW YORK CITY. The East River docks at the intersection of South Street and Maiden Lane in 1828.

For one thing, they accepted the auction sale of merchandise favored by British manufacturers, whereas in a self-preserving effort Philadelphia and Boston importers legally restricted auctions, since they eliminated the need for American importers. However, New York merchants quite correctly realized that the efficient auction system would in time make lesser ports, including Philadelphia and Boston, reliant on New York and New York middlemen for British manufactures. (Also, clever Erie Canal promoters saw a flourishing auction system as a means of generating revenues for canal building; in 1817 they helped engineer a state auction law that both encouraged auctions and earmarked most of the auction tax revenue for the canal.) New Yorkers secured another advantage by developing a regularly scheduled shipping service between New York, Liverpool, and other European ports. Four Quaker merchants introduced the "packet service" (the carrying of persons, cargo, and mail on a regular schedule) of the Black Ball Line in 1817, and it became a rapid and substantial success; both exporters and importers profited from dependable transoceanic service. The willingness of the New York merchants to innovate, coupled with their growing competitive power, gave them a lead in developing trading connections with newly independent Latin American nations and in achieving control over a growing portion of the buoyant cotton trade. Since their agents in southern ports offered cheaper service in financing, insuring, and shipping cotton exports, New York merchants gained a dominant share of the cotton passing through northern ports.

Finally, sheer size and concentration of both population and trade-related activity provided economies of scale that equipped New York with additional advantages as a commercial center. All told, the various assets enjoyed by New York as a trade center brought its mercantile community control of almost two-thirds of the nation's foreign imports and almost 50 percent of total foreign trade by 1840.

Meanwhile, sluggish development of an agricultural hinterland slowed the growth of Boston, and prompted considerable emigration from New England, much of which swelled the population of New York State. Boston suffered also from the contraction of West Indian trade after the War of 1812 and from the loss of the lumber and fish trade to the British maritime colonies to the north. Still, the city held its own. Well-established connections in trade with Europe and European colonies as well as supremacy in the China trade preserved the relative position of Boston among the great cities. But Bostonians were unable to compete with New Yorkers in the cotton trade, despite the heavy use of cotton in New England's mills.

Baltimore prospered before Jefferson's embargo, but thereafter its growth was handicapped by difficulties similar to but more serious than those of Boston. The basic factor was that its hinterland did not grow rapidly enough to maintain the relative position of the city among Atlantic ports. A sharp decline in the demand for Chesapeake tobacco and wheat, caused by the decline of the West Indian trade, constrained the growth of agriculture in the area tapped by Baltimore merchants. At one time, as the major East Coast port closest to the West Indies and as one capable of tapping interior wheat lands, Baltimore benefited the most from the West Indian trade. And of all the Atlantic ports it suffered the most from the deterioration of that trade during and after the war. Also, it found itself cut off from the growing interior, since it was impossible to build a canal linking Baltimore to the West. The city did have the Cumberland Road, which was completed through to Wheeling in 1818, but travel on the road was not as easy or as inexpensive as on waterways elsewhere, and Baltimore merchants did not begin construction on the Baltimore and Ohio Railroad, conceived as an alternative to land transport, until 1827. Finally, Baltimore was unable to compete with New York as a result of the physical liabilities of its port.

In addition to having the same physical drawbacks as a port as did Baltimore, Philadelphia likewise suffered from the slack international market for wheat, a staple that had supported strong performance of the city at the end of the colonial period. Besides that, Philadelphia lacked the international connections possessed by New York and Boston that might have made it a world entrepôt; and as if that were not enough, of all the Atlantic cities, Philadelphia most directly faced New York in competition for the trade of the interior.

Commerce was the central element in the growth of the largest American cities through the decade of the 1830s. Their dependence upon the expansion of the agricultural sector explains their relatively slow growth, that is, their failure to grow significantly faster than the nation as a whole. Furthermore, their various complements of advantages and disadvantages external to the marketplace, in particular their physical setting within the nation's transportation system and their position with regard to the location of agricultural enterprise, explain their growth relative to each other. During the period 1790–1840 the Atlantic seacoast cities thrived, stagnated, or underwent declines according to the advantages they possessed for the development of commerce.

The Commercial City in the West, 1790–1860

As the agricultural frontier moved westward, there was a general redistribution of population—urban as well as rural. The growth of interior cities in the coastal states and, most dramatically after 1810, the growth of interior western cities accounted for the declining share of urban population within the four giant seaboard ports. These western cities contained almost 20 percent of the nation's urban dwellers by 1840. (See Table 14, p. 216.) Just as was the case on the seaboard, a handful of cities dominated overall urban growth in the West. In 1830 New Orleans, Pittsburgh, Cincinnati, and Louisville accounted for almost three-quarters of urbanized population in the West, nearly 20 percent even in 1840. The commercial city remained the predominant urban form in the West not only before 1840, as in the East, but throughout the entire ante-bellum period. For a longer period western manufacturing was directed at local markets, and western cities mainly supported the exchange of exports and imports that sustained the expansion of agriculture. As in the coastal states, the relative size and importance of western cities altered as the farm population shifted.

The largest and most important mercantile town in the West was, without question, New Orleans. Situated at the mouth of the Mississippi, the only major western water exit to the ocean until the 1820s, the city was in an ideal position to manage the trade of both the explosive cotton frontier of the Southwest and, to a lesser degree, the expanding settlement of the Ohio River valley. Although its relative growth weakened as northern connections between the Ohio valley and the seaboard improved, New Orleans did grow rapidly. By 1840 the city exceeded Boston and Philadelphia in size and trailed Baltimore closely, making it the third largest city in the nation. But New Orleans remained immature; it never branched into the diversified kind of trading activity or trade services that characterized, and consistently earned higher incomes for, the eastern seaboard ports. Instead New Orleans merchants specialized in cotton. More than one-quarter of the nation's exports were shipped from New Orleans during the cotton boom of the 1830s, but only 20 percent, roughly, of total imports entered there, consistently less than at New York or Boston or Philadelphia. The concentration on cotton exports meant that New Orleans trailed behind most of the largest seaboard cities in income and incremental population growth, despite the fact that its volume of exports rivaled even that of New York. Later, in the 1840s and 1850s, it would mean that New Orleans merchants were less likely to innovate in the building of import-competing industries.

One reason for the minimal growth of indigenous commercial services was that New Yorkers, Bostonians, and, most important, Europeans, especially Liverpool merchants, were more efficient in providing those services necessary to bring cotton to market, including production capital, than were New Orleans traders. Prior to the introduction of the steamboat in 1815, ascent of the Mississippi was extremely difficult, a condition that eliminated New Orleans as a center for imports to the Mississippi and Ohio River valleys. Then with the creation of direct and efficient connections between the interior and the eastern seaboard during the 1820s and 1830s New Orleans again found itself at a competitive disadvantage.

The remaining western cities played only minor roles within the national communications network, and their development and growth reflected their inferior situation. Until the 1840s the primary interior cities—most notably, Pittsburgh, Cincinnati, Lexington, Louisville, and St. Louis—were service centers for the upper Mississippi and Ohio valleys. Although neither was officially urban until the 1810 Census, Lexington and Pittsburgh were the foremost interior cities as long as land transport reigned over the East-West connections. Lexington, ideally located at the juncture of an Ohio River connection and the Wilderness Road (the prime link between the West and the upper South), became the trade center where the agricultural goods of Kentucky and Tennessee—hemp, grain, and tobacco—were exchanged for eastern manufactured goods. Similarly, Pittsburgh functioned as a center of exchange for the newly settled regions upstream and as a focal point of westward migration, since the town was the first place where overland immigrants reached downstream water transport.

After 1815 the steamboat transformed western water transport by making upstream travel practicable. The result was a sharp alteration in the pattern of urban growth. In particular, landlocked Lexington stagnated, despite local efforts to promote internal improvements. After 1810 its decennial rates of growth were substantially lower than those of competing cities and considerably below the rate of population growth in the nation as a whole. (See Table 16.) The commercial position of Pittsburgh weakened when the National Road, completed to Wheeling in 1818, provided an alternate connection with the East and when the Erie Canal and the developing North-South canal system in Ohio further diverted East-West trade. Yet during the 1820s and 1830s the growth rate of Pittsburgh surged to about twice that of the nation as a whole. Improving road connections with Philadelphia, promoting the canal-river connection with Philadelphia, and developing the water passage through the city enabled Pittsburgh to enhance its role as a focal point of East-West exchanges. By 1820, however, its downstream neighbor Cincinnati had assumed leadership among the interior western cities by almost quadrupling in size between 1810 and 1820, then more than doubling during the 1820s. Before the 1830s and the completion of the Erie Canal, the hinterland of Cincinnati contained the most rapidly growing portions of the West—the area west of the Muskingum in Ohio, most of Indiana, and large sections of Kentucky, Illinois, and Missouri. The role of Cincinnati as import distributor was especially important to its continuing prosperity and growth.

The location of Louisville on the falls of the Ohio, a stretch impassible to steamboats, made the city a necessary transshipment point and was the central fact in explaining a growth rate matching that of Cincinnati during the 1820s. (Nevertheless, Louisville was still a small town, half the size of Cincinnati in 1830 and smaller than

TABLE 16 POPULATION OF THE LARGEST INTERIOR CITIES, 1810–1840: DECENNIAL RATES OF INCREASE

	1810– 1820	1820– 1830	1830– 1840
Pittsburgh	52.0%	73.4%	68.0%
Lexington	22.0	14.2	16.1
Cincinnati	279.6	157.5	86.6
Louisville	—	157.8	105.1
St. Louis	—	—	230.9
New Orleans	57.6	69.6	121.8

Source: Taylor, *op. cit.*, pp. 311–315.

Pittsburgh.) In time, however, mercantile activity became self-generating, so that Louisville grew even after the city built a canal around the falls in 1830; the city more than doubled in size during the following decade.

Apart from that of Cincinnati between 1810 and 1820, the growth of St. Louis during the 1830s provided the most dramatic decennial increase for any pre-1840 western city. St. Louis more than tripled in size as a result of the dynamic fur trade of the trans-Mississippi (especially when the federal government lifted the ban on direct trade with the Indians in 1822), the thriving lead industry of Illinois and southwestern Wisconsin, which provided lead to the glass factories and shot mills of Philadelphia, and trade with the expansive Southwest. In 1840, nonetheless, the city was only about half the size of Louisville and ranked behind Lexington and Nashville.

After 1815 steamboating on the Mississippi and Ohio had changed the pattern of urban growth in the interior. Then the Erie Canal, by permitting the integration of the upper Northwest into the national economy, again altered the development of western cities. The canal shifted the locus of economic activity in the West to the Great Lakes and brought about a relative decline in the importance of the river cities. With the canal came the growth of the Great Lakes ports, beginning in the 1830s and accelerating during the 1840s and 1850s. Cities like Buffalo, Cleveland, Detroit, Chicago, and Milwaukee came to dominate western urbanization because they were at breaking points in water transport, as was Buffalo, or, more typically, because they could tap the agricultural hinterland through both canal and rail transport.

Throughout the ante-bellum period the development of western cities depended on the growth of the agricultural sector, linked to western expansion, and the development of the transportation network designed to support the growth of agriculture. The relative growth of western cities depended on their varying capacities to service western farmers, specifically, by their locations within the network of water and, increasingly, rail transport.

Railroads became more independent of water transport during the 1850s, and this development reinforced the preexisting pattern of Great Lakes urbanization. Cities, especially Chicago, which were in a position not only to receive feeder lines into the interior but to serve as important points of juncture in the developing trunk lines, became the prime beneficiaries of an agricultural expansion linked to the proliferation of rail networks. And then, as the trans-Mississippi west grew, so did the Great Lakes ports, especially Chicago, with rail linkages to the new west, and so did St. Louis, which was well placed to take advantage of both water and rail connections to

CINCINNATI, 1848. This Ohio River steamboat (probably the first ever photographed) signifies the importance of river commerce to western cities.

the trans-Mississippi. As early as 1860 St. Louis and Chicago overtook Boston and Baltimore, thereby moving into the third and fourth positions, respectively, in the ranking of the nation's cities.

Urbanization and Industrialization, 1790–1860

In the early stages of industrial modernization, the period when large-scale enterprises reached more widely dispersed markets and combined labor and capital more efficiently, industrialization resulted in growing concentrations of people but did not always proceed within preexistent cities. Early industry, particularly in the most modern sectors like textile production, became located either near supplies of raw material or, more commonly, near water-power sites, and rather than relying on existing population concentrations, firms often brought labor to the locations of raw materials and water power. The founding of almost all company towns, during and after the period of early industrialization, was a response to the occasional rationality of bringing people to the location of other resources. The mill operators who brought New England farm girls to factory dormitories (the Waltham system) were responding to the immobility of their water-power sources and to the mobility of the population. Soon, however, a mobile, urbanized factory labor force of independent migrants replaced the Waltham system and the company towns, and that pool of labor itself became a magnet for new industries. While the availability of labor encouraged further manufacturing growth, the demands of the textile industry for standardized machinery in particular spurred the growth of manufactures, incomes, and population. Industrialization in its earlier stages grew independent of urban forces but, once under way, fostered urban growth. Urban centers, then, independently stimulated the progress of industrialization.

Before 1840 mercantile activities dominated the development of cities; and despite the fact that commercial cities, through their concentrations of population, accumulations of imports and exports, holdings of capital, and supplies of entrepreneurial talent, became centers of manufacturing activity even in the early decades of the century, manufacturing in absolute terms remained secondary to other forms of enterprise. Even as late as 1860 manufacturing employment occupied less than one-third of the total labor force in the largest cities. Manufacturing employment was higher for New England and the Middle Atlantic states as a whole (43 percent and 35 percent of total employment, respectively), but it was still less than half of the labor force.[10] None of the large northeastern cities departed significantly from the general pattern of commercial dominance.

Throughout the ante-bellum period, manufacturing in the largest port cities grew out of the commercial functions of those cities. More specifically, the port cities specialized either in the processing of goods for export, an activity dependent on imports from the hinterland or from the West Indies, or in the manufacturing of goods that could compete with foreign imports for the growing domestic market, particularly in and around the cities themselves. Much of the port manufacturing was a response to the necessity of transshipment of goods within these ports, either because of physical necessity or because of a change of ownership; transshipment offered an opportunity to process efficiently. New York, for example, had growing and prosperous sugar-refining, tobacco-milling, and leather-working industries. Industry in Boston was similarly directed, with the most important difference being its large distilleries. Also, supplied in part by the China trade, it worked more exotic materials; the umbrella and cane industries, for example, utilized ivory, silks, buckhorn, linen, rattan, ebony, and boxwood. Such manufacturing of imports for export accounted for at least 20 percent of both value added in manufacturing and employment in Boston.

Concentrations of population and economic activity in the major ports also encouraged the development of manufacturing during the period of industrial revolution. Just as during the colonial period, commercial activities generated demands for certain service industries, especially shipbuilding, probably America's first truly modern industry. When New York passed Philadelphia as the largest city, it also became the nation's foremost shipbuilder, yet so thriving was the industry in the other major ports that New York accounted for no more than a quarter of United States production of ships in the 1830s. Similarly the printing and publishing industry grew in response not only to the expansion of urban population but to commercial activities as well, with their large demands for business and legal paper. In terms of employment it was the leading industry in New York in 1840. The biggest group of urban manufacturers, however, produced goods strictly for the sustenance of a growing population. Each of the port cities contained large and evenly distributed industries that produced construction materials, such as glass, nails, bricks, and paint, and consumption goods, such as clothing, carriages, furniture, and food products. In Boston, for example, in the early 1830s, about half of both total employment and value added in manufacturing stemmed from such manufacturing for the local market. Even when commerce dominated the development of the nation's largest cities, manufacturing activity grew as a result of the demands created by both commerce and the needs of growing populations.

The processes linking urbanization and industrialization widened their imprint on the economy in the 1840s and 1850s. The increase in the proportion of the population that was urbanized was about the same in the 1830s as in the 1820s, but between the 1830s and 1840s there was a sharp break. The incremental change in urbanized population during the 1840s and 1850s was more than double that experienced in the two preceding decades. Moreover, the incremental change for New England states reached its all-time high during the

1840s, with the Middle Atlantic states attaining a similar peak a decade later.[11] The acceleration of urbanization was clearly associated with the thrust of industrialization, which was also rapidly increasing in tempo during the boom of the late 1840s and early 1850s. As the interior developed, the pattern followed by the larger but still more commercial seaport cities emerged with the industrial cities: accumulation of population provided opportunities to manufacturers for exploiting economies of scale, thus stimulating industrialization, which, in turn, induced further urbanization. In addition, with the proliferation of the stationary steam engine, which released the most modern manufacturing, such as the textile industry, from its dependence on fixed water-power sites and which manufacturers adopted on a large scale in the 1850s, manufacturing increased in relative importance in the seaport cities. But the final victory of steam over water did not occur until the 1870s. Even then, steam was most important in the West where water power was either more expensive or nonexistent, and coal for steam-engine fuel was cheaper.

The interrelationships between industrialization and urbanization became cemented by mid-century, each process clearly reinforcing the other. Most important, because of declining costs of transportation and the development of alternative power sources, the manufacturing advantages of an urban location were growing rapidly compared to those available in locations near sources of cheap power and natural resources. In addition, proliferation of manufacturing within cities and their suburban satellites was encouraged by a number of other attractions, including ready availability of labor, highly developed capital markets, ready access to mercantile savings, ease of information gathering, economies of bulk purchase and handling, sophisticated trading services, easy access to the services of social overhead capital (such as warehousing), and the availability of a large, effective marketplace characteristic of population concentrations. The most important growth of manufacturing came within the largest cities, which had previously established their position and size within world trading networks. The positive elements of large urban size more than offset the negative externalities of urban scale, that is, the costs to persons and firms that resulted from large concentrations of people and economic activity. Congestion in the urban core, increasing transportation difficulties, resource pollution, and social disorder, all resulting to a large extent from inadequate investment in social overhead capital, would not raise manufacturing costs significantly until the latter part of the century. During the first half of the century, and especially after 1840, urbanization itself was a positive force in the progress of economic modernization and the concomitant achievement of high, sustained rates of real economic growth.

THE GOVERNMENT AND THE MARKETPLACE

The United States found itself enmeshed in the industrial revolution without having consciously or deliberately chosen "modernization." Rather than a core of self-conscious, powerful developers with access to political power launching the economy on an upward pattern of growth linked to modern industrial and agricultural development, it was the thousands of mobile Americans of modest means whose collective decisions gave weight to the forces of industrialization. In more general terms, the central institution of American economic development in the nineteenth century was the competitive marketplace. The mobility of men and their capital was necessary to the extension and refinement of market institutions and responsible for the atomistic character of economic life in the first half of the century.

Reliable measures of the aggregate level of government activity in the ante-bellum United States do not exist, and even if they did, they would not necessarily reveal the importance of the public sector during early industrialization. There is no measure of the *comparative* role of government in the United States—as contrasted with other nations at similar points in their development. Nonetheless, some evidence, albeit impressionistic, suggests that in Great Britain and the United States the government was far less important in the initial stages of industrialization than in nations that followed in the process of modernization, most notably France, Germany, and especially Japan and the Soviet Union—latecomers in development who were more likely to rely on a small group of farsighted developers able to mobilize resources through the use of governmental instruments.

Those measures of United States governmental activity that do exist reveal only limited facts about the public sector in the nineteenth century. We know that state and local governments were the most important agencies throughout the nineteenth century, that the federal government did not increase its activities materially until the Civil War decade, and that the significant enlargement of government, as compared with the private sector, occurred only in the last decade or two of the century. Regional variations in governmental activity also existed. Areas with higher incomes and greater levels of urbanization tended to spend more money per capita than lower-income and more sparsely settled regions. And within areas similar in income and degree of urbanization the level of government activity varied as a result of interlocal and interstate differences in the configuration of political power.[12] But we have no way, as yet, of judging the significance of these variations, including the impact of regional or local variations on economic performance.

The complexity and variety of governmental activity at all levels, local, state, and federal, defy quantification in any comprehensive way. Indeed, accurate measures of governmental activity nationally and by regions would not necessarily reveal very much about the significance of the polity in the development of economic life. They might reveal the actual and potential influence of government expenditures on the movement of the business cycle, but they could not suggest even the outlines of the impact of government on long-term economic growth. Government activity cannot be evaluated solely or even mainly in terms of its dollar cost, since plainly two programs with the same cost might well have widely varying impacts on the economy. Nevertheless, we can and should look at the indirect ways that government shaped the structure of the economy. More specifically, we need to examine the ways in which government provided or fostered innovations in economic organization that effected a more efficient utilization of resources.

Free Banking and the Mobilization of Capital

Efforts to mobilize capital and to provide for orderly capital markets that would permit maximization of returns on capital investment did find encouragement by government during the first half of the nineteenth century. The most obvious example is the promotion of uniform commercial banking arrangements by the federal chartering and financing (20 percent) of two national banks. The influence of these banks extended over four of seven decades between 1790 and 1860, including the expansive 1790s and, most significantly, the transitional 1820s. The creation of national banks was directed toward the fostering of order rather than the mobilization of capital per se. But the commercial banks that ordered local and regional affairs were obviously more important than the federally sponsored initiatives, since the expansion of the late 1840s and early 1850s occurred in the absence of a national banking institution. After 1820 state governments encouraged commercial banks in various ways. Some states owned stock in chartered commercial banks, several supported the acquisition of banking capital through pledges of credit, and eight states owned and operated banks between 1819 and 1837. The trend, however, was toward less state *control*, reduced state participation, and greater ease of incorporation, coupled with greater state *regulation* in the more urban-industrial regions, as in the body of state banking legislation framed in New York after 1838, when the state made bank incorporation more accessible (the establishment of free banking). The accumulation of all such legislation served to foster regularity and to build confidence in the banking system. As the movement toward free banking matured, that is, as state legislatures exercised restraint in the process of incorporation, they promulgated positive support for orderly commercial banking. Except for the few smaller bankers and wildcatting entrepreneurs who saw opportunity in loose practice and unpredictability, this legislation was desired by everyone in the business community of the metropolitan areas. Government thus provided a legal and institutional framework for the ante-bellum departure from an emphasis on personal relations in the workings of capital markets. Consequently capitalists found the costs of risk reduced and themselves better able to judge the returns from promising new investments.

Incorporation and Expansive Public Policy

Incorporation became available to forms of enterprise other than banking, a trend that had begun during the colonial period and culminated before the Civil War in making the ability to incorporate a right rather than a privilege. In procedural terms, this meant that an incorporator would have only to satisfy an executive authority that he had fulfilled certain statutory requirements; he no longer was obliged to seek a special act of the legislature. In widening access to corporate charters, competing states were responding, in part, to the demands of businessmen and to the lack of state funds, particularly after the Revolution, for investment in enterprises serving traditional public functions. But they were moved as well by Revolutionary ideology, the commitment to make the advantages stemming from government available to all groups and individuals in the society. As a result the states created some 200 corporations between 1776 and 1789, with the effect of spreading the benefits of the corporate form among many citizens being to cause the privileges that had accompanied the old quasi-monopolistic charters to lose their meaning. (By way of contrast Britain, without a federal system or the ideology of the Revolution, had less than twenty modern corporations in 1800, when the United States had more than 300.) Subsequently, the states reduced the conditions necessary for incorporation to a minimum, and largely in the 1830s legislatures replaced the granting of individual charters with general incorporation acts. At the same time, however, protection was granted to such privileges as were actually extended by state government. That principle was established clearly by the outcome of the *Dartmouth College* case (1819), which prevented the state legislature of New Hampshire from altering the terms of the original college charter. Thus the states encouraged business enterprises by lowering barriers to incorporation, thereby facilitating more-effective mobilization and management of capital, and by creating a general framework of laws guaranteeing stability to corporate enterprise.

To the extent that the changing legal setting of the corporation constituted a microcosm of the development of governmental polity, a widening of opportunity was characteristic of the framework of law during the first half of the nineteenth century. This characteristic was not new or associated solely with the onset of the industrial revolution. The general incorporation laws of the 1830s grew out of the Revolutionary and eighteenth-century experience as much as they stemmed from the increasing economic utility of the corporate form of business organization. Finally, this policy was hardly one of laissez faire; it was not neutral, but positive. To be sure, government extended a freer hand to corporations and reduced the kind of involvement that had been characteristic under the special charters. Nevertheless, the refinement of corporate policy is better seen as government actively seeking to encourage economic development, and economic equality, through the creation of a very favorable climate for entrepreneurial activity.

The Market for Labor

The labor market developed with far less intervention by political agencies; government did little to alleviate the basic labor shortages. During the colonial period and until the 1840s the expansion of the labor supply depended almost entirely on the natural increase of the population, rather than immigration. When the natural rate of increase declined in the early decades of the century, there was no significant governmental reaction, such as an effort to promote and subsidize large-scale immigration. The levels of immigration that were attained in the 1840s were a response mainly to the growing shortage of native labor rather than to any governmental program of support. States frequently set up immigration commissions to propagandize, or they sent agents to foreign ports to recruit new settlers; but the clear disparity between returns to labor in Europe and those possible in the United States was the major force in attracting immigrants, a force that did not require any concomitant changes in existing labor institutions.

Nor did state and local governments do much to alleviate the shortage of skilled labor. During the first half of the nineteenth century, Americans considered investment in education as a means of relieving a scarcity of skilled labor to be far less important than investment that went directly into productive activity. Even as late as 1860 the resource cost of education (including direct expenditures and earnings from employment foregone by students while enrolled in school) accounted for less than 1.5 percent of national product, as contrasted with almost 2 percent in 1880 and 3 percent in 1900. Not only was educational investment a small diversion of resources, but the bulk of direct educational expenditure came from private sources, despite the fact that the common schools enjoyed increasing enrollments before the Civil War. Even by 1850 less than half of such expenditures came from public sources, and by 1860 the public's share was only barely dominant. (During the 1880s and 1890s education was to consistently receive almost 80 percent of its support from government.)[13]

The one striking departure from the general pattern of government detachment in the labor market was its prohibition of the international slave trade. Because of the increasingly large monopoly profits implicit in slaveownership, the flow of slaves from Africa and the West Indies would very likely have been substantially larger if such trade had not been prohibited in 1807, as authorized by the Constitution. The restrictive action was taken before the cotton frontier became reality, and thereafter the support for reopening the slave trade was insufficient to overcome the highly stringent requirements for a Constitutional amendment. Abolitionist sentiment, widespread Northern opposition to both the extension of slavery and the movement of black populations into the West, and the desire of slave-breeding areas of the Old South to protect both their markets and their high returns by limiting the supply of slaves precluded the reestablishment of a truly free market in slaves.

The Abundance of Land: The Governmental Contribution

Far more important than participation in capital and labor markets was the role of the federal government in enlarging and dispensing the nation's physical resources, especially the supply of agricultural land. Beginning with the period of the Confederation, the national government assured Americans that land would be available in a regular fashion and on increasingly liberal terms. It provided physical order, as in the elaboration of the prior, rectangular survey, and guaranteed political and social stability as well. Furthermore, it consistently enlarged the territory available to land-hungry Americans by negotiating the Louisiana Purchase, conquering vast Mexican territories during the Mexican War, acquiring Oregon, and, where necessary, removing and destroying Indian populations. Land policy

was another part of the effort of government to provide an environment in which expansion and the search for opportunity could be
fruitful. Taken in the aggregate, it constituted a subsidization of
western agriculture and a fillip to westward expansion. The results
promoted real gains in agricultural productivity through an improvement in the quality of agricultural land, the realization of economies
of regional specialization, and a dramatic growth in the resources
available to the developing national economy.

Exploitation of the nation's massive landed resources was made
possible by an enormous transport system. And, in a variety of ways,
the government contributed to the construction of the network of
railroads and waterways. In the case of turnpikes and canals, support
ranged from the mere chartering of companies to forcing mutual
savings banks to invest in public enterprise and to assuming outright
ownership of internal improvements.[14] And public investment dominated canal construction. The essential ingredient of public interest,
once again, was the provision of a stable yet flexible environment for
expansion. Direct public support to transport was less important
after the 1830s, on the order of 25 to 30 percent during the vast
expansion of railroads in the 1840s and 1850s.[15] One reason for diminished public involvement was the crisis of confidence in internal-
improvement subsidies created by the Panic of 1837. Also, the
conquest of the midwestern prairies in the 1840s and 1850s was less
risky for private enterprise than the conquest of the Appalachian
barrier, which took place largely before 1837. Finally, by the 1840s
both capital markets and corporate structures had become better
equipped to mobilize and manage the large units of capital required.
Nonetheless, governments, especially state and local, were important promoters of transport systems in the Old Northwest, especially
during the earliest days of railroad building there, that is, the period
of construction of lines that served as feeders to lakes, rivers, and
canals. At the urging of urban promoters, governments located at
crucial water junctures made private, eastern investors more confident of future returns to their railroad investments by mobilizing
public support for initial railroad construction. Thus, before the Civil
War, the government played a significant role in reducing transportation costs by mobilizing capital, removing bottlenecks to continuing development, and creating an economic climate favorable to
private capital formation.

Tariff Policy

Government also contributed to the reduction of the costs of transactions and consequently to the accumulation of interregional and
international exchanges by reducing tariff barriers after the Tariff of

1828, a process culminating in the passage of the Walker Tariff of 1846. Just when American manufacturers were developing the ability to compete effectively in international markets, the federal government reduced tariff barriers to stimulate trade and, on the verge of the Civil War, Americans seemed ready to choose free trade. The question of the impact of tariffs before 1846 is, as yet, lightly explored territory for economic historians, but the high tariffs culminating in 1828 probably served only to redistribute income toward protected industries; they did not in all probability contribute to economic growth by subsidizing new industries in need of less expensive capital or by protecting infant enterprise against more-efficient foreign competitors until it could compete on its own. If the large New England textile firms are typical, modernizing industry enjoyed a favored position in the imperfect capital markets of the nineteenth century independent of the impact of the tariff. Although modernizing industries may well have gained much of their competitive power through learning by doing, they probably would have achieved the same efficiencies without the brief period of high-tariff protection.[16]

An Overview

An inescapable fact is that a marketplace of individual enterprise and profit maximization was the dominant institution of American economic life during the decades that witnessed the entrenchment of the industrial revolution, just as it had been during the period of preindustrial expansion. That marketplace was never self-sufficient. Economies as we know them are influenced and, in the case of American development, sustained by noneconomic institutions, an important part of which are, in the usual sense of the word, political in character. The basic pattern of governmental activity in the nineteenth century was one of positive reinforcement of marketplace decisions. We must realize that although the impact of the functions of government as yet cannot be rigorously assessed, the broadly based activities of government in the early-nineteenth-century economy were part of a societal framework that provided positive, sustained impetus for development and growth. In particular, government sought and succeeded in providing an institutional setting that reduced the costs of risks, innovation, raw materials, and transportation to those who were investing their labor and especially their capital in American economic development.

Because governmental arrangements reinforced the social processes advancing economic growth, government contributed to the increasing concentration of wealth holding in the first half of the nineteenth century. Federal, state, and local governments assumed no significant responsibility for those whose lack of skills or property placed them at the lower end of the economic spectrum, or even for those who had difficulty maintaining a subsistence level of living. Significant public assumption of a welfare responsibility or involvement in augmenting the bargaining power of labor did not develop until the last decades of the century; nor did significant political support develop for altering the trends of income distribution—at least after the expiration of the artisan-based labor movement of the 1830s. The fundamental assumption of governmental policy was that expansion of the marketplace and increasing efficiency would redound to the benefit of every citizen. And most upwardly mobile Americans participating in the marketplace were very probably fearful of the high costs of a public welfare responsibility. To lower-middle-class German immigrants, who predominated in the *Auswanderung* of 1830–1845, for example, a strong element of the appeal of the American dream was the promised freedom from the taxes on land necessary to support a large class of poor; and those same Germans, transplanted in America, proved, subsequently, to be socially conservative on the issues of taxation and poor laws.[17] The commitment of small landowners, skilled workers, and small manufacturers and tradesmen to social conservatism is obvious, but one suspects that the continuing scarcity of labor and the attendant opportunities for upward economic mobility blunted the potential radicalism of even unskilled factory workers, those tied to domestic service, and the landless tenant farmers and farm laborers.

NOTES

1. For the contribution of railroads I rely very heavily on Albert Fishlow, *American Railroads and the Transformation of the Ante-Bellum Economy* (Cambridge, Mass.: Harvard University Press, 1965). See also Robert W. Fogel, *Railroads and American Economic Growth: Essays in Econometric History* (Baltimore: Johns Hopkins University Press, 1964).

2. For a critique of this estimate of the direct benefits of ante-bellum railroads, which is Albert Fishlow's, see Peter D. McClelland, "Railroads, American Growth, and the New Economic History: A Critique," *Journal of Economic History*, 28 (March 1968), 102–123.

3. Carter Goodrich, "Internal Improvements Reconsidered," *Journal of Economic History*, 30 (June 1970), 297.

4. Arthur M. Johnson and Barry E. Supple, *Boston Capitalists and Western Railroads: A Study in the Nineteenth Century Investment Process* (Cambridge, Mass.: Harvard University Press, 1967).

5. The ability of banks to create money refers to their power to expand loans beyond the money they receive as deposits. This power prevails so long as business confidence remains high and bankers invest prudently. Under such conditions the flow of net deposits (or the purchase of new bank notes in the nineteenth century) tends to balance out withdrawals (or the redemption of bank notes), and bankers need keep only a small fraction of the value of demand deposits (or borrowed capital) as reserves to protect against withdrawals (or note redemptions).

6. To assess further the contribution of the second national bank to economic stability one should turn to Peter Temin, *The Jacksonian Economy* (New York: Norton, 1969).

7. Jean A. Wilburn, *Biddle's Bank: The Crucial Years* (New York: Columbia University Press, 1967).

8. J. Van Fenstermaker, *The Development of American Commercial Banking, 1782–1837* (Kent, Ohio: Kent State University Press, 1965), especially p. 68.

9. Allan R. Pred, *The Spatial Dynamics of United States Urban-Industrial Growth, 1800–1914: Interpretive and Theoretical Essays* (Cambridge, Mass.: M.I.T. Press, 1966), p. 148.

10. This and following estimates of the size and structure of post-1840 urban manufacturing are from Pred, *op. cit.*

11. Eric E. Lampard, "The Evolving System of Cities in the United States: Urbanization and Economic Development," in Harvey S. Perloff and Lowdon Wingo, Jr. (eds.), *Issues in Urban Economics* (Baltimore: Johns Hopkins Press, 1968), pp. 116–125.

12. For a description of such variations see Lance E. Davis and John Legler, "The Government in the American Economy: A Quantitative Study," *Journal of Economic History,* 26 (December 1966), 514–555.

13. Albert Fishlow, "Levels of Nineteenth-Century American Investment in Education," *Journal of Economic History,* 26 (December 1966), 418–436.

14. For the suggestion that state governments constrained the investment opportunities of mutual savings banks to subsidize the construction of internal improvements see Alan L. Olmstead, "New York City Mutual Savings Banks in the Ante-Bellum Years: A Dissertation Summary," *Journal of Economic History,* 31 (March 1971), 272–275.

15. For data on the public contribution to railroad investment see Goodrich, *op. cit.,* p. 297.

16. For a pioneering effort to explore the contribution of experience and training effects on industrial efficiency, and suggestions on the impact of early tariff protection, see Paul A. David, "Learning by Doing and Tariff Protection: A Reconsideration of the Case of the Ante-Bellum United States Cotton Textile Industry," *Journal of Economic History,* 30 (September 1970), 521–601.

17. Mack Walker, *Germany and the Emigration, 1816–1885* (Cambridge, Mass.: Harvard University Press, 1964), pp. 42–69.

SUGGESTED READINGS

Transportation

Books

Chandler, Alfred D., Jr. (ed.). *The Railroads: The Nation's First Big Business.* New York: Harcourt, Brace and World, 1965.

Fishlow, Albert. *American Railroads and the Transformation of the Ante-Bellum Economy.* Cambridge, Mass.: Harvard University Press, 1965.

Fogel, Robert W. *Railroads and American Economic Growth: Essays in Econometric History.* Baltimore: Johns Hopkins University Press, 1964.

Goodrich, Carter, *et al. Canals and American Economic Development.* New York: Columbia University Press, 1961.

Johnson, Arthur M., and Barry E. Supple. *Boston Capitalists and Western Railroads: A Study in the Nineteenth Century Investment Process.* Cambridge, Mass.: Harvard University Press, 1967.

Articles

Lebergott, Stanley. "United States Transport Advance and Externalities," *Journal of Economic History,* 26 (December 1966), 437–461.

McClelland, Peter D. "Railroads, American Growth, and the New Economic History: A Critique," *Journal of Economic History,* 28 (March 1968), 102–123.

Commercial Banking

Books

Fenstermaker, J. Van. *The Development of American Commercial Banking, 1782–1837.* Kent, Ohio: Kent State University Press, 1965.

Haites, Erik E., *et al. Western River Transportation: The Era of Internal Development, 1810–1860.* Baltimore: Johns Hopkins University Press, 1975.

Hammond, Bray. *Banks and Politics in America from the Revolution to the Civil War.* Princeton, N.J.: Princeton University Press, 1957.

Smith, Walter B. *Economic Aspects of the Second Bank of the United States.* Cambridge, Mass.: Harvard University Press, 1935.

Temin, Peter. *The Jacksonian Economy.* New York: Norton, 1969.

Wilburn, Jean A. *Biddle's Bank: The Crucial Years.* New York: Columbia University Press, 1967.

Articles

Davis, Lance E. "Capital Immobilities and Finance Capitalism: A Study of Economic Evolution in the United States, 1820–1920," in *Purdue Faculty Papers in Economic History, 1956–1966.* Homewood, Ill.: Irwin, 1967, pp. 581–595.

La Force, J. Clayburn. "Gresham's Law and the Suffolk System: A Misapplied Epigram," *Business History Review,* 40 (Summer 1966), 149–166.

Schur, Leon M. "The Second Bank of the United States and the Inflation After the War of 1812," *Journal of Political Economy,* 68 (April 1960), 118–134.

Timberlake, Richard H., Jr. "The Specie Standard and Central Banking in the United States Before 1860," *Journal of Economic History,* 21 (September 1961), 318–341.

Urbanization

Books

Albion, Robert G. *The Rise of New York Port.* New York: Scribner, 1939.

Gilchrist, David T. (ed.). *The Growth of the Seaport Cities, 1790–1825.* Charlottesville, Va.: University Press of Virginia, 1967.

Handlin, Oscar, and John Burchard (eds.). *The Historians and the City.* Cambridge, Mass.: M.I.T. Press and Harvard University Press, 1963.

Knights, Peter R. *The Plain People of Boston, 1830–1860.* New York: Oxford University Press, 1971.

Pred, Allan R. *The Spatial Dynamics of United States Urban-Industrial Growth, 1800–1914: Interpretive and Theoretical Essays.* Cambridge, Mass.: M.I.T. Press, 1966.

Thernstrom, Stephan, and Richard Sennett. *Nineteenth-Century Cities: Essays in the New Urban History.* New Haven: Yale University Press, 1969.

Wade, Richard C. *The Urban Frontier: Pioneer Life in Early Pittsburgh, Cincinnati, Lexington, Louisville, and St. Louis.* Chicago: University of Chicago Press, 1964.

Warner, Sam Bass, Jr. *The Private City.* Philadelphia: University of Pennsylvania Press, 1968.

Articles

Cohen, Ira. "The Auction System in the Port of New York, 1817–1837," *Business History Review,* 45 (Winter 1971), 488–510.

Crowther, Simeon J. "Urban Growth in the Mid-Atlantic States, 1785–1850," *Journal of Economic History,* 36 (September 1976), 624–644.

Lampard, Eric E. "The Evolving System of Cities in the United States: Urbanization and Economic Development," in Harvey S. Perloff and Lowdon Wingo, Jr. (eds.), *Issues in Urban Economics.* Baltimore: Johns Hopkins Press, 1968, pp. 81–139.

Taylor, George Rogers. "American Urban Growth Preceding the Railway Age," *Journal of Economic History,* 26 (September 1966), 309–339.

Warner, Sam Bass, Jr. "If All the World Were Philadelphia: A Scaffolding for Urban History, 1774–1930," *American Historical Review,* 74 (October 1968), 26–43.

Williamson, Jeffrey G. "Ante-Bellum Urbanization in the American Northeast," *Journal of Economic History,* 25 (October 1965), 592–608.

————, and Joseph A. Swanson. "The Growth of Cities in the American Northeast, 1820–1870," in *Explorations in Entrepreneurial History,* 4 (Supplement, 1966).

Government

Books

Carstensen, Vernon (ed.). *The Public Lands.* Madison, Wis.: University of Wisconsin Press, 1963.

Fogel, Robert W. *The Union Pacific Railroad: A Case in Premature Enterprise.* Baltimore: Johns Hopkins University Press, 1960.

Goodrich, Carter. *Government Promotion of American Canals and Railroads, 1800–1890.* New York: Columbia University Press, 1960.

Handlin, Oscar, and Mary Flug Handlin. *Commonwealth: A Study in the Role of Government in the American Economy, Massachusetts, 1774–1861.* New York: New York University Press, 1947.

Hartz, Louis. *Economic Policy and Democratic Thought: Pennsylvania, 1776–1860.* Cambridge, Mass.: Harvard University Press, 1954.

Heath, Milton S. *Constructive Liberalism: The Role of the State in Economic Development in Georgia to 1860.* Cambridge, Mass.: Harvard University Press, 1954.

Hibbard, Benjamin H. *A History of Public Land Policies.* New York: Smith, 1939.

Hurst, James Willard. *Law and the Conditions of Freedom in the Nineteenth Century United States.* Madison, Wis.: University of Wisconsin Press, 1964.

————. *The Legitimacy of the Business Corporation in the Law of the United States, 1780–1970.* Charlottesville: University Press of Virginia, 1970.

Robbins, Roy M. *Our Landed Heritage: The Public Domain, 1776–1936.* Princeton, N.J.: Princeton University Press, 1942.

Scheiber, Harry N. *Ohio Canal Era: A Case Study of Government and the Economy, 1820–1861.* Athens, Ohio: Ohio University Press, 1969.

Articles

Broude, Henry W. "The Role of the State in American Economic Development," in Hugh G. J. Aitken (ed.), *The State and Economic Growth.* New York: Social Science Research Council, 1959, pp. 4–25.

Cochran, Thomas C. "The Business Revolution," *American Historical Review,* 79 (December 1974), 1449–1466.

David, Paul A. "Learning by Doing and Tariff Protection: A Reconsideration of the Case of the Ante-Bellum United States Cotton Textile Industry," *Journal of Economic History,* 30 (September 1970), 521–601.

Davis, Lance E., and John Legler. "The Government in the American Economy: A Quantitative Study," *Journal of Economic History,* 26 (December 1966), 514–555.

Fishlow, Albert. "Levels of Nineteenth-Century American Investment in Education," *Journal of Economic History,* 26 (December 1966), 418–436.

Lively, Robert A. "The American System: A Review Article," *Business History Review,* 29 (1955), 81–96.

Mercer, Lloyd J. "Land Grants to American Railroads: Social Costs or Social Benefit?" *Business History Review,* 43 (Summer 1969), 134–151.

———. "Rates of Return for Land-Grant Railroads: The Central Pacific System," *Journal of Economic History,* 30 (September 1970), 602–626.

Slavery and the Civil War, 1790-1870

THE ECONOMICS OF SLAVERY

Viability, Profitability, and Slave Welfare

Except for those in that now virtually extinct minority who believed in the racial inferiority of slaves, the fundamental evaluation of slavery has been an easy task for all historians. The moral condemnation of the institution of slavery has appealed to a society that has always placed a high value, at least in theory, on individual liberty. But because of that moral commitment, historians have had difficulty understanding the powerful attachment of slaveowners, and southern society, to an institution so at odds with the norms of the wider society. To the enterprise of explaining the setting of slavery in American life, and thus to the endeavor of understanding an infamous record of human failing, economic historians can offer an assessment of the significance of the forces of the marketplace.

The expansiveness of southern agriculture and slavery suggests the validity of considering the institution of slavery primarily as an economic institution. (See Figure 15 for the shift in the geographic distribution of the slave population between 1790 and 1860.) Nonetheless, because of the way that slavery impinged upon the totality of life in southern society, the institution was clearly more than just economic in character. One description of slavery popular a generation ago, and recently revived, emphasizes that slavery was most significant as a means of social control, indeed, that as an economic institution it was secondary, becoming even less important as the

241

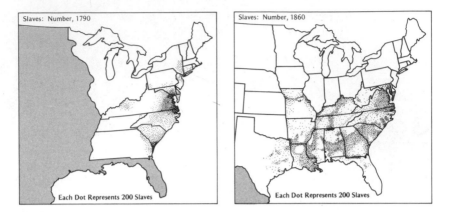

FIGURE 15: *The Distribution of the Slave Population in 1790 and 1860*

Civil War approached.[1] If the Civil War could have been forestalled, goes the theory, slavery would have expired eventually as a result of its lack of economic feasibility or viability.[2]

The viability of slavery as an economic institution, however, is amenable to measurement, and slavery was viable, it is clear, as long as there was a continuing incentive to raise slaves, both by slave breeders and by planters raising them for their own use. Stated in somewhat different terms, so long as the market value of slaves remained equal to or greater than the costs of reproducing those slaves, the system was viable.[3]

One application of this framework to available data finds that the difference between the market value of slaves and the costs of rearing them actually increased between 1820 and 1860 and that rearing costs became a larger portion of market value. The margin between market price and the costs of rearing, or economic rent, is the measure of the potential fall in slave values that could have occurred without making slavery unprofitable to the slave economy as a whole. Incredibly enough, in the last half of the 1850s the market price of slaves could have fallen almost 100 percent before slavery would have been no longer viable. Economic rent as a share of market value rose in three spurts, from about 60 percent during the 1820s to its peak for the period in the late 1850s. Market price would have to have fallen relatively twice as far in the late 1850s as in the 1820s for slavery to have been no longer viable as an economic institution.[4]

There is no evidence that a decline in the viability of slavery was imminent at the onset of the Civil War or even that southern planters anticipated such a decline. If they had had serious doubts about the future of slavery, their desire to own slaves would have diminished, and as a consequence, the market price of slaves would have fallen relative to net rearing costs. The increasing margin of economic rent is accounted for not only by the strong demand for slaves but also by the rigidity, or inelasticity, of the supply of slaves. Slaves from West Indian and African sources were no doubt available after the closing of the slave trade in 1808, but in reduced quantities.[5] Since the current prevailing rate of interest was included as a cost in calculating the costs of reproducing slaves, the increasing margin of economic rent meant that the rate of return based on the reproduction costs of slaves was above that rate of interest. Consequently both the returns to planters from slave breeding and the price of slaves were artificially inflated. Because of the way in which the restricted supply of slave imports contributed to higher slave prices, it is understandable, at least in economic terms, that the desire to reopen the slave trade intensified in the lower South and in newer agricultural areas during the 1850s.

If we accept the fact that economic rent of slaves was increasing, we should not necessarily conclude that southern planters, or any investors in southern agriculture, were making a return on their investment in slaves that was comparable to the return possible on investment elsewhere. Other values, such as the quest for greater social status within southern communities or the perverse gratifications possible with absolute control of human beings, might have supported slave prices as much as expectations of monetary income. These social possibilities lead to the question, distinct from the one of the viability of slavery as an economic system, of the economic profitability of slavery to individual planters. What was the return made by planters on their investments in slaves? A rather definite consensus on the best answer to that question has emerged from extensive inquiries by economic historians.[6]

Calculations based on the *market value* of slaves have shown that returns on investments in slaves, both male and female, on all but the poorest of land averaged about 10 percent. Rates of return varied little according to the sex of slaves or geographic region. Moreover, these rates of return equaled or exceeded returns on alternative investments available to southern planters. Southern railroads, for example, earned substantially less than 10 percent on investments even during the dynamic 1850s. For that matter, even the most successful of the New England textile firms rarely produced rates of return larger than 10 percent during the 1840s and 1850s. Hence, one need not invoke prestige or "psychotic" needs for slaves in order to explain the level of demand for them, although these needs were quite likely present in some measure. Of course, the profitability figures are averages, and we cannot know from them how many slaveowners earned normal profits. Some planters may well have paid too much for their slaves or bought too many slaves in order to satisfy needs for conspicuous consumption or to gratify perverse impulses. But they were not sufficiently numerous to reduce the average profitability of owning slaves below that of owning other assets.

The relative profits of slaveowning depended heavily on slave ages. A recent study indicates that in the Old South in 1850 male slave prices and the average annual profits that male slaves yielded varied greatly according to their age. Profits were negative until age eight, increased until a peak during the mid-thirties, and then declined, although remaining positive, until the late seventies. The pattern for female slaves was closely parallel.[7] Despite the variations, owners obtained significant value from slaves over almost all of an average slave's life span. This finding suggests that slaveowners had a distinct vested interest in maintaining the physical well-being of slaves, old and young alike. A minority of slaveowners may well have worked slaves to death at early ages, but more typical behavior appears clearly to have been a determined protection of investment through the fostering of physical health. Corroborating this inference is the fertility and mortality experience of slaves in the United States. Slaves reproduced more rapidly and survived longer in the United States than elsewhere in the Western Hemisphere. In fact, during the eighteenth century the rising rate of natural increase of the North American slave population closely paralleled that of the white population. By the 1820s, after the fertility of whites had begun to decline, rates of natural increase were approximately the same for both slaves and whites. Thereafter the rate of natural increase of slaves tended to surpass that of whites.[8] More adequate food, clothing, and shelter, as well as a salubrious climate and the rewards that planters offered to fecund slaves, contributed to the high rate of natural increase.

Caution should be exercised in concluding that the patterns of profitability reflected favorably on the economic welfare of slaves. The study of slaves' economic well-being remains uncertain despite recent claims that slaves enjoyed a great deal of upward mobility, a high degree of family stability, adequate medical care, and light punishments, as well as diets, clothing, and housing that were good by the standards of the day.[9] A balanced judgment, based on the full range of current research, would admit that North American slavery provided slaves with material benefits that kept fertility and mortality rates close to national norms but would also question whether those benefits placed slave welfare on a par with that enjoyed by free people, even those living in the South. The key to the economic

SLAVES ON AUCTION IN VIRGINIA, 1861. Contributing to the "psychic costs" of slavery was the slaves' forced migration to the Southwest.

appeal of slavery was the ability of slaveowners to expropriate income from slaves, to deny them a portion of the income that they had earned. Employers of free labor with monopsony power can exploit their employees in this same manner. But the combination of the legal sanctions available to planters, including those that encouraged physical coercion, and the relative isolation of rural plantations allowed American slaveowners to keep an unusually large share of the income earned by slaves. The best estimate of this rate of exploitation places it at about 50 percent.[10] The coercive power available to slaveowners also allowed them to force slaves to work in gangs—the typical work unit on the fields of large plantations. The resulting economies of scale reinforced the rate of expropriation to make slavery even more attractive to planters. But in achieving these economies of scale planters further diminished the welfare of their slaves. After Emancipation, slaves demonstrated their antipathy to gang labor by choosing, where possible, sharecropping and tenant farming instead, despite the exploitative nature of those institutions. Thus, evaluation of the welfare of slaves must recognize not only material well-being but also the unquantifiable psychic loss that slaves suffered from being denied the range of social choice available to free people.

Slaves responded to the denial of social freedom in a variety of ways. A unique religion and family structure developed as support mechanisms.[11] Concerted slave rebellions were rare, but passive resistance and low-level sabotage became common. Malingering, carelessness, damage to property, stealing, arson, and escape were among the slaves' repertoire of defensive tactics.[12] But the use of these tactics did not undo the economic efficiency of slave labor on plantations. Efficiency remained high because of gang labor, high rates of expropriation, and the large revenues that the sale of cotton on the world market produced. But one may not conclude on the basis of the high revenue-producing efficiency of slave labor that slaves worked as enthusiastically and as effectively as they would have under freedom.[13]

Southern Economic Growth

Even though slavery was both viable and profitable, the possibility remains that the long-run effect of slavery was to retard the economic development of the South. This possibility is important in terms of developing and refining our concept of the basic processes underlying economic growth in the nation as a whole; if slavery did not retard the long-run performance of the South's economy, our emphasis on free labor and its mobility in explaining the productivity of the economy would be misplaced.

Descriptions of the ante-bellum southern economy have often begun with the implication that the South was a low-income, sluggishly growing region. But the actual pattern was more complex. It is true that per-capita income in the South failed to keep pace with that in the nation at large in the period 1840–1860.[14] But even in 1860, the level of southern per-capita income was respectably high: almost three-quarters of the national average. Moreover, per-capita income in the South was higher than per-capita income in the North Central region in both 1840 and 1860. Further, estimates of per-capita income treat slaves as consumers and the costs of feeding, clothing, and housing slaves as slave income. When slaves and slave "incomes" are excluded, per-capita income in the South falls only slightly short of the national average and the average for northern states in 1840. And in 1860, it exceeded both averages.[15] For the twenty-year period before the Civil War the South, although losing ground, was not a low-income region and the South's economy generated for freemen income benefits that were increasingly impressive by national standards.

Per-capita levels of income and wealth reveal nothing, however, of the distribution of wealth and income. Obviously it is possible that high levels of per-capita income in the South reflected only unusually high returns made by the largest owners of slaves and land; it is conceivable that a large, extremely depressed class of small, non-slaveowning farmers swarmed beneath them on the social ladder. Using the distribution of wealth among people employed in agriculture, North and South, as the most appropriate standard provides some evidence for such a conclusion. The concentration of both holdings of improved farmland and slaves was substantially greater in all portions of the cotton South than in the agricultural states of the North. But extending the comparison to urban-industrial America as well as the rural-agricultural North yields a different result; the distribution of wealth among freemen in the cotton South in 1860 was *much* more equal than in large cities. Finally, the distribution of wealth among the free members of the ante-bellum South was not substantially different from the distributions of wealth recorded in the twentieth century.[16]

The level of both urbanized population and industrialized labor force in the South was far less—indeed, less than half that of national levels. Even in the most industrial southern states—Virginia and Kentucky—manufacturing output per capita was only about half the national level and less than a quarter of the New England level in both 1850 and 1860. Although by this measure, manufacturing in those two states gained slightly on manufacturing in the Northeast during the 1850s, manufacturing in the maturing Great Lakes region increased at a substantially more rapid pace.[17] Given the elevated levels of southern income before the Civil War, it is clear that urbanization-industrialization was not always necessary to achieve significant levels of economic growth. But the South should have industrialized for long-term growth, for success in the twentieth-century economy; even during the ante-bellum period, per-capita incomes in the industrializing Northeast were substantially higher than those in the South. Thus, from the standpoint of sustained, fully modern economic growth, southerners failed to invest sufficiently in manufacturing. More-rapid industrialization would have offered greater promise of relieving southern society from the moral burden of slavery.

The failure of southern investors can be explained in a variety of ways but not in terms of lack of modernity or lack of flexibility. The wealthiest slaveholders were by no means narrow or highly specialized in their business activities. Besides producing staple crops, they engaged in mercantile activity, speculated in urban real estate, established banks, built railroads, and even owned factories and mines. To some, a more attractive and influential explanation for the failure of southern investors to lead industrialization has been that southern demand for manufactured goods was insufficient to sustain a vibrant manufacturing sector. In this accounting, plantation slavery is seen as so limiting the purchasing power of the South, by fostering a highly concentrated distribution of income, that any industry that did develop lacked a home market large enough to sustain large-scale production. According to this argument, then, southern manufacturers were incapable of competing with northern firms whose development had been based on the existence of much wider markets.

The theory emphasizing limited markets cannot be maintained, however, in the light of data on the total purchasing power in the South and the optimal size of manufacturing plants in the Northeast. Of course, the distribution of income was less equitable than in northern agricultural districts. But for the purposes of calculating southern demand for goods and services, all cash expenditures, including those made for slaves by their owners, should be treated as income. An estimate of such cash expenditures and a calculation of the optimal size of manufacturing plant reveal that the region could have supported over 50 cotton-textile plants and more than 200 large boot and shoe establishments in 1860.[18] Furthermore, the distance of southern markets from northern factories served as an artificial tariff barrier against northern manufactured goods and gave southern manufacturers a competitive edge.

If we accept the potential for manufacturing activity within the South, how do we explain the failure of modern manufacturing to develop more rapidly in the midst of the plantation economy? One part of the answer lies in a simple yet powerful economic fact: the sizable comparative advantage and high returns available in the production of cotton. It was not slavery that inhibited the development of manufacturing in the ante-bellum period so much as the capitalistic tendency of southern planters to concentrate on their most rational, profit-maximizing course, cotton monoculture. Southern planters behaved no differently in responding to the short-run demands of the marketplace than their northern cousins who relied on free labor. Certainly some southerners did invest in manufacturing in their region, and a considerable number of large-scale manufacturing firms proved successful. Nevertheless, these enterprises, with a few notable exceptions, either failed to sustain their success or catered their activities to the special tastes of a local market. Only in periods of unusually low cotton or staple prices, when investment in land and field hands brought a reduced return, did the number of such enterprises increase rapidly. With the exception of the period 1783–1815 and the decade of the 1840s, manufacturing activity grew more slowly in the South than elsewhere. The profitability of investing in the system of cotton production, including the raising of slave labor, made it impossible for southern manufacturers to mobilize the capital required to match the performance of manufacturers in the most rapidly growing areas of the nation or to gain significantly on those established in the Northeast.

The high profitability of investments in cotton agriculture was not the only reason for the slow growth of southern manufacturing. Also significant was urbanization's erosion of the ability of urban slave-holders, including manufacturers, to expropriate slave income and, as a consequence, the weakening of their ability to bid against plant-ers for slaves, whose supply was fixed by the closing of the slave trade in 1808. Urban employers used slaves in a wide variety of enterprises and were able to organize them in large factory units in order to take advantage of economies of scale. Slaves worked in textile mills, iron works (led by Tredegar Iron Company of Richmond, Virginia, which employed over 400 slaves by 1861), tobacco factories, hemp mills, sugar refineries, and rice and flour mills.[19] Urbanization brought increased economic freedom for slaves, who found themselves more subject to the forces of the marketplace in all aspects of their life than did their rural counterparts. Urban slaves took advantage of the more disorganized quality of urban life to seize a greater measure of independence. In response, to make rebellion and escape less likely, urban masters granted more lenient terms. By the 1850s urbaniza-tion had so weakened the ability of masters to capture income earned by slaves that planters were easily able to outbid urban employers for slaves, despite the fact that the cities had more buoyant demands for labor in general. During the 1850s the urban slave population actu-ally declined in absolute terms. To fill their labor needs, the urban employers increasingly shifted to rural southern whites and immi-grant labor. However, immigrants were highly reluctant to compete with slaves. Consequently, urban employers could not afford to mobi-lize the labor force they desired and, thus, to raise output to the levels they desired. Because slavery offered the most attractive profits to planters and at the same time discouraged immigration, slavery raised the price of labor to manufacturers and retarded the growth of southern manufacturing. With Emancipation, however, urban em-ployers found that they could more easily lure labor from southern rural areas. During the 1860s, despite high cotton prices, the urban black population increased sharply. But slavery had already biased the southern economy toward agriculture.[20]

Although slavery inhibited urbanization and manufacturing de-velopment, it is inescapable that slavery, joined with the large-scale plantation, supported the attainment of high levels of income in the ante-bellum South. Also, it is undoubtedly true that plantation agri-culture, dependent on labor institutions such as sharecropping and tenant farming, which varied little in substance from those of slavery, was vital after the Civil War. After the 1870s levels of income in the South began to converge with the national average. Also, the expansion of cotton agriculture would most probably have continued into the 1860s had there been no Civil War. World prices for cotton continued to climb and elicited a large increase in the supply of cotton from areas outside the United States. Without the inevitable loss of markets during the Civil War, southern per-capita income probably would have been substantially higher in the 1860s and 1870s. Taking a somewhat longer view, relentless focus on cotton was economical because the demand for American cotton was strong; the real price of cotton was increasing up to the early 1920s. Furthermore, after severe structural problems during the 1920s virtually precluded continued growth, the region over the next twenty years developed an economy that was capable of yielding respectable growth rates once again.

Despite this appearance of prosperity and flexibility, an early shift to family-farm cultivation—even of cotton—on a northern pattern or a more decisive effort to expand manufacturing would have improved the economic performance of the South following the war. Perhaps a greater concentration on manufacturing and family-farm agriculture would have meant more rapid convergence of regional incomes after the war. Certainly the emphasis on surprisingly high levels of southern income masks the cost to the nation resulting from the lack of adequate investment in human capital. Much of the efficiency of the plantation is undoubtedly attributable to its ability to exploit labor by maintaining levels of living lower than those common under a free-labor, family-farm style of agriculture. (To take just one example, slave codes, made more rigid during the 1830s, forbade education for slaves.) Because the skills demanded of slave laborers were of the lowest quality, their acquisition did little to make the southern labor force more receptive to the diffusion of improved technology after the Civil War. The lack of a skilled labor force was instrumental in the failure of the South to transform itself after the demise of slavery and, indeed, lies at the heart of the contemporary poverty problem. The heritage of slavery is seen most clearly when we define our modern problem as one of absorbing the unskilled and undereducated into a society that places prime value on the attainment of skills and whose growth is tied to high levels of investment in people. If ante-bellum agriculture had been organized on a free-labor basis while still maintaining the high degree of specialization in staple production for export, per-capita income levels probably would have been lower in 1860, but the opportunities for developing indigenous industry would have come sooner than the 1930s and

1940s. Specialization per se, when it takes into account a calculation of regional comparative advantage, is not necessarily undesirable. But, tragically, by delaying real modernization until almost midway in the twentieth century, the South left the nation with the problem of coping with several centuries of neglect of the development of human resources.

THE IMPACT OF THE CIVIL WAR

Abolition of Slavery

Emancipation of the more than 3.8 million slaves would not have taken place immediately if there had been no Civil War. Slavery probably would have survived in the South for another generation. But the declining world demand for cotton during the last decades of the century, the inability of southern farmers to occupy new lands after 1890, and the collapse of the fortunes of specialized cotton farming during the 1920s guaranteed that demand for agricultural labor could not sustain the economic incentives that had supported slavery at mid-century. Of course, if slavery had survived to the end of the century, it might have spread to the North and West. Certainly, slaves could have been used profitably in both large-scale agricultural and extractive enterprises, such as cotton farms in California and western silver mines. But it is highly likely that free laborers in the West and morally concerned sectors of the growing middle class would have prevented slavery from extending into new territory, just as such a coalition did in the northern states earlier. Lieutenant Governor Oliver P. Morton of Indiana, in 1860, summed up the economic content of the popular Free-Soil sentiment: "Free labor languishes and becomes degrading when put in competition with slave labor, and idleness, poverty, and vice, among large classes of non-slaveholders, take the place of industry and thrift and virtue."[21] Whatever directions federal law might have taken, western communities could have refused to supply slaveowners with protective laws, much as Senator Stephen A. Douglas of Illinois suggested in his program of "popular sovereignty." The opportunity for slavery to expand into the developing manufacturing sector was highly unlikely. Even in the South during the buoyant 1850s urban slavery was on the wane, partly because of the difficulty that urban employers faced in expropriating income. Falling profits in agriculture would possibly have allowed urban employers to compete more effectively for slaves. But the continuing shortage of skilled labor would have created incentives for urban slaveowners, particularly manufacturers, to offer slaves the incentives of an opportunity to buy their freedom in order to improve their productivity. Moreover, the weakening economic position of slavery, the growing recognition of the need for governmental action to increase the supply of skilled labor, and increasing distaste for the institution of slavery among the free classes might well have led to programs of emancipation, most likely with compensation, undertaken by the federal government and the states, especially in the upper South.[22] At the same time that American society took steps to eradicate child labor in the factories (through child-labor and compulsory-education laws), it might have moved also to emancipate the remaining slave population. In fact, governments could have purchased all of the nation's slaves in 1861 for less than the direct costs of fighting the Civil War. (See p. 255, below.) Although the Civil War may have been the most rapid and certain way to eliminate slavery, it was not the only or least costly means to that end. The inclusion of the benefits and costs of Emancipation in a reckoning of the economic impact of the Civil War must be highly qualified and extremely tentative.

The effects of Emancipation, then, should be analyzed independently of the impact of the Civil War. The long-run benefits of the elimination of slavery are clear. Emancipation enhanced economic growth by removing slavery as a threat to the nation's system of free labor. Modern economic growth in the United States has depended heavily on individual mobility, investment in human capital, and the ability to attain improved knowledge and skills. For the South, Emancipation was the first step in a long-term restructuring that would accelerate during the 1930s. For the nation as a whole, Emancipation initiated the restoration of a massive segment of the labor supply to the ambit of the free marketplace.

The full long-term benefits of Emancipation for the welfare of the labor force were not reaped immediately. Given the impacted quality of the institution of slavery, its legal death did not guarantee that the South would make an instantaneous, smooth transition to a system of free labor. In a technical sense, Emancipation meant an enormous redistribution of capital. The ownership of over $3 billion of human capital passed from slaveowners to former slaves. But real control over that human capital did not pass as readily from slaveowner to ex-slave. Presidential Reconstruction under Andrew Johnson granted a great deal of latitude to the planters in reorganizing southern society, and the brief period of radical Reconstruction that followed had only a fleeting impact. The national government was unwilling to counter the power of the Ku Klux Klan and the other ex-Confederate guerrilla forces with sufficient Union troops. Also, it was not disposed to go beyond the constructive, but limited, experiments of the Freedmen's Bureau (which expired in 1869) to radically enhance the economic position of the ex-slaves. As a consequence, during Johnson's Reconstruction and, later, under "redeemer" governments, planters had a free hand in colluding to use the legislative process for the restriction of the economic freedom of the ex-slaves.

Under Johnson's plan of Reconstruction, state legislatures supported planters with the passage of the Black Codes. These codes regulated all aspects of the lives of the ex-slaves. They included provisions for restriction of entry into nonagricultural employments, prohibitions on landowning, arrest and hire to landlords for unemployed laborers, the requirement of signing twelve-month, binding contracts with landlords during the first ten days of January, restriction of laborers to their employer's property, and the prescription of arrest and forced labor for striking employees. The specific enactments varied from state to state but had in common the intent of continuing the expropriation of income from slaves through coercion designed to inflate the supply of agricultural labor (thus reducing the price of labor to planters) and to limit the ability of ex-slaves to bargain for higher real wages. These codes formed the basic legal framework for the participation of blacks in the southern labor market during the formative period of Reconstruction. In general they were revived after radical Reconstruction (despite the intent of the Fourteenth Amendment to the Constitution) and were phased into the Jim Crow laws of the 1880s and 1890s that limited blacks to agriculture or, in the cities, to common labor and domestic service.

The degree of exploitation of the post-bellum population remains unmeasured, but the rate of expropriated income was lower than it was under slavery. For one thing, despite the force of the Black Codes and Jim Crow laws, many ex-slaves withdrew altogether from the labor force, refused to work in labor gangs, and in other ways reduced their work effort. Women, children, and the elderly were especially apt to leave the labor force. According to one estimate, the reductions in labor-force participation and hours worked caused the per-capita work effort of the black population to fall by around one-third between 1860 and 1870.[23] It appears that ex-slaves were able to take advantage of Emancipation by taking more of their real income as leisure time—another measure of the exploitative nature of slavery as well as an indicator of the benefits of Emancipation for the slaves.

The institutions of sharecropping and tenant farming, moreover, offered some advantages to the ex-slaves, who actively sought such arrangements to enhance their control over their working conditions.[24] Under sharecropping contracts the sharecroppers typically turned over between one-half and two-thirds of their harvested crops to their landlords. The landlord's share appears quite large but the landlord provided land, seed, fertilizer, tools, food, and managerial advice (including marketing advice). And it must be remembered that ex-slaves were largely illiterate, slightly skilled (perhaps only one-sixth having even a minimal skill), lacking in managerial experience, and bereft of material assets. Thus, sharecropping bound together laborers and the owners of land and capital in a common sharing of risks and returns.

No one has measured in a compelling way the exploitation possible under sharecropping, but it appears that the share of agricultural income sharecroppers earned came far closer to what their productivity earned than did slave "wages." The combination of increased freedom of action for the ex-slaves, despite the Black Codes and other restrictive laws, and the incentives that landowners had for increasing the productivity of agricultural labor yielded significant relative gains to the ex-slaves.[25] One indication of these gains is the fact that a large number of ex-slaves were able to earn enough to accumulate savings for the purchase of the land they worked. By 1910, black farmers owned close to one-third of the land they cultivated.

Despite the improvements that Emancipation brought to the welfare of the ex-slaves, their levels of living remained substantially lower than that of agricultural labor in general. That was so not only because of exploitation and low productivity but also as a consequence of a slowdown in the rate of growth of world-wide demand for cotton. As a result of retardation in the British textile industry, demand for cotton increased more slowly than before the war. Cotton remained the most profitable crop for southern farmers, but its sale could no longer keep per-capita income growing as rapidly in the South as elsewhere in the nation. Between 1860 and 1880, the sluggish demand for cotton, as well as the declining supply of labor, contributed to a fall in southern per-capita income from 72 percent of the national average in 1860 to only 51 percent in 1880. British demand recovered during the last two decades of the century but only slowly. Consequently, while per-capita income in the South increased between 1880 and 1900, it remained at about 51 percent of the national average.[26] Often, Emancipation has taken the blame for the poor postwar performance of southern income. But the decline would have taken place anyway as a consequence of the continued dependence of southern agriculture on international demand for its key commodity. On the whole, Emancipation significantly advanced the economic well-being of the ex-slaves and, indeed, of the South at large.

Costs of the War Effort

The Civil War had its most direct impact on the economic life of the nation through the destruction it wrought. There can be no doubt that the devastation handicapped the growth of the economy. The costs of the military enterprises and wartime destruction, including over 600,000 soldiers dead and more than 500,000 wounded (together more than 3.5 percent of the U.S. population in 1860), were staggering. A recent study estimates the direct costs: military expenditures and the cost of lost property and lives (calculated by estimating the value of the wages those who died could have expected to earn had they survived). The sum is $3.4 billion for the North and $3.3 billion for the South. Added together, they equal the entire national product for at least one and a half years at the end of the 1850s.[27] Incomplete as such estimates necessarily are—particularly as estimates of the human wastage—they still indicate the great damage the economy suffered from the war. And it should be remembered that although, in time, American society replaced the physical capacity destroyed and paid the debts that had to be incurred in order to rebuild the economy, the wartime losses were permanent. Moreover, the growth of the nation's productive capacity and income suffered a marked retardation largely as a consequence of wartime destruction. The setback was marked during the 1860s. In that decade the rates of growth of commodity output, value added in manufacturing, labor productivity, and per-capita output were lower than during any other decade of the century. In fact, the productivity of labor actually declined—a unique phenomenon for a decennial period.

A complete inventory of the economic cost of the wartime disruption defies an accurate evaluation. In addition to the direct costs, one must count the less measurable, but no less real, costs of the prolonged departure from normal economic life, the extended political instability, and the untold opportunities precluded by concentration on the war effort. An example of these disruptions is the loss by northern manufacturers of their large southern markets. Southern demands for consumer goods used by both slave and freemen had supported the development of northern industry, and the sharp reduction of such demands retarded the rate of growth of manufacturing. Another example is the distortion of the labor market caused by the manpower needs of the Union army. At the same time that manufacturers had to meet wartime needs, they had to employ men who were inexperienced or lacked adequate skills. A severe reduction in labor productivity resulted. A recent estimate is that all of these "indirect" costs totaled almost $15 billion. But such estimates must rely heavily on the uncertain guesswork required to speculate about the rates at which the American economy might have grown had there been no Civil War. Precise estimates add little to the powerful impressionistic evidence that the chaos of the Civil War seriously interrupted the processes of economic growth.[28]

A "Second American Revolution"?

Some historians attach great significance to the indirect influence of the Civil War on the long-run course of the American economy. Most influential are Charles A. Beard and Mary R. Beard, who regard the Civil War as a "social war" important enough in its impact to be called the "Second American Revolution." The results of the war included, in their words, "the unquestioned establishment of a new power in the government" and "vast changes in the arrangement of classes, in the accumulation and distribution of wealth, in the course of industrial development." More specifically, the Beards suggest that "the supreme outcome of the civil strife was the destruction of the planting aristocracy which, with the aid of northern farmers and mechanics, had practically ruled the United States for a generation," and "the undisputed triumph of a new combination of power: northern capitalists and free farmers who emerged from the conflict richer and more numerous than ever."[29] The embodiment of this triumph for the Beards was the passage of a wide range of federal legislation, including the creation of a national banking system, the adoption of a greenback currency, the raising of high tariffs to protect domestic manufacturing, the subsidizing of transcontinental railroad building with massive federal land grants and loans, the passage of the Homestead Act, and the provision of a contract-labor program. Collectively, these measures constituted the Republican economic program, a program long discussed in Congress and in the nation but enacted only after secession had truncated Democratic opposition.

Historians have cast a great deal of doubt upon the political dimensions of the Beards' interpretation, pointing out that the Civil War had a far more modest effect on political alliances, that economic interest groups were not nearly as coherent or cohesive as the Beards suggest, and that the enactment of the Republican program would have occurred eventually without a Civil War. For example, political historians have noted the agreement of northern and southern conservatives, even representatives of the planter class, on many principles of the Whig economic program (including the need for federal subsidies for transcontinental railroads). As early as 1876 these conservatives were able to reestablish a national coalition behind the Republican economic program. Economic historians have also tended to discount the Beards' interpretation, arguing that America's commitment to industrialization was both firm and long-standing by the time the nation was rent by civil strife and that the Republican program had little impact on economic growth.

Economic historians who dismiss the Beards' argument must confront, however, the acceleration of per-capita income and, to a lesser extent, industrialization after the Civil War. The key fact is that per-capita output grew more rapidly between 1870 and 1900 than it had grown between 1840 and 1860. The annual rate for the end of the century was 2.1 percent, as contrasted with 1.45 percent for the last two decades of the ante-bellum period. This acceleration probably meant that the economy was, in part, making up for lost time, resulting from the release of pent-up southern demand for northern manufactured goods after the resumption of a healthy rate of growth during the 1870s and the reduction of high wartime excise taxes on virtually all major articles of popular consumption. A catching-up phenomenon is also suggested by the fact that annual rates of per-capita commodity output were the same for the entire period 1860–1900 as for 1840–1860. In other words, for the nation as a whole the unusually high growth rate of the 1870s was offset by the sluggish performance of the 1860s. But in the northern states a different pattern emerged in that the increases of the 1870s more than made up for the slackness of the 1860s. In the North, however, the unusually high annual rate of growth (2.6 percent) during the 1870s produced a rate of growth for the period 1860–1880 that was substantially higher (1.75 percent) than for the prewar period 1840–1860 (1.3 percent), suggesting that the North's economy in the 1870s was growing much more rapidly than was necessary to catch up to a "normal" rate of growth. In fact, the high northern growth rate continued, averaging 1.9 percent annually between 1880 and 1900.[30]

The acceleration of industrialization is limited only to the 1880s. No evidence of catching up appears since the incremental increase in the share of the labor force industrialized was less during the 1870s than in any other decade since 1810 (with the exception of the 1860s). But the 1880s recorded one of the two most dramatic incremental changes in the share of the labor force industrialized: during the decade, the proportion of the labor force in nonagricultural employments increased from 48.7 percent to 57.3 percent.[31]

Trying to explain the acceleration in the pace of economic growth and industrialization in terms of the various aspects of the Republican program, however, yields only meager results. The Homestead

Act, although encouraging the migration of free labor into certain areas of the trans-Mississippi West, did little to reduce the costs of settlement and capital formation necessary in an increasingly "industrial" agricultural sector. In national terms, the acts of subsidy to farm-building entrepreneurs may well have retarded growth by luring romantic Americans away from more productive opportunities in agriculture, as well as from manufacturing, to the settlement of marginal lands. High postwar tariffs also did little to increase productivity. They probably did protect the wages and jobs of workers in certain uncompetitive industries, but the economy was mature enough to have proceeded along the path toward free trade, which had been pointed out in the 1850s. By and large, American manufacturers could compete successfully with their European counterparts, and the Republican tariffs served only to induce misallocations of resources and reduce real incomes without providing any genuine protection for infant industries. The benefits of contract laborers were also obscure. Although used in prominent labor disputes as strike breakers, their numbers were insignificant. The operation of the marketplace for labor received virtually no aid from the institution of contract labor to meet the needs of manufacturers. It is reasonably clear that federal land grants to railroads were justified as public investments in that the rate of return realized by society at large from the diversion of resources represented by the grants was high. On the other hand, these grants made only a very modest contribution to economic growth. For example, the grants to the Union Pacific Railroad, the major recipient of federal land, apparently produced an increase of only .01 percent of national product.[32] Moreover, although the Civil War hastened the decision to build the transcontinentals, it was not a necessary political prerequisite for the land grants; the pre-Civil War North-South debate was over the location of the first transcontinental, not over its desirability. It is equally difficult to find any major growth impetus in most Civil War financial legislation. The greenback issues to finance government wartime expenditures undoubtedly eased the monetary pinch of the war years, but in the expansive postwar years their issue was sharply curtailed. Also, the creation of a national banking system undoubtedly brought greater order and dependability to national capital markets, but it was not a drastic departure from the regional and local efforts that characterized the ante-bellum period. The new system still failed to provide a lender of last resort (an institution for bailing out banks with emergency loans in periods of crisis) and, in fact, itself contributed to economic instability and possibly a dampening of economic growth.

The strongest case that can be made for the Civil War's role in accelerating economic growth rests on the effects of the deficit financing of the war and the subsequent effort to pay off the wartime debt. Tax revenues paid for only a minor portion of the federal wartime costs. In the main, Lincoln's administration resorted to borrowing, and because the Treasury was faced with the problems of a poorly developed domestic market for federal securities and a lack of European confidence in Union victory, the federal government in organizing bond-sale drives came to rely heavily on the services of a single entrepreneur of capital markets, Jay Cooke. Cooke's highly successful promotional campaigns helped to educate the American public to save at higher rates; by the 1880s that higher rate of saving would support the capital needs of massive new enterprise. At the same time, techniques of marketing emerged from the process of placing the federal debt which, when institutionalized, would bring together investors and capital seekers on a scale hitherto unrealized in America. Supported by such innovations in capital markets, the economy maintained the great increase in the share of national product absorbed by capital investment that occurred between 1834–1843 and 1899–1908. Nonetheless, the precise impact of Civil War finance on capital market innovation must remain obscure, for historians have been unable to determine what progress this innovation would have taken had there been no Civil War. However, since financiers had been active in devising tactics for mobilizing savings as early as the 1850s, one can quite reasonably speculate that the capital-hungry economy of the late nineteenth century would have induced financial market improvements even without the Civil War experience.

Liquidation of the massive war debt, begun in 1866, also may have promoted capital investment. By using consumption taxes (excises) to finance the debt and interest payments, according to the argument, the Republican national leadership transferred significant amounts of capital to investors. In effect, this tax system produced forced savings that would not have been generated otherwise. Moreover, the debt retirement allowed individuals to replace nonproductive war debts with claims on more productive assets. This argument proceeds to link Civil War policies with an increased supply of capital, a decline in the relative price of investment goods, a rise in the rates of capital formation, and the enhancement of labor productivity and per-capita output. One estimate suggests that debt retirement and interest payments accounted for as much as one-half of the rise in the share of the national economic product devoted to capital formation between the 1850s and the 1870s.[33] But this estimate is tentative. It is not based on a full consideration of other factors that may have increased savings rates and, hence, levels of capital formation. For example, the growing importance of a middle-class population meant that American society was shifting its spending preferences away from current consumption to saving for future spending. Also, middle-class families may have acquired stronger tastes for saving and, therefore, saved at higher rates. And even if the Civil War debt-retirement program affected the supply of capital in an important way, its impact on capital formation may have been substantially less than the effects of the shifting *demand* for capital goods. Technological changes focusing on the mechanization of manufacturing activities encouraged manufacturers to favor capital more heavily—quite independently of the falling price of capital induced by its increasing supply.[34] In sum, while the retirement of the Civil War debt quite likely accelerated rates of capital formation, the importance of the effect must be regarded as highly uncertain.

There is relatively little solid evidence to suggest that the Civil War caused a marked acceleration in the rate of growth following the war. Only government activity in financial markets remains as a possible candidate for accelerating per-capita output, and the case for it remains tentative, at best. Even if the creation, management, and liquidation of the public debt did accelerate growth rates somewhat, a historian would be hard pressed to revive the concept of the Civil War as the "Second American Revolution" on the basis of that evidence alone. Even if the Civil War should be regarded as an event that helped quicken the nation's rate of growth, the war cannot be said to have freed the nation from a semifeudal past, thus paving the way for a new industrial order. Moreover, the significant structural departures that came to characterize the late nineteenth century developed independently of the Civil War.

NOTES

1. The classic statement of the "traditional" view of the economic character of slavery is to be found in the recently reprinted Ulrich B. Philipps, *American Negro Slavery* (Baton Rouge: Louisiana State University Press, 1966). The modern restatement of this general analysis, *without* Philipps' implicit assumption of Negro inferiority, is best expressed in Eugene D. Genovese, *The Political Economy of Slavery* (New York: Pantheon, 1965).

2. This conclusion does not necessarily follow, however, from a finding that slavery was not particularly "economic." If southern whites, under sanction of the federal government, had deemed preservation of slavery important enough, for nonpecuniary reasons, they could have continued to ignore any economic irrationality of their labor system.

3. Market value is construed as equivalent to expectations of future flows in income, discounted to obtain present value, resulting from the ownership of slaves.

4. Yasukichi Yasuba, "The Profitability and Viability of Plantation Slavery in the United States," *Economic Studies Quarterly*, 12 (September 1961), 60–67.

5. The latest and best estimate is that between 1808 and 1861, slave imports into the United States averaged around 1,000 per year, or about one-third of the rate during the eighteenth century. Philip Curtin, *The Atlantic Slave Trade: A Census* (Madison, Wis.: University of Wisconsin Press, 1969), pp. 231–234, 265–269.

6. The standard analysis remains Alfred H. Conrad and John R. Meyer, *The Economics of Slavery* (Chicago: Aldine, 1964), pp. 43–114. Refinements and reinforcement are found in Edward Saraydar, "A Note on the Profitability of Ante-Bellum Slavery," *Southern Economic Journal*, 30 (April 1964), 325–332; Richard Sutch, "The Profitability of Ante-Bellum Slavery Revisited," *Southern Economic Journal*, 30 (April 1964), 365–377; Robert Evans, Jr., "The Economics of American Negro Slavery," in National Bureau of Economic Research, *Aspects of Labor Economics* (Princeton, N.J.: Princeton University Press, 1962), pp. 185–243; James D. Foust and Dale E. Swan, "Productivity and Profitability of Antebellum Slave Labor: A Micro-Approach," in William N. Parker (ed.), *The Structure of the Cotton Economy of the Antebellum South* (Washington, D.C.: Agricultural History Society, 1970), pp. 39–62.

7. Robert W. Fogel and Stanley L. Engerman, *Time on the Cross: The Economics of American Negro Slavery* (Boston: Little, Brown, 1974), pp. 67–78.

8. Jack E. Eblen, "Growth of the Black Population in *Antebellum* America, 1820–1860," *Population Studies*, 26 (July 1972), 273–289, and "New Estimates of the Vital Rates of the United States Black Population During the Nineteenth Century," *Demography*, 11 (May 1974), 301–319.

9. Fogel and Engerman, *op. cit.*, pp. 107 ff.

10. Paul A. David and Peter Temin, "Slavery: The Progressive Institution?" *Journal of Economic History*, 34 (1974), 739–783.

11. See Eugene D. Genovese, *Roll, Jordan, Roll: The World the Slaves Made* (New York: Pantheon, 1974; and Herbert G. Gutman, *The Black Family in Slavery and Freedom, 1750–1925* (New York: Pantheon, 1976).

12. For the best survey of these tactics, see Kenneth M. Stampp, *The Peculiar Institution: Slavery in the Ante-Bellum South* (New York: Knopf, 1956), pp. 86–140.

13. Fogel and Engerman, *op. cit.*, pp. 192 ff., infer too much about the slave experience from their measure of efficiency of slave labor, and, in any case, their estimates of efficiency are too high as a consequence of their underestimate of both the length of the southern growing season and the participation rates of slaves. See also David and Temin, *op. cit.*

14. For the specific data consult Richard A. Easterlin, "Regional Income Trends, 1840–1950," in Seymour Harris (ed.), *American Economic History* (New York: McGraw-Hill, 1961), pp. 525–547.

15. For estimates that exclude slaves and slave incomes, see Stanley L. Engerman, "The Effects of Slavery upon the Southern Economy: A Review of the Recent Debate," *Explorations in Entrepreneurial History*, 4 (Winter 1967), 71–97.

16. Robert E. Gallman, "Trends in the Size Distribution of Wealth in the Nineteenth Century: Some Speculations," in Lee Soltow (ed.), *Six Papers on the Size Distribution of Wealth and Income, Studies in Income and Wealth*, Vol. 33 (New York: National Bureau of Economic Research, 1969), pp. 22–23; Gavin Wright, " 'Economic Democracy' and the Concentration of Agricultural Wealth in the Cotton South, 1850–1860," in Parker, *op. cit.*, pp. 63–93.

17. Fred Bateman *et al.*, "Large-Scale Manufacturing in the South and West, 1850–1860," *Business History Review*, 45 (Spring 1971), 1–17.

18. Engerman, *op. cit.*, p. 91.

19. Robert Starobin, *Industrial Slavery in the Old South* (New York: Oxford University Press, 1970), pp. 3–34, 146–189; Charles B. Dew, *Ironmaker to the Confederacy: Joseph R. Anderson and the Tredegar Iron Works* (New Haven: Yale University Press, 1966).

20. The standard history of urban slavery remains Richard Wade, *Slavery in the Cities: The South, 1820–1860* (Chicago: University of Chicago Press, 1964). One should also consult Claudia Goldin, *Urban Slavery in the American South, 1820–1860: A Quantitative History* (Chicago: University of Chicago Press, 1976).

21. Quoted by Eric Foner, *Free Soil, Free Labor, Free Men: The Ideology of the Republican Party Before the Civil War* (New York: Oxford University Press, 1970), p. 57.

22. For the argument that during the 1850s the Old South's stake in slavery in the New South waned, see Laurence J. Kotlikoff and Sebastian E. Pinera, "The Old South's Stake in the Inter-Regional Movement of Slaves, 1850–1860," *Journal of Economic History*, 37 (June 1977), 434–450.

23. Roger Ransom and Richard Sutch, "The Impact of the Civil War and of Emancipation on Southern Agriculture," *Explorations in Economic History*, 12 (January 1975), 1–28.

24. For a close study of the development of sharecropping, see Roger Ransom and Richard Sutch, *One Kind of Freedom: The Economic Consequences of Emancipation* (New York: Cambridge University Press, 1977).

25. For analyses emphasizing the position contribution of sharecropping and tenant farming, see Joseph D. Reid, Jr., "Sharecropping as an Understandable Market Response—the Postbellum South," *Journal of Economic History*, 33 (March 1973), 103–130, and Stephen De Canio, "Productivity and Income Distribution in the Post-Bellum South," *Journal of Economic History*, 34 (June 1974), 422–446.

26. On the significance of the demand for cotton, see Gavin Wright, "Cotton Competition and the Post-Bellum Recovery of the American South," *Journal of Economic History,* 34 (September 1974), 610–635.

27. Claudia G. Goldin and Frank D. Lewis, "The Economic Cost of the American Civil War: Estimates and Implications," *Journal of Economic History,* 35 (June 1975), 299–326.

28. Goldin and Lewis, *op. cit.,* are responsible for the estimate of indirect costs. Peter Temin has pointed out the uncertainties that necessarily attend such estimation procedures by suggesting that Goldin and Lewis grossly underestimate the effects of Emancipation and of the declining demand for cotton in calculating the indirect costs to the South. Peter Temin, "The Post-Bellum Recovery of the South and the Cost of the Civil War," *Journal of Economic History,* 36 (December 1976), 898–907.

29. Charles A. Beard and Mary R. Beard, *The Rise of American Civilization,* Vol. II (New York: Macmillan, 1930), pp. 53, 99.

30. A thorough discussion of the rates of economic growth, 1840–1900, can be found in Stanley L. Engerman, "The Economic Impact of the Civil War," *Explorations in Economic History,* 3 (Spring 1966), 176–199.

31. Eric E. Lampard, "The Evolving System of Cities in the United States: Urbanization and Economic Development," in Harvey S. Perloff and Lowdon Wingo, Jr. (eds.), *Issues in Urban Economics* (Baltimore: Johns Hopkins Press, 1968), p. 117.

32. Lloyd J. Mercer, "Land Grants to American Railroads: Social Costs or Social Benefit?" *Business History Review,* 43 (Summer 1969), 134–151, and "Rates of Return for Land-Grant Railroads: The Central Pacific System," *Journal of Economic History,* 30 (September 1970), 602–626.

33. Jeffrey G. Williamson, "Watersheds and Turning Points: Conjectures on the Long-Term Impact of Civil War Financing," *Journal of Economic History,* 34 (September 1974), 636–661.

34. The outward shift in the demand function for capital helps explain why the long-term interest rate did not drop as dramatically as one would predict simply from looking at the increasing supply of long-term capital. For a suggestion of this, see Moses Abramovitz and Paul A. David, "Reinterpreting Economic Growth: Parables and Realities," *American Economic Review,* 63 (May 1973), 428–439.

SUGGESTED READINGS

Slavery

Books

Bruchey, Stuart (ed.) *Cotton and the Growth of the American Economy.* New York: Harcourt, Brace and World, 1967.

Conrad, Alfred H., and John R. Meyer. *The Economics of Slavery.* Chicago: Aldine, 1964.

David, Paul A., *et al. Reckoning with Slavery.* New York: Oxford University Press, 1976.

Fogel, Robert W., and Stanley L. Engerman. *Time on the Cross: The Economics of American Negro Slavery.* Boston: Little, Brown, 1974.

Genovese, Eugene D. *The Political Economy of Slavery.* New York: Pantheon, 1965.

Goldin, Claudia. *Urban Slavery in the American South, 1820–1860: A Quantitative History.* Chicago: University of Chicago Press, 1976.

Parker, William N. (ed.). *The Structure of the Cotton Economy of the Antebellum South.* Washington, D.C.: Agricultural History Society, 1970.

Starobin, Robert S. *Industrial Slavery in the Old South.* New York: Oxford University Press, 1970.

Woodman, Harold D. (ed.). *Slavery and the Southern Economy.* New York: Harcourt, Brace and World, 1966.

Articles

Conrad, Alfred H., *et al.* "Slavery as an Obstacle to Economic Growth in the United States: A Panel Discussion," *Journal of Economic History,* 27 (December 1967), 518–560.

Engerman, Stanley L. "The Effects of Slavery upon the Southern Economy," *Explorations in Entrepreneurial History,* 4 (Winter 1967), 71–97.

Evans, Robert, Jr. "The Economics of American Negro Slavery," in National Bureau of Economic Research, *Aspects of Labor Economics.* Princeton,.N.J.: Princeton University Press, 1962.

Foust, James D., and Dale E. Swan. "Productivity and Profitability of Antebellum Slave Labor: A Micro-Approach," in William N. Parker (ed.), *The Structure of the Cotton Economy of the Antebellum South.* Washington, D.C.: Agricultural History Society, 1970, pp. 39–62.

Gunderson, Gerald. "Southern Ante-bellum Income Reconsidered," *Explorations in Economic History,* 10 (Winter 1973), 151–176.

Rothstein, Morton. "The Ante-Bellum South as a Dual Economy: A Tentative Hypothesis," *Agricultural History,* 41 (October 1967), 373–382.

Wright, Gavin. " 'Economic Democracy' and the Concentration of Agricultural Wealth in the Cotton South, 1850–1860," in William N. Parker (ed.), *The Structure of the Cotton Economy of the Antebellum South.* Washington, D.C.: Agricultural History Society, 1970, pp. 63–93.

Yasuba, Yasukichi. "The Profitability and Viability of Plantation Slavery in the United States," *Economic Studies Quarterly,* 12 (September 1961), 60–67.

Civil War

Books

Andreano, Ralph (ed.). *The Economic Impact of the American Civil War,* 2nd ed. Cambridge, Mass.: Schenkman, 1967.

Gates, Paul W. *Agriculture and the Civil War.* New York: Knopf, 1965.

Gilchrist, David T., and W. David Lewis (eds.). *Economic Change in the Civil War Era.* Greenville, Del.: Eleutherian Mills-Hagley Foundation, 1965.

Ransom, Roger, and Richard Sutch. *One Kind of Freedom: The Economic Consequences of Emancipation.* New York: Cambridge University Press, 1977.

Articles

Goldin, Claudia G., and Frank D. Lewis. "The Economic Cost of the American Civil War: Estimates and Implications," *Journal of Economic History,* 35 (June 1975), 299–326.

Temin, Peter. "The Post-Bellum Recovery of the South and the Cost of the Civil War," *Journal of Economic History,* 36 (December 1976), 898–907.

Williamson, Jeffrey G. "Watersheds and Turning Points: Conjectures on the Long-Term Impact of Civil War Financing," *Journal of Economic History,* 34 (September 1974), 636–661.

part three

THE ERA OF INDUSTRIAL MATURITY

Most of the central economic trends established during the early industrial revolution continued after the Civil War. Most importantly, per-capita income continued to increase rapidly. In fact, during the period between the Civil War and World War I, the rate of growth accelerated over the period 1840–1860. Nonetheless, during the postwar era the industrial revolution showed distinct signs of maturing. The birth rate underwent a marked deceleration and the rate of population growth eased. After a period of growing instability, which extended into the 1890s, the economy became significantly more stable. The pace of structural change—industrialization, urbanization, and the settlement of new land—slowed and provided less of an explanation of the gain in per-capita income than it had during early industrialization. Meanwhile, imbalanced technological change and sharp jumps in rates of saving dominated the process of economic growth. As the economy came to rely on higher rates of capital formation, it developed a stronger need for skilled labor and rewarded that labor accordingly. Largely as a consequence, American society reversed the trend toward an increasing concentration of income that had prevailed since colonial times. And efficiency in mobilizing capital led America to begin significant export of capital abroad. Accompanying all of these developments were institutional changes that contributed to the economic discontinuities and further justify designation of the era as one of maturation—of passage to the character and pace of economic change that have tended to prevail until the present day.

9

The Substance and Structure of Industrial Revolution, 1870-1914

THE PACE OF ECONOMIC GROWTH

Commonly, the waning decades of the nineteenth century have not received kind treatment from historians. The period has been depicted as one of spiritual malaise, fraught with inner corruption and bleak in comparison with bordering eras of moral enthusiasm and crusading for social justice. However valid such characterizations of the moral tone of the era might be, the period was certainly one of widening economic opportunity and substantial prosperity. In fact, the period was one of passage to a higher plateau for the rate of increase in per-capita output. Economic growth had, of course, been impressive before the Civil War, but per-capita output increased only slightly more than 1 percent per year during the years 1800–1860, reaching an average of 1.45 percent per year during the dynamic 1840s and 1850s. By way of contrast, the annual rate of per-capita output growth reached 2.1 percent for the period 1870–1900. During this period the growth of per-capita output reached the "modern" rate of between 1.5 and 2.0 percent per year—"modern" in the sense that the economy has tended to maintain that rate down to the present.

The passage to the new plateau was not entirely smooth, however. The most rapid period of growth in per-capita product occurred during the 1870s and early 1880s. (See Table 17.) To some extent this high rate resulted from the process of compensation for Civil War disturbances. But during the late 1890s, after a period of decelerated growth and the depression of the mid-1890s, per-capita product resumed a rate of increase well above mid-nineteenth-century levels. A recession in 1914–1915, the disruptions of World War I, and the serious depression of 1920–1921 intervened, but the 1920s witnessed another return to the modern rate.

Gains in per-capita product can come from either an increase in an average person's ability to produce goods and services or an increase in the amount of time an average person works. Most of the gains registered in this period came from increasing productivity per man-hour. (See Table 17.) Before World War I the number of hours worked per person did contribute to increases in per-capita product as a consequence of the growing share of women who worked outside the home and the high concentration of immigrants in those age groups that worked at the highest rates. (Two-thirds were between the ages of fifteen and forty.) But even during the late 1890s and the early part of the next decade, when these factors were most influential, their contribution was less than half that of productivity per hour of work. After World War I, the declining significance of immigration and the growing ability of workers to take real income gains in the form of money led to declines in the number of hours an average person worked. Dominating the growth of per-capita product throughout the period was the growth of product per hour worked.

The advance of product per hour worked was more stable than the growth of per-capita product, which was influenced by the volatile fluctuations in worker effort. Although suffering some retardation in the late 1880s and adversely affected by the depression of the 1890s, product per hour grew relatively steadily until the recession of 1914–1915 and the period of economic troubles produced by

TABLE 17   GROWTH OF THE U. S. PRIVATE ECONOMY (AVERAGE ANNUAL RATES)

	National Product Per Capita	Man-Hours Per Capita	National Product Per Man-Hour
1874–1884	3.8%	0.6%	3.2%
1884–1894	0.6	0.0	0.6
1889–1899	2.3	0.0	2.3
1894–1904	2.9	0.9	2.0
1899–1909	2.2	0.4	1.8
1904–1914	1.1	−0.1	1.2
1909–1919	0.8	0.1	0.7
1914–1924	1.4	−0.6	2.0
1919–1929	1.8	−0.7	2.5

Source: U.S. Bureau of Economic Analysis, *Long Term Growth, 1860–1970* (Washington, D.C.: U.S. Government Printing Office, 1973), pp. 107 ff.

World War I. Subsequently, during the 1920s, it resumed its assured growth.

CAPITAL FORMATION AND TECHNOLOGICAL CHANGE

Behind the gains in per-capita output and the productivity of labor were massive additions to the nation's stock of capital goods. Of course, much of the capital formation was for net additions to that stock. But as the stock of capital goods grew, an increasingly large share of both national product and capital formation was necessary to replace capital goods, especially industrial equipment, that were either worn out or obsolete. Consequently, a decreasing share of savings was available for net additions to capital stock. In fact, beginning in the late nineteenth century the share of national product devoted to *net* capital formation has declined—a reversal of the upward trend of the mid-nineteenth century, which peaked in the 1880s. The growing demands for replacement of capital goods has frequently created doubts that savers and investors would be able to mobilize a constantly increasing share of national product for capital formation and fears that worker productivity and per-capita income would cease to grow as a result. However, the expansion of national product has been swift enough, in contrast with the growth of the labor force and population, to sustain not only a rising level of capital stock but also a continuing substitution of capital for labor. Between 1869 and the onset of the Great Depression, the capital stock available to average members of the labor force grew roughly 20 percent each decade. In 1869 the average worker had available over $2,000 of capital goods; by 1919 he had well over $5,000.

The era deserves to be dubbed the "age of capital"; the process of industrial revolution during the period could be described largely in terms of the substitution of capital for labor. Certainly it would have been, in theory, possible to enjoy increasing per-capita production without changes in the ratio of capital to labor. The quality of labor and capital might have improved at comparable rates, or technical and organizational improvements might have drawn equally heavily on capital and labor. But the available evidence suggests that capital formation accounted for most of the growth of real product during the period 1869–1919.[1] Some recent studies have tended to reduce emphasis on the general contribution of capital to economic growth and to augment the role played by labor. But these studies fail to adjust their measures of capital input for the quality of capital services, thus underestimating the contributions of that factor.[2] Another set of studies, which make such adjustments, suggests that the role of capital input explains almost half of the increase of national product even for the period since 1929, when tangible capital has played a diminished part in the growth of output.[3]

Much of the capital formation during this period supported the rapid build-up of the nation's transportation system. In three great waves of expansion (1868–1873, 1879–1883, and 1886–1893), railroad construction more than quadrupled the railroad mileage that had been in place before the Civil War. (See Figure 16.) The construction projects elaborated existing systems in older regions and increasingly brought railroad services to less developed areas, particularly through the building of the transcontinental lines. After 1893 the rate of increase in mileage declined, but track mileage still almost doubled by 1920 and railroads made heavy investments in better equipment. Among the items of improved equipment were freight cars that were larger and made of steel, locomotives that were also larger and had more efficient boilers, Pullman cars, and George Westinghouse's package of air brakes, car couplers, and a switching system. With the last items, railroads were able to run longer, swifter trains. Much of the new mileage was devoted to building passenger lines in and around the nation's largest cities. By 1920 in this preautomobile era, most of the nation's working people relied on these lines for a round trip each day. And the rapidly growing urban transit lines required massive investments in the electrical facilities from which they drew their power.

The building of urban transit lines and their supporting equipment were part of the larger development of an infrastructure that served the needs of the burgeoning urban populations and required the investment of large quantities of capital. Beginning in the 1870s, road systems in large urban areas expanded, and, at the same time, capital-intensive asphalt began to replace the more labor-intensive bricks and cobblestones on city streets. In the 1890s, Portland cement, which was structurally stronger than asphalt, came into use, particularly for bridges and drainage systems. Cities also began to build elaborate water and sewage systems, lighting systems (relying first on gas and then, beginning in the 1890s, on electricity for the incandescent lamps invented by Thomas Alva Edison in 1882), bridges, and, after the refinement of steel reinforcement during the 1880s, structures that rose over ten stories.

Most important to the growing capital intensity of the economy were the efforts of manufacturers to substitute capital for labor and to improve the quality of capital goods. Of course, to some extent the increasing amount of capital available per worker simply reflected the fact that manufacturing, with its heavy capital requirements, grew more rapidly than the economy as a whole. Moreover, within

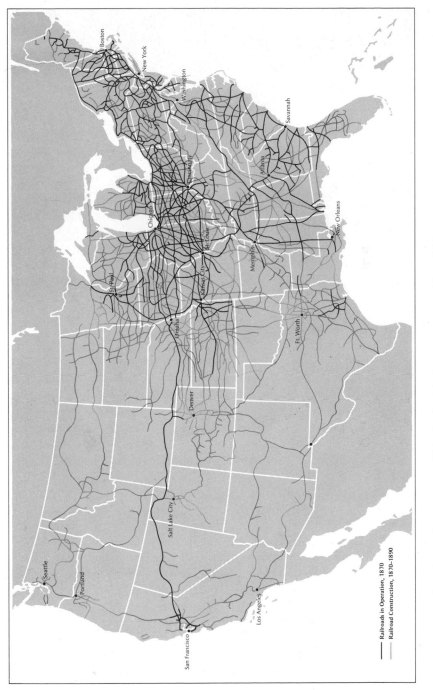

FIGURE 16: *Railroads in Operation, 1870; Railroad Construction, 1870–1890*

Railroads in Operation, 1870
Railroad Construction, 1870–1890

RAILROAD COACH CAR, 1886. Speed, convenience, and low cost produced a dramatic increase in railroad travel by people of modest means.

the manufacturing sector the most rapidly growing industries were
the iron and steel industries, which were unusually intensive users of
capital. But the general increase in capital intensity also resulted
from the new labor-saving machinery adopted by the "growth" industries. In the steel industry, for example, the introduction of the
Bessemer and open-hearth processes, increases in the scale of blast
furnaces, and the use of conveyors and hoists not only augmented the
quantity of capital used per worker but also enhanced worker productivity. Before World War I the modern automobile industry appeared and utilized new labor-saving, capital-intensive methods.
Most important was the moving assembly line, introduced by Henry
Ford in 1913. It promoted capital intensity by requiring electric
power and machine tools that could rapidly cut and stamp out the
parts of automobile bodies. Such changes, focused on the mechanization of production, affected less capital-intensive, more traditional
industries as well. In the textile industry, the adoption of the North-
rup automatic loom in 1895 reduced labor requirements by allowing
empty bobbins to be replaced automatically and to stop looms automatically when threads broke. The clothing industry had begun to
use sewing machines during the 1850s, but after the Civil War it
adopted higher-speed machines and supplemented them with cutting machines that could slice through several thicknesses of cloth

BROOKLYN BRIDGE, 1881. After fourteen years of construction and the deaths of twenty workmen, the Brooklyn Bridge opened in 1883 as the world's longest suspension bridge.

HENRY FORD'S MOVING ASSEMBLY LINE, 1913. Here, at the end of the line, the stamped bodies were dropped on chassis.

and thus facilitate mass production of garments. In shoe production, a variety of machines assumed almost all of the basic tasks. In the meat packing industry, the development of refrigeration techniques allowed the expansion of assembly (or disassembly, more correctly) line practices and meant an increase in capital investment per worker. All such innovations stimulated the growth of the machine tool industry, which also intensified the use of capital in its operations. The industry adopted high-speed cutting tools and presses that were driven by electricity. Adoption of the capital-intensive innovations required mechanization, which in turn shifted the demand for power away from low capital-intensive horse and water power toward steam and electrical power. The shift to steam necessitated the building of larger, more efficient steam engines. The shift to electricity required electrical power plants (the first major one being Edison's New York plant completed in 1882), dams for hydroelectric power, and capital-intensive techniques in coal mining, which met at least 80 percent of industrial energy needs until 1920. (These techniques included the use of compressed air power, the mechanization of drilling and hauling, and blasting with dynamite.)

The development and adoption of these capital-intensive techniques were responses both to the intrinsic bias of late nineteenth-century technological change toward capital and to shifts in the relative prices of the factors of production. The relative importance of these two elements remains undetermined, but both were at work. Even if the relative prices of capital and labor had not shifted, employers would have increased the ratio of their capital inputs to their labor since this method of reducing total factor costs was the primary one provided by nineteenth-century advances in technology. Reinforcing the bias of technological change toward capital was a decline in the price of capital relative to that of labor and of land, a decline that persisted until the first decade of the twentieth century. Within a given level of technological achievement, these shifts created incentives for adopting labor-saving techniques and facilitated the heavier use of landed resources, such as iron ore and coal, which capital-intensive methods of production often required.

The shift in relative prices resulted partly from the increasing willingness of members of the economy to save. By the 1880s people were withholding from consumption a greater share of the nation's gross national product to sustain the higher rates of economic growth. While savers and investors devoted only 14 to 16 percent of national product to capital formation prior to the Civil War, by the 1870s they devoted almost one-quarter to capital formation, and by the 1880s they had increased the rate to 28 percent.[4]

The remarkable rise in the savings rate, so obviously important to the substitution of capital for labor, lacks a full explanation. Certainly, some of that increase resulted from capital-market improvements, which provided potential investors with better information about likely rates of return. (See Chapter 10 for a survey of the institutional factors that shaped the accumulation and mobilization of capital.) The dramatic widening of middle-class status between the Civil War and World War I, a widening that was itself largely a product of the intensification of capital use, also contributed to increasing savings rates; upward economic mobility allowed a growing share of the population to earn more than was necessary to meet their consumption desires. Reinforcing this trend was an increase in the average age of the population. Older people tended to save at higher rates than younger people, perhaps because a higher proportion were married, had children, and were concerned about saving in order to pass on a legacy to the next generation. And, in the corporate sector, the development of large corporations with their better access to accurate information may also have enhanced the savings rate.

The bias of technical change and the falling relative price of capital created incentives not only for swift capital formation but also for marked improvements in the quality of labor. More skilled labor was needed to operate the rapidly growing stock of machines. And as the machinery became more complex and massive, as the scale of production consequently increased, as work became more specialized, the demand grew for people who were able to coordinate and control work processes. The relative scarcity of labor, coupled with these needs, increased the rate of return on investments in human capital to a level quite possibly above that of the returns on investments in physical capital.[5] Americans responded by undertaking a wide assortment of measures to upgrade the quality of labor. These measures included new investments in formal education, prohibitions on child labor in factories, improvements in urban health and sanitation conditions, and encouraging families to raise better educated children.

The expansion of education programs—professional schools, public and private trade schools, public elementary and secondary schools, and public literacy training for recent immigrants—is easy to document. Between 1860 and 1900 the share of its resources American society devoted to education (through direct expenditures and earnings forgone by students) more than doubled—from 1.4 percent to 2.9 percent. This probably was an acceleration, based on the fact that before the 1860s the expenditures by individuals and institutions on formal education increased only slowly relative to national product. (The earnings forgone by students are unknown before 1860.) The total resource costs of schooling showed a particularly sharp acceleration, relative to national product, during the 1880s and 1890s. The basis for this acceleration was twofold. First, expenditures within the public sector of education expanded rapidly, more rapidly than within the private sector, accounting for the acceleration of direct expenditures. Second, the earnings forgone by students were a rapidly growing share of the total resource cost of education.[6]

After 1900, the contribution of increased investment in people to the growth of national product and productivity grew more than the contribution of physical capital but did not surpass it until the 1920s, when the end of immigration placed an even higher premium on the development of a skilled labor force. Nonetheless, the significance of educational investments, and of investment in human capital during the maturing industrial revolution in general, even when physical capital dominated, is unquestionable.

Some of the gains in per-capita income and the productivity of labor were produced by institutional innovations that raised the productivity of more than one factor of production. For example, improvements in communications made it possible to employ all the factors of production with greater sensitivity to differentials in rates of return. Most important, perhaps, the portion of the nation's people and economic activity organized in concentrated urban settings grew in large increments. The share of the population living in urban places was 19.8 percent in 1860; by 1910 it had grown to 45.7 percent; and by 1920 it was 51.2 percent. More people, relative to the total size of the population, were added to the urban population during the 1880s and the decade 1900–1910 than during any other inter-Census decade in the nation's history. (See Table 18.) As had been the case before the Civil War, urbanization provided a means, through the enhancement of communication, to organize economic life more efficiently. However, with the rapidly falling costs of communication, particularly transportation, the pace of urbanization slackened. The share of the population urbanized had increased with assured rapidity beginning in the 1820s and continued to do so through the 1860s. But the rate at which the level of urbanization increased tended to decline from the 1870s through the 1920s. Altogether, the improvements in economic efficiency, which the separate measures of capital and labor productivity cannot capture, contributed no more than about one-quarter of the annual rate of increase in output per capita. The growth of per-capita income dur-

TABLE 18   GROWTH OF URBANIZATION

	Level of Urbani- zation*	Decennial Increase in Share of Population Urbanized**	Rate of Increase in Share of Population Urbanized
1800–1810	7.3%	1.2	19.7%
1810–1820	7.2	–0.1	–1.4
1820–1830	8.8	1.6	22.2
1830–1840	10.8	2.0	22.7
1840–1850	15.3	4.5	41.7
1850–1860	19.8	4.5	29.4
1860–1870	25.7	5.9	29.8
1870–1880	28.2	2.5	9.7
1880–1890	35.1	6.9	24.4
1890–1900	39.7	4.6	13.1
1900–1910	45.7	6.0	15.1
1910–1920	51.2	5.5	12.0
1920–1930	56.2	5.0	9.8

Source: Eric E. Lampard, "The Evolving System of Cities in the United States: Urbanization and Economic Development," in Harvey S. Perloff and Lowdon Wingo, Jr. (eds.), *Issues in Urban Economics* (Baltimore: Johns Hopkins Press, 1968), pp. 108, 112.

* End of decade.
** Percentage point increment.

ing this period was dominated by the mobilization of greater amounts of capital per worker and, to a lesser extent, by improvements in the quality of labor.[7]

STRUCTURAL CHANGE

During the last half of the nineteenth century, the pace of structural change—the shift of resources and products among the various sectors and regions of the economy—slowed. The absolute levels of incremental structural change remained large simply because the economy grew so rapidly in size. But the relative importance of the structural shifts diminished.

This retardation occurred not only in urbanization but also in industrialization, or in the rate at which the labor force became more industrial in its employment. (See Table 19.) During the 1880s and the decade 1900–1910, there was an acceleration in the growth of the nonagricultural labor force associated with short-term accelerations in urbanization and immigration. But even then the rates of increase were substantially lower than those during the period 1810–1850.

The shift in the geographic distribution of population provides another example of decelerating structural change. During the years between the Civil War and World War I, the areas to the west of the Mississippi River—the Great Plains, the mining regions of the Rocky

TABLE 19 INDUSTRIALIZATION OF THE LABOR FORCE

	Level of Industrial- ization*	Incremental Change in Share of Labor Force Industrialized	Rate of Change in Level of Industrial- ization
1810–1820	21.2%	4.9	30.9%
1820–1830	29.4	8.2	38.7
1830–1840	36.9	7.5	25.5
1840–1850	45.2	8.3	22.5
1850–1860	47.1	1.9	4.2
1860–1870	47.5	0.4	0.8
1870–1880	48.7	1.2	2.5
1880–1890	57.3	8.6	17.8
1890–1900	59.8	2.5	4.4
1900–1910	68.6	8.8	14.7
1910–1920	74.1	5.5	8.0
1920–1930	78.4	4.3	5.8

Source: Stanley, Lebergott, *Manpower in Economic Growth: The American Record Since 1800* (New York: McGraw-Hill, 1964), p. 510.
* End of decade.

TABLE 20   DISTRIBUTION OF POPULATION BY REGION

	East Coast	East Central	West Central	West	U.S.
1790	97%	3%	0%	0%	100%
1860	51	35	12	2	100
1910	41	29	22	8	100
1960	40	27	18	15	100

Source: U.S. Bureau of the Census, *Census of Population: 1960, United States Summary* (Washington, D.C.: U.S. Government Printing Office, 1963), pp. 1–19.

Mountains, and the West Coast—grew more rapidly than the population as a whole. (See Table 20.) But these shifts were less dramatic than the shifts of population that had taken place before 1860, reducing the *relative* size of the East Coast's population by half. And, in the decades following World War I, the pace of geographic redistribution was even more modest. By the late nineteenth century, the settlement of western lands had begun to diminish in its impact on the rate of shift in the geographic distribution of population.

At the same time that the distribution of population became more stable, the occupational structure of the regions converged. The regions had begun the process movement toward homogeneity of industrial profile. And, as occupational structure converged, the interregional differentials in per-capita income tended to decline. With a few deviations, particularly in the South, levels of personal income per capita in the various regions moved toward the U.S. average. (See Table 21.) The late nineteenth century marked the end of the sharp regional divergence of per-capita income that characterized early industrialization. Yet another modern trend had begun.

Urbanization and other shifts in the structure of the economy contributed powerfully to economic growth in the first half of the nineteenth century. (See Chapter 5.) Such shifts, however, appear to have been less important to the dynamics of growth during the late nineteenth and the twentieth centuries. The rate of increase in per-capita product reached a higher level while the pace of structural change decelerated, and the association between productivity advance and structural change became weaker. Gains in productivity came less from the increasing importance of particular sectors or regions and more from an increasingly widespread diffusion of the process of per-capita growth throughout the economy.

THE CHANGING POPULATION

The strong gains in per-capita income between the Civil War and World War I were possible in part because the rate of population growth slowed significantly. Population growth remained rapid, but

TABLE 21   PERSONAL INCOME PER CAPITA, 1860–1920*

	1860	1880	1900	1920
United States	100%	100%	100%	100%
Northeast	139	141	137	132
New England	143	141	134	124
Middle Atlantic	137	141	139	134
North Central	68	98	103	100
Great Lakes	69	102	106	108
Plains	66	90	97	87
South	72	51	51	62
South Atlantic	65	45	45	59
East South Central**	68	51	49	52
West South Central†	115	60	61	72
West	—	190	163	122
Mountain	—	168	139	100
Pacific	—	204	163	135

Source: Richard A. Easterlin, "Regional Income Trends, 1840–1950," in Seymour E. Harris (ed.), *American Economic History* (New York: McGraw-Hill, 1961), p. 528.

*   Each region's level given as a percentage of the U. S. average.
** Alabama, Kentucky, Mississippi, and Tennessee.
†   Arkansas, Louisiana, Oklahoma, and Texas.

not so rapid as to dissipate gains in real product. Indeed, the marked deceleration meant that the growth in real product more easily raised the levels of per-capita income.

During the 1840s and 1850s, the population had grown at a rate in excess of 3 percent per year—a rate comparable to that reached during the expansive population surge of the eighteenth century. (See Table 22.) During the Civil War decade, the rate of growth dropped to slightly more than 2 percent per year. While undoubtedly a result partly of high Civil War mortality and a decline in immigration, the decline proved to be more than a short-run phenomenon. Although the rate underwent subsequent increases—during the early 1870s and early 1880s, for example—the long-term trend was one of deceleration. Even before World War I's disruption of immigration sharply reduced the rate of growth, the rate of population increase declined to a level that fell consistently below 2 percent per year. The decline in the population's growth rate, which would continue after being interrupted by the "baby boom" of World War II, was well under way by the 1870s.

A persistent, remarkable decline in the birth rate was responsible for the long-term trend of growth-rate deceleration. The decline in the birth rate (births per hundred per year in Table 22) was sufficient to offset the impact of a falling death rate. Mortality remained relatively stable through the 1880s, holding at a level close to that which

TABLE 22 GROWTH OF POPULATION: AVERAGE ANNUAL RATES

	Total Increase	Net Migration	Birth Rate	Death Rate
1820–1830	2.87%	0.11%	—	—
1830–1840	2.81	0.33	—	—
1840–1850	3.04	0.71	—	—
1850–1860	3.02	0.94	—	—
1860–1870	2.35	0.58	—	—
1870–1875	2.55	0.67	4.08%	2.18%
1875–1880	1.83	0.34	3.88	2.38
1880–1885	2.54	1.01	3.69	2.10
1885–1890	1.99	0.58	3.53	2.06
1890–1895	2.01	0.45	3.43	1.95
1895–1900	1.63	0.28	3.16	1.88
1900–1905	1.85	0.60	3.00	1.76
1905–1910	1.98	0.69	2.96	1.66
1910–1915	1.75	0.53	2.75	1.47
1915–1920	1.05	0.11	2.61	1.62
1920–1925	1.69	0.36	2.50	1.13
1925–1930	1.25	0.20	2.15	1.06

Source: Warren S. Thompson and P. K. Whelpton, *Population Trends in the United States* (New York: McGraw-Hill, 1933), pp. 1, 303; Richard A. Easterlin, *Population, Labor Force, and Long Swings in Economic Growth: The American Experience* (New York: Columbia University Press, 1968), p. 189.

had prevailed since the late colonial period. But it began a marked decline in the 1890s that became rapid by the time of World War I. It clearly moderated the deceleration in the overall growth of the population. The increase in life expectancy came largely in major cities, which were undertaking massive improvements in public health. The installation of sewers and the provision of central supplies of pure drinking water had a particularly spectacular effect in reducing the incidence of bacterial diseases. Largely as a consequence, the life expectancy at birth for males increased. In Massachusetts, for example, it rose from 38.7 years in 1855 to 54.1 years in 1919–1920.[8] The decline in the birth rate was also high enough to offset in most years the impact of high levels of immigration. While the rate of immigration did not increase consistently, as had been the case before the Civil War, it reached its all-time peak in the early 1880s and attained very high levels throughout the period, except during the depressions of the late 1870s and 1890s and during World War I. Immigration accounted for most of the short-run variations in the rate of population growth but in the long run was outweighed by the impact of the falling birth rate.

The birth rate fell during this period for largely the same reasons that it fell before the Civil War. For one thing, the cost of women's time rose sharply; the growth of real wages for women accelerated. This had the effect of increasing the rate at which women worked. The age of marriage rose as women delayed marriage to take advantage of the growing demand for their services, and married women worked outside of the home at increasing rates. By 1910 nearly 40 percent of all single women and about 10 percent of all married women worked outside the home. (See Table 23.) The married women most likely to work were those who were black; nearly one-third of them had employment by 1920. And the vast majority of all working married women, both white and black, were of child-bearing age. The consequence was a decline in the average number of births per marriage.

Reinforcing the growing inclination of women to work outside their households was the same impulse to rear better educated children that had contributed to the early nineteenth-century fertility decline. The high returns that the acquisition of skills could earn, coupled with the proliferation of middle-class status, led a growing number of families to enhance the social competency of their children. It is arguable that while investments in public education and public health services grew rapidly, beginning in the 1880s, they did not increase swiftly enough to satisfy the desires of the burgeoning middle-class populations. In response, those families sought to shift the resources of women into child rearing. However, this proved to be expensive because the rising real wages for women raised the opportunity cost of mothers and older daughters specializing in child rearing. Families responded to the rising relative cost of child rearing in two ways. First, like factories and farms, they made their activities more capital-intensive. They mechanized, relying on an array of

TABLE 23 PARTICIPATION OF WOMEN IN THE AMERICAN LABOR FORCE, 1870–1930

	Women's Share of Labor Force*	Working Women in the Female Population
1870	14.8%	13.7%
1880	15.2	14.7
1890	17.0	18.2
1900	18.3	21.2
1910	20.0	24.8
1920	20.4	23.9
1930	22.1	24.4

Source: W. Elliot Brownlee and Mary M. Brownlee, *Women in the American Economy, a Documentary History, 1675 to 1929* (New Haven: Yale University Press, 1976), p. 3.

* Includes females over age fourteen.

consumer durable goods (including washing machines, wringers, and sewing machines) that became available as early as the 1870s, well before the electrification of the home that began in earnest during the 1910s. However, the expenditures for these goods and the other consumption goods that were becoming increasingly popular in the late nineteenth century made investment in children more difficult. Not only were the goods expensive, but new generations became conditioned to demand the luxury goods of their parents as items of necessity.[9] Second, in order to cope with rising family expenditures and be able to devote more attention and care to each child, families limited their size.

Families throughout the social spectrum restricted the growth of family size. Black families, for instance, reduced fertility and, after 1880, did so more swiftly than did white families. To some extent they were simply catching up. Under slavery blacks had had little control over marital choice and faced planter-created incentives to enhance their fertility. After Emancipation, however, black women were able to choose to devote less of their lives to childbirth, to pay more attention to each child, and to work more extensively outside the home to supplement meager family incomes.[10] Farm families also limited family size. They sought to maintain or increase the amount of physical capital that they passed on to their children. At the same time, they tried to produce skilled children who could take advantage of new urban employments. The growing scarcity of new land propelled the fertility decline both by making it more difficult to bequeath adequate legacies and by enhancing the appeal of alternatives to farming.

Despite the wide dispersion of family limitation, it was the cities, as the foci of the service activities that supported the buoyant middle class, that experienced the most rapid fertility declines. And urbanization as a social process may have contributed to the deceleration. In the same way that cities fostered communication with regard to opportunities for investment in factories and service activities, they eased communication among families about relative opportunities for investments in their children and, in addition, about the best methods of birth control. Birth-control techniques became less expensive and more reliable in the late nineteenth century, and the diffusion of these more efficient methods was an urban phenomenon. Crucial were the rise of mass-produced condoms made of vulcanized rubber and the increasing resort to quasi-professional abortions. Beginning in the 1860s medical societies became acutely concerned about the high incidence of abortions in cities and launched the effort that led to effective regulation and prohibition of abortions in the early decades of the twentieth century. Meanwhile, observers noted the ease of access that urban women had to abortions. The Michigan

Board of Health, for example, guessed that in 1898 fully one-third of all pregnancies in the state ended in abortion.[11] However, like its role in the general advance of productivity, urbanization as a process that contributed to a more efficient organization of the marketplace was less important than shifts in technical change and in the relative prices of the factors of production—in this instance, the market forces that encouraged families to increase their investment of human capital in their children.

THE DISTRIBUTION OF INCOME AND WEALTH

The era between the Civil War and World War I appears to have been a watershed in the history of the distribution of the fruits of economic growth. It is true that disparities in the distribution of income and wealth remained great. For example, according to one set of estimates, the wealthiest 2 percent of the nation's families owned over one-third of the nation's physical wealth in both 1860 and 1900, the richest 10 percent owned almost three-quarters, and the richest 50 percent owned all the nation's physical assets.[12] Thus, the continued industrialization of 1870–1914 stimulated no drastic changes in the distribution of physical wealth. But with the increasing premiums attached to the possession of skills and the spread of middle-class status and occupations, the ownership of physical capital was becoming an increasingly poor measure of an individual's ability to earn income. No adequate measurement of the full distribution of this ability has been made for this period. But preliminary accountings of the distribution of current incomes (not identical, of course, with the present values of future flows of income) do exist. They suggest that the distribution of current income—the earnings from the ownership of human as well as physical capital—improved between the Civil War and World War I.[13] Moreover, the distribution of physical wealth clearly appears to have been stable in the late nineteenth century. Certainly, there is no reliable evidence to support the notion that, in relative terms, the rich got richer and poor got poorer. This era of maturing industrial revolution appears to have marked the halt of the pre-Civil War trend toward a higher concentration of the wealth in the hands of the rich.

This dividing point was, in fact, a rather remarkable achievement of the institutions shaping economic growth in the United States, given the strong tendency of urbanization and immigration to worsen the distribution of wealth and income. Nonhuman wealth (tangible assets such as structures and equipment) and income tended to be more poorly distributed in the cities than on the countryside. And the immigrant population tended to be poorer, in terms of both assets and skills, than native Americans. And since the population was becoming increasingly urban and included an increasing percentage of foreign-born, other conditions remaining unchanged, income and wealth actually should have been less evenly distributed. Therefore, one has to conclude that between the Civil War and World War I the distribution of wealth in the cities, although worse at any given time than that on the countryside, was improving strongly.

The trend toward greater equality did not proceed swiftly, however. Clear, unambiguous signs of such movement would come only after World War I. During the depression of the 1890s, for example, inequality tended to become more extreme in that middle- and upper-income people suffered less from unemployment and, in fact, found their real incomes rising during the severe deflation if their pecuniary incomes remained relatively stable. Subsequently, during the expansion that ensued during the late 1890s and extended until World War I, the combination of price inflation bearing more heavily on the lowest income groups, the resumption of heavy immigration increasing the supply of unskilled labor, and the demands for skilled labor raising the wages of the skilled relative to the unskilled, all prevented any dramatic movement toward greater equality. However, the rapid entry of new people into the middle-class ranks of the skilled produced the observed trend toward more equal distribution of income.[14]

The fact that income and wealth distributions did not become strikingly more even in this period should not be surprising. Apart from the impacts of immigration, depression, rising cost of living (after 1897), and widening wage differentials between skilled and unskilled, the requirements for capital investment were unusually high. A highly uneven distribution of wealth and income was necessary in order to generate the savings required to sustain economic growth. If social institutions had yielded a dramatically more uniform distribution, a much larger share of income very likely would have been devoted to current consumption and the advance of per-capita income would have been severely retarded. But, at the same time, the general stability in the distribution of wealth and income argues that enjoyment of the benefits of economic growth was by no means limited to the rich. All income groups benefited from economic growth, even though the poorer sectors failed to gain ground relatively, and may have lost ground relative to the growing middle class during the years 1898–1914. Thus, the patterns of wealth and income distribution point to solid signs of increasing economic opportunity in industrial America from 1870 to 1914.

ECONOMIC INSTABILITY: LONG SWINGS AND THE BUSINESS CYCLE

Accompanying the extremely rapid rates of growth attained between 1870 and 1914 was severe instability, one kind in particular being of a long-term character—that produced by the long swings in economic growth. All the long swings of the period began with a phase of increasing demand for goods and services enhancing the demand for labor. The tighter labor market, with its offer of higher returns, brought about an accelerated rate of migration from the countryside to the foci of urban opportunity. The resulting increase in the growth rate of labor force, population, and households and the larger accumulation of people further augmented buoyant demands for both services (like housing and urban transport) and products (such as consumer goods). Investment in the production of newly demanded goods and services—especially in housing, railroads, and manufacturing—pushed the upward surge even further. But the long swing began its descent when new additions of capital failed to maintain the growth of productivity, the rate of output growth declined, and the rate of growth of total demand fell.

The key to the timing of long swings since the industrial revolution has been the timing of the growth of the productivity of capital. Rates of capital productivity growth have tended to rise and fall in waves that precede those of the rates of output change by a short interval. Increases in productivity seem to be the necessary elements in initiating the upward movement of long swings. Once again, attention should be drawn to the analytical power of the concept of capital formation.

More severe in their fluctuations than the long swings were the business cycles. And in the late nineteenth century, it appeared that the extended phases of slack were becoming deeper and more prolonged. The depressions of 1873–1878 and 1892–1896 were unprecedented, generated progressively more unemployment, retarded the progress of urbanization, industrialization, and immigration, and slowed significantly the growth of per-capita income. The reasons for the increasing severity of business-cycle variations are complex. To some extent, they are rooted in the increasing capital intensity of the era. The scale of capital units and the consequent growth in the scale of economic organizations grew more rapidly than the ability of economic planners in either the private or the public sector to maintain economic stability, to match supply with demand in a smooth, consistent fashion. The public sector appears to have been more culpable in that much of the instability, particularly during the 1890s, resulted from mismanagement of the nation's monetary policies. With sounder economic management, the nation would have avoided the excessive hardships of economic contraction. However, it would have been unreasonable to expect success in curing the basic instability that has been and remains inherent to all economies actively participating in the large and highly unpredictable world marketplace.

Increasing instability had a marked influence on the development of American economic institutions. The instability touched almost everyone. The workingman faced increasing threats of joblessness, the farmer risked being squeezed between low prices and high fixed costs, and the businessman encountered the real possibility of over-production and an income-price squeeze similar to that faced by the farmer. All suffered from retardation in the advance of per-capita incomes. All affected groups sought to restructure economic institutions, both public and private, to provide a more stable framework for economic growth.

The following chapter examines the institutional innovations that were central to this period of maturing, industrial revolution. These innovations affected the patterns of economic growth but more heavily influenced the pace and timing of economic fluctuations. It should be clear that American society found it much easier to follow through on its commitment to economic growth than to provide a more dependable and orderly economic environment.

NOTES

1. For examples of the current revival of interest in capital as the crucial determinant in the economic growth of this period, see Moses Abramovitz and Paul A. David, "Reinterpreting Economic Growth: Parables and Realities," *American Economic Review*, 63 (May 1973), 428–439; and Jeffrey G. Williamson, *Late Nineteenth-Century American Development: A General Equilibrium History* (London and New York: Cambridge University Press, 1974).

2. See especially Edward F. Denison, *The Sources of Economic Growth in the United States and the Alternatives Before Us* (New York: Committee for Economic Development, 1962).

3. Zvi Griliches and Dale W. Jorgenson, "Sources of Measured Productivity Change: Capital Input," *American Economic Review*, 56 (May 1966), 50–61; and Laurits R. Christensen and Dale W. Jorgenson, "U.S. Real Product and Real Factor Input, 1929–1967," *Review of Income and Wealth*, 16 (March 1970), 19–50.

4. The rate has probably remained about the same for the entire period since, with the exception of the sustained depression of the 1930s. See Robert E. Gallman, "Gross National Product in the United States, 1834–

1909," in Conference on Income and Wealth, National Bureau of Economic Research, *Output, Employment, and Productivty in the United States After 1800,* Vol. 30, *Studies in Income and Wealth* (New York: Columbia University Press, 1966), p. 11; and Simon Kuznets, *Capital in the American Economy: Its Formation and Financing* (Princeton, N.J.: Princeton University Press, 1961), p. 521.

5. See, for an example, Edward Meeker, "The Social Rate of Return on Investment in Public Health, 1880–1910," *Journal of Economic History,* 34 (June 1974), 392–421.

6. For this data, see Albert Fishlow, "Levels of Nineteenth-Century American Investment in Education," *Journal of Economic History,* 26 (December 1966), 418–436; and Lewis C. Solmon, "Estimates of the Costs of Schooling in 1880 and 1890," *Explorations in Economic History,* 7 (Supplement, 1970), 533–581.

7. Christensen and Jorgenson, *op. cit.,* are able to account for about three-quarters of the gain in per-capita output from 1929 to 1967 in terms of increases in the productivity of capital and labor. The remainder, or one-quarter, might be regarded as an upper boundary for technological and organizational changes that were neutral toward capital and labor. Such changes have probably been more important since 1929 than before, so this estimate of one-quarter is also a reasonable upper boundary for the period 1870–1920 as well.

8. U.S. Bureau of the Census, *Historical Statistics of the United States, Colonial Times to 1957* (Washington, D.C.: U.S. Government Printing Office, 1960), p. 24.

9. A popular interpretation of the long-term fertility decline focuses almost exclusively on children as "consumer" goods. It views families as "consuming" rather than "producing" children and argues that the increasing competition between children and other consumption goods led to declining marital fertility rates between generations. The classic statement of this is Richard Easterlin's. See his "On the Relation of Economic Factors to Recent and Projected Fertility Changes," *Demography,* 3 (1966), 131–153. Recently, Easterlin has modified his views, at least for the rural fertility decline. See, for example, "Factors in the Decline of Farm Family Fertility in the United States: Some Preliminary Research Results," *Journal of American History,* 63 (December 1976), 600–614.

10. For evidence on systematic slave breeding, see Kenneth M. Stampp, *The Peculiar Institution: Slavery in the Ante-Bellum South* (New York: Random House, 1956), p. 250; and Richard Sutch, "The Breeding of Slaves for Sale and the Westward Expansion of Slavery, 1850–1860," in Stanley L. Engerman and Eugene D. Genovese (eds.), *Race and Slavery in the Western Hemisphere: Quantitative Studies* (Princeton, N.J.: Princeton University Press, 1975), pp. 173–198. On nineteenth-century black fertility trends, see Jack E. Eblen, "New Estimates of the Vital Rates of the United States Black Population During the Nineteenth Century," *Demography,* 11 (May 1974), 301–319; and Reynolds Farley, "The

Demographic Rates and Social Institutions of the Nineteenth-Century Negro Population: A Stable Population Analysis," *Demography*, 2 (May 1965), 386–398.

11. For scattered evidence on the difficult problem of the relative incidence of various birth-control techniques, particularly the use of the condom, see Norman E. Hines, *Medical History of Contraception* (New York: Gamut Press, 1963), especially pp. 201–205 and 335 ff. On the rate of abortion and on the antiabortion movement, see Carroll Smith-Rosenberg and Charles Rosenberg, "The Female Animal: Medical and Biological Views of Woman and Her Role in Nineteenth-Century America," *Journal of American History*, 60 (September 1974), 344.

12. Robert E. Gallman, "Trends in the Size Distribution of Wealth in the Nineteenth Century: Some Speculations," in Lee Soltow (ed.), *Six Papers on the Size Distribution of Wealth and Income* (New York: Columbia University Press, 1969), p. 6.

13. Lee C. Soltow, "Evidence on Income Inequality in the United States, 1866–1965," *Journal of Economic History*, 29 (June 1969), 270–286.

14. One economist has characterized the trend between 1896 and 1914 as the "last great surge in American inequality." However, he refers to the pay and cost-of-living differentials between skilled and unskilled workers. He does not consider how the more even distribution of skills within the population would tend to offset the impact of widening wage and cost-of-living differentials on measured inequality. Jeffrey G. Williamson, "American Prices and Urban Inequality Since 1820," *Journal of Economic History*, 36 (June 1976), 303–333. For data suggesting that during this period "upward mobility both from blue-collar to white-collar callings and from low-ranked to high-ranked manual jobs was quite common," see Stephan Thernstrom, *The Other Bostonians: Poverty and Progress in the American Metropolis, 1880–1970* (Cambridge, Mass.: Harvard University Press, 1973). (The quotation is taken from p. 257.)

SUGGESTED READINGS

Books

Easterlin, Richard A. *Population, Labor Force, and Long Swings in Economic Growth: The American Experience.* New York: Columbia University Press, 1968.

Higgs, Robert. *The Transformation of the American Economy, 1865–1914: An Essay in Interpretation.* New York: Wiley, 1971.

Kuznets, Simon (ed.). *Population Redistribution and Economic Growth: United States, 1870–1950.* 3 vols. Philadelphia: American Philosophical Society, 1957–1964.

Thernstrom, Stephan. *The Other Bostonians: Poverty and Progress in the American Metropolis, 1880–1970.* Cambridge, Mass.: Harvard University Press, 1973.

Williamson, Jeffrey G. *Late Nineteenth-Century American Development, a General Equilibrium History.* London and New York: Cambridge University Press, 1974.

Articles

Abramovitz, Moses. "The Passing of the Kuznets Cycle," *Economica,* 35 (February 1968), 349–367.

————, and Paul A. David. "Reinterpreting Economic Growth: Parables and Realities," *American Economic Review,* 63 (May 1973), 428–439.

Easterlin, Richard. "Factors in the Decline of Farm Family Fertility in the United States: Some Preliminary Research Results," *Journal of American History,* 63 (December 1976), 600–614.

Fishlow, Albert. "Levels of Nineteenth-Century Investment in Education," *Journal of Economic History,* 26 (December 1966), 418–436.

McCormick, William W., and Charles M. Franks. "A Self-Generating Model of Long-Swings for the American Economy, 1860–1940," *Journal of Economic History,* 31 (June 1971), 295–343.

Meeker, Edward. "The Improving Health of the United States, 1850–1915," *Explorations in Economic History,* 9 (Summer 1972), 353–373.

Soltow, Lee C. "Evidence on Income Inequality in the United States, 1866–1965," *Journal of Economic History,* 29 (June 1969), 270–286.

Uselding, Paul J. "Factor Substitution and Labor Productivity Growth in American Manufacturing, 1839–1899," *Journal of Economic History,* 32 (September 1972), 670–681.

Williamson, Jeffrey G. "American Prices and Urban Inequality Since 1820," *Journal of Economic History,* 36 (June 1976), 303–333.

10

Institutional Sources of Economic Change, 1870-1914

A full explanation of economic change during maturing industrialization must include a consideration of central institutional developments. As the last chapter indicated, the most important were those that affected the mobilization of capital resources and the stability of the economy. This chapter examines these developments in detail. It suggests that as the nation approached World War I, institutional innovation provided cause for considerable optimism about the economy's future health. A set of maturing financial institutions had been successful in generating a high level of capital formation. Corporate managers, especially the manufacturers, were refining their abilities to make the most productive use of their resources. While economic institutions could not yet guarantee orderly growth, the emerging facility of producers in matching supply with demand augured well for the future, and reforms of the nation's banking and monetary arrangements offered at least the possibility of creative management of the business cycle. Meanwhile, between the late 1890s and World War I, the economy enjoyed a period of prosperity characterized not only by high rates of growth but also by freedom from serious economic reversal.

THE REFINEMENT OF CAPITAL MARKETS

The economic expansion of the late nineteenth and early twentieth centuries had a voracious appetite for capital. Indeed, the nation's capital stock grew more rapidly than did its level of output until the

1920s. Strong demands arose for capital to complete the modern railroad network; to supply agriculture, undergoing its own industrial revolution, with machinery and equipment; to provide roads, housing, schools, and sewers, meeting the needs of the rapidly expanding urban populations; and, most important, to build the plant capacity necessary for manufacturing, which was not only growing rapidly but also increasing greatly in its scale of operations. The strength of such demands clearly distinguishes the period from the preceding era of economic growth.

The major source of that capital, and, in fact, of all capital formation in both the nineteenth and twentieth centuries, has been the savings of the institutions that were themselves the users of the capital.[1] But a most significant innovation appeared during the nineteenth century, especially during the last decades, when investors probably obtained a greater share of their capital from external sources, such as stock markets. This institutional development was part of a more general modernization of the process of capital formation, which included, as well, the increasing resort to both corporate forms and to massive corporate reorganizations.

The development of external markets, crucial to the rapid pace of growth and central to instability, involved the search for a greater measure of two key elements, specialization and regularity, which together provided investors with improved means for judging the potential returns on alternative investment opportunities and supported the continuing search for the optimum return on investment. The specialization of capital markets, or the movement away from a highly personalized capital market, had been under way since the onset of the industrial revolution in the early decades of the century. For example, stock exchanges had long been established in New York and Boston, and private investment bankers with specialized activities had proliferated in those cities. Also, savings banks had been growing since the second decade of the century and by 1860 had received some $150 million in deposits. Insurance companies, which invested in securities, loans on collateral, and mortgages on real estate, grew as well, handling over $250 million by 1860; by 1900 their assets would expand to almost $1.75 billion. These financial intermediaries became increasingly important in the mobilization of capital, owning some 17 percent of the nation's physical assets by 1890. At the same time, individual sources diminished in significance. This trend continued into the twentieth century until, by the 1940s, financial intermediaries accounted for over two-thirds of all external capital, as contrasted with about one-half for the first decade of the century.[2]

The most significant aspect of this continuing specialization was the increasing interest of investment bankers in new issues of industrial stocks and bonds. The rising industrial giants had massive demands for external capital: almost half of capital formation accounted for by nonfinancial corporations (primarily manufacturers) came from external sources during the first decade of the twentieth century—about twice the share common by mid-century—and the proportion was very likely higher in the preceding decades.[3]

Nonetheless, bankers and investors both tended to view industrial issues with a skeptical eye, even in the latter part of the century. In fact, bankers declined to receive industrial securities as collateral on the same basis as they did railroad issues until the 1920s, by which time railroading had become a stagnant enterprise. Moreover, bankers tended to look more favorably on bonds, which had to be periodically repaid or refunded, than they did on stocks. Many stocks were not listed on the New York exchange but were sold instead on the Curb Market, which was a more loosely organized market that accommodated new issues. (The Curb actually lived up to its name until 1921, when it finally acquired a roof.) And the charter terms of many banks and insurance companies prevented them from purchasing common stocks to hold as assets. Nonetheless, industrials increased rapidly in acceptability and popularity among a growing number of investment bankers after the Civil War.

The intermediaries for most industrial issues were the international firms, which had descended from the Anglo-American investment bankers who, in turn, had descended from the old eighteenth-century merchant bankers. (J. Pierpont Morgan, for example, had begun his career before the Civil War as a New York agent of the Anglo-American merchant banker George Peabody.) Activity in new industrial issues developed strongly after 1873, when the panic of that year led European investors to question the wisdom of buying into American railroads at former levels. (The proximate cause of the collapse of 1873 was the failure of Northern Pacific bonds and the investment house of Jay Cooke.) Partly as a result, the center of gravity shifted within the transatlantic investment houses; Americans generally acquired a dominant voice in those houses.

Despite the rapid growth of investment bankers with a strong, specialized interest in manufacturing, their numbers were few. Industry was still considered a fairly risky proposition, and not many outsiders invested in manufacturing. As a result their capital found a high return in manufacturing enterprises, accounting in large part for the very impressive earnings that corporate financiers like J. P. Morgan received. Their success stemmed also from the fact that they proved to be the leading force in promoting industrial innovation. The investment bankers not only engineered the organization of the largest manufacturing combinations of the day but also led the internal reorganizations that were designed to maximize the returns from the use of the new, large accumulations of capital.

Investment bankers were in an unusually strategic position to take initiatives in corporate restructuring and, in effect, in the management of the business cycle. Before 1873 they had been very heavy investors in the nation's largest railroads. After the panic of that year the competitive situation among railroads worsened; many roads became overextended, found operation impossible, and passed into the hands of the investment bankers, who became attentive to the development and operation of the lines in order to ensure the underlying net worth of the securities. In managing railroad investments, bankers gained unique insights into the special requirements of managing enterprises with large-scale capital commitments, along with considerable practical experience in facilitating the requisite kinds of corporate reorganization. Subsequently, especially in the late 1890s and early 1900s, they acquired a vast amount of industrial securities, presenting opportunities very similar to those they had faced within the transportation sector a decade or two earlier. J. P. Morgan, for example, having managed the restructuring of the New York Central in the 1870s, became a powerful figure in the reorganization of United States Steel, General Electric, and International Harvester. In short, the investment bankers became the first organizers of the modern industrial economy, as they sought to establish system and regularity in the interest of protecting their investments. By 1912 the House of Morgan, the First National Bank of New York (controlled by Morgan), and the National City Bank (controlled by John D. Rockefeller) held 341 directorships in 112 corporations worth $22.2 billion.

The nation's increasingly specialized financial system operated with little strong, overall regulation until 1914, such order as there was coming from the efforts at self-regulation on the part of various sectors of the financial community. The failure to provide adequate regulation of the banking system, which was at the core of the nation's financial markets, was especially important in exaggerating the normal fluctuations of the business cycle, although the regional devices—especially those associated with the New York City Safety Fund system—did lend a greater measure of stability. The most visible important instrument for promoting banking stability was the national banking system created in the Civil War banking acts. Apart from the short-run objective of creating a market for federal wartime securities, the primary objective was to provide a more uniform national currency by taxing state bank notes out of circulation and by creating national bank-note currency. Like the state banking laws that preceded, the federal acts sought to regulate banking by setting standards for membership in the new system, in particular, establishing minimum capital requirements, reserve levels, and cash requirements as necessary conditions for the granting of federal charters.

However, neither the private banks nor the public arrangements of the late nineteenth century were potent enough to ameliorate the fluctuations in the business cycle. Certainly the national banking acts did not cure the feverish instability that resulted from the concentration of bank reserves in the highly skittish New York *call fund* market (the market for funds that the banks could call in at will). The acts allowed national banks to keep three-fifths of their reserves as deposits in national banks located in regional financial centers. Banks in these reserve cities, of which there were seventeen, in turn, could keep half of their reserves with national banks in New York, which was designated the central reserve city. Given their ties to Wall Street, the New York City banks paid relatively high interest rates and strongly attracted these excess reserves, which they invested in stock-market securities as call funds. A pinch came, however, whenever the stock market weakened. The country banks and reserve city banks outside New York would tend to call back their deposits in New York, and the New York banks, in turn, would be forced to call in their security loans and thus augment the downward pressures on the stock market. In addition, the seasonal demand for cash in the hinterlands produced an annual crisis in the spring, followed by a recovery beginning in the summer. The recurrent, and frequently reinforcing, need to liquidate stocks to meet the demands of loaners of call funds created waves of selling and persistent market collapses. In the post-Civil War period the market seriously panicked in 1873, 1884, 1893, 1903, and 1907, with the demand for cash frequently becoming too great for New York banks to meet, resulting in bank collapse and a worsening of financial crisis. Given the centrality of New York in the nation's capital markets, the impact of such crises radiated rapidly throughout the economy.

After almost every one of these panics the federal government sought some revision in the national banking system that would eliminate or moderate financial instability. Before the creation of the Federal Reserve System the most important was an 1887 amendment of the Banking Act of 1864 designed to reduce the influence of the New York financial market and thus dilute the source of instability. The amendment permitted an increase in the number of central reserve cities, and shortly thereafter St. Louis and Chicago joined New York in the system. They both sought to become holders of reserves and develop as money markets, but found themselves facing severe competitive liabilities in coping with the advantages available to the New York banking community. A well-developed stock market, long-established investment houses, proximity to the home offices of major corporations, and the unquestioned preeminence of New York as a trade center precluded any serious challenge to its banking dominance. In fact, the St. Louis and Chicago banks themselves continued to keep large deposits at New York banks to maintain access to Wall Street and the market for short-term funds.

Be that as it may, the failure of the banking system to provide for economic stability and an orderly investment market resulted, not from the economic strength of New York, but from the lack of a true central bank. The banking system provided no means for eliminating or reducing reliance on cash reserves during panics; order demanded a bank that could act as a lender of last resort, one that had the ability to create reserves through its credit-granting power and thus support banks that were in acute danger of failing during panic. At last, in 1907, after no less than the fifth serious panic since the Civil War, a central-banking movement gathered force, supported by the recommendation of the National Monetary Commission of Senator Nelson Aldrich of Rhode Island. However, the commission's suggestion of one central bank did not meet with congressional favor. The belief that the root of instability was the financial power of New York persisted and found reinforcement in the populistic belief, which had some basis in fact, that Eastern control of the nation's banking structure deprived the West and South of sufficient credit at low rates.[4] Indeed, reflecting the political leverage of the relatively less developed portions of the nation, the Federal Reserve Act, which capped the movement in 1914, provided for not one central bank but *twelve* regional central banks. Proponents assumed that a regional bank would be more responsive to local credit needs than would a bank at a distance in New York or Washington, D.C. The act divided the nation into twelve reserve districts, each with its own central bank and subject only to the loose supervision of the Federal Reserve Board. On the governing board of each central bank were three appointees of the board and six elected representatives of the member banks, no more than three of whom could be bankers. The Federal Reserve Board was composed of the secretary of the Treasury, the comptroller of the currency, and five presidential appointees. The act required all national banks to join the system and permitted state banks to join if they met the federal standards. Like the Civil War banking acts, the new act set certain reserve requirements for the various categories of banks and maintained minimum capital requirements, although lowering them in response to western and southern pressure.

The most important departure was the endowment of the new

central banks with the power of money creation. Each district Federal Reserve Bank could issue a new currency—Federal Reserve notes—with which it could purchase securities in the open market. (The district banks could also contract the nation's currency supply by selling off its holdings of government bonds, taking up and withholding Federal Reserve notes.) Much more important in the eyes of the creators of the Federal Reserve System was the ability of the central banks to use Federal Reserve notes to buy up, at a discount, commercial paper already discounted and held by member banks. Indeed, the initial anticipation was that this process of rediscounting commercial paper, including manipulation of the rediscount rate around the market rate of interest, would be the primary means for controlling credit and promoting financial stability. (In 1916 an amendment expanded the money-creation powers of the Federal Reserve further by allowing the central banks to make direct loans, or advances, which were secured by eligible commercial or governmental paper to member banks at the rediscount rate.)

The creation of the Federal Reserve System, however, did not mean the automatic achievement of a significantly higher degree of economic stability. The basic machinery of the system did offer an opportunity for the achievement of greater financial order and regularity, but the effectiveness of the system depended on the quality of information available to those in control and on their understanding of the economic processes involved in the use of rediscounting and open-market operations. As it turned out, sufficient knowledge and understanding were lacking, and although the nation's capital markets were probably more orderly than they had been previously, substantially more monetary instability prevailed after 1913 than earlier, under the nineteenth-century gold standard. The periodic crises in the New York banking community always had had national ramifications, but the crises induced by the Federal Reserve had an impact that far outweighed in fundamental monetary instability those that occurred under the aegis of the Civil War banking legislation.

The Federal Reserve Act marked, within the public sector, the maturing interest in refining institutions that would promote industrial stability and regularity. In terms of the continuing desire to create more-orderly capital markets, a line of continuity connects the Civil War banking acts with the creation of the Federal Reserve. The establishment of a national banking system was a response to the need for a more geographically uniform capital market. Similarly, the creation of the Federal Reserve implied a search for the more dependable operation of capital markets. Such interest, in both the public and private sectors, contributed to the development of more-mature financial markets. By World War I, investment flows responded with greater sensitivity to interregional and interindustry variations in return, with capital flowing much more easily from low- to high-return areas. This contribution to economic development and growth was extremely important in that the mobilization of capital was the most vital element in the accelerating growth of the late nineteenth century. However, progress was much slower in using the new institutions of financial regulation to achieve a higher degree of economic stability, or to ensure that the fruits of economic growth could be enjoyed without significant disruption. It would take a crisis of catastrophic proportions—the Great Depression—to bring about institutional reform and the development of sufficient planning expertise to confront and ultimately, perhaps, solve the most difficult problems of economic instability.

REORGANIZATION OF THE MANUFACTURING CORPORATION

During the last quarter of the nineteenth century the growth of regional and national markets resulting from the increasing effectiveness of communications systems and technological changes such as the introduction of the Bessemer process created opportunities for manufacturers to enhance the rates of return on their investments by enlarging the scale of production. Accordingly intensifying their search for more-efficient means of mobilizing capital and managerial skills, manufacturers reorganized their activities in a variety of ways, beginning with the incorporation of their enterprises.

The corporate form of enterprise had historically provided benefits to investors by lowering risk, and that protection had facilitated the mobilization of capital. For the most part it was large-scale investments extending over a wide physical expanse and requiring some degree of public protection that most frequently called for the cover of a corporate charter. Prior to the late nineteenth century, corporate enterprise was much more likely to encompass schools, banks, canals, and turnpikes than manufacturing activity, which tended to be small-scale, rooted in discrete locations, and family-owned, with little need for public support in its efforts to mobilize capital. However, beginning in the 1870s, manufacturing firms resorted increasingly to incorporation as the customary way of doing business. And in the early 1890s the number and relative importance of corporations within the manufacturing sector swung sharply upward.[5]

After incorporation, manufacturers found in their encounters with serious new problems arising from the competitive instability

Alexander Graham Bell making the first long distance call between New York and Chicago, 1892. The telephone as well as the railroad dramatically improved interregional communication.

endemic to the period that existing corporate structures were flimsy supports. The dynamic growth of urban markets and the falling costs of transport brought many new entrants into manufacturing and placed many older manufacturers in face-to face competition for the first time. As manufacturers tried to meet this heightened competition by making increasingly heavy capital commitments to expand production and take advantage of economies of scale, overhead costs, such as interest payments on capital borrowed to finance plant expansions or to build up inventories necessary for effective interregional marketing, took up a rising share of total costs. However, the price level was falling from the 1860s until the late 1890s, and this worked to increase the burden of fixed costs; debts contracted at a high price level were more difficult to repay as the real value of the dollar increased. (Deflation has the effect of transferring wealth from debtors, whether large or small, to creditors.) Manufacturers had to meet such fixed charges regardless of the level of production. As a result, a significant number of businessmen became more willing to make price cuts to meet their overhead costs and thus at least keep afloat. Such price cutting, in turn, forced other businessmen to make similar cuts and, ultimately, place their massive new accumulations of assets in jeopardy. Further, manufacturers had to cope with the exigencies created by a highly variable level of demand, marked by extreme lows during the depressions of the 1870s and the 1890s. Earlier, when a depression or recession struck, a firm could usually ride out the contraction easily by shutting down production and temporarily laying off workers. But the larger-scale, more capital-intensive factories of the late nineteenth century, with their large bills for fixed charges, needed to maintain a more steady level of production in order to survive.

As a result of the pressures exerted by growing markets and increasing instability, manufacturing corporations began altering organizational patterns, achieving by the end of the century the essential structure within which the American corporation developed in the twentieth century.[6] The basic thrust of these innovations was to give an added measure of control of assets to corporate managers in order that they might plan for the long term, lend greater stability and dependability to their operations, and, in particular, gauge future demand more accurately. The objective was not so much to put competitors out of business or to achieve monopoly power as to create a more comprehensible environment; that is, the strategy of reorganization was less one of combining activities in a horizontal direction (by merging a number of competitors engaged in a common enterprise) than one of meshing operations in a vertical direction (by combining all the processes involved in producing a single product or set of products under the aegis of a single corporation).

The initial impetus for the reordering movement was the sharp deflation of the 1870s and, as one would expect, arose first among those firms undergoing the sharpest competition—the producers of consumer goods. By the early 1890s vertical integration among such firms had made giant strides, with the acquisition of raw material production (plantations, mines, and wells), manufacturing, transportation (railroads, pipelines, and steamship companies, for example), distribution, and finance generally housed under a single corporate roof.

Reorganization usually followed one of two paths within the consumer-goods industry. The first type was adopted by the manufacturers of products that were new to late-nineteenth-century consumers. For example, Edwin and Gustavus Swift, taking advantage of the little-exploited possibilities of refrigerator cars, formed a partnership in 1878 to ship fresh western meat to the East and during the 1880s built a nationwide system of distribution and marketing. Then, to provide the necessary measure of stability and regularity, the brothers, between 1888 and 1892, extended and coordinated purchasing procedures and, in effect, produced a fully integrated, vertically organized corporation. The Swifts were not particularly interested in horizontal integration, and, in fact, they never monopolized the meat-packing industry.

Another "new" product was the cigarette, and the innovating manufacturer was James B. Duke. Whereas the Swift brothers had expanded their distribution system beyond the capacity of their purchasing operations, Duke extended his production capacity beyond his marketing ability. As a pioneer in the mechanical production of cigarettes, Duke found that effective demand was far too limited to remove his product from the market and still render an adequate return. Consequently, just as the Swifts strove to expand and reorganize their purchasing, Duke moved to create demand through extended advertising and to structure a national selling organization, moving his home office from Durham, North Carolina, to New York City in the process. His reorganization of the 1880s was more important than the merger with five smaller competitors (in 1890) which marked the creation of the American Tobacco Company.

The other path of reorganization in the consumer-goods industry was closer to the stereotypic pattern of monopoly-seeking businessmen but was, nonetheless, significantly distinct, involving those firms that produced items familiar to nineteenth-century consumers (leather products, sugar, biscuits, petroleum lighting fuel, fertilizer, etc.) and that, at the same time, faced the most severe competition. Numerous older such firms that had enjoyed the protection that high costs of transportation provided against more efficient producers now faced potentially fatal competition, and even healthy firms in this industry found themselves sorely tested. Consequently the first reponse of the smaller firms producing familiar goods was to combine in order to organize the marketplace. Thereafter, however, these firms became much more interested in vertical organization, as was the first group of reorganizing corporations. Rather than trying to drive competitors out of business, they sought to create more-orderly flows of product to the consumer, creating large distribution and purchasing departments, centralizing administration, regularizing the flows of information throughout the bureaucracy, designating responsibility in a clearer fashion, specifying objectives more sharply, and, in general, decreasing reliance on personal relationships in the exercise of authority and the exchange of information. The formation of the National Biscuit Company is a useful case in point. Formed as a merger of three regional companies in 1898 to counter a state of ruinous competition among older biscuit companies, the company initially sought to control prices and output in a monopolistic fashion. But soon thereafter this loose collection of firms decided to devote their energies to the integration of production with marketing. In the process, the company built a vastly improved marketing organization and created a brand-name product (the Uneeda biscuit).

The restructuring of corporations engaged in the manufacture of producer goods, that is, intermediate goods such as machinery used in the production of consumer articles or the manufacture of equipment used in the provision of services, came later than the reorientation of consumer-goods manufacturers. Almost all of the reorganizations occurred after 1897, when the nation was emerging from the depression of the 1890s. (This reorganization movement formed the core of one of the three great merger waves in American economic history—this one beginning in 1898, reaching a peak in 1899, and continuing through 1902.[7]) One reason for the delay was the obvious fact that the urban market for producer goods developed later than a comparable market for consumer goods. Indeed, the growth of the production of consumer goods was responsible, in large part, for the enlargement of the demand for producer goods. The delay also underscores the secondary role of reorganizing in order to exert monopoly power: the surge of mergers in the producer-durables industry came well after the conclusion of the contraction of the 1890s, whereas if the quest for monopoly profits had been predominant, such reordering would have made more sense during the contraction. Finally, the buoyant stock market from 1897 onward made merger reorganization much easier in that investors found ample new opportunities for capital gains in the upward movement of security prices.[8]

The pattern of reorganization of producer-goods industries was basically uniform. The most important thrust was toward the attainment of more secure control over previously uncertain sources of supply of raw materials, or of components for finished products. For example, John D. Rockefeller's Standard Oil Company, built around the refining and marketing of oil, became interested in the production of crude only in the 1880s, to assure a steady supply of raw material and to preclude an imminent combination of producers against the giant. Andrew Carnegie acted in a similarly defensive fashion in the late 1890s when he purchased ore lands in the Mesabi range. In the reorganization of these producer-goods companies one finds little evidence of interest in the promotion of markets through advertising and large sales organizations. These industries suffered far less from a kind of overproduction than was the case for the consumer-goods manufacturers, moving toward market dominance or price collusion to even a lesser degree than the consumer-goods producers. Firms like American Tin Plate, American Bridge, American Can, Allis-Chalmers, and International Harvester were interested far less in exerting greater control over prices and output than in consolidating and coordinating their complex operations to obtain greater regularity and efficiency and, ultimately, a higher return on investment.

Subsequent to these reorganizations the structure of corporate institutions remained fundamentally unchanged. After World War I important structural and strategic innovations would continue in industries such as chemicals, automobiles, petroleum, and distribution, but would be based in large part on earlier models. All such reorganizations had their most important long-run impact on the management of the business cycle and the upward movement of productivity. During the period 1870–1914 sustained expansion of production with its high initial demands for capital would have been impossible without extensive efforts to reshape corporate institutions. Although the industrial corporation did not experience immediate success in smoothing economic fluctuations, it did make fluctuation more bearable and laid the foundation for future innovation which by the 1940s would result in very dramatic successes in matching supply with demand.

The emergence of the modern industrial corporation during this period encompassed not only a revolution in internal structure but also a revision of the relationships among firms, especially through various strategies of combination which were, clearly, essential to the success of corporate reform and, ultimately, the attainment of economic stability. Depending on the legal environment, the types of consolidations available to firms included pools, or informal agreements providing for the sharing of markets, trusts and holding companies, which linked managements through financial arrangements but maintained the legal integrity of the original corporations, and, most important, mergers, which involved direct, complete linkages of both management and capital and the removal of the legal identity of at least one of the older firms.

For the most part, government at various levels and in various ways promoted and reinforced the consolidation effort. At the state level, for instance, especially from the 1890s, corporations found that the common-law tradition which restricted monopolies had become less forceful. Moreover, certain strategically located states went out of their way to encourage the new corporate forms. New Jersey legalized holding companies in 1888 and in 1896 granted them the right to do business anywhere in the United States. (In response to this accommodating policy, John D. Rockefeller incorporated Standard Oil in New Jersey in 1899, moving it from Ohio where his combination was still illegal under the common law.) New Jersey also reduced corporation taxes and provided for a more expeditious amendment of corporate charters. Delaware, in particular, was quick to follow the example of New Jersey. No individual state could do very much to prevent consolidation, given the interstate mobility of capital, but states could provide distinct competitive advantages for large firms by lowering legal barriers to consolidation.

On the federal level virtually no opposition to corporate consolidation emerged during the first wave of mergers. Even the trusts largely escaped prosecution, despite the declaration of the Sherman Antitrust Act of 1890 that "every contract, combination in the form of a trust or otherwise, or conspiracy, in restraint of trade or commerce" was illegal. Between 1893 and 1903 the federal government initiated only twenty-three cases under the act. Neither the presidents nor their attorneys general were interested in such action, and Congress, for its part, appropriated no special funds for antitrust enforcement. As a result the Cleveland administration presented a very shoddy case to the Supreme Court in 1895 in its suit against a sugar manufacturer (E. C. Knight) alleged to be in restraint of trade; the Court had virtually no choice but to rule that manufacturing, as defined by the government, did not fall under the rubric of interstate commerce and was therefore outside the aegis of the 1890 act.

Not until Theodore Roosevelt's presidency did the federal government initiate vigorous antitrust prosecutions. That series of attacks culminated in the dissolution of J. P. Morgan's Northern Securities in 1904 and both Standard Oil and American Tobacco in 1911. These decisions clearly demonstrated the potential force available to those with a serious interest in stemming or reversing the tide of consolidation. And in the short-run the decisions discouraged some consolidations. But in the long-run they actually served to reinforce the consolidation movement. For one thing, the judiciary claimed that not every restraint of trade was illegal in terms of the Sherman Act. The Court held that the rule of reason would hold sway; that is, only combinations that restrained trade unreasonably could be considered illegal. For another, mergers fell outside the usual interpretation of the Sherman Act. In the *Addyston Pipe and Steel Company* case (1899), for example, the Supreme Court ruled illegal only the combination of *independent* companies to fix prices. Thus, mergers rather than trusts carried the thrust of the consolidation movement after the offensive of the Roosevelt and Taft administrations. Finally, the Rooseveltian assault convinced the public that the federal government was taking decisive action against the combinations and thus cooled anticorporation passions.

In 1914 the Clayton Act reinforced the impression of federal antitrust activism further but also served, in fact, to reinforce the efforts of large manufacturers to achieve a more reliable economic and governmental environment. The Clayton Act defined and outlawed certain unfair practices: discrimination in prices among various buyers, exclusive and tying contracts, intercorporate stockholdings, and interlocking directorates. The Federal Trade Commission was established to enforce the act. The setting of certain unfair practices beyond the pale of legality actually constrained competition, thus providing the kind of restriction of competition many businessmen had vigorously sought through the consolidation movement; the "civilizing" of competition was as much a part of the antitrust movement as it was of the consolidation effort. The Clayton Act undoubtedly contributed to the protection of the public against corporate abuses and probably protected a degree of competition by discouraging practices that supported the formation of monopolies. But by helping to eliminate some of the more obnoxious characteristics of corporate behavior the act also lent sanction to the creation of the industrial giants during the period. Combinations of unprecedented scale followed the Clayton Act, including the formation of General Motors, and there was no tradition of effective opposition to combination that would stand up against either the second great merger wave, that of the 1920s, or a third, beginning after World War II. Indeed, the nation would never experience a significant reduction in the degree of industrial concentration that had been achieved by the turn of the century. The durability of the corporate innovations of the late nineteenth and early twentieth centuries has testified to the success of the corporate movers of that era, sustained by the public authorities, in fabricating an institutional base for realizing both an advanced degree of economic stability and the relentless advance of productivity.

THE MONEY SUPPLY: THE ROLE OF THE GOLD STANDARD

During the late nineteenth century the instability that the economy so gracelessly displayed resulted from more than the *inventory cycle,* that is, flux produced by the inability of firms to match supply with demand, and the imperfections in banking institutions and capital markets. In particular, variations in the size of the money supply had a powerful impact on changes in the level of total demand for goods and services. And behind the volume of money available for economic exchange at any particular time was the operation of the international gold standard and significant American modifications of that standard, both threatened and real.[9]

The major impacts of changes in the size of the money supply were on short-run variations in total demand and on the long-run movement of prices. Sharp monetary contractions intensified the depressions of the 1870s and 1890s, thereby retarding the growth of real product. But the gradual phases of the monetary stagnation that began in the mid-1870s did not interfere with the long-term expansion of output. Even when the money supply contracted, if it did so gradually, people could adjust their behavior appropriately without disrupting the processes of economic expansion. However, the monetary stagnation, coupled with continuing output growth, resulted in a declining price level into the late 1890s. With the available money supply failing to keep up with the expansion of production, the only way for output to expand was for prices to decline.[10]

The institutions that shaped the development of the money supply between the Civil War and the late 1870s sprang from Civil War monetary experimentation. To begin with, in financing the war, the Union government created a large volume of greenbacks, which subsequently became the single largest component of the nation's currency, and at the same time temporarily took the nation off the gold standard, placing it instead on a *fiduciary* standard, or one founded on public confidence in the currency itself rather than on a precious, physical standard supporting the currency. The Union took that step in 1862 by discontinuing its conversion of Union currency into specie, thus allowing the marketplace for greenbacks to set their value; until 1875, therefore, there was no established parity between the dollar and other world currencies, so that whereas the British pound, for instance, had been worth $4.86 earlier, it was worth $12.00 in 1864. However, even though the nation abandoned the gold standard, gold continued to circulate within the nation's borders and formed a substantial element in the money stock.

Another new form of money in circulation during the period was the national bank note. In becoming part of the national banking system banks lent their initial capital investments to the federal government, receiving federal bonds in return. Then, in exchange for their bonds, through the Currency Act of 1863–1864, the federal government issued national bank notes.

When the federal government created the national banking system and bank notes, it sought to drive state bank notes from circulation and, in effect, to create a more uniform national currency. Accordingly, the national banking acts prevented state banks that obtained national charters from issuing notes and placed a 10-percent tax on the issues of state banks. These actions did eradicate state bank notes but neither destroyed state banks nor curtailed their influence over the money supply. Although state-chartered banks comprised only about one-sixth of all banks in the 1860s, they accounted for almost two-thirds by 1910. Most significantly, demand deposits, highly convenient as a form of money and as a mechanism for extending credit, were already growing in importance relative to state bank notes, and consequently the 10-percent tax only mildly retarded the growth of the money-creating ability of state banks.

Thus, during the Civil War these different forms of money brought a rapid increase in the stock of money, but from the end of the war to 1879 produced a smaller rate of increase, amounting to an annual rate of 1.1 percent—very sluggish given the fact that almost all of the rise occurred during a very short period of time, 1870–1872. In fact, the stock of money actually decreased from 1875 to 1879.

On the side of expansion during this period was the commercial banking system and confidence in banks on the part of the public, which was increasingly willing to hold its assets as bank deposits, generally increasing those deposits in relationship to its currency holdings. At the same time banks increased their deposit-reserve ratios; that is, they expanded their deposits more rapidly than their reserves for those deposits. Working in opposition to the growth of commercial banking, however, were two major factors. For one thing, since the stock of national bank notes in circulation depended on the size of the national debt, the federal government, in contracting the size of its long-term debt, restricted monetary growth. More significantly, in 1875 the federal government enacted the Resumption Act, which pledged resumption of specie payments for greenbacks on January 1, 1879, and fixed the stock of greenbacks at $347 million. For the government to be able to convert greenbacks into gold it was necessary to promote an increase in the value of the greenback (in terms of gold) with a vigorous policy of contraction. By selling bonds for gold, the government achieved the capacity to cover later specie demands, created greater confidence in the promise of the monetary authority, increased the willingness of people to hold on to dollars in anticipation of their appreciation in terms of gold—in effect, exerted a strong deflationary force on the money supply.

The net result of the interaction of the forces of expansion and those of contraction was a failure of the money supply to expand as rapidly as the national product. Since the public was unwilling to spend its dollars at a more rapid rate (in comparison with its expenditures), a long-term deflation inevitably followed.[11] The deflation had large redistributional effects, those individuals and firms with heavy debt obligations facing the most severe long-term difficulties. Also, the contraction reinforced the inventory cycle to contribute to a severe depression between 1873 and 1878. However, monetary contraction was not dramatic at any particular time. Consequently, the depression of the 1870s was less severe than those of the 1890s and 1930s.

With the resumption of specie payment in 1879 the nation moved into a period of monetary history in which the international gold standard once again dominated. Under the system created during the Civil War, domestic policy could exercise virtually complete control over the nation's stock of money. But under a gold standard, with its fixed exchange rates between dollars and other currencies, external circumstance took control of the size of the money stock. Moreover, since most of the important trading nations operated on a gold standard, and the position of the United States in that gold-standard world was still rather limited, the United States had even less influence over its own monetary policy. (Until 1973, except for several brief periods, the gold standard has been the nation's monetary standard since 1879, although the nation abandoned the standard for domestic purposes in 1934.)

Under the gold standard, between 1879 and 1897, the stock of money grew more rapidly than it had under the fiduciary standard of the preceding period—at an annual rate of about 6 percent. Even so, this new rate of growth was still very slow when compared with the increase in production. As a result, the long-term secular decline in prices that began in the 1860s continued past 1879, with prices falling at an annual rate of about 1 percent between 1879 and 1897. Return to the gold standard, then, did not bring significantly more expansive monetary instruments than those worked out under the temporary fiduciary standard. The rate of increase of the world's stock of gold had slowed and the demand for available gold had increased as the use of the gold standard spread. Consequently the money supply failed to keep pace with economic output throughout the world and was even more sluggish in contrast to the expansion of production in the United States.

Between 1879 and 1897 the nation's money stock consisted of essentially the same components as during the preceding period— with one important exception, that of silver coinage. The nation had minted silver coins since 1834, but during the 1840s silver had virtually disappeared from circulation and silver coinage was sharply restricted in 1853. Then in 1873 Congress made the demise of silver official by demonetizing it (i.e., by ceasing to mint silver coins). However, in 1878 Congress reversed directions by passing the Bland-Allison Act, which permitted the limited coinage of silver (between

$2 million and $4 million per month at the market value of silver). Under this act the Treasury's monetary silver grew to almost $380 million by 1890.

The reappearance of silver in the national money stock meant that the nation was edging toward a modification of the gold standard as a result of political pressure on behalf of monetary expansion and price inflation. That pressure during the 1860s and early 1870s focused on expanding the nation's stock of greenbacks. But, after the Resumption Act buried the greenback movement by tying the greenback to gold, those desiring inflation (or an end to deflation) turned to the resumption and expansion of silver coinage.

Although a variety of proposals were in the air, the leading exponents of expansion usually focused on a system that would utilize two monetary standards, gold and silver, with the value of gold set at sixteen times the worth of silver. In other words, under this bimetallic standard a holder of dollars could redeem them in either gold or silver, according to his choice, receiving sixteen times as much silver (in weight) as gold for those dollars. Also, producers of gold and silver could sell to the mint and receive dollars in return, according to the 16-to-1 ratio. Before the late 1870s such a system would not have been expansionary. At a fixed mint ratio of 16 to 1, silver miners would have been better off taking their silver to industrial users (in other words, as a result of the pattern of supply and demand, the real ratio was lower than 16 to 1), and the mint would have had no silver to mint. In fact, something like this had happened during the 1840s, as silver came to bring a higher dollar return when sold for purposes other than coinage. But beginning in the mid-1870s the domestic supply of silver increased rapidly, with the discovery of new sources in the West, such as the famous Comstock Lode. Consequently the market price of silver fell and gold became relatively more valuable until the ratio of 16 to 1 became too low to reflect market conditions accurately. If the nation had adopted bimetallism at a ratio of 16 to 1, it would have been extending a subsidy to the silver miner for selling his output to the mint rather than to private users and, if the mint had coined all that silver, the nation's money stock would have grown just as rapidly as silver miners hauled silver to the mint. How much inflation would have resulted is anyone's guess, but clearly the price level would have risen until the market price for silver rose to meet the mint price.

It was the anticipation of this decline in silver prices that led key people—the secretary of the Treasury, a high mint official, and the chairman of the Senate Finance Committee—who were interested in protecting the gold standard and monetary stability to persuade Congress to demonetize silver in 1873. During the 1890s silverites characterized that act as the Crime of '73, and in a sense they were absolutely correct; the act had followed a conspiracy of gold-standard supporters, and it did prevent the money supply from becoming substantially more expansive in the late 1870s. However, Congress as a whole did not view the elimination of silver coinage as a restrictive act; knowledge of the incipient decline in silver prices was not widely circulated, even in governmental quarters. Indeed, much more national and congressional support existed for silver than was indicated by the 1873 legislation. Certainly the public, with its rather mystical attachment to "hard money," was fundamentally more receptive to expansion based on a precious metal such as silver than one founded on a paper issue (such as greenbacks). Reflecting the popularity of silver expansion was the Bland-Allison Act, which was in essence a compromise between the proponents of the unalloyed gold standard and those supporting bimetallism.

In 1890 Congress again responded to the desires for a more flexible currency by passing the Sherman Silver Purchase Act. This measure required the secretary of the Treasury to purchase 4.5 million ounces of silver monthly, to be paid for with silver certificates—a new currency created for the occasion—which could be redeemed in either gold or silver according to the seller's preference. All silver purchases, under both the Bland-Allison and Sherman Silver Purchase acts, added a rapidly increasing volume of currency to the

PROPAGANDA FOR BIMETALISM, 1894. This political cartoon appears to suggest, incorrectly, that the supply of silver in 1872 was extensive.

nation's money supply. By 1893 the 1890 act had added about $150 million, bringing the silver contribution to more than $500 million.[12]

The Sherman Silver Purchase Act had a dramatic impact on monetary conditions in the nation far beyond the simple expansion of silver money. At the same time, during the depression of the 1890s the nation's trade balance was worsening, reducing its ability to acquire foreign exchange and purchase gold imports necessary to support the dollar. This problem would have disappeared, however, if America had enthusiastically embraced the gold standard. Instead, the simultaneous political attacks on the gold standard, successful in enacting the Sherman Act and subsequently carried forward by radical farm groups (such as the Populists), joined with the balance-of-payments difficulties to produce an international crisis of confidence in America's allegiance to the gold standard. Speculators in gold anticipated the abandonment of the gold standard and the depreciation of the dollar relative to the value of other currencies. Consequently, they tended to turn their dollar holdings to gold, causing a flow of gold out of the country. Gold reserves fell drastically and reinforced international doubts about the ability and willingness of the government to support the dollar.

But just as public policy produced a crisis of confidence in gold, policy action restored the viability of gold. For one thing, in 1893 President Cleveland induced Congress to repeal the silver-purchase clause of the Sherman Act and thereafter engaged in a broad set of deflationary actions. Further, in February of 1895 the Cleveland administration, with the aid of a J. P. Morgan–August Belmont syndicate, launched an extensive sale of bonds for gold that protected the American gold reserve and restrained American gold exports. In a period of rudimentary public institutions for the management of international monetary systems, the active participation of the most prominent American investment bankers on behalf of the nation was not extraordinary and continued well into the next century. Moreover, their contribution was real. However, it should not be ignored that a syndicate did in fact exploit a financial crisis for the benefit of its members (by manipulating exchange rates at levels above the point at which gold would be exported from the United States), protected the European customers who bought bonds through their houses, and guaranteed a continuing, strong European market for American securities.[13]

As a result of the Cleveland administration's restrictive policies, the nation's stock of money remained essentially unchanged between 1890 and 1896. The costs of such a policy were high. It made the long-term squeeze between fixed costs and income more difficult and exaggerated the distributional impact of the long-term secular decline in prices of the late nineteenth century. Moreover, the monetary contraction contributed to and worsened the depression of the 1890s. Nonetheless, to keep the nation on the gold standard it was necessary to take just the action that the Cleveland administration followed. If it had been possible to adopt bimetallism in a decisive fashion, that would indeed have provided a more expansive currency, eased the problems of the depression of the 1890s, and reversed the long-term price decline. In this sense the proposals of the silverites were rational. But the silverites erred in their assumption that such a course of action was politically realistic. They grossly underestimated popular support for the gold standard and the price stability it promised and usually delivered. The free-silver movement split the Democratic party in two because of the adherence of the Cleveland forces to the gold standard, and handed the election of 1896 to the Republicans, who stuck firmly to traditional monetary policies. In fact, the Republicans used their popular position on the money question to overcome their image as anti-immigrant and anti-Catholic and to attract massive support from urban workers. The voter coalition that the Republicans assembled through an emphasis on economic issues—espousal of protective tariffs as well as the gold standard—in 1896 provided them with victories in every presidential election, save those of 1912 and 1916, until their loss to Franklin D. Roosevelt. After the 1896 elections the Republicans affirmed the gold standard and, in effect, the policies of the Cleveland administration. In net, the Populists and other silverites succeeded only in worsening the contraction. Their challenge to the gold standard seriously weakened confidence in the dollar and directly necessitated the contraction adopted by Cleveland beginning in 1893.

The final segment of our period, the years between 1897 and 1914, was marked by a dramatic change in the external conditions that governed the size of the money supply. In large part as a result of the appreciation of gold in the 1890s, gold miners exploited new gold sources in South Africa, Alaska, and Colorado. At the same time they developed an improved mining and refining technology, the chief innovation being the cyanide process for extracting gold from the ore. The result of the new supplies was a falling price of gold and the overvaluation of gold at the United States mint. In other words, gold producers found it more profitable to take their gold to the mint for sale (and eventual coinage) than to sell it for industrial purposes. As a result the stock of money grew extremely rapidly, at an annual rate of 7.5 percent. Accompanied by a slower rate of output growth, the monetary expansion produced an annual rate of price increase of about 2 percent.

Thus the gold standard proved capable of supporting monetary expansion and moderate price inflation. Ironically, the expansion of the money supply was exactly what the silverites had advocated in the 1890s. And if they had achieved the adoption of bimetallism, they would have found no appreciable change in domestic monetary conditions during the following decade. The economic base for the silverite movement had been removed, and this permitted the official affirmation of the gold standard in 1900 and the congressional adoption of the requirement that the government hold gold reserves of a fixed amount ($150 million). Even so, interest in monetary reform, linked more explicitly with the desire to establish a greater degree of political control over the nation's money supply through greater control of the banking system, became stronger until the passage of the Federal Reserve Act of 1914. However, as a postscript to the workings of the gold standard between 1879 and 1914, it should be noted that although the institution involved harsh distributional problems in the late nineteenth century, it provided for greater monetary stability than that enjoyed within the context of the Federal Reserve System. In fact, the fluctuations in the money supply became more severe after 1914, and the depression of the 1930s— which was essentially monetary in origin—was far more severe and protracted than those of either the 1870s or the 1890s. The contribution of the Federal Reserve Act was in providing the *potential* for a more orderly management of the nation's monetary system.

NOTES

1. The data are quite imperfect for the nineteenth century, but for the twentieth century, between 60 and 78 percent of gross capital formation has stemmed from internal sources. Simon Kuznets, *Capital in the American Economy: Its Formation and Financing* (Princeton, N.J.: Princeton University Press, 1961), p. 264.

2. *Ibid.*, p. 306.

3. The demand of manufacturers for external capital was unusually high. In contrast with capital formation in manufacturing, more than three-quarters of *all* capital formation was generated internally during the decade 1900–1909. *Ibid.*, pp. 178, 265.

4. As late as the turn of the century interest rates remained substantially higher throughout the West and South than in the Northeast and Great Lakes region. Even in 1914 the differentials persisted for the Great Plains, the Mountain states, and the South. One recent study suggests that the differential resulted in part from monopoly power held by national bankers in country districts. (The monopoly power resulted from restrictions on entry into the national system and the taxation of state bank notes.) See Richard Sylla, "Federal Policy, Banking Market Struc-

ture, and Capital Mobilization in the United States, 1863–1913," *Journal of Economic History*, 29 (December 1969), 657–686. However, other studies have explained the persistent differentials in terms of other market imperfections. See Lance Davis, "The Investment Market, 1870–1914: The Evolution of a National Market," *Journal of Economic History*, 25 (September 1965), 355–399; and John A. James, "The Development of a National Money Market, 1893–1911," *Journal of Economic History*, 36 (December 1976), 878–897. Still others argue that interest rate differentials were entirely compatible with perfect markets. See, for example, Richard H. Keehn, "Federal Bank Policy, Bank Market Structure, and Bank Performance: Wisconsin, 1863–1914," *Business History Review*, 48 (1974), 1–27; and George Stigler, "Imperfections in the Capital Market," *Journal of Political Economy*, 25 (1967), 287–292.

5. George H. Evans, *Business Incorporations in the United States, 1800–1943* (New York: National Bureau of Economic Research, 1948), pp. 10–35, 50–74.

6. In my discussion of this aspect of institutional change I have drawn very heavily on the pioneering work of Alfred D. Chandler, Jr. See especially *Strategy and Structure: Chapters in the History of American Industrial Enterprise* (Cambridge, Mass: M.I.T. Press, 1962).

7. The disappearance of firms as a result of mergers increased from 69 in 1897 to 303 in 1898 to 1,208 in 1899. Although the level dropped, it remained between about 350 and 425 through 1902. Ralph L. Nelson, *Merger Movements in American Industry* (Princeton, N.J.: Princeton University Press, 1959), p. 37.

8. One author has gone so far as to suggest that this was the most important factor promoting industrial mergers. *Ibid.*, pp. 116–126.

9. In the following description and assessment of monetary arrangements I am most heavily indebted to Milton Friedman and Anna J. Schwartz, *A Monetary History of the United States, 1867–1960* (Princeton, N.J.: Princeton University Press, 1963).

10. Another possibility is that people could have spent what money was available more rapidly, purchasing the same volume of goods and services but bidding up the price level. This possibility is only theoretical, however, since the velocity of money, or the ratio between the market value of output and the money stock, remained roughly constant during the period.

11. In terms of the fundamental monetary equation $p \cdot Q = M \cdot v$, if the velocity of money (v) is constant and real product (Q) increases more rapidly than the money (M), then the general price level (p) must fall.

12. Also in 1890 Congress allowed the payment of customs duties to take place in silver as well as gold, thus further weakening the gold standard.

13. Matthew Simon, "The Morgan-Belmont Syndicate of 1895 and Intervention in the Foreign-Exchange Market," *Business History Review*, 42 (Winter 1968), 385–417.

SUGGESTED READINGS

Books

Chandler, Alfred D., Jr. *Strategy and Structure: Chapters in the History of American Industrial Enterprise.* Cambridge, Mass.: M.I.T. Press, 1962.

————, *The Visible Hand, The Managerial Revolution in American Business.* Cambridge, Mass.: Harvard University Press, 1977.

Davis, Lance E., and Douglass C. North. *Institutional Change and American Economic Growth.* Cambridge, Eng.: Cambridge University Press, 1971. See especially Chapters 6 and 8.

Evans, George H. *Business Incorporations in the United States, 1800–1943.* New York: National Bureau of Economic Research, 1948.

Faulkner, Harold U. *The Decline of Laissez-Faire, 1897–1917.* New York: Holt, Rinehart and Winston, 1951.

Friedman, Milton, and Anna J. Schwartz. *A Monetary History of the United States, 1867–1960.* Princeton, N.J.: Princeton University Press, 1963.

Kirkland, Edward C. *Industry Comes of Age, 1860–1897.* New York: Holt, Rinehart and Winston, 1961.

Kolko, Gabriel. *The Triumph of Conservatism.* Chicago: Quadrangle, 1967.

Krooss, Herman E., and Martin R. Blyn, *A History of Financial Intermediaries.* New York: Random House, 1971.

Myers, Margaret G. *The New York Money Market.* New York: Columbia University Press, 1931.

Nelson, Ralph L. *Merger Movements in American Industry.* Princeton, N.J.: Princeton University Press, 1959.

Thorelli, Hans B. *The Federal Antitrust Policy: Organization of an American Tradition.* Baltimore: Johns Hopkins University Press, 1955.

Unger, Irwin. *The Greenback Era: A Social and Political History of American Finance, 1865–1879.* Princeton, N.J.: Princeton University Press, 1968.

Articles

Davis, Lance E. "Capital Immobilities and Finance Capitalism: A Study of Economic Evolution in the United States, 1820–1920," *Explorations in Entrepreneurial History* (Fall 1963), 88–105.

Hessen, Robert. "The Transformation of Bethlehem Steel, 1904–1909," *Business History Review,* 46 (Autumn 1972), 339–360.

James, John A. "The Development of a National Money Market, 1893–1911," *Journal of Economic History,* 36 (December 1976), 878–897.

Keehn, Richard H. "Federal Bank Policy, Bank Market Structure, and Bank Performance: Wisconsin, 1863–1914," *Business History Review,* 48 (1974), 1–27.

Simon, Matthew. "The Morgan-Belmont Syndicate of 1895 and Intervention in the Foreign-Exchange Market," *Business History Review,* 42 (Winter 1968), 385–417.

Sylla, Richard. "Federal Policy, Banking Market Structure, and Capital Mobilization in the United States, 1863–1913," *Journal of Economic History,* 29 (December 1969), 657–686.

❀ 11
Economic Growth and Labor, 1865-1914

THE WELFARE OF THE WAGE EARNER

Life during the industrial revolution, especially in the late nineteenth and early twentieth centuries, can easily appear harsh, barren, and degrading. There is no doubt, for example, that for those who toiled in the nation's factories, mines, and railroads, the risks to life and limb were high; not until the war and the 1920s were there laws that protected workers against the cost of injuries or induced manufacturers to provide a safer working environment.[1] In addition to the increasing risk of injury, the worker faced a growing chance of unemployment. A good estimate of average decennial unemployment finds that about 10 percent of the labor force was unemployed during both the 1870s and the 1890s—significant increases over the rates for the depressed decades of the years before the Civil War.[2]

In addition to the risks inherent in industrial employment, the urban resident had to cope with housing, sanitation, and public services of dismally poor quality in cities that were congested and diseased. Put more analytically, costs external to the cost-reckoning process of the marketplace for the first time began to be an important element in urban development (not only for individuals but for all decision-making units, including business firms). By the late nineteenth century, government would respond by drastically expanding the level and quality of public services. By 1900, for example, Washington, D.C., and Buffalo had become perhaps the best-paved cities in the world (directing national attention to the use of asphalt), followed closely by Boston and New York. Also, in the last two decades of the nineteenth century, cities, led by Boston and Washington, greatly expanded their sewer systems, drawing on improvements in sewer construction and methods of waste disposal. In those same two decades the number of cities with public waterworks increased sixfold, many cities introduced filtration systems, and the largest cities expanded their facilities, with such achievements as the construction of the New Croton Aqueduct, which provided New Yorkers with water far safer to drink than before. As a result spectacular reductions in death rates occurred in many overcrowded districts. In spite of such governmental initiatives and the effort to force firms to bear a share of external costs through increased taxes, individuals had to bear high personal costs resulting from the character of the urban environment. And although perhaps there is always the temptation to romanticize preindustrial rural life, urban costs were undoubtedly higher than those incurred in the countryside. There seems to be little question, for instance, that the mortality rate, especially for infants, was higher in urban places than in rural, despite the improvements in the public-health overhead during the period. But if one focused purely on the disadvantages of urban life one would fail to comprehend why a flood tide of population continued to flow into the nation's cities.

Immigration resists a complete explanation unless one rests heavily on the attractive force of American economic opportunities.[3] And it is more difficult still to explain the prolonged and sustained movement out of a highly productive American agricultural sector unless one recognizes that the city offered real opportunities for upward economic mobility. Indeed, the greatest waves of rural-urban migration within the United States came, not during periods of agricultural depression, but during times of farm prosperity, when nonfarm economic booms created new demands for *both* labor and farm products. In short, the phenomenal urbanization and immigration of our fifty-year period bears witness to the strength of marketplace considerations in the decisions of millions of individuals to participate directly in the industrial revolution.[4] In effect, urban migrants set monetary remuneration ahead of the physical and psychological costs inherent to urban life of the late nineteenth and early twentieth centuries.

Data on real wages during this period highlight the reality of increasing economic opportunity associated with industrialization. The period between 1860 and 1920 was one of increasing real incomes for American wage earners. Although there was an increasingly large increase in the cost of living during the Civil War, a long decline ensued in 1865 which eventually eliminated the impact of Civil War inflation, and by 1890 real wages and earnings in manufacturing were some 50 percent higher than they had been in 1860. Further, there is little doubt that real earnings increased very rapidly during World War I (or between 1914 and 1920), and there is also little question that money earnings increased strongly throughout the period. Disagreement on the earnings of labor has turned, not on these issues, but on the extent of the increase in the cost of living between 1890 and 1914. The general price level was rising from the late 1890s; hence the possibility exists that increases in the cost of living canceled out dollar gains in earnings. However, the best study at hand finds that the consumer price index rose more slowly than earnings, the real earnings of manufacturing wage earners rising 37 percent between 1890 and 1914, or at an annual rate of about 1.3 percent.[5]

The slight retardation in the growth of real wages between 1890 and 1914 can be explained largely in terms of the mild slowdown in the growth of productivity—a consequence of the depression of the 1890s and the massive immigration of unskilled workers at the beginning of the century. For the period 1860–1920 as a whole, wages and productivity were closely associated. Thus, industrialization appears not to have involved extensive exploitation of labor during that period—wages increased very close to the rate justified by productivity gains. Between 1890 and 1914 the rate of increase in real earnings of manufacturing workers (1.3 percent) was slightly less than the measured rate of increase in worker productivity (1.5 percent). However, in light of the difficulties in developing reliable measures of productivity, in particular ones that accurately reflect changes in the quality of labor, the similarity between the two figures ought to be given greater weight than their difference.

Wages are not the only element to measure in determining the real earnings of workers. Workers can take real income in leisure time as well as in dollar earnings. In other words, by forgoing earnings in taking leisure time, the worker places a real value on the leisure time. In this period, despite the fact that his average hourly real earnings were increasing, the worker was taking greater amounts of leisure time and reducing his working day and week. After 1860 the number of hours the average worker worked declined steadily; by 1890 the average workweek in manufacturing industries was 60 hours and by 1914 it was down to 55.2 hours. The hours worked by skilled labor tended to be even less: the skilled building trades, for example, attained a 50-hour week by the 1890s and a 44.7-hour week by 1914.[6] What is more, the average workweek figures do not reflect the amount of leisure time taken informally—for example, the Blue Monday absenteeism that before Prohibition often followed Saturday payday.

Manufacturers' realization of the contribution of shorter hours to increased efficiency did not blossom until the 1920s; but, in fact, the most rapid declines in hours worked had come well before then. The predominant factor was not the employer's search for efficiency or higher-quality labor but the desire of the average workingman to take a greater portion of his increasing real income as leisure rather than as dollars paid for his services. The inescapable implication is that the industrial revolution provided workers with sufficient monetary returns (transformed into housing, clothing, food, transporation, etc.) to permit them to sacrifice additional returns for the rewards of family, self-education, and recreation. It was no coincidence that this period marked the expansion and specialization of urban entertainment industries. The circus, vaudeville, burlesque, popular theater, and the legitimate stage developed as distinct forms. Saloons, beer gardens, houses of prostitution, dance halls, and billiard parlors offered a complex of complementary yet increasingly specialized services to occupy urban leisure. Rapid-transit companies, in conjunction with suburban amusement parks, offered new opportunities for Saturday and Sunday outings, and spectator sports, such as horse racing, prize fighting, and especially baseball, acquired a larger share of the workingman's dollar.

MINORITIES WITHIN THE LABOR FORCE

Aggregate data provide unmistakable signs of increasing economic opportunity. However, this conclusion must be tested against the experience of important groups whose national origin, race, sex, or age may have caused them to fail to participate fairly in the fruits of economic growth.

Immigrants

Natural increase accounted for the major growth of population as a whole throughout the period, but immigrants contributed heavily to the growth of population, labor force, and the manufacturing-service sectors of the cities. During the dynamic 1880s and the first decade of the twentieth century, net arrivals (gross arrivals less departures) of immigrants accounted for about 40 percent of population increase. More immigrants pressed to American shores in those two decades than in any two others. Correspondingly, those decades witnessed larger increments in the share of the labor force industrialized and the share of the population urbanized than did any others. The foreign-born, at least three-quarters of whom before World War I were European, increased as a share of the total population in the late nineteenth and early twentieth centuries, only to subside in relative importance after the federal government restricted immigration during the 1920s. By then the foreign-born had increased to about 14 percent of the population (from about 10 percent in 1850); thereafter they declined to 11 percent in 1930 and to 6 percent in 1950. The impact of immigration on the continuing industrial revolution was even more marked than the overall figures suggest since the bulk of immigrants settled in cities rather than in the countryside and a disproportionate share of them took on manufacturing employment. Of the 6.5 million foreign-born males in the labor force in 1920, fully 80 percent held urban-located occupations. By 1920 immigrants and their children comprised about half of the nation's total urban population, almost two-thirds of the population residing in large cities (those with over 100,000 people), and an even larger share of the large cities of the New England, Middle Atlantic, and Great Lakes states. And they held more than one-half of the nation's manual jobs in the nonfarm sector.

Immigration depended heavily on the forces of "push." In other words, the number of people potentially available for immigration depended to a great extent on conditions internal to the nations sending populations. Mass flights, such as those of the Irish, of the Jews from Russia, and of Slavic groups from Austria-Hungary, illustrate the point. Discrimination was often a factor, and a very visible one, but the conditions contributing to "push" were usually heavily economic in character. From the mid-nineteenth century, the nations undergoing the more massive reorganization of their traditional agricultural sectors under the pressure of industrialization tended to be the heavier donors of people—immigrants drawn heavily, at their source, from rural areas and nonmanufacturing employments.[7] And among these nations, those with the highest rates of natural increase (and thus greatest pressure on available resources) and the lowest per-capita income (and thus the weakest ability to support their populations) tended to produce emigrants at the highest rates.[8] In this period, these were largely the nations of southern and eastern Europe, particularly Italy, Portugal, and the Austria-Hungarian empire, and Scandinavia, particularly Norway and Sweden. (It must be remembered that in terms of impact on the United States, the size of the donor nation was significant. Thus, Russia, with a very low rate of emigration because of the vitality of its own frontier and restrictions on emigration, still contributed significantly to American population increase.) However, an explanation of immigration that focuses on the donor nations fails to capture the high sensitivity of the immigration patterns to relative levels of economic opportunity on both sides of the Atlantic, and especially to economic conditions within the United States. (The flexibility of the international labor force, made possible by low costs of ocean travel, is suggested by the fact that a high proportion of immigrant arrivals, perhaps as high as one-third on the average during the period, invariably returned to their place of origin.) Indeed, the strength of the attraction of American opportunity is strongly indicated by the fact that long swings in immigration lagged behind long swings in the demand for labor in the United States; an increase in the rate of immigration was usually preceded by a rising rate of growth in wages and a decline in the rate of unemployment.[9] Immigrants poured into American cities, not because they were ignorant of other, better opportunities elsewhere or because they were duped by transportation companies, but because they were cognizant, perhaps mainly through friends and relatives already in the United States, of the relatively high wages even their unskilled labor could command in the nation's cities and factories.

Immigrants found enhanced economic opportunities in the New World, but they may well have exerted a depressing effect on the general wage level. Despite its ambiguity, empirical evidence suggests this conclusion. Specifically, the periods of more rapid real-wage increase coincide with the decades of small immigrant contribution to labor-force expansion.[10] Even without direct evidence, it is clear that the large increase in the supply of labor made possible by immigration reduced the price of labor in the short run. This initial short-run impact was largely on the price of unskilled labor, since the late nineteenth- and early twentieth-century immigrants, particularly those from southern and eastern Europe, tended to be less skilled and often more illiterate than were native white Americans.

Discrimination against immigrants probably added to the downward pressure on wages. Some evidence points toward systematic discrimination against immigrants from southern and eastern Europe.[11] Such evidence consists of findings that some groups of immigrants received lower pay than did native Americans who possessed comparable skills. The mechanisms appear to have been discriminatory hiring and firing practices, which reduced access of immigrants to skilled positions and put immigrants in unusual jeopardy during periods of economic contraction. As a consequence of exclusion from some skilled job opportunities, southern and eastern Europeans crowded into unskilled jobs in artificially large numbers, thereby reducing their wages below that justified by their productivity. Reinforcing this crowding were the proclivities of the first generation of immigrants: for example, a preference for residential segregation that limited full access to employment opportunities and a distaste for agricultural employments that swelled the ranks of immigrants in manufacturing and service jobs. (In 1910, less than 20 percent of first-generation immigrants worked on farms. In contrast, about one-half of native Americans were in agricultural employments.) And, first-generation immigrants tended not to question wage levels, despite their discriminatory content, which were far higher than those prevailing in their home lands. Nonetheless, even the studies that point to discrimination find that most, by far, of the wage differential between immigrants and native Americans can be explained in terms of differences in skill. Moreover, discrimination in hiring and firing practices had little bearing on wage differentials between second- or third-generation immigrants and those workers with a more extensive American ancestry. By 1910, about the same percentage of second-generation immigrants who were nonfarm workers had white-collar or other skilled occupations as did native Americans who were in the nonfarm sector.[12] Extensive discrimination beyond the first generation appears to have been limited to certain groups of southern and eastern Europeans (Armenians, Greeks, and Syrians, for example), Mexicans, Chinese, Japanese, and, among domestic migrants, blacks.[13] Racial prejudice was the most potent instrument for establishing sustained discrimination. In sum, although some of the prejudiced employers and competition-conscious skilled workers discriminated in employment, for most immigrants, including those from southern and eastern Europe, the impact of discrimination was largely mitigated by profit-maximizing employers who pursued the advantages of opening skilled positions to competition among all those workers who were qualified.[14] Thus, the marketplace, with its reward structure that favored measurable productivity, worked, in time, to erode the influence of irrational anti-immigrant prejudice.

A balanced assessment of the contribution of immigration to economic welfare would point out that the massive arrivals of the 1880s and 1900–1910 kept down real wages in the short run. At the same time, however, it would stress that the expansion of the supply of unskilled labor quickened industrial development, facilitated an enlargement of the scale of enterprise, and thus encouraged productivity gains and growing real wages. In the short run, then, immigration expanded the opportunities available to new arrivals. In the long run, all portions of the labor force, foreign-born and native, unskilled and skilled, benefited from the flexible supply of labor that immigration provided.

Blacks

The major source of labor continued to be adult white males, but the employment of women, children, and nonwhites was increasing. The nonwhite population accounted for about 10 percent of the net increase in the labor force between 1870 and 1910. Although surges of Asian, especially Chinese, and Mexican immigration appeared, particularly in the 1870s and during the decade of World War I, the absolute size of these population movements was small and their impact was limited to California and the Southwest. From the national standpoint the fundamental source of the nonwhite population was native blacks, the character of whose employment was basically unchanged from that of slave days. In 1900, for example, some 86 percent of all blacks were still employed in agriculture or in personal-domestic service. However, these employments were, in fact, declining in importance, especially during World War I with its high demand for labor in manufacturing, and by 1920 agriculture and personal-domestic service accounted for only two-thirds of the black labor force, while manufacturing, mechanical, trade, and transportation accounted for the remainder. Most of these jobs were in mining, lumbering, and construction, were located primarily in the South, involved only the heaviest, lowest-skilled work, and drew the lowest wages. Economic opportunities for blacks were widening, but they were more restricted than for whites who had the same skills, or lack of skills.

As the structure of the black labor force changed, its distribution over the country began to shift as well. The first important migration of blacks was to the North from the cotton South during World War I, with virtually all of those northward-bound blacks locating in cities. By 1920 over 80 percent of all blacks in northern and western states lived in urban places. Also, by that time, fully 34 percent of the nation's entire black population lived in urban places, whereas only 23 percent did in 1900. Typically, like other American population movements, the black migration was a response to real changes in the patterns of economic opportunity—changes, in other words, in the patterns of the price of labor. In this case the enormous demand for labor created by rapid mobilization for war and later, during the 1920s, the relative decline of cotton agriculture accelerated the northward movement. But one fact about the black migration stands out as unique: it was a one-way movement; few blacks migrated *back* to the South. Even though whites migrated from the South at the same time as blacks, their migration exhibited the much more usual pattern of an ebb and flow—a characteristic of a labor force sensitive to changing regional differentials in wage earnings. The strong implication is that the black migration was a response not simply to higher wages in the North but also to greater, persistent discrimination in the South. As limited as the opportunities in northern cities were for the black immigrant from the southern countryside, they were still wider than those open in the South. Thus the pattern of black migration argues that the push of southern circumstance was stronger than the pull of northern opportunity for blacks.[15]

Women

The huge demand for labor that sustained immigration and helped to carry the black population into the industrial labor force also attracted large numbers of women. From 3.75 million in 1870, the number of women employed at full-time jobs increased to about 8 million in 1910, accounting for over 20 percent of the labor force, as contrasted with less than 15 percent in 1870. Agriculture and manufacturing remained large employers of women throughout the period, but their share of the total employment of women declined. (See Table 24.) Meanwhile the service sectors increased in importance. The relative shift of employment to service occupations was slow, but significant changes were hidden within that sector. Domestic service declined dramatically as an employer of women, particularly after 1900. But employment as store clerks and saleswomen (included in "trade and transportation") increased rapidly between 1890 and 1900, as did employment as office clerks, stenographers, typists, bookkeepers, cashiers, teachers, social workers, and nurses

TABLE 24   OCCUPATIONAL DISTRIBUTION OF WOMEN, 1890–1920

	1890	1900	1920
Agriculture	17.4%	15.9%	11.2%
Manufacturing	26.2	24.8	22.8
Service	56.4	59.3	66.0
Trade and Transportation	5.8	10.0	10.5
Domestic and Personal Service	42.6	40.4	26.0
Professional Service	8.0	8.9	29.5
Total	100	100	100

Sources: U.S. Bureau of the Census, *The Report on Population of the United States at the Eleventh Census*, 1890, Vol. 1, Part 2 (Washington, D.C.: U.S. Government Printing Office, 1897), pp. 414–431.

U.S. Bureau of the Census, *Statistics of Women at Work: 1900* (Washington, D.C.: U.S. Government Printing Office, 1907), pp. 170–174.

U.S. Bureau of the Census, *Fourteenth Census of the United States, Populations*, Vol. 4, *Occupations* (Washington, D.C.: U.S. Government Printing Office, 1923), pp. 708–750.

AUDIT DIVISION OF THE METROPOLITAN LIFE INSURANCE COM-
PANY, 1897. Insurance companies and banks led in hiring young women as
clerks and typists.

(all included under "professional service"), especially during World
War I. Only with the war did women move into white-collar jobs in
significant numbers. The wartime mobilization, involving exhorta-
tion to women to work as their patriotic duty, and the widespread
adoption of the typewriter created new demands for the labor of
women, and to an increasing extent men and women became interchangeable in service occupations. Although many women lost their
jobs when the men returned from war, the trend of greater participation was not reversed. When immigration slackened in the last of the
1920s, women, primarily young and unmarried, filled a large part of
the unsatisfied demand for labor: in a sense, women began to replace
the immigrant in the labor force.

As a result of World War I, the end of immigration, and the
accelerated demand for service workers, the contribution of women
to the gainfully employed increased to 25 percent by 1930 and the
share of women employed in "professional service" continued to
increase dramatically. Without this expansive source of female labor

mainly white, the nation would have had to look abroad once again for its labor supply, make heavier investments in enhancing the quality of labor, introduce further labor-saving technological and organizational change, or accept a slower pace of economic growth.

Economic opportunities for women clearly grew during this period, and the changing character of women's employment—particularly the shifts away from farm work and domestic service toward professional service—clearly represents an enhancement of the economic status of women who worked. Moreover, where women did the same work as men, they appear to have received the same pay. But such a circumstance was unusual, involving transitory situations where women were in the process of replacing men, as they were in the Pittsburgh stogy sweatshops or in New York insurance offices, for example. Typically, women worked in a more narrow range of occupations and in less skilled positions than men. Men were more than twice as likely as women to work as professionals, proprietors, managers, officials, foremen, or skilled laborers. Moreover, certain jobs—clerking and typing, for example—became stereotyped as women's work; the labor marketplace appeared to have become segmented or "Balkanized" by sex. This stereotyping occurred in manufacturing also, where women concentrated in a few industries, notably textiles, boots and shoes, food products, and tobacco products.[16]

The extent to which discrimination contributed to these job patterns is unclear. Certainly, the modest ambitions of many women workers contributed. Most women who worked were either young, unmarried, and simply pursuing short-term employment, or married and seeking to supplement the inadequate income of their husbands. Some concentration in lower-skilled jobs should have been the inevitable consequence. But this cannot fully explain the segmentation of the labor market. An explanation must rely, in part, on the phenomenon of "crowding." Discrimination, if practiced through denial of equal access to job opportunities, should have led some women to crowd into the occupations that they found open. That crowding would have meant that women in the open occupations offered their labor services at wages lower than would have prevailed in a discrimination-free economy and lower than competing men were willing to accept. Employers or industries willing to eschew discrimination would have enjoyed a marvelous opportunity to increase their profits by paying wages lower than the productivity of their workers warranted. Indeed, employers in the service sector would have found such employment particularly attractive since so many young American women had acquired a solid competence in arithmetic and language skills. (In 1890 two-thirds of the nation's high-school graduates were women.) Even a relatively small amount of job discrimination could have produced a large amount of crowding, given the hyper-sensitivity of employers to wage differentials in the labor-scarce economy. However, a puzzle remains: Why didn't discriminating employers recognize the extra profits that nondiscriminating employers earned and seek to bid away the underpriced labor of women until wages returned to levels justified by productivity? The answer probably is that significant numbers of employers, particularly in manufacturing, pursued sexist hiring and firing practices in order to maintain harmony among male employees. Nonetheless, this conclusion must be regarded as tentative until more is known about the extent and distribution of job discrimination.

Children

In addition to the increase of women in the work force after the Civil War, there was a rise in child labor. By 1910 nearly one-quarter of all children between the ages of ten and fourteen had full-time jobs. Here again, the shortage of unskilled labor sharply altered the social composition of the labor force. In this case, however, strong, moralistic middle-class resistance mounted to the pressures exerted by industrialization, and by the end of the century, states were becoming more active in passing legislation to eliminate child labor. In itself, such legislation was generally unsuccessful in keeping children out of the marketplace. But when the child-protection movement effectively merged with the movement to impose compulsory education, the results were much more satisfactory.[17] By 1920, primarily as a result of those movements, the employment of children fell below 1 million (less than half as high as it had been in 1910 and only about 2.6 percent of the labor force), most of them employed in agriculture. In the case of child labor, one can argue, society decided not only that the industrial employment of children was immoral but also that long-run growth would be promoted by forcing families to forgo the earnings that children could make as full-time members of the labor force and require their children to improve their skills and capacities, that is, to acquire a larger increment of human capital. To the extent that those interested in compulsory education were following an economic strategy, they were assuming that the shortage of skilled labor was a more crucial problem than an insufficiency of unskilled workers. Those who promoted educational programs or touted the nuclear family as a vehicle for increasing investment in human capital made the same assumption. As a result of the increasing attention to the welfare of children, the labor force became better trained for specialized occupations, more competent in the basic skills of com-

CHILD TENDING SPINDLES IN A NORTH CAROLINA TEXTILE MILL, 1909. Such photographs helped mobilize northern middle-class opposition to child labor.

munication and thus more able to take advantage of new opportunities and to cope with changing technologies and modes of social organization, and healthier and longer-lived.

In short, examination of the participation of those groups most likely to have been denied full participation in the maturing industrial revolution should not alter a fundamentally positive evaluation of the contribution of the marketplace to labor-force welfare. The marketplace worked efficiently to mesh the collective quest of millions to raise their material standards of living with the huge appetite of the American industrial revolution for their labor. Discrimination, carried forward by noneconomic forces, limited the economic success of immigrants and women, but even these groups found the impact of the marketplace more powerful than cultural restrictions on economic opportunity.

THE LABOR MOVEMENT

The optimistic view that the marketplace effectively rewarded most workers, even those who were not white, native American males deserves scrutiny in the light of the history of the labor movement between the Civil War and World War I. Is it possible to square this interpretation with the efforts of workers to organize collectively?

During the late nineteenth century, the profile that would distinguish the labor movement in the twentieth century clearly emerged. Labor organized in national units on a scale appropriately large to contest the power of corporations in labor markets. Taking advantage of the falling costs of communication, some nineteen national unions formed in the 1860s and ten more joined before 1873. These unions acquired experience in managing large organizations and thereby eased the formation of the Federation of Organized Trades and Labor Unions in 1881 and its successor, the American Federation of Labor (A.F.L.) in 1886. Under Samuel Gompers, this union and its member locals were devoted almost exclusively to the representation of skilled workers by "pure and simple" unionism: concentration on gaining more pay and better working conditions through collective bargaining with employers and, when necessary, the strike. The A.F.L. for the most part eschewed involvement in politics, only rarely endorsing political candidates or parties and scrupulously steering clear of political and economic reform movements. National unions that involved themselves in politics, such as the National Labor Union (1866–1872) and the Knights of Labor (with a career that began in 1878 but ended rapidly after its zenith in 1886), failed to develop a base of permanent supporters. After the depression of the 1890s, the A.F.L. made rapid, sustained gains in organizing skilled workers. During the depression, union membership had fallen to about 1 percent of the labor force, but by World War I nearly 6 percent of the labor force belonged to unions, largely those affiliated with the A.F.L.

Despite the organizational gains of the union movement, it had far less impact on the terms and conditions of work than did factors like immigration, which affected labor supply and demand. Unions never represented large segments of the working population. Even at their pre-New Deal peak of membership during World War I, unions organized only about 20 percent of the nonagricultural labor force.[18] However, after 1897, when the craft unionism of the American Federation of Labor under Samuel Gompers became well established, unions may indeed have bargained effectively on behalf of segments of skilled labor and had an important influence on the upward course of wages in certain trades and industries.[19] Most im-

SAMUEL GOMPERS. His attire and bearing suggest the success of the A.F. of L. and its absorption with the interests of skilled labor.

portant were unions in industries with a long history of union activism—those with A.F.L. unions representing printers, cigar makers, molders, brewers, and machinists, for instance. But in crucial industries like steel, automobiles, agricultural machinery, electrical products, cigarettes, and meat packing, to say nothing of public utilities, the organization of labor made virtually no headway. And if unions achieved short-run victories of significance, their wage increases often encouraged employers to shift to more capital-intensive production, which eliminated the jobs of many union members. For example, after some 50,000 shoemakers joined the Knights of St. Crispin in the late 1860s, employers hastened their adoption of sewing machines to replace the craftsmen. The consequence was the demise of the Knights of St. Crispin. When skilled steel workers gained marked organizing strength during the 1880s, U.S. Steel replaced them more rapidly with mechanical controls, other equipment, and engineers who were more skilled. Largely as a result, unionization of the steel industry failed to advance significantly until the 1930s.[20] It was difficult, indeed, for labor unionists to overcome the forces of the market. For the period as a whole and for industry in general unions demonstrated little power to increase the real income of labor.

The weakness of the labor movement and of the cohesiveness of the nation's workers stemmed from a complex set of factors. Most fundamental was the success of the marketplace in rewarding labor with wages that closely approximated levels justified by labor productivity. American workers enjoyed rapidly rising real wages, which were basically commensurate with productivity gains, despite the fact that the marketplace was essentially free of combinations of labor. Upward economic mobility, while not breathtaking in its swiftness, was rapid enough—particularly between the first and second generations of immigrants—to temper the desire of workingmen for class-oriented action. Skilled workers experienced the most rapid increase in wages, grew rapidly in their relative numbers, tended to aspire to middle-class status, and, consequently, tended to adopt readily prevailing values. Those values, reinforcing the reality of economic mobility, included the widespread assumption that America was fundamentally a land of opportunity and that economic failure was a product of the mistakes or inadequacies of the individual rather than society at large.

The low level of class action was not entirely a consequence of the economic successes of the period. The rapid growth of the labor force, the rapid entry and exit of immigrants from the labor force, the high degree of geographic mobility of workers, and the disorganized quality of urban life during the period all sapped the organizing force of the labor movement. The rapid pace of technical change continuously undermined the organizing base of labor by rendering old job categories obsolete and by creating new job opportunities for both skilled and unskilled labor. Recurring episodes of high unemployment also retarded or reversed the course of unionization. The depressions of both the 1870s and 1890s contributed to marked declines in union membership. Depressions enhanced economic incentives for organization but simultaneously produced labor surpluses that led individuals to be more willing to undercut their fellow workers in order to obtain employment. Also, since unskilled workers tended to suffer more from depressions than skilled workers, economic instability tended to drive a wedge between the interests of skilled and unskilled workers, reinforcing differences that were already great. It is hardly surprising that organization of the unskilled made little progress and that the Knights of Labor, drawing heavily on the ranks of the unskilled for its members, met an early end.

The ethnic and religious tensions, which had divided labor during the 1840s and 1850s, intensified as immigration from southern and eastern Europe crested. If anything, Protestant America grew more nervous about the imagined threat of Catholics. On the one hand, German and Scandinavian Lutherans added to Protestant strength while, on the other, Italians, Poles, and German Catholics added to the Catholic population and to the swift accretion of national political power by the Democratic party during the 1880s and early 1890s. Moreover, native Americans and immigrants from northern Europe often regarded the "new" immigrants as inferior social types—degraded in their living standards, corrupt in their political practices, criminal in their public behavior, and responsible for all the problems facing the cities of the late nineteenth century. There were economic issues at stake as well. Native Americans and recent immi-

ANTI-CHINESE RIOTING IN DENVER, 1880. Antagonism to Chinese workers culminated in 1882 with congressional closing of Chinese immigration.

grants from northern Europe tended to be more skilled than the "new" immigrants. Consequently, the divisions between skilled and unskilled, which usually became more acute in depressions, often took on ethnic dimensions. Further, many native Americans resented the opposition of some immigrant politicians and church leaders to the expansion of public-school systems and requirements that English be the language of instruction. Disputes over the nature of public education became especially bitter on the local and state level. The significance of ethnic differences in the factories is unclear, but in some industries employers deliberately mixed up various nationalities in order to raise the cost of communication among workers and thus impede unionization. All of these issues contributed to the movement of the A.F.L. toward support of immigration restriction. During the first decade of the twentieth century, as the immigration from southern and eastern Europe reached new heights, the A.F.L. and Samuel Gompers embraced a literacy test for all immigrants. (Such a test had been passed by a Republican Congress in 1895 but the Democratic president, Grover Cleveland, had vetoed it.) Those who were embroiled in these issues, whether they were immigrants whose primary political allegiance was to their ward bosses or native Americans committed during the 1880s to the fanatic Minute Men, the Loyal Legion, or the Sons of America, diverted their energies from the organized labor movement. Thus, in the extended, intense, and unusual social flux that massive immigration brought to the United States, ethnicity and religion worked to accentuate economic differences and hamper unionization, both within skill groups and across skill lines.

Only one important national union, the Knights of Labor, tried to bridge the gaps between skilled and unskilled, native American and immigrant, northern European and southern European, Catholic and Protestant. (Not even the Knights, however, developed a serious organizing interest in the growing numbers of women and blacks who were part of the urban work force.) Attracted by a charismatic Irishman, Terence V. Powderly, encouraged by an accidental strike victory over Jay Gould's railway system, and frustrated by the slow, narrow gains of "pure and simple" unionism, large numbers of unskilled or low-skilled workers flocked to the Knights. By 1886 nearly 700,000 had joined. The Knights proposed to end the wage system and to introduce cooperative enterprises that would share the wealth, but they recognized that this would take time. Meanwhile, they promoted a variety of social reforms, focusing on the adoption of legislation insuring the eight-hour day for all workers. With a vague program and a highly disorganized membership, the leadership of the Knights had great difficulty in exercising control. Wildcat strikes became rife, and the Knights, in order to create an impression of central direction, called for a nationwide general strike on May 1, 1886. In the third day of a strike against the McCormick Reaper Works in Chicago, at a meeting called to protest the killing of four strikers at the plant, someone threw a bomb which touched off the Haymarket riot. Ten more people were killed, and some fifty were injured. When it turned out that a small group of anarchists on the fringe of the Knights of Labor had organized the meeting, a wave of anti-immigrant, antiunion hysteria swept the nation. A jury convicted eight of the Chicago Knights of murder, many states passed laws restricting the ability of workers to organize, other states prosecuted union members for conspiracy, and large sectors of rural America and the middle classes, including skilled workers, identified the organization of unskilled workers, particularly if they were recent immigrants, with unnecessary violence and with revolutionary activism. Support for the Knights quickly evaporated. The Haymarket Riot had brought latent ethnic and economic divisions among workers to the surface. Another massive effort to unite workers across skill and ethnic boundaries would wait until the 1930s. Until then, the future of organized labor lay with the A.F.L. and Samuel Gompers, who largely ignored the unskilled worker and predicated his program on the fundamental hostility of the American middle class to unionization.

The internal divisions within the labor movement and the unpopularity of unionization with the middle class allowed employers to have easy access to the power of governments in order to suppress unions. Efforts of the federal and state governments to break strikes and blunt organizing drives were particularly popular with the burgeoning middle class of the large cities, which identified with corporate leaders and sought social cohesion in a period of social change.[21] Thus, President Rutherford B. Hayes won national acclaim when he called out federal troops and successfully broke the Railroad Strike in 1877, the first interstate strike in the nation's history. And President Grover Cleveland won similar accolades in 1894 when he invoked the use of federal troops to break the Pullman Strike, another interstate strike of railroad brotherhoods which had nationwide support from the American Railway Union. Besides the use of troops, employers were able to use a variety of other techniques sanctioned by government. A favorite was the "blacklist"—a list of union organizers circulated among employers within cities. Another was the "yellow dog" contract—an agreement written into a worker's contract proscribing union activity. A third was the injunction—a court order restricting strike activity. In the 1894 Pullman Strike, for example, employers and the federal government found they had to resort to the injunction to supplement their military force. Turning to the federal courts, they obtained an order forbidding the railroad workers from engaging in virtually any action that might hamper the business of the twenty-three railroads involved. Nonetheless, the American Railway Union maintained a boycott of Pullman cars, and the federal government subsequently arrested the president of the union, Eugene V. Debs, and convicted him of contempt of court. Employers were able to maintain their legal advantages until the 1930s, when a dramatic narrowing of economic opportunities, a waning of the divisive power of ethnicity, and a shift in the climate of middle-class opinion would contribute to encouraging large-scale unionization. Meanwhile, the A.F.L. would seek a conservative, businesslike image for the labor movement, an image designed to win gradually the confidence and cooperation of corporations in the process of collective bargaining with skilled workers.

In sum, the history of the labor movement before World War I confirms an optimistic view of the role of the marketplace in determining the welfare of wage earners. The weaknesess of the movement and its emphasis on "pure and simple" unionism, grounded as they were in the prosperity of the era, the growing importance of skilled labor, and the vitality of the middle classes, reinforce an emphasis on the success of the marketplace in adequately rewarding labor for its contribution to economic growth. Even the violent ethnic divisions, which weakened the movement, support that emphasis. One can reasonably speculate that under conditions of chronic economic stringency workers would have been more willing to set aside their national and religious differences. Indeed, one can argue that they did so in the 1930s largely because of the exceptionally protracted nature of the Great Depression.

THE WELFARE OF FARMERS: POLITICS AND MARKET FORCES

No convenient measure such as real wages exists to chart the degree to which farmers successfully participated in economic growth. Farmers included not only wage earners but also small businessmen, who frequently were small capitalists as well, more interested in calculating the return on their investment than in gauging the return on their own, and their family's, labor. Given the consequent difficulty of determining the income of farmers during this period, historians have tended to focus instead on the very high degree of political activism that characterized substantial portions of the farming population, especially during the last decades of the nineteenth century. The highly visible movements of the 1870s and 1890s—the Grange, the Greenback party, the Farmers' Alliance, and, finally, the Populist party—have in large part shaped a historical judgment of this period that finds the farmer's lot to have been an extremely difficult one. Moreover, it is tempting, as a result of that intense political activity, to view the condition of agriculture in the late nineteenth century as having been a function of political developments. The Populists, in particular, explained the apparent farm depression of the post-Civil War years as resulting from their failure to gain access to the political system, or their inability to counter the economic power of the nonproducers who sought, in the view of the Populists, to monopolize economic activity.

The most difficult economic problem that the farmers faced during the last decades of the century, especially the 1870s and 1890s, was the same one that faced all those businessmen who had gone into debt to expand production—the contraction of the money supply. The monetary contraction resulted in a failure of demand to expand as rapidly as was possible, and as demand failed to keep up with the rate of increase of real product, the price level declined. If the failure of the money supply to expand adequately to support demand was a political failure of the post-Civil War generation, it was also a failure of the nineteenth-century gold standard, a failure that bore as hard upon small businessmen as it did upon the farmers. In a period of a secular decline in prices, all debtor capitalists who had little control over the prices they received for their production were caught between fixed costs, stemming largely from the costs of borrowing capital, and uncertainty of future incomes. It was difficult to pay off investments while income was shrinking; and the burden of fixed costs was growing during the period. The sharpest price downturns, as well as the sharpest monetary contractions, came in the 1870s and 1890s; it is no accident that these decades marked the peaks of farm protest and the peaks of the interest of small business in expanding foreign markets to supplement domestic demand.[22] Compounding the problems posed by the income–fixed cost squeeze was the instability of farm prices during the late nineteenth century. More primary producing nations such as Australia, Argentina, South Africa, and Russia (the Ukraine) joined the United States in competition for metropolitan markets, and that competition, along with the climatic irregularities endemic to agriculture, enhanced price instability for American farmers. The 1870s were particularly difficult for farmers in the Great Lakes region and the upper Mississippi valley, while the 1890s proved unusually troublesome for farmers in the Great Plains.

The farmer found the income–fixed cost squeeze especially difficult to bear, for both economic and psychological reasons, because during that same period he was becoming substantially more productive and, in fact, was contributing to his income problem by enlarging his productive capacity. Between 1870 and 1900 the productivity of farm workers increased by about 45 percent. Given the prevailing deflation, it seems almost certain that during this period the rate of increase of per-capita farm income lagged substantially behind the rate of increase of farm productivity.

The trends of expansion and heightened productivity stemmed from the redistribution of agricultural activity, the stimulation of new demands, increasing efficiency in transportation and marketing, and the widening spread of improved technology. During the 1870s southern production resumed a rapid rate of growth, and southern per-capita income began to move toward the national level. Through the opening of newer lands within the boundaries of the old South, the increasing use of commercial fertilizers, and the rapid proliferation of farm machinery, southern agriculture may well have realized productivity gains. The most expansive agricultural section, however, was the Great Plains, which received the bulk of new agricultural settlement after 1870 and where commercial agriculture was the rule. Wheat production, centered in the Great Plains and prairie states, more than doubled between 1870 and 1900. Eight of the ten leading wheat-producing states were west of the Mississippi, and older wheat states, such as Wisconsin, developed new specialties.

COMBINES ON A PACIFIC NORTHWEST WHEAT FARM, 1908. The heavy machinery and horse power suggest the growing capital-intensity of agriculture.

Real investment in implements and farm machinery, especially drills, reapers, and threshers, increased dramatically; expenditures for fertilizers also grew rapidly. The production of meat animals, much of which was also located in the Great Plains, increased from $984 million in 1870 to $1.6 billion in 1900. The expansion of Great Plains agriculture was facilitated by the expanding railroad network, and by the increasing efficiency of the services offered by middlemen. Despite the farmer's tendency to condemn the bankers, railroads, grain handlers, shippers, and owners of grain elevators, their services of finance, transport, and marketing did indeed become more efficient and in the long run contributed in an important way to the ability of American farmers to compete effectively in world markets.[23] (Indeed, due to America's advantaged position because of both increased efficiency and the falling price level, European farmers had extreme difficulty meeting the competition of American agriculture, so much so that the foreign market regularly absorbed almost 20 percent of United States agricultural produce during the period.)

Efficiencies aside, however, transportation costs remained high relative to all costs of farmers—as much as half of the value of crop production in some areas—and farm prices tended to fall more rapidly than the costs of transportation and other services during the downturns of the 1870s and 1890s. It is, therefore, easy to understand the agitation of farmers over the costs of middlemen's services during these periods of adversity.[24]

The most rapidly growing sector of American agriculture was that which produced specialized crops more keyed to the growth of urban markets and per-capita income than were the staple commodities—poultry and eggs, dairy products, vegetables and fruits rather than wheat, corn, and meat. Because of fast-rising demand, producers of these crops, generally located in the eastern and North Central states, did not suffer the price–fixed cost squeeze experienced by staple producers and, by and large, eschewed the more radical politics of the 1870s and 1890s. To the extent that such farmers went to the political system for advancement of their economic interests, they sought support, including subsidies, for their efforts to become more productive. They were simply participating in the wider social recognition of the importance of investment in human capital to the heightening of productivity.[25]

Agricultural education expanded rapidly during the period, receiving both state and federal support. In 1890 Congress passed the second Morrill Act, which markedly increased the federal contribution to agricultural colleges. Farmers' institutes received the support of state governments and agricultural colleges, and in the 1890s the colleges developed extension programs and short courses. Beginning in the 1860s various states developed agricultural experiment stations, and in 1887 Congress passed the Hatch Act, which provided for an annual appropriation of $15,000 (from public land sales) to each state and territory for the establishment of experiment stations. By the 1890s a pattern of cooperation had developed between the Department of Agriculture, the experiment stations, and the agricultural colleges in the promotion of increased productivity. Within the Department of Agriculture the Division of Chemistry conducted research in new crops and methods of increasing the yields of old ones; the Division of Statistics conducted production surveys; the Division of Entomology worked to perfect means of insect control; the Bureau of Plant Industry and the Bureau of Animal Industry conducted research in plant and animal diseases, with the latter developing a successful vaccination program for hog cholera; the Division of Pomology tested the adaptability of orchard trees to various locales; and the Division of Soils did pioneering work in the development of a soil science. State experiment stations and the agricultural colleges developed a professional elite of innovators and disseminators of scientific knowledge in agriculture. Both educating the nation's more prosperous farmers and reinforcing their desire to increase productivity, this group became the nucleus of leadership for further expansion of farm programs in the twentieth century, culminating in the revolution in agriculture brought about by the

BARN RAISING IN OHIO, 1888. Cooperative as well as individualistic traditions were important to nineteenth-century rural culture.

application of chemical and biochemical knowledge in the 1930s and 1940s.[26]

To some extent, increased subsidies to agricultural research were defended as necessary alternatives to more radical solutions to the farmers' marketplace problems. These proposals, which developed from the Farmers' Alliance and Populist movements and were supported by most farmers who took to politics, fell in two basic categories: achieving greater control of the institutions for marketing farm output; and promoting a more expansive money supply to support domestic demand for farm products and, hence, the level of farm prices and farm income. The former included the sub-Treasury system favored by southern Populists for extending credit on harvested cotton and holding cotton off the market until the highest possible price could be attained; the Granger cooperative efforts and proposals for railroad regulation; and the Populist program for nationalization of the railroads. The monetary solutions were essentially those of the greenback and free-silver movements (see pp. 307–315). Regardless of the merits of the various programs, the farmers achieved virtually none of their more radical objectives, and the marketing of farm products remained essentially unchanged. The Populists, in particular, suffered a decisive political defeat in 1896 which actually worked to affirm the gold standard. Nonetheless, beginning in the late 1890s the economic situation changed drastically in favor of the farmer. Although this economic success in the face of political defeat did not deny the validity of the Populist solutions, especially the monetary ones, it did attest to the fact that the marketplace could very definitely work in the interests of the farmer, without drastic institutional alterations. At the same time farm hostility to the corporations and middlemen waned, and concepts that emphasized the contributions of the corporations to material progress became more typical of farmers' attitudes.[27]

The vastly improved situation of the farmer was a result of change in conditions of both supply and demand. In the first place, the gold standard again provided an expansive money supply (in a sense, the Populists achieved their goal of a monetary expansion, even though their specific proposal had failed). On the demand side, the nonrural population grew far more rapidly between 1900 and 1910 than it had during the 1890s. Reinforcing the positive impact of buoyant demand on farm income was an inability of agriculture to expand to new lands as rapidly as had been the case previously. Farm acreage increased only about 5 percent, with output per acre showing little increase between 1900 and 1910. Corn acreage increased about 10 percent, but wheat acreage actually declined almost 15 percent. Also, the supply of farm laborers was about constant, approximately

11 million in both 1900 and 1910. In short, demand far outstripped supply during this period. Indeed, domestic demand was such that domestic prices increased much more rapidly than foreign prices, with the exports of foodstuffs falling off sharply. As a result of the changing configuration of supply and demand, corn prices increased from 35 cents per bushel to 52 cents per bushel. Wheat prices increased from 62 cents per bushel to 91 cents per bushel, and the index of farm wholesale prices (1926 prices equaling 100) increased from 50.5 in 1900 to 74.3 in 1910, for a gain of almost 50 percent. At the same time, however, all wholesale prices increased only about 25 percent. As a result of growing farm income, the value of farmland and buildings almost doubled (the average price per acre of farmland increased from $19.81 in 1900 to $39.60), an unprecedented rate of increase for the late nineteenth century.

This very favorable supply-and-demand situation continued without interruption until a recession intervened in 1913–1914 to retard the rate of increase in farm values. But while it lasted, the relative prosperity farmers achieved after the late 1890s, and especially between 1910 and 1913, was unmatched, before or after. Never were farm prices and farm incomes so high, relative to other prices and incomes. Consequently, it is not surprising that this period, especially 1910–1913, has been called the golden age of agriculture and has been the period to which farmers have looked in trying to establish parity between themselves and other groups. Despite the political setback of 1896, the period thereafter was one in which the American farmer fared better in relationship to other members of the economy and one in which he participated more extensively in the fruits of economic growth than at any other time in the nation's economic history.

NOTES

1. Under the common law, which prevailed in most cases during the period, management could claim that a worker accepted employment with full knowledge of possible hazards, or it could pass the blame for an accident off to a fellow employee rather than to the management. New York and New Jersey did enact successful worker-protection laws that were upheld by the Supreme Court; Congress applied the Employers' Liability Act to railroads in 1908 and to all public employees later; and many other industrial states followed the example of New York and New Jersey during the war and during the 1920s.

2. Those high rates, however, would not be reached again until the decade of the Great Depression. Stanley Lebergott, *Manpower in Economic Growth: The American Record Since 1800* (New York: McGraw-Hill, 1964), pp. 187–190.

3. For recent studies that emphasize the pull of economic circumstance in determining the pattern of international migration and the significance of information provided by previously landed friends and relatives to the functioning of the international labor market, see Lowell E. Gallaway and Richard K. Veder, "Emigration from the United Kingdom to the United States: 1860–1913," *Journal of Economic History*, 31 (December 1971), 885–897; and John A. Tomaske, "The Determinants of Intercountry Differences in European Emigration: 1881–1900," *Journal of Economic History*, 31 (December 1971), 840–853.

4. Eventually historians may be able to say that the entire pattern of population movements in the United States has been determined, most fundamentally, by patterns of opportunity. For example, a recent study finds very high rates of mobility within nineteenth-century Boston, within the city and out of the city to other urban areas. But apart from observing that poor people were not trapped in particular ghettos, the authors are unable to determine whether mobility within the urban sector meant increased welfare, as did the rural-urban and transatlantic movements. See Stephan Thernstrom and Peter R. Knights, "Men in Motion: Some Data and Speculations About Urban Population Mobility in Nineteenth-Century America," *Journal of Interdisciplinary History*, 1 (Autumn 1970), 7–35.

5. The best studies for 1860–1914 are Clarence D. Long, *Wages and Earnings in the United States, 1860–1890* (Princeton, N.J.: Princeton University Press, 1960); and Albert Rees, *Real Wages in Manufacturing, 1890–1914* (Princeton, N.J.: Princeton University Press, 1961). For World War I see Paul H. Douglas, *Real Wages in the United States, 1890–1926* (Boston: Houghton Mifflin, 1930).

6. U.S. Bureau of the Census, *Historical Statistics of the United States, Colonial Times to 1957* (Washington, D.C.: U.S. Government Printing Office, 1960), p. 91.

7. See Simon Kuznets, *Economic Growth and Structure: Selected Essays* (New York: Norton, 1965), pp. 45–46.

8. See Richard A. Easterlin, "Influences in European Overseas Emigration Before World War I," *Economic Development and Cultural Change*, 9 (April 1961), 331–351.

9. Richard A. Easterlin, *Population, Labor Force, and Long Swings in Economic Growth: The American Experience* (New York: Columbia University Press, 1968), p. 30 ff.

10. Lebergott, *op. cit.*, p. 162.

11. See, for example, Paul F. McGouldrick and Michael B. Tannen, "Did American Manufacturers Discriminate Against Immigrants Before 1914?" *Journal of Economic History*, 37 (September 1977), 723–746.

12. E. P. Hutchinson, *Immigrants and Their Children, 1850–1950* (New York: Wiley, 1956), pp. 138–142, 201–216.

13. On discrimination against urban blacks, see Clyde Griffen, "Making It in America: Social Mobility in Mid-Nineteenth Century Poughkeepsie," *New York History* (October 1970), 497–499; and Stephan Thernstrom, *The Other Bostonians: Poverty and Progress in the American Metropolis, 1880–1970* (Cambridge, Mass.: Harvard University Press, 1973), pp. 176 ff.

14. For an elaboration of this argument, see Robert Higgs, "Race, Skills, and Earnings: American Immigrants in 1909," *Journal of Economic History,* 31 (June 1971), 420–428.

15. Ray Farley, "The Urbanization of Negroes in the United States," *Journal of Social History,* 1 (Spring 1968), 241–258; C. Horace Hamilton, "The Negro Leaves the South," *Demography,* 1 (1964), 273–295; Simon Kuznets (ed.), *Population Redistribution and Economic Growth: United States, 1870–1950,* Vol. III, *Demographic Analyses and Interpretations* (Philadelphia: American Philosophical Society, 1964), pp. 90–107, 123–129, 209–210.

16. Edith Abbott, *Women in Industry* (New York: Appleton, 1909); The National Manpower Council, *Womanpower* (New York: Columbia University Press, 1957), pp. 110–142; Robert W. Smuts, *Women and Work in America* (New York: Columbia University Press, 1959); U.S. Bureau of the Census, *Historical Statistics of the United States, Colonial Times to 1957* (Washington, D.C.: U.S. Government Printing Office, 1960), pp. 71–74; U.S. Bureau of Labor Statistics, *Boot and Shoe Industry as a Vocation for Women,* Bulletin No. 179 (Washington, D.C.: U.S. Government Printing Office, 1915).

17. On the intimate linkage in New York between the abolition-of-child-labor and compulsory-education movements which yielded the Compulsory Education Law of 1894 and subsequent enforcement measures, see Moses Stambler, "The Effect of the Compulsory Education and Child Labor Laws on High School Attendance in New York City, 1898–1917," *History of Education Quarterly,* 8 (Summer 1968), 189–214.

18. Leo Troy, "Trade Union Membership, 1897–1962," *Occasional Paper No. 92* (New York: National Bureau of Economic Research, 1965).

19. Unions' effectiveness was probably greatest during the two surges of membership between 1897 and 1904 and between 1914 and 1920.

20. See David Brody, *Steelworkers in America* (New York: Russell & Russell, 1960).

21. At the same time unions of skilled workers frequently received vigorous support from local authorities and elites in small and middle-sized cities. See Herbert G. Gutman, "The Workers' Search for Power," in H. Wayne Morgan (ed.), *The Gilded Age* (Syracuse: Syracuse University Press, 1970), pp. 31–53.

22. For the most thorough survey of the interest of farmers in redeeming themselves through foreign trade, see William A. Williams, *The Roots of the Modern American Empire* (New York: Random House, 1969).

23. For suggestions of this contribution see Allan G. Bogue and Margaret Beattie Bogue, " 'Profits' and the Frontier Land Speculator," *Journal of Economic History,* 17 (March 1957), 64–72; Eric E. Lampard, *The Rise of the Dairy Industry in Wisconsin: A Study in Agricultural Change, 1820–1920* (Madison, Wis.: State Historical Society of Wisconsin, 1963), pp. 121–144, 294–332; Douglass C. North, "Ocean Freight Rates and Economic Development, 1750–1913," *Journal of Economic History,* 18 (December 1958), 537–555; Morton Rothstein, "America in the International Rivalry for the British Wheat Market, 1860–1914," *Mississippi Valley Historical Review,* 47 (December 1960), 401–418.

24. For an outline of the relative movements of farm prices and railroad rates, 1867–1915, see Robert Higgs, "Railroad Rates and the Populist Uprising," *Agricultural History,* 44 (July 1970), 291–297.

25. This political interest, quite remote from that characterizing the Populist movement, is exemplified by the "Wisconsin Idea of Dairying." See Lampard, *op. cit.,* pp. 333–351.

26. On the relationship between farmers and the experiment-station scientists, see Charles E. Rosenberg, "Science, Technology, and Economic Growth: The Case of the Agricultural Experiment Station Scientist, 1875–1914," *Agricultural History,* 45 (January 1971), 1–20.

27. An approach to measuring this attitudinal change is found in Louis Galambos, "The Agrarian Image of the Large Corporation, 1879–1920: A Study in Social Accommodation," *Journal of Economic History,* 28 (September 1968), 341–362.

SUGGESTED READINGS

Books

Barger, Harold, and H. H. Landsberg. *American Agriculture, 1899–1939: A Study of Output, Employment, and Productivity.* New York: National Bureau of Economic Research, 1942.

Brody, David. *Steelworkers in America.* New York: Russell & Russell, 1960.

Commons, John R., *et al. History of Labor in the United States,* Vols. III and IV. New York: Macmillan, 1935.

Easterlin, Richard A. *Population, Labor Force, and Long Swings in Economic Growth: The American Experience.* New York: Columbia University Press, 1968.

Kuznets, Simon (ed.). *Population Redistribution and Economic Growth: United States, 1870–1950.* 3 vols. Philadelphia: American Philosophical Society, 1957–1964.

Lampard, Eric E. *The Rise of the Dairy Industry in Wisconsin: A Study in Agricultural Change, 1820–1920.* Madison, Wis.: State Historical Society of Wisconsin, 1963.

Lebergott, Stanley. *Manpower in Economic Growth: The American Record Since 1800.* New York: McGraw-Hill, 1964.

Long, Clarence D. *Wages and Earnings in the United States, 1860–1890.* Princeton, N.J.: Princeton University Press, 1960.

Rees, Albert. *Real Wages in Manufacturing, 1890–1914.* Princeton, N.J.: Princeton University Press, 1961.

Ringenbach, Paul T. *Tramps and Reformers, 1873–1916: The Discovery of Unemployment in New York.* Westport, Conn.: Greenwood Press, 1973.

Shannon, Fred A. *The Farmer's Last Frontier.* New York: Holt, Rinehart and Winston, 1963.

Thernstrom, Stephan. *The Other Bostonians: Poverty and Progress in the American Metropolis.* Cambridge, Mass.: Harvard University Press, 1973.

———, and Richard Sennett (eds.). *Nineteenth Century Cities: Essays in the New Urban History.* New Haven: Yale University Press, 1969.

Ward, David. *Cities and Immigrants: A Geography of Change in Nineteenth Century America.* New York: Oxford University Press, 1971.

Articles

Fishlow, Albert. "Levels of Nineteenth-Century American Investment in Education," *Journal of Economic History,* 26 (December 1966), 418–436.

Gallman, Robert E. "Trends in the Size Distribution of Wealth in the Nineteenth Century: Some Speculations," in Lee Soltow (ed.), *Six Papers on the Size Distribution of Wealth and Income.* New York: Columbia University Press, 1969.

Gutman, Herbert G. "Work, Culture, and Society in Industrializing America, 1815–1919," *American Historical Review,* 78 (June 1973), 531–588.

Haraven, Tamara K., and Maris A. Vinovskis. "Marital Fertility, Ethnicity, and Occupation in Urban Families: An Analysis of South Boston and the South End in 1880," *Journal of Social History,* 8 (Spring 1975), 69–93.

Higgs, Robert. "Race, Skills, and Earnings: American Immigrants in 1909," *Journal of Economic History,* 31 (June 1971), 420–428.

Laurie, Bruce, *et al.* "Immigrants and Industry: The Philadelphia Experience, 1850–1880," *Journal of Social History,* 9 (Winter 1975), 219–248.

McGouldrick, Paul F., and Michael B. Tannen. "Did American Manufacturers Discriminate Against Immigrants Before 1914?" *Journal of Economic History,* 37 (September 1977), 723–746.

Meeker, Edward. "The Improving Health of the United States, 1850–1915," *Explorations in Economic History,* 9 (Summer 1972), 353–373.

Soltow, Lee C. "Evidence on Income Inequality in the United States, 1866–1965," *Journal of Economic History,* 29 (June 1969), 270–286.

Sutch, Richard, and Roger Ransom. "The Ex-Slave in the Post-Bellum South: A Study of the Economic Impact of Racism in a Market Environment," *Journal of Economic History,* 33 (March 1973), 131–148.

Towne, Marvin W., and Wayne D. Rasmussen. "Farm Gross Product and Gross Investment in the Nineteenth Century," in National Bureau of Economic Research, *Trends in the American Economy in the Nineteenth Century,* Vol. 24, *Studies in Income and Wealth,* Princeton, N.J.: Princeton University Press, 1960, pp. 255–312.

※ 12
Industrial America
in an Expanding World Economy

THE PATTERN OF EXPANSION

The continuing industrial revolution in the United States transformed not only the structure of the domestic economy but also the structure of the country's international trading relationships. However, primarily because of America's unusually large and productive agricultural sector, this transformation was not nearly so marked or so important to domestic development as was the case for the industrializing nations of Europe and Japan. Thus it continued to be the widening domestic marketplace rather than exchanges abroad that dominated the attention of almost every important group in the economy and shaped the central institutional changes of the period.

Between the Civil War and World War I the swift growth in the productivity of the domestic economy helped to work significant changes in the patterns of American trade with the rest of the world. For one thing, American exports soared, roughly tripling (in current dollar value) between the late 1860s and the late 1890s and then more than doubling during the rest of the period up until World War I. (See Table 25.) This expansion reflected both the growing efficiency of American producers and, in the period prior to the late 1890s, falling prices, which declined more dramatically than those of any other country in the world, making American products available at bargain prices. Then, beginning in the late 1890s, as American prices moved in line with world prices, exports became less buoyant. During the long surge of exports, American imports were also highly

TABLE 25   MERCHANDISE BALANCE OF TRADE, 1866–1915

Period	Exports	(Millions of Dollars) Imports	Exports Less Imports
1866–1870	1,605	2,042	−437
1871–1875	2,508	2,889	−381
1876–1880	3,383	2,463	920
1881–1885	3,960	3,337	623
1886–1890	3,692	3,585	107
1891–1895	4,462	3,925	537
1896–1900	5,786	3,708	2,078
1901–1905	7,270	4,861	2,409
1906–1910	8,894	6,724	2,170
1911–1915	11,853	8,561	3,292

Source: U.S. Bureau of the Census, *Historical Statistics of the United States, Colonial Times to 1957* (Washington, D.C.: U.S. Government Printing Office, 1961), pp. 537–538.

expansive. Again, the strength of the domestic economy was responsible. Increasing levels of per-capita income stimulated Americans to demand more foreign imports. But as long as high foreign prices prevailed (that is, until the late 1890s), imports did not grow as rapidly as exports, roughly doubling between 1860 and the late 1890s, as opposed to tripling. With the resumption of domestic expansion in the late 1890s, one might have expected the balance of trade to have moved, once again, in an unfavorable direction, as a result of domestic demand for imports growing more rapidly than foreign demand for exports. Yet even though world prices proceeded to fall relative to domestic prices, increasing American productivity resulted in the persistence of a *favorable* balance of trade. (In fact, until 1971 the annual merchandise trade balance since 1896 had always been favorable.) The size of that favorable balance of trade remained fairly constant after 1900 until World War I approached, when it again increased sharply. Despite fluctuations in the trade balance, the dominant element in America's international commercial relations, from the Civil War through World War I, was the strength of her highly efficient export sector.

Implicit in the boom in American trade was a change in the nature of both imports and exports, though the change was more pronounced in exports, with manufactured goods providing the leading edge in export growth. Manufacturers of a wide range of products, including reapers, sewing machines, typewriters, electric lamps, telephones and telegraphs, drugs, and explosives, were particularly able to compete with their European counterparts and came to dominate the growth of the export sector, especially after 1897.[1]

Although manufactured goods accounted for only 20 percent of all exports in the late 1860s, they increased to about 30 percent three decades later and then continued to grow, at a faster rate, amounting to almost one-half of exports just before the outbreak of World War I. Agricultural exports, such as grains and cotton, suffered commensurate declines. The structure of imports also changed but was more stable than that of exports. As American producers of manufactures increased specialization and productivity and as the domestic price level moved upward again, Americans tended to import more raw materials and unprocessed food and fewer finished manufactures and manufactured foodstuffs. Imports of crude materials (e.g., rubber, hides, wool, long-staple cotton, tobacco, and tin) and of food increased from about one-third of all imports in the 1870s and 1880s to almost one-half by 1914.

Most of the structural changes in the trade sector were associated with changes in the relative importance of America's trading partners. The European nations remained the primary trading partners throughout the period and, in fact, bought most American goods sold abroad. However, with the nation exporting more manufactured goods and importing more raw materials, dependence on Europe declined. In the 1880s the United States still drew over 55 percent of its imports from Europe, but the proportion was already falling and by the outbreak of World War I, had fallen to about 47 percent. Making up most of the difference were Asian imports, largely raw materials, which grew from about 10 percent of all imports in the 1870s to over 15 percent by 1911–1915.

Just as growth and structural change were more dramatic in exports than in imports, the shift away from Europe was more marked for exports. Europe's share of American exports fell from 83 percent in 1876–1880 to 80 percent in 1891–1895 to 64 percent in 1911–1915. The acceleration of decline after the late 1890s was due to the rise of American prices, which drove Europeans to seek primary products elsewhere, especially in Australia, Argentina, Russia, and parts of Asia. Concurrently the United States was expanding its exports to the non-European world—especially of manufactured goods. Whereas Canada and Mexico took only about 10 percent of United States exports in 1876–1880, they absorbed more than 20 percent by 1915. The other growth sector was the Asian market, which increased its share of all exports from only about 2 percent in 1876–1880 to over 5 percent in 1911–1915. South America's share, however, was fairly constant at 4 or 5 percent. Although Europe remained the major trading area of the United States, the nation was becoming more dependent on the non-European world, especially for exports of manufactured goods, and relatively less involved in the European world, especially in its exports of manufactures.

An increasing flow of capital also went from the United States to certain new trading areas. By the end of the nineteenth century the United States was well on its way to becoming a net exporter of capital, although exports did not outweigh imports of capital debts until 1908, and even then the nation still paid out more interest than it received. The shifting flow of capital roughly corresponded to the changing pattern of exports because short-term investments or extensions of credit were necessary to open up new markets and to enable foreigners who did not export goods and services to the United States to purchase American exports. Capital exports were generally not for the purpose of *producing* abroad but for aiding nations with unfavorable trade balances with the United States to expand their imports. Canada and Mexico had the most unfavorable American trade balances and consequently received the lion's share of capital exports; Asia's trade balance being more favorable, little capital flowed there from the United States.

The American export of capital, even for purposes of trade promotion, was slight compared to the European. Few American firms engaged in international competition, and the capital exports of those firms that did were very limited in scale. As a result, the flow of capital from the United States worked no drastic transformation in the nation's capital accounts until World War I. Between 1874 and 1895 Americans received a net of $1.5 billion of capital, largely from Great Britain, about the same in absolute terms as for the previous twenty-year period, but relative to domestic capital flows, a much smaller amount. The declining role of foreign capital continued into the period 1896–1914, when the nation exported a net of $700 million. But even this net increase was far less than the shift experienced in the following five years, embracing World War I, when the nation's net capital exports totaled over $14 billion.[2]

The expansion of American trade with other nations was part of a world-wide growth of trade that began in the 1840s; it reflected not only domestic development but also the reduction of the costs and risks of international trade through such innovations as the laying of the first transatlantic cable in 1869, the completion of great canals (such as the Suez, in 1869), the spreading of railroad networks throughout the world, the adoption of power-driven docking equipment, the growth of steamship transport, and the wide acceptance and use of refrigeration techniques on both railroads and ships. As a consequence of such changes and the widening of trade, the costs of ocean transport, especially on long hauls, fell after the mid-1870s, and international economic interchange became more intense.[3] In the case of the United States these trends reinforced gains in productivity and, until the late 1890s, the relative decline in prices, which created a real price advantage in world markets.

The industrialized nations of Europe developed a far more pronounced international dependency than did the United States, de-
spite the rapid change in the international position of the United
States between the Civil War and World War I. Although the United
States increased its share of world trade in the nineteenth century,
from about 6 percent in the 1820s to around 8 percent during the
Civil War years, and then to around 10 percent in the 1880s, it failed
to do so thereafter until World War I.[4] The shares of the United
Kingdom and Germany were consistently larger than that of the
United States, and the United States did not surpass France until the
early 1890s, nor Holland and Belgium until the late 1890s. At the
same time the shift toward dependence on less-developed nations
was not nearly as great for the United States as for the European
nations. Great Britain, for example, imported about half of its food
and fuel by 1900, whereas the United States, of course, possessed a
very large internal supply of food, fuel, and raw materials. Thus the
United States still had a limited stake in world trade. (Although some
American producers, especially farmers and small manufacturers
who had little control over the marketing of their output, tended to
blame depressions and falling prices on what they believed was an
unnecessarily flaccid export sector, exports were not significant in
sustaining long-run growth in the United States.) In the years just
before World War I, for instance, foreign trade constituted only
about 11 percent of national product in the United States, while it
was 44 percent in the United Kingdom, 54 percent in France, 38
percent in Germany, 30 percent in Japan, and 32 percent in Canada.
What is more, since an early phase of the industrial revolution, that
ratio for the United States had declined (from 13 percent during the
period 1834–1843), while the ratio for other nations moved strongly
upward as industrialization progressed.[5] Although the United States'
share of world trade was growing between the 1830s and World War
I, trade was not growing any faster than the economy as a whole; it
was probably growing less rapidly. The experience of other rapidly
industrializing nations provides a sharp contrast to the internal focus
of American trade.

THE POLITICAL ECONOMY OF EXPANSION

The Tariff and the Manufacturers

One of the paradoxical political facts of rapid growth in trade and
increasing American productivity, particularly within the manufacturing sector, was the enactment of high tariffs on imports of manufactures and agricultural products. The Union government needed

higher tariffs both to raise revenue and to protect producers whose goods were now laboring under high wartime excise taxes; it was an opportune time for farmers and manufacturers with an interest in protection from foreign competition to work for the reversal of the ante-bellum trend toward free trade. With the way broken by the Morrill Act of 1861, the tariff act of 1864 imposed duties that were almost half the total value of all dutiable imports. Although the wartime excises were lowered rapidly during the 1860s, the high tariffs were retained. Revisions in 1867, 1872, 1875, 1883, 1890 (the McKinley tariff), 1894 (the Wilson-Gorman Act), 1897 (the Dingley Act), and 1909 (the Payne-Aldrich Act) failed to change the fundamental structure of the tariff system, and until the Underwood-Simmons Tariff of 1913 significantly reduced the Civil War rates, the ratio between duties and the value of dutiable goods rarely dropped below 40 percent and was frequently close to 50 percent. The highest rates were imposed on manufactured goods, particularly on metals and metal products, especially those of the iron and steel and related industries, cotton textiles, and certain woolen goods; on many such items the rate of protection was as high as 100 percent.

Adherence to tariff orthodoxy among manufacturers went far beyond the few somewhat inefficient industries, such as chemicals or high-quality textiles, which may have received genuine protection against their own weaknesses. But one can easily conclude that American manufacturers, because of their growing capacity to compete effectively in world markets, and because of the obvious benefit in having no duties on their growing imports of raw materials, would have profited from freer trade. Indeed, most of the duties were irrelevant to the pattern of competition. If they had been removed, American efficiency, low raw-material costs, and cheap land would have prevented foreign imports from penetrating the domestic market. It was extremely unlikely, for example, that most iron and steel products, agricultural machinery, the cheaper cotton goods, or boots and shoes would have been imported into the United States even if there had been no tariff. In 1909, when Congress made significant reductions in iron and steel duties, no appreciable increase in imports resulted. And after 1913, even taking the onset of World War I into consideration, the increases in imports were far less than might have been predicted from the drastic reductions in tariff rates, especially inasmuch as the free list included pig iron, iron in slabs and blooms, Bessemer steel ingots, barbed and galvanized wire, steel rails, and most agricultural implements. (Such tariffs were even more irrelevant, since those on goods that did not enter the country, either because of the tariff or because of their high cost, raised no revenue.)

The resolution of this paradox lies partially in the fact that some manufacturers (and many farmers) supported free trade, and while they did not usually work for full-scale tariff reform, they either opposed increases in tariffs, as did most New England manufacturers during Reconstruction, or supported the movement to achieve reciprocal trade agreements involving mutual lowering of trade barriers. Especially to placate farmers with a free-trading interest, the McKinley Tariff of 1890 gave the president power to impose duties on sugar, molasses, tea, coffee, and hides (all admitted without duty otherwise) in order to coerce other nations into reducing their barriers to "the agricultural or other products of the United States." Between 1890 and 1894 the administrations of Harrison and Cleveland sought concessions for exports, largely of agricultural goods (especially grain, flour, and provisions) but also of iron and steel and agricultural machinery to Latin America. Although successful in the British West Indies, Cuba, Puerto Rico, and Brazil, the reciprocity program expired in 1894, when Congress decided to admit tea and coffee on an unconditional free basis and to restore a sugar duty. Although the 1897 act revived reciprocity in a limited way, the act of 1909 once again wiped out this approach to promoting trade. (In 1897 Congress provided for the retaliatory taxation of tea, coffee, tonka beans, and vanilla beans but not sugar; the suspension of taxation on certain French imports to prevent retaliation for new, high tariffs on silk; and the arrangement of commercial treaties for general reduction of duties, culminating in agreements with France, Germany, Italy, and Portugal.[6]) While interest in reciprocity did reflect some heightening of concern with Latin American expansion, it was a result far more of the efforts of farmers to expand traditional exports than of manufacturers to change the structure of exports, and it did not result in any significant departures from the existing tariff system.

The adherence of manufacturers to a protectionist orthodoxy stemmed more fundamentally from inertia in a policy area that many considered unimportant, uncertainty about the results of repealing a framework of law that by 1900 was a generation old, and recognition that the favorable impact of tariff reduction depended on a complex of factors not easily shaped by Congress, including the responses of other nations. The vast majority of manufacturers who competed abroad did not find themselves handicapped by the tariff. They competed successfully and extended credit to compensate for limited American imports of foreign products. Others, who imported foreign raw materials, felt no significant pinch, either because tariffs on their raw materials failed to raise raw-material prices or because Congress had protected their products with a tariff compensating for high raw-material prices. And besides, most manufacturers had primarily domestic interests and failed to develop much concern about the character of international trade in the first place. In addition to expansion at home, their chief concern in the latter part of the century was in creating more-stable domestic markets to protect their investments better. For most manufacturers there appeared to be no risk or cost, in terms of ordering the domestic marketplace, in leaving tariffs essentially unchanged.

Manufacturers' lack of interest in any significant expansion of tariffs, either in rate or in scope, contributed to a certain stability in the tariff system. Tariffs were not increased appreciably between 1864 and 1913 and were not applied to any significant new imports. The ratio of the value of duties to the value of *total* imports consequently underwent an intermittent but persistent decline from the late 1860s on, decreasing from over 40 percent to about 18 percent, even before the impact of the Underwood-Simmons Tariff registered. (With regard to the lowering of tariffs in 1913, manufacturers may well have been rather passive politically, because of the slowing down of the rate of growth of exports associated with the rise of United States prices, relative to world prices, after the late 1890s.)

Finally, many Americans of diverse employments and interests, but especially labor, either supported the high-tariff system or, like the manufacturers, were uncertain about the results of tariff reform.[7] The American workingman came to attribute his high wages (relative to European wages) not so much to productivity gains as to protectionism, that is, to the supposed ability of the tariff to shield him from the competition of cheap foreign labor. Indeed, the Republicans cemented their hold on national power by attracting large numbers of workers to their ranks with their consistent support of the principle of protectionism. Neither disgruntled middle-class consumer interests nor farmers who opposed tariffs on manufactured goods (but favored tariffs on grain, flax, wool, hides, and beet sugar) were able to offset the political power wielded by the coalition of the few inefficient producers, the much larger group of timid or apathetic manufacturers, and the politically potent force of labor on behalf of the tariff system.

The impact of protective tariff legislation on the progress of economic growth remains, as yet, undetermined. But by the late nineteenth century there were scarcely any infant industries that required paternal treatment to survive foreign bullies during their period of modernization. Consequently it is reasonable to conclude that during this period the tariff promoted some international misallocation of resources and, to a degree, inhibited economic growth by shifting income to the protected industries. For the most part, however, tariffs did not alter patterns of activity. Perhaps only in the production of certain higher-quality goods in which Europeans had a cost advantage, such as silks, did the tariff encourage wasteful manufacturing activity in the United States. But again, the international sector was not crucial to economic growth during this period anyway. To the extent that trade fostered American growth, it was still internal trade, through the promotion of regional specialization, that was fundamentally responsible, not international exchange.

The American Empire

From the limited and secondary role of foreign trade during this period one can conclude that American policies of colonialism and imperialism were not central to the nation's economic development. The expansion and organizational-technological sophistication of the domestic economy determined the basic patterns of growth, and businessmen were far more interested and successful in expanding their domestic markets than in expanding abroad. Nevertheless, to those manufacturers who were, in fact, enlarging their activities to include foreign markets and sources of supply, the show, and use, of American military power and the support of politically vigorous departments of state and commerce could prove to be real assets in shaping local political conditions. Thus the shift of economic interest toward the less-developed world, limited as it was in the United States, contributed to the popular support accorded to the international expansion of government power and, at various times, may well have decisively shaped the character of that expansion.

There were, without doubt, American exporters who sought the support of their government in reaching new markets. In the depressed 1890s, in particular, producers of all sorts, manufacturers and farmers alike, frequently assessed their difficulties as having grown from overproduction rather than from monetary constraint and instability. To compensate for the deficiencies in domestic demand they sought foreign outlets for their products. This feeling was particularly intense among farmers and smaller businessmen, including small manufacturers represented by the National Association of Manufacturers (organized in 1895), who never had substantial control over the marketing of their output and found that handicap to have severe consequences during a period of depression. More generally, those producers who faced the squeeze between fixed costs and falling prices during the entire deflationary period of the late nineteenth century, and were unable to shape the marketplace to meet their needs, were more likely to seek recourse through an expanded export effort.

The continuing lure of the China market led export-minded manufacturers, especially in the 1890s, to seek to enlist governmental support in weaving through the political maze created by imperial rivalries in the western Pacific. Exporters of iron and steel (including Bethlehem Iron), cotton and woolen textiles, and kerosene (including Standard Oil), in particular, sought the support of the McKinley administration in widening trading privileges in China; supported the open-door policy, that is, the effort to prevent the partitioning of China, as a necessary means of support for American traders in the competition for spheres of influence; and saw the acquisition of the Philippines (1898) as necessary to expansion in China. And later they favored the building of the Panama Canal (opened in 1914) to improve communications between Asia and the United States. In Latin America, American traders also supported the Isthmian canal and found much to applaud in the development of an American sphere of influence facilitated by the Roosevelt Corollary (1904–1905), which interpreted the Monroe Doctrine as sanctioning American seizure and management of custom houses in Caribbean nations threatening to default on European debts.

But expansionist businessmen were not sufficiently motivated, numerous, or powerful to shape policy successfully to their ends, despite the likelihood that economic and, consequently, political power were more concentrated among firms doing more business abroad than at home.[8] The strongest corporations, such as Standard Oil, needed little support from the public sector. More typically, it was the weak firms that were disappointed by the failures of reciprocity in Latin America, the disarray within the consular service in Asia, and, in general, the discovery that governmental support usually meant little more than verbal encouragement. Not surprisingly, the governments of Great Britain, France, Germany, Russia, and Japan, recognizing their heavier reliance on foreign trade, were far more willing to lend active support to business enterprise abroad. To the extent that the nation followed an expansionist course desired by business, it did so, basically, as a result of a more broadly based expansionist dream. People of all walks of life, with only a rudimentary conceptualization of their economic interests abroad, were moved by ideals of national superiority and the lure of invigorating international competition as a Darwinian mechanism for demonstrating that superiority. Certainly Theodore Roosevelt's zest for international competition, to take the most prominent example, cannot be understood solely or mainly as an outgrowth of international capitalism. President William Howard Taft's dollar diplomacy, to take another example, was a policy of inducing reluctant bankers to expand their foreign interests for the sake of the expansion of American *political* influence in Latin America. But even with such broadly gauged support, the imperialist posture of the United States was, as yet, fairly modest. Reflecting that fact, and the limited interest of business in foreign expansion, was the unwillingness, after the acquisition of the Philippines, to incur the costs and risks implicit in further colonialism or the political absorption of foreign territory. The American empire was still largely informal in character and, although rudimentary in structure, was, if anything, more than equal to the nation's economic needs abroad. Those requirements were limited; political rhetoric and activity on behalf of expansion neither revealed structural weaknesses in the economy nor provided evidence of a weak domestic market. On the contrary, domestic expansion was extraordinary in the late nineteenth and early twentieth centuries, and as a result, the United States was able to hew much more strictly to old trading patterns than were Europeans.

NOTES

1. For a description of the activities of representative manufacturers, see Mira Wilkins, *The Emergence of Multinational Enterprise: American Business Abroad from the Colonial Era to 1914* (Cambridge, Mass.: Harvard University Press, 1970), pp. 35–109.

2. Those capital exports between 1896 and 1914, joined with interest payments to Europeans on their still massive American investments, the remittances of immigrants to Europe, and the purchase of services from Europeans (e.g., ocean transport and mercantile services), produced a markedly worsening balance-of-payments situation. The result was a drain on the nation's stock of gold; more than three times as much gold flowed out of the nation during 1896–1914 as during the preceding twenty years. U.S. Bureau of the Census, *Historical Statistics of the United States, Colonial Times to 1957* (Washington, D.C.: U.S. Government Printing Office, 1961), pp. 562–565. (Virtually all of the data on international exchanges in this chapter come from this invaluable compendium.)

3. Douglass C. North, "Ocean Freight Rates and Economic Development, 1750–1913," *Journal of Economic History,* 18 (December 1958), 537–555.

4. For a discussion of these data and those that follow on the contribution of foreign trade to national product, see the innovative comparative study of Simon Kuznets, *Modern Economic Growth: Rate, Structure, and Spread* (New Haven and London: Yale University Press, 1966), pp. 285–358.

5. During comparable early periods of industrialization (like the 1830s and 1840s in the United States) the ratio for the United Kingdom was 22 percent, for France, 18 percent, and for Japan, 10 percent. *Ibid.,* pp. 312–313.

6. In 1911 Taft pushed through the Senate a Canadian reciprocity tariff which provided for the free importation of grain and cattle from Canada —action desired by American millers, packers, and leather manufacturers—but Canada, fearful of economic annexation, refused to consummate a treaty.

7. Perhaps reflective of this uncertainty was the extremely low quality of the economic content of the congressional tariff debates in 1894. See Richard C. Edwards, "Economic Sophistication in Nineteenth Century Congressional Tariff Debates," *Journal of Economic History*, 30 (December 1970), 802–838.

8. For a suggestion of the significance of the fact that, among Americans, ownership of foreign assets tends to be more highly concentrated than the ownership of domestic assets for the determination of foreign policy, see Robert Zevin, "An Interpretation of American Imperialism," *Journal of Economic History*, 32 (March 1972), 349–350.

SUGGESTED READINGS

Books

Ashworth, William. *A Short History of the International Economy, 1850–1950.* New York: Longmans, Green, 1952.

Kuznets, Simon. *Modern Economic Growth: Rate, Structure, and Spread.* New Haven and London: Yale University Press, 1966.

La Feber, Walter. *The New Empire: An Interpretation of American Expansion, 1860–1898.* Ithaca, N.Y.: Cornell University Press, 1963.

McCormick, Thomas J. *China Market: America's Quest for Informal Empire, 1893–1901.* Chicago: Quadrangle, 1967.

Taussig, F. W. *The Tariff History of the United States.* New York: Capricorn Books, 1964.

Varg, Paul A. *The Making of a Myth: The United States and China, 1897–1912.* East Lansing: Michigan State University Press, 1968.

Wilkins, Mira. *The Emergence of Multinational Enterprise: American Business Abroad from the Colonial Era to 1914.* Cambridge, Mass.: Harvard University Press, 1970.

Williamson, Jeffrey G. *American Growth and the Balance of Payments, 1820–1913.* Chapel Hill, N.C.: University of North Carolina Press, 1964.

Articles

Coben, Stanley. "Northeastern Business and Radical Reconstruction: A Re-Examination," *Mississippi Valley Historical Review,* 46 (June 1959), 67–90.

David, Paul A. "Learning by Doing and Tariff Protection: A Reconsideration of the Case of the Ante-Bellum United States Cotton Textile Industry," *Journal of Economic History,* 30 (September 1970), 521–601.

May, Ernest R. "American Imperialism: A Reinterpretation," *Perspectives in American History,* 1 (1967), 123–283.

North, Douglass C. "Ocean Freight Rates and Economic Development, 1750–1913," *Journal of Economic History,* 18 (December 1958) 537–555.

Simon, Matthew. "The United States Balance of Payments, 1861–1900," in Conference on Research in Income and Wealth, National Bureau of Economic Research, *Trends in the American Economy in the Nineteenth Century,* Vol. 24, *Studies in Income and Wealth.* Princeton, N.J.: Princeton University Press, 1960.

Zevin, Robert. "An Interpretation of American Imperialism," *Journal of Economic History,* 32 (March 1972), 316–360.

⁂ part four

THE RISE OF A MANAGED MARKETPLACE

Since 1914 the economy has closely resembled that of the late nineteenth century. For example, the growth of per-capita output and income has remained close to the high level reached during the last century. Moreover, the sources of economic growth have not changed in any basic way, although the contribution of efficiency gains, as opposed to the utilization of more capital and labor per capita, has increased. What truly distinguishes the period since the onset of World War I has been the marked intensification of efforts to manage the development of the marketplace. Although competition has remained a widely embraced ideal and, to a significant extent, has continued to govern economic relationships, private and public endeavors to plan for economic growth, stability, and equity have become commonplace. Whereas the period 1870–1914 had been free of both major wars and economic calamities, the extended post-1914 era has included the nation's most severe economic disaster and at least three enormous military enterprises, including the cold war. It thus has provided the nation's political leadership and economic elites with unique opportunities for a wider diversity of experiments in economic planning, particularly for stability but also for growth and social justice. Without the Great Depression and certainly the wars, American economic society could have realized its successes more easily. But the period of turmoil since 1914, primarily the Great Depression, has resulted in institutional arrangements that have lent the economy a greater measure of protection against external shocks and, quite possibly, an enhanced capacity to cope with current distributional and environmental problems.

❖ 13
The Experience of World War I

THE UNITED STATES IN THE WORLD ECONOMY: THE LEAP TO DOMINANCE

World War I catapulted the United States into its modern position within the world's economy. The nation's startling rise to dominance, however, was firmly rooted in its growing economic strength—a strength that permitted Americans to compete with increasing effectiveness in world markets and to dominate the finance of international trade. Because the nation, with a large internal supply of raw materials, did not match its exports with comparable levels of imports, the extensive shipment of American capital abroad was essential to the growth of American exports. To enable foreigners to sustain their purchases of American exports, American bankers, merchants, and manufacturers had to provide them with loans, at the same time reducing the foreign debt acquired during the great expansion of the nineteenth century. By 1908 more capital flowed out of the United States than flowed into it, although the nation's debts still outweighed her credits. Thus World War I did not initiate the transformation of the nation from a debtor to a creditor, but it did accelerate its pace (to such an extent, in fact, that within the short course of the war, New York replaced London as the financial center of world trade).

The voracious demands of the Allies for armaments, guns, ammunition, food, and clothing provided an enormous stimulus for American exports. At first many Americans traded with both sides, but after the United States accepted the British blockade of the Central Powers, trade with Germany virtually disappeared, declining from $169 million annually in 1914 to slightly more than $1 million in 1916, while the Allied trade of $824.5 million in 1914 almost quadrupled to $3.2 billion in 1916, well before American entry into the war.

To suggest the dimensions and distribution of this increase some examples are in order. During the three years ending in June 1917 the investment-banking firm of J. P. Morgan alone, acting as an agent for the governments of Great Britain and France, shipped them goods valued at $3.1 billion, a sum that accounted for more than one-quarter of American exports to all countries. Another single contract, which the British government placed with the American Locomotive Company in April 1915, called for $63.7 million of shells. Another one for ammunition, placed with Bethlehem Steel at about the same time, came to $83.2 million, followed by another three months later for $64 million. In September 1916 du Pont accepted a $96.4 million contract for powder. Also in September the Allies jointly contracted for 448 million pounds of copper to be delivered during the first six months of 1917, the whole order representing one-third of the total copper production in the United States for that period. Although manufacturers benefited more, farmers enjoyed favorable markets as well. Demand for agricultural output expanded rapidly; between 1914 and 1917 shipments of wheat to the Allies were almost seven times as great as in the preceding three years.

To pay for their purchases, the Allies, hard-pressed by the demands of war and consequently unable to send goods and services in return, had either to borrow from Americans or to liquidate their American investments and use the proceeds for commodities. The Allies pursued the latter course vigorously, foreign investments falling from $7.2 billion in 1914 to less than $4 billion in 1919 and foreign investment in corporate securities declining from $5.46 to $1.6 billion in the same period. Those foreign holdings that remained were usually those of nonbelligerents; both Britain and France sold off about 70 percent of their holdings by the end of 1919. As for the Germans, they found the British very closely supervising their transactions, seizing securities, if possible, and blacklisting brokers or bankers dealing with Germany. As a result Germany was not able to use foreign securities as a basis for loans and had to sell its holdings outright, through neutral countries. When the United States entered the war, the Office of Alien Property finally confiscated and then liquidated whatever German holdings remained. (By amendments to the Trading with the Enemy Act [up to 1928], however, the United States returned the proceeds of these sales to dispossessed German owners—part of a policy of extending very favorable economic treatment to Germany during the 1920s.) The result of all the foreign sales of American securities was an acceleration of the already rapid pace by which the nation moved from international debtor to international creditor.

By the end of 1915 the Allies had sold some $1.5 billion worth of securities, receiving United States currency in return and applying it to purchases of American products. It was obvious, however, that the Allies could not rely indefinitely on the liquidation of assets to keep goods flowing across the Atlantic, and many Americans whose basic concern was to support the Allied war effort searched earnestly for more effective means of providing supplies. Included in that American group were influential commercial and investment bankers, located primarily in New York City, and two important Wilson administration figures, Secretary of the Treasury William G. McAdoo and Secretary of State Robert Lansing, who believed, as well, that there were compelling economic reasons for developing new means of Allied finance.

In the first place, the heavy sale of European securities exerted a downward pressure on the stock market, making the marketing of new issues more difficult and, in fact, threatening general confidence in the economy. In the second place, once the Allies had expended their limited assets, the export trade would collapse, with the very likely result of a domestic depression. Finally, although the bankers never admitted it publicly, they believed there were attractive profits to be earned as middlemen in the Allied trade, if the administration would only let them export capital.

The Wilson administration initially resisted any such economic arguments. Until the fall of 1914 the government interpreted neutrality rigidly and frowned on American extension of credit to the belligerents. In August of 1914 William Jennings Bryan, then secretary of state, announced that "in the judgment of this government loans by American bankers to any foreign nation which is at war are inconsistent with the true spirit of neutrality." As a result J. P. Morgan and Company dropped plans to lend $100 million to the French government. In the autumn the Wilson administration made a rather tentative movement away from that kind of restriction by not objecting to the extension of commercial credits—that is, entries of short-term debt on the books of a corporation—to Russia ($5 million) and to France ($10 million) by John D. Rockefeller's National City Bank. Then in February 1915 the Wilson administration overlooked a credit of $50 million extended to France by J. P. Morgan and Company. These initiatives by private banks, however, covered only a small part of the purchase of supplies during most of 1915. In view of the heavy sales of American securities, a weak stock market, and the onset of depression, economic leaders pressed Wilson for a more generous loan policy, one that would permit not only the extension of credits but also the sale of the notes of Allied governments in American capital markets. In support of such a policy, McAdoo wrote to Wilson in August 1915, reminding him that Great Britain had always been the United States' best customer and that Britain's demand for food had brought prosperity to farmers and its demand for war munitions, a boost to industry. He concluded: "Great prosperity is coming. It is, in large measure, already here. It will be tremendously increased if we can extend reasonable credits to our customers." The new secretary of state, Robert Lansing, echoed McAdoo's view, telling Wilson that if the Allies were unable to find the means to maintain their unfavorable trade balances with the United States, they would have to stop buying and the result would be industrial depression. The various arguments of McAdoo, Lansing, and the bankers found a receptive audience in Wilson, who was convinced that the earlier policy of no loans was contrary to the conventional rules of neutrality and that singling out only one commodity—money —for embargo was senseless. Thus in October the administration approved the floating of a large, unsecured $500 million loan to the British and French by J. P. Morgan and Company. The noninstitutional public, however, proved unenthusiastic about the loan, registering its lack of confidence in Allied prospects by taking only $33 million of bonds and by forcing the underwriting banks to purchase the last $187 million of the issue in December. Nonetheless, the capital sustained Allied purchases and, along with the continued extension of credit by the banking system, contributed to a stock-market recovery and the initiation of a year of significant domestic prosperity.

Earlier, in September 1915, the Federal Reserve System agreed to rediscount the foreign acceptances (the evidence of trade debts incurred by foreigners) of member banks, a move that enabled New York bankers to surpass their London competition and play a preeminent role in international capital markets, especially the financing of international trade. The ties of the American manufacturers of munitions and war materiel, farmers who shipped grain and foodstuffs to the Allies, and exporters who served as middlemen to markets in the Allied countries tightened, and their stake in an Allied victory intensified. More generally, by the end of 1916 the entire economy had become dependent on the export trade with the Allies as a way of maintaining full employment and short-run stability. In light of the limited expertise in the management of fiscal policy or in the operation of the Federal Reserve System, the nation could hardly have been expected to forgo the full-employment economy provided by an extremely buoyant export market.

As powerful as the economic ties between the United States and the Allies were by 1917, it does not necessarily follow that the nation entered the war for economic reasons. In the first place, the initial choice of Britain as the nation's major trading partner, in 1914, was more a response to military realities (the chief one being British control of the seas) than to economics. Moreover, Wilson's diplomacy of 1916, which involved pressuring American bankers to dampen their enthusiasm for Allied loans, would have been given credit for keeping America out of the war if the British had sued for peace or the Germans had abstained from unrestricted submarine warfare against American ships. And in making the final decision Wilson, Congress, and the nation acted in response to a wide assortment of hopes, fears, and objectives, beyond those economic.

With American entry into the war, war finance moved into a new phase, one in which the federal government was obligated to support the export trade with its credit and, in effect, protect the private investment that had preceded. The first Liberty-loan act came as early as April 1917 and authorized the secretary of the Treasury to purchase the notes of Allied governments. By the end of the year the secretary had advanced $3.7 billion to the Allies, and in 1918 he lent an additional $4 billion (these loans were made on terms favorable to the Allies—a kind of subsidy for the war effort—and on no security, apart from good faith). By January 1919 Allied governments owed the United States government about $9.5 billion, and the American prewar net debt to foreigners of $3.7 billion had dissolved into a net credit of $12.5 billion. That shift would have occurred eventually anyway, but much more slowly. Because the change was so rapid, most Americans, including those with economic and political power, failed to comprehend it. As a consequence, Americans would face grave difficulty in managing their role in the international economy of the 1920s and would contribute, unwittingly, to the severity of the world-wide collapse that ensued at the end of the decade.

WARTIME PLANNING: DISORDER FOLLOWS INNOVATION

For almost three years Americans welcomed the massive Allied requirement for exports and capital. But after intervention in the European war, the nation had to strain to meet the heightened demands, both internal and foreign, for the resources of war. The nation's markets became so pinched that the federal government had to adopt a vastly expanded role in the determination of national economic priorities, resulting in substantial departures from traditional reliance on the marketplace. After the war, the departures lapsed, with disastrous results for postwar stability, but they stimulated the private sector into the attainment of production efficiencies realized during the 1920s and thereby accelerated the trend toward industrial order that began in the late nineteenth century.

Just prior to America's extensive economic involvement in the European war, late in 1915, economic activity was in the doldrums. By the fall of 1916, however, the economy worked up to full capacity and continued to do so throughout the war. Nonetheless, there was no evidence of significantly increased capacity for production until two years later, in the autumn of 1918; between 1916 and 1918 real product increased by far less than 1 percent. However, between 1914 and 1916 physical production increased about 14 percent, with mining, manufacturing, and railroads the most buoyant. Manufacturing, for example, increased its share of national product from 18.8 percent in 1914 to 22.9 percent in 1916. But manufacturing production did not continue to rise rapidly; in fact, it actually declined somewhat from the middle of 1917 to the fall of 1918.

The sluggish growth of the economy after American entry into the war placed severe handicaps on the government's war effort. Once having joined the hostilities, the government found itself competing with not only the Allies but also American civilians, who were not subject to rationing for available goods and services. The pressing requirements of war left insufficient time for producers to increase capacity, achieved through new investment, in order to meet the needs of all sectors. Indeed, it was the hectic scrambling to order the conflicting demands of domestic consumers, the military, and the Allies that caused the decline of economic output in 1918. Consequently the government stepped in to provide the necessary order and divert resources into production with a military purpose. Quite simply, the result was a set of innovative departures into economic planning.

The Wilson administration created over 5,000 agencies, staffed with dollar-a-year men, primarily from large corporations, who possessed varying, often conflicting powers and responsibilities to set national economic priorities. Much experimentation and considerable disruption followed as a result of public and private inexperience with mobilization for a modern war. Finally, in the spring of 1918, Wilson fixed coordination of war industry with the War Industries Board (WIB) under the cunning but scrupulously unpartisan leadership of Bernard M. Baruch. A figure already proven capable of encouraging cooperation and compromise among business leaders, Baruch had the role, not of economic dictator, but of conciliator among powerful organizations, particularly the large corporations. Although its mandate was vague, the WIB held ultimate authority over all industrial matters except the fixing of prices. That was left to a committee of the board directly responsible to Wilson. The WIB's fundamental function was to match supply with demand and to reconcile the various buyers to accepting the limited supply of goods. It had the power, when necessary, to seize and operate plants, but it used this discretion rarely; in general, industry cooperated voluntarily, although it was doubtless mindful of the possibility of government takeover. Indeed, for the most part, industry welcomed Baruch's management of the WIB as a necessary step in bringing rationalization to a mobilization effort that previously threatened economic chaos. Less enthusiastic was the military; it accepted coordination only grudgingly. Most officers working with the WIB were won over, including General Hugh S. Johnson of later New Deal significance. But the War Department was able to maintain control over the purchasing of munitions rather than submitting to a munitions ministry, as proposed by Baruch and other industrial leaders.[1]

Another crucial agency was the Food Administration, under Herbert Hoover. With congressional sanction (the Lever Act, passed in August 1917), Hoover bought and sold all American foodstuffs for the Allies, trying in the process to increase production by guaranteeing returns to the nation's farmers. The Food Administration achieved particular success in the nation's wheat markets by guaranteeing minimum prices through the transactions of the United States Grain Corporation, owned and financed by the federal government. Wheat production increased from about 620 million bushels in 1917 to about 904 million bushels in 1918. Hoover also stimulated production of sugar through the Sugar Equalization Board and encouraged hog production by reaching price agreements with the packers, the number of hogs slaughtered increasing from about 56,000 in 1917 to over 65,000 in 1918. To the benefit of the consumer, Hoover encouraged such increases without significant price inflation; this success served the Wilson war effort by reducing consumer discontent with high prices—a discontent that had produced urban food riots led by housewives in February 1917. (Although farm prices doubled between 1915 and 1919, 80 percent of that increase occurred before the intervention of the Food Administration.[2]) However, although farmers found more-secure markets under Hoover's reign as food czar, they experienced a worsening of their income position (relative to other groups) as a result of the slowing of price gains. Also, in order to increase production, farmers had moved production on to poorer, previously uncultivated land, especially in the Great Plains and the northern Great Lakes states, and thus used land less efficiently. (See Figure 17.) Unit costs of production then rose rapidly, reinforcing the impact of sluggish prices. The nation's 6.5 million farmers, while

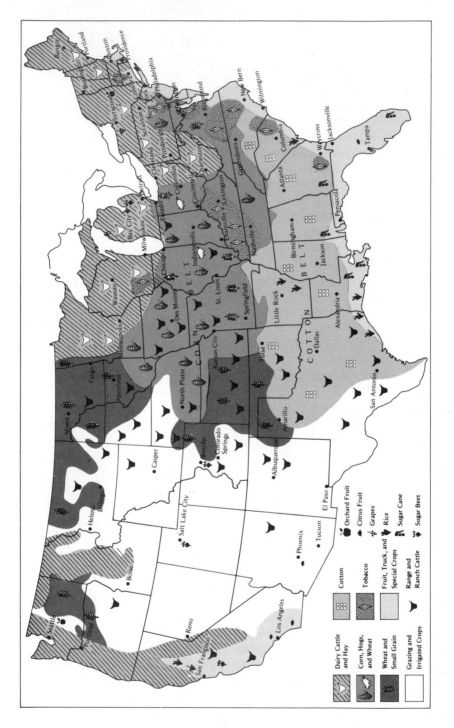

FIGURE 17: *Patterns of Agricultural Production, 1920*

losing some of the ground they had gained during the golden age of agriculture, found Hoover's efforts to meet wartime demands and check inflation consistent with their own continuing prosperity. After the war, however, many farmers would find that they had overexpanded in response to wartime needs and had entered a major depression long before the nation as a whole.

The government actively entered labor as well as product markets, first by creating acute labor shortages in the process of building an army. The war diverted about 16 percent of the male labor force, predominantly unskilled laborers, to military employment (those with war-industry jobs could receive deferments under the Selective Service Act of May 1917). To take up slack, in May 1918, the chief of the selective service system ordered the unemployed to assume a useful job or hit the trenches. It was an era of high demand for labor, and the bargaining power and appeal of unions soared. To minimize loss of production from strikes, and to ensure continued cooperation of industry in the war effort, President Wilson created the National War Labor Board in April 1918, charging it with the responsibility of settling disputes that went beyond the capacities of other agencies. The board did not accept the validity of strikes, but it recognized the

WOMEN WORKING ON FUSES FOR ARTILLERY SHELLS. The industrial employment of women increased sharply, but only temporarily, during World War I.

right of unions to organize and bargain collectively and supported the eight-hour day. Samuel Gompers and the A.F.L., the major beneficiary of Wilson's support, responded by exercising extreme restraint in calling strikes. As a consequence of the tight labor market and government support, union membership soared. By 1920 over 12 percent of the labor force had joined unions—more than twice the percentage in 1910. This growth in union membership was dominated by the A.F.L., which accounted for more than 80 percent of all union members in 1920. Reinforced by government-sanctioned union power, the strong demand for labor caused real wages to increase more rapidly during the war than they had previously, and, in fact, at a rate larger than the rate of productivity advance. Another aspect of wartime labor policy was the sponsorship by the Department of Labor of the first national employment service to ease the scarcity of unskilled labor that had resulted from the draft and a slowing of immigration.[3] Finally, in May 1918, Wilson created the War Labor Policies Board, under the chairmanship of Felix Frankfurter, to coordinate the various labor agencies (the war ended before the board had time to effectively impose itself).

In addition to shifting resources from civilian to military uses, the government promoted the more efficient use of existing resources. The agency most active in this endeavor was the WIB, which encouraged industrial efficiency by standardizing products and reducing the number of product designs, especially those for weaponry but also those for such diverse products as typewriter ribbons, plows, baby carriages, and coffins. Perhaps most striking were the efficiency gains that planners induced in the transportation industry. Through the Emergency Fleet Corporation, another government-owned corporation, the Shipping Board worked to expand the fleet. In the process the board contributed significantly to the development of modern mass-production techniques in ship construction. In the provision of railroad services, the United States Railroad Administration, under Secretary of the Treasury McAdoo, made striking gains in efficiency by operating all the railroads as a single unit, guaranteeing a return to each road, and exploiting much unused capacity within the system. In most areas, however, especially in the manufacturing sector, the real payoff from government initiatives in the promotion of improved productivity came substantially later, during the 1920s.

Through these agencies the Wilson administration achieved its primary goal of shifting the focus of production from civilian to military purposes. War output made up less than 1 percent of national product in 1914, remaining at about that level through 1916; then it increased to 9.4 percent in 1917 and to 23.3 percent in 1918.

Along with the diversion of resources, the nonwar portion of national product fell by 22 percent between 1916 and 1918. In spite of successfully reordering national priorities to meet the needs of war, Wilson and the Congress failed to preserve economic stability. The wartime situation was fraught with inherent inflationary pressures, as producers became increasingly hard-pressed to meet demands. At first increasing demand affected just production; and between 1914 and 1915 the wholesale price index rose only 2 percent. But further growth in demand tended to result in higher prices rather than increased production. The wholesale price index climbed about one-quarter between 1915 and 1916, then jumped by almost 40 percent between 1916 and 1917. The rate of increase moderated somewhat between 1917 and 1918 but, nonetheless, was still a very substantial 12 percent.

The government had three major options in facing inflation. First, the WIB could have attempted to exercise greater control over prices. Instead, the committee responsible for price fixing relied exclusively on voluntary agreements. Not only that, but the committee faced the obstacle of poor cost accounting, which meant it never had adequate information on the impact of its efforts. Only at the very end of the war did the WIB seriously investigate the possibility of controlling consumer prices directly rather than working through industrial agreements. But, in any case, effective price control was very likely beyond the administrative capacities of the day.

Second, the government could have used fiscal policy (the manipulation of governmental expenditures and receipts). The fiscal actions of the Wilson administration, however, presented no resistance to the rapidly rising price level. In fact, the federal budget encouraged inflation by augmenting the nation's demand for goods and services. The basic source of the upward pressure was the vast expenditure associated with the war effort, beginning in December 1915 and extending until 1920. The most dramatic increase came between April 1917 and June 1920, with the government spending some $31.5 billion. At the peak, military expenditures accounted for about one-quarter of national product.

Coupled with the high increase in expenditures was the general unwillingness of the Wilson administration to make an increase in tax rates that would bring about a comparable increase in tax revenues. By reducing civilian demands through higher taxes, effective total demand could have been reduced and inflationary pressures eased. When the administration, with Congress, did raise taxes, it settled on the rather low figure of one-third as the proportion of expenditures to be financed by taxes—rejecting the advice of economists such as Irving Fisher of Yale and Secretary of the Treasury McAdoo to impose higher taxes. Wilson was less concerned with inflation than with preserving the popularity of his administration and public support for the war, and he feared a sharper tax increase would erode both. Also, in response to public unease over the war and, in particular, to the radical critiques of American war motives made by Robert M. La Follette, William E. Borah, and the Socialists, among others, Wilson moved the nation's tax structure in a more progressive direction, that is, more toward a structure in which a person's or a corporation's tax rate increases as his income increases. The revenue act of October 1917 increased income tax rates, which had previously extended from 1 to 13 percent, to a graduated scale reaching from 4 to 63 percent on individuals and it also imposed an excess-profits tax on business incomes. The latter tax meant that businesses paid from 20 to 60 percent of their net incomes, according to the ratio of excess profits to invested capital, on profits that exceeded the average net earnings of 1911–1913. While the tax was more equitable, it increased the cost of using capital to manufacturers and consequently retarded the effort to increase production through higher levels of investment. Not only did the wartime tax system retard investment; it left taxes on low- and middle-income groups at fairly modest levels, thus further encouraging inflationary tensions by failing to restrain consumer demand in a significant fashion.

Heavier taxation having been rejected, borrowing—the only other way for governments to acquire resources—became the primary mode of financing the war. Just when inflationary pressures were worst, during 1917, and despite the fact that the economy was already operating at a full-employment, or full-capacity, level, the government began incurring considerable deficits as a result of tax revenues lagging behind expenditures. Whereas the federal budget had been almost in balance during 1915 and 1916, by 1919 the deficit at full employment reached more than $13 billion. Meanwhile the government increased its debt, through short-term borrowing from banks and bonds sold in Liberty-loan drives, from a little over $1 billion to more than $25 billion. The result of that stimulation was a severe episode of inflation, which Wilson and the Congress could have avoided by adopting the tax increases recommended by numerous fiscal experts. However, the objective of reducing the political cost of the war by keeping taxes down dictated otherwise and prevailed.

Third, the government could have used monetary policy (the manipulation of the nation's money supply) to resist inflation. But the Federal Reserve Board, which had responsibility for regulating the money supply, simply reinforced Wilson's inflationary fiscal policy. To provide the Treasury with the means for financing the public debt Congress amended the Federal Reserve Act in 1916 to permit reserve banks to rediscount loans that were made on the collateral of government bonds, in addition to the rediscounting of commercial paper provided for in the original act. Empowered by this amendment, the Federal Reserve willingly became the bond-selling window of the Treasury, seeking to make borrowing to buy bonds extremely easy. The process would begin by a member bank in the Federal Reserve System making a loan (either in Federal Reserve notes or as a deposit) to a customer who, in turn, would use the proceeds to purchase a government security. If the bank needed more reserves to cover increased loans, it could rediscount the customer loan or rediscount its own collateral note secured by the bond. In contrast to the financing of the Civil War, the government did not print greenbacks, but both the Federal Reserve notes that were lent out and the Federal Reserve deposits that were created as needed to purchase bonds fulfilled the same function. By the end of the war, Federal Reserve notes and deposits at Federal Reserve banks dominated the nation's money supply. The impact of this rapidly expanding money supply was sharply increased competition for a limited supply of goods. Unfortunately, hardly anyone, especially within the Wilson administration, conceived of the Federal Reserve Board as an independent factor in the economy, seeking to stabilize conditions. Rather, most viewed it as an agency whose primary obligation was to the Treasury and, ultimately, to the goals set by the administration in power.

In mobilizing the nation for war, the federal government demonstrated both its ability to reshape production priorities and the willingness of the public to accept such redirection if the emergency warranted. In the process, planners such as Baruch learned a good deal about operating a more coercive economy; big businessmen developed a greater appreciation of the benefits of government-sponsored cooperation; and the Wilson administration accomplished a good part of its war program. Nonetheless, stabilization of the economy eluded the war makers—between 1914 and 1918 the price level almost doubled—and their failure would plague the nation both immediately after the war and during the Great Depression.

With the end of hostilities the government only hesitantly and sporadically used the instruments of wartime mobilization to fashion a greater measure of order and efficiency in the peacetime economy. Wilson and most of his key advisers considered the boards, agencies, and special corporations to be merely emergency efforts, justifiable in time of war but unwarranted departures from a competitive marketplace during peacetime. Their strong distaste for long-range economic planning conducted by the public sector extended even to the way in which they coped with demobilization, virtually ignoring any planning for reconversion of the economy to the needs of peace.

Many agencies closed up their operations immediately. War agencies canceled substantial amounts of contracts, ended the construction of public housing that was being built near shipyards and munitions plants, and neglected the task of finding peacetime employment for the 4 million men in the armed forces and for the 9 million persons in war industries.

Surprisingly enough, employment and production hardly suffered in the first months after the war. True, the war component of national product fell by almost half between 1918 and 1919, but the nonwar sector more than took up the slack. National production held steady between 1918 and 1919, an improvement over the decline registered between 1917 and 1918, when mobilization policy was floundering. By the last quarter of 1919 a boom began that lasted into the second quarter of 1920.[4]

To account for the continuing strength of the economy, despite the collapse of public planning, it is tempting to emphasize pent-up demand for consumer durables—a force that would produce much of the prosperity immediately following World War II—but the market for such goods immediately after World War I was too limited to be credited. Support for the economy stemmed from other sources, one being the construction industry, which when released from wartime rationing of building materials, experienced immediate recovery and contributed to the boom, although not as dramatically as it would during the mid-1920s. More important was the market for American exports, which continued as a vital source of expansion, European demand for American foodstuffs compensating, in large part, for the disappearance of demand for war materiel. American merchants, bankers, and manufacturers continued to provide effective short-term financing for exports of a wide range of goods. The American Relief Administration, managed by Herbert Hoover, and the United States Grain Corporation did their part to encourage exports by selling supplies on credit to a Europe whose agriculture had not recovered from the ravages of war.

Probably the most important source of expansion was an inflationary psychology that pervaded the American buying public. Because prices had virtually doubled during the four years of war, consumers anticipated further hikes and, in turn, increased their purchases. Consequently domestic consumption of nonwar goods was strong during the boom. In other words, people chose to hold less money, which was depreciating in value, and more assets, such as consumer goods, which were increasing in dollar value. Making the same calculation as did consumers, manufacturers sought to build up their inventories; likewise farmers increased their holdings of land, not only in response to continued demand for food but also to invest in an asset whose supply was fixed. This kind of inflationary buying, in turn, contributed to further price increases, thus making forecasts of continued price increases self-fulfilling prophecies. As both cause and effect, wholesale prices accelerated their advance. Whereas the price level had increased 12 percent in 1918, it rose a startling 29 percent during the following year. And despite the downturn that finally ensued in 1920, prices were 11 percent higher in that year than they had been in 1919. In 1920 prices were almost three times as high as they had been only six years earlier.

Although the federal government had relinquished almost all of the control it might have exercised over stability by means of wartime planning agencies, it still could have moderated the postwar expansion through the appropriate use of fiscal and monetary remedies. Instead, the fiscal and monetary devices it pursued only stoked the fires of inflation. Most strikingly, in fiscal 1919, while the economy was at full employment, the federal government, still paying for the war, incurred the largest deficit of the war. Meanwhile the Federal Reserve continued to hold itself very closely to the interests of the Treasury by seeking to reduce the cost of borrowing money to the Wilson administration, which was then extending both long- and short-term debt throughout 1919. To make money readily available for purchasers of federal securities the Federal Reserve kept the discount rate well below current market rates and, in the process, contributed strongly to the inflation.[5]

Only toward the end of 1919 did the Treasury and the administration act to control and subdue the persistently rising price level. In September 1919 Benjamin Strong, the dynamic governor of the Federal Reserve Bank of New York, became an exponent of decisive action by arguing for an increase in the discount rate. But at that point Secretary of the Treasury Carter Glass was preoccupied with debt management; he prevailed upon the board to take no action. Following Glass's success Strong rebelled in October and raised the rates of the New York bank. The governors of the board rejected Strong's action, but a few weeks later the Treasury finally approved such an increase, and the discount rate at New York rose to 4.75 percent. By that point Strong already had begun to have doubts about restrictive policy, suspecting that the time to induce a gentle cooling of the economy had already passed, but a grave illness prevented him from exerting his influence against contraction. Meanwhile the overanxious Treasury urged and achieved a further increase in the discount rate to 6 percent in June 1920, the largest single increase in the history of the Federal Reserve System, before or since. Virtually simultaneously the federal government reduced the level of its expenditures to bring about a budget that was in balance and thus reinforced the restrictive action of the Federal Reserve.

If either the first increase in the discount rate or the budget tightening had occurred earlier in 1919, the public authorities might have eased the expansion with finesse. But because of the overexpansion of inventories, the boom was already on the verge of tapering off, having peaked in January 1920. The contraction was mild at first, but restrictive policy, especially the curtailment of the growth of the money supply by the Federal Reserve, brought about a more rapid collapse.[6] Prices began declining in May, continued falling for several months, and then, with the added downward pressure of the Federal Reserve's June restriction, nose-dived. By June 1921 prices were scarcely above half their level of May 1920. More than three-quarters of the decline occurred between August 1920 and February 1921, which makes this the sharpest price collapse in American economic history. Production declined, dropping precipitously in the fall of 1920. As a result nearly 10 percent of the labor force was unemployed at the bottom of the depression.

The trough came in July 1921, some eighteen months after the downturn had begun. Businessmen had liquidated short-term debts and absorbed their losses; in the winter, they began building up their inventories once again. The recovery to prosperity gathered momentum and continued on through the 1920s, with only very brief pauses in 1924 and 1927 before the collapse of 1929.

In sum, inflation was the major problem that faced the economy during the period of reconversion. The people in Washington essentially did nothing to plan for this situation and failed to act appropriately, once they were enmeshed in the inflationary net. As had happened after earlier wars, the economy finally took the route of sharp deflation, returning prices to something approximating prewar levels. Earlier the national government could have moderated the inflation, thus making the deflation easier to endure; or once in the deflation, it could have taken the opportunity to cushion the decline. Instead, the agencies of stability encouraged expansion and exacerbated the contraction.

The prosperity that followed during the 1920s was real enough. But the performance of the stabilizing instruments of federal management between 1915 and 1921 were a grim foreboding of what was possible when the marketplace failed to ensure the maintenance of economic order or when well-intentioned public authorities intervened without being able to gauge the impact of their actions with any significant degree of accuracy.

World War I left its imprint on the American economy. No measure of the resource costs of World War I equals the quality of the measures available for the Civil War. However, the most easily calculated costs were high, particularly in light of the limited duration of direct participation of America in the war. From 1917 through 1920 the additional public expenditures required for the war (including credits to the Allies) amounted to $17.1 billion (in 1913 pr ces), or about 40 percent of national product in 1913. Great Brilain and Germany spent more on the war, but not much more—$21.2 billion and $19.9 billion, respectively.[7] The increasing capital intensity characteristic of the domestic economies of the United States and western Europe had also dramatically affected the techniques of war. The high financial contribution of America to the war represents in part the capital intensity of the war effort and the great capacity of the American economy to produce the machines and equipment for war as well as for peace.

America's human contribution to the war was far less than its financial effort. American casualties were extremely light in view of the scale of the killing. Close to 120,000 servicemen died, and more than 200,000 were wounded. Losses of this magnitude must be regarded as significant. But about three times as many soldiers died in the Civil War, close to four times as many died in World War II, and more than three times as many men were wounded in World War II. Also, by way of contrast, each of the major European powers (except Italy) lost between 1 and 2 million men. In total, the war cost the lives of 10 million soldiers. In short, although the American financial contribution to the war was relatively large, its total contribution (including an evaluation of the losses of human capital) was far less than that of the other major belligerents.

More important in the long run to the American economy were structural changes that the war induced. Most significant was a dramatic enhancement of America's position in the world—in part a consequence of the magnitude of the human and physical devastation that the war wrought in Europe. One estimate is that without the war the European economies would have reached their 1929 levels of food and manufacturing output in the early years of the decade.[8] Had there been no war, America would have acquired preeminence in world markets eventually. But the war pushed America to dominance so swiftly that serious international instability resulted. It is quite possible that without the war's disruption of the international economic order, America and the world would have avoided both the Great Depression and World War II.

NOTES

1. For a reexamination of the role of Baruch, the WIB, and the dollar-a-year system, see Robert D. Cuff, "Bernard Baruch: Symbol and Myth in Industrial Mobilization," *Business History Review*, 43 (Summer 1969), 115–133; and Paul A. C. Koistinen, "The 'Industrial-Military Complex' in Historical Perspective: World War I," *Business History Review*, 41 (Winter 1967), 378–403.

2. Prices would have risen even more slowly, however, if the government had not abstained from rationing food to domestic consumers during the war. The Food Administration did place restrictions on processing foods considered expendable, like liquor and candy, and did force consumers to purchase substitutes for wheat and rye flour, but the program fell far short of the strict rationing of World War II.

3. Only in 1907 did the immigrants arriving outnumber those arriving in 1914. From well over 1 million in 1914, immigrant arrivals dropped off to about 325,000 in 1915 and declined to around 110,000 in 1918. Not until 1920 did the level of immigration begin to rise appreciably.

4. National product was down about 4 percent in 1920 from 1919, but the decline resulted from depressed conditions in the latter half of the year.

5. Although realizing that it was contributing to inflation by creating an incentive to borrow from the Federal Reserve, the board declined to take decisive countercyclical action. The board could have acted, for example, by selling its substantial holdings of assets in open-market operations to restrict monetary expansion. But this action would have exerted a downward pressure on the price of government bonds, made financing the debt more difficult for the Treasury, and squeezed commercial banks which still had substantial amounts of the Victory Loan—the final war loan, not floated until after the armistice—on account and had extensive loans outstanding to their customers secured by those bonds.

6. The stock of money declined steadily from September 1920 until July 1921. The total decline was 9 percent, the largest percentage decline up to that time.

7. H. Mendershausen, *The Economics of War* (Englewood Cliffs, N.J.: Prentice-Hall, 1941), p. 305.

8. W. A. Lewis, "World Production, Prices and Trade, 1870–1960," *The Manchester School of Economic and Social Studies*, 20 (1952), 105–138.

SUGGESTED READINGS

Books

Clark, John M. *The Costs of the World War to the American People.* New Haven: Yale University Press, 1931.

Faulkner, Harold U. *The Decline of Laissez-Faire, 1897–1917.* New York: Holt, Rinehart and Winston, 1951.

Friedman, Milton, and Anna J. Schwartz. *A Monetary History of the United States, 1867–1960.* Princeton, N.J.: Princeton University Press, 1963.

Gilbert, Charles *American Financing of World War I.* Westport, Conn.: Greenwood, 1970.

Hardach, Gerd. *The First World War, 1914–1918.* Berkeley and Los Angeles: University of California Press, 1977.

Link, Arthur. *Wilson: The Struggle for Neutrality, 1914–1915.* Princeton, N.J.: Princeton University Press, 1960.

———. *Wilson: Campaigns for Progressivism and Peace, 1916–1917.* Princeton, N.J.: Princeton University Press, 1965.

Samuelson, Paul A., and Everett E. Hagen. *After the War, 1918–1920.* Washington, D.C.: National Resources Planning Board, 1943.

Soule, George. *Prosperity Decade: From War to Depression, 1917–1929.* New York: Holt, Rinehart and Winston, 1947.

Wilson, Robert W. *How America Went to War.* New Haven: Yale University Press, 1931.

Articles

Cuff, Robert D. "Bernard Baruch: Symbol and Myth in Industrial Mobilization," *Business History Review,* 43 (Summer 1969), 115–133.

Hall, Tom G. "Wilson and the Food Crisis: Agricultural Price Control During World War I," *Agricultural History,* 47 (January 1973), 25–46.

Koistinen, Paul A. C. "The 'Industrial-Military Complex' in Historical Perspective: World War I," *Business History Review,* 41 (Winter 1967), 378–403.

☷ 14
The 1920s: A Glimpse of Modernity

THE HIGH-PERFORMANCE ECONOMY

To understand the economy during the 1920s, we should view it, not as a sick decade, full of foreshadowing of the depression to follow, but as a period that bears a strong resemblance to the best years of the post-World War II era in its rising standard of living, sustained high employment, stable prices, and strong market for articles of mass consumption. Indeed, the record of the 1920s in providing jobs and price stability surpassed that of the period from 1945 to the present. Despite our retrospective awareness that a major depression was to follow, the prosperity was unprecedented and was sustained from 1922 through much of 1929, with only modest pauses in 1924 and 1927.

Traditionally, economic historians have emphasized the structural weaknesses of the economy during the 1920s. That such weaknesses existed is indisputable, but historians of the 1920s have usually exaggerated their dimensions and their contribution to the collapse of the economy in 1929. The successes of the period were at least as important as the failures, and by examining those strong areas we see that the more recent episodes of stability and growth are based on the accomplishments of the 1920s just as well as on the New Deal and the mobilization for World War II. To a large extent the organizational and technological basis of post-Great Depression prosperity developed from the innovations of the 1920s.

384

The most significant feature of the prosperity of the 1920s for the average American was solid income growth. National income, per-capita income, and wages per member of the labor force increased rapidly. Per-capita income jumped from an annual average of $517 during the decade between 1909 and 1918 to $612 between 1919 and 1928. During the 1920s national income and product grew at rates of almost 2 percent per year, close to the rate obtained during the first decade of the century. Real earnings also grew steadily for employees and at rates substantially greater than even those during the two preceding decades. Between 1900 and 1910 the real earnings of employees increased about 20 percent, and in the following decade, about 12 percent. But during the 1920s these earnings increased about 23 percent. The position of the average employee was also improving more rapidly. Between 1900 and 1920 the average real income of employees increased by roughly 25 percent, but during the 1920s alone the increase was about 30 percent. Moreover, the rate at which workers took real income in the form of leisure increased sharply. By the end of the decade, production workers in manufacturing, for example, were close to realizing the forty-hour week. Largely as a consequence, man-hours worked per capita began to decline steadily. The end of massive immigration contributed to the decline since immigrants worked at higher rates than did native Americans. But the decline in hours worked per capita began in the early 1920s and amounted to more than 1 percent annually.[1]

No direct, reliable evidence exists that accurately describes changes in the distribution of income and wealth during the 1920s. However, the trend toward more even distributions, which began in the late nineteenth century, appears to have continued during the 1920s. All of the factors that contributed to the earlier trend prevailed during the 1920s. Particularly strong were shifts toward higher demand for skilled labor, higher premiums attached to the acquisition of human capital, and a larger skilled population in relation to the entire population. These shifts were reinforced by an epoch-ending change in the structure of the economy and, indeed, of the larger society. This change resulted from the legislative restriction of massive immigration. Wartime conditions had seriously inhibited the flow of immigrants from Europe. Then, in 1921, Congress began a program of limitation with temporary legislation and, in 1924, completed it with the National Origins Act. The act's national quotas succeeded in reducing the annual flow of immigrants to about 250,000 by the end of the decade; in 1914, well over a million had arrived. As a consequence of the war and immigration restriction, the ratio of immigration to labor-force growth was only 40 percent between 1914 and 1930, whereas it had reached 73 percent between 1900 and 1914. Since the restriction fell more heavily on unskilled people, the end of massive immigration tended to raise the wages of unskilled workers, encourage the convergence of the wages of skilled and unskilled labor, and contribute tö an equalization of income and wealth distributions.

Offsetting these powerful trends to some degree were severe problems of imbalanced growth that blemished the prosperity of the 1920s. Certain enterprises experienced severe structural problems in the 1920s, and these problems constituted the source of regional depression—depression that would only become more severe during the 1930s. The New England textile industry, for example, suffered from the shift of firms to the lower-cost labor markets of the South. Railroads faced stiff competition in freight and passenger service from publicly subsidized highways (including a trunk system initiated by the Federal Aid Road Act of 1916), suffered from uncoordinated and inefficient management, and thus incurred declining passenger revenues, stagnant freight revenues, and subnormal rates of return. Extractive industries, particularly mining, having experienced overexpansion as a result of wartime demands, suffered from depletion and severe new competition. Coal mining was especially unhealthy, barely surviving the competitive inroads made by hydroelectric power, fuel oil, and natural gas: between 1923 and 1929, wages in coal mining fell some 14 percent. The lumber industry faced overexpansion and depleted resources, especially in the northern portion of the Great Lakes states. Finally, agriculture, containing the most severe defects, faced problems of war-induced overexpansion and, in the regions of severest hardship, extreme overpopulation. Significant regional problems resulted from these afflicted industries, and regional income levels diverged during the decade, reversing the trend of the late nineteenth century. Per-capita income in New England rose relative to that in the nation as a whole, despite the sluggishness of textiles, but the West North Central states (containing much of the Great Plains), the South, and the West were not as fortunate as a result of the hard times in lumbering, mining, and agriculture. (See Table 26.)

Certainly the distribution of income would have been more favorable and the upward movement of per-capita income even more impressive with a better-balanced growth. But the really significant phenomenon for reaching an understanding of the 1920s is the high earnings per employee, despite per-capita earnings declining in some significant industries and in several regions of the nation.

Accompanying the high levels of income was an unusual degree of price stability and an exceptional record of employment. Con-

TABLE 26   PER–CAPITA PERSONAL INCOME: THE REGIONS
              COMPARED

	1920	*1930*
United States	$100	$100
Northeast	132	138
New England	124	129
Middle Atlantic	134	140
North Central	100	101
Great Lakes	108	111
West North Central	87	82
South	62	55
South Atlantic	59	56
East South Central	52	48
West South Central	72	61
West	122	115
Mountain	100	83
Pacific	135	130

Source: Richard A. Easterlin, "Regional Income Trends, 1840–1950," in Seymour
Harris (ed.), *American Economic History* (New York: McGraw-Hill, 1961), p. 528.

sumer prices were extraordinarily stable after the collapse of 1920–
1921 and were scarcely any higher in 1929 than they had been in
1922. (See Table 27.) (The average annual rate of increase in prices
was less that 1 percent between 1922 and 1929.) The nation enjoyed
the unusually stable price level without incurring a high rate of
unemployment; over the same period, strong demand for goods and
services caused unemployment to drop to an annual average of only
3.7 percent. That was a significant improvement over the performance of the two preceding decades and was a record unmatched
during the presumably more enlightened 1950s and 1960s.[2]

The glitter of newness associated with the 1920s was real. Consumers purchased strikingly greater quantities of durable goods,
mainly automobiles and electrical appliances, than they had previ-

TABLE 27   CONSUMER PRICE INDEX

(1947–1949 = 100)			
All Prices			*All Prices*
1920	85.7	1925	75.0
1921	76.4	1926	75.6
1922	71.6	1927	74.2
1923	72.9	1928	73.3
1924	73.1	1929	73.3

Source: U.S. Bureau of the Census, *Historical Statistics of the United States, Colonial
Times to 1957* (Washington, D.C.: U.S. Government Printing Office, 1960), p. 126.

ously and demanded higher levels of services. Although electrical appliances and automobiles had been available during the decade of World War I, large numbers of people demanded them only in the 1920s. Consequently, the production of radios increased over 25 times between 1923 and 1929; that of refrigerators, over 150 times between 1921 and 1929. And passenger-car registrations grew from 9.3 million in 1921 to 23.1 million in 1929. Helping to make all this possible was the finance company, newly emergent and extending consumer credit on a large scale, primarily on automobiles but on furniture and appliances as well. By 1929 outstanding installment debts reached over $3 billion, with almost half that representing automobile paper.

The increases in consumer spending on durables were not only absolute gains but gains relative to spending on all consumer goods. These relative increases were possible in part because real and substantial growth in incomes permitted consumers to shift away from

One of the twelve million families who owned a radio in 1929.

purchases of food and clothing, which still accounted for well over half of the flows of goods to consumers. Another aid to the shift in purchasing patterns was the low level of food prices of the 1920s, largely a product of the war and postwar overexpansion of production. In terms of electrifying the household and putting the family in an automobile the 1920s clearly marked a revolution. However, in structural terms this consumer revolution was actually quite modest. In the decade 1909–1918 durable goods accounted for 9.2 percent of consumption purchases; by the next decade their share had increased only slightly, to 10.6 percent.[3] In other words, consumers increased their purchases of other goods and services during the 1920s almost as rapidly as they increased their spending on durables: they purchased not only more radios, automobiles, and kitchen appliances, but also more food, clothing, education, entertainment, and perhaps even gin. Thus, although consumers bought new kinds of durable goods, they did not drastically increase their purchases of durable goods relative to other goods and services. If there was a real revolution in the character of consumption patterns, it was in the early and middle portions of the nineteenth century rather than the 1920s.

PRODUCTIVITY, STABILITY, AND PLANNING

The prosperity that Americans enjoyed during the 1920s rested on the more efficient use of capital and labor. The growth of national product per man-hour accelerated sharply to 2.5 percent annually— a rate unequaled since the dynamic "catch up" years following the Civil War. Workers employed in manufacturing led in this productivity gain, contributing an average annual rate of 5.6 percent per worker during the 1920s. Gains in the productivity of capital were even more striking, growing at an annual rate of 4.3 percent.[4]

The productivity gains of the 1920s rested more heavily than those of earlier decades on technological change that enhanced the efficiency of both capital and labor and less heavily on either the utilization of more capital per worker or the enhancement of the quality of capital. Most crucial to this technological change was the application of scientific information rather than the results of mechanical ingenuity and the accumulation of practical experience. Manufacturers pursued innovations that promoted full mechanization of their activities, in particular, new techniques for mass production and the electrification of factories. Prior to the 1920s manufacturers tended to invest in enlarging their plants or in the building of new facilities, but during the 1920s they more often updated existing manufacturing plants, with an eye toward using capital more efficiently, particularly by the exploitation of scientific knowledge. This was especially true with those manufacturers who faced extraordinary demands for their output: producers of automobiles, electrical appliances, and synthetic fibers, along with those in the related areas of the chemical and petroleum industries—gasoline, paints, lacquers, solvents, and chemicals used in rayon manufacture.

Several circumstances favored this particular response to the pressure of demand on existing plant capacity. For one thing, manufacturers could now tap low-cost reserves of electric power as a result of the refinement of the electricity-generating steam turbine engine and electric motors. For another, they acquired a large backlog of process inventions, such as catalytic cracking (the breaking up of the hydrocarbons of petroleum into lighter chemicals with the use of high heat, intense pressure, and a catalyst), which enhanced plant efficiency. In addition, wartime mobilization had taught some manufacturers how to expand production without increasing investment in new plants. Further, as competition among new products (especially chemicals) intensified during the 1920s, manufacturers searched more intently for cost-saving methods.

Among those innovators in mass production and industrial electrification were the manufacturers of glass products, who adopted automatic feeding devices. Producers of rubber tires and tubes introduced extensive conveying systems. In the tobacco industry, machine-made cigarettes and cigars were the two major trends. Iron and steel mills increasingly used production flows arranged in more efficient straight lines and controls powered by electricity.

The contribution of these innovations to gains in capital productivity is not easily measured. However, one study has found that the introduction of the fully continuous cracking process alone increased the efficiency of capital in petroleum refining about 42 percent between 1919 and 1929, for an annual average rate of increase of 3.6 percent. And in the paper-manufacturing industry the same study finds that fully 48 percent of the advance in the productivity of capital resulting from all factors could be explained as the result of increasingly sophisticated applications of electric power to paper-manufacturing processes. Even without precise data for most industries, the basic trend is clear. A close association existed between the highly rapid advance of the productivity of manufacturing capital and the widespread application of refinements in mass-production techniques.[5]

Accompanying the technological advances of the 1920s was a set of organizational innovations designed to equip firms to deal with the broad problems posed by very rapid expansion. The structural change most closely connected with technological advance was the institutionalization of research and development. Firms created and budgeted departments to develop new products and to reduce production costs of old products. More generally, in order to manage rapidly growing operations, firms practiced heightened diversification and, led by the electrical manufacturers, sought to reorganize themselves around specialized divisions. These new structures, departmentalized by functions such as production and sales and coordinated by a central office, provided improved financial control over increasingly complex operations and consequently stabilized highly erratic unit costs. Further, firms continued to use techniques of vertical integration, just as they had two decades earlier, to ensure steady flows of resources from mines, wells, farms, and forests to consumers. To sort out the complex intrafirm relationships necessary to vertical integration, first du Pont and then other companies developed the practice of interdivisional billing at full market prices and established a more general refinement of accounting procedures for individual units within the firm. More ambitious cost control also meant an increased sensitivity to differentials in state and local tax costs, which were rising rapidly during the 1920s as a result of the hard-pressing demand for more schools and roads.[6] The establishment of organizational changes directed toward more rational production was by no means complete in the 1920s, even within the consumer-durables industry. Rather, the departures of the 1920s were a significant prelude to the more thoroughgoing adjustments in corporate organization and strategies following the Great Depression.

Supporting both the technological and organizational changes of the 1920s was the increasing level of skill of the population. Perhaps most important was the significant increase in the nation's public-education effort. In less than ten years, between 1920 and 1928, the share of gross national product devoted to direct expenditures on public education almost doubled: from 1.17 percent to 2.22 percent. Much of this increase was at the secondary level. By the end of the decade 29 percent of the population of seventeen years of age were high-school graduates—in contrast with 16.8 percent in 1920. Financed by both public and private resources, institutions of higher education also increased their enrollments rapidly. By 1928 over 12 percent of the population between eighteen and twenty-one years of age were enrolled in such schools. Only 6 percent had been enrolled in 1918. The resulting increase in people with high-level skills meant that producers were able to meet more easily the growing requirements for coordination and control created by technological innovation and the increasing scale and complexity of production units.

When manufacturers reorganized production to meet the conditions of demand, they also began, in the 1920s, to predict more accurately, and even to shape, demand for their products. Increasingly manufacturers attempted systematically to forecast future market conditions; that is, they tried to match supply and demand more effectively. General Motors and the electrical manufacturers were the first to develop their own statistical approaches for such estimations. Other manufacturers aided in financing private, nonprofit agencies such as the National Industrial Conference Board and the National Bureau of Economic Research to develop useful market projections. To stimulate and stabilize consumer demands, manufacturers engaged in extensive experimentation with advertising, which they saw as a way of both enhancing investment opportunities and reducing investment risk. And for manufacturers faced with increasing competition, especially those in the consumer-durables industry, advertising was also a means of exaggerating the differences between their products and those of their competitors. To augment demand, producers introduced rapid style changes and promoted those changes with advertising, hoping to fix the image of their particular product in the consciousness of the consumer. By 1928, for example, the Ford Model T in basic black had become the Model A, available in four colors and in seventeen body styles, and to promote the style changes, in one exceptionally expansive week Ford spent about $2 million on advertising. More generally, national brands proliferated during the 1920s; the number of national advertisers selling a standard brand increased from about 5,000 in 1925 to 8,500 in 1930. One result of this multifaceted absorption with controlling demand was that advertising expenditures reached $3.4 billion by 1929, or more than 3 percent of national product—a share comparable to that diverted to advertising after World War II.

Another expression of the desire of manufacturers to attain a greater control over the marketplace was the new wave of mergers during the 1920s, the second of the three great periods of merger in American economic history. Beginning in 1924 the number of mergers rose from 368 to 1,245 in 1929.[7] The firms that made the most fervent efforts to promote mergers were those that experienced most rapid growth of production during the 1920s, one of their important objectives being leverage over prices. The competitive equilibrium established in the first merger wave between 1898 and 1904 had disappeared during the early 1920s, and the movement of the late 1920s was in part an effort to restore it. Another objective of merger was diversification into the production of new products. Diversification, through the acquisition of smaller companies, permitted the large-scale application of similar technological and organizational processes to the manufacture of dissimilar products and the consequent attainment of productivity gains. The new, larger companies had a greater ability to develop new products, in large part because they had more capital available to finance research and development. A buoyant stock market, offering extremely attractive opportunities for capital gains, facilitated the efforts of manufacturers to contain competition and to diversify through merger.[8] As a result of the merger movement, the production of transportation equipment (e.g. automobiles by General Motors), chemicals, and electrical machinery (e.g., household appliances by Westinghouse and General Electric) became significantly more concentrated in the hands of a few firms. However, for industry in general the degree of the concentration—the extent to which production emanated from the largest firms—remained more or less unchanged during the 1920s.[9]

The success of the merger movement depended in no small part on the sanction and support of the federal government, whose guideline remained the rule of reason. In 1920 the Supreme Court ruled that although the United States Steel Company had restrained trade by its size and power, it was not in violation of the Sherman Act, since it had not restrained trade in an unreasonable fashion—by coercing competitors. Henceforth, firms merging during the 1920s met with no government interference unless they created a formal monopoly; in fact, the 1920 ruling of the Court prevailed until 1945. The Federal Trade Commission, still harboring a remnant of Wilsonian antitrust activism, was the only source of opposition. Although the FTC occasionally issued cease-and-desist orders, businessmen could appeal them, and usually found that they had a friend in Secretary of Commerce Herbert Hoover. Not only did Hoover support the merger movement among large firms, he vigorously promoted the formation of trade associations, largely within industries containing relatively small-scale firms.

The origins of the trade-association movement of the 1920s went back far beyond Hoover, however, for trade associations, or cooperative organizations of businessmen within the same industry, had nineteenth-century origins. Further, it was World War I rather than the competitive difficulties of the 1920s that gave the associations a degree of real power. Wartime mobilization put a premium on cooperation, and the associations, working with wartime agencies, made that cooperation more effective. Most important were the efforts of William C. Redfield, Wilson's secretary of commerce, to promote cooperation in industry, one of which was the creation, in February 1919, of the Industrial Board of the Department of Commerce. The board sought to stave off price declines in case of a threat of depression and to provide a way for manufacturers to write "reasonable trade agreements," but railroad supporters in the Wilson administration and the strong antitrust convictions of Wilson and others on his cabinet brought a premature end to the board.[10] From this wartime experience many businessmen learned the value of cooperation to promote efficiency and push up prices. Interest in cooperation languished during the economic collapse of 1920–1921, but after a judgment of the Supreme Court in 1925 that competitors could exchange information if they did so without the explicit purpose of raising prices, Hoover enthusiastically directed the Department of Commerce in promoting the growth of trade associations and their activities.

The impact of the trade associations was in fact slight. Associationism probably did little more than mildly reinforce the oligopolistic trend of the middle and late 1920s; the merger wave had little or nothing to do with the trade-association movement. Besides that, the areas in which Hoover succeeded in promoting cooperation were precisely those that needed it the least. Departing from the conservatism of President Coolidge, Hoover proposed cooperative reorganization of the industries, particularly agriculture and coal mining, that World War I had afflicted. Although these industries suffered from overproduction and excessive competition induced by wartime conditions, they were far from enthusiastic about his approach. Coal-mine operators, for example, refused to disown the ethos of individualism, even when they joined associations. It took more than two years of the Great Depression to convince the National Coal Association that it should sponsor and test the legality of district cooperatives, and even in 1933, after the establishment of the National Recovery Administration, heroic efforts were required to get mine operators to agree to an industrial code regulating prices, production, and employment. Although achieving little in themselves during the 1920s, however, Hoover's policies did in fact pave the way for the formation of industrial codes in the 1930s, thereby providing an essential link between the wartime experiments, such as the Industrial Board, and the National Industrial Recovery Act of 1933.

Thus the pace of industrial reorganization quickened during the 1920s as manufacturers adapted their institutions and business practices to promote productivity and to predict, or to control more effectively, the rapid growth of demand. Resulting was the proliferation of important technological innovations, substantial investment in research and development, advances in vertical integration and diversification, growing sophistication in projecting market trends, an enlarged use of advertising, and a new surge of merger activity: in all, an economy that could function in a more predictable and productive fashion.

AGRICULTURE IN THE 1920S: A TARNISHED AGE

As farmers entered the decade of the 1920s they had almost every reason to believe that they would continue to enjoy a prosperity much like that of the golden age of agriculture. Favorable conditions had persisted for almost two decades after the late 1890s, stretching even into the war and through 1919. Conditioned to expect strong demands, rising farm prices, and buoyant farm incomes, farmers anticipated continued prosperity after the war by making an enormous investment in farmland, much of it marginal, partially in expectation of growing demand for farm production and partially in anticipation of a dramatic, inflation-fed appreciation of the value of farmland. In so doing, farmers were behaving much like manufacturers who built up inventories during the same period.

The dreams and fortunes of the optimistic farmers evaporated when farm prices dropped sharply in May and June of 1920, at the onset of the postwar depression. Farmers who had expanded production and land holdings during the preceding months now found themselves heavily in debt without the ability, in many cases, to cover their fixed expenses. As costly as the economic collapse was in the short run, its long-term impact on agriculture would have been minimal if farm prices had returned to their earlier level and buoyancy. But during the 1920s they remained well below the relative position they had occupied since the late 1890s. The decline reduced purchasing power of farmers in the 1920s to about three-quarters of the wartime level. Net farm income also fell to about 40 percent of the 1919 level and in the 1920s never returned to more than about three-quarters of that level.[11] Consequently, agriculture's share of national income was also in drastic decline. In short, agriculture never fully recovered from the postwar depression before it suffered further blows in the 1930s.

The economic maladies of the farmers that the war had produced were compounded by marketplace forces, by the patterns of supply and demand. The most damaging element was the slackening of demand for agricultural products, relative to demand for all goods and services. European demand, a strong force for growth during the war, fell off sharply after 1919, as Europeans raised effective tariffs against American produce in order to aid the recovery of their own agriculture. And within the United States the increase in incomes during the 1920s failed to produce a proportionate increase in the demand for agricultural products. Demand for agricultural goods increased rapidly during the 1920s, given the fact that the population growth was rapid—more rapid even than during the previous decade—but the declining share of income spent on farm products helps to account for the worsening position of the nation's farmers.

(Generally speaking, as people experience increasing incomes, they at some point choose to devote more of their incomes to the purchase of nonagricultural goods and services than they had previously, a phenomenon known as the low income elasticity of the demand for farm products.)

Once demand slackened, farmers could not unite to restrict supply in a way that would have maintained prices and incomes. Not only did farm production and farm acreage equal or exceed wartime levels during the 1920s, but farm productivity increased more rapidly than during the preceding decade. Just as manufacturers responded to increasing competition by seeking to use capital more efficiently, farmers sought to undersell their competitors not only by increasing their use of farm machinery and equipment, particularly tractors, motor trucks, and automobiles, but also by using that equipment more effectively. But where manufacturers succeeded, farmers failed; they were unable to develop the same ability to match supply and demand that large corporations had fostered so consciously. The marketing of farm products remained almost totally beyond the farmers' control, whereas manufacturers were, by the middle of the 1920s, gauging the marketplace more successfully. In response, farmers began their first serious departures from the free market, as they sought to develop a public policy that could serve, in a sustained fashion, to maintain prices and incomes.

The government had never sought to provide the farmer with the tools for gaining control over the marketing of his products to augment his income. The wartime experiments with policies to stabilize farm prices, like Herbert Hoover's Food Administration program, were directed more at combating inflation and encouraging production than at enlarging farm income. Moreover, very few politicians or farmers construed even those measures as permanent in character, and, indeed, the end of the war marked the intended end of government involvement in farm markets. But the depression of 1920–1921 revived interest in finding means to regulate farm prices —now with the central objective of protecting the farmer's place in the economy. Those politicians with the welfare of the farmer at heart began to face the problem of determining what the farmer's fair share was. Farm representatives came to agree that the government should strive to restore the farmer to a parity position defined in terms of the halcyon years 1910–1914.

The many proposals put forward to restore parity fell under the rubric McNary-Haugenism (representing the contributions of Senator Charles L. McNary of Oregon and Representative Gilbert Haugen of Iowa). A typical program included protective tariffs for farm products; the chartering of a federal corporation, as in World War I, to buy farm products at pegged higher prices; and the selling at world prices rather than at the artificially raised United States price of surpluses acquired by the corporation. If, as anticipated, the government experienced losses from its buying and selling of surpluses, it would pass those losses to farmers through the imposition of an equalization fee on all sellers. The government corporation, in other words, would buy and sell farm products at supported prices, that is, at prices higher than those prevailing before the entry of the government. However, at these higher prices consumers would be apt to buy fewer farm products than they had previously, so the government corporation would be left with a surplus. To recoup, the corporation would dump the surplus wherever it could, accepting whatever price prevailed (the world price). But the returns from these sales could not cover the costs of purchasing the domestic surplus. (The fact that the government corporation would find it necessary to rid itself of surpluses indicates that the world price would be lower than the support price.) The remaining costs of purchasing the surplus would be distributed among farm producers, thus reducing their gross incomes.

Twice Congress passed bills creating a McNary-Haugen program, but each time President Coolidge vetoed them. He acted, in large part, on the advice of Secretary Hoover, who understood a serious, probably fatal flaw in the McNary-Haugen proposals: the omission of production controls, specifically, limits on the levels of production that farmers could achieve. The implication of this omission was that farmers would have an incentive to produce as long as the support price afforded increasing income. There was a strong likelihood, therefore, that surpluses would continue to mount, depressing world prices to the point that the cost of equalization fees would cancel out any gains realized from supported domestic prices. The farmer was likely, in short, to return to his earlier equilibrium position.

Hoover favored limiting farm production but opposed outright government controls to achieve this goal. He believed on ideological grounds that federal controls were an undesirable limitation on economic freedom. Consequently, he wanted to channel government interest into the pursuit of an alternate program, a second basic approach to the farm problems of the 1920s—government-sponsored, cooperative marketing. As in the McNary-Haugen proposals, there was no place in this program for compulsory production controls, but the objective was to limit production rather than to encourage surpluses. Such limitation would emerge from voluntary agreements, similar to the ones Hoover favored in his endeavors to stimulate the trade-association movement. His objective was to provide farmers with the degree of control over production that he recommended for business through the trade associations. Although his proposals lacked elements of compulsion, they were closer to the New Deal approach to managing commercial agriculture than was the abortive McNary-Haugenism.

Hoover's program and McNary-Haugenism, even if successful, would have alleviated the difficulties of only a small minority of the nation's farmers. Problems of farm prices and income were the domain primarily of the nation's commercial farmers, roughly speaking, that half of all farmers that accounted for over 90 percent of farm production. A substantial portion of the other half were trapped in patterns of production that offered virtually no chance for welfare gains without significant structural changes in the economy.

The social problem in agriculture was the overpopulation of certain regions in relationship to their supply of natural resources. Areas of the Great Plains, the southeastern cotton belt, southern Appalachia, and the cutover region of the northern Great Lakes states (Minnesota, Wisconsin, and Michigan) contained large populations who were unable to participate effectively in the marketplace. High wheat and livestock prices stimulated an expansion of acreage and production into the Great Plains during and after the war. But demand was insufficient to maintain those who had moved onto marginal lands. Then, in the 1920s, droughts affected this region severely, foreshadowing the dust-bowl conditions of the 1930s. Similarly, the cutover region faced difficulties that began with the overexpansion of agriculture during World War I. Although people had previously streamed onto lands made available by new cutting of forests, wartime demands, reinforced by subsidies of state governments for settlement, were the most significant impetus to settlement in the northern portions of the Great Lakes states. Here farm builders, accustomed to an orderly transformation of forest to farmland, expected their dreams to materialize. However, these twentieth-century pioneers, lured on by pockets of excellent farmland, first had to subdue a terrain that was rough and heavily seeded with rocks and boulders. The supply of good land was just enough to keep the flow of settlers coming, but not enough to provide the means for those settlers to support themselves. In Wisconsin, for example, northern counties had to rely almost exclusively on state aid to finance their public services, because they lacked an economic base to generate sufficient taxes of their own. A more orderly, planned development was necessary before this region became successfully integrated within the Great Lakes economy.

In the South the problems of overpopulation were more severe in that the inhabitants' attachment to their traditional locations and occupations was considerably stronger. Much of the agriculture of Appalachia was only self-sufficient in character. Even though production in the older cotton belt was more commercial, that area had severe problems resulting from an insufficiently mobile population, a decline in world demand for cotton, a labor-intensive kind of cultivation that brought heavy soil erosion and burdensome fertilizer costs, competition from more-efficient southwestern cotton producers, the ravages of the boll weevil, which began during the 1920s, and a heavy burden of debt which the postwar price collapse had left resting on tenant farmers.

The plight of farmers in all these regions was a common one: the failure of the nation's social institutions to allow the transfer of human resources from a less productive to a more productive sector or area of enployment. In all these regions, but especially in the South, the process of migration was too costly, in the face of farmers' income problems, for enough farmers to take advantage of buoyant urban opportunities. The out-migration from the South that began during World War I continued into the 1920s, but it was not large enough to have any significant impact on per-capita incomes in the South by reducing the pressure on existing opportunities. Even in the Great Plains and the cutover, where people had arrived recently and were more geographically mobile, it took considerable coercion and inducements during the 1930s to move them to centers of greater opportunity.

The most difficult aspect of the farm problem of the 1920s was this set of social rigidities, not the price and income problems of commercial farmers. Indeed, the same was true of the depression years of the 1930s. But public policy in both decades took as its primary objective the resolution of the more manageable market problems of the commercial producers. The resistance of the social problem to corrective medicine partly explains the emphasis of public policy, but the more important factor influencing the choice of policy objectives was the decisive political weight of the commercial farmers.

Although certain farmers (such as the California fruit growers) experienced a decade of rising demands and incomes, most had to shoulder the burdens of the overexpansion that World War I had induced. The structural weakness of agriculture was not sufficient to alter the basically prosperous appearance of the economy during the 1920s, but it was responsible for the regional disparities of the decade and would make the impact of the Great Depression even more severe for the nation's farmers.

THE WORLD ECONOMY: A HOUSE OF CARDS

As has been indicated, by the 1920s the United States was the world's largest creditor, and the fact that it had become the world's largest, most productive economy meant the reinforcement of its creditor position. Advancing the nation ever more as a creditor was the growth of American private investment abroad—a growth of more than two and one-half times between 1919 and 1930. Some of this investment served to facilitate international trade and, in this sense, was an extension of the wartime interest in supporting Allied purchases of supplies. As in wartime, the New York banking community played a crucial part in supplying short-term credit. To some extent federal legislation eased the way. The Federal Reserve Act as amended in 1916 allowed national banks to establish foreign branches and to own, in whole or in part, special foreign banking corporations. After the war, Congress passed the Edge Act (December 1919) to expedite the creation of foreign banking corporations involved in the financing of exports. Previously, such investment corporations, under law, required state charters, although national banks could invest in them. The concept behind the act was that corporations created under its provisions would sell their own bonds in the United States and then lend the proceeds to foreign importers, taking long-term foreign obligations as collateral. Thus the Edge Act authorized federal incorporation of investment trusts that would act as instruments to support American export trade. Associations formed under the act included Morgan's American and Foreign Banking Corporation and Rockefeller's International Acceptance Bank, which worked out short-term arrangements with Credit Anstalt, the great Austrian bank. By 1931, American investment in such banking organizations totaled about $125 million.[12]

Along with the expansion of government-promoted international banking on behalf of trade went an even stronger growth of long-term private investment, especially after 1925 when European stability seemed assured. In the mid-nineteenth century, American promoters had canvassed Europe for foreign lenders, but in the last half of the 1920s they scoured the world, including Europe, for foreign borrowers. Typically, twenty-nine representatives of American financial houses in Colombia all tried to negotiate loans for the national government and other parties; some thirty-six houses, mainly American, competed to make a loan to the city of Budapest; and fourteen scrambled for a loan to the city of Belgrade. American agents discovered a Bavarian hamlet to be in need of about $125,000 and persuaded the town to borrow $3 million. American promoters relied heavily on insiders to smooth the way for foreign deals. In Cuba, the son-in-law of the president received a well-paid position in the Cuban branch of the Chase bank while the bank competed successfully with other American banks seeking to finance the Cuban government. Meanwhile the Chase bank extended the president himself a large personal line of credit. In another instance, the son of the president of Peru received $450,000 from J. and W. Seligman Company and the National City Bank for services rendered in arranging a $50-million loan, which these houses marketed for Peru.[13] The private banks had free reign, since the federal government played a rather limited role in this vigorous and heated expansion of long-term investment capital. The administration looked favorably on the migration of private capital, and although it reviewed prospective loans, it rarely exerted any decisive influence against the loans on behalf of either political or economic considerations. Whether or not the investments were rational is virtually impossible to determine, since the Great Depression wiped out good and bad loans alike. The year 1927 marked the peak of America's foreign loan activities and the onset of depression in some parts of the world. By the time of the collapse of Credit Anstalt in 1931, world-wide financial disorder prevailed.

As American banking expanded, American manufacturing became more of an international force—promoted by a national policy of maintaining a favorable balance of trade. The Webb-Pomerene Act of 1918 suspended the antitrust laws to permit manufacturers to organize export associations so that they might compete more effectively in international trade and thus enlarge exports. Government support for banking organizations to provide short-term credits was also an aid to American exporters. Tariff policy, as implemented by the Emergency Tariff of 1921 and the Fordney-McCumber Tariff of 1922, meant significantly higher barriers against European goods and worked to enlarge the favorable balance of trade. Proponents of higher tariffs were advocating a policy that would have made sense only if the nation had still been an international debtor and seeking a favorable balance of trade to acquire foreign exchange that would balance out capital imports. Furthermore, the United States, at least for the time being, was the principal source of shipping services in the world, which brought in even more foreign exchange. The result of private and public efforts was that the United States consistently reaped a favorable balance of trade, most of which was accumulated in Europe.

Europeans, in particular, welcomed American capital, but they found serious obstacles in obtaining it. Specifically, the United States government used the demand for capital as a bargaining point to obtain repayment of the Allies' debts, which by 1919 totaled $9.5 billion. During the 1920s government policy began to make it impossible for public authorities and private enterprises in France, Belgium, Italy, Greece, Rumania, and Yugoslavia to borrow in the United States until the governments of those countries settled their accounts with the Treasury. Among the debtor countries, France was the most stubborn, and persistently failed to reach even a quasi-permanent agreement about the terms of payment. Until 1927, as a result, France had to rely almost exclusively on unpoliced and indirect ways of borrowing dollars instead of the public borrowing supervised by the Department of State. The French had little time to support their economy before the Great Depression intervened. Then, in 1934, with the passage of the Johnson Act, the United States closed its loan market to those governments in default on their war-debt payments.

Although Europe was in dire need of capital for economic recovery, and American private-investment bankers favored refunding interest on the wartime debt, refinancing the public loans, and keeping tariffs low, the American government insisted on repayment of the wartime debt without providing any means, other than encouraging private loans, to assist Europe to make its payments. Few Americans, particularly taxpayers of modest means, were willing to forgive the debt and accept the cost as a necessary part of waging the war; the United States persistently viewed money lent to the Allies as money invested rather than spent. In 1919 Washington rejected the proposals of private bankers to modify the debt and in 1922 ignored the protests of the American Bankers Association against the Fordney-McCumber Tariff and also disregarded the British proposal for outright cancellation of the debts.

Yet some compromise was ultimately necessary, given the weakness of the European economy and American insistence on maintaining high tariffs. Consequently Congress set up a debt commission, under Secretary of the Treasury Mellon, which eased the formerly intransigent position somewhat between 1923 and 1926. In the course of scaling down debts according to ability to pay, the commission wrote off 20 percent of the British debt, 53 percent of the French, and 75 percent of the Italian. (The Russian debt had already been repudiated by the Soviet government.) The commission extended the repayment period from twenty-five to sixty-two years to make the debt easier to service. Under this plan, which itself was quite demanding, the United States got back about $200 million per year up to the Hoover moratorium on debt payments in 1931. With the exception of continued payments from Finland, that year marked the virtual end of debt repayment. The Allies had discharged about 20 percent of the debt.

One way Europeans could have more successfully paid back the debt was to have sold more goods to Americans than they purchased. In other words, if the United States had wished to facilitate debt repayment, it could have run an unfavorable balance of trade. (In fact, this was the way Finland, that supposed paragon of financial virtue, was able, alone among all the Allies, to pay back its debt, buying very little from the United States and selling it far larger quantities of newsprint.) However, Washington held a favorable balance sacrosanct, and Europe was left to borrow.

The American policy that encouraged a return to the gold standard also forced Europeans to the American loan market. Liquid gold reserves were limited in Europe, so gold proved no more useful than dollars as a medium for repayment. Very few nations were able to go back on a working gold standard after 1919, and those that were found themselves faced with the possibility of serious deflation if they used gold for repayment. (Just such a deflation struck Britain after 1925, the result, in part, of using gold stocks to repay the debt.) Only by 1928–1929 did an international system of free conversion of currencies into gold at fixed exchange rates effectively govern American-European trade.

Given the American policies of rapid debt repayment, maintaining a favorable balance of trade, and returning swiftly to the international gold standard, the functioning of the international system depended on a sustained and continuing flow of private American investment dollars abroad. The crucial element in this international pattern was heavy American lending to Germany. American private investment was very widely distributed, but only a small portion of it went to the Netherlands, Great Britain, and France, the principal recipients being Germany, Canada, Australia, and the South American nations. For the most part, the extensive American export of capital was neither directed toward the largest wartime debtors nor conceived of as a way of relieving the burden of wartime debt. Rather, the central objective behind American loan policy was the economic and political recovery of Germany.

American aid to Germany began as an attempt to withdraw French troops from the industrial Ruhr valley in 1924. The French occupation, designed to guarantee reparations, was unpopular in Great Britain and the United States and, in fact, proved an obstacle to rebuilding the German economy. To remove the troops, General Charles G. Dawes, acting as chairman of a subcommittee of the Reparations Committee of the League of Nations, proposed a plan to reform the German economy that would ensure recovery and the payment of reparations. The essence of the Dawes Plan, as adopted, was to scale down the reparations payments. The plan also recognized that it was necessary to restructure the German financial system, including a return to gold exchange, the introduction of a new mark, and the creation of a transfer committee to oversee the payment of reparations.

The plan worked quite well, especially for Germany, as was its intention. During the five years following 1924 the Germans made their payments regularly and transferred them to their creditors without difficulty, for one thing, because the reparations were by no means burdensome. During the last half of the 1920s the highest percentage of national income required for their payment was only 3.3 percent due to Germany's prosperity during the same period.[14] The main reason for German success, however, was the massive thrust of American capital into Germany. Americans loans to Germany were far in excess of the level necessary to finance reparations. After the mark had been stabilized, foreign capital poured in, amounting to more than three times the gross amount of reparations payments. Germans sold some 180 stock and bond issues in the United States, raising $1.5 billion. The reparations were paid, quite literally, with the money of foreign investors, not with the savings and taxes of the German people, which, in conjunction with foreign investment, largely American, were used to renovate German industry during the late 1920s. Ironically, at the same time that the United States was building up the economic capacity of Germany it was hindering the general recovery of western Europe through short-sighted policies.

Thus the international economic system, particularly with reference to Europe, depended on the flow of American capital to Germany, reparations payments from Germany to the former Allies, and the repayment of debts to the United States. The system, convoluted as it was, worked reasonably well after the Dawes Plan, but it was inherently unstable. If the outflow of capital from the United States ceased, the international house of cards would collapse. This is, in fact, what happened toward the end of the decade. Short-term lending abroad declined in 1928, and long-term lending followed suit a year later.[15] When the loans stopped, the creditors of Germany met again and this time adopted the plan of Owen D. Young, chairman of the General Electric Company. His plan once more sharply reduced the reparations payments. Meanwhile the former Allies were forced to default on their promised debt-repayment schedules, evoking the Hoover moratorium of 1931, which effectively canceled all debt and reparations payments once and for all. At the same time European demand for American exports fell off drastically, reinforcing the domestic depression. The end result was an unusually serious and prolonged hiatus in the international flow of funds and international trade.

The instability of the international economy of the 1920s was rooted in failures of American policy. Although the United States had undergone an enormous transformation in its international role since the nineteenth century, dominant political opinion still assumed that preserving the vitality of the export sector was the key to upholding prosperity at home and that pursuing a short-run policy of squeezing the most out of foreign investments would have no long-term costs. The fact is that if the United States had canceled the debts or had modified them while providing the means to repay the debt through trade, the European economy would have been stronger, Europeans would have had less urgent demands for American capital, American investments in Europe would have been sounder, and the international economy would have rested on a much firmer foundation than was the case in 1929, when it was overly dependent on the health of the United States. The economic and political devastation of World War I clinched the basic, inescapable fact of American superiority in the marketplaces of the world. But the short-sighted American policies of trade promotion, imposing fidelity to wartime contracts, and a firm adherence to the gold standard turned the fact of superiority into a severe problem for maintaining economic stability and growth throughout the world.

In conclusion, although the economy of the 1920s was in numerous significant ways remarkably prosperous and stable, and although the refinement of corporate strategies and structures during the 1920s would prove of inestimable value in the future to an economy seeking higher rates of growth and a larger measure of stability, there were serious exceptions to the generally sturdy pattern—distortions created largely by World War I. The war and public policy had forced an overexpansion of agriculture that resulted in low prices, low incomes, a heavy burden of debt, and an increase in the number of small farmers trapped on marginal, unproductive land. The war also warped the international role of the United States by too rapidly accelerating its transition from debtor to creditor nation. The pace of change was so swift that Americans failed to comprehend the implications of the transition and to recognize the nation's economic self-interest, enacting policies that placed the world economy in an exceedingly precarious position. Both of these structural weaknesses resulting from the war would prolong and intensify the course of the Great Depression.

NOTES

1. Simon Kuznets, *National Income: A Summary of Findings* (New York: National Bureau of Economic Research, 1946), p. 32; Stanley Lebergott, *Manpower in Economic Growth* (New York: McGraw-Hill, 1964), pp. 163, 523.

2. Lebergott, *op. cit.*, p. 512.

3. Harold G. Vatter, "Has There Been a Twentieth-Century Consumer Durables Revolution?" *Journal of Economic History,* 27 (March 1967), 1–16.

4. John W. Kendrick, *Productivity Trends in the United States* (Princeton, N.J.: Princeton University Press, 1961), pp. 152–153, 166–167.

5. John H. Lorant, "Technological Change in American Manufacturing During the 1920's, *Journal of Economic History,* 27 (June 1967), 243–246.

6. With the exception of the response to the expanding government service-state, these organizational changes are discussed at length in Alfred D. Chandler, Jr., *Strategy and Structure: Chapters in the History of American Industrial Enterprise* (Cambridge, Mass.: M.I.T. Press, 1962).

7. Willard L. Thorp, *The Structure of Industry,* Temporary National Economic Committee, *Investigation of Concentration of Economic Power, Monograph No. 27* (Washington, D.C.: U.S. Government Printing Office, 1941), p. 233.

8. Another, less thoroughly investigated factor behind some corporate reorganizations was the sharply increasing rates of state and local taxation during the 1920s. Not uncommonly, manufacturers formed holding companies to manage their tax obligations. One example was the 1923 reorganization of Wisconsin's Palmolive Company around a Delaware holding company to pass profits beyond the reach of that state's income tax. For a general discussion of the uses of the holding company during the 1920s, see James C. Bonbright and Gardiner C. Means, *The Holding Company: Its Public Significance and Its Regulation* (New York: McGraw-Hill, 1932).

9. Alfred D. Chandler, Jr., "The Structure of American Industry in the Twentieth Century: A Historical Overview," *Business History Review,* 43 (Autumn 1969), 255–298.

10. Robert F. Himmelberg, "Business, Antitrust Policy, and the Industrial Board of the Department of Commerce, 1919," *Business History Review,* 42 (Spring 1968), 1–23.

11. U.S. Bureau of the Census, *Historical Statistics of the United States, Colonial Times to 1957* (Washington, D.C.: U.S. Government Printing Office, 1960), p. 283.

12. For a discussion of the origins of the Edge Act in the context of the often conflicting aims of the Treasury and private bankers, see Paul P. Abrahams, "American Bankers and the Economic Tactics of Peace: 1919," *Journal of American History,* 56 (December 1969), 572–593.

13. See Cleona Lewis and K. T. Schlotterbeck, *America's Stake in International Investments* (Washington, D.C.: Brookings Institution, 1938), for these and other examples.

14. Étienne Mantoux, *The Carthaginian Peace; Or, The Economic Consequences of Mr. Keynes* (London: Oxford University Press, 1946), pp. 94–179.

15. Arguing that the rapid reduction of American capital exports was the central element in the collapse of the international economy in 1929–1933 does not rule out the possibility that independent conditions triggered economic downturns elsewhere in the world. On the initiation of the German collapse see Peter Temin, "The Beginning of the Depression in Germany," *Economic History Review*, 24 (May 1971), 240–248.

SUGGESTED READINGS

Books

Barger, Harold, and H. H. Landsberg. *American Agriculture, 1899–1939: A Study of Output, Employment, and Productivity.* New York: National Bureau of Economic Research, 1942.

Bernstein, Irving. *The Lean Years: A History of the American Worker,* 1920–1933. Boston: Houghton Mifflin, 1960.

Chandler, Alfred D., Jr. *Strategy and Structure: Chapters in the History of American Industrial Enterprise.* Cambridge, Mass.: M.I.T. Press, 1962.

Cochran, Thomas C. *The American Business System, 1900–1955.* Cambridge, Mass.: Harvard University Press, 1965.

Feis, Herbert. *The Diplomacy of the Dollar, 1919–1932.* Baltimore: Johns Hopkins University Press, 1950.

Friedman, Milton, and Anna J. Schwartz. *A Monetary History of the United States, 1867–1960.* Princeton, N.J.: Princeton University Press, 1963.

Lebergott, Stanley. *Manpower in Economic Growth.* New York: McGraw-Hill, 1964.

Lewis, Cleona, and K. T. Schlotterbeck. *America's Stake in International Investments.* Washington, D.C.: Brookings Institution, 1938.

Lewis, W. Arthur. *Economic Survey, 1919–1939.* London: Allen and Unwin, 1949.

Mantoux, Étienne. *The Carthaginian Peace; Or, The Economic Consequences of Mr. Keynes.* London: Oxford University Press, 1946.

Soule, George. *Prosperity Decade: From War to Depression, 1917–1929.* New York: Holt, Rinehart and Winston, 1947.

Articles

Abrahams, Paul P. "American Bankers and the Economic Tactics of Peace: 1919," *Journal of American History,* 56 (December 1969), 572–593.

Chandler, Alfred D., Jr. "The Structure of American Industry in the Twentieth Century: A Historical Overview," *Business History Review,* 43 (Autumn 1969), 255–298.

Himmelberg, Robert F. "Business, Antitrust Policy, and the Industrial Board of the Department of Commerce, 1919," *Business History Review,* 42 (Spring 1968), 1–23.

Lorant, John H. "Technological Change in American Manufacturing During the 1920's," *Journal of Economic History,* 27 (June 1967), 243–246.

Vatter, Harold G. "Has There Been a Twentieth-Century Consumer Durables Revolution?" *Journal of Economic History,* 27 (March 1967), 1–16.

✦ 15
The Great Depression and the New Deal: The Expansion of Public Planning

THE SOURCES OF THE GREAT DEPRESSION

The high-income, high-employment economy of the 1920s vanished in 1929. National product and income declined by one-third between 1929 and 1933, and unemployment reached a record peak of 25 percent in 1933, the bleakest year of the Great Depression. In the intensely industrialized portions of the nation—the formerly expansive cities—the toll of the unemployed was even more staggering. To take only Ohio cities as examples, in Cleveland 50 percent of the labor force was jobless, in Akron, 60 percent, and in Toledo, 80 percent. Many city dwellers existed in primitive conditions much like those of a preindustrial society stricken by famine. Conditions in the countryside, while not quite as bad as those in the city, were severe enough to thrust farmers into a position probably worse in real terms than that of the 1890s. Especially hard-hit were those agricultural regions—Appalachia, the cotton Southwest, the Great Plains, and the northern Great Lakes—that had been faced with depression since the early 1920s.

The nation's worst economic collapse, which followed on the heels of exceptional prosperity, shook Americans' faith in their economic system, and convinced many that the flaws in the nation's economy were fundamental in character. However, that conviction reflected the terrible contrast between the 1920s and the early part of the 1930s rather than the reality of economic experience during the twentieth century. To be sure, the economy had flaws, but they were not serious enough to account for the scale of the Great Depression. Rather, that severity resulted from the failure of public officials to use effectively the stabilization instruments at their disposal, particularly those of the Federal Reserve System; the public's primitive understanding of the economy, which focused almost exclusively on the vagaries of the stock market; and the distortions that World War I had imposed on the nation's economic life. While these were problems with very serious results during the 1930s, they were not fundamental to the economy and were, therefore, yielding to solutions well within traditional modes of institutional reform in the interests of stability. By encouraging such solutions, the Great Depression forced an acceleration of the quest for successful management of a modern, industrial economy—a quest that had begun at least a half-century earlier.

Structural Problems: Underconsumption

Darker explanations for the extreme harshness and protraction of the Great Depression dwell upon the supposed inability of the American public to consume the fruits of increasing productivity. Such theories point to the unequal distribution of income as restricting total demand; the minority earning the lion's share of national income is said to have saved at rates that prevented consumption sufficient to bring the economy to full employment and provide adequate investment opportunities. Reinforcing such underconsumption, according to this line of argument, was extreme business concentration that led to inordinate market power and a tendency for manufacturers to keep prices at a level too high for maximum consumption to be realized. As a result of the income maldistribution, monopolistic pricing, and a decline in the rate of population growth, demands—especially for the growth products of the 1920s (automobiles, radios, refrigerators, etc.) and for residential housing (particularly apartments) and commercial structures—had become saturated, resulting in the collapse of industries central to the prosperity of the 1920s; quite simply, demand fell behind supply. Members of the underconsumptionist school of thought proposed a massive redistribution of income to favor consumption and a rigorous suppression of monopoly pricing. But neither was forthcoming during the New Deal. Therefore, according to the underconsumptionists, only massive support of demand by the federal government (through the World War II mobilization effort) and the consequent growth of new demands (such as for the products of the aerospace industries) can account for postdepression prosperity.

However, the explanation resting on underconsumption is not

easily supported by the historical record. First, the characteristics that the structuralists emphasize in describing the economy of the 1920s are, if anything, more descriptive of the period 1898–1914. During those earlier years, the distribution of income was less even, government spending provided less economic stimulation, and business concentration was probably higher. Thus, if the structuralist theory were valid, the period 1898–1914 should have witnessed the onset of severe economic stagnation. Second, the economy achieved a rapid rate of recovery even during the supposedly afflicted decade of the 1930s—well before the stimulating intervention of World War II. At the end of the 1920s the automobile and appliance industries had a very great future for rapid growth; only one family in six owned an automobile, only one family in five owned a fixed bathtub or had electricity in its home, and only one family in ten had a telephone. In fact, increased demand for and consumption of such goods provided the basis for the very considerable degree of economic recovery during the last half of the 1930s and for the strong persistence of high levels of demand after the war, despite a sharp decline in government purchases of the goods and services for making war.[1] Third, it is arguable that had there been no defense establishment to maintain after the war, resources supporting defense industries in the postwar years would have been allocated by the private sector in such a way as to better promote economic stability. Yet even though economic planning in the twentieth century could have been more effective in an environment of stronger price competition and more even distribution of income, as the underconsumptionists suggested, one lesson of the 1930s is that such conditions are not *necessary* to the fostering of stability. As will be seen, the view of the Great Depression as a fairly short-run problem stemming from external accidents, especially those associated with World War I, and institutional flaws is one that seems much more plausible.

The Stock Market

Even if insufficient demand (or underconsumption) cannot explain the unusual severity of the Great Depression, it does account for the initial onset of the downturn, inasmuch as manufacturers of automobiles and appliances grossly overestimated the ability of the American consuming public to buy their products in 1929.[2] The result was a pileup of excessive inventories, and beginning in the summer of 1929, cutbacks in production, the laying-off of workers, reduced incomes and buying power—in short, recession. However, it was only a garden-variety business contraction; the economy had tolerated many such inventory cycles in the past without suffering long periods of excessive unemployment and low incomes. Previously, in fact, once many factories had sold off their inventories, they had customarily resumed production.

With a recession well under way, the stock market collapsed in October and November, adding a second and much more significant force to the economic slide, and in a fashion rather unique in American business cycle history, prolonging and intensifying the course of the Great Depression.

Since the latter part of 1927 the stock market had been in a grotesquely inflated condition. The investing public ignored the pace of industrial growth and became wedded to the conviction that, in the short run, stock prices would rise much more rapidly than any measure of industrial-corporate progress. Credit for stock-market transactions was readily available, margin requirements (the requirements for down payments on stock purchases) were low, and stock prices were strongly buoyant. This constellation of factors allowed traders to increase the number of shares they held, as well as their equity in those shares, without expending any additional amounts of their own funds. The attractions were irresistible: the market recorded price increases of over 60 percent between December 1927 and September 1929.

Various sources of unstable growth influenced the behavior of the market. One was the influx of money from investors new to Wall Street who were attracted by the high return that short-term funds, or call money, could earn in the bull market; the rate of interest on such money doubled during the boom, reaching 12 percent by the end of 1928. Although some share of this money originated in the commercial banking system, the greater portion emerged from foreign banking agencies, corporations with large cash balances, and brokers and individuals possessing idle funds who sought short-term opportunities. Such investors added a large measure of instability in that they could recall their loans at will and were the first to flee the market once a downturn began.

Another source of weakness was the investment trust, a new financial institution drawn to the market by buoyant conditions. Each of these nonoperating companies traded in a variety of stocks and offered its own stock as a way for the small investor to diversify his holdings. The concept proved popular: some 160 of these firms had emerged by 1927, and 140 more joined them in that year alone. However, the novelty of the investment trusts shielded them from public regulation and they relied very heavily on debt financing, thereby making their own stocks very attractive in a bull market. Consequently, these stocks were vulnerable to any hint of weakness in the market, and the trusts tended, at the slightest suggestion of trouble, to sell off their better securities in order to protect their position. They contributed to the burst of unstable growth and, in the process, made the structure of the market even more top-heavy. Further, owned and promoted by commercial banks, the investment trusts would carry the impact of the stock-market crash to the commercial banking system.

A final source of weakness was the lack of regulation over the activities of stock-market "insiders." Commonly, groups of exchange members representing pools and syndicates of large investors would agree to boom a particular stock, with no reference to the earnings performance of the company concerned, thus attracting both national attention and investors to that stock. Then, the insiders, sometimes buying early and selling as investors bid up the price or other times letting publicity alone carry the price upward and then selling short before the price dived, used their privileged connections with brokers to reap large gains. Lack of regulation of brokerage firms allowed the insiders to feed the bull market of 1927–1929, added a further measure of instability to the market, and jeopardized the capital of many investors, small and large alike, who had been duped by the insiders and their brokers.

The public had allowed the distortions of the stock market to develop by tolerating its collection of serious institutional flaws. But then, the stock market had never before been the center of the nation's economic attention; consequently, its problems had never had a sufficiently wide impact to motivate reform interest. Once having experienced the Great Crash, the government would, in the course of the New Deal, regulate margin buying, separate investment from commercial banking, and sharply restrict the activities of insiders, creating the Securities and Exchange Commission to regulate the market. These reforms, although not particularly radical inasmuch as they served primarily to make the stock market function as a more effective marketplace, would have prevented the stock-market crash of 1929 and would have significantly diminished the Great Depression.

As it was, the stock-market crash reinforced a recession already well along, and in an important way contributed to the unusual failure of the economy to recover from an economic reversal within one or two years. The stock market during the late 1920s had become to Americans of all walks of life the symbol of the nation's prosperity and economic strength and the embodiment of the faith of millions in the ability of corporations to sustain that well-being. Business leaders found their own self-confidence amply reinforced by the high prices that the public was willing to pay for their securities. When the inevitable pinprick of doubt burst the bubble, those same Americans became pessimistic about the future not only of the stock market but also of the economy, in regard to both its long-run potential to grow and its shorter-run ability to return to high levels of production and income. The impact of the crash was to sharpen and prolong the crisis of confidence that grew worse as depression dragged on between 1929 and 1933. In a sense the depression became self-feeding: the longer it continued, the more dismal were the prospects for recovery, and expectations of extended depression inhibited the consumption and investment necessary to stimulate the economy. The stock-market crash became part of that nexus of paralysis by providing a tangible form for the dashing of economic anticipations.

The Federal Reserve System

Despite the pessimism created by the collapse of what seemed to be the nation's central financial institution, the federal government even then possessed sufficient power and the appropriate institutions for stimulating the economy to recovery, indeed, for preventing the crash in the first place. The Federal Reserve System, in particular, must incur culpability for failing on both counts.[3]

The disastrous policy making of the Federal Reserve System passed through three phases. In the first phase, with powerful tools at its command—open-market operations (the buying and selling of government securities to expand or contract the money supply) and manipulation of the discount rate—the system could have taken decisive action in either 1928 or early 1929 to stem overexpansion. Instead it was passive, allowing the boom to continue unchecked. In the second phase, between 1929 and 1931, the system did nothing effective to encourage economic revival, despite signs in the first half of 1931 that revival was imminent. (It only very moderately lowered the discount rate and undertook only the most limited purchase of government securities.) Then, after pursuing exactly the wrong policy in 1928–1929 and acting only hesitantly thereafter, the system in 1931 took a gravely incorrect turn. In October the Reserve Bank of New York greatly increased its discount rate and the Reserve Board sharply restricted its open-market purchases (for reasons explained below). As a result the Federal Reserve severely limited the ability of the nation's banking system to meet domestic demands for currency and credit by making borrowing much more expensive and by reducing the size of the available money supply, which fell at an incredible, unprecedented annual rate of about 31 percent into 1932. Beginning in February 1932, the Reserve somewhat relaxed its policies, even engaging in modest open-market purchases between April and July, but thereafter returned to restriction, which increased the rate of monetary contraction to an annual pace of 78 percent by early 1933. All told, as a consequence of the Federal Reserve System, the stock of money fell by fully a third from August 1929 to March 1933, when the economy reached the trough of the Great Depression.

To gauge the full impact of this contraction we should realize that with a drastically reduced supply of money available, Americans could have staved off a sharply falling national income only by more rapidly spending the dollars they did have. In other words to sustain income, fewer dollars would have had to do much more work. But, in fact, the strong inclination of Americans was to defer spending and remove their deposits from commercial banks, thereby holding more cash, in relation to income, than they had previously. That increasing preference for cash rather than other forms of assets resulted from prevailing expectations that prices would continue to fall and thus augment the value of money and from a lack of faith in the ability of banks to protect deposits.

The combination of monetary policy and public expectations turned financial panics into serious banking crises in October 1930, March 1931, and January 1933. In the face of monetary restriction, the heavy withdrawal of deposits in each crisis produced a wave of bank failures, often initiated by failures of the unusually weak banks that served distressed agricultural areas. The failures reinforced public distrust of banks, causing each crisis to become worse than its predecessor, and accelerating the contraction of the money supply through a vicious reversal of the process of multiple-deposit creation.[4]

Certainly, money policy was not the only cause of the severity and persistence of depressed conditions between 1929 and 1933, but just as certainly, it was a sufficient cause. Given the restrictive approach of the Federal Reserve, recovery was virtually impossible before 1933. And if the Reserve had applied its very considerable powers of money creation effectively, particularly avoiding the disastrous turn taken late in 1931, it could have prevented the contraction of the money supply and hastened recovery.

In 1928–1929, through a lack of internal agreement on how the board should respond to fluctuations in the business cycle, the Federal Reserve arrived at its fateful decisions. Disagreement within the system was nothing new. During the 1920s the New York Reserve Bank promoted the idea (which economists now generally endorse) that their system had a primary responsibility to actively work against the business cycle. Other financial centers tended to believe that the system ought only to respond to the needs of business for credit, thus reinforcing the business cycle. However, that disagree-

A RUN ON A NEW YORK CITY BANK. Between 1930 and 1933, banking panics cost depositors more than $1.3 billion.

ment became low-keyed as the New York bank, under the skillful leadership of Benjamin Strong, proved able to turn its central location in national and international capital markets to a position of command in the Reserve system. Most significantly, Strong successfully applied his chairmanship of the five-member Open Market Investment Committee (created in 1923, the OMIC guided the Reserve banks and the board in managing open-market operations) to the moderation of swings of the inventory cycle in 1923–1924 and again in 1926–1927. In that countercyclical activity, Strong reinforced his hand with the informal power he had obtained by leading the board to consistently rubber-stamp the discount rate set by the New York Reserve.

After Benjamin Strong's death in 1928, the New York bank failed to find a leader of comparable intellectual force, personality, and reputation. Consequently, the center of political gravity within the system shifted to the other Reserve banks, which welcomed an opportunity to advance their influence within the system. Unfortunately, their parochial setting in the nation's capital markets led to increased enthusiasm for a monetary policy that reinforced cyclical movements and resulted in a period of indecision for the board. Strong had ended his life plumping for higher discount rates and open-market sales to cool the bull market, but the board, deadlocked in the manipulation of both policy tools, in effect sanctioned the boom.

Indecision as to the appropriate domestic role of the Reserve system continued as the economy moved into the depths of the Great Depression, but in the period 1931–1933 that factor shared culpability with the preoccupation of the system with protection of the international gold standard. That concern had appeared in a beneficial way during the first two years of depression as the system responded to an increase in the pace at which gold flowed into the nation (a flow that resulted from heightened purchase of exports by Europeans and a lessened demand by Americans for imported goods). The desire to reduce the pressure on European gold reserves and thereby to shelter the increasingly shaky gold standard led the board to take a favorable attitude toward New York's interest in lowering discount rates (which would reduce the short-term interest rate and encourage the flow of short-term investment capital to Europe) and expanding open-market purchases (which would exert an upward pressure on domestic prices and reduce America's favorable trade balance). So until mid-1931, international concerns pushed the Reserve toward a policy of encouraging domestic recovery. However, the reluctance of most of the Reserve banks to embrace countercyclical monetary policy reduced the impact of that pressure on policy formation, sharply limiting the expansion of open-market purchases desired by New York.

In September 1931 England went off the gold standard, inducing holders of pounds sterling to trade them for gold. The world demand for gold jumped. The English devaluation also produced widespread fear that the United States might itself go off the gold standard, and this led to a movement to trade dollars for gold. Consequently, gold began to flow out of the United States, in turn exaggerating concern that the United States might devalue the dollar or abandon gold as a monetary standard. The necessity of shoring-up the gold system led the Reserve to sharply raise the discount rate to increase the short-term interest rate and so make short-term investments in dollars more attractive than those elsewhere, in other currencies.

Raising the discount rate succeeded in stemming the external demands for gold and in temporarily restoring international confidence in the gold standard, but it had deleterious effects on domestic recovery. It is true that halting the gold flow protected the banking system, whose integrity had been threatened by the stiff pressure foreign demand for gold made on its reserves. But at the same time increasing discount rates hampered the banking system in its efforts to meet internal demands for currency. The Reserve might have been able to offset the impact of raising the discount rate through open-market purchases, which would create bank reserves, as the leadership of the New York bank suggested, but the board, having assumed greater power over open-market operations (widening the membership of the OMIC in March 1930 to include all the bank governors), was reluctant to adopt a policy of working against the business cycle.[5] Consequently, the Reserve had worsened the depression by increasing pressure on the banking system and causing money supply to contract drastically. Thus, a rigid commitment to preserve the converting of dollars into gold freely at a fixed exchange rate that was untempered by sufficient understanding of the requirements for domestic recovery led the Federal Reserve to smother the small flame of recovery. It is, of course, possible that open-market purchases could not have offset the increase in the discount rate. But the 1931 turn of policy meant that the Reserve had rejected any possibility of a compromise between domestic and international responsibilities. When the flow of gold out of the banking system resumed late in 1932 (in response to belief that President-elect Roosevelt intended to devalue), the Reserve once again was forced to restrictive-discount action. And true to the pattern of 1931, the Reserve abstained from any relief that open-market purchases might have provided to the banking system, which was moving into the crisis of 1933. As it turned out, sustained recovery began only when policy makers cut their ties to the gold standard in 1933.

RECOVERY POLICY: HERBERT HOOVER

In 1931 the deflationary policy of the Federal Reserve Board not only reduced the money supply but also fed the depression by tying the hands of the fiscal authorities, including President Hoover and Congress. Judged by the standards of the day, Hoover was an activist in the manipulation of tax rates and levels of federal spending to stimulate investment[6] and reduce unemployment; in fact, he was ready to do far more to move the economy in 1931 than the Federal Reserve Board allowed him to do. Soon after the stock-market crash, Hoover managed to cut taxes payable in 1930, called on state and local governments, and public utilities as well, to increase capital outlays, and during 1930 and the first half of 1931, pushed up the federal public works budget (undertaking projects such as the building of Hoover Dam). As a result of Hoover's policy and congressional action, federal fiscal policy had taken a distinctly expansive turn between 1929 and 1931, a turn definitely promoting recovery; between 1929 and 1931 a full-employment budgetary surplus of $1 billion had become a full-employment deficit of well over $3 billion.[7] (Not until 1936 would the full-employment deficit be as large, and not until World War II would the rate of change in the deficit be as substantial in an expansionary direction.)

After the monetary restriction of 1931, however, Hoover became concerned that federal fiscal policy would have little impact on recovery in the face of the drastic decline in the stock of money. He realized that an expanded budgetary deficit would mean greater competition between government and private borrowers for available credit, a consequent increase in the long-term interest rate, and an inhibition of private investment. Furthermore he recognized that an increase in long-term interest rates brought about by a larger deficit would mean a further depression of security prices and a reduction in the value of bank assets, thus undermining further the public's faith in the banking system. Finally, Hoover believed, probably incorrectly, that the wavering confidence within foreign quarters stemmed in part from the persistent deficits of his administration. By reducing the deficit, he felt that he would reduce the gold flow and thus relieve the pressure exerted on the Reserve Board to tighten the monetary screws.

As a direct response to the action of the Reserve Board and international conditions, Hoover, in December 1931, invoked a new phase of his fiscal policy—the phase that has tended to predominate in the public's memory. He asked Congress for tax increases that promised to raise tax revenues by one-third, and received in return the Revenue Act of 1932, enacted in June. This measure, which to date is the largest peacetime tax increase in the nation's history, raised income tax rates, lowered exemptions, increased surtaxes on the upper-income brackets, and boosted corporate rates. Subsequently, as a direct result of Hoover's effort to balance the budget, the full-employment deficit decreased for two consecutive years in 1932 and 1933. The central point is not that Hoover's fiscal policy hampered recovery after 1931, although it certainly had that effect, but that no administration could have vigorously stimulated the economy, given the preconditions set by the Federal Reserve System.[8] Indeed, Hoover strongly desired a more inflationary monetary policy in 1931 and 1932, and if he had had his way with monetary policy, he might well have promoted an expansive fiscal policy. As Hoover realized, recovery would ensue only when monetary conditions eased. But he was too conservative to take the necessary steps, fearing that abandoning monetary orthodoxy would worsen the international depression and hoping that an improvement in international conditions would promote recovery in America. Ultimately, ease in the American money supply would result not so much from a reversal of international conditions as from a restructuring of the monetary system designed to bring about both monetary expansion and a liberated fiscal policy, a restructuring that Hoover might have opposed had he still been president in 1934–1936.

Although in retrospect it is clear that Hoover failed to promote recovery effectively because he was too inclined to accept the existing institutional arrangements, he did smooth the way for future institutional reform by committing the federal government to the task of engineering a return to prosperity. Such a commitment was implicit not only in the Revenue Act of 1932 but also in a series of other recovery measures that Hoover initiated in 1931–1932. In the early summer of 1931 he declared the moratorium on the payment of international loans and reparations; his objective was to help ease the crisis of international liquidity (initiated in May by the collapse of Credit Anstalt as a result of heavy foreign liabilities) and thereby to ease the foreign pressure on the dollar, which ultimately led the Federal Reserve to take a restrictive turn of policy. (Earlier, also to relax pressure on the dollar by way of reducing American demands and payments for European goods, Hoover supported the highly protective Hawley-Smoot Tariff of 1930, the highest tariff enacted since 1828.) To the same end, and to preserve the integrity of the nation's financial system, he proposed in December 1931 the formation of the Reconstruction Finance Corporation (RFC), an instrument designed to guarantee a steady flow of credit to the nation's banks. It would, he hoped, offset the policy change of the Federal Reserve by protecting funds for private investment and shoring up the banking system. Under Charles G. Dawes (of the Dawes Plan) the RFC in 1932 engaged in bailing out banks, particularly those holding the bonds of bankrupt railroads, with tax receipts. The act proved to be an effective way to ensure soundness at the center of the nation's system of money and credit, and the New Deal quickly adopted an expanded RFC as a fundamental element of its own recovery program.

RECOVERY POLICY: FRANKLIN D. ROOSEVELT

After the economy reached its nadir in 1933, the pace of recovery was remarkable. National product grew steadily and rapidly, with the exception of a sharp downturn in late 1937 and early 1938. The rate of increase in product from 1933 to the peak of expansion in 1937 was an astounding 12 percent per year; the nation has never had another four-year period with such a rapid growth of real product and income. Moreover, the period of recovery, 1933–1937 (fifty months), was the longest period of peacetime expansion until the 1960s.[9] (The implication is that one should not have an image of the economy lying prostrate *throughout* the 1930s, with Franklin Roosevelt and the New Deal frantically but unsuccessfully trying to breathe new life into it.) But given the extent of the depths in 1933, even an extremely rapid pace of recovery did not mean an immediate return to 1929 conditions. Real income was only 3 percent higher in 1937 than it had been in 1929, and per-capita income did not reach its 1929 peak until 1939. Even at the height of the first surge of recovery, in 1937, about 14 percent of the civilian labor force— over seven million people—were still without work. Obviously recovery was incomplete even in 1937, but a decline to 14 percent unemployment constituted a massive improvement over the dismal low of 25 percent registered only four years earlier. To put the dimensions of recovery another way, almost half of the people without jobs in 1933 had found work by 1937. After the 1937–1938 recession, recovery resumed at its former pace. Without that break, full recovery might well have been reached by 1939 or 1940—before the impact of World War II mobilization.

Government-Sponsored Planning

The fundamental source of the post-1933 recovery was an improvised, often contradictory, but ultimately effective set of New Deal policies. Nonetheless, Roosevelt began his attack on the recovery problem in a discouraging fashion, the least effective of his approaches to reawakening the economy being his very first: government-sponsored planning that bordered on the use of compulsion to reopen factories, enlarge the employed labor force, expand production, increase the nation's payroll, and increase consumption. The National Industrial Recovery Act provided the organizational framework of this program by instituting over 700 industrial codes that sought to stabilize production, employment, and prices. Although the NIRA program was one of bewildering complexity, certainly one of its central objectives was to cause the price level to turn upward. If enough people were convinced that deflation had ceased, or anticipated price increases, they would decide to increase production or spend their cash holdings before prices went up even further. The result, it was hoped, would be a speedy recovery. The ambitious effort at industrial coordination appeared to work for a time; production, employment, and income grew during much of 1933. But planning as a solution to the recovery problem never got a long-run test because the political difficulties of reconciling the conflicting interests of large manufacturers, small businessmen, and labor broke the back of NIRA—long before the Supreme Court added the *coup de grâce* by declaring the act unconstitutional in 1935.

Monetary Reform and Expansion

Even in 1933 Roosevelt turned away from planning and adopted what proved to be the most successful avenue of recovery policy: monetary reform and expansion. Roosevelt was able to establish the expansive monetary policy that Hoover had desired in 1931 by, among other things, playing the gold-standard game according to his own rules and by exerting political pressure on the Federal Reserve Board (courses of action that Hoover had not even considered). At the same time this monetary reform freed his hand for implementing expansionary fiscal policies that external events and Hoover's reluctance to tinker with the monetary system had precluded in 1931.

The New Deal began to promote monetary expansion with a program of banking reform that augmented public confidence in the banking system. In March the bank holiday and the Emergency Banking Act closed all banks for at least one week to protect the system from massive deposit withdrawals, provided a plan for the orderly reopening of most banks, and asserted Roosevelt's leadership in the banking crisis. In June 1933 the Banking Act of 1933 created the Federal Deposit Insurance Corporation, which for the first time insured the nation's depositors against bank collapse, making them once more willing to put their funds in the custody of banks. With increased deposits banks were able to expand their loan activities and the process of multiple-deposit creation and monetary expansion could take its hold on the economy.

The pressure applied to the Federal Reserve System by Roosevelt and Congress was both direct and indirect. Most pointed was the Banking Act of 1935, which centralized control of the system in the hands of the board and moved the board's locus of power from New York to Washington to be more responsive to the desires of politicians. Then, too, the 1933 demonstration of decisive administrative-legislative action was somewhat chastening, and the board, wary of encouraging more-radical initiatives, including the nationalization of the banking system, avoided any action that would restrict monetary expansion. It, therefore, abstained from raising the discount rate or engaging in open-market sales.[10]

The restraint of the Federal Reserve System permitted Roosevelt to achieve his most significant successes through an improvised program of manipulation of the nation's monetary standard. Beginning in the winter of 1933, in response to the sluggish pace of recovery, Roosevelt and the Congress made a series of moves that drastically altered the nation's gold standard and produced a high degree of monetary growth. With the initial objective of promoting price increases (just as intended in the NIRA), Congress, in May 1933, authorized the president to reduce the gold content of the dollar by as much as 50 percent. From November through January 1934 Roosevelt kept the announced price of gold, in terms of dollars, greater than the price abroad. Subsequently, the Gold Reserve Act of 1934 made the devaluation official by fixing a buying and selling price for gold of $35 an ounce rather than the $21 an ounce adhered to formerly. The act first called in all domestically held gold at $21 an ounce to prevent its holders from reaping enormous windfalls; thereafter the federal government would pay $35 an ounce for all gold offered to it. Selling gold would be more limited, however, in that the federal government would sell gold only for foreign payments and would prevent the domestic circulation of gold. If a person acquired gold in some manner, by exporting goods to Europe, or by digging it up in South Africa, for example, he could take it to the Federal Reserve Bank (in New York), receive a check for it (representing Federal Reserve notes) amounting to $35 per ounce of gold, and deposit that check in his bank. (The Federal Reserve Bank, in turn, handed the gold over to the Treasury, to be placed in Fort Knox, and was paid in gold certificates.)

The new price provided a bonanza for foreigners holding gold and for world gold production because this pegged price was substantially higher than the world price. Consequently, both gold production and the importation of gold into the United States soared, the stock in Fort Knox more than tripling between early 1934 and the end of 1940. Correspondingly, deposits of Federal Reserve notes paid out for gold imports underwent a large increase, enabling banks to increase their reserve holdings and thus expand their loan activities while still maintaining reserves in excess of legal requirements (a position which banks, highly security-conscious after 1933, generally desired). In sum, the sharp devaluation of the dollar had enlarged the nation's gold stock, which in turn expanded deposits of Federal Reserve notes and thus initiated the powerful money-creating mechanism of multiple-deposit expansion.[11] If, on the other hand, the New Deal had allowed the Federal Reserve System to be an independent agent during the 1930s, and if the system had operated upon the assumptions that had governed its policy during 1929–1933, it would have taken action to offset the large influx of gold and thus forcefully inhibit the resulting expansion.

The strong inflow of gold had a decisive effect on overall monetary expansion; from April 1933 through March 1937 it forced an expansion of the stock of money at the extremely rapid rate of almost

11 percent per year. And it is this monetary expansion that seems to have been the fundamental factor in the nation's economic recovery. Movements in the stock of money roughly corresponded with and led movements in national income. People and institutions, especially banks, suddenly found that they had more money than they needed and decided that prices were going to go up. Hence they began to spend; that spending stimulated demands for goods and services; idled manufacturers resumed production and hired workers; and those workers tended to spend their new earnings. In short, as a result of the rapid growth of the money supply, the economy was on a recovery path.

Roosevelt's Fiscal Policy

With the accomplishment of monetary reform, Roosevelt won considerably more leeway in adopting an expansionary *fiscal* policy than Hoover had enjoyed, and to a limited extent Roosevelt took advantage of that latitude to reinforce monetary expansion. But only in 1937–1938 did he invoke the appropriate fiscal policy with force and purpose. His deficits, prior to 1938, were largely inadvertent, a result of a depressed tax base; he would have preferred to have avoided them had he been able.

Any stimulative effect from Roosevelt's early fiscal policy sprang from the urgency with which the New Deal advocated a series of expenditure programs. Until 1937, but especially in 1933 and 1935, Roosevelt and Congress rapidly increased the level of federal expenditures by financing a vast array of programs—in 1933, relief through the Reconstruction Finance Corporation, the NIRA and the Agricultural Adjustment Act, the Public Works Administration (supporting large-scale public construction), the Civil Works Administration (a relief-employment program providing jobs, primarily unskilled, on small-scale public projects), the Tennessee Valley Authority, and in 1935, Social Security and the Works Progress Administration (a more permanent employment program replacing the CWA). However, Roosevelt embarked on these programs, *not* as a means to spend money and thereby energize the economy, but for the substantive merit of the programs. Indeed, the objective of the most expensive New Deal activities tended to be the relief of the unemployed and the structural reform of the economy rather than recovery. Moreover, Roosevelt continually sought to cover expenditures with tax receipts by increasing taxes, largely because he never departed from a belief in the high virtue of balanced budgets and he thus muted the expansionary effect of his ambitious expenditures. The Economy Act of 1933, the provisions within NIRA and AAA for self-funding, the

Tax Revenue Act of 1934, and the taxes imposed under Social Security all reflected Roosevelt's obeisance to the traditional morality of balanced budgets. Therefore, about half of Roosevelt's budget deficits resulted, not from deliberate policy, but from the depression of the nation's tax base. Nevertheless, Roosevelt did not raise taxes as much as he might have; if the economy had been at full employment, achieving a fully expanded tax base, annual deficits still would have been on the order of $2 billion. In other words, Roosevelt did pursue a mildly expansionary fiscal policy. Even with his sizable tax effort, Roosevelt's fiscal policy encouraged rapid recovery.

Despite Roosevelt's belief in the desirability of balanced budgets, his fiscal policy was substantially more expansive than Hoover's had been in 1932 and 1933. Roosevelt was able to accept larger deficits for a variety of reasons. The demand for high levels of emergency spending was stronger than in Hoover's years and, in fact, it was given shape and form by Roosevelt the politician. But his desire for greater public services would not have expanded fiscal policy if he had not first restored a financial system that was capable of holding the public's confidence and if monetary authority, largely under Rooseveltian reform pressure, had not been extremely cooperative. In contrast with Hoover in 1931, Roosevelt did not have to fear that deficits would aggravate a financial crisis and ultimately worsen the depression.[12]

Roosevelt's reluctance to pursue as vigorous a fiscal policy as economic circumstances permitted implies that he and his administration had not chosen to seek salvation in the economics of John Maynard Keynes; countercyclical fiscal policy was not part of Roosevelt's policy repertoire, although Roosevelt's performance unintentionally earned moderately strong Keynesian applause. But Roosevelt's economic thought did advance toward an explicitly Keynesian position after the chastening experience of the recession of 1937–1938. The administration could not ignore the fact that poor policy caused the downturn. The recession had begun when both it and the Federal Reserve Board changed policies to reflect their concern that recovery was taking place too rapidly. In an extreme reaction, the Federal Reserve had sought to restrict monetary growth, and the Roosevelt administration had attempted to balance the budget.[13] After musing over the disappointing setback to recovery that resulted, Roosevelt launched, with a vengeance, an energetic new spending policy. In March 1938 he asked Congress for substantial increases in WPA, Farm Security Administration, Civilian Conservation Corps, public works, and housing expenditures, justifying them in terms of what they would add "to the purchasing power of the Nation." Consequently the full-employment deficit surged upward in both 1938 and 1939, and recovery was under way once again at its rapid 1933–1937 rate, substantially before the initiation of heavy wartime spending.

Even by 1939 the nation had not experienced a conversion to deficit spending as a tool for management of the business cycle. But never again would a national administration cut expenditures or the Federal Reserve Board take sharply restrictive action in the face of a recession. Indeed, through the medium of the New Deal the nation institutionalized the maintenance or extension of spending programs during economic reversals. There was, as yet, no explicit adherence to recovery programs with clearly specified techniques and magnitudes, but progress had been substantial. Most important, key groups, such as commercial farmers and organized labor, and certain national leaders had come to expect a positive government response in periods of economic adversity. In addition, economic experts in government service were more decisively in favor of deficits than was the case in 1933, and they had begun to discover a rationale for their political position in the work of John Maynard Keynes. The public as well grew more accustomed to, if not enthusiastically in favor of, continued deficits to manage economic recovery. It was clear to most that no disaster had befallen the nation as a result of the doubling of the federal debt between 1932 and 1937.

Thus the accomplishments of the New Deal in fiscal management lay not so much in the vigorous use of compensatory fiscal policy as in the creation of an institutional environment free of an overbearing and dominant monetary authority, one that would promote the use of more finely tuned fiscal instruments in the future. New Deal fiscal and monetary measures not only encouraged recovery in the 1930s but opened the way for the implementation, after World War II, of policies that assure a higher degree of orderly economic growth. In effect, New Deal recovery policy became a significant part of the New Deal reform program.

The International Economy

Roosevelt's efforts on behalf of recovery must be evaluated also in terms of his success in restoring international economic stability. The task that faced Roosevelt in 1933 was enormous, for by the end of that year the Great Depression had destroyed even those limited arrangements for maintaining world economic stability that the United States had fostered during the 1920s. Once American capital exports, especially to Germany, dried up, the network of reparations and debt repayment jammed; ultimately nations defaulted on their debts and, in the case of Germany, on reparations as well. In addition, the capital scarcity caused many to raise tariff barriers in the hope of decreasing purchases of imports, thereby conserving gold and international exchange. The resulting restriction of trade of course only deepened the character of the international depression. Further disorder resulted when, in response to the scarcity of exchange, all the major trading nations, beginning with Great Britain in September 1931, seriously modified or, in the case of Britain, abandoned the gold standard. By 1932 the gold standard was suspended in twenty-four countries and rendered inoperative in seventeen others. Consequently, by 1933 no orderly system existed for adjusting the values of international currencies; unstable exchange rates meant an even more acute restriction of international intercourse. Debt defaults, increased tariffs, and abandonment of gold fed international distrust which, in turn, stifled the flow of international capital, especially from the United States, and accelerated the dissolution of international order. Thus, the nations of the world wrestled with the problems of depression without any significant degree of international organization.

The Roosevelt administration, however, was not entirely responsible for the American contribution to instability. After all, the fostering of an inherently unstable postwar payments system by the Harding and Coolidge administrations was the most important element in the American contribution to the international breakdown. Nonetheless, Roosevelt must bear primary responsibility for the scuttling of the London Economic Conference in 1933, which developed new rules and procedures to revive the gold standard and international trade, and the drastic changes in the gold standard undertaken in 1933–1934. These actions encouraged domestic American recovery but at the same time they guaranteed that the world would not quickly develop international arrangements to restore and preserve economic stability. Roosevelt's signing of some twenty reciprocal trade agreements between 1934 and 1938 under the Reciprocal Trade Agreements Act of 1934 had little effect on international recovery and could not offset the impact of his earlier actions. However, even if the United States had pursued more internationalist policies along the lines suggested by Herbert Hoover, it is by no means clear that the rest of the world would have responded cooperatively. Even before the collapse, each nation had bound itself to limited concepts of national self-interest, and to that extent the international trading community shared responsibility for the collapse. Having reached extreme proportions between 1931 and 1933, the debacle was beyond the control of any single trading nation.

After 1933 a world order of even modest proportions was attainable only with the greatest difficulty. Economic cooperation did increase at the same time that recovery began or continued in many nations. But a number of economies, including that of the United States, remained depressed and turned inward in search of relief, a tendency reinforced by the fact that rates of recovery varied rather greatly from nation to nation, with each nation believing that its own particular problems and opportunities precluded international economic cooperation. The U.S.S.R. and Japan led the way to recovery. By 1932, Soviet production, dependent only to a very limited extent on dealings with the outside world in any case, had doubled its 1929 level and continued its almost uninterrupted industrial growth through the 1930s. Japan, exercising strict financial control over a very large portion of Far Eastern trade, almost equaled its 1929 production by 1932. Although recovering more slowly, even Germany and the United Kingdom had returned to predepression levels by 1936, whereas the United States, with the greatest potential economic force, had yet to do so by that date. (As a result of the depth of the Great Depression in the United States and the New Deal preoccupation with internal solutions to the recovery problem, American foreign trade shrank relative to world trade. For example, while American exports had accounted for 17 percent of all world imports during 1924–1927, they accounted for slightly more than 12 percent during 1933–1938, despite the attainment of a rapid rate of recovery during that period.)

Because of the severity of the collapse and the slowness of the international marketplace to recover, a maze of political modifications of the competitive market persisted during the 1930s. Accordingly, bilateral trade agreements, import quotas, tariffs, and restrictions on the movement of foreign exchange hampered international trade. The dilution of the rules governing international competition had political as well as economic implications. Nations that had suffered less from the depression, were more dependent on trade, and were capable of pursuing their national self-interest abroad had an opportunity to expand their ambit of influence without the check of external economic competition. Germany and Japan, in particular, took advantage of unusual opportunities for expansion. After British efforts to create a Danubian customs union had failed in 1932–1933, Germany moved into the woefully depressed and unorganized regions of central and eastern Europe, using a combination of military threats and restrictive financial devices to obtain food and raw materials at exceptionally low prices. Meanwhile, with similar tactics, Japan extended its economic power toward a weakened China. The future Allies, especially the United States and the Soviet Union, lacked an economic incentive and the will to check such expansion, given the inward focus of their own policies. In the 1920s both Japan and Germany had extended their influence under the loose control of the United States; cooperation with those nations was then part of the American approach to international order. Once American influence lifted, Germany and Japan had a freer hand not only to expand but also to exercise restrictive political control over their economic spheres of influence. As it turned out, not only was their expansion territorial (in other words, colonial in a real sense), it was also designed to promote national self-sufficiency—in defiance of the nineteenth-century tradition of fundamentally free international competition. One of the reasons that the world ultimately went to war again was the desire of the older industrial powers to restore a more dependable, orderly economic environment. In 1941, when Roosevelt met with British Prime Minister Churchill at the Atlantic Conference, they agreed that their two countries should "further the enjoyment by all states . . . on equal terms, to the trade and to the raw materials of the world which are needed for their economic prosperity"; promote "the fullest collaboration between all nations in the economic field"; and seek a peace that would "enable all men to traverse the high seas and oceans without hindrance."

The war merely prolonged the disorganized condition of world trade and investment, although it did change the international distribution of economic power, especially by enhancing the strength of the United States. As it had done twenty-five years before, America became an Allied supply base, thereby lifting itself completely out of the depression. But the financial contribution of the United States to the Allied cause was much greater than during World War I. At the outset Britain, as a result of the Johnson Act of 1934 (which forbade loans to nations that had defaulted on their World War I debts), had to pay cash for war goods and, in fact, had not been allowed to purchase arms at all until November 1939 (under the terms of the Neutrality Act of 1935). However, after the collapse of France and severe British financial problems during the winter of 1940–1941, it became clear that Britain would be drained of dollars without massive American support. The response was the lend-lease program of 1941, which deferred the question of financial settlement until after the war, when the United States, in contrast to its posture following World War I, accepted the costs of financing the Allies as the price of victory. In terms of physical and human destruction, however, the American share of wartime costs was relatively small. The United States escaped physical destruction at home and suffered relatively few casualties. (The only major belligerent with fewer losses of military personnel, even in absolute terms, was France. In contrast with the roughly 300,000 Americans killed or missing, 7.5 million Russians, 2.8 million Germans, 2.2 million Chinese, 1.5 million Japanese, 400,000 British, and 300,000 Italians were lost.) Consequently, the United States at the end of the war was in a commanding position to shape the institutions of the postwar marketplace.

THE NEW DEAL AND STRUCTURAL REFORM

Roosevelt's reform program went far beyond either institutionalizing more-effective monetary and fiscal policies or undertaking structural innovation designed to promote recovery. However, despite the ambitious contours of Roosevelt's reform efforts, his first serious attempt to reshape fundamental institutions, the National Industrial Recovery Act of June 1933, primarily embodied recovery objectives. Propelled by the conviction, rather prevalent during the early New Deal, that a restructuring of industry would be necessary before a full recovery would be possible, the NIRA provided that under a compulsory trade association and a code of fair practice, firms in a particular industry would plan the overall direction of the industry and coordinate production plans in conjunction with their collective estimates of future demand. The basic assumption behind NIRA was that a greater degree of planning and a departure from competition, sponsored and enforced by federal policy, would provide a stronger measure of economic stability. In the context of 1933 the assumption was that such coordination would bring about an increase in the price level and stimulate recovery. The consequent loss of economic freedom would be acceptable if the economy moved upward and, ultimately, matched the successes of the 1920s.

NIRA found support among a wide range of economic groups; even small businessmen of the United States Chamber of Commerce and the National Association of Manufacturers and labor leaders, particularly men like John L. Lewis and Sidney Hillman, who were promoting industrial unionism, welcomed the NIRA. (Section 7a of the NIRA had offered a guarantee of collective bargaining, which many large employers were willing to accept in return for greater control over pricing and output.) Despite the breadth of initial support, reform of industrial structure, in contrast with reform of financial institutions, failed. Small business, labor, and eventually the consuming public became disenchanted with NIRA; the declaration of NIRA's unconstitutionality merely officially sealed the administration's prior steps to abandon this approach. After the termination of NIRA, federal efforts to reform the conditions of competition fell into disarray. There was some effort to impose planning on the failing industries of the 1920s and 1930s, especially coal mining. A wave of fairly vigorous antitrust prosecutions emerged from the Justice Department under Thurman Arnold. But Roosevelt made no effort to reconcile the divergent approaches toward business concentration represented by centralized planning and the restoration of competition. The investigations launched by the Temporary National Economic Committee in 1938 truly revealed the character of New Deal business policy: indecision resulting from a political deadlock. After a long period of experiments, the nation had an antitrust policy that differed little from that at the end of the nineteenth century. At the conclusion of the New Deal in 1939 the degree of concentration within industry was substantially greater than it had been ten years earlier.[14]

The New Deal reform impulse won its greatest victories in two other areas, the restructuring of agriculture and the reordering of labor relations, with commercial farmers and industrial, organized labor gaining greater bargaining power. The AAA, like the NIRA, developed initially as a recovery measure, but it involved significant reform in that it gave commercial farmers, for the first time, a significant degree of control over the marketing of their crops. In essense AAA programs lent a compulsory aspect to Hoover's limitation of production which he proposed in response to McNary-Haugenism and implemented in the voluntary Farm Board. However, only World War II restored parity (that is, returned the purchasing power of the farmer to the relative position during the golden age of agriculture).

The AAA did indeed raise incomes of those farmers for whom its programs were designed, but in general the New Deal farm policy involved little attempt to confront the most serious structural difficulties facing the American farmer. Although allotment payments to farmers for reduction in acres in cultivation provided for by the first AAA and price-support payments legislated by the second AAA (1938) relieved, to a significant degree, the income problems inherent in the extremely depressed Great Plains region, the farm programs were much less successful in easing the burdens that the depression had placed on the already troubled southern economy. Under the first AAA, allotment payments for acreage reduction in the South went, not to the tenant farmers and sharecroppers who worked the land, but to the landowners. Thus, instead of challenging the existing distribution of economic and political power in the South by redistributing income in the direction of those at the very bottom of the economic ladder, the New Deal subsidies in many instances enabled southern planters to finance mechanization of their operations and force their tenants off the land. By accelerating the outward movement of population from the overpopulated portions of the cotton South the AAA may have benefited long-run income growth in the South and, also in the long run, coerced migrants into taking advantage of economic opportunities of which they might otherwise have been ignorant. But in the 1930s the cities were even less prepared to deal with the social problems posed by large inflows of migrants than they have been subsequently. Reflecting this is the fact that substantial numbers of people in the 1930s fled the cities to take temporary refuge in the countryside. Many of these migrants were simply young people who had left farms during the 1920s and, having lost their jobs, were returning home. Others were looking for an opportunity to take up subsistence agriculture and tended to move to the most depressed agricultural counties where they had a better chance to find free land and abandoned shacks. While many undoubtedly established a greater degree of independence, others— probably most, as the Michigan Relief Association concluded—soon found themselves on the public assistance rolls. Nonetheless, they formed a large proportion of the depression migrants and their numbers in the early 1930s were sufficient to cause rural areas in almost all states to grow markedly while urban areas made little or no population gains.

The New Deal also promoted population migration out of the overpopulated cutover region of the northern Great Lakes states and Great Plains, but without the kind of short-run costs to the migrants inherent in the AAA approach. The Resettlement Administration (RA), in effect, subsidized out-migration and, where it had funds and state and local cooperation, such as in Wisconsin, which had adopted rural zoning (restricting agricultural use of poor land), accomplished a great deal by moving impoverished farmers onto good soil that provided a future. The lack of support for resettlement in Appalachia, however, vitiated any New Deal efforts in that region. In general, the RA accomplished little as a result of sustained opposition of southern leaders. Such opposition in Congress to subsidies for tenant farmers and sharecroppers forced the RA to scale down its relocation aspirations from 500,000 families to a mere 4,441.

In 1937, the RA was replaced by the Farm Security Administration (FSA), which extended rehabilitation loans to farm owners, made low-interest loans to tenant farmers to enable them to purchase their own land, and established clean, well-run migratory labor camps. Although the FSA had spent more than a billion dollars by the end of 1941, most of that expenditure was in the form of loans, the loans tended to be to low-risk farmers who were in only mild distress, and, as it turned out, the rate of repayment was extremely high. In the long run, large-scale farmers looking for a cheap labor force and the taxpayer proved effective opponents of the FSA and other measures designed to redistribute income to marginal farmers.

THE HUMAN DIMENSION OF MIGRATION. A migrant family from the Rio Grande Valley, Texas, camping near Haltville, California, 1937.

While the RA and FSA amounted to significant, if only experimental, departures in using planning to solve the structural problems of the economy, the New Deal made its most striking assault on those problems by establishing the Tennessee Valley Authority. The enactment of TVA was at once a solution to an extended controversy over the disposition of a power dam and two nitrate plants built by the federal government at Muscle Shoals, Alabama, and the initiation of a massive effort to plan for the resolution of the impacted problems of the 40,000-square-mile area of the valley of the 650-mile-long Tennessee River. While the former purpose accounted for the early adoption of the reform measure (May 1933), the latter lent TVA its long-run significance. Over the 1930s the agency built (or bought) and managed a score of dams by which it provided flood control, navigation, and power production serving almost all of Tennessee and large areas of Mississippi, Alabama, Georgia, and Kentucky (see Figure 18), engaged in the production and sale of fertilizer, reorganized the use of land by reforestation and promotion of soil conservation, improved the health and educational services available to residents of the valley, encouraged industrialization, and, more generally, according to its congressional mandate, worked to foster "orderly development" of the region. While a more economical program probably would have been one that concentrated on moving people to the foci of economic opportunity, TVA undoubtedly brought a substantially higher standard of living to the valley, and a resettlement effort would have had to face the ingrained hostility within Appalachia to significant changes in residential patterns. But TVA, like AAA, had its shortcomings. Most significantly, there was wholesale racial discrimination in the hiring practices of TVA (involving 14,000 jobs by 1940), and its failure to use its economic power to alter the pattern of race relations was costly in economic as well as in human terms. In net, however, TVA was an inspiring experiment in mobilizing the power of government to correct the failures of the competitive marketplace to conform with its theoretical promise. Yet its example has since been ignored more than followed, and it seems clear that the failure to adopt creative, economically effective regional planning in the United States has been a result, not of

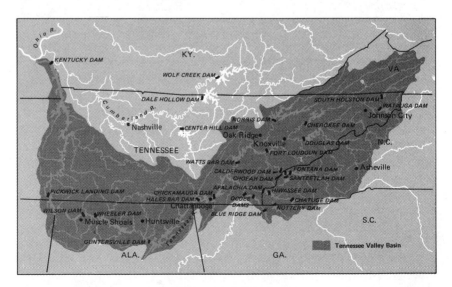

FIGURE 18: *The Tennessee Valley Authority, 1933*

flaws in TVA or the New Deal, but of the political limitations imposed on such experimentation so that subsequent administrations have been less adventuresome than Roosevelt's.

Paralleling the New Deal's efforts on behalf of farmers, particularly those with a strong commercial interest, were programs to extend greater economic leverage to organized labor. The labor movement had declined in intensity and success after World War I and the participation of organized labor in the mobilization effort. In the 1920s unions were no longer needed by the government to fulfill a public objective, the public was more sympathetic to employers than to unions (just as had been the case during earlier periods of prosperity), the A.F.L. was unwilling to organize low-skilled workers, and, given the buoyancy of labor earnings, unions lacked issues to form the basis for organizing drives. As a result trade-union membership fell off precipitously during the 1920s. (See Table 28.) But the Great Depression created the political support necessary to institutionalize, in a fairly permanent fashion, a strong union movement. For one thing, many middle-class people, formerly with white-collar occupations, found themselves unemployed or having to accept work of a lower status. This phenomenon of downward mobility undoubtedly bred greater sympathy for the union movement. With falling wage levels, unions also were able to make a more powerful appeal to those who were still employed, although that organizing drive might not have accomplished any more than earlier ones that took place in depressions if the federal government had not lent its support to union leaders interested in organizing low-skilled workers.

In keeping with its sympathy to the cause of labor, its belief that the cooperation of labor was necessary to promote effective economic recovery, and its recognition of growing public support for unions, the Roosevelt administration came to the aid of organized labor at several critical junctures. Section 7a of the NIRA first encour-

TABLE 28   LABOR UNION MEMBERSHIP BY AFFILIATION*

	All Unions	A. F. L.	C. I. O.	All Other
1920	5.0	4.1	—	0.9
1925	3.6	2.9	—	0.7
1930	3.6	3.0	—	0.6
1935	3.8	3.2	—	0.6
1940	7.3	4.3	2.2	0.8
1945	12.6	6.9	3.9	1.8

Source: Bureau of the Census, *Historical Statistics of the United States, Colonial Times to 1970*, Part 1 (Washington, D.C.: U.S. Government Printing Office, 1975), p. 177.

* Expressed in millions of members.

aged the reawakening of labor between 1933 and 1935, particularly the efforts of new leaders like John L. Lewis, Sidney Hillman, and David Dubinsky, who were seeking to organize whole industries rather than specific crafts or trades within a variety of industries. That industry-wide group formed the Committee for Industrial Organization within the old American Federation of Labor in 1935, but in 1937 when the A.F.L. expelled eight industrial unions, those unions, in turn, became the Congress of Industrial Organizations. The most significant breakthrough came in March 1937, when, with the essential aid of the National Labor Relations Board, created by the Wagner Act of 1935, the C.I.O. succeeded in extracting a contract from United States Steel. Shortly thereafter General Motors capitulated as well.

The ease with which the industrial giants yielded suggests another element that worked in the favor of labor. Large firms, though by no means enthusiastic about unionization, could see, from the standpoint of labor management, certain advantages in dealing with one large union rather than a myriad of small craft unions. Industrial unionism was more efficient and proved to be an effective tool in providing industrial discipline, in that corporations were able to delegate much labor-management responsibility to these unions. Large firms had a sense of this, and although they would have clearly preferred their own company unions, most were willing to accept the C.I.O. without strenuous opposition. With a few exceptions, such as the war between the United Auto Workers and the private army of the Ford Motor Company, the real violence of the labor movement of the 1930s occurred in the organizing effort directed at smaller firms, climaxed by the shooting of ten Republic Steel Company strikers in Chicago in 1939. By that time, however, the major battles, such as with United States Steel and General Motors, were over and had been resolved for the most part without violence or even the threat of violence, given the provision of a legal framework by the Roosevelt administration.

Supported by the favorable set of political circumstances, and paced by union giants such as the United Steel Workers of America, the United Mine Workers, the United Auto Workers, the United Electrical, Radio, and Machine Workers, and the Amalgamated Clothing Workers, union membership soared during the 1930s, with that of the C.I.O. reaching about half of that of the A.F.L. by World War II. In the longer run the accelerated union drive of the 1930s has meant more-efficient labor relations and a significant enhancement of the power of organized labor in corporate decision making. At the same time, however, despite organization around industries, the skilled and already prosperous workers have reaped the lion's share of the benefits gained by augmented bargaining power in labor markets. In fact, by effectively raising the cost of labor, unions have contributed to increased unemployment of the unskilled, and this effect has reinforced the impact of the minimum-wage legislation of the 1930s to price much unskilled labor out of the market. In coal mining, for example, John L. Lewis, to obtain significantly higher wages for the skilled miners, agreed to cooperate with the operators in their promotion of technological progress—but at the cost of unemployment for a very large segment of the coal-mining labor force. Nonetheless, to the extent that raising labor productivity has augmented output and incomes, in turn creating new labor demands (especially in the service sector), the unfavorable impact of unionization and minimum-wage legislation on the employment of unskilled workers has been mitigated.

New Deal labor policies focused on those workers whose services would have been strongly in demand in normal times and on those who usually were able to find employment even during the 1930s. But the Roosevelt administration made an effort to solve the problems of those whose participation in the labor force was only marginal. In particular, a system of national social insurance emerged via the Social Security Act of 1935, which included three broad programs: (1) a system of social insurance for old age, administered entirely by the federal government; (2) a set of joint federal-state assistance programs for the blind, deaf, and the dependent children of the unemployed; and (3) a program of unemployment relief financed by the federal government but designed by the individual states.

Because the act decisively redistributed income toward at least some of those people on the fringe of the economy, it clearly constituted an important advance over the system of more limited, scattered, state, local, and voluntary efforts. Nonetheless, the coverage of the Social Security programs was so limited that the New Deal eased neither the short-run problem of relief nor the long-run problems resulting from structural flaws in the labor market. For one thing, the act left large numbers of laborers uncovered, the most severe omission being those who were permanently unemployed, and it excluded from coverage certain others, such as farm laborers. Another deficiency was that the act permitted the states to determine the character and extent of unemployment benefits without federal standards. Some of the variations that resulted reflected interregional differences in industrial structure and consequent differences in the nature of unemployment, especially that of a seasonal character. But much of the variation resulted from large differences in the degree of effort states were willing to make, in conjunction with industry, to protect the unemployed and significant differences in the ability of states in low-income regions to provide benefits comparable in real terms to those offered by states in more prosperous regions.

Still another limitation of the program was its reliance on the insurance formula implemented by payroll taxes. The framers assumed that unemployment would only be temporary in character and that, therefore, there would be no class of people frozen almost permanently into unemployment. Rejecting the alternative of funding current unemployment benefits out of current income-tax revenues, the New Dealers passed up an opportunity to redistribute income and restricted the ability of the Social Security system to treat the postwar problems of the hard-core unemployed.[15] Still, all of these limitations resulted partly from political calculations, which must be weighed in the balance when evaluating the New Deal's welfare record. The framers of Social Security introduced conservative features partly to protect the system from later conservative efforts to dismantle it. Insurance funding, for example, was designed to give the public a sense of proprietorship in the system. The longevity of Social Security perhaps testifies to the correctness of the New Deal's political judgment.

National social insurance came late to the United States, having been undertaken by Germany in 1888, by France in 1905, and by Great Britain in 1908. Moreover, it was born somewhat grudgingly. Its programs were handicapped by the political limitations of federalism, its supporters had little interest in reaching the lowest-income workers or the chronically unemployed, and its traditional welfare approach was insufficient to eradicate structural poverty. Even so, the New Deal provided the most marked advances, before or since, in protecting the worker from the vagaries of the business cycle.

A final approach to structural reform of the economy that ran throughout the 1930s was the effort, obscured at times by other New Deal policy objectives, to redistribute income through the instruments of taxation. In particular, the Roosevelt administration sought to raise a greater share of revenues from the use of progressive income taxation. Because of the relatively depressed, albeit rapidly increasing, levels of income during the 1930s, the resort to income taxation did not immediately have a dramatic impact on the federal revenue structure. (It was not until World War II that revenues generated by income taxes came to dominate federal revenues.) But if the reform of federal taxation had an impact on the distribution of income, that impact was realized by the 1930s. However, since reliable measures of income distribution exist only for the period since 1929 and the links between the complex policies of the New Deal and the distribution of income are inherently obscure, no definitive judgment on such an impact is possible. Yet given the importance of the question, exploration of possibilities is important.

From the onset of the Great Depression in 1929, the trend of income distribution is clear: a movement toward a wider distribution of income, at least until the 1950s. The magnitude of change, however, is not revolutionary in scale. The only dramatic change was in the share of family personal income received by the 5 percent of the families with the highest incomes; it declined from 30 percent of such income in 1929 to 24 percent in 1941 and continued to fall to a relatively stable share of about 21 percent in 1946. (See Table 29.) Similarly, the share of income earned by the 20 percent of families with the largest incomes declined from about 54 percent in 1939 to about 46 percent in 1946. Gaining at the expense of the top 20 percent throughout the period was the middle 60 percent of families. The share of the bottom 20 percent appears nearly constant until World War II. Although there was no relative progress of the bottom decile, the share of the middle three deciles grew from 41.5 percent in 1929 to 44.2 percent in 1935–1936, 47.1 percent in 1941, and 49.1 percent in 1946. Quite striking is the consistency of this pattern with the general political thrust of New Deal legislation: the orientation of policy toward the interests of middle-class labor and agriculture, coupled with neglect of those who found themselves excluded from effective participation in the economy.

In short, measures of income distribution since 1929 are compatible with the interpretation that the New Deal promoted a more equitable but not revolutionary redistribution of income. Yet we cannot make out a clear-cut case for the impact of the New Deal,

TABLE 29 DISTRIBUTION OF FAMILY PERSONAL INCOME BY EACH FIFTH AND TOP 5 PERCENT OF FAMILIES FOR SELECTED YEARS

	Lowest Fifth	Second Fifth	Middle Fifth	Fourth Fifth	Highest Fifth	Total	Top 5 Percent
1929	—12.5%*—		13.8%	19.3%	54.4%	100.0%	30.0%
1935–1936	4.1	9.2	14.1	20.9	51.7	100.0	26.5
1941	4.1	9.5	15.3	22.3	48.8	100.0	24.0
1946	5.0	11.1	16.0	22.0	46.0	100.0	20.9
1950	4.8	10.9	16.1	22.1	46.1	100.0	21.4
1955	4.8	11.3	16.4	22.3	45.2	100.0	20.3
1960	4.6	10.9	16.4	22.7	45.4	100.0	19.6
1962	4.6	10.9	16.3	22.7	45.5	100.0	19.6

Source: Herman P. Miller, *Income Distribution in the United States* (Washington, D.C.: U.S. Government Printing Office, 1966), p. 21.

* Figure represents percentage for sum of lowest two-fifths; finer distribution is unavailable.

since there are other factors that might satisfactorily explain the trend of improvement since 1929. In the first place, one can by no means be certain that the trend toward greater equity began as late as 1929; it may have started with the 1880s or the decade 1900–1910 or the prosperous 1920s. Explanations that emphasize the end of immigration, increasing per-capita levels of social investment in human capital, and an expanding redistributional role of government (beginning in the late nineteenth century) would place the reversal earlier than the 1930s. A tentative conclusion should be that the New Deal reinforced trends already in existence to even out the distribution of income, thereby accelerating a movement already under way.

The set of institutional changes wrought by the New Deal very probably worked to grant greater economic leverage to large groups than that which the marketplace had accorded them. Commercial farmers and organized labor in particular attained significantly enhanced economic power, while those who were excluded found, at best, little improvement in their economic situation as a consequence of New Deal policy. Although the search for economic justice was a central element in the New Deal, more important than reform of basic economic institutions was the search for an economy that would operate in a more rational, dependable manner, one in which conflicts between contending groups could be controlled with greater ease and in which successful long-term planning for orderly growth could be implemented.

NOTES

1. Expansion of the demand for automobiles during the last half of the 1930s yielded a per-capita ownership of automobiles in 1940 greater than that in 1950—even after the five-year period of expansion 1945–1950, in which the rate of ownership had almost tripled. G. C. Chow, "Statistical Demand Functions for Automobiles and Their Use for Forecasting," in A. C. Harberger (ed.), *Demand for Durable Goods* (Chicago: University of Chicago Press, 1960), pp. 157, 164.

2. For the automobile industry see Lloyd J. Mercer and W. Douglas Morgan, "Alternative Definitions of Market Saturation: Evaluation for the Automobile Industry in the Late Twenties," *Explorations in Economic History*, 9 (Spring 1972), 269–290.

3. The discussion of the role of the money supply that runs throughout this chapter relies heavily on the data available in Milton Friedman and Anna J. Schwartz, *A Monetary History of the United States, 1867–1960* (Princeton, N.J.: Princeton University Press, 1963).

4. The process of multiple-deposit creation refers to the way in which the banking system creates money (in the form of demand deposits) after its receipt of new deposits. Money creation by banks is possible because,

under conditions of public confidence in commercial banking, bankers need keep only a small fraction of the value of demand deposits as reserves to protect against withdrawals. Upon receipt of new deposits, they will loan out a large fraction of those deposits. The loans, in turn, will appear in the money supply as demand deposits and these deposits will themselves engender further loan activity. The ultimate result will be an increase in the money supply determined by the product of the initial deposit and a factor set by the prevailing reserve ratio. However, the process can operate in reverse: if deposits are withdrawn from the banking system, the result will be a reduction of the money supply determined by the product of the value of the withdrawal and a reserve-ratio factor.

5. It has often been suggested that the Reserve was unable to increase open-market purchases because of the probability that those purchases would cause the system to violate the requirement that it cover Federal Reserve notes with a reserve of 40 percent gold and 60 percent gold or eligible paper. The eligible paper did not include government bonds, and, consequently, the Reserve's holdings of eligible paper were usually too small to allow the Reserve to let its gold reserves fall to 40 percent. Hence, in conjunction with the gold drain, open-market purchases might have expanded the volume of Federal Reserve notes to a point threatening required reserves. Indeed, congressional desire to promote a more expansive monetary policy led to the adoption of the Glass-Steagall Act in February 1932 that allowed government bonds to be substituted for gold as reserves against Reserve notes. (That congressional interest also pressured the Reserve into its brief period of monetary ease in 1932.) However, Milton Friedman has argued convincingly that the threat to reserves was not a leading element in the Reserve's 1931 calculations and that if it had been it would have been an irrational concern. Friedman and Schwartz, *op. cit.*, 399–406.

6. Hoover was well aware of the success of the large tax cuts of 1924, 1926, and 1928 in both augmenting investment in domestic enterprise and, as a result, enlarging government revenues. For a recent, partial restatement of the neo-Keynesian view, which minimizes the role of money, see Peter Temin, *Did Monetary Forces Cause the Great Depression?* (New York: Norton, 1976).

7. To measure federal fiscal policy one could look merely at the actual budgetary surplus or deficit of the federal government. However, that measure reflects not only change in policy but change in the *level of national income as well.* For example, revenues and taxes will fall as national income falls, given the importance of income taxes to the federal tax system, *even though there has been no tax cut or expenditure increase.* In short, looking only at the real budget makes fiscal policy self-justifying. But we can exclude the influence of income changes by using the full-employment surplus (or deficit) as our measure of fiscal policy. This is the surplus (or deficit) that would be attained *if the econ-*

omy were operating at full employment. (If this surplus changes, it has to be because of changes in policy rather than changes in economic conditions.)

8. Another constraint on federal fiscal action was the accumulation of policy judgments by state and local governments. Not being able to print money, they had to seek to preserve their solvency in the Great Depression crisis and, consequently, took even more restrictive action than did the federal government. The weight of such decisions was great; state and local budgets were more massive than that of the federal government.

9. G. H. Moore and J. Shiskin, "Indicators of Business Expansion and Contraction," *N.B.E.R. Occasional Paper No. 103* (New York: National Bureau of Economic Research, 1967), p. 113.

10. The rediscount rate at New York, after a series of declines in 1933 and early 1934, remained at 1.5 percent for more than three years. During the same period the system's portfolio of assets remained essentially unchanged as it conducted virtually no open-market operations.

11. The fact that the massive flow of gold into the United States continued for such an extended period of time resulted from an unusual set of circumstances. Indeed, Roosevelt's gold policy would not have succeeded without a very fortunate coincidence of international events. Ordinarily one would expect devaluation to have been followed by a rapid depreciation of the dollar, or a marked increase in American prices as the expanded supply of dollars provided by the government bid up prices. But instead, at the same time that the United States was offering more dollars for gold, large, wealthy groups of Europeans demanded to exchange their assets for dollars. Those in Germany, especially Jews, who feared Hitler's rise to power and people in the rest of Europe who believed their assets threatened by the outbreak of war sought to convert their European assets to dollars held in a secure haven. They traded their capital for gold and then transformed the gold into dollars in the United States.

12. By this same argument, of course, one can suggest that Roosevelt could easily have moved fiscal policy in a more expansive direction (by financing an expanded WPA program through deficits, for example) and thus have achieved an earlier recovery, if his ideological opposition to deficits had not been so powerful.

13. Roosevelt sought to balance the budget not only to cool the economy but to avoid high costs of financing deficits unavoidable with the Federal Reserve tightening the supply of money and exerting an upward pressure on interest rates. Even the administration's staunchest defender of deficit spending, Marriner Eccles, advocated balancing the budget for these reasons.

14. Alfred D. Chandler, Jr., "The Structure of American Industry in the Twentieth Century: A Historical Overview," *Business History Review*, 43 (Autumn 1969), especially p. 259.

15. The reluctance to impose federal standards for unemployment benefits or to use the unemployment program as an opportunity to redistribute income by no means indicates that the framers of Social Security were insensitive to the economic limitations of their social justice program. On the contrary, by recognizing the power of conservative state governments and by tying unemployment benefits to insurance contributions, they believed that they were protecting the political future of the program, including the level of benefits. Interestingly, both opponents of Social Security and those to the political left of the framers of the program favored financing benefits out of income-tax revenues: conservatives hoped to be able to slash benefits in the future by cutting taxes; the framers of Social Security sought to preclude that possibility. For a discussion of the political and intellectual environment of the engineers of Social Security see Theron F. Schlabach, *Edwin E. Witte: Cautious Reformer* (Madison, Wis.: State Historical Society of Wisconsin, 1969).

SUGGESTED READINGS

Books

Chandler, Lester V. *American Monetary Policy, 1928–1941.* New York: Harper & Row, 1971.

Cochran, Thomas C. *The American Business System: A Historical Perspective, 1900–1955.* Cambridge, Mass.: Harvard University Press, 1965.

Friedman, Milton, and Anna J. Schwartz. *A Monetary History of the United States, 1867–1960.* Princeton, N.J.: Princeton University Press. 1963.

Galbraith, John K. *The Great Crash, 1929.* Boston: Houghton Mifflin, 1954.

Hawley, Ellis W. *The New Deal and the Problem of Monopoly: A Study in Economic Ambivalence.* Princeton, N.J.: Princeton University Press, 1966.

Kindleberger, Charles P. *The World in Depression, 1929–1939.* Berkeley and Los Angeles: University of California Press, 1973.

Lekachman, Robert. *The Age of Keynes.* New York: Random House, 1966.

Leuchtenburg, William E. *Franklin D. Roosevelt and the New Deal, 1932–1940.* New York: Harper & Row, 1963.

Lilienthal, David E. *TVA: Democracy on the March.* Chicago: Quadrangle, 1966.

Mintz, Ilse. *Cyclical Fluctuations in the Exports of the United States Since 1879.* New York: Columbia University Press, 1967.

Mitchell, Broadus. *Depression Decade: From New Era Through New Deal, 1932–1940.* New York: Harper & Row, 1969.

Stein, Herbert. *The Fiscal Revolution in America.* Chicago and London: University of Chicago Press, 1969.

Temin, Peter. *Did Monetary Forces Cause the Great Depression?* New York: Norton, 1976.

Articles

Brown, E. Cary. "Fiscal Policies in the 'Thirties: A Reappraisal," *American Economic Review,* 46 (December 1956), 857–879.

Chandler, Alfred D., Jr. "The Structure of American Industry in the Twentieth Century: A Historical Overview," *Business History Review,* 43 (Autumn 1969), 255–298.

✵ 16
Managing the Business Cycle, 1939-1977

Since the depression, economic stability has been the preeminent economic issue. While the nation has avoided any major economic reversals, it has experienced recurring recessions, particularly during the 1950s, and bouts of inflation, which were especially severe during World War II reconversion and mobilization for the Indochina involvements. In fact, only for a brief, heady period in the mid-1960s did the economy appear to be operating at a high level of employment without significant price inflation. Consequently, even during the 1960s and 1970s, when the issue of the quality of economic growth pressed forward, the problems of economic instability remained paramount. Indeed, it is arguable that American society can deal effectively with the problems of economic justice, the environment, and the distribution of economic power only when it learns how to provide a framework of continued productivity growth and sustained economic stability.

PRIVATE PLANNING AND STABILITY

Any postdepression achievements in taming the business cycle came from an ongoing refinement in the private management of market conditions as well as from growing expertise in countercyclical public policy. The private sector has refined its fundamental institutional structure, placing a contemporary emphasis on diversifying products and markets, especially among industries, such as electronics and chemicals, that draw heavily on scientific knowledge and can easily adapt and exploit their knowledge for the manufacture of new products.[1] And within those industries diversification has been most sustained among the largest firms whose profits provided capital for research and development. In addition, corporations have further systematized strategic decisions and regularized product development, an institutionalization of diversification that has included the concentration of general office managements on only the most essential planning decisions and the formulation of research divisions to develop a steady flow of new products.

The roots of the diversification movement go back to the 1920s and the Great Depression, when firms that had assembled massive stocks of skills and equipment found their markets weak and, eventually, evaporating. As pressure to develop new products with growth markets intensified, only the largest, most technologically advanced corporations could respond. In the 1920s electrical-equipment manufacturers diversified into household appliances, automobile companies began to turn to the production of diesels, appliances, and tractors, and rubber companies developed new products through chemistry. World War II stimulated this trend by creating needs for synthetic rubber, radio and other new electronic equipment, high-speed aircraft, and new drugs, such as antibiotics. After the war the patterns of demand, both private and public, favored the continuation of the strategy, particularly as practiced by producers of chemicals and electrical, electronic, and transportation equipment, but also with regard to manufacturers of foods, metals, and petroleum. By 1960 the vast majority of large manufacturers operated in more than five industries, and over thirty giant firms produced in more than ten distinct industries. To take only one example, until the 1920s General Electric was basically a manufacturer of power- and light-generating machinery. During the 1920s it expanded its activities to enter the consumer market, not only to answer high demand for electrical appliances but also to utilize the products of research, including refined tubes, wires, and insulation, initially designed to improve power and light equipment. By the 1930s, responding to weak markets, General Electric was producing full lines of appliances, lamps, X-ray machines, elevators, and generating machinery. World War II reinforced that diversification by creating stronger demands for electrical products of all types, and thereafter General Electric continued to expand its activities, moving into nuclear power, jets, computers, and industrial automation systems, among other product lines.

Reinforcing product diversification has been the third great merger wave, which began in the early 1950s and became particularly intense in the late 1960s. Differing in character from those of the 1890s and 1920s, it emphasizes conglomerate mergers, or the merging of firms with distinct and often seemingly unrelated product lines, rather than the accomplishment of horizontal or vertical integration. To take one example of a conglomerate, International Telephone and Telegraph at one point had acquired firms engaged in baking (Continental Baking), hotel keeping (the Sheraton Corp.), car renting (Avis), home building (Levitt and Sons), food sales (Canteen Corp.), and insurance (Hartford Fire Insurance); and, to mention other examples, W. R. Grace and Co., a steamship company, diversified into food and chemicals; R.C.A. bought Random House and tried to purchase Hertz; the Singer Co. moved from sewing machines into air conditioning, office equipment, and textile machinery.

It is too soon to render a definitive judgment on the significance of this movement, but its intensity and uniquely long duration suggest that its impact on the organization of American business has been considerable. The recessions of 1969–1970 and 1974–1975 exposed the financial weakness of many of the conglomerate mergers, but a tentative overall judgment would be that such mergers generally enhanced the maximization of the net worth of capital, facilitated the search for productivity gains, and rescued many failing corporations with doses of capital and profit-maximizing management.[2] More generally, despite the obvious differences between the earlier merger waves, the latest has been propelled by a similar, traditional desire on the part of merging firms to put resources to more efficient use or to protect resources threatened by uncertain markets.

Just as in the first great merger wave, federal antitrust policy reinforced the thrust of the marketplace. During the Johnson administration there was but one notable antitrust prosecution, and even that resulted in only the modest prohibition of mergers of companies in *related* product lines.[3] By the early 1970s it became clear that the Nixon administration, despite lingering Justice Department activism and concern among many large corporations about certain conglomerate abuses, had failed to assume a more aggressive posture. If the pattern of the past held throughout the 1970s, any anticonglomerate offensive that developed would restrain only the most obvious departures from free competition and leave the vast bulk of new mergers unchallenged.[4]

This merger wave and, more generally, the success of giant, diversified corporations have boosted overall concentration in American industry since World War II. By 1963 the nation's 200 largest corporations accounted for 41 percent of value added by manufacturing, whereas their share had been only 30 percent in 1947. But

heightened overall concentration by no means implies a diminution
of concentration and competition in any particular industry. In fact
in the central, science-based industries, containing the nation's largest corporations, concentration has actually declined. Thus in each of
the chemical, electrical, machinery, instrument, and rubber industries, for example, the largest firms accounted for *less* of total production in 1963 than they had in 1947. And in each of those industries
in 1963, the giant firms (no fewer than six in each industry) accounted
for no more than 45 percent of product value.[5] Diversification has
meant that large firms moved into new industries and offered new
competition, based on their research-and-development capacities, to
older firms in those industries. (One important example has been the
movement of oil companies into the production of chemicals and
synthetic rubber. In the future, one might find the example of firms
like General Electric or Westinghouse producing electrical automobiles.) And the conglomerate movement may well have enabled certain weaker firms to compete more effectively in their industries by
providing them with the resources, both human and material, of the
acquiring companies.

A useful element in implementing the strategy of diversification
has been the development of apparatus and expertise for estimating
future demand. Within the consumer-goods industry corporations
have not only more effectively anticipated changes in demand but
have also become more vigorous in shaping its character, expending
an increasing share of national product to create distinctions between their own products and those of their competitors and to
stimulate markets for them.[6] Those firms engaged in the manufacture of producer goods, including a major portion of the electronics
industry, although relying much less on the power of advertising,
have been equally expert in gauging demand and creating an environment of increasing stability. Further, these companies have made
the most significant private contributions to increasing efficiency and
to stimualting long-term economic growth. Other groups within the
private sector—certain large banks, for example, and research foundations such as the Brookings Institution—have developed and applied models of the economy that have made the management of the
inventory and investment cycles far more effective. Large corporations, in a sustained effort to determine a consensus about future
economic conditions, have widely supported these private research
foundations and sponsored a considerable volume of communication
among business economists. The federal government, for its part, has
sanctioned and indirectly encouraged such activity through the extension of tax-exempt status to foundations and by the judgment of
the Department of Justice that discussions of corporate economists

concerning market forecasts do not constitute collusion in violation of the antitrust laws.

Not only has the corporate central management acquired more clearly delegated responsibility for essential policy decisions and strengthened its ability to estimate future demand for new and old products; it has also made routine the basic production decisions, given estimates of future prices. With the comprehensive input-output analysis made possible by electronic data processing, the modern corporation is able to allocate human and material resources among different production processes (usually with various geographic locations) and different, highly diversified combinations of output to effectively maximize profits, thus contributing to economic growth and supporting a stable economic order.

PUBLIC PLANNING AND STABILITY: THE ROLE OF MILITARY SPENDING

Private initiatives in planning for stability have received slight reinforcement from the public sector, apart from its fitful effort to provide a predictable fiscal and monetary environment. Indeed, the conduct of public activities in general has been disorderly and, if anything, has aggravated problems of economic instability.

The most profoundly destabilizing influence of the federal government has been through its management of spending for war and defense. The impact of military expenditures on the economy has clearly been substantial. Since World War II defense spending has dominated the spending of the federal government and has often amounted to close to 10 percent of national product. The relative level of spending has been even higher in certain regions. The South and West have been the heaviest recipients of defense spending, California heading the list of contract recipients by value, followed by Texas, which moved up from seventh place during the Kennedy and Johnson administrations. Defense spending has influenced the behavior of a vast number of economic units. In 1968, for example, Pentagon contracts yielded about 22,000 prime contractors and 100,-000 subcontractors and qualified some seventy-six industries as "defense-oriented" or having at least one-third of their sales accounted for by defense contractors. In general, airplane manufacturers and shipbuilders have derived more than half of their sales from defense work. Also in 1968 about 5,300 cities and towns boasted at least one defense plant or company doing business with the armed forces; and about 10 percent of the labor force found employment in the armed services or with defense-oriented industries. Further, defense spending has had a multiplier effect, generating income for those who provide services for the military and military contractors. Finally, military needs have powerfully influenced national spending on research and development. The stake of the federal government in science grew rapidly during World War II, continued to expand during the cold-war era, and by the late 1960s accounted for about two-thirds of the funds spent on research and development within colleges and universities and about half of that spent within industries. And about 90 percent of the federal research-and-development funds fell under the control of the Department of Defense, the National Aeronautics and Space Administration (NASA), and the Atomic Energy Commission.

This enormous spending has destabilized the economy for several reasons. First, the military needs of the nation have often run counter to the search for greater short-run economic stability. Each major postwar military enterprise has produced a bout of inflation, accentuated by an unwillingness to raise taxes, and then an episode of recession. Second, defense spending, financed through varying combinations of taxation and inflation, has subtracted resources from enterprises that might well have enhanced the nation's economic efficiency more effectively and thus alleviated inflationary pressures. No doubt the research-and-development aspects of defense programs have had important effects in developing the modern electronic, chemical, and aircraft industries, promoting advances in jet propulsion and computer technology, in particular. But it is arguable that society could have achieved the same benefits more efficiently by relying more heavily on private resources and by selecting more carefully the risks that justified public subsidies. Third, lucrative defense contracts have tended to protect a small, but significant sector of American industry from the discipline of the marketplace. Relieved of the necessity of relying on its own resources for new investment, this sector, composed primarily of the aerospace companies, has lagged in the refinement of management expertise. It has been strikingly unsuccessful in judging the scale of private demand for its products, particularly in the area of commercial aircraft, has had extreme difficulty in realistically projecting future costs, has operated with great uncertainty as to the return from its research-and-development investments, has often failed to make its operations as efficient as possible, and has been unwilling or unable to make meaningful efforts, when necessary, to convert or reconvert its capabilities to peacetime enterprise. Conversely, the corporations most committed to private planning, including most of the electrical, chemical, and transportation industries, although receiving some stimulation from public investment, have received far less governmental support and coordination.[7] In fact, these are the corporations that have been the most significant force in improving public planning. Sponsoring the Committee for Economic Development to research new programs and coordinate their legislative efforts, many of these corporations became particularly active in the 1960s, promoting the tax cut of 1964, reorganizing defense planning, and instituting more effective budgetary controls and foreign trade and investment policies designed to promote stability in the developed world.[8]

PUBLIC PLANNING AND STABILITY: FISCAL AND MONETARY POLICY

The profoundly disruptive influence of military spending made it impossible for the New Deal's initiatives to begin a revolution in the character of federal economic planning on behalf of stability. The experience of the 1930s did, of course, push to the fore the issue of government responsibility for maintaining economic stability—for preventing another depression on the one hand and staving off inflation on the other. But a clear and operational definition of the mission of the government developed slowly, even after the instructive impact of expansive public policy following the recession of 1937–1938 and especially during World War II.

World War II, 1939–1948: Another Episode of Conversion and Reconversion

In the spring of 1940 the American economy began to react to events in Europe. The result would be a decisive acceleration of the process of recovery from the depression of 1929–1933 and the recession of 1937–1938, manifested by the rise of per-capita income and production above the levels that had been attained during the 1920s.

The stimulation of the economy from abroad began prior to United States entry into World War II, with the Allied, mainly British, large-scale purchases of war materiel between May 1940 and March 1941. Beginning with Germany's assault on the Low Countries and France, these purchases totaled some $2 billion and were made with gold. Almost simultaneously, the nation launched an expanded program of national defense, causing an increase in the budgetary deficit from $3.9 billion to $6.2 billion between 1940 and 1941, despite a rapid increase in receipts. The inflow of gold, which neither the Federal Reserve nor the Treasury discouraged, coupled with an expansive fiscal policy, produced a sharp increase in total demand, industrial production, employment, and income. However, prices were quite stable as the expansion took place, largely through the utilization of slack capacity that still remained from the 1930s. The sources of expansion remained relatively unchanged throughout the period of neutrality (through November 1941), except that the rapid increase in the flow of gold, which had begun in 1938, ended in April 1941. A month earlier the government began its lend-lease program, under which the United States paid for much of the war supplies used by the Allies, especially Britain, in return for services rendered by the Allies in fighting the Axis powers. During the course of the war the United States spent some $50 billion under the program, without any intention of receiving cash repayment, thereby reinforcing the expansiveness of fiscal policy.

The major source of expansion during the period of belligerency was the enormous demand for goods and services of war. Energized by Pearl Harbor, governmental expenditures soared and continued to increase through 1945, the federal deficit going from $6.2 billion in 1941 to $21.5 billion in 1942 and then to $57.4 billion in 1943. (Because tax receipts increased rapidly, the deficit remained at about the 1943 level through the remainder of the war.) The expansionary wartime fiscal policy received reinforcement on the monetary side from the actions of the Federal Reserve Board which, as in World War I, focused its activities on enlarging the money supply and easing credit to finance bond purchases.[9] As a result of the fiscal and monetary stimulus to demand, unemployment declined to 1.2 percent of the labor force by 1944.

The war program meant a sizable advance in the growth of the economy and an enormous transfer of resources from peacetime to wartime needs. The average level of federal expenditures from 1942 through 1945 amounted to roughly half of net national product. Indeed, this was a more massive shift of resources than was the case during World War I; in addition, it was faster and more prolonged. The period of American neutrality, during which adjustment to wartime pressures could take place, was short in contrast with the long period preceding American entry into World War I, and the period of belligerency was much more extended than during World War I. The organizational basis for that swift and prolonged diversion of resources remains unexplored in most of its aspects, but the bureaucratic experience of World War I joined with the development of administrative expertise during the 1920s and 1930s within both public and private sectors probably accounted for the successes of the Controlled Materials Plan (1942), the Components Schedule Plan (1942), the direction of the War Production Board (WPB), and the coordination of the Office of War Mobilization.[10]

Another striking difference between the mobilization experiences of the two world wars was the much slower rise of prices

SHIPYARD OF HENRY J. KAISER, PORTLAND, OREGON. During World
War II this shipyard and six others like it each produced a ship per day.

during World War II, despite the larger and more sustained war
effort. During the brief neutrality period, 1939–1941, the wholesale
price index rose at an annual rate of about 9 percent and during the
period of direct participation, at a relatively modest 4 percent. The
source of this very favorable price experience lies in a variety of
factors, including a sounder public policy.

The federal government, in contrast with its performance during
World War I, determinedly sought to retard inflation. The Roosevelt
administration initiated a program of price controls and rationing in
January 1942 and made it more stringent in May 1943; the Truman
administration maintained it until June 1946. The primary vehicle
for implementing price control was the Office of Price Administration (OPA). Its fundamental charge was to set and enforce maximum
prices in order to prevent high wartime incomes and shortages of
goods from resulting in rampant inflation. Also, to reduce the arbitrariness of the pattern of distribution that would result from artificially low prices, the OPA rationed very scarce goods such as
gasoline, tires, fuel oil, sugar, coffee, meat, and processed food. In
imposing its counterinflation measures, the OPA received considerable support. It was able to spend over $185 million and to employ,
during its peak effort in 1945, more than 60,000 men and women.

Moreover, the OPA received aid from the federal judiciary. In fiscal 1946 appeals and prosecutions of OPA rulings accounted for over half of all civil cases and nearly 10 percent of all criminal cases begun in U.S. district courts.

On the surface, the record of this massive effort was impressive. Prices rose 6.4 percent per year over the nine-year period between August 1939 and August 1948 and 12.5 percent per year between June 1946, when controls were lifted, and August 1948. But during the period of most effective controls, between May 1943 and June 1946, prices increased only 2.1 percent per year. However, the *recorded* consumer price index is not a completely reliable measure of real price increases during a period of price control. For one thing, many people were able to evade OPA restrictions through black marketeering. Illegal trade was especially rampant in meat and gasoline, but there is no record of the prices people actually paid for these rationed items. For another, there were changes in the quality of goods and services and the elimination of discounts that did not register in price indexes. Some consumers purchased higher-quality goods when they found preferred, lower-priced items unavailable ("forced uptrading"). Such behavior meant, in effect, unrecorded price increases. The upward movement of real prices was undoubtedly larger than the increase recorded by the price index, and a substantial part of the inflation ensuing in 1946 may have been simply the belated recording of wartime increases. But that inflation is as yet unmeasured, and it may be assumed that the vigorous federal control program, supported by public opinion, markedly restrained inflation. Whether the probable success of the OPA should encourage contemporary policy makers to embrace price controls is highly dubious. Whatever overall success the OPA achieved resulted not simply from an effective enforcement campaign but also from the high popularity of the general war effort and the unusual willingness with which Americans accepted price controls and rationing.[11]

Another important factor in retarding the rise of prices during the war was the desire of people to increase the amount of money held relative to expenditures. (The ratio of the stock of money to national product increased by about one-third between 1942 and 1946.) Part of the reason was the public's willingness to postpone expenditures for consumer durables. The Supply, Priority, and Allocations Board (a forerunner of the WPB) began to restrict the production of consumer durables during the summer of 1941, and in 1942 ended the production of automobiles, trucks, refrigerators, washing machines, and other electrical appliances for civilian use. Saving was the result. Instead of households and individuals spending their augmented incomes by purchasing consumer durables, they invested in other assets, including United States savings bonds and money itself. Part of the public's restraint stemmed from its eagerness to support the war effort. But more significant was its anticipation that the relative prices of consumer durables would fall after the war. Also important was the fear that economic collapse would follow the war. The experience of the 1930s was fresh in everyone's mind, and many remembered as well the serious depression that had followed World War I in 1920–1921. These memories left many Americans doubting that the nation had found a formula for maintaining the economy at full employment in a peacetime environment.[12]

To the contrary, however, the conclusion of hostilities began a dramatic departure in the history of reconversion following major wars. The most striking discontinuity was the failure of the economy to undergo an economic contraction of any significant magnitude. Despite the fact that demobilization did mean a turning of fiscal policy toward restriction, no serious recession or heavy level of unemployment ensued.[13] Although wartime production peaked early in 1945, the subsequent decline in output lasted only until October 1945, when another upward trend set in, persisting until November 1948.

One of the curiosities of the postwar expansion was that it defied a restrictive fiscal policy. The curtailment of expenditures that began in 1946 continued throughout 1948, with expenditures declining to about one-third of what they had been in 1945, but with receipts diminished by less than 10 percent. The 1946 deficit of $20.7 billion had become a surplus of $8.4 billion by 1948. Yet in the face of widespread concern about the possibility of economic collapse and stagnation, and despite the demonstration of the capacity of fiscal policy during the war and some abatement of public fear of deficits, the federal government adopted a budgetary policy that made economic reversal more likely. The expansion of government necessary to stage American participation in World War II was regarded as appropriate only for the most extreme emergency; expenditures were scaled down, not to restrain expansion, but because there were no social objectives considered worthy of such fiscal effort. However, the federal government did not lower its receipts as rapidly as it did expenditures. Behind this action was a strong belief in the wisdom of balancing the budget as a way of preserving confidence in the economy. Indeed, the Truman administration wedded itself more to budget balancing than had the Roosevelt administration. Reflecting the lack of enthusiasm for countercyclical fiscal policy were the important qualifications and limitations written into the Employment Act of 1946. Although Congress agreed to pledge the government to the *encouragement* of employment, it failed to make a guarantee of

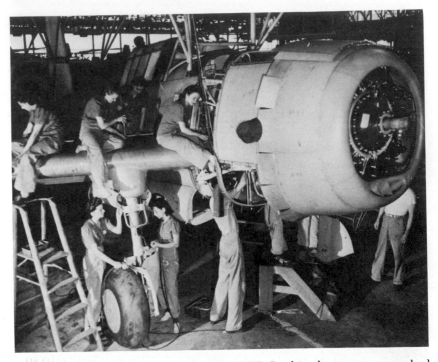

WOMEN ASSEMBLING A DIVE BOMBER. In this plant women worked with men and operated heavy machinery.

full employment, announced it would take only those actions consistent with other economic objectives, and avoided defining what appropriate policy might be. The act did create the Council of Economic Advisers, but its function was only to advise the president. Additionally, there was no guarantee that the council members would be able to agree on coherent policy recommendations. In short, the act did little more than record officially the responsibility for stimulating employment (under certain vague conditions) that the federal government had implicitly recognized since the Hoover administration.

Largely by chance, however, Truman and Congress adopted a set of postwar policies that were closer to being correct than a more expansive set would have been. In fact, one can argue that fiscal policy should have been even *more* restrictive to stem the inflation that followed hostilities. After the third quarter of 1945 the wholesale price index continued upward and then in the middle of 1946, after the removal of price controls, took off. The annual rate of increase between June 1946 and August 1948 was 16.4 percent—more than five times that registered during the period of price controls. Quite obviously, larger full-employment surpluses would have been desirable during the period to retard the price advance.

The problem remains, however, of explaining how the nation broke the pattern of postwar depression, despite the very contractionary fiscal policy. The answer lies primarily in the release of pent-up consumer demand following the lifting of wartime restrictions, especially with regard to consumer durables and housing. Indeed, because of the large accumulation of money and other highly liquid assets to support this pent-up demand, the public would have spent a great deal more on peacetime goods and services had the government not run a surplus.

As just suggested, another expansive force was the increase in the stock of money, which grew at a rate of slightly more than 4 percent per year between January 1946 and August 1948: a steady, strong upward pressure on the level of total demand for goods and services. A significant source of this increase was an inflow of gold, a result primarily of the expenditures of former belligerents (in excess of the expenditures financed through United States loans and the Marshall Plan) and of neutral nations desiring goods not available during the war. Also working to expand the money stock was the increasing willingness of the public to hold more of its money as deposits and less as currency. In addition, the Federal Reserve continued to support Treasury issues as it had during the war.[14]

Indeed, monetary conditions, more than fiscal policy, contributed to the persistence of high levels of economic activity after the conclusion of the war. But the expansionary monetary policy, like the restrictive fiscal policy, happened largely by political accident. The role of the Federal Reserve was dictated by the assumption that the primary mission of the system was to support the Treasury in its role of managing the government debt rather than by a belief in the necessity of using monetary instruments to maintain full employment and stem inflation.

The resulting monetary policy, despite its contribution to high employment, was immodest. When coupled with pent-up consumer demand, its cost was a large accumulation of higher prices. Overly expansive monetary policy contributed heavily to a 50-percent increase in prices between the end of the war and the price peak in August 1948. (Only a minor part of the increase was simply the delayed recording of wartime inflation.) This extended inflation constituted a sharp departure from the habits of earlier postwar periods, which had been marked by a restoration of prices to their prewar levels through a severe deflation. Thus, although the war mobilization produced less inflation than had the more modest effort for World War I, the absence of postwar deflation meant that average indexes were stabilized at roughly twice their 1939 levels. Particularly to those who had anticipated a postwar contraction, the stabilization of prices at a higher level usually meant a loss of real wealth. Perhaps largely as a result of inflationary losses, the period after 1948 until at least the early 1960s was marked by a politically potent fear of inflation. To a large extent that fear shaped public policy after 1948 and contributed to a long period of fairly stable prices. Thus most of the inflation incurred since 1939 has been generated during the periods of converting to and converting from a wartime economy.

The Abandonment of Full Employment and the Overkill of Inflation, 1948–1960

The years 1948 through 1960 provided only modest support for those who believed that the New Deal and World War II experiences had advanced the art of countercyclical policy management in a striking fashion. A recession in 1949 followed by three others during the Eisenhower administration—in 1953–1954 (after the Korean War), in 1957–1958, and in 1960–1961—created doubt about the ability of public policy to control the business cycle, especially in view of an average annual rate of growth of gross national product of only 2.9 percent (the comparable rate for Japan was 8.7 percent; for Germany, 7.2 percent; for Italy, 5.8 percent; for France, 4.2 percent; for Sweden, 3.7 percent; for Canada, 3.6 percent; and for Great Britain, 2.7 percent)[15] and an unemployment rate that was around 5 percent beginning in 1953 and close to 7 percent in 1957–1958 and again in 1960–1961. Both the problems of slow expansion and unemployment stemmed largely from failures of stabilization policy.[16] The postwar economy, as a result of New Deal reforms on behalf of stabilization and private-sector advances in planning, was intrinsically more stable. Given those institutional reforms, frequent changes in fiscal and monetary policy carry primary responsibility for exaggerating the normal fluctuations in income and employment since World War II.[17]

The weakness of policy during the late 1940s and 1950s was more in the management of fiscal policy than in the use of monetary mechanisms. The Federal Reserve Board maintained a rather consistent posture throughout the period, in effect working to keep the nation's money stock growing at a reasonably stable rate, one upon which other institutions and individuals could depend.[18] The exaggerated instability and high unemployment to a great degree came from the techniques and, in part, the objectives of fiscal policy. Large deficits appeared in the public accounts, leading some people to suggest that even the Eisenhower administration had discovered the profound power of fiscal stabilization policy and had accepted the necessity of incurring deficits to stimulate the economy. However, the deficits of the 1950s resulted, not from expansionary budget policy, but from sluggish demand weakening the income-tax base and thereby causing revenues to fail to cover expenditures. Fiscal policy undercut demand at three crucial points during the 1950s— by failing to maintain an easy transition from the Korean War, by overreacting to the threat of inflation in 1957, and by an undue concern with the outward flow of gold in 1960–1961. In the last contractionary episode the full-employment surplus grew from about $3 to $5 billion to over $13 billion in 1960. The last recession was purely a "policy recession," and although the preceding two stemmed from the fluctuations of the inventory cycle as well, the managers of the nation's fiscal policy could have acted to avert or ameliorate the downturns. By so doing, they would have not only reduced unemployment but stimulated a more rapid rate of expansion.

The mediocre record in policy making, one inferior to that of New Deal recovery planning, developed from various sources. Among the foremost was the pressure to insulate the international economy from shocks, both political and economic, like those of the 1930s and 1940s—pressures that encouraged American policy makers to adhere to a set of deflationary policies at home (see pp. 467–473). Furthermore, disagreement sharpened among both economists and policy makers over the character of policy, even over the basic terms of definition and measurement of fiscal and monetary policy. This intellectual and ideological turmoil led to the popularity of the notion that given limited information and uncertain theoretical frameworks, the government was best advised to remain passive and permit the private sector to plan effectively for stability, a bland prescription warmly received by the Council of Economic Advisers. In part, the problem arose from the political maze through which coherent programs had to pass before implementation. At least three competing authorities (the executive, Congress, and the Federal Reserve Board) shaped policy, all with different sources of information, experts, policy definitions, and political constituencies. Nonetheless, such agencies reliably reflected the ideological disposition of the nation. There was by no means widespread acceptance of the desirability of a more vigorous planning role for the federal government, even in the name of maintaining stability. In fact, during and after the war there was a political turn to the right. Congress abolished the National Resources Planning Board in 1943 and the Bureau of Agricultural Economics in 1944 and prescribed only a bromide in its Employment Act of 1946. In addition, a strong ideological opposition to budget deficits and national debt persisted. Both Truman and Eisenhower associated themselves more closely with the objective of budget balancing than Roosevelt had done, and the public continued to be attracted by analogies between family and federal budgets, despite the facts that families and businesses were themselves heavily in debt and that after 1946 the national debt was declining in comparison with national product. President Eisenhower was fond of using such analogies as well as of asserting his fear of enlarging the burden of debt that the present generation's "grandchildren" would have to bear. Finally, and most important, public opinion strongly supported policies that were directed at fighting or preventing inflation rather than promoting full employment. Unemployment of even 7 percent was a considerable improvement over the 1930s; consequently the issue of unemployment lost a good deal of its political sting, especially with the doubling of the price level between 1939 and 1948. During much of the 1940s and 1950s, public preoccupation with the threat of inflation offered an opportunity, which the Eisenhower administration accepted, to make political capital. In fact, that administration succeeded in preventing inflation; consumer prices increased only about 1.6 percent per year between 1948 and 1963. (However, in light of the tendency of price indexes to overstate price increases and given the difficulties in adjusting for the improvement in the quality of goods, that 1.6-percent rate may well have amounted to *deflation,* rather than a moderate rate of inflation.) To the extent that the Eisenhower administration was fiscally active, it either permitted a recession to drag on somewhat longer than it should have or cut short a period of expansion, as in 1960.

In sum, public fear of continued inflation, the willingness of the Eisenhower administration to exploit that fear, widespread disenchantment with public planning (including vigorous countercyclical policy), public distaste for budget deficits, a chaotic set of institutions for making fiscal policies, a lack of consensus among professional economists as to the appropriate use of stabilization instruments, and the internationalist pressures of the 1950s produced an episode of business-cycle management that marked a regression from the example set by the New Deal, especially after 1937. However, stabilization policy was not nearly as disastrous as that of 1929–1933 (largely as a result of monetary stability) and should be seen as part of a long-term trend toward the development of effective planning for orderly growth.

The Revival of Growth and Inflation, 1961–1977

The administration of John F. Kennedy committed itself far less to a continuing fight against inflation than to the task of overcoming sluggish rates of expansion. Fiscal policy consequently eased during the first year of Kennedy's administration, but since monetary policy worked in the opposite direction, little acceleration in the rate of expansion of national product appeared. Then in 1962–1963, as part of an effort to stem an increasing outward flow of gold, fiscal policy took a restrictive course, just as it had in 1960–1961 for the same reason. Thus the full-employment surplus rose from $5 billion to about $12 billion. Fortunately for the health of the domestic economy a very strongly expansionary monetary policy more than compensated for the reversal, and the rate of growth of the economy accelerated rapidly near the end of 1962. Monetary policy tightened somewhat thereafter. But in 1964 fiscal policy took a sharply expansive turn, not from a dramatic expansion of the welfare state, but from a massive reduction of taxes.

That tax cut, proposed by Kennedy in 1962 and signed into law by Lyndon B. Johnson in February 1964, was the nation's most decisive step toward the development of a coherent countercyclical fiscal policy—the first time in the nation's fiscal history that the federal government deliberately slashed taxes in the face of large deficits. Recognizing that the deficits resulted from economic slack, proponents of the tax cut argued that the action would stimulate total demand, increase incomes, augment federal income-tax revenues, and, in fact, serve to reduce the government deficit. The 1964 tax cut marked the first dramatic use of compensatory fiscal policy to prevent a recession and stimulate the economy to grow in a sustained fashion. And if one had to date the conversion of federal budgetary policy to a "Keynesian revolution," it would be in 1964 rather than in 1939, or at any earlier time. As a result of that departure the full-employment surplus declined to about $1 billion, or the level attained in 1958, and the rate of growth in output accelerated, bringing unemployment down close to 4 percent in 1964–1965 without significant inflation.

The Kennedy-Johnson tax cut held out hopes for a fiscal policy effectively attuned to the interests of rapid growth, high employment, and price stability. Apart from its favorable results (including the probable avoidance of a recession), the tax cut reflected closer agreement among the nation's economists, represented by the Council of Economic Advisers, as to the impact of fiscal policy on spending and incomes. Also, it signified that a powerful consensus existed between those favorably disposed toward the expansion of the activities of the federal government and an important sector of the nation's largest corporations, represented intellectually and politically by the Committee for Economic Development, on behalf of a vigorous fiscal policy.[19]

But there were indications of future difficulty for the liberal-center coalition that had joined forces under the banner of Keynes. Although Kennedy and crucial portions of the business community had reached agreement as to the desirability of a tax cut by June 1962, conservative opposition (led by Senator Harry F. Byrd of Virginia, who accused even the United States Chamber of Commerce of "fiscal irresponsibility") delayed enactment for almost two years. Moreover, much less agreement had been reached among economists on the appropriate use of monetary policy to promote economic stability. At the extremes, many thought that variations in the size of the money supply had little impact on economic stability, whereas others had exaggerated confidence in their ability to manage the money supply in the interests of stability. Further, some, including those who were skeptical of the influence of monetary policy, still denied that variations in the money supply provided a useful basis for measuring monetary policy. These divisions among the nation's intellectual forces for fighting recessions and inflation were rudely exposed during the late 1960s and early 1970s.

In 1965 the nation vastly expanded its military effort in Indochina, requiring a sharp increase in federal expenditures. That increase reinforced the expansive impact of the tax cut and the Federal Reserve Board added its own stimulus. In so doing the Federal Reserve adhered to a policy that had almost always disrupted orderly economic management—a policy of reducing the costs of Treasury borrowing by increasing purchases of federal securities, thereby increasing their price. In the process the Federal Reserve exerted a strongly expansive influence on the size of the money supply and, hence, on the size of the demand for goods and services. At the same time that the full-employment surplus continued to increase, the rate of growth of the money stock increased. From May 1965 until April 1966 the stock of money increased about 6.6 percent and then, after a "credit crunch" lasting for the remainder of the year, when the Federal Reserve held the money supply essentially constant, grew at an even more rapid rate until June 1969.

The result of the conjunction of expansive fiscal and monetary policies was the attainment of an exceptionally low rate of unemployment, but at the cost of a very rapid rate of price increase. At the beginning of 1966 unemployment moved below 4 percent for the first time since 1957 and remained below until the first quarter of

1970, even closely approaching 3 percent in 1968. However, the rocketing demand that reduced unemployment also placed pressures on the existing capacity of the economy to produce. That phenomenon of too much money chasing too few goods accelerated the rate of price increase and created an inflationary psychology, that is, a widespread anticipation of further price increases. Even with the sharply restrictive action of the Federal Reserve Board in 1966, the annual average rate of price increase for 1965 through 1968 was 3.4 percent, rising to 4.7 percent in 1968. In 1969 the rate increased even further to 6 percent.

In the middle of 1968, fiscal policy turned in a contractionary direction with the enactment of a 10-percent surtax on incomes, sponsored by the Johnson administration, followed by cutbacks in defense spending, designed by the Nixon government. Then in the last half of 1969 the growth of the money supply virtually halted. During the last quarter of 1969, after those actions, national product peaked and the economy moved downward into the recession of 1969–1970. But even the convergence of restrictive monetary and restrictive fiscal policies failed to contain the rapidly rising consumer price index; the prospect of "stagflation," or the unusual conjunction of sluggish expansion and inflation, faced the economy. The period of price increase had extended for such an unusually long period of time—almost nine years elapsing between the 1961 recession and the 1969 recovery peak—that the public strongly anticipated continued inflation. In expectation of relentless price increases, people continued to reduce their dollar balances, purchase commodities, and thus hedge against future inflation. That tendency, coupled with cost-push inflation, that is, inflation resulting from wage settlements and price increases fostered by labor unions and businessmen with inflationary expectations and exercising monopoly power, maintained the upward pressures on prices. Even though restrictive fiscal and monetary policies produced high rates of unemployment (reaching 6 percent by the end of 1970), prices continued to increase, tapering off in their rate of advance only toward mid-1970. Before restrictive policy could restore stable prices, in response to high levels of unemployment, monetary policy eased during the first half of 1970 and became exceptionally expansive during early 1971. Fiscal policy, as well, became buoyant before the end of 1970. Consequently, economic activity had begun to revive by early 1971.

The recession, however, had not proceeded long enough to reverse inflationary expectations and subdue price increases. Thus when the economy recovered slowly from the recession of 1969–1970 and high unemployment consequently persisted, prices continued to increase at rates only slightly lower than during the late 1960s.

Aware of the political threat posed by a combination of rapid inflation and high unemployment, the Nixon administration in August
1971 instituted the first peacetime program of price and wage controls to retard inflation without hampering economic expansion, beginning with a ninety-day freeze on all wages and prices. Following
the freeze, the Nixon administration (under Phase 1 of its anti-infla-
tion program) created extremely rudimentary machinery for price
control, relying heavily on voluntary compliance and the alertness of
consumers to support the Price Commission, and experienced severe
difficulty in fostering the development of a consensus among business, labor, and consumer interests on the issue of wage controls
through the operation of the Pay Board. Nonetheless, with the assistance of a restrictive monetary policy, the rate of consumer-price
increase declined to an annual rate of less than 3 percent in the last
half of 1971. Meanwhile, fiscal policy had acquired a highly expansive
posture, reducing unemployment to less than 5 percent by the end
of 1973 but once again exacerbating inflationary pressures.

The period of moderated inflation continued into 1972 but after
a sustained period of monetary expansion throughout 1972 (with the
money stock increasing at a rate of more than 8 percent) and a
reduction of the stringency of wage and price controls in January
1973 (Phase 2), the rate of price increase assumed the exceptionally
high annual rate of nearly 25 percent before the administration, in
June, reversed directions again, freezing prices for as long as 60 days
(Phase 3). During the subsequent period amidst increasing widespread uncertainty as to the future, growing disrespect among both
economists and the public at large for wage and price controls, and
continuing inflation, it appeared that the administration wished to
return to traditional formulas. As 1973 drew to a close a new, very
weak program of inflation control had emerged (Phase 4), but fiscal
and monetary policy, in conjunction, assumed a restrictive form.
Restrictive monetary policy continued into 1974 and was joined by
Ford administration efforts to reduce the deficit. This policy shift was
aimed at offsetting the impact of a quadrupling of oil prices, an
explosion of food prices resulting from crop failures throughout the
world, and a slowing of the growth of productive capacity. All of
these developments reinforced the persistent hold of inflationary
expectations to produce a rate of price increase that reached 11.5
percent per year during the third quarter of 1974. Finally, by mid-
1974, budget policy and Federal Reserve policies had become so
restrictive that a recession ensued.

The recession, which began in mid-1974, became the worst economic reversal since the Great Depression. The contraction lasted a
full year, and unemployment rates climbed to 10 percent. Restrictive

policies played a part in prolonging the recession. Both the administration of Gerald Ford and the Federal Reserve Board pursued restrictive policies after the onset of the recession. Their calculations were deliberate. Extending the recession was a tactic to bring under control the high inflation that the hyperexpansion of demand during the previous decade had produced. The only other options open were rigorous, probably ineffective price controls and sharply accelerating inflation. Consequently, the choice of severe recession appears to have been a reasonable, though dismal one. Responsibility for the higher unemployment that resulted rested primarily with the Johnson administration and with Congress, which failed to check the expansion before it soared out of control, and the Nixon administration, which failed to allow the much milder recession of 1969–1970 to continue until inflation had subsided. Moreover, the recession of 1974–1975, like that of 1957–1958, was unusually severe not simply because of restrictive policy but also because of the international quality of the recession. Of all the recessions since the 1930s, those of 1957–1958 and 1974–1975 were the only ones suffered simultaneously by all the major trading nations. The various domestic recessions reinforced each other and, as a consequence, the recessions were unusually severe. Finally, exculpating the Ford administration was the fact that by January 1975, when the rate of price increase began to moderate, the Ford administration turned to wage war against unemployment by endorsing the biggest budget deficit— more than $50 billion—in peacetime history. Subsequently, Congress passed, and Ford approved, a tax cut of more than $22 billion, the largest ever in the nation's history. The final deficit for fiscal 1976 totaled nearly $60 billion. That program of fiscal stimulation, coupled with a permissive monetary policy, contributed to the strong economic recovery that had begun by summer of 1975 and continued, although more slowly, through 1977. If anything, Ford, Congress, and the Federal Reserve erred by undertaking policies that were too stimulating. Prices continued to increase rapidly even in 1975, increased more slowly in 1976 (at an annual rate of 4.4 percent during the fourth quarter), and accelerated once again during the first half of 1977 in anticipation of fiscal stimulation by Jimmy Carter's administration. Powerful inflationary expectations never died, despite the severity of the recession. These price increases helped maintain rates of unemployment at historically high levels. Unemployment was high because the inflationary damage to family budgets led to a sharp increase in the efforts of women and teen-age children to seek employment in order to offset the erosion of their families' real income. Despite the strength of the recovery and a dynamic rate of job creation that pushed the percentage of working-age people who were employed to an all-time high, the surge of new entrants into the labor force was so exceptionally great that the rate of unemployment remained about 7 percent even at the end of 1977.

The management of countercyclical policy since 1965 has shown that it is extremely difficult to keep the economy on a path that affords *both* price stability and low unemployment. Probably more difficult than the problem of insufficient information and inadequate forecasting tools are the problems of separating political consider-ations from the determination of policy. For example, the 10-percent income surtax enacted in 1968 found advocates within the adminis-tration and, indeed, the support of President Johnson as early as 1966. But as some critics of the Kennedy-Johnson tax cut (like Sena-tor Paul Douglas of Illinois) had predicted, it proved to be much easier to lower taxes to stimulate the economy than to raise them to cool off an expansion: fearing the unpopularity of increasing taxes, especially taxes designed to finance a heightened war effort, Con-gress denied approval to the increase until the inflation had become severe. Thereafter, once policy makers had been impaled on infla-tionary spikes, severe restriction to produce a lengthy recession or effective wage and price controls threatened only to intensify the political agony.

Sensitivity in the use of fiscal and monetary instruments was sub-stantially higher during the 1960s than in the preceding decade. But the outcome of policy decisions was only slightly more favorable, the thrust of error, largely for political reasons, now being toward exces-sive price inflation (rather than excessive unemployment). The one brief period of successful stabilization during the first half of the decade, when contrasted with the dismal years thereafter, illustrates how much policy is dependent on political choices that have little to do with the objectives of economic stability and also on fundamental institutions, like Congress and the Federal Reserve, that cannot iso-late the making of countercyclical policy from the working out of the nation's other goals. Most importantly, during the last half of the 1960s a choice was made to fight a politically unpopular war, a deci-sion that led to the renunciation of orderly economic growth at home.

Monetary and fiscal policies have become more constructive since the Great Depression, but progress has been slow, incomplete, and offset by the destabilizing aspects of defense spending. It has been fashionable to dwell periodically upon the lack of centralized planning in the United States. The serious recession of 1974–1975 and the high rates of unemployment that have persisted since have led to intensified calls for national economic planning. To be sure, the record of the federal government in planning for stability remains weak, in contrast with the governments of Japan and some of the nations of western Europe, particularly Germany, France, and the Scandinavian countries. And it is equally true that public activities in general have been carried on in a highly disorderly fashion in the United States ever since the massive but chaotic efforts of the Roosevelt administration to cope with the exigencies of serious depression and major war. Nonetheless, preoccupation with the failures of public planning should not lead to discouragement with the overall record of planning for stability in the United States. Within the private sector institutional reforms have made significant advances in promoting a more orderly marketplace. Indeed, overall, the record of planning for stability in the United States equals that made by European societies with their tendency to rely more heavily on the public sector.[20] Proponents of more centralized national planning for stability ought to consider carefully how to preserve the important advances made by private planning initiatives during the postwar years as well as how to enhance the effectiveness of public planning.

THE UNITED STATES AND INTERNATIONAL MONETARY ORDER, 1944–1977

An evaluation of American planning for stability must weigh heavily the nation's efforts to restore the order that international economic relations had lacked for more than a decade. The main thrust of that effort was the creation of a stable international monetary system. The political instability that had resulted during the breakdown of the international monetary order during the 1930s lent a particular urgency to that task.

Planning among the Allied nations for the postwar economic order began as early as 1941 and reached a climax with the United Nations conference held at Bretton Woods, New Hampshire, in 1944. The explicit goal of the conference was to find mechanisms that would help surmount the kind of narrow economic and political nationalism that had become endemic during the 1930s. However, the conference failed in its attempt to overcome decisively the dead weight of the past. Unwillingness on the part of all major participants —not just the United States—to delegate any significant portion of national sovereignty to an international body prevented the adoption of the proposal of John Maynard Keynes (among others) for the creation of a true international central bank that could provide the same kind of stability and flexibility for the world economy as that offered a national economy by a central bank.

Instead of creating a new international currency and an international bank, the architects of stability designed a system that improved upon but left fundamentally intact the gold-standard system of the 1920s. Intended to effect a compromise between the preservation of national economic independence and the creation of a powerful supranational financial agency, the Bretton Woods Conference agreed on a system of moderately flexible currency exchange rates supported by a new institution, the International Monetary Fund (the IMF), designed to be a central currency pool on which member national central banks had limited borrowing rights to meet temporary deficits. Its central objective was to spare any nation the necessity of running a persistently large deficit in its balance-of-payments account, thereby staving off restrictions on the movement of foreign exchange and preventing currency devaluations (IMF rules, however, did provide for some limited, orderly exchange rate adjustments). Despite the new institution, each member nation was committed, just as under the old gold standard, to maintain convertibility of its currency at the current agreed-on exchange rates.

In practice the IMF has provided short-run stability in the movement of exchange rates and thus stability in world capital markets. But it has failed to check the persistence of massive payments deficits —from the United States, in particular. As a result the IMF has not, in fact, acted as a real international central bank; instead, the United States has performed that function, manipulating and managing a very large volume of dollars in circulation abroad, dollars generated by an unbalanced payments account. Since Bretton Woods, the large flow of dollars abroad as private investment, public credit, and military expenditures has been substantially in excess of dollars returned, such as in the purchase of American exports. These dollars have served as the world's primary medium of international exchange, much more important in volume than either gold or the pound sterling. Their volume has been determined by the size of the American balance-of-payments deficit, which, in turn, has been determined by an array of American policies: regulation (or, nonregulation) of foreign investment, spending programs for economic development and military programs abroad, the management of the balance of trade, domestic countercyclical policies, and, most fundamentally, the determination of the value of the dollar in terms of gold. Whereas other nations have commonly devalued their currencies, the United States has usually adhered to a fixed exchange rate, in terms of gold, with the precise objective and result of maintaining a large pool of dollars circulating abroad.

Despite the fundamental failure of the IMF, under American management, the alternative has worked to ensure a much higher degree of stability in world capital markets than existed during the

1920s and a substantially more favorable environment for world trade and economic development. For one thing, the United States has been more restrained in using its power to enlarge world markets for American products, in sharp contrast with public policy during the 1920s. Unwillingness to devalue the dollar has curtailed the growth of exports, and the lowering of tariff barriers has permitted the expansion of imports. Although some threat of a departure toward protectionism appears possible in the 1980s, American policy since World War II has been rather consistently one of promoting international competition by removing obstacles hampering international trade. By 1947 the United States had already signed some twenty-nine pacts under the Reciprocal Trade Agreements Act of 1934. Then in response to an American proposal, twenty-three nations pledged themselves to a code of commercial policy promising to reduce barriers to trade, especially tariffs, on a multilateral basis. Largely under this General Agreement on Tariffs and Trade (GATT), the United States by 1960 had lowered the average level of its import duties to about 12 percent (from over 50 percent in 1930–1933), thus lending a degree of permanency to the reversal of protectionism that had begun in 1934. When the Reciprocal Trade Agreements Act finally expired in 1962, it was replaced by another act conceived in the same spirit, the Trade Expansion Act of 1962, designed primarily to enable the United States to bargain with the European Common Market. It authorized the president to negotiate for tariff reductions on broad categories of goods (not just on single items, as under the 1934 act), to offer tariff reductions amounting to as much as 50 percent of 1962 rates, and to eliminate altogether tariffs on articles for which the Common Market and the United States account for 80 percent of world exports.

Another contribution to stability came from the Marshall Plan, which pumped about $13 billion of capital, in the form of public grants, into the recovering European economy during the crucial period 1948–1951. In addition to enabling European industrial and economic growth, that capital promoted the expansion of the crucial United States trade with Europe by making the purchase of American exports to Europe easier to finance. At the same time, with its regional focus, the Marshall Plan encouraged the trend toward European unity and the construction of a strong European economy more fully able to utilize economies of scale and national comparative advantages. Clearly, American planners had taken the lessons of the 1920s and 1930s seriously.

Despite the favorable record of postwar international stability, the dollar system has been potentially unstable, inasmuch as the dollar must take a back seat to gold as a bona fide standard of exchange.

The effectiveness of the dollar as a standard for international exchange has depended on the belief among money traders that the United States would continue to convert dollars freely into gold at the fixed exchange rate. If that confidence in the dollar waned, as a result of a sharp increase in the balance-of-payments deficit in relationship to the nation's stock of gold and an ensuing fear that the United States would be forced to devalue the dollar, a run on the dollar, expressed in an increase in the flow of gold out of the United States, resulted. Runs on the dollar recurred in the postwar period, and although they have not been calamitous, given the commitment of central banks around the world to maintaining stability, they did demonstrate the instability inherent in the institutions created at Bretton Woods and finally forced the United States, in February 1973, to abandon any effort to convert dollars into gold. In slightly different terms, after 1944 the world came to rely on a continued, large balance-of-payments deficit run by the United States to provide an effective medium of exchange; at the same time, it became highly sensitive to changes in the size of that deficit. At last, the runs on the dollar, accompanied by dollar devaluations, became serious enough to force at least temporary abandonment of the Bretton Woods system. Without the substitution of a more orderly system the world might well face a period of deflation and contraction during the 1970s.

Potential international instability has been one cost of the dollar system. Another has been that the United States, in order to manage the world's money supply effectively, has chosen a policy of restraint in pursuing full employment during much of the postwar period. This was particularly so during the 1950s, when the Eisenhower administration, adhering to an internationalist posture, adopted successful deflationary policies to maintain confidence in the dollar abroad (in part, deflationary policy consisted of an effort to keep short-term interest rates at high levels, thereby attracting mobile capital to this side of the Atlantic). Deflation, by moderating increases in the prices of American goods, served to promote the expansion of American exports (especially nonmanufactured goods) thus curbing the outward flow of dollars for imports. The Kennedy administration coped with the problem of maintaining the dollar system by first adopting rather restrictive fiscal policies and then by restricting the flow of American capital abroad, by a system of selective taxation, to reduce the size of the payments deficit. The Johnson administration imposed mandatory limits on the outflow of enterprise capital. However, the rapid increase in the size of the payments deficit during the Johnson and Nixon administrations, largely as a result of rapid domestic inflation and the overseas expenditures to

THE MARSHALL PLAN'S SETTING: WARTIME DESTRUCTION, 1945.
Civilians (directed by Russian soldiers) clear rubble from a Berlin street.

maintain the military in Indochina, made monetary crises, although
still fairly mild, more frequent in the late 1960s and early 1970s. In
1971, in response to a heightened run on the dollar, the Nixon administration abandoned the long effort to maintain an inflexibly stable
dollar by rejecting the course of action that dictated high domestic
interest rates and deflation. It devalued the dollar for the first time
since 1934. First, in August, the administration temporarily discon-
tinued the convertibility of dollars into gold, thus floating the dollar
(that is, allowing the supply and demand for dollars at any time to set
the price of the dollar in terms of gold and other currencies); then
in April 1972 Congress officially devalued the dollar by increasing
from $35 to $38 the price the United States would pay for an ounce
of gold. The new price was designed to reflect more accurately the

market for dollars and to redress an unfavorable balance of trade in 1971—the first since 1896—by effectively lowering the relative price of American exports.[21] However, the devaluation provided no visible improvement in the balance of trade. In fact, the deficit for 1972 proved to be three times as large as that for 1971. Consequently, the value of the dollar abroad slumped drastically and the administration, in February 1973, devalued again (to an official rate of $42.22) and once more, this time for an indefinite period, allowed the dollar to float unsupported in world currency markets (where it already had sunk to a value of less than half the official but now virtually meaningless rate). By the end of 1973 the value of the dollar had somewhat stabilized, perhaps because of signs of improvement in the trade balance, and world trade had not suffered, at least in the short run, from the floating dollar.

The more flexible international monetary system faced its first serious test when the enormous increase in the price of oil in late 1973 and early 1974 produced a massive flow of revenue to the handful of oil-exporting nations in the Middle East. These nations began to run gigantic trade surpluses while the oil-importing countries began to incur large, sustained trade deficits. Despite the disruption of trading patterns, none of the developed nations incurred a persistent balance-of-payments deficit. The developed countries have been successful in adjusting their trade and attracting investments from the petroleum nations sufficient to bring their balance of payments into equilibrium. The less developed nations that lack oil have had more difficulty in making similar adjustments. Yet they, too, have generally succeeded with the assistance of direct economic aid from other countries (including the petroleum nations), private credits extended by American and European banks, which draw on the surpluses of the Organization of Petroleum Exporting Countries (OPEC), and aid from the World Bank and the IMF. The system passed another major test during the world-wide recession of 1974–1975. Despite the slowdown in world trade that accompanied the recession, the crisis predicted by many who criticized the flexible system never materialized. Indeed, if anything, the world's monetary system appeared to have become more stable than it was during the late 1960s. In fact, ironically, the dollar appeared to have gained strength as a key currency, despite its float. In 1976, the strength of the American recovery and the stability of the nation's balance of payments kept the dollar as a reasonably stable point of reference for other currencies. But in 1977, because domestic inflation accelerated and the deficit in the nation's balance of trade increased (a result, in large part, from growing purchases of foreign oil), the value of the dollar declined significantly against other key currencies. Given the great volume of dollars held abroad (primarily as "Eurodollars"), concerns grew that this weakening of the dollar might seriously destabilize the international economy. Thus, by the end of 1977 it had not become clear whether the new, more liberal system would serve the world adequately in the long run. Future international crises might lead the greatest economic powers in the world to resume movement toward a transfer of key economic decisions from national to international government. Specifically, they might resume movement toward the creation of an independent monetary authority with the ability to supply a stable and flexible currency for the world's traders and investors.[22]

NOTES

1. For an analysis of the institutional adaptation of the corporation to the marketplace, see Alfred D. Chandler, Jr., *Strategy and Structure: Studies in Industrial Enterprise* (Cambridge, Mass.: M.I.T. Press, 1962), and "The Structure of Industry in the Twentieth Century: A Historical Overview," *Business History Review*, 43 (Autumn 1969), 255–298. The data presented below on degrees of concentration and diversification are taken from the latter work.

2. For evidence that conglomerates have provided the firms they acquired with more highly professional managerial talent and greater strength in the application of new technologies to product development, see Harry H. Lynch, *Financial Performance of Conglomerates* (Boston: Graduate School of Business Administration, Harvard University, 1971).

3. In 1967, as a result of this prosecution brought by the Federal Trade Commission, the acquisition of the Clorox Chemical Company by Procter and Gamble was in violation of the Clayton Act by tending to create a monopoly through a merger of firms producing closely related products—in this case, soaps and liquid household bleach.

4. An example of conglomerate-bred competition that was viewed as unfair within the Nixon administration was that of collusive, reciprocal trading relations. Thus the administration sought to break up the Ling-Temco-Vought conglomerate because it contained a large producer of steel (Jones and Laughlin) and a large car-rental system (National Car Rental). By virtue of its power to purchase large quantities of automobiles, the conglomerate, presumably, was in a position to force automobile manufacturers to buy its steel. For similar reasons the Justice Department brought suit against International Telephone and Telegraph because of its acquisition of Canteen Corporation and Hartford Fire Insurance, forcing ITT to agree out of court to relinquish the former holding.

5. It should be noted that concentration was even less in many other industries. In the textile, paper, fabricated-metals, machinery, and food industries, the largest firms accounted for less than 20 percent of output in

1963, while for the leather, publishing and printing, lumber and wood, furniture, and clothing industries, the share of the largest producers was no more than 3 percent.

6. For an engaging effort to minimize consumer choice and maximize manipulation of demand by the large corporations in explaining contemporary expansion, see John K. Galbraith, *The New Industrial State* (Boston: Houghton Mifflin, 1967). On the role of advertising see pp. 198–218.

7. Although firms like General Electric, Westinghouse, American Telephone and Telegraph, International Telephone and Telegraph, International Business Machines, Radio Corporation of America, General Motors, and Ford have been among the largest defense contractors, their contracts amounted to well under one-quarter of total sales of each of those companies during the 1960s. (In fact, contracts were less than 10 percent for American Telephone & Telegraph, General Motors, Ford, and IBM.) In contrast, defense orders constituted more than two-thirds of total sales of Lockheed Aircraft, General Dynamics, McDonnell Douglas, Grumman Aircraft, AVCO, and Ling-Temco-Vought.

8. A typical sample of the corporations represented on the Research and Policy Committee of the CED included no aerospace firms but did include large companies such as Ford, General Motors, Bank of America, Standard Oil of New Jersey, Cowles Communications, Eastman Kodak, and American Telephone & Telegraph. See, for example, Committee for Economic Development, "Budgeting for National Objectives," January 1966. Also see Karl Schriftgiesser, *Business and Public Policy: The Role of the Committee for Economic Development* (Englewood Cliffs, N.J.: Prentice-Hall, 1967).

9. The support of United States securities was even more direct, however, than it had been during World War I; in World War II the Federal Reserve itself bought government securities. In general, the Federal Reserve committed itself to protecting the prices of government securities by guaranteeing to buy whatever amounts were necessary to keep the yield of securities from rising (i.e., to keep their prices from falling). The Federal Reserve, in effect, relinquished control over the quantity of money to the Treasury, which found that Federal Reserve protection transformed its issues into the equivalent of money.

   As in the preceding chapter, I have relied heavily on the discussion of Milton Friedman and Anna J. Schwartz on the role of monetary policy. See *A Monetary History of the United States, 1867–1960* (Princeton, N.J.: Princeton University Press, 1963), especially pp. 546–638.

10. For suggestions of the advance of bureaucratic capabilities over World War I mobilization, see Alfred D. Chandler, Jr., and Louis Galambos, "The Development of Large-Scale Economic Organizations in Modern America," *Journal of Economic History*, 30 (March 1970), 212–216.

11. Even Professor Friedman, highly skeptical of the effectiveness of wage and price controls, agrees that despite the imperfections in the available

measures of real prices, "prices rose more slowly during the war than before or after." See Friedman and Schwartz, *op. cit.*, p. 558. However, the only systematic analysis of the effects of price controls is that of a wartime committee of economists led by Wesley C. Mitchell. The economists found that the downward bias of the consumer price index was only 2 to 3.2 percent in December 1943, but they ignored the effects of black markets and could not study the period of most intense inflationary pressures. See Wesley C. Mitchell *et al.,* "Prices and the Cost of Living in Wartime—an Appraisal of the Bureau of Labor Statistics Index of the Cost of Living in 1941–1944: Report of the Technical Committee Appointed by the Chairman of the President's Committee on the Cost of Living," in *Report of the President's Committee on the Cost of Living* (Washington, D.C.: U.S. Government Printing Office, 1945).

12. In contrast with this behavior, when World War I commenced, people were living under a rising price level and conditions that had been essentially prosperous since the late 1890s. They consequently acted as if they expected the upward trend to continue, perhaps even at a more rapid pace. Furthermore, during World War I the government made no serious effort to stem inflation. Finally, consumers and investors during World War I did not find significant federal obstacles presented to the purchase of real assets, except insofar as inflationary policies raised the price level. With inflation, purchase of consumer and producer durables became more attractive, and such purchases did not meet with imposed rationing.

13. The share of the civilian labor force unemployed for 1946 was still only 3.9 percent. But it should be pointed out that the economy maintained a high rate of employment and successfully integrated the members of the armed forces (whose numbers declined from 12.1 million in May 1945 to 1.9 million in December 1946) not only because civilian employment expanded but also because many people left the labor force. Over 5 million people abandoned the job market in 1945 and over 2 million followed in 1946. Some of those exiting the labor force were men who were retiring, but the vast bulk were women, primarily younger married women with young families, whose employment had been sought only as a last-resort emergency measure to meet the needs of the war effort.

14. It was not until August 1947 that the Federal Open Market Committee lowered the support prices somewhat. But even so, the Federal Reserve intervened to prevent any serious deterioration in the price of long-term securities, increasing the stock of money in the process.

15. It is tempting to attribute the higher European and Japanese rates to the process of catching-up after wartime destruction. But it should be borne in mind that wartime destruction of productive capacity was surprisingly limited. Furthermore, no extensive land warfare took place in western Europe between 1940 and 1944, and the impact of strategic bombing on Axis economies was, despite the protestations of the air

force to the contrary, relatively limited. See the United States Strategic Bombing Survey, *The Effect of Strategic Bombing on the German War Economy* (Washington, D.C.: U.S. Government Printing Office, 1945).

16. During the 1950s fears waxed that the persistence of high rates of unemployment was the inevitable result of the processes of automation; that is, that high unemployment was structural or technological in origin. But the experience of the high employment of the mid-1960s served to allay such concern and to attribute a major portion of the unemployment of the 1950s to poor public policy.

17. For a detailed argument of this point that takes into account and minimizes the destabilizing role of private investment, see C. A. Blyth, *American Business Cycles, 1945–1950* (New York: Praeger, 1969), especially pp. 19–59.

18. The most significant institutional change in the determination of monetary policy was the freeing of the Federal Reserve System from the support of the market for United States bonds. When another military emergency intervened, with its heightened pressures on the federal budget, and strong inflationary pressures resulted, the system resisted the desire of the Treasury to have nothing but docile cooperation. In the accord of 1951, and in the implementation of that agreement during the next two years, the system gained the acquiescence of the Treasury in its desire to abstain from supporting prices of government securities, and thus facilitating the financing of the Korean War, as objectives of policy. Also, because the system now had more detailed information about changes in the stock of money (having monthly data from 1944), it was more responsive to variations in monetary conditions. As a result of its new independence and a heightened sensitivity to the need for smoothing fluctuations in monetary conditions, the rate of growth of the money supply was unusually stable during the period 1948–1960.

19. Founded in 1942 under the intellectual leadership of Beardsley Ruml (treasurer of Macy's but also formerly a dean at the University of Chicago and close to New Deal economists) with the explicit objective of promoting full employment, the CED became the leading edge of Keynesian analysis within the business community and an important force in converting the nation on account of the representation of some of the largest manufacturers, mercantile houses, and bankers in the leadership of the CED. For an institutional and intellectual history of the organization see Schriftgiesser, *op. cit.*

20. For a stimulating discussion of planning in the United States and western Europe, see Andrew Shonfield, *Modern Capitalism: The Changing Balance of Public and Private Power* (New York: Oxford University Press, 1965). For a survey of planning in the United States since the New Deal that emphasizes the public sector, see Otis L. Graham, Jr., *Toward a Planned Society: From Roosevelt to Nixon* (New York: Oxford University Press, 1976).

21. At the same time, the Nixon administration engineered the imposition of a 10-percent tax on the value of foreign imports. Sustained into December 1971, the tax appeared to have been successful in assisting the administration to compel the Japanese and German governments to increase the value of their currencies in terms of dollars and thus raise the relative dollar price of those nations' exports.

22. A significant step in that direction was the creation in 1969 of Special Drawing Rights (SDR) on the International Monetary Fund. Distributed among nations by agreement, SDR circulate among central banks like cash and are convertible into an IMF member's currency. The objective, sharpened by a rise in the demand for gold as confidence in the dollar waned in the winter of 1967–1968, was to reduce the reliance of the payments system on gold.

SUGGESTED READINGS

Books

Ashworth, William. *A Short History of the International Economy Since 1850.* London: Longmans, Green, 1962.

Benoit, Emile, and Kenneth E. Boulding (eds.). *Disarmament and the Economy.* New York: Harper & Row, 1963.

Chandler, Alfred D., Jr. *Strategy and Structure: Studies in Industrial Enterprise.* Cambridge, Mass.: M.I.T. Press, 1962.

Clayton, James L. (ed.). *The Economic Impact of the Civil War.* New York: Harcourt, Brace and World, 1970.

Friedman, Milton, and Anna J. Schwartz. *A Monetary History of the United States, 1867–1960.* Princeton, N.J.: Princeton University Press, 1963.

Galbraith, John K. *The New Industrial State.* Boston: Houghton Mifflin, 1967.

Heller, Walter W. *New Dimensions of Political Economy.* New York: Norton, 1967.

Kuznets, Simon. *Modern Economic Growth: Rate, Structure, and Spread.* New Haven and London: Yale University Press, 1966.

Lekachman, Robert, *The Age of Keynes.* New York: Random House, 1966.

Lewis, W. Arthur. *Economic Survey, 1919–1939.* London: Allen and Unwin, 1949.

Shonfield, Andrew. *Modern Capitalism: The Changing Balance of Public and Private Power.* New York: Oxford University Press, 1965.

Stein, Herbert. *The Fiscal Revolution in America.* Chicago and London: University of Chicago Press, 1969.

❧ 17
Planning and Problems of Distribution

POVERTY: THE HISTORICAL AND ECONOMIC DIMENSIONS

With the publication of Michael Harrington's *The Other America* (1962) the nation began to rediscover poverty, or the social and economic fact that a substantial portion of the nation's people had an inadequate standard of living—at least by contemporary standards. Because of a favorable set of political circumstances, that kind of exposure has led to a redirection of public policy toward an amelioration of poverty. To evaluate the significance of that redirection and the possibilities for innovation in future policy making it is useful to consider the historical and economic setting of poverty and the policies designed to favor those at the bottom of the economic ladder.

Traditionally, or at least since the beginning of the industrial revolution, the nation has relied almost exclusively on the marketplace to raise levels of living, not only for the average worker but for those who at any particular time might be considered impoverished. The fundamental assumption of public policy has been that continued economic growth, with its relentless augmentation of per-capita incomes, was a sufficient means of ensuring that all members of the economy adequately participate in it and its rewards. If those people toward the lower end of the economic scale could not or were not allowed to improve their *relative* position, they were to receive compensation from larger real incomes and more generous standards of living. In any case, the assumption has been that those who received low incomes were being paid according to their productivity. Rarely have makers of public policy felt any compelling need to intervene by way of redistributing income from richer to poorer. The only exceptional departure was during the Great Depression, when the collapse of the economy provided unusually strong incentives for various groups—primarily organized labor and commercial farmers —to use political instruments to redistribute income and created a political environment tolerant of such deviations from the marketplace.

In fact, economic growth has been the most significant historical force in mitigating the problem of poverty, and the United States has a good long-term record in relying on economic growth to raise general levels of living. Per-capita income has advanced steadily since at least the early decades of the nineteenth century, with only occasional breaks associated with periods of economic slack and high unemployment. Moreover, since 1929 the distribution of income and wealth has improved, and that improvement actually began at the end of the last century as a consequence of the high premiums attached to the attainment of skills and the widening distribution of human capital. Even if the distribution of income had remained unchanged, increasing per-capita incomes would have meant that all income and wealth classes were moving upward at the same time, without the wealthier gaining at the expense of the poorer. Even the long-term trend in the distribution of wealth strongly suggests a high degree of upward economic mobility. Quantitative measures of the concentration of ownership of physical wealth have remained relatively stable in the twentieth century, but one might reasonably have expected them to show sharply increasing concentrations in light of the advantage the wealthy can have in accumulating more wealth. Tax collectors, charities, and improvident families appear to have played a significant role in preventing a growing concentration of physical wealth.[1]

Even since the rise of interest in structural solutions to poverty, economic growth has made significant inroads on poverty. During the 1960s, as a consequence of the rapid rate of per-capita income growth, reinforced by the absence of serious recessions and the slow growth of the labor force (which raised wage levels in the short run), the number of poor people declined substantially. At the end of the 1950s 38.9 million Americans, or slightly more than one-fifth of the population, were poor. But by 1967, less than a decade later, the absolute number of those poor had declined to about 26 million, representing a reduction of the share of the population below the poverty line to slightly more than 10 percent. This estimate of the poor, based on definitions used by the Department of Health, Education, and Welfare, has been more severely criticized for being too high than for underestimating the size of the poverty-stricken population.[2] But whatever the measure of poverty employed, one finds that the process of economic growth can, without a rapid redistribution of income or wealth, move large numbers of people out of poverty in a brief period of time, as the record of the 1960s demonstrates.

The record of the 1970s has been more mixed. The severe recession of 1974–1975, increases in the relative prices of food and fuel (which bore more heavily on lower-income groups), an increase in the rate of labor-force expansion (resulting in part from the post-World War II baby boom), and preoccupation with fighting inflation during the recovery from the recession have offset, to some degree, the poverty-reducing power of economic growth. Consequently, unemployment remained at nearly 7 percent even at the end of 1977 (almost double the rate attained during the 1960s). But that did not imply a reversal in the amelioration of poverty. The unusually high rate of unemployment for a period of strong recovery resulted largely from the rapid growth of the labor force. While the teen-agers and married women who sought work at much higher rates kept wages down and unemployment up, they also tended to bring second and third incomes to families, thereby relieving the pressures of rising prices on family incomes.

An interpretation of the character of current economic opportunity that emphasizes the fairly steady advance of per-capita income, although fundamentally accurate even for the 1970s, fails to describe the situation of a significant sector of the population at the lower reaches of the economic order and, for that reason, fails to elicit appropriate prescriptions of public policy. Most centrally, the present rate of upward economic mobility of people in the poorest one-fifth of the population is not as rapid as we might expect—at least by historical standards—and this aspect of poverty is significant not only for the measure of economic opportunity it suggests but also for the way it reflects the changing character of the labor requirements of the modern industrial economy.

From the standpoint of assessing the character of poverty, the most striking economic change over the course of the last generation has been the declining demand for unskilled labor. The migrants coming to the cities from both the American and the European countryside during the century before World War II were no more skilled than the rural-urban migrants of 1940–1970. If anything, the migrant of the earlier period came with less developed talents and abilities; indeed, a very high proportion of immigrants from southern and eastern Europe were illiterate in all languages. But those earlier waves of rural-urban migrants moved upward not only in terms of per-capita income but also with regard to their relative economic position, more rapidly than the post-World War II generation of such migrants. (This is not to say that the bottom 20 percent of the earlier period improved their relative position any more rapidly than the bottom 20 percent is presently doing. The turnover of the earlier bottom one-fifth was indeed more rapid, given that the average rates of upward mobility and upward exit from the ranks of the poor were higher than is currently the case. But as families and individuals in the bottom one-fifth moved upward, their numbers were more rapidly replaced, chiefly by new European immigrants.) The slower rate of exit is explained by the character of labor needed. Before the Great Depression, people came to the city with capabilities that were assured of great demand because of the formidable appetite for unskilled labor that characterized the continuing industrial revolution. In contemporary America, however, a man or woman with severely limited education and training is apt to be redundant and, more significantly, possesses narrower opportunity for relative improvement in economic position.

The most difficult structural problems connected with the uneven distribution of income are posed by the hard-core unemployed, a cadre of rural-urban migrants and their children who comprise perhaps one-third of the poor and are unemployed virtually continually as a result of their educational deficiencies. From a welfare standpoint, the hard-core unemployed would benefit from being exploited in the sense that wage earners may have been in the period 1890–1914, insofar as their productivity outpaced their wages; being underpaid can be preferable to not being paid at all, to being irrelevant and expendable. One has to be very skeptical of the possibilities that economic growth alone can move this group out of poverty. Furthermore, the finding that the relative income position of the poorest fifth of the population has remained unchanged over the last generation ignores the strong possibility that the gap between those outside the marketplace and the remainder of the population is widening rather than remaining unchanged. Less serious as part of the poverty tangle is the situation of the working poor, those below the poverty line who have full-time employment. In the post-World War II era, urban unemployment would have been enormous in scope without the very rapid growth of the service sector—providing cleaning, cooking, and selling jobs for low-skilled people. Almost all of the working poor—probably about two-thirds of the poor—were employed in this category of low-productivity, low-paying jobs that offered little opportunity for upward economic mobility.

The cultural isolation of the hard-core unemployed and the immobility of the working poor are in large part the legacy of slavery, in terms of both racial barriers to equal opportunity and more than a century of the South's inadequate investment in human capital. Whereas the North, with its bourgeois values, its large, politically influential middle class which valued education as a means to upward mobility, and its economic leadership which believed in the necessity of enlarging the pool of skilled labor, invested heavily in education through taxation, familial contributions, and foregone earnings, southern economic elites, rooted in the traditional plantation economy until the 1930s, had no incentive for investing in people, either white or black, as long as a supply of unskilled, uneducated labor was adequate to their needs.[3] When southern agriculture entered a technological revolution in the 1930s, the migration of unskilled whites and blacks northward began in earnest and reached its most rapid rate with the exaggerated wartime demand for labor. About 1.6 million blacks moved to northern states during the 1940s, followed by 1.5 million during the 1950s and about 900,000 during the 1960s. Yet geographic mobility was not sufficient to move people to jobs of higher productivity; large numbers of people remained in the southern countryside, receiving even less real income than they might have as working poor or near-poor in northern cities. Consequently, most of those below the poverty line live in the countryside, primarily in the South, rather than in the cities. Only about one-quarter of the white poor live in central cities; and although the black poor tend to be more urban, less than half reside in the central cities. In the North, the cities have inherited the problems associated with the underinvestment in people that had been created by southern society.

Despite the predominance of whites among the poor, the burden of poverty and economic disadvantage has been heavier on black people. Whereas in 1967 about 10 percent of white families were impoverished, over one-third of nonwhite families found themselves in that condition. Also, it is likely that within the poverty sector blacks tend to be poorer than whites. Indeed, the elevation of the poverty problem among the nation's priorities in the 1960s was the result of the black civil rights movement, accentuated by a concurrent growth pace of the economy that raised expectations for some, and for others increased the gap between the reality and the ideal. To the extent that black poverty rests on racial discrimination, good public policy must, of necessity, entail not only programs designed to enhance the growth rate of the economy but also the removal of racial barriers to effective economic participation. Quite obviously it will be helpful to have the support of open-housing legislation, effective prohibitions against job discrimination applying to both employers and labor unions, and the provision of equal educational opportunities at all levels.[4] But elimination of discrimination will not suffice to remove the handicaps under which the black poor toil. The problem of underinvestment in people will remain until society generates the resources for programs designed to augment the human capital owned by those below the poverty line. If racial barriers are significant in obstructing escape from poverty, they are so primarily by virtue of being obstacles to the enactment of programs that chiefly benefit racial minorities.

Because of the legacy of underinvestment in human beings, optimal public policy must, in some fashion, go beyond accelerating the pace of growth to redistribute wealth, in the form of human capital, toward people below the poverty line. One approach, gaining support rapidly during the late 1960s and the 1970s, is that of direct supplementation of the incomes of the poor, either by means of a guaranteed annual wage or income, an income-maintenance program, or a negative income tax. Interest in income support emerged in a significant way during the 1950s, when the persistence of high rates of unemployment evoked fears that American society was on the verge of experiencing massive unemployment from structural causes related to automation. Its proponents urged that society seek to break the connection between work and income, arguing that if a civilized society cannot employ everyone, it must find alternative ways to support those outside the marketplace. The resulting proposal in the 1950s and early 1960s was for the provision of guaranteed annual income, or a federal program to raise incomes below the poverty line to a level adequate to provide a decent standard of living.

Although concern with the severity of structural unemployment declined when public policy in the 1960s successfully reduced unemployment to 4 percent and below, the notion of the guaranteed annual income survived, grew stronger as interest in poverty intensified, and increasingly took the form of the negative income tax. Under such a program a broad range of people, extending well above the poverty line, would receive a rebate from the federal government in excess of their taxes paid, with the amount of return becoming progressively larger as one descended in income. Like the guaranteed annual income, this proposal assumes that the obstacles standing between the worker and the private job, such as lack of education and racial discrimination, can be overcome only with great difficulty, making attractive the prospect of lifting people out of poverty swiftly through the direct and simple provision of income support. Unlike the guaranteed annual income, however, the negative income tax offers an incentive for the low-productivity, low-wage worker to continue to work even though he receives a subsidy, since with the subsidy, it would allow a worker whose income fell below the poverty line to advance his total income substantially beyond the poverty level, whereas under the guaranteed annual income, he would attain an income just above the poverty line, regardless of whether he was employed, and could hope for no more than the decent minimum.

Many opponents of the guaranteed annual income and the negative income tax emphasize the costliness of such programs. Certainly, the costs would be substantial, would require redistribution of income, and would thus raise considerable political opposition to the enactment of a generous program. The redistribution of income required might amount to as much as 3 percent of national product (in 1966).[5] However, such a program would be highly effective for the working poor and the near-poor, both of which groups already participate in the economy to a substantial degree and might well be able to advance their relative position as a result of realizing a more adequate standard of living. Such people have a demonstrated commitment to the work ethic and would most probably not be subverted by a large public subsidy. And such a program might produce substantial savings by permitting the reduction of other welfare programs which are less efficient and, in many instances, subsidize people who do not require support. Finally, direct income support could eliminate the need for programs such as rent subsidies, food stamps, and birth-control subsidies, which are designed to meet significant but only partial needs of the poor and are paternalistic and degrading in that they assume that the poor will be unable to spend augmented incomes in the most appropriate fashion. Moreover, a negative income tax would facilitate elimination of locally administered welfare programs, with their debasing attempts to determine the consumption patterns and, more generally, to monitor the life style of the poor, help end the Aid to Dependent Children (ADC) program, with its incentive for fathers to flee their families in order to qualify them for support, and possibly bring about the phasing out of the nation's system of unemployment insurance, with its programs of regressive taxation and its exclusion of significant portions of the labor force.

The objections to negative income taxation as a cure-all for poverty stem from the possibility that the program might well fail to provide the means for those outside the marketplace to participate in the economy effectively. Merely providing money to those at the very bottom of the distributional scale—those perhaps trapped by what Michael Harrington calls a "culture of poverty"—might still leave them without health, education, social competence, or jobs and, at the same time, little income. Moreover, their children might well find themselves locked into the same narrow cycle of life.

The most significant alternative supplementary approach to income maintenance is a continuation of a very traditional approach to poverty: public support of education, with particular attention to those with the most limited resources. As dramatically as taxation programs, educational programs offer the opportunity to redistribute wealth. The most important source of wealth for the advancement of the average person, and probably for the economy as a whole, is human capital; indeed, the maldistribution of human capital is at the very heart of the current poverty problem.[6] By taxing middle-class incomes at a higher rate (perhaps requiring reform of the manner in which schools are financed, including substitution of taxation of income for property taxation), or by forcing middle-class families to bear a higher percentage of the costs of their education (by, for example, increasing tuition at state universities serving largely middle-class students), or by shifting budgetary priorities at the federal level to free resources now committed to national defense and related programs, American society could redistribute income by enhancing educational investment designed to release people from a poverty culture and to give people of limited productivity a greater degree of leverage over their economic participation in society. The question of what sorts of education programs are and will be appropriate to both the needs of the economy at large and those of the poor can best be determined within a process of experimentation over an extended period of time. In that sense the great variety of programs enacted during the 1960s were extremely productive. The Manpower Development and Training Program, Community Action programs, Job Corps, Neighborhood Youth Corps, Head Start programs, Area Redevelopment Training, Operation Mainstream, Work Experience Program, Indian Manpower Activities, New Careers, Veterans On-the-Job Training, Opportunities Industrialization Centers, and the Educational Opportunity Program all provided experience useful to future efforts to redirect education, and some programs, especially Head Start and EOP, significantly widened the availability of educational services, bringing not only a substantial private return to the recipients but a respectable return to society as well. On the whole, however, the wide assortment of programs appeared to the American public to be overly costly, especially because of the element of income redistribution but also because of the minimal short-run returns of most of the programs and because of the manner in which the programs seemed to become embroiled in contests for political power in the nation's cities. Given the tendency of the Kennedy and Johnson administrations to place substantial responsibility for education programs in the hands of the poor themselves, these expenditures tended to create a base of power within the cities that challenged traditional political structures and power distribu-

HEAD START CLASSROOM, 1966. This program, which has survived into the 1970s, recognizes the importance of early childhood education to later success in school.

tion. While the challenges were successful in numerous cities, they created a severe backlash in other cities and in the nation at large. Thus, for future success, proponents of such programs will have to deal more effectively with the political problems associated with controlling them, either by maintaining the power of existing political elites over new programs or by winning significant support among middle- and upper-class Americans for altering the distribution of political power to favor the poor.

Whether the approach adopted by government is income maintenance in some form, expanded educational services, or a combination of both, it will be a movement away from traditional welfare programs. The major alternative to the innovations mentioned so far would be one inherited from the New Deal: guaranteed employment. In other words, the government would guarantee work, and thus some kind of an income, to the poor, thereby allaying the fear of many that a guaranteed annual income or even the negative income tax might be exploited by those unwilling to work. At the same time, it is argued, such employment might be directed toward valuable social ends, such as cleaning up the countryside or revamping the physical structure of the modern city under a contemporary, urban version of the New Deal's Civilian Conservation Corps, which provided both employment for young people and the means for significant improvement of the countryside. The difficulty with such an approach is that the employment provided would be only glorified, low-paying service jobs and would offer an even more limited future to those reached than would the guaranteed annual income. At least under the latter program an individual would have time available to upgrade his own training or education. To be sure, the existing Social Security system could be maintained with effectiveness, especially for the sustenance of the aged, perhaps for relief of those who suffer from temporary unemployment, and possibly for the provision of comprehensive health insurance. But one should see Social Security mainly as a patchwork effort to provide for emergencies rather than for the poor, particularly the hard-core unemployed, and as a program that currently either ignores or makes more difficult the situation of those in the most severe need.

POVERTY: OBSTACLES TO STRUCTURAL CHANGE

The record of post-World War II reform should not make one optimistic about the likelihood of new departures in undertaking redistributional policies. Since the New Deal, structural reform in the spirit of Social Security, minimum wage, and the expansion of income taxation has been minimal. As indicated by the character of its expenditures, public policy since the New Deal, particularly at the federal level, has *not* been designed, in any significant way, to redistribute income or to cope with the social problems attendant upon the inability of a large share of the population to participate in the marketplace. It is true that the size of the federal government, as measured by dollars of expenditure, has increased since the 1930s, but most of the increase resulted from large spending on weapons and armies: there was no significant increase in federal transfer payments (Social Security and veterans benefits) in comparison with national product. In 1939 transfer payments amounted to about 4 percent of gross national product but barely expanded during the next two decades, reaching only 4.4 percent in 1960. In fact, transfer payments and federal civilian expenditures, taken together in comparison with national product, declined—from 7.4 percent in 1939 to only 6 percent in 1960. In effect, any momentum toward the attainment of the welfare state gained during the New Deal largely disappeared during the 1940s and 1950s. During the Kennedy and Johnson administrations a movement to elaborate the welfare state revived. Federal expenditures on training of all sorts, for example, grew from about $65 million in 1963 to over $1.5 billion in 1969. By 1969, transfer payments, rapidly enlarged by the enactment of the Medicare program, had increased to 6.6 percent of national product, and the ratio between all federal civilian expenditures (including transfer payments) had increased to 9.1 percent. Still, the War on Poverty, including the traditional Social Security programs, never amounted to more than 2 percent of national product. Furthermore, during the 1960s, social-overhead expenditures, including those for education and highways, were carried increasingly by state and local governments, heightening the pressure on the state and local tax base which, by and large, did not include incomes, given the inability of state and local governments to use income taxation as extensively as did the federal government.[7] Growing tax demands on property owners stoked potent hostility to increased educational expenditures, and the more frequent resort to state sales taxes lent an increasingly regressive cast to the nation's tax system. Thus even in the 1960s, movement toward an expanded governmental response to domestic needs faced serious limitations. By the end of the 1960s any movement toward a larger and more effective welfare state met further barriers in the economic demands created by the commitment to prosecute the war in Indochina. In particular, the Nixon administration, supported politically by the impact of the economic distortions created by that war, sought to restrict growth of federal social services. Since the New Deal, then, the nation has rarely departed from the diversion of only a limited share of national resources to social problems. Most fundamentally, the nation continually chose to adhere to the notion that the marketplace was a sufficient determinant of the most socially useful investment.

Failure to mobilize a larger share of resources to alleviate poverty has been the most regrettable humanitarian shortcoming of post-World War II America, one that rests on a wide array of social facts. Of those with an economic content, perhaps the most prominent has been the slowness of the progress that the nation's planners have made toward the stabilization of the economy at near full employment and price regularity. (It is no coincidence that the only period of significant change in the orientation of national policy came in the mid-1960s, when for the first time since World War II, planners had contributed to the emergence of a promising period of price stability and near full employment.) But other obstacles to structural reform were present as well, most massively, the claims of national defense on the nation's resources and the limitation of the condition of poverty to a rather small, politically weak sector of the nation's population.

A basic prerequisite for the solution of all problems of economic structure, including those of poverty, is the guarantee of national security. But acknowledging the importance of national security and the defense spending required to provide it does not advance one very far toward evaluating the precise contribution of specific levels of spending to the attainment of security. Such a determination obviously lies beyond the ambit of marketplace analysis. However, a strong skepticism about the benefits of massive defense spending in terms of protection is in order in light of both the enormous vested interest that many individuals, institutions, groups, and localities have developed in defense industries and of the concomitant reluctance of those economic factors to fall back on the rigors of the competitive marketplace. The strength of political support for the continuation of defense programs, independent of the benefits provided for national security and at the expense of education and health programs, is, therefore, rather easy to visualize.

In calculating the costs of the defense sector one must consider the opportunity cost of *not* meeting other social priorities, including those posed by the problems of poverty. Even a modest reallocation of the vast resources taken up by the defense enterprise (as much as three-quarters of the federal budget during the 1960s) would significantly enlarge the investment made by society in human capital. And, it is more than likely that the multiplier effect of such spending would be higher than that of investment in the research, development, and delivery of weaponry and defense services.

The final obstacle to structural reform is the uneven distribution of income and wealth (including human capital). The distribution of power is likewise unequal, and although the degree of conformity of political with economic power remains unknown, it is clear that both economic and political elites contribute most heavily to the decision-making process. That characteristic seems to be true of all modern industrial societies, including those of western Europe, the Soviet Union, and Japan. And even with a large degree of democratic political participation, as in the United States, there are significant obstacles to a greater redistribution of income and wealth through political instruments. Specifically, poverty programs directly benefit only a politically small and weak minority—no more than one-fifth of the total population. In contrast, the New Deal succeeded in devising programs to redistribute income on behalf of farmers and labor because those groups comprised large sectors of the population with a strong potential for wielding political power. To be optimistic about the future of income redistribution in the United States one has to be confident either that the marketplace, with its emphasis on the social returns from education, will continue to work a gradual but significant redistribution, extending finally to those of the bottom fifth, or that those in the wealthiest four-fifths will see it as being in their self-interest, perhaps from a purely moral standpoint or, more likely, in the interests of social order, to encourage that redistribution through political mechanisms.

RELATIONS WITH THE LESS DEVELOPED WORLD: AN IRONIC VIEW

Since World War II many nations have joined the older industrial powers in attaining significant economic growth, in discovering how to increase per-capita income steadily. But many others have failed in this same endeavor. It has been charged that the advanced nations, through the exercise of monopoly power, are responsible for those failures and now bear a responsibility to redistribute wealth to favor the less developed nations.

Monopolistic abuses certainly appear in the history of relations between the developed and the less developed worlds. But their relative importance remains as yet unmeasured. And most recently, led by the Organization of Petroleum Exporting Countries (OPEC), many less developed countries that have the ability to exercise a high degree of control over supplies of raw materials have shown a growing interest in and a willingness to use their monopsony power in setting prices. Moreover, many nations that have found paths of sustained growth have done so by relying heavily on income earned from the export of raw materials, food, and simple manufactures. And the problems of developing nations include a wide array of internal obstacles to growth—ones that have little to do with foreign exploitation.

The United States, however, has contributed to the problems of the developing nations. But the means have been quite different than the exercise of monopoly power. More important than exploitation has been the preoccupation of the United States with the expansion of trade and investment with the nations of the developed world. While U.S. involvement in Europe and the other developed nations has grown, its relative interest in trade and investment in the less developed world has diminished sharply. Behind this eclipse lies not only the great benefits the developed nations have reaped from

TABLE 30   DOMESTIC CONSUMPTION OF RESOURCE PRODUCTS AS PERCENTAGE OF DOMESTIC PRODUCTION

	All	Agricultural Products	Fishery and Wildlife	Forest Products	Minerals Total	Metallic Ores	Mineral Fuels	Other Minerals
1900	91%	88%	116%	98%	98%	101%	94%	115%
1920	98	97	132	101	101	116	97	106
1940	105	105	157	104	103	139	97	103
1950	105	101	164	110	112	174	104	104

Source: U.S. Bureau of the Census, *Statistical Abstract of the United States: 1956* (Washington, D.C.: U.S. Government Printing Office, 1956), Table 906, p. 731.

mutual trade and investment but also the continuing ability of the American environment to provide the nation with resource products (agricultural products, fish, forest products, and minerals), although it is true that during the twentieth century the nation moved from a net exporter to a net importer of resource products and that American dependency on a few resource imports grew dramatically during the same period. In particular, domestic consumption of fish, certain metallic ores, and crude petroleum grew far more rapidly than domestic production. (See Table 30.) For example, by 1950 net imports of metallic ores equaled almost three-quarters of the production of the nation's mines, whereas net imports of metallic ores had been virtually nonexistent in 1900. However, for resource production in general, American dependency is rather slight and the trend toward that dependency has been modest, reaching a peak before World War II. As late as 1950, domestic consumption exceeded domestic production of resource products by less than 5 percent. Further, even with the growing importance of foreign oil production, domestic consumption of all mineral fuels was only 4 percent greater than domestic production. In addition to enjoying an abundance of domestic raw materials, producers of finished products have used their imports with increasing efficiency (including the recycling of tin, lead, and copper) and have relied to a growing extent on synthetic products as replacements for crude materials.

As a result of the expansiveness of the domestic primary sector and the efficiency of manufacturers, United States imports of resource commodities have lagged far behind the growth of the economy. Moreover, consumption of raw materials, both imported and domestic, has risen much more slowly than national product. Since 1900 national product has increased about one and a half times as rapidly as total raw-material consumption, and manufacturing production has grown more than three times as rapidly.[8] Further, as a reversal of the nineteenth-century trend, finished goods have come to occupy an increasingly large portion of the nation's imports: over two-thirds of current imports are manufactured or semimanufactured articles. At the same time close to three-quarters of imports come from Canada, western Europe, Australia, and Japan.[9] Despite the buoyancy of such imports of finished articles, the ratio of imports to national product (in real terms) has failed to increase since the late nineteenth century as a result of the low demand for foreign raw materials.[10]

For underdeveloped nations the very sluggish pace of increase in demand for raw-material and food imports by the United States and other more industrial nations has contributed to low prices and earnings for their commodities. However, the range of performance has been wide, with those nations specializing in food production often facing stiff competition from highly efficient agriculture in the advanced nations and thus faring the worst, and those nations blessed with ample ore deposits and oil resources experiencing greater success with their exports than food-producing nations. One escape from weak markets for many agricultural nations is to develop a capacity to manufacture for export simple finished goods that require a high input of labor, such as cheap textiles. (Hong Kong, Taiwan, India, and Pakistan have had some success in such a venture.) But while the American, European, and Japanese economies are tending to specialize in the production of capital goods, electronics, chemicals, and other goods (and services) requiring a large component of human capital, the political strength of the older industries in the developed nations, such as that of the American textile industry, has successfully restricted imports of low-cost competitors. Consequently, these industries have reduced the attractiveness of specialization in simple finished goods by the less developed world.

The lukewarm trading interest in the less developed economies has contributed as well to a lack of enthusiasm for the export of American capital to these economies. Although export of private, long-term capital to the underdeveloped nations has increased since Bretton Woods, it has grown much less rapidly than the export of private capital to western Europe. In the nineteenth century, exports of long-term capital from the advanced nations went largely to the developing nations. In 1913, for example, some two-thirds of British investment abroad was in the primary producing regions of the Western Hemisphere and Australia. But currently only about one-quarter of long-term capital exports from the industrial nations goes to the underdeveloped countries, and the bulk of this extends to the richest of the developing nations, especially the oil producers. Africa and Southeast Asia, for instance, together have received scarcely more than 25 percent of such exports. American investments abroad have conformed to the general pattern. Since World War II, American investment in the advanced nations has grown rapidly. By the mid-1960s almost two-thirds of American-owned assets abroad were located in Europe and Canada. Of the remaining third, fully half were invested in the petroleum sector. Trade and investment are joined today, as they were in the nineteenth century, but they now tend to bind the developed nations rather than providing powerful linkages for the export of economic growth to the less developed nations.

In general the scarcity of private capital has been reinforced by a lack of public interest in providing long-term capital to the developing nations. However, as the accomplishments of the Marshall Plan became clear in the early 1950s, they briefly generated enthusiasm for exporting the plan to the rest of the world. During 1954–1957 there ensued a rapid expansion of public development grants and "soft" loans (uncompetitive loans which extended over longer time periods, carried lower interest charges, and provided for more-liberal repayment terms than those available privately). In addition, the International Bank for Reconstruction and Development (the World Bank) gave shape to the desire to enhance capital exports by providing a vehicle for American public capital. Funded by member contributions and bond sales (both largely American), the World Bank extended loans to developing nations, largely for construction of power and transport systems. However, the urge to export public capital was impulsive and hardly a reasoned response to the development problem. In particular, exporters of public capital discovered in their experiences with developing nations as culturally disparate as Brazil and India that capital alone did not turn preindustrial economies into modern, competitive economies. And if policy makers believed that dramatic structural reform of developing economies was necessary to obtain modernity, they were unwilling to act on that assumption by encouraging the redistribution of political and economic power. Even at the peak of interest in exporting public capital in the mid–1950s, the guiding principles of American policy were to keep capital exports small, to keep them under American control, and to avoid offending private investors, whose interests were often closely tied to economic and social status quo. For its part, the World Bank has always operated in a very cautious fashion, selecting only good risks, making modest loans, and requiring a high level of repayment of principal.

Faced with significant obstacles to real growth in the underdeveloped world, the lack of American interest in social reconstruction in foreign lands, and the waning concern with the less developed nations, American enthusiasm for public participation in economic development of disadvantaged countries virtually vanished after the mid–1950s. Public grants were essentially abandoned, soft loans fell into disfavor, and little sustained support emerged for President Kennedy's reform and capital-export program for Latin America, the Alliance for Progress. Currently, public assistance to the low-income countries comes to less than 0.5 percent of national product, about one-fifth of the resources devoted to the war in Indochina at its peak and less than one-fourth of the share of national product extended to western Europe at the height of the Marshall Plan. For the entire post-World War II period, and especially since the mid-1950s, the vast bulk of aid to underdeveloped nations has been for military rather than developmental purposes. One can accept that choice with equanimity only if one believes that external threats to international stability in the less developed nations were sufficiently severe to inhibit development and that such military aid has not precluded economic modernization and improvements in levels of living by reinforcing the grip of tradition-bound leadership.

Given that American public interest in the less developed nations since World War II has been far more political than economic in character, the fundamental source of public policy has been the competitive impulses motivating the United States and the Soviet Union—even though the policy direction taken has frequently supported the interests of certain corporations, chiefly the firms engaged in extractive enterprise, such as the petroleum companies. Certainly, it is ironic that at the same time that the more advanced nations have grown less interested in the economies of the underdeveloped world, their political and military involvement and competition in the colonial areas of the world have become much more intense; and that competition has had only marginal economic benefits for either the underdeveloped or the metropolitan nations. The best microcosm of that ironic situation has been the war in Indochina.

For economic development to occur among the majority of the world's societies, a significant reorientation of policy will be necessary, both in the developed and developing nations. In particular, a delicate balance of cooperation will be necessary. From the standpoint of the less developed nations, the problem is one of restructuring their own societies and also of interesting the advanced nations in their development, although ultimately many may have to band together in their own partially restricted development areas if they wish to emulate the wealthier nations. In general, without the trade, capital, and knowledge of the advanced nations, significant economic advance is, at best, exceedingly difficult. At the same time, the challenge for the advanced nations is not only to invoke policies that encourage development (such as removing trade barriers to cheap manufactures) but also to cope realistically with reform and revolution in the less developed world. The degree of social reconstruction necessary is variable and uncertain, but, without doubt, if the advanced nations are to develop a sustained interest in the underdeveloped nations, they must accept the fact that the transition will be highly costly and frustrating to the developed nations and may well require a larger, more enlightened participation of government in the development process. The obstacles to accommodation within the advanced nations are twofold: concentration on profit maximization has led to a diminished interest in the underdeveloped world in general and social reform in particular, and the attainment of an effective public policy on behalf of development, including a reasoned program of capital exports, is handicapped by the possibility that the public, on account of a narrow determination of short-run economic interest, will fail to see such policies as beneficial to national welfare. The metropolitan nations must come to view the short-run costs of an effective development policy as justified by the long-term benefits of world economic (and political) stability.[11]

NOTES

1. For an exploration of this point, see Stanley Lebergott, "Are the Rich Getting Richer? Trends in U.S. Wealth Concentration," *Journal of Economic History*, 36 (March 1976), 147–162.

2. If anything, the HEW definition of poverty, relying on annual income, tends to exaggerate the number of poor. For one thing, it does not take into account the size of *expected lifetime* incomes as well as *current* incomes. For another, the estimate fails to take into account wealth holdings, counting as poor many retired individuals whose incomes are low but whose assets are fairly substantial.

3. One result of the South's underinvestment in people, regardless of race, is a body of white poor larger than that of impoverished blacks. Relative to total population of each group, more blacks were poor in 1967, but there were more than twice as many poor whites as poor blacks. Even in the central cities, there were about 20 percent more poor whites than poor blacks.

4. It should be noted that with the very strong demand for skilled labor, the increased supply of such labor that would result from the elimination of racial barriers would not result in a significant lowering of wage rates. The financing of almost all of the higher wages paid to nonwhites in more highly productive jobs would come, not from the wages of skilled whites, but from the resulting addition to national product.

5. James Tobin *et al.*, "Is a Negative Income Tax Practical?" *Yale Law Journal*, 77 (November 1967), 1–27.

6. It is arguable that as educational opportunity is made more equally available to all, and as education continues to be more highly prized in society, the distribution of income will move toward the distribution of competitive economic abilities, which is most certainly closer to that of a normal bell-shaped curve.

7. The problem evoked proposals such as the Heller plan, which was designed to assist state and local governments, particularly those in urban areas, in meeting social-overhead expenses, providing for the sharing of federal income-tax revenues and the adoption of a federal value-added tax to aid local school finance. Revenue sharing was enacted in 1972, and its performance since 1973 has suggested promise for easing pressure on the instruments of property taxation, providing additional revenues for areas and people in greatest need, and even encouraging local and state initiatives in social planning. But fears of either reducing the efforts of state and local governments or losing control over federal revenues to more-conservative state governments appear to limit the program's future.

8. Ragnar Nurske, "Patterns of Trade and Development," in *International Trade and Finance: A Collected Volume of Wicksell Lectures, 1958–1964* (Stockholm: Almquist and Wiksell, 1965), pp. 58–60.

9. The pattern of the nation's exports is much the same: Canada takes about one-quarter, western Europe approximately one-third, and Japan about one-tenth of United States exports. For current data, see Department of Commerce, *Survey of Current Business* (Washington, D.C.: U.S. Government Printing Office, monthly).

10. Robert E. Lipsey, *Price and Quantity Trends in the Foreign Trade of the United States* (Princeton, N.J.: Princeton University Press, 1963), p. 44.

11. It is a heroic though plausible assumption that the problems of the long-run costs of world environmental degradation, not to mention the higher resource prices, that will inevitably result from the spread of economic growth will be more easily solved in a world atmosphere of greater economic stability. For discussion of economic growth and the environmental issues, see pp. 498–513 in this book.

SUGGESTED READINGS

Books

Gordon, Kermit (ed.). *Agenda for the Nation.* Garden City, N.Y.: Doubleday, 1968.

Harrington, Michael. *The Other America*, New York: Macmillan, 1962.

Maizels, Alfred. *Industrial Growth and World Trade.* Cambridge, Eng.: Cambridge University Press, 1963.

Mansfield, Edwin. *The Economics of Technological Change.* New York: Norton, 1968.

Miller, Herman P. (ed.). *Poverty, American Style.* Belmont, Calif.: Wadsworth, 1966.

Moynihan, Daniel P. *Maximum Feasible Misunderstanding.* New York: Free Press, 1969.

Report of the National Advisory Commission on Civil Disorders. Washington, D.C.: U.S. Government Printing Office, 1968.

Theobald, Robert. *Free Men and Free Markets.* Garden City, N.J.: Doubleday, 1965.

U.S. Department of Labor and U.S. Department of Commerce. *Social and Economic Condition of Negroes in the United States.* Washington, D.C.: U.S. Government Printing Office, 1967.

Ward, Barbara, *et al.* (eds.). *The Widening Gap: Development in the 1970s.* New York: Columbia University Press, 1971.

✸ 18
Planning and the Environment

During the 1960s a significant portion of the American public came to realize that the process of economic growth had not only failed to eradicate poverty but had, to a perilous extent, depleted and degraded the earth's natural resources. That realization arose from a wider concern, phrased most aptly by John Kenneth Galbraith in *The Affluent Society* (1958), that per-capita national product provided an inadequate measure of the quality of life in a mature industrial nation. Galbraith focused on what he considered to be the low quality of much of the market basket of private goods and services and the meager quantity of public goods. A similar critique developed of society's treatment of its physical environment. Accordingly, it was asserted that the marketplace failed to reckon the environmental costs of an increasing national product and that because of the American cultural fixation on the primacy of the marketplace, governmental action had not been forthcoming on a scale sufficient to take account of such costs and move economic development onto a less costly path, for this and future generations. More critical than Galbraith's book was *The Limits of Growth,* published by the Club of Rome in 1972, which persuaded many of the truth of this argument and of the urgency of the problem. The book predicted the collapse of modern society by the mid–twenty-first century unless the growth of population, depletion of resources, and pollution were not strictly controlled. The specific predictions have been heavily criticized as unsubstantial guesswork based on unrealistic, unduly pessimistic assumptions. But the book, combined with the visible damage of pollution and the rising costs of energy and raw materials

498

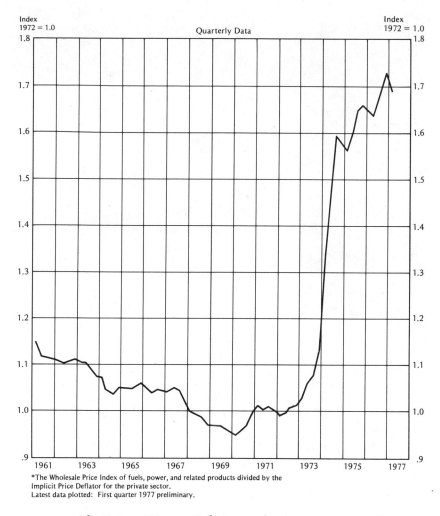

Index
1972 = 1.0

Quarterly Data

Index
1972 = 1.0

*The Wholesale Price Index of fuels, power, and related products divided by the
Implicit Price Deflator for the private sector.
Latest data plotted: First quarter 1977 preliminary.

FIGURE 19: *The Price of Energy Relative to the Price of Output**

(see Figure 19), markedly sharpened the public's sense of "crisis."[1]

This chapter surveys the tentative knowledge that we have of the
extent of environmental costs of economic growth and the prospects
for appropriate reckoning of those costs.

POPULATION TRENDS

No one can question that the quantity of resources on the earth is
finite, that degradation of resources by pollution has increased
dramatically since World War II, or the attendant possibility that the

CARS LINED UP FOR SCARCE GASOLINE, FEBRUARY 1974. The gasoline shortage in the winter of 1973–1974 gave many Americans their first sense of an "energy crisis."

optimal size for the earth's population may be close to what it is currently. Nevertheless, scientists have not been able to make firm estimates of the degree of pressure on the world's physical resources and the seriousness of pollution. Consequently, they have not been able to calculate the earth's optimal population. Nonetheless, the central part of any public policy designed to reduce the pressure on the environment, including retarding the depletion of finite resources, has to be one promising to discourage or restrict the size of the population, both in the advanced nations and in the remainder of the world. In the United States, the Soviet Union, Japan, and western Europe such a policy would offset the high per-capita demands for fuel, food, and mineral resources, and, in the less developed nations, it would enable societies to provide a larger measure of income to their people beyond that necessary for mere survival. In fact, viewing economic growth only in terms of per-capita product implies that a nation can enjoy the fruits of economic growth while having a population that remains constant or even declines in size. A nation, therefore, can have rapid, real economic growth even with a sharply reduced rate of growth of gross national product, if it manages to retard sufficiently its rate of population growth. Although the choice of optimal birth-control policy lies beyond the competency of economics, economists can offer advice on the relative efficacy of various measures, such as tax incentives for family limitation, a system of negotiable licenses for children beyond a family's first or second, or subsidies for research into and distribution of birth-control devices, medication, and operations. Ethical-normative considerations concerning the proper degree of public intervention in family-planning decisions will obviously weigh heavily in the ultimate choice of policy. Effective population control can also lie outside the realm of public policy. The extent to which this is so depends on people's willingness and ability to plan their families in light of the environmental factors affecting their economic welfare.

It has been suggested that the increase in marital fertility that followed World War II in the United States casts doubt on the reliability of voluntary population adjustments for limiting population. Certainly the "baby boom" was large and was a marked departure from a long-standing trend. During the 1930s, the rate of population growth resulting from the birth rate had reached an all-time low—less than 2 percent per year—but throughout the period 1945–1960 it hovered close to 2.5 percent per year. This high rate, joined with a moderate decline in the death rate and a small increase in the rate of net migration, produced a sharp increase in the rate at which the population grew. During the 1930s, the rate of population increase had fallen to about 0.7 percent per year, but by the 1950s the rate had more than doubled—to about 1.7 percent per year, or close to the rates of increase typical of the early decades of the century. Thus, it appeared that the long-term decline in rates of fertility and population increase might have come to an end.

Despite the rather prolonged nature of the baby boom, predictions of sustained fertility increases proved erroneous. Toward the end of the 1950s, marital fertility rates once again began to decline, and by the late 1960s they had fallen once again to the levels reached during the Great Depression. Moreover, research into the causes of the baby boom revealed influential factors that were only temporary in their impact. Most telling among the economic circumstances that produced the boom was the sequence of unusually high postwar prosperity following an unusually protracted period of relative economic scarcity. The Great Depression had begun in 1929, and although recovery had resumed during the 1930s it was not until 1946, when reconversion to peacetime began, that consumers could make optimum use of their increasing incomes. This had the simple effect of prompting families to believe that they could afford to enlarge their families or, in the case of young couples, to have more children than their parents had. The depression had rendered temporarily ineffective the tendency of one generation to treat the luxuries of its predecessor as necessities, to increase its consumption accordingly, and, consequently, to restrict family size. And large accumulations of cash enabled families not only to consume houses, cars, refrigerators, and televisions in larger quantities but also to raise more children. Reinforcing economic conditions was the surging impulse of "togetherness," a cultural mood that turned families away from the crises of depression, war, and atomic diplomacy to family satisfactions, particularly those obtained from consumption goods. Thus, the fertility increases of the 1940s and 1950s were products of the very unusual conditions created by twentieth-century crises and should not be used as evidence demonstrating the unreliability of voluntary population control.

More revealing of the long-term consequences of using voluntarism as an instrument of population policy is the sharp decline in birth rates in the United States that began in the 1960s and continued into the 1970s. The decline must be regarded as a hopeful sign. It suggests that limitation of the population's size may be accomplished without resort to coercive planning measures. The decline in fertility appears to have been the same kind of individualistic adjustment to economic processes that characterized the nineteenth-century fertility decline. Perhaps most powerful in encouraging the decline was the continuing desire of parents to produce children who would have more opportunity than they had enjoyed. As the children of the baby boom came of age, finished their schooling, and entered the labor market, they, and parents who were just forming families, came to recognize that the parents who had created the baby boom had erred in believing that their children would enjoy the same relative degree of economic opportunity that they had experienced. The baby boom had crowded young people into education and the labor market during the 1960s and 1970s. Despite the buoyancy of the economy and its overall success in providing educational opportunities and jobs, young people as a whole faced frustration in seeking chances for upward economic mobility that were as attractive as those their parents found in the 1940s and 1950s. This disjuncture of opportunity no doubt accentuated the "generation gap" and the intergenerational conflict, which became especially acute during the late 1960s and early 1970s.

Other factors as well contributed to the decline in birth rates. One was the decreasing cost of effective birth-control technology—particularly the "pill." Another was the dramatic increase in the rate at which women participated in the economy. The increase was especially significant for young married women who postponed having children or abstained from having additional children. A third was the environmental "crisis" itself, which was, to some extent, the product of the baby boom. The dramatic upsurge of population after World War II and the associated acceleration of suburbanization contributed to highly visible increases in pollution and conversion of land from agricultural uses to housing developments, shopping centers, industrial facilities, and highways. To some extent, perceptions that high rates of population growth not only threatened to limit job opportunities but also endangered environmental quality contributed to the decisions of young couples to limit family size. All of these factors joined to produce a birth rate that, if sustained and not offset by immigration, would in time, after the number of women of child-bearing age declined, result in a *declining* population.

Optimism created by birth-rate trends must be guarded, especially in light of recent immigration trends. Rates of immigration, particularly illegal immigration, increased during the 1970s, especially during the strong recovery from the recession of 1974–1975. This immigration was heavily from the West Indies, particularly Puerto Rico, and from Mexico. The Mexican economy, although having enjoyed substantial long-term gains in per-capita income since World War II, experienced a severe financial crisis in 1976, which produced unemployment rates in excess of 25 percent and a large population eager to take advantage of opportunities in the boom

LONG ISLAND, NEW YORK, 1950s. Using mass production techniques, New York builders turned potato fields into densely populated housing developments.

economy of the "sun belt" states. The close proximity of depressed areas in Mexico to metropolitan areas in the United States (especially Los Angeles and San Diego), the lack of a welfare program for the unemployed in Mexico, and the virtual impossibility of effectively enforcing immigration restrictions produced a rate of immigration that, although unmeasurable because of its illegality, appeared unprecedented, at least for the recipient American cities. However, it was reasonable to assume that this immigration would subside once the forces of long-term economic growth resumed their hold on the Mexican economy, creating new job opportunities and inducing families to restrict their size.

In sum, the history of fertility trends, including those in the United States since World War II, indicates that increasing per-capita income remains a potent method of reducing fertility and, consequently, of moderating, and even eliminating, population increases voluntarily. Even fertility in developing nations demonstrates that point. During the early 1970s, the growth rate of the world's population finally began to decline, reflecting more the impact of economic development on attitudes toward fertility than the efficacy of organized family planning. Indeed, promoting gains in per-capita income may well be the only certain means of engineering controlled fertility. The historical record suggests that those who would invoke governmental instruments in order to protect the environment should proceed cautiously. Solutions that would disregard the power of economic growth to limit population expansion might well prove ineffective or counterproductive.

RESOURCE DEPLETION

The economic history of the United States, especially during the twentieth century, offers a basis for some optimism in planning for the avoidance of a confrontation between economic growth and finite resources. American economic growth has always relied heavily on the more efficient use of resources, including "land" (embracing all resources for food, fuel, and fabrication). Especially during the twentieth century, the economy has reduced its reliance on the exploitation of larger per-capita amounts of natural resources. With the exception of the period of World War II and its aftermath, the trend during this century has been for the value of raw materials consumed per capita to *decline* in the United States. The average American consumes a lower value of raw materials than he or she did at the beginning of the century; the larger value of national product enjoyed by that average member of the economy has grown because of the growing ability to combine and process raw materials with larger inputs of labor and capital, including capitalized knowledge, relative to the value of raw materials.[2] The question of whether or not technological and organizational progress that permits a more efficient use of natural resources will continue is, of course, moot. Some consider that kind of adaptation to the reality of scarce and finite resources as providing no long-run solution; they see it, rather, as merely a quest for a "technological fix." Although this view is doubtless correct in foreseeing a potential ultimate clash between resources and growth, it may tend to ignore the historical experience of growth based on efficiency rather than on exploitation and thus underrate the medium-term possibilities for continued success in technological-organizational adaptation. In the medium term it may well be reasonable to predict technological change permitting, for example, the feasibility of continuing increases in food yields of lands without the use of pesticides in the developed regions, a markedly enlarged use of the food-producing capacity of the coastal-shelf waters of the oceans, the development of new energy sources, particularly through atomic fusion and solar energy, and not only the more efficient utilization of untapped or lower-grade mineral resources but also virtually complete recycling of waste materials. For the long term it is arguable that we could sustain a population of constant size

SOLAR HEATED HOME, CORRALES, NEW MEXICO. During the 1970s many homes, even ones that were conventionally designed, found solar power to be a feasible source of energy.

(perhaps not much larger than that currently in existence, however) which fed itself adequately for an indefinite period, consumed constant or increasing per-capita levels of energy indefinitely, made use, with only negligible losses, of the existing supply of nonreproducible resources, and, at the same time, continued to enjoy economic growth because it performed tasks more efficiently (e.g., by transporting itself with smaller cars or with a radically different system or by communicating with a minimum of transportation, reserving travel for the purpose of recreation or exercise).

If the feasibility of continued technological-organizational adaptation to continued growth is reasonably clear, assuming sufficient population control, the likelihood is far more subject to uncertainty. Nonetheless, we can reasonably conjecture that the marketplace itself will be a powerful force toward such adaptation as the costs of depleted resources rise (especially as less developed nations continue to seek economic growth) and induce cost-saving innovations that promote the use of less scarce resources or the more efficient utilization of more expensive resources. Reinforcing the marketplace, public policy in the developed nations, informed by more-accurate assessments of future resource availabilities, can provide investment in appropriate research-and-development projects with a rate of return insufficient to have justified private investment. And with a significant portion of the nation's resources now committed to national defense, the nation could undertake more than an adequate beginning in a new environmental-engineering effort. Because environmental pressures can affect, in a very direct fashion, the entire population, the prospects for the development of programs for governmental action appear more likely than in the solution of the problem of poverty.

Formulation of policies to deal with the pressures of population upon resources will undoubtedly be complicated by some severe political obstacles, especially in the less developed nations. Planning in western Europe faces the problem of a high dispersion of political power. Soviet planners, with their more abundant supplies of unexploited resources, will probably be slower to plan for greater efficiency. Similarly, Japan may well look forward to heavy reliance on untapped Asian resources—land no less than labor. Meanwhile the developing nations, in their effort to catch up with the pace-setting nations, are likely to have enormous difficulty curbing both their populations and their appetites for raw materials. Consequently, it is highly probable that before effective world-wide planning for technological-organizational adaptation occurs, serious regional ecological disasters will appear, with the higher probability of calamity being in the less developed world, given the relatively larger significance of food shortages there.

It should be remembered, however, that America has a surprisingly rich history of efforts to conserve scarce resources through governmental action—surprising in light of America's marvelous resource endowment and traditional recognition of land as the most abundant factor of production. Certainly, generations of American settlers and land developers enjoyed the luxury of landed resources which appeared to be in infinite supply. But even in the colonial period agricultural communities occasionally recognized the need for conserving resources for future use. Plymouth Colony, for instance, enacted an ordinance (1626) that prohibited the cutting of timber on colony lands without official permission, and William Penn required (1681) that one acre in trees be left for every five acres cleared. Plymouth and Pennsylvania were observing that their landed resource most vulnerable to depletion was timber and were striving, in a mercantilist fashion, to preserve a source of public revenue. Only in the late nineteenth century, however, did pressures on the nation's timber resources become sufficient to begin the development of government policies to conserve and protect them.

Beginning in the 1870s, with the waxing support of timber users, the federal government gradually instituted a substantial program for the creation of forest reserves. As a result of the cumulative contributions of Secretary of the Interior Carl Schurz (1877–1881), the Forest Reserve Act (1891), Presidents Benjamin Harrison, Grover Cleveland, and Theodore Roosevelt, and, in particular, of Gifford Pinchot, chief of the Division of Forestry, the Bureau of Forestry, and the Forest Service (1898–1910), the nation's forest reserves amounted to 150 million acres by 1910, and the federal government had become committed to management of those reserves for conservation and multipurpose use. This first conservation movement raised the price of timber products (relative to other prices) in the short run, but because of its preservation of forests for future use and its encouragement of reforestation, recycling of waste wood, and shifts to wood substitutes, contributed to the stabilization of the price of timber products (relative to other prices) that has occurred since the 1920s.[3]

Although no natural resource shortage was as severe as that of timber, public interest in conservation expanded in other directions during this period of accelerating industrialization. In 1872 the federal government recognized the need to set aside land for recreational use by creating Yellowstone National Park. In 1879 it began to inventory public lands, particularly those containing mineral resources, by establishing the Geological Survey and appointing John

Wesley Powell as its first director. His survey of the arid lands of the West sparked interest in governmental responsibility and investment in irrigation, leading to the Reclamation Act of 1902, which formed the Bureau of Reclamation in the Department of the Interior to initiate federal reclamation efforts. One earlier effort to make more productive use of land was the passage of the Hatch Experiment Station Act of 1887, providing federal support for agricultural experiment stations based at the agricultural colleges already supported by the Morrill Act. Perhaps the most tantalizing initiative of the period was Pinchot's and President Theodore Roosevelt's effort to suggest that resource problems were not only interrelated but continental and global in scope. In 1908 Roosevelt convened a White House conference to promote planning on all fronts for total resource conservation, organized the North American Conservation Conference for continental planning, and sought to convene world powers at The Hague to expand that effort. War in Europe precluded any global departure, but the National Conservation Commission appointed by Roosevelt began, under Pinchot's leadership, the fundamental task of inventorying the nation's resources (1909).

With the exception of acts permitting the creation of national forests in the East (1911), the establishment of the National Park Service (1916), the restriction of the hunting of migratory birds (1918), federal licensing of hydropower development on public lands (1920), regulation of the use of federal coal, sulphur, phosphate, oil, and oil-shale lands (the Mineral Leasing Act of 1920), and the first designation of an extensive wilderness area (1924), no significant conservation planning measures appeared until the crisis of the Great Depression impressed American society with the fragility of a healthy economic life and promoted a variety of efforts to make more-efficient use of the nation's resources. However, without the personal commitment of Franklin Roosevelt to conservation, little would have resulted. His New Deal included the creation of the Civilian Conservation Corps (1933), which contributed greatly to the improvement of public parks and forests, the creation of a permanent national soil and water conservation program (with the initiation of the Soil Erosion Service in 1933 and the passage of the Soil Conservation Act of 1935, which established the Soil Conservation Service in the Department of Agriculture), the subsidizing of county-level conservation programs (under the Agricultural Adjustment Act), the institution of stricter federal regulation of the use of the unreserved public domain (under the Taylor Grazing Act of 1934), the development of a national flood-prevention policy (under the Omnibus Flood Control Act of 1936), the provision of federal funds to states for wildlife protection (the Pittman-Robertson Act of 1937), the subsidizing, under the Resettlement Administration, of the relocation of farmers in the northern Great Lakes states and the dust-bowl areas of the Great Plains states, and, of course, the establishment of the Tennessee Valley Authority (1933), which planned for the integrated development of an entire river basin. Although New Deal initiatives resulted in agencies and centers of power with overlapping and conflicting jurisdictions, Roosevelt made a serious effort to coordinate planning for national resource development by the creation of the National Planning Board (1933) and its successors, the National Resources Board (1934) and the National Resources Committee (1935). The nation inherited from these centralizing agencies a comprehensive survey of its natural resource base, but interest in meeting the priorities of wartime mobilization (including heavy exploitation of minerals and a disruption of orderly cropping systems that had been developed during the 1930s) and a postwar ideological reaction against planning precluded continuation of a centralized conservation agency.

After World War II, only slight advances in planning to husband scarce resources occurred until the 1960s, when rising public concern with the preservation of wilderness combined with a responsive national administration represented by Secretary of the Interior Stewart L. Udall. Secretary Udall was less concerned than his predecessors with keeping the costs of natural resources low to those who wished to exploit them rapidly. A significant result was the National Wilderness Preservation Act of 1964, which for the first time firmly established the principle of preservation of lands for their aesthetic qualities—preservation for preservation's sake. Then began the development of procedures for protecting wilderness areas, including initially some 9.1 million acres of public land.

The 1970s, however, have seen few departures in public planning for protecting exhaustible resources. To be sure, rising energy and raw material costs, with their skewed distributional effects, widened public concern with protecting resources. Nonetheless, by 1978 little public planning had emerged to guarantee future supplies of such resources. Reliance continued to be on the marketplace—on price mechanisms that would reflect scarcities, induce conservation, and make production dependent on alternative energy sources and supplies of raw materials.

POLLUTION

The problem of pollution, or the degradation of the earth's physical resources, as a result of high concentrations of population and industrial activity, is analytically separable from the problem of the depletion of nonreproducible resources and is also more amenable to study by economists. The social costs of pollution are measurable as the price society is willing to pay to redress and prevent resource degradation. Moreover, these costs—the costs external to the money-reckoning processes of the marketplace—can be taken into account by forcing firms and public agencies to include the cost of eliminating pollution (the cost of disposal, or of preparation for recycling, or of restoring water used in processing to its original pristine condition) in the costs of goods produced and services rendered. If the consuming public comes to value environmental quality sufficiently, it will demand that producers of both public and private goods avoid or eliminate pollution and will either pay for the resulting costs in the form of higher prices or, in the case of pollution created by privately produced goods and services, seek to force firms to internalize such costs by taxing them appropriately. In response, manufacturers and public agencies would seek less costly ways of producing the same fundamental goods and services. In the central case of air pollution created by the automobile, the public could force automobile manufacturers and public agencies alike to accept the necessity of developing a lower-cost mode of transport. In this instance the outcome might well be a public or quasi-public mode of transport, with Detroit engaging in production for urban and federal governments (under contract) or consumers or both.

Needless to say, the automobile manufacturers, for example, with their enormous capital investment in the production of cars, have so far successfully blunted societal interest in developing a cleaner transport system. But one should argue that the power of the automobile companies stems from inadequate public demand for alternative transport systems. Consumer demand has been insufficient to induce competitor firms to produce pollution-free vehicles (assuming that to be technically feasible) or, the more promising possibility, to bring about public research, sponsorships, and implementation of innovative forms of public or quasi-public transport. Once again, however, the prospects for a political or a marketplace solution in this area are better than for the poverty problem, because of the wider impact of the social costs of pollution. The American public, as consumers and as taxpayers-voters, clearly possesses the power and is, no doubt, beginning to possess the will to demand solutions. More generally, the American public has the power to improve drastically the quality of life, regardless of its definition, through its consuming and voting functions.

Quite obviously the costs of diverting resources to cleanse the environment and develop cleaner production processes may result in growth that in the short run is slower in pace than would be the case without an effort to account for the social cost of pollution. But in the long run the cumulative social gain would undoubtedly outweigh the short-term costs. However, it is the short-term costs of such social action that will impede world-wide progress on pollution control—particularly in the developing nations that are eager to catch up with the pace-setters and therefore apt to view environmental concern as a luxury of the affluent nations. Most significantly, the pollution problem does not demand an abandonment of the social goal of economic growth. In fact, the reverse is true. An increasing per-capita rate of growth will make society's decision to free a meaningful portion of its resources to cope with pollution easier to bear. While it would be theoretically possible to clean up pollution in the context of a no-growth economy, it is thoroughly impractical; without a dramatic cultural transformation, no-growth would only diminish interest in pollution control. It is realistic to believe that as the more advanced nations continue to grow in productivity, and as the less developed nations build a significant margin of welfare above that necessary to provide only subsistence, society will find it easier to recognize the costs resulting from resource degradation.

Finally, the historical record of public policy in the United States suggests that American society, through the mobilization of public action, has made significant progress in coping with environmental pressures and, more generally, the reality of costs and benefits external to the marketplace requiring governmental intervention for their elimination or realization. Despite the primacy of the marketplace in American economic development, significant ventures in public investment that yielded high social returns yet provided only minimal private returns have dotted American economic history. We need only mention early-nineteenth-century canals, the transcontinental railroads, the Tennessee Valley Authority, and, most important of all modern governmental activities, the expansion of public education. Moreover, to a significant extent state and local governments of the late nineteenth and early twentieth centuries forced firms to bear the costs of services those governments provided them (and, thus, to internalize negative externalities associated with urban crowding and pollution) through the expansion of corporate taxation. Only the most naïve capitalist would deny the existence of externalities—whether costs not accounted for or benefits not provided by the marketplace—and the consequent necessity for appropriate governmental intervention.

Americans have no doubt made less advance in recognizing environmental negative externalities than in isolating and acting upon externalities associated with the scarcity of labor and capital, such as those, for example, implicated in investment in public education, public health, and sewage disposal. But for that reason the departures of the past are impressive and strongly suggest the possibilities for future political movement in coping with the degradation of air, water, and soil. Indeed, even during the 1960s important antipollution measures were adopted. These measures included the setting of federal standards for clean air, including the first effort to control automobile emissions (Motor Vehicle Air Pollution Control Act of 1965), and the subsidization of cooperative programs to reduce air pollution. Then the elaboration of federal standards for clean water (the Water Quality Act of 1965 and the Clean Water Restoration Act of 1966) and the creation of effective regulation of radiation levels (the Radiation Control for Health and Safety Act of 1968) followed. In a resumption of New Deal coordination measures, the federal government sought to unify and more efficiently expand programs of environmental control. Under the National Environmental Policy Act of 1969 Congress made a commitment to protect and improve the environment and, in fact, specified the general content of such a policy and provided initial but specific standards for the enforcement of environmental control, creating the Council on Environmental Quality in the Executive Office to monitor on behalf of the public the environmental impact of all types of governmental actions. The act also created the Environmental Protection Agency as an instrument for bringing together all the environmental control functions of the federal government. Through the medium of these bodies the 1969 act attempted to require all agencies to assess the environmental consequences of their proposals and current policies. It also set specific, albeit incomplete, legal definitions of environmental quality.

Although the pace of structural-environmental reform quickened in a promising manner during the 1960s, the future of such planning in the United States without any doubt remains uncertain. Recent legislative and executive efforts, coupled with heavy reliance on price mechanisms, may well foster appropriate technical-organizational responses to the environmental crisis; certainly contemporary society holds the intellectual competency to solve that constellation of problems. What is less clear is whether enough people are concerned in sufficient depth to provide American society with the will to confront environmental problems in a sustained and rational fashion. The historical perspective suggests that the will exists. Economic growth, through the raising of standards of living, has itself contributed to the growing taste for amenities and to the development of environmental sensibilities. The shift of values toward enhanced environmental quality began not in the 1970s but a century ago with the rise of the conservation movement. This long-term shift of values, joined with the continued power of the market to solve problems of scarcity (now of land, rather than labor) and to restrain population growth, creates the strong possibility of effective resolution of the environmental "crisis."

NOTES

1. For examples of criticisms of the Club of Rome report, see William D. Nordhaus, "World Dynamics: Measurement Without Data," *Economic Journal,* 83 (December 1973), 1156–1183, and "Resources as a Constraint on Growth," *American Economic Review,* 64 (May 1974), 22–26.

2. Harold J. Barnett and Chandler Morse, *Scarcity and Growth: The Economics of Natural Resource Availability* (Baltimore: Johns Hopkins University Press, 1963), pp. 164–201.

3. *Ibid.,* pp. 170–172, 184, 194–198.

SUGGESTED READINGS

Books

Barnett, Harold J., and Chandler Morse. *Scarcity and Growth: The Economics of Natural Resource Availability.* Baltimore: Johns Hopkins University Press, 1963.

Commoner, Barry. *The Poverty of Power: Energy and the Economic Crisis.* New York: Knopf, 1976.

Cooper, Chester L. (ed.). *Growth in America.* Westport, Conn.: Greenwood, 1976.

Hays, Samuel P. *Conservation and the Gospel of Efficiency: The Progressive Conservation Movement, 1890–1920.* Cambridge, Mass.: Harvard University Press, 1959.

Mishan, E. J. *The Cost of Economic Growth.* Harmondsworth, Eng.: Penguin, 1969.

Murdoch, William W. (ed.). *Environment, Resources, Pollution, and Society.* Stamford, Conn.: Sinauer Associates, 1971.

Nash, Roderick (ed.). *The American Environment: Readings in the History of Conservation.* Reading, Mass.: Addison-Wesley, 1968.

Nordhaus, William, and James Tobin. *Economic Growth.* National Bureau of Economic Research, *Fifteenth Anniversary Colloquium V.* New York: Columbia University Press, 1972.

Passell, Peter, and Leonard Ross. *The Retreat from Riches: Affluence and Its Enemies.* New York: Viking Press, 1973.

Rosenberg, Nathan. *Perspectives on Technology.* Cambridge: Cambridge University Press, 1976.

Swain, Donald C. *Federal Conservation Policy, 1921–1933.* Berkeley: University of California Press, 1963.

❖ Index

515

❈ About the Author

W. Elliot Brownlee is an Associate Professor of History at the University of California, Santa Barbara. He received his Ph.D. from the University of Wisconsin. His area of specialization is U.S. Economic History.

Professor Brownlee received a Haynes Foundation Fellowship in 1969 and a Regents Humanities Fellowship in 1977. He is currently a Fellow at the Charles Warren Center. His published works include *Progressivism and Economic Growth: The Wisconsin Income Tax, 1911–1929* and *Women in the American Economy: A Documentary History, 1675 to 1929.* In addition, he has contributed to professional journals that include *Economica, Economic History Review, Explorations in Economic History, Journal of American History, Journal of Economic History, Journal of Interdisciplinary History,* and *Wisconsin Magazine of History.*

A Note on the Type

The text of this book is set in a computer version of the Linotype face CALEDONIA designed by W. A. Dwiggins. It belongs to the family of printing types called "modern face" by printers—a term used to mark the change in style of type-letters that occurred about 1800. Caledonia borders on the general design of Scotch Modern but is more freely drawn than that face.

This book was composed by Datagraphics. The text was designed by Susan Phillips and the cover by Deborah Payne.

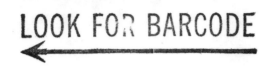